THE HONEST
COURTESAN

WOMEN IN CULTURE AND SOCIETY
A Series Edited by Catharine R. Stimpson

THE HONEST
COURTESAN

VERONICA FRANCO
CITIZEN AND WRITER
IN SIXTEENTH-CENTURY
VENICE

Margaret F. Rosenthal

THE UNIVERSITY OF CHICAGO PRESS
Chicago & London

THE UNIVERSITY OF CHICAGO PRESS, CHICAGO 60637
THE UNIVERSITY OF CHICAGO PRESS, LTD., LONDON

08 07 06 05 04 03   8 9 10

ISBN (paper): 0-226-72812-9

Library of Congress Cataloging-in-Publication Data

Rosenthal, Margaret F. 3117 8642 11/04
    The honest courtesan : Veronica Franco, citizen and writer in
sixteenth-century Venice / Margaret F. Rosenthal.
        p.   cm. — (Women in culture and society)
    Includes bibliographical references and index.
    ISBN: 0-226-72812-9 (pbk.)
    1. Franco, Veronica, 1546–1591. 2. Venice (Italy)—Intellectual
life. 3. Courtesans—Italy–Biography. 4. Authors, Italian—16th
century—Biography.   I. Title.   II. Series.
DC678.24.F73R67   1992
945'.3107'092—dc20   92-14540
    [B]   CIP

♾ The paper used in this publication meets the minimum requirements of the
American National Standard for Information Sciences—Permanence of Paper for
Printed Library Materials, ANSI Z39.48-1992.

Contents

Foreword

An extraordinary woman, Veronica Franco was born in 1546 in Venice. Because they were citizens of Venice by birth, members of her family had a secure legal identity. They were, however, neither rich nor powerful. Indeed, Franco's mother was a penurious courtesan. Following a tradition among economically vulnerable Venetian mothers and daughters, Franco, too, became a courtesan. She made a success of her profession: visiting Venice, a future king of France called on her. Veronica was also a brilliant woman whose gifts compelled her to develop them. She educated herself and then invented herself as a literary figure. Here, too, she succeeded. Between 1570 and 1580, she wrote poetry and public letters. She took on editorial projects. Tintoretto, the Venetian painter, did her portrait. Regrettably, when she died in 1591, much of the wealth she had earned was gone, a lot of it apparently stolen. Yet, Franco's life, on balance, was a dramatic narrative of the exercise of will and talent.

Now Tita Rosenthal has written *The Honest Courtesan,* the first major study of Veronica Franco in English. Massive and meticulous, the result of both scrupulous archival research and elegant textual readings, *The Honest Courtesan* places Franco in the culture and society of Venice, the native city that she left perhaps twice, once to embark upon a pilgrimage to Rome, once to go into exile because of a shattered relationship. Within Venice, alluring, exciting, and beautiful though it was, Franco had to manage—with skill, imagination, and energy—her own life, children and family, and profound cultural tensions concerning sex and gender.

In brief, although female figures dominated the city's public iconography, few women could actually enter into the city's public discourse. Fortunately for Franco, Venice, the center of European publishing, provided as many opportunities for writers of both genders as any city might have. Moreover, Venetian iconography adapted and burnished a common Western polarity in the representation of women, the polarity between angel and witch, virgin and whore, Virgin Mary and Eve, or, in Venice's self-presentation, between an immaculate, pure, virtuous city and a luxury loving, bejewelled, voluptuous one. In part to ensure the purity of its women, especially the wives and daughters of the elite, Venice regulated them strenuously. Their space was to be private, not public. Because "good women" were so restricted, "bad women" had this social role of playmate and source of sexual release. As Rosenthal notes, the Venetian courtesan, like the Japanese geisha, was expected to provide cultivated company and good conversation as well. However, during periods of grave social and economic danger, such as mid-1570s when the plague infected Venice, the courtesan and prostitute were conveniently available as symbols of disorder and vileness.

Franco had her patrons and supporters, especially Domenico Venier, who conduted an influential salon. She could not have survived without them. However, she also seems to have been very much her own woman, the author of her own self-promotions and self-justifications. She had two, inseparable tasks: to defend the courtesan and to take on a public role forbidden to the conventional woman. The voice that she created was that of "honest courtesan and citizen poet" (MS 108). In careful detail, Rosenthal shows the twists, turns, and rhetorical strategies of this voice; its parallels to and divergences from that of the male courtier; and, significantly, its reworking of the genres and motifs of classical and Renaissance literature in order to permit a woman's voice to flourish. For, Franco—talking with men, working with men, sleeping with men, giving birth to three surviving sons—forgot neither women nor the realities of prostitution. Indeed, two wills leave money for poor women.

If powerful men helped Franco to survive, powerful men also opposed and abused her. Some were fellow writers, among the most vicious a relative of her patron, Domenico Venier. They projected their own social, professional, and psychological anxieties onto women in general, the figure of the courtesan/prostitute in particular, and, most particularly, onto Franco herself. Then, in 1580, the courts of the Inquisition summoned her on charges of performing heretical incantations, charges that the male tutor of her children had first filed. The language of her self-defense when she was on trial was similar to that of her self-defense against poets when they attacked her. Once again, she won out, though at an unquantifiable cost. After the trial, the charges against her were dropped.

In one of the poems in which Franco confronts a male poet who is her adversary, she pictures herself as an Amazon warrior, an image that women writers have frequently used. She is leading her tribe into battle. She writes,

"When we too are armed and trained, we can convince men that we have hands, feet and a heart like yours; and although we may be delicate and soft, some men who are delicate are also strong. . . . Women have not yet realized this, for if they should decide to do so, they would be able to fight you until death; and to prove that I speak the truth, amongst so many women, I will be the first to act, setting an example for them to follow; and on you who have sinned against them all, I turn with whichever weapon you may choose, with the wish and hope of throwing you to the ground" (MS 351). Strong, clever, bold, cunning, Veronica Franco refused to be exiled from language and literature. Because of *The Honest Courtesan,* we now realize how grateful we must be for this strength, cleverness, boldness, and bountiful refusal.

Catharine R. Stimpson
Rutgers University

Acknowledgments

I have enjoyed immensely writing this book on Veronica Franco because the nature of the subject has brought me into contact with many people and scholars from disciplines far from my own. I have come to realize that the pleasure I have derived over these years of thinking, researching, and speaking on the Venetian courtesan as writer has much to do with the collaborative nature of interdisciplinary research. The excitement for interdisciplinary study was first kindled while I was a graduate student in Italian literature at Yale University. In an art history seminar on Italian renaissance and baroque portraiture, Professor Gloria Kury asked me to investigate the woman who was constructed in ubiquitous Venus and toilette paintings of the early to late sixteenth century. Using sixteenth-century conduct books on manners, I tried to decipher the half-clothed images of women, grandiosely dubbed Venuses. Little did I know then, nor did she, that this initial inquiry into female representation in Italian renaissance portraiture would open up to me the richly enigmatic world of Venice and the Venetian courtesan—one that has taken hold of my imagination for many years. I am enormously grateful to my professors at Yale University—Margaret W. Ferguson, Giuseppe Mazzotta, and Paolo Valesio—who first encouraged me to pursue the topic of the Venetian courtesan, Veronica Franco, for my dissertation.

I owe, more than to any other person, a special debt of gratitude to Ann Rosalind Jones, who from the time I was a graduate student until now has provided me with lively encouragement and unstinting critical assistance. She has been a mentor to me, standing as a model of the best kind of intellectual and academic collaboration. Her generosity and support, and the attentiveness with which she offered her critical expertise as a reader of my work on Franco from graduate school days until now, are immeasurable and invaluable. Over the years we have shared a passion for the works of Veronica Franco and have by now amassed an epistolary correspondence of which Franco could only be proud.

I would like to thank the Gladys Krieble Delmas Foundation (1980–81) and the Woodrow Wilson National Fellowship for Women's Studies (1982–83) for their financial aid which first enabled me to travel to Venice and to begin the primary research for this study. I am also grateful to the staffs of the Biblioteca Nazionale Marciana and the Biblioteca Civico Correr in Venice for their generous assistance. To the archivists and my friends at the Archivio di Stato in Venice, especially Alessandra Schiavon, who shares with me an interest in Veronica Franco, Michela Dal Borgo, and Alessandra Sambo, I am indebted for their patience and good cheer in explaining to me year after year the mysterious but intriguing world of the state archive. To Tiziana Agostini Nordio I am especially indebted for sharing with me her findings on Domenico and Maffio Venier. To all my Venetian friends, and especially to James Mathes, warm thanks for the many years of hospitality, Prosecco, and spirited conversation walking along the Zattere.

The list of friends, colleagues, and students who have read or listened to portions of this book, or from whom I have received ideas, constructive advice, and bibliographical suggestions, which have contributed to my thinking in fundamental ways, is so long as to constitute an autobiography of my adult life. It is with enormous pleasure that I now have the opportunity to thank them for invariably leading me to clearer thinking and refinement of style. The wide variety of disciplines they embrace reflects my own wide-reaching investigation into the subject of this book—a subject that has taken me from my own expertise in literary criticism into the realms of art history, social history, and feminist research. If it had not been for meeting Sherrill Cohen and Laurie Nussdorfer in the early 1980s, who were at the time graduate students of Professor Natalie Zemon Davis in the Department of History at Princeton University, my research would not have taken a turn toward social history. They and others, especially my friends Carlo and Luisa Ginzburg, first inspired me to push beyond the confines of literary criticism to examine the social, political, and economic context of cinquecento Venice, particularly with regard to women's work and social status.

I especially value the lively world of social historians of Venice for all of the critical guidance and encouragement I have received from them over the years. The Venetian scholarly community is extraordinarily friendly—from the personal generosity of archivists to the warmth of Venetianists working collectively in the archives and libraries, often puzzling out issues which feed into one another's projects. Many thanks to a host of Venetianists with whom I have enjoyed sharing ideas about sixteenth-century Venice: Linda Carroll, Stanley Chojnacki, Paul F. Grendler, Margaret L. King, Patricia H. Labalme, John Martin, Edward Muir, Dennis Romano, and David Rosand. I gratefully acknowledge the unfailing encouragement and support of Guido Ruggiero, whose conversation and friendship have meant a great deal to me over the years. To many friends I owe more than I can say: Florine Bruneau, Libby and Tom Cohen, Theresia De Vroom, Donna Landry, Aine O'Healy, Hilary Schor, James G. Turner, and Nancy Vickers. To my colleagues in the Department of French and Italian at the University of Southern California, I owe many thanks. I wish to thank Albert Sonnenfeld, the chair of my department, for his generous support and encouragement throughout the writing of this book. To Marshall Cohen, dean of the Humanities, I am grateful for leave time from teaching responsibilities and for financial assistance. Many thanks to Silvia Herzog for her excellent photographs and to Giulio Ongaro for his expert assistance with deciphering archival documents. I appreciate the financial assistance from the following institutions which allowed me to complete the writing of this book in Trieste, Venice, and in the glorious pastoral setting of the Black Forest in Freiburg, Germany: Gladys Krieble Delmas Foundation (summer 1987), USC Faculty Research and Innovation Fund (1987), NEH Summer Fellowship (1988), and ACLS (1989) Award for Recent Recipients of the Ph.D.

Without the extraordinary stimulus from Catharine R. Stimpson, who first recognized the project's potential for a book for her Women in Culture and Society series, and who spurred me to articulate my feminist views more forcefully than I had in my dissertation, and without the encouragement I have received along the way from Karen Wilson, editor at the University of Chicago Press, this book would not be what it is today. Without the generous and imaginative assistance of Haidy Scafetta, whose artfulness in translating the knotty, syntactic snarls of Franco's terze rime and the many difficult aspects of sixteenth-century Italian and Venetian dialect poetry, the task of translation would have been extremely difficult.

There is one friend and colleague (formerly at USC, now at the University of Chicago) whom I must single out: Martha Feldman. Together we share a love of Venice, Venetian poets of the sixteenth century, and all things Venetian. Most importantly, she responded with conviction about the book's merits in moments of crisis, and with extraordinary critical acumen and meticulous commentary when editing and reading the final manuscript. My family, too, has been a constant source of encouragement.

I thank my father, Raymond Rosenthal, for his encouragement and for his interest in the subject of this book. To Robin Shakeshaft, my husband, who reminded me every time I said I was not writing the book I wanted that this was the sign that I was, I owe many thanks and much love for bolstering my spirits with his wonderful sense of humor, and for just keeping me going. Finally, I will never be able to express fully the extent of my appreciation to my mother, Elsa Rosenthal, whose passion for Italian culture, unfailing generosity, and intellectual curiosity were models to me in my youth. I hope that this book will convey, in some small part, the measure of my affection for her.

For my Mother and Father

INTRODUCTION

In this book I present a study of one Venetian honest courtesan, Veronica Franco (1546–91), a writer and citizen of Venice who offers to the modern reader an intriguing and eloquent testimony to a courtesan's interaction with the Venetian patriciate and with leading intellectuals in Venetian society. Franco's literary works dramatize a courtesan's life through unconventional choices in literary style and genre. Through the multiplicity of genres that the lyric *capitolo* in terza rima embraced (elegy, poetic debate, love lyric, dialogic exchange, verse epistle), Franco points to the many difficulties that a Venetian courtesan encounters when seeking public recognition.

In Veronica Franco's published poems and familiar letters, she exposes the mechanisms of upward social mobility and the processes of negotiation and accommodation required of all early-modern writers in Venice when they seek public acclaim. But, and I share here the view first put forward by Ann Rosalind Jones with regard to early modern women writers, for women authors "a 'negotiated' viewer position is one that accepts the dominant ideology encoded into a text but particularizes and transforms it in the service of a different group."[1] Jones's theoretical paradigm has called important attention to how levels of conformity and negotiation in a woman-authored text of the early modern period constitutes for women a positive and hence productive set of contradictions. For a writer such as Franco, who viewed herself as a *cittadina* (see chap. 2 n. 16) and courtesan poet of Venice, she makes use of her "negotiated" position within Venetian culture to identify herself with other Venetian women as a group and to speak in support of women previously silenced by male authors. Despite the relative freedoms afforded by a merchant city such as Venice, where social and class hierarchies presented fewer obstacles than the Italian courts in Tuscany and other regions of Italy, I contend throughout this study that Venetian courtesans rose neither with ease nor without considerable difficulties through the ranks of Venetian society.

As a courtesan writer, Franco openly competed with male contemporaries for public visibility. She negotiated a literary profession by relying on, as Jones says, "the support of powerful men and a framework of political and class flexibility more available in international merchant cities such as . . . Venice."[2] Franco reveals in her literary works and in the events of her life the complexity of this balance between negotiation and accommodation, required especially of women writers of the early modern period, if they hoped to secure patronage from male mentors. Franco accepts the terms of literary contest as a challenge which she faces with unusual courage and bravura, especially when defending herself from vicious assaults to her public honor. Her success at self-defense and her artistic ability to present a compelling self-portrait in her published works, one that radically overturns received assumptions about the Venetian courtesan, is the story that this book will tell.

Indeed the Venetian courtesan has long captured people's imagination as a female symbol of sexual license, elegance, beauty, and social unruliness. This fascination with her multiple allures first emerges powerfully during the sixteenth century, when foreign visitors to the island republic often traveled great distances to observe the famed *cortigiane oneste* (honest or honored courtesans) within their specific social milieus. The accounts left by early-modern tourists praise honest courtesans for their beauty, for their talents as highly sophisticated conversationalists and cunning rhetoricians, and for their dexterity at navigating their way through a loosely organized maze of social structures and class hierarchies.

English and French visitors, such as Thomas Coryat, Fynes Moryson, Sir Henry Wotton, Michel Montaigne, John Evelyn, and others, noted, at times with paternalistic surprise, that the honest courtesan rose to public acclaim and social parity with the upper echelons of Venetian society owing to what seemed to them a movement of relative ease from their nonpatrician status to striking levels of refinement that vied with the elegance and grandeur of the Venetian patriciate. Unlike the patriciate, they were quick to add, the courtesan flaunted an unbridled taste for sensuous extravagance and luxuries which elicited moralizing comments from her bedazzled observers regarding her provocative and hence disruptive sexuality. Honest courtesans' social mobility, at which they marveled, was all the more compelling precisely in light of the often severe patriarchal injunctions that weighed so heavily upon aristocratic women, restricting the ornamentation of their dress and their freedom to circulate and participate in Venetian public life.

Early-modern travel diarists and chroniclers thus delighted in the paradoxical nature of a city that indulged on the one hand in lavish public spectacles while maintaining a sober image of republican restraint and judicious modesty on the other. These reports have spawned a wealth of wonderfully descriptive anecdotal narratives of Venetian courtesans at all levels. The effect of such descriptions has been to obscure, however, the important distinctions between cultural myth and operative realities at work in the Venetian republic; they bolster rather than demythologize the republic's own carefully constructed presentation of Venice as a city founded on principles of equality, magnanimity, domestic harmony, and justice for all of its citizens. Invariably the honest courtesan thus stands, for the foreign observer, as a cultural code or cipher through which Venice, the secular city, publicized itself in the sixteenth century. They offer her as eloquent proof of the republic's progressive social policies, its tolerance of foreign immigrants and marginal groups, and its reputation for pleasure seeking in early modern Europe.

This idealizing view of the courtesan's profession took hold not only in a period when Venice was intent on projecting throughout Italy and abroad a message of social freedom and tolerance but also in latter-day cultural and historical treatments of the subject. The honest courtesan, according to this perspective, not only embodied a city immersed in luxury, spectacle, disguise, commercialization, voluptuousness, and sensuality but also had a hand in bringing about the republic's subsequent decline.

Correcting romanticized notions about a courtesan's livelihood has necessitated returning to an examination of the primary documents housed in the Venetian state archive that shed light on the courtesan's position and practices in sixteenth-century Venice. Archival sources, however, never tell the whole story. For this reason, I have sought throughout this study to find a synthesis of literary text and historical document which has entailed reconstructing in the opening chapters the layers of cultural myth and anecdotal legends surrounding the honest courtesan when they first appeared in the sixteenth century.

In many chapters I align an examination of a primary document with a specific textual reading. Indeed one of the basic premises of this study is that social and cultural pressures cannot be separated from Veronica Franco's literary production but intersect significantly in all of her literary works. I view the events of Franco's personal history as a narrative that il-

3

luminates in a reciprocal fashion her rhetorical self-presentation and self-construction in her poems and letters. Franco's biography reveals the extent to which her strategies of survival as an honest courtesan in a society dominated by men are analogous to the textual maneuvers she employs in her published works.

The organization of the book reflects my belief that it is necessary first to demythologize the courtesan as legend before we can understand successfully the terms of one courtesan's, Veronica Franco's, self-construction not as a cultural anecdote but as a literary figure engaged socially, politically, and intellectually in Venetian public life. One of my main premises is that the honest courtesan's profession is best understood as socially and intellectually defined rather than limited to sexual activity.

To study the literary works of a courtesan is therefore to examine the conjunction of social and textual issues within a broader articulation of class and gender concerns. Early nineteenth- and twentieth-century scholars have repeatedly overlooked this perspective and have focused instead on the erotic levels of a courtesan's poetics as inextricably connected, in the case of Veronica Franco, to her personal biography. Antiquarian historians such as Giuseppe Tassini and Arturo Graf, and liberal idealist historians such as Benedetto Croce, who have all written influential works on Veronica Franco to which I am indebted for the wealth of historical and cultural material they first made available, reveal many critical prejudices that have served as important catalysts for this study.[3] I depart, however, from their belief that Franco's literary works can only be read as strictly tied, in a cause-and-effect relation, to her profession as courtesan. The effect of such a reading has been to flatten the complex layers of rhetorical self-presentation evident in her literary works and to render her infamous as a sexual performer rather than famous as an accomplished writer. I argue, rather, that a reading of Franco's published poems and letters as mere autobiographical records or, as Benedetto Croce would have it, as the confessions of a repentant magdalen, is fundamentally shortsighted.[4] These critics have fallen prey precisely to the persuasive force of the Venetian cultural myth and the anecdotal lore surrounding the courtesan which has resulted in either romanticizing the honest courtesan's talents as exceptional, or in other words, as unique to Veronica Franco, or in criticizing her sexual exploits as morally reprehensible.

The first serious textual scholarship began with Riccardo Scrivano's important essay, which was an effort to locate Franco's work within an albeit too rigidly conceived Petrarchan and anti-Petrarchan framework.[5] This tendency to fit Franco's poems and letters into predefined literary categories has been questioned recently in the highly informative published studies of Sara Maria Adler, Fiora A. Bassanese, and Francesco Erspamer, who prefer to speak of Franco's poetic style as a-Petrarchan, a term first coined by Riccardo Scrivano.[6] To date, however, there exists no full-length study in English devoted to Veronica Franco, although important contributions have appeared in recent years from Italian scholars (Alvise Zorzi, Marcella Diberti Leigh) which have enriched the field.[7]

I adopt in this study the tools of materialist, feminist and social historians (Judith Brown, Natalie Davis, Michele Barrett, Judith Newman, and Carlo Ginzburg, among others), who read archival documents and literary texts together in order to reconstruct gender, or marginal groups as an identity, in the analysis of culture. Rather than use historical documents simply as background material for Franco's life, I ask how all documents intersect in Franco's literary production. With the enormous advances in what we now know about women's social history in Italy in the early modern period, and about the construction of gender as a combination of class relations and textual processes, owing to the influential research of Stanley Chojnacki, Guido Ruggiero, Margaret L. King, Dennis Romano, Patricia H. Labalme, and others, I, as a literary historian, focus on the textuality of archival documents. I attempt to pay careful attention to the inarticulated tensions between literary document and archival record.

Veronica Franco uses certain literary genres and poetic forms to register social conflict while she transforms them often with a subversive twist. All of Franco's literary works were written and published within a ten-year period. Although I discuss her familiar letters (*Lettere familiari a diversi*, 1580) before her edition of poems (*Terze rime*, 1575), both the letters and the poems, I believe, were written in the same period. Her familiar letters often gloss the content of her poems. I also place an analysis of Franco's letters before the poems (chapter 4) in order to help document some of the confusion of identities in the literary exchange of capitoli between male and female authors in Franco's *Terze rime*.

In the opening two chapters I set out in general terms the collective need in sixteenth-century Venetian patriarchal society for such a refined yet sexualized version of the aristocratic woman. Although there were many attempts throughout the period to restrict the courtesan's appropriation of patrician women's sartorial privileges, they were most often unsuccessful. The republic tried in vain to reconstruct the social boundaries that had eroded between social classes by enforcing sumptuary laws that monitored the lavishness of a courtesan's dress and by proposing regulations that re-stricted her circulation in public. Owing to a belief in the early modern period that women's speech led to sexual temptation, or that eloquence was tantamount to promiscuity, it is not surprising that courtesans embodied for sixteenth-century male courtiers the living proof of their moral injunc-tions.

Indeed to achieve the position of honest courtesan in Renaissance society meant to enter a public world denied to most upper-class Renaissance women; the honest courtesan offered social and intellectual refinement in return for patronage. Playing music, singing, composing poetry, and pre-senting a sophisticated figure were the courtesan's necessary, marketable skills. Much like the courtier, Franco's texts were appeals for social connec-tion and public recognition. Her poetic texts often equate sexual perfor-mance with poetic bravura.

A courtesan's appropriation of the courtier's strategies for self-advancement is what accounts for the paradoxical term *cortigiana onesta*, or honest courtesan. The honest courtesan redefines the male humanist category of *virtù* as a woman's intellectual integrity. She calls attention to her acquisition of intellectual, not mercenary, capital by dissociating it from the selling of one's body for financial gain. The honest courtesan's capital, Franco reminds her male interlocutor and her reader, is acquired by "honest" means alone, that is, through intellectual and literary projects. Because the Venetian honest courtesan often lived outside the strictly defined marital relations that severely limited the economic and social free-doms of aristocratic women in Italy, she had, in theory at least, the oppor-tunity to manage her own capital. This fact is precisely what left the upwardly mobile courtesan especially vulnerable to the political and legal authority of men who vied at times with her for public recognition.

As I have already indicated, Veronica Franco promoted her literary career in much the same manner as the sixteenth-century courtier projected a rhe-torical persona for political and social advancement. Her search for male patronage resembles, in the most general sense, the ambitious upward mo-bility of the male courtier; verbal expertise and a sophisticated social de-meanor were essential to courtesan and courtier alike. This similarity, however, bred contempt. Franco's successful self-advancement in Venetian society fueled acrimonious slurs from male contemporaries who competed with her for literary acclaim. I view the Venetian republic's contradictory attitudes toward the courtesan in relation to the textual stereotype of the courtesan. That stereotype, the venal prostitute, is set in the satirical dialogues and plays of Pietro Aretino, in the moralizing treatises and orations of Tomaso Garzoni and Sperone Speroni, and in the misogynist Venetian dialect poems of Lorenzo and Maffio Venier. They use the honorific civic image of Venice as sublime female ruler to denigrate the courtesan as a vulgar whore. Their negative satirical representations of Venetian courtesans in general, and Veronica Franco in particular, point instead to male intellectuals' uneasiness about their own relationship to patronage in Venetian society. When they denounce the courtesan's activities on moral grounds, they mask, I argue, a fear of the potentially threatening challenge a courtesan writer posed to their own profession. Ironically, the male courtier's repudiation of a courtesan's manipulation of authority points to his own painful awareness of the often depraved and brutal treatment inflicted on him by his own patrons. Thus, these male writers see themselves as both victims of the deceiving courtesan whom they attack and victims of the patronage system on whose support they all depend.

In chapter 2 I move from this satirical tradition to a reconstruction of Franco's involvement in Venetian civic practices and literary projects in honor of the Venetian republic. In this chapter Veronica Franco takes center stage. I read, for example, the republic's laws on prostitution and regulations against courtesans alongside Franco's wills and tax report, and in relation to her self-definition as an honest courtesan and *cittadina* in her civic patriotic verses. The two wills of Veronica Franco were first unearthed and transcribed by Giuseppe Tassini in the 1860s. He also alluded in his monograph, *Veronica Franco: Celebre poetessa e cortigiana del secolo XVI,* to the Inquisition trial proceedings brought against Franco in 1580 but never transcribed them. The trials were recently first transcribed by the Venetian archivist Alessandra Schiavon. Since then, other historians have produced alternative readings and transcriptions, to which I add, in this study, my own versions.

Veronica Franco challenges and rewrites the textual stereotype of the venal, greedy, and deceitful courtesan made popular by her male contemporaries. Thus, I return repeatedly to the terms of the satirical presentation first proposed in chapter 1. In chapter 2, more specifically, I concentrate on Franco's reaction to this social climate when I trace her movement into the public spheres of Venetian life and in particular her affiliation with the prestigious literary academy of Domenico Venier. With Venier as her male patron and literary counselor, Franco composed verses in praise of the republic and its heroes. But she transforms the honorific female figure of the republic to suit her own self-elevating designs: she identifies herself, as loyal

Venetian citizen, with the female ruler at the same time that she calls attention to the social inequalities at the heart of the Venetian patrician and patriarchal founding myth.

Chapters 1 and 2 therefore ask general questions that I qualify and attempt to answer in chapters 3, 4, and 5. All five chapters are meant to interact with one another and to add further layers to what is already an extraordinarily complex tangle of received attitudes regarding the courtesan. Indeed Franco's self-presentation in her literary works grows out of, and must be seen as a reaction to, the Venetian satirical tradition, both literary and social, ridiculing women. Franco, as a courtesan writer, exposes the practice of Venetian male authors who use women as literary commodities to advance their careers but then discard them when they are no longer useful to their self-promotion.

In chapter 3 I analyze Franco's participation in Venetian charitable public institutions—for the protection of and assistance to maidens too poor to support themselves—in light of her reworking of the humanist familiar letter. Franco's epistles address women's social and economic needs. Veronica Franco recasts the humanist familiar letter in order to present a public version of the courtesan's private self. In so doing she counters the textual representation of the venal whore by insisting that a courtesan can provide useful moral, social, and ethical counsel to male correspondents who fail to adhere to the same advice they have given others. Her *Lettere familiari a diversi* shed further light on her recognition of social inequalities between the sexes in Venetian society. These letters act as correctives to Venetian patriarchal rule.

At times Veronica Franco openly competed with men for public commissions. This provoked the kind of vindictive attacks that we witness in her poetic debate with an anonymous male accuser. In chapter 4 I invoke the satirical tradition first proposed in chapter 1 when I read the poetic debate in Franco's edition of poems, the *Terze rime*, together with her self-defense in a series of Inquisition trials charging her with witchcraft and superstitious magic. In both literary and political arenas, Franco faced down male detractors who sought to denigrate her profession as courtesan and to humiliate her publicly. The records of the trial proceedings, combined with the poetic debate, illuminate the varieties of self-defense Franco employed to protect herself from acrimonious accusations.

Finally, in chapter 5 I discuss Franco's elegiac verses, written while in "exile" from an aggressive lover, in relation to the plague which ravaged Venice from 1575 to 1577. I examine Franco's reworking of Ovid's amorous epistles in the *Heroides* in light of the Venier academy's interest in, and experimentation with, the uses of classical meters, forms, and genres. This experimentation marks an important departure from the Petrarchan love lyric tradition. As the academy's program (the *Somma delle opere*) attests, a close investigation of the ancient elegists' (Ovid, Catullus, and Propertius) uses of rhetorical and artificial devices, together with a study of the expressive and emotional nature of the elegiac love lament, took precedence over a formal study of the Petrarchan-style sonnet. Franco's elegiac love lyrics publicize the sensuality of classical elegy while empowering her voice with learned allusions to ancient authors. I argue that a reading and translation of Ovid's *Heroides* into *capitoli* in terza rima by academy members, precisely during the period when Franco was composing her poems, must have provided her with a powerful rhetorical model. The Ovidian double letters between male and female lovers in the *Heroides* present Franco with interesting dialogic, epistolary, and polemical strategies for her poems.

Franco's election of the elegiac form is also an appropriate response to the effects of the plague that struck Venice and the Veneto region from 1575 to 1577. A collective sense of shame overwhelmed the Venetian people and made its way into the lyrics of Venetian poets, who elegiacally yearned for a delivery into a golden age. All citizens felt implicated in a crime which challenged the core of the republic's myth of virginal origins. They tried to purge their souls as a group by constant prayer, good deeds, and acts of penitence. Thus, Franco's attempt to purge her own soul connects her poems with the wider sociohistorical context and with her dialogic engagement with her city. She records her exile from her cruel lover as a flight from plague-infested Venice. She laments her involuntary banishment in the concluding *capitolo* by contrasting the idyllic beauty of this pastoral retreat with allusions to the epidemic that defiles her virginal city. The classical vernaculars discussed here in relation to the literary concerns of the Venetian Accademia della Fama and Domenico Venier's literary salon counteract Maffio Venier's misogyny and the challenge of Venetian dialect which I discuss in relation to the poetic debate in chapter 4.

When I first read Veronica Franco's poems and letters many years ago, I was struck, as I still am, by her forthright polemical stance. She writes passionately in support of women unable to defend themselves. She writes with conviction about social and literary inequalities. Deploying an eroticized language in her epistolary verses, Franco calls attention to the performative, seductive nature of all poetic contests—courtesanry, like courtiership, relies on debate, contest, and competition. It is Franco's insight into the power conflicts between men and women, and her awareness of the threat she posed to her male contemporaries, who were also aspiring writers, that makes her literary works and her interaction with Venetian intellectuals so forceful and so extraordinarily modern. Franco is dramatic in her indignation—comic, coy, and vehement in her repudiation of social injustices. She adopts the epistolary form in all of its literary manifestations in the Renaissance—as poetic debate, familiar letter, verse epistle, elegy— to engage in a conversation with her male contemporaries.

The goal of this book, then, is to present the many paradoxical layers in sixteenth-century portrayals of the honest courtesan by reconstructing, with the aid of a variety of historical, textual, visual, and archival mate- rials, the specific relations between one honest courtesan and the cultural, social and economic contexts in which she lived. Sixteenth-century male representations of the courtesan's livelihood have obscured the important connections between the difficult material conditions of a courtesan's life and the terms of a courtesan's literary self-presentation. This has also been true of latter-day cultural historians and literary critics of Franco's oeuvre. Thus I have asked throughout this study what was at stake, and for whom, in viewing the courtesan as merely a sexual commodity rather than as a writer who participated in important intellectual coteries in Venice and who published her works.

Veronica Franco understood that to enter the public arena as a woman and a courtesan was to take part in a "theater of public competition," nor- mally denied to Renaissance women.[8] She calls attention in her *Terze rime* to this public stage by reminding her masked male antagonist that for him to enter into direct battle with her is to risk losing face not only in the social but also in the textual arena. In capitolo 16 in the *Terze rime,* for example, Franco proudly denounces her antagonist's poetic and linguistic arsenal that he used to vilify her as a vulgar whore. She performs a critical reading of his vituperative poem; most importantly, she insists on defending other women and on setting "an example for them to follow."

One

SATIRIZING THE COURTESAN: FRANCO'S ENEMIES

La nutrice de l'altre città {Venice} e la madre eletta da Dio per fare più famoso il mondo, per raddolcire le consuetudini per dare umanità a l'uomo e per umiliare i superbi, perdonando a gli erranti. *
Pietro Aretino, *Il primo libro delle lettere* (1537)

Più minacciosa della folgore, più orrenda del terremoto, più velenoso del serpe . . . perché è cosa troppo chiara e manifesta che l'amor delle cortigiane non cagiona altro che miseria e infelicità per fine de' suoi piaceri. Vadino dunque tutte le cortigiane in chiasso, e gli huomini saggi e prudenti attendono ad altri studi. †
Tomaso Garzoni, *La Piazza universale di tutte le professioni del mondo* (1585)

When foreign travelers visited Venice throughout the early modern period, few failed to marvel at the large numbers of courtesans in the city. The eccentric Englishman, Thomas Coryat, exclaimed with astonishment that there were as many as twenty thousand courtesans in Venice in 1608: "As for the number of these Venetian Cortezans it is very great. For it is thought there are of them in the whole City and other adiacent places, as Murano, Malomocco, &c. at the least twenty thousand, whereof many are esteemed so loose, that they are said to open their quivers to every arrow." [1] Already in the early sixteenth century, Marin Sanuto, a Venetian patrician and famed Venetian diarist, recorded with alarm that there were 11,654 prostitutes in a city of 100,000 people. [2] And yet hearing of the large number of prostitutes in Venice will not surprise anyone familiar with the city's long-lived image as a haven of loose morals and beautiful women. Contributing to this image, perhaps by exaggerating the numbers of prostitutes and courtesans

---

*A nurse to their cities and a mother elected by God to add to the world's fame, to soften mores, to bestow humanity on mankind, and to humble the haughty by forgiving the errant.

†More menacing than a lightning bolt, more horrifying than an earthquake, more venomous than a snake—for it is only too clear and manifest that the love of courtesans brings nothing but wretchedness and unhappiness in the wake of its pleasures. So leave all courtesans to the brothel and let wise and prudent men devote themselves to other studies.

in their reports, early modern travelers' diaries, letters, and travel accounts feature the courtesan as one of the republic's obligatory, although suspect, tourist attractions. Propelled by an insatiable curiosity, male tourists allegedly traveled great distances just to verify for themselves whether the courtesans' reputed beauty was fiction or fact. Coryat remarked that "so infinite are the allurements of these amorous Calypsoes, that the fame of them hath drawn many to Venice from some of the remotest parts of Christendome, to contemplate their beauties, and enjoy their pleasing dalliances."[3]

Paradoxically, foreign travelers' descriptions of the scenes of Venetian daily life, in which the courtesan assumes a prominent place, often follow their praises of Venice as an exemplum of civic and social concord.[4] Organized as a multitude of magistracies and councils, the republic was ruled by a doge, elected for life by a closed corporation who formed the membership of the Maggior Consiglio (Great Council)—the patricians' corporate body—and other lesser offices. The Collegio was the most authoritative body, including twenty-six members by the sixteenth century. It acted as the steering committee of the Senate and was made up of the doge, six councillors from each district in Venice, three heads of the Quarantia (the forty-man appeals court for criminal and civil cases), sixteen *savi,* the Council of Ten (the most prestigious of Venetian magistracies), which by the sixteenth century dealt not only with state security but also foreign policy and finance, and the Pregadi, or the Senate. The Venetian Senate (from 150 to 200 members), with its "College of Sages," included five *savi grandi* (great sages), five *savi agli ordini* for maritime affairs, and five responsible for military affairs on the mainland or *terraferma.* In theory all political decisions were made in the name of a government agency or a council, with the authority of the entire government supporting them. Individual opinion was subordinated to a collective will, thereby giving the impression of unity and common will. While the "unruly" presence of courtesans in Venice might appear to be at odds with the view that the republic epitomized a well-governed state, many English Commonwealth visitors over the centuries regarded the city as a model of wise leadership, constitutional excellence, and careful law enforcement.[5] Indeed this paradoxical combination of social and political fictions endured until the time of Casanova.

Both the social myth of Venetian pleasure seeking and the civic myth of Venice's unmatched political harmony place a symbolic female figure in central position.[6] In the sixteenth century, the female icon of Venice, depicting the republic's unmatched social and political concord, joined in one civic figure a representation of Justice or Dea Roma with the Virgin Mary and Venus Anadyomene.[7] Prominently displayed in all public forms of Venetian life—the visual arts (painting, sculpture, and public buildings), musical settings, ritual and pageantry, occasional and patriotic poetry— this icon was designed to remind all visitors and citizens that Venice was founded miraculously, according to legend, on the day of the Annunciation to the Virgin (25 March), and born like a Venus Anadyomene from the sea, pure and inviolate.[8] Further, the myth asserts that the city was divinely chosen as Christian successor to ancient Rome for having successfully combined three forms of government (democracy, oligarchy, and monarchy) into one well-balanced state.[9]

The artistic decorations adorning Venice's government and religious buildings in Piazza San Marco celebrate this transcendent female icon and the singular properties of the Venetian republic. Located at the heart of Venetian public, ceremonial, and political life—a domain restricted to men—representing the Christological and secular components of the civic myth, this polyvalent icon appears on the facades and in the interiors of the Basilica of San Marco, the adjacent Ducal Palace, the Loggetta, and the Libreria Sansoviniana.[10] Commemorating the Serenissima's divine origins, this icon also celebrates Venus, the secular goddess of love.[11] In Paolo Veronese's ceiling allegory, *The Apotheosis of Venice,* painted in 1579 for the Sala del Maggior Consiglio in the Ducal Palace, the room where the doge welcomed foreign dignitaries, the female personification of the republic assumes her secular powers; she sits majestically on an elevated throne surrounded by her loyal and adoring citizens and flanked by flying Victories. Exalted to the status of virginal ruler, and crowned with a laurel wreath by a figure representing victory, "Venetia" triumphantly wields power, with staff in hand, over the cities and provinces (represented directly below her) that she oversees and protects. As a conflation of sacred and secular icons, this secularized Venus occupies the sacred role of Virgin intercessor. Indeed she shields her citizens from the irruption of foreign invasions and guards them from potential corruption from outside and alien forces.[12] Created by Venetian patricians in support of their claim to natural heredity, but "championed as well by adopted foreigners, conquered subjects and parvenù citizens," the Venetian civic myth during the Renaissance took hold over contemporary imaginations.[13]

This idealized female icon portraying the founding myth of Venice welcomed Thomas Coryat on his architectural, artistic tour through the island republic. Immediately upon his return to England, he published a tantalizing account of his five-week Venetian sojourn as: "My observations of the most glorious, peerlesse, and mayden citie of Venice: I call it mayden because it was never conquered." Also distracted, however, by certain of the republic's more profane citizens, who infiltrated the public spaces restricted to upper-class male use, Coryat offers, in addition, more than ten pages in his *Crudities* to, as he calls it, "a deciphered and as it were anatomized description" of the Venetian courtesan's profession. Perhaps because he exhibits such an inordinate fascination with the courtesan's activities, he ensures that he excuses himself in his closing remarks so as to ward off "scandalous imputations of many carping Criticks," who "will taxe me for luxury and wantonnesse."[14] After his foray onto illicit ground, Coryat returns obediently to his initial purpose of summarizing, at the end of the section devoted to Venice, the city's most prized characteristics. His summary includes all of the civic myth's most traditionally acclaimed virginal attributes: "and so at length I finish the treatise of this incomparable city, this most beautifull Queene, this untainted virgine, this Paradise, this Tempe, this rich Diademe and most flourishing garland of Christendome."[15] If the presence of women at the symbolic center of Venetian patriarchal life appeared to be a sign of their increased presence in Venetian society, it was only a mythical presence. Indeed as late as 1651 an English visitor "recapitulated the mythical attributes," this time calling attention, however, to the republic's unparalleled beauty, its profane Venus. James Howell's vision of Venice ("Upon the Citty and Signorie of Venice") in his *S.P.Q.V., a Survey of the Signorie of Venice, of Her Admired Policy, and Method of Government . . .* places comic emphasis on Venice as impregnable sovereign and sexualized Venus, playing as well with allusions to the Roman Republic's motto SPQR (Senatus Populusque Romanum):

> Could any State on Earth Immortall be,
> Venice by Her rare Government is she;
> Venice Great Neptunes Minion, still a Mayd,
> Though by the warrlikst Potentats assayed;
> Yet She retaines Her Virgin-waters pure,
> Nor any Forren mixtures can endure;
> Though, Syren-like on Shore and Sea, Her Face
> Enchants all those whom once She doth embrace,
> Nor is ther any can Her beauty prize
> But he who hath beheld Her with his Eyes:
> Those following Leaves display, if well observed,
> How she so long Her Maydenhead preserved,
> How for sound prudence She still bore the Bell;
> Whence may be drawn this high-fetched parallel,

Venus and Venice are Great Queens in their degree,
Venus is Queen of Love, Venice of Policie. [16]

The power of the virginal queen depicted in Veronese's allegory at the one extreme of this mythic icon and the unruly licentiousness of Venus at the other contrast sharply with the highly regimented and restricted lives of most sixteenth-century Venetian women of all classes. Women possessed virtually no political power of their own, owing to an oligarchy dominated by men, and the laws passed by men reveal not only a class bias but a special arrogance toward women. [17] Upper-class married womens' activities were carefully regulated by their husbands, and government officials, who feared political and social disturbance, repeatedly monitored courtesans' dress, expenditures, and public appearances, apparently not always with success. [18] Indeed sixteenth-century women's lives were hardly immune to, or protected from, social and personal oppression. Contrary to the mythical image of the courtesan as irresponsible or wayward that was presented in European travelers' accounts, Venetian courtesans, whether of the *cittadino* or lower classes, did not choose prostitution over other professions but were forced into it principally out of economic necessity. In a society in which arranging a reputable marriage for a young woman had become increasingly, even prohibitively, expensive as a result of the inflation of dowries, not to mention politically problematic for the upper classes, many Venetian girls were introduced to prostitution at a very young age by their aging mothers, who were in need of financial assistance. Veronica Franco was herself the daughter of an impoverished courtesan. [19]

While the highly visible female icon purportedly announced to Venetian citizens and foreign travelers Venice's unparalleled social and political freedoms, women themselves were far from free to participate in Venetian public and civic life. When it served the republic's civic needs, however, both the elegant aristocratic woman and the sophisticated honest courtesan were fêted as symbols of Venice's liberty, justice, and splendor. But courtesans were seldom championed by their fellow citizens as earthly Venuses worthy of praise. Frequently they were the victims of envious men who competed with them for public attention and in some cases literary acclaim. Unleashing their anger toward the upwardly mobile courtesan, Venetian men, especially those insecure in their own social standing, sought to expose the courtesan's "misdeeds" by denouncing her in legal arenas or defaming her in satirical invectives.

The Venetian civic myth tells a powerful story about Venetian male patricians' image of themselves and others. The role that the myth played as an idealized and ideologically motivated cultural fiction that the Venetian republic adopted about itself, repeated and promoted in countless patriotic panegyrics and rhapsodic tourist accounts, is a subject that has received a great deal of scholarly attention.[20] Although recent historical studies advocate skepticism toward the civic myth as a historical measure for Venetian practices and government politics in the early modern period, no studies to date have spoken about the symbolic resonance of the immaculate icon for a woman citizen and writer at that time. When we look at the civic myth from this point of view, many elements of the myth take on different meanings. Veronica Franco, a *cittadina* and a courtesan poet, adapts courtly encomiums to civic pride;[21] she uses the immaculate female icon to overturn male satirical representations of the vulgar courtesan and to protect a public persona, while reminding her reader of the enormous difficulties a woman encounters when she seeks access to public arenas traditionally reserved for men.[22] Because the honest courtesan attempted to position herself at Venice's public center, both in her literary activities as writer and editor and in her public interactions with celebrated visitors to the republic, she provoked negative responses from many male contemporaries. They denounced the courtesan's participation in Venetian public and intellectual life. And to do so, they drew their satirical arsenal from the polarized extremes of angel and whore embodied in the civic icon. As we shall see, in Franco's life and in her literary works, she seeks to counter negative representations of the courtesan's profession by questioning the ideological separation of woman into angel or whore and by instead investing each term with positive meaning. In her self-representation she insists on intellectual and social freedoms to satisfy emotional and economic needs—a right often denied Renaissance women.

To a considerable extent, however, the social myths announcing Venetian pleasure seeking did, on the face of it, mirror the general permissiveness of Venetian daily life that most certainly would have struck any visitor to the Serenissima. From the vantage point of foreign travelers, there were increasing numbers of Venetian prostitutes and courtesans in the city, a circumstance seemingly tolerated by Venetian officials. Despite this scene of "misrule," when compared to other Italian cities, Venice enjoyed relative peace, stability, and social cohesion in the sixteenth century—a period when the rest of Italy was divided by citizen uprisings, and when Europe was in violent battle for territorial expansion.[23] But even when Venetian social and political fictions diverged from historical truth, they nonetheless sustained a tenacious grip on foreigners' and Venetians' ways of understanding the truth. The dualism of the Venetian civic icon in post-Tridentine Italy fostered either adulatory verses in praise of idealized, chaste women or punitive, defamatory charges directed against immoral ones.[24]

Thus, rather than being championed by many male contemporaries, the courtesan was used repeatedly in late sixteenth-century Venice as a satirical outlet for male authors increasingly uneasy about their own relationship to Venetian authority and patronage. Further, Venetian male authors' satirical representations of the courtesan reveal a mistrust, even envy, of the courtesan's claim to public estimation and her desire for literary acclaim. Franco's interactions with the prestigious Venier academy and her affiliation with patrician intellectuals often engendered spiteful and injurious attacks.

The complexity of attitudes regarding the Venetian courtesan's public entrance into Venetian society is nowhere more evident than in the complicated web of interactions between members of the patrician Venier family triangle. At the summit of this hierarchical triangle was the patriarch, Domenico (1517–82), and at the two opposite points below him, his nephews Marco (1537–1602) and Maffio (1550–86). It is difficult to disentangle the complicated interactions between male family members, but it is certain that Veronica Franco was caught between Venier patriarchs in a struggle for power and authority.[25] Perhaps because she captured the attention of the prominent literary patron Domenico Venier and profited from his tutelage, Maffio, the self-appointed outcast of the family, was bitterly envious and thus mercilessly sought revenge. One of the most powerful noble clans of Venice, the Venier family continually occupied important political and intellectual positions throughout the sixteenth century. After relinquishing his duty as senator in 1546 because of his physical infirmity, Domenico Venier became the central figure in an informal literary academy that met regularly at his private home, Ca' Venier. In many of Franco's letters, presumably to Domenico Venier, which she published in her *Lettere familiari a diversi* in 1580, she refers to "insulse" (insults) directed against her, and to legal "cause" (cases) for which Domenico presumably offered his "cortese protezzion" (courteous protection).[26]

Venice was certainly not unique in fostering literary attacks on prostitutes. However, few Italian cities posit an immaculate and profane icon at their mythical center. The representation of the Venetian courtesan in male authors' texts intersects with the virginal civic icon signifying Venetian "libertà." Equating the evils and vanities of the court and courtier with the courtesan, sixteenth-century authors residing in Venice exalted their own social and intellectual stature by degrading hers. This situation parallels the one Alvin Kernan attributes to eighteenth-century antifeminist satirists, who combined wit with aggression in order to rein in, yet legitimate, their own destructive impulses.[27] It also echoes Felicity Nussbaum's analysis of misogynist satire of the Augustan period, in which such satire is permitted only if it is directed "against the things [the satirist] most fears": "Aside from the motives of the particular historical moment, there may be within satire an atemporal motive to cope with the satirist's deepest fears through attacking his victim with wordplay. The satirist may be attempting to expel, or at least to project, that portion of his self which he finds most reprehensible."[28]

Similarly, Venetian authors of the sixteenth century (as Michael Seidel claims about English satirists of the same period), "attempt to expel, or at least to project," their ambivalent feelings about the dynamics of patronage onto the courtesan. They transform her from the celebrated Venus Anadyomene (born from the waters) into the embodiment of a world fueled by an unrestrained desire for wealth, profit, and personal ambition. Far from the idealizing civic icon—the Virginal Venus who protects Venetian male citizens' self-acclaimed "libertà"—the portrait of the Venetian courtesan promoted in the works of Pietro Aretino and of Lorenzo and Maffio Venier bespeaks anarchy. Hers is a world, they contend, where corruption, deceit, and lasciviousness reign.[29]

Pietro Aretino's pornographic dialogues, the *Ragionamenti*, or *Sei giornate*, published in 1534 and 1536, and the scurrilous satirical poems of his protégé, Lorenzo Venier, both use the courtesan as a symbol of moral, economic, and social disruption. Their formulation of a new genre of pornographic writing, which pointed to the ambiguous status of prostitutes and courtesans in Venetian society, provided a paradigm for subsequent writing both on prostitutes and by courtesans. Aretino and Lorenzo Venier spare no one in their attacks: the Church, the court, the chastity of the clergy, and the prostitute all receive satiric blows. To the question of whether the young woman Pippa should follow the "profession" of nun, married woman, or prostitute, Nanna, the former prostitute and mother of the girl in question, responds unwaveringly that the only "honest" profession is that of the prostitute. Lorenzo's son's bawdy verses, composed in the 1570s in Venetian dialect, take the generalized social criticism of his father and transform it into increasingly personalized invectives. No longer broad satirical reproaches, they are now directed at identified victims. Indeed he points his venomous verses specifically against the courtesan Veronica

Franco. Further, Maffio Venier's satirical invectives denounce the profession of the courtesan at the same time that they parody the discourse of the Petrarchan male-lover poet as used in Franco's *Terze rime*.[30]

In all of these authors' works we can trace both a growing mistrust and hatred of the courtesan and a maturing literary genre that used the courtesan as an object of satiric and parodic reproach. Aretino uses the courtesan to denounce both the abject servility of the courtier he so abhors and the moral corruption of the court. Similarly, the courtesan provided Lorenzo and Maffio Venier with a literary pretext: onto her they deflected their personal anxieties regarding patronage, poverty, and disease. When they did so, they found a chorus of disapproval to support them, especially among certain moralistic foreign visitors, who voiced dismay at the republic's tolerance of such "wayward wantons." Canon Pietro Casola, a Milanese pilgrim on his way to the Holy Land, as early as 1494 commented with dismay not specifically on a courtesan's dress and demeanor but on all Venetian women's lascivious dress, which he separates into distinct categories of "high" and "low":

> They paint their faces a great deal, and also the other parts they show, in order to appear more beautiful. . . . Above all,—at least indoors. These Venetian women, both high and low, have pleasure in being seen and looked at; they are not afraid of the flies biting them, and therefore they are in no great hurry to cover themselves if a man comes upon them unexpectedly. . . . Perhaps this custom pleases others; it does not please me. I am a priest in the way of the saints, and I had no wish to inquire further into their lives.[31]

Certainly Casola's wish not to "inquire further into their lives" distinguished him from most male visitors, who preferred to see the courtesan as a symbol of the Venetian myth of social freedom. While many did not welcome the Venetian courtesan's participation in public, civic affairs, either because they simply disapproved of her livelihood on moral grounds or because they feared succumbing to her seductive allure, few failed to inquire into the "nature" of her profession. Sir Henry Wotton, English ambassador to Venice for over ten years, reportedly fled the city in 1591, during his first trip there, because "he found the climate of the city unwholesome, and 'not being made of stone' he felt he could not trust himself among the famous Venetian courtesans."[32] Montaigne, a traveler who wanted to verify for himself the legend of Venetian women's unparalleled beauty, was less shocked by the courtesan's licentiousness than surprised by her exacting professionalism. He begrudgingly noted in his *Journal de voyage* (1580) that Venetian courtesans not only charged a standard fee for the "négotiation entière" (whole deal) but charged a separate fee for conversation alone.[33] Further, as his travel companion and secretary reported, they were not even the celebrated beauties Montaigne had hoped to find: "Il n'y trouva pas ceste fameuse beauté qu'on attribue aus dames de Venise" (he did not find there the famous beauty that is attributed to Venetian women).[34] Montaigne admired courtesans' commercial success, evident, among other things that he notes, in their lavish costumes: "et vit les plus nobles de celles qui en font traficque; mais cela lui sembla autant admirable . . . d'en voir un tel nombre, comme de cent cinquante ou environ, faisant une depense en meubles et vestemans de princesses; n'ayant autres fons a se maintenir que de ceste traficque" (and he saw the prominent among those who are active in the profession; but it still surprised him—that there should be such a huge number of them, close to 150 who splurge on furnishings and garments worthy of princesses; for they had no other source of income than this profession).[35] Coryat, instead of marveling at the courtesan's success, purportedly sought to protect the innocent traveler, like himself, from her seductive "arts," by offering his reader the advice "Lipsius did to a friend of his that was to travell into Italy":

> As for thine eyes, shut them and turne them aside from these ven-
> ereous Venetian obiects. For they are double windowes that con-
> veigh them to thy heart. Also thou must fortifie thine eares against
> the attractive inchauntments of their plausible speeches. . . . so
> doe thou only breath a few words upon them and presently be gone
> from them: for if thou dost linger with them thou wilt finde their
> poyson to be more pernicious than that of the scorpion, aspe, or
> cocatrice.[36]

Worthy of marvel but more often viewed as an object of moral reprehension, the Venetian courtesan in both travelers' accounts and Venetian male satirists' texts often receives much of the blame for the republic's lavish displays of wealth and power throughout the sixteenth century. When, in 1575, the plague killed a large percentage of the population, forcing all citizens to pray to God to release them from what they perceived to be his vindictive wrath, male poets transformed the virginal icon into a bejeweled venal whore. Maffio Venier, one of Franco's most vehement attackers, wrote a canzone on the plague in which he decried this moral and physical corruption:

Or le tue belle membra e 'l crine adorno
d'oro, di perle e d'ostro
forman di vaga ninfa orrido mostro.

Now your beautiful limbs and tresses adorned with gold
and pearls and crimson cloth turn a lovely nymph
into a horrid monster.

The Venetian upper classes were much less chastised for *luxuria*.[37]

For foreign traveler and envious Venetian writer alike, the courtesan embodied the evils of a mercantile society concerned principally with making a profit—a world where the allure of money corrupted human relationships and even the basic fabric of society. For Coryat the courtesan was the single blemish on an otherwise perfect city. He remarks, "A most ungodly thing without doubt that there should be a tolleration of such licentious wantons in so glorious, so potent, so renowned a City." Yet he chastises the woman, not the city, for flaunting her "wantonness" shamelessly.[38] Confessing, at the end of his description of Venice, that he did indeed succumb to his curiosity by visiting a courtesan during his stay in the Serenissima, he hurriedly informs his reader that this meeting afforded him the welcome opportunity to test the power and efficacy of his oratorical arts (for which he was admired by his contemporaries). Although unsuccessful in persuading the courtesan, Margarita Emiliani, to live a more "virtuous" life, his visit with her permitted him a close-up scrutiny of the courtesan's style of life: "In like manner I both wished the conversion of the Courtezan that I saw, and did my endevour by perswasive termes to convert her, though my speeches could not take the like effect that those of Panutius did to Thais."[39]

The acute foreign observer of Venetian social practices attempted to offer his reader more than a voyeuristic description of the courtesan's profession. Not all observers were satisfied that the city's aesthetic facade and social life based on pleasure and leisure activities were entirely what they seemed on the surface. On closer inspection, Fynes Moryson (1566–1630), in his *Itinerary Containing his Ten Yeeres Travell* (London, 1617), perceived that the overwhelming presence and demand for female prostitutes, not to mention the more refined *cortigiana onesta,* was not merely a product of the republic's reputed sexual license but rather was tied to the repressed physical desires of young or married men.[40] He observed that "men of all sortes" are driven

> with fierce affections to forbidden lusts, and to those most which
> are most forbidden, most kept from them, and with greatest cost
> and danger to be obtayned. And because they are barred not only

the speech and conversation but the least sight of their love (all which are allowed men of other nations) they are carryed rather with a blynde rage of passion . . . to adore them as Images, rather than love them as wemen. And as nowe they spare no cost, and will runne great dangers to obtayne their lustfull desyres, so would they persue them to very madnes, had they not the most naturall remedy of this passion ready at hand to allay their desyres, namely Harlotts, whom they call Curtizans, having beauty and youth and whatsoever they can imagine in their mistres.[41]

Coryat had also taken note of the unusually severe restrictions imposed by Venetian husbands on their wives' movements, "For the Gentlemen do even coope up their wives alwaies within the walles of their houses for feare of these inconveniences. . . . So that you shall very seldome see a Venetian Gentlemans wife but either at the solemnization of a great marriage, or at the Christning of a Iew, or late in the evening rowing in a Gondola."[42] Wanting to protect their wives' chastity, which was tantamount to their own honor, Venetian men confined them, he notes, to the private space of the palace complex: "For they thinke that the chastity of their wives would be the sooner assaulted, and so consequently they would be capricornified."[43] And yet if Venetian patricians were truly intent on ridding the city of corrupting influences on noblewomen, all they would have to do, Coryat adds, is to eliminate the presence of courtesans from Venice. But as he shrewdly observes, the Venetian government sought to profit from this "most ungodly thing" by collecting a sizable tax from courtesans, and "the revenues which they pay unto the Senate for their tolleration, doe maintaine a dozen of their galleys, (as many reported unto me in Venice) and so save them a great charge."[44]

Recent sociohistorical studies confirm many of these early reporters' observations. Young Venetian men were forced to channel their sexual needs into areas of sexuality unsanctioned by the state, but at the same time Venetian authorities tolerated courtesans' "corrupting" influence because it provided the republic with a commercial asset.[45] Official sexual ideologies restricted respectable women's movements, and the sociopolitical, economic, and familial constraints governing marriage (especially for the upper classes)—the institution most favored by the Venetian republic—made licit outlets for sexuality difficult.[46] An exploitative use of female sexuality in the form of the courtesan, in particular the more common and less well paid prostitute, was intended, as Guido Ruggiero demonstrates in his sociohistorical study on sexual crimes in Renaissance Venice, to "meet the sexual needs of young males and partially to keep adolescent sexuality from doing even greater damage to society and family."[47] Leah Lydia Otis's observations regarding prostitution in medieval Languedoc, although pertaining to earlier centuries and a different country, are nonetheless pertinent for understanding the social climate in sixteenth-century Venice. She claims that the ever-increasing demand for female prostitutes owed as much to the urban context as to the specific economic exigencies of a mercantile, port city:

> The amplitude of the demand comes from the nature of the social groups there (communities of traveling merchants, large groups of unmarried young men) as well as from the scale of the population, and payment is facilitated by cash flow, characteristic of urban exchange economies. These conditions are, of course, not sufficient unless there is a greater tolerance for male than for female sexual activity.[48]

The growing numbers of female prostitutes in sixteenth-century Venice, although certainly tied to the practice of late marriage for men (especially at the upper social levels) and to the increasing mercantile fluidity of an urban, capitalist economy, can also be explained in terms of a government that tended to overlook female prostitution when faced with other sexual crimes—adultery, fornication, and rape—which they deemed more serious. But rather than interpret Venetian authorities' acceptance or tolerance of prostitutes and courtesans as a sign of an unusually liberal social policy, I would argue, following Ruggiero's lead, that female prostitution was less severely punished because it eased the severe socioeconomic problems facing sixteenth-century Venetian society. In Ruggiero's words, "by capitalizing on the sexuality of young women who did not have the economic status to fit into society through the normal dowry system . . . society created a secondary sexual economy that safely incorporated the sexuality of young women too poor to participate in the primary system."[49] Although officials regarded all illicit sexuality as deviant, they did so "not so much because [it] threatened public morals," as Ruggiero reminds us, "but because [it] undermined society's most basic institutions of marriage and family."[50]

The comparatively light punishments for heterosexual offences such as fornication and adultery, in contrast with those for sodomy, make it clear that officials viewed adultery, fornication, and rape as relatively permissible outlets for male desire. Similarly, they regarded adultery and fornication as necessary evils because both sexual crimes created, paradoxically, quasi-familial relationships.[51] Further, rape was, they believed, a substitute for courtship because the offender could escape penalty by marrying his victim. Only sodomy was seen as a severe threat to the patrician civic myth of social harmony and concord. Considered a direct offense to God, and hence radically subversive of the stability of the republic, sodomy was the object of legislative rulings throughout the early modern period, in contrast to much less serious efforts to resolve the exploitation of women's sexuality.[52] This commercialization of eros and the commercialization of a woman's body stem from a society, Otis claims, that has "an ambivalent attitude to sexuality . . . an ambivalent attitude toward material gain . . . and an ambivalent attitude toward women (honored for Mary's sake, despised for Eve's).[53]

In this sense the female civic icon of Venice may be seen as harboring negative content. Indeed the very ideology that insists on exalting Venice as a female paragon of transcendent virtue is the same one that condemns women. In the sixteenth century Venice witnessed an unprecedented rise in the number of women from differing social classes who published their works. Notwithstanding this, the dominant cultural myths regarding women as angel at the one extreme and whore at the other continued to shape the standard ways in which early modern authors conceived of and represented female sexuality in their published works.[54]

II

While certain foreign tourists to Venice attempted to explain to themselves and to their readers the reasons underlying Venetian libertinism, Italian travelers to Venice, newly settled residents, and Venetian patricians publicly pronounced their moral condemnation of the courtesan's profession. Local observers were deeply troubled by the courtesan's crossing of invisible social boundaries. In Venetian patricians' treatises and citizens' literary dialogues of the latter half of the sixteenth century, they counseled unsuspecting young male visitors to Venice against falling into the courtesan's seductive trap. Francesco Sansovino's *Ragionamento . . . nel quale brevemente s'insegna a giovani huomini la bella arte d'amore* (Lectures . . . by which young men are taught briefly the beautiful art of loving) (Venice, 1545) reminds the young male listener that while he must always respect women ("tu le sia riverente, benigno, piacevole, liberale, modesto, e leale" [you shall be reverent with her, pleasant, generous, modest, and honest]), he must also be careful to avoid any association with courtesans:

24

quelle donne che per picciol pregio vendano lor medesime indegnamente ap-
pellate Cortegiane, che usurpano l'altrui roba, che stanno sommersi e per-
duti nell'otio, che son lievi e volubili come le foglie, che con le parole
offendano l'Ott. Mass. Dio che hanno pronta la lingua a i vituperi di
questo o di quello. [55]

Women who sell themselves for a small price, [are] unworthy of
being called courtesans; [they] usurp the property of others, live
immersed and lost in idleness, their words offend our supreme,
most Excellent Lord, hav[ing] a quick tongue when it comes to vi-
tuperating this person or that.

And in Sperone Speroni's *Orazione contra le cortegiane* (1575), directed to
an imaginary courtesan whom he intends to denounce and to a reading
public whom he wants to persuade of her wrongdoing, he reduces courtesanry,
"una antica, ma vile e sozza professione" (an ancient, but vile and filthy,
profession) to a vulgar and pathetic level. Indeed the often excited, moralistic commentary that began to appear in the sixteenth century praising or
decrying the courtesan's freedom of social movement reflected Renaissance
authors' uneasiness about their own relationships to social hierarchies not
always working in their favor. Speroni, for example, was forced by Roman
censors to rewrite his earlier *Dialogo d'amore* (1542), in which the courtesan
Tullia d'Aragona is a central speaker. Thus, this oration contains all of the
most typical Counter-Reformation charges brought against courtesans.
Written on demand in order to appease his Roman patrons ("Ne però debbo
tacere, sì perché il de mi è commesso, e tocca a me ubbidire" [nor may I
remain silent, for those are my orders and I must obey]), Speroni's oration
points to the obstacles he faced in the increasingly reactionary climate of
Rome in the 1570s when he tried to reprint his *Dialoghi.* He denounces in
the courtesan his own failed desire for, and efforts toward, autonomy. Further, this oration offers us an interesting reversal not only of Speroni's earlier dialogue, written in the first half of the century before the restrictions
of the Index of Prohibited Books were enforced in 1571, but also a reworking of an earlier, more optimistic oration in praise of courtesans by the Venetian poet Antonio Brocardo. [56]

The first part of Speroni's oration charges the courtesan with evil practices by contrasting her to virtuous women throughout history:

Quanto mal faccia la Cortigiana, mentre falsando con rei costumi incivili
la sua natia gentilezza, vive una vita sì vergognosa, che bene, o male, che
glie ne avvegna, diviene indegna egualmente di compassione, e d'invidia.
(169)

> So much evil is done by the courtesan when betraying her innate
> sweetness with depraved and uncivilized behavior; she lives such a
> shameless life that whether she profits or loses by it she becomes
> equally undeserving of compassion and of envy.

Like Boccaccio before him, Speroni cites female worthies (Penelope, Artemisia, Zenobia, Diana, and others) who through their chastity, heroic virtue, or wifely fidelity have warranted the praise of centuries.[57]

In the second part of the oration, he claims that the courtesan is unworthy of "cotal voce" (her name), for it exalts her to the level of the courtier with whom she shares, in Speroni's polemic, no similarities:[58]

> *chel nome di cortigiano vien veramente da corte; e corte è albergo di cortesia, e*
> *cortesia è virtù . . . or non è dubio, che da niuna delle virtù della cortesia,*
> *non che da molte così adunate non prende il nome la Cortigiana; la quale è*
> *vuota di ogni bontà e colma di tutti i vitii . . . hor, non so come, o per qual*
> *cagione l'uso del mondo, che in fatto, e in detto è corrotto, le voglia dir*
> *Cortegiane: questo so bene, che cotai mostri infelici non sono degni di cotal*
> *voce.*

> that the name of courtier surely derives from the word court, and
> the court is the abode of courtesy, and courtesy is a virtue. . . . now
> there is no question that the courtesan does not derive her name
> from the virtues of courtesy or any others thus acquired for she is
> devoid of all good and chock-full of vices. . . . Now I do not know
> how or why it is customary for the world in which both word and
> deed are corrupt to insist on calling them courtesans. I know with-
> out a doubt that those wretched monsters are unworthy of such a
> name.

They are motivated only by a fear of poverty: "lor vita vituperosa dicono alcune non esser altra, che la paura, che si de' haver della povertà, fonte e principio d'ogni materia, e però degna di essere fuggita" (some of them claim that their shameful life is nothing but a fear of poverty, the source and root of all misery [187]). But they are incapable of finding a remedy to this predicament through art, as does the courtier: "fugge ogni artista colla sua arte la povertà, et la fame" (all artists try to escape poverty and hunger by their art [187]). The courtesan, he writes, wants merely to satisfy her appetites and vanity: "non tanto fugge la fame quanto ella segue l'amor del gusto (189–90) . . . ma ella dura sì fatta pena per guadagnarsi da empier la golla di cibo, et vini a sua scielta, et parte ancora per addobarsi superbamente" (she is not so much trying to escape hunger as following her love for pleasure . . . to fill her gullet with food and choice wines and also to adorn herself superbly [191]). However, instead of embodying fullness or abundance, she represents merely deprivation and sickness.

After a vicious condemnation of her many "immoral" practices, where the potential for men's attraction to "destructive" elements are turned into attacks on the female sex, he concludes by turning his pointed remarks directly to one of these "miserelle" (poor wretches). In the course of the oration, he has lowered her still further, from courtesan to prostitute:

> *Cortegiana non vuol dir altro che meretrice . . . la Cortegiania delle peccatrici è in molti luoghi per tutta Italia, ove hora Corte non ha; ma ben vi ha case, et palazzi, et ove ha principe, et Corte sua, già non son proprie de Cortigiani le meretrici; ma allor communi, e alla plebe (192).*

> Courtesan means nothing but prostitute . . . the courtesanry of these sinners is to be found all over Italy where, at present, it cannot lay claim to a Court but indeed owns houses and palaces, and wherever there is a prince with his court, the prostitutes do not belong to the courtiers but are shared by them and by the populace.

He feels no measure of compassion for the pitiable state he has just described but rather strikes one final walloping blow: he mocks her for believing that the profession of courtesan can ever afford her the independence or status of "signora" she so desires:

> *Credi tu forse, che la tua vita licentiosa si debba dir signorile, perché l'hai sciolta dalla ragione, et fai di lei a tua voglia? Veramente troppo t'inganna questa credenza, perciochè in tale et sì fatta vita, tu non sei libera pur un punto, non che signora. (206–7)*

> Do you think perhaps that your licentious life can be called genteel because you have released it from reason and do with it as you please? This belief of yours is most certainly deceiving you because within your present kind of life you are not at all free and much less are you a lady.

By daring to disdain the patriarchal institutions made available to her—marriage, charitable institutions, or religious seclusion[59]—she has subjected herself and her body to another's desires, whom he also accuses of being "servo" (servant) to the devil; she has become forever servile to another's tyranny; "ben sei tu serva e in prigione di tanto numero di tiranni, quanti ha dimoni un inferno" (but you are enslaved and the prisoner of as many demons as there are in hell [206–7]). Using a sociopolitical rhetoric that Venetians proud of their self-acclaimed "libertà" would appreciate, but that Speroni himself was forced to relinquish in rewriting his oration, he denounces her for believing that she has gained personal freedom:

> *Libera tu Signora, tu miserella? Non hai membro sulla persona, che non sia servo di tutto 'l popolo: Forse ti vanti di dominarlo, che dì et notte ti viene a casa ad ogn'hora con mani piene di ariento et oro? . . . non è tributo, ma pagamento per comperarti. Dunque tu servi, non signoreggi: è ben vero, chel tuo patrone è anche servo con esso teco al dimonio, che tien legati ambedue; lui col diletto, che egli ha di te; et te coll'utile, che ne traggi; l'oro et l'ariento, che tu li costi, son per te ceppi, et catene perché ti paia di trionfar nella servitù, e non ti caglia di liberarti. (208)*

A free woman, you lady, you poor wretch? And yet there is not a limb of your body that is not at the service of an entire populace. Perhaps you flatter yourself that you are in command and that in the night he comes to your house at all hours with hands full of silver and gold? . . . That is no tribute but rather your payment for your services: therefore you are a servant and not a master, although it is true that along with you also your master is a servant of the devil who holds you both in thrall: him through the pleasure that he takes from you, and you by the profit that you extract from him: the gold and silver that you cost him are your shackles and chains, and believing yourself triumphant in your servitude, you have no desire to free yourself.

Unlike Erasmus's dialogue between a young gentleman and a prostitute in which the male speaker demonstrates some empathy for the downtrodden prostitute whom he tries to convert, Speroni's stringent, preachy oration has a single focus and a single aim—to condemn mercilessly. Erasmus's "Dialogo di un giovane e di una meretrice" (Dialogue of a young man and a whore) (1549) even reaches comic heights when the prostitute acknowledges that her interlocutor has himself only recently "converted" from the "ciancitore" (blowhard) she once knew to a man of earnest "santità" (sanctity).[60] Further, although he has recently been in Rome, none of the corruption of the Roman court, she marvels, has diverted him from his missionary zeal:

> LUCRETIA: *Gli è il vero ciò, che tu di: ma donde ti è venuta cotesta santità; il quale solevi essere un ciancitore? Niuno veniva a me più spesso e fuori d'ogni tempo. Odo che sei stato a Roma.*

> What you say is true but how did you come by such saintliness? you who used to be such a blowhard. Nobody came to see

28

me more often and at the most inopportune time. I hear you
have been in Rome.

SOFRONIO: *Vi sono stato.*

I have been there.

LUCRETIA: *Sogliono gli huomini ritornare d'indi peggiori, non so come di
te sia avvenuto il contrario.*[61]

Men usually return from there worse than they were before; I
do not understand why the opposite has happened to you.

Thus the focus of satirical reproach in this dialogue is double, as it was also
for Pietro Aretino in his *Ragionamenti,* which he certainly bases upon this
dialogue. Prostitutes are condemned for their corrupt practices, but so are
Roman prelates, or preachers in Venice, who while hiding behind a pretense of sanctity, commit the most nefarious acts. This version of satire, as
Felicity Nussbaum has noted, hopes to correct rather than to condemn:

> Satire may be a bitter wind, painful as well as comic. In order for
> the satire to have a corrective effect, the satirist must indicate that
> women's vices do not arise so much from nature as from social and
> cultural pressures. Once this empathy with the satiric victim is
> voiced, however, the tragic turns to comic, the ill wind blows more
> kindly, and the satirist acknowledges that he too may be flawed.[62]

When Sofronio offers at the end of the dialogue to assist the prostitute in
leaving "cotesta guisa di vivere" (this type of life), he lists many of the same,
albeit limited, options dictated by Venetian patriarchs (marriage, charitable institutions, service in a patrician household, or the convent) that Speroni notes are available to a woman in sixteenth-century Venice. Each one
depends, however, on the financial generosity of either a male figure or a
well-placed noblewoman, both of whom must be committed to protecting
a young girl's honor:

LUCRETIA: *Che vuoi, ch'io faccia?*

What would you have me do?

SOFRONIO: *Che ti parti tantosto da cotesta guisa di vivere: sei ancora
giovanetta, puorsi lavare la macchia, che hai contratta; overo mari-
tarti; e io ti darò alquanto della dote; o entra in un monastero che
riceve tali fallite; overo entra in casa di qualche matrona honesta. Io ti
prometterò d'affaticarmi perché ti riesca.*[63]

Give up your way of life immediately: you are still young, the
stain that has contaminated you can still be cleansed; you

> could get married, and I shall give you part of the dowry; or
> enter one of those nunneries that take in such fallen girls, or
> become part of some honorable matron's household. I promise
> that I will make every effort to help you succeed.

While we may consider Speroni's oration as a "bitter wind," Erasmus's dialogue is "the ill wind [that] blows more kindly." What the two have in common, however, is an insistence that human dignity depends on never subjecting oneself to the irrational will of another. In this sense, the satirical topoi in these dialogues and treatises, and the language employed to ridicule the courtesan and prostitute, echo the anticourtier discourse so popular among Venetian writers proud of their self-appointed "libertà."[64]

Pietro Aretino, choosing to live in Venice near the Rialto bridge, having rejected the corrupt demands made of him by greedy Roman prelates and power-hungry princes, decried throughout his works the enforced servility of the courtier. Always careful to condemn courts in general rather than specific individuals who inhabited them, Aretino managed to protect himself from personal attack or intrigue.[65] In his letters to Venetian political leaders from whom he sought, and eventually won, overwhelming respect and support, and in his comedies and satirical dialogues, he enthusiastically embraced the social and intellectual freedom that Venice offered him. How Aretino achieved this freedom is yet another story; his letters certainly demonstrate that it required a measure of "prostituting" himself to powerful urban patrons and political leaders in order to win their approval and trust. Aretino is often read with circumspection as a slippery, meretricious, contradictory, and opportunistic character. I want also to expose Aretino's power-seeking strategies as a foil employed against other courtiers and courtesans eagerly searching for patronage and support. Aretino's famous claim that he follows only nature, taking his models from "life and truth," was extremely well received by Venetian patrons eager to promote the myth of Venetian freedom.[66] Indeed, once having firmly secured Doge Andrea Gritti's affections, Aretino wrote him a letter (1530) in which he lauded the republic's unparalleled justice by denouncing the depraved conditions at court he now so vehemently disavowed:

> *Ma io, che, ne la libertà di cotanto stato, ho fornito d'imparare a esser*
> *libero, refuto la corte in eterno, e qui faccio perpetuo tabernacolo agli anni*
> *che mi avanzano: perché qui non ha luogo il tradimento, qui il favore non*
> *può far torto al dritto, qui non regna la crudeltà de le meretrici, qui non*
> *comanda l'insolenza dei ganimedi, qui non si ruba, qui non si sforza e qui*
> *non si amazza.*[67]

> But I, who in the freedom of this state have succeeded in learning to be free, renounce the court for ever and ever, and I build here an everlasting tabernacle for my remaining years. For here treachery has no place, here favor cannot conquer right, here reigns neither the cruelty of harlots nor the insolence of the effeminate, here there is no theft, or violence, or murder.

Similarly, Tomaso Garzoni (1549–89), born in Bagnocavallo, a student in Verona and Siena, and a monk in Porto di Ravenna, dismantles the idealizing portrait of Castiglione's courtier, echoed in Speroni's praise. He insists that none of his vices may be found among "i virtuosi" (the virtuous) in Venice.[68] He would not have included Aretino, however, in such distinguished company. Indeed, in his *Teatro de vari, e diversi cervelli mondani* (1581) he criticized vehemently the lack of decorum not only in Aretino's books but also in the satires of Nicolò Franco and Ortensio Lando. They signaled to his mind the corruption evident in a society that lacked an appreciation of learning and scholarly pursuits. Garzoni uses the same opprobrious topoi he aims against courtiers to denigrate the Venetian courtesan and prostitute. Just as the courtesan devises treacherous schemes in order to acquire the capital she purportedly covets and deceives male lovers into believing that her affections are devoted to them alone so as to secure some personal gain, in the same way the court cultivates intrigue, deception, and venality. The court ratifies the courtier's flagrant pursuit of power and prestige. Further, the courtier, hypocritical in his adulation of his prince and untrustworthy in all human interactions, will undermine anyone, even one who was once his friend, if it is necessary to secure the power he covets:

> *Ma se tu trovi oggidì un cortigiano, che non sia ambitioso, et che per rispetto solo, non stenti la vita sua come un cane nelle corti de signori, bramando pur qualche ufficio, o dignità, che al fine lo rilevi, et consoli; et che oltra di ciò non sia uno adulatore, e un lusinghiere . . . per secondar la volontà del Prencipe con aperta simulatione . . . che non sia venditore della sua lingua, e de suoi passi, come un vilissimo bezzaruolo; et che facci esteriormente dell'amico, et del buon compagno con tutti al principio, per acquistar credito nella corte, e impadronirsi del Prencipe: et che non sia un malitioso e sofistico machinatore d'inganni, di calonnie, e di trovate, per sbatter questo, et ruinar quell'altro emulo . . . (529)*

> But if today you should find a courtier who is not ambitious, who merely out of self-respect, refuses to eke out a living like a dog at a gentleman's court, while he yearns for some office or title that

might at last afford him a measure of relief and comfort . . . and who besides all this is not a flatterer and a toady deferring to the prince's will with blatant simulation . . . who does not sell his tongue and his steps like some contemptible two-bit beggar; and at the outset does not pretend to be everyone's good friend and companion in order to acquire credit at court and captivate the prince; and is not a malicious and cunning fabricator of deceptions, slanders, falsehoods for the sake of beating and ruining a rival of the same ilk . . .

Furthermore, the courtier's excessive vanity emasculates him, while the courtesan's obsession with her appearance exposes her moral depravity:

> . . . che non sia tutto lindo e profumato, come un Spagnol di Valenza . . . lascivo ne' vestimenti, affettato nel passo, morbido di persona, ocioso, vano, giocatore, mentitore, bestemmiatore, dishonesto, leccardo. (529)

> . . . who is not all polished and perfumed like a Spaniard from Valencia . . . lewd in his attire, affected in his walk, with a flabby body, lazy, vain, a gambler, a liar, blasphemous, dishonest, a glutton.

Because the courtesan aligned herself with powerful patrons in order to advance in her career, and because she advertised this fact in her literary works, her rivals denounce her for mimicking the courtier's self-promoting strategies they so despise.[69] Unlike the Venetian republic, the court, Garzoni implies, is a haven of corruption, nurturing sinfulness and rewarding unleashed ambition:

> . . . oggidì molte corti non sono altro, che un collegio d'huomeni depravati, una raunanza di volpi malitiosi, un theatro di pessimi satelliti, una scuola di corruttissimi costumi, et un rifugio di dishonestissime ribalderie . . . è un naufragio di tutte le virtù, una oppressione di tutte le bontà . . . la libertà che si perde nelle corti, l'inquietudine de desideri ambitiosi, le spese intolerabili per farsi honorare . . . (529)

> . . . today many courts are nothing but a congregation of depraved men, an assembly of malicious foxes, a theater of evil satellites, a school for the most corrupt mores and a haven for the most dishonest ribaldry . . . and the shipwreck of all virtues, the suppression of all that is good . . . the freedom one forfeits at court, the anxiety engendered by ambitious desires, the intolerable expenses one must face in order to secure honor . . .

Immediately following this anticourt and anticourtier harangue, Garzoni inveighs against the "meretrici, et de' loro seguaci" (whores and their followers) who receive twelve pages of similar acrimonious treatment, conjoined with a generous dose of virulent misogyny:

> *Quanto da loro si riceve, e acquista, non è altro, che mille immondezze, e sorditezze, le quali honestamente nominare non si ponno, e s'abbellisce il concetto descrivendo quanto son brutte, sporche, laide, infami, furfante, pidocchiose, piene di croste, cariche di menstruo, puzzolenti di carne, fetenti di fiato, ammorbate di dentro, appestate di fuori, che le Gabrine in comparatione son più desiderabili che loro. (601)*

> Whatever one receives and acquires from them is nothing but a thousand filthy and sordid things that cannot be called by their name with any decency, and indeed one does embellish the concept by describing how ugly they are, how dirty, foul, infamous, crooked, full of lice, full of scabs, drenched in menstrual fluid, with stinking flesh, fetid breath, diseased within, polluted without, so that by comparison Gabrine [dishonest women] are more desirable than they.

What both courtier and courtesan as prostitute share, in the minds of Garzoni, Sansovino, and Aretino, is abject servility. What were the courtier's attributes become hers; furthermore she embodies all of the negative characteristics of the court that these writers have so proudly and vehemently rejected.

The Venetian civic myth worked in this sense in consort with these writers' claims to independence. It assuaged in part their anxieties about securing patronage in a world where enlisting a patron's sympathies was becoming increasingly difficult. Like a mother who comforts her child's fears, this Venetian female icon purportedly oversaw her (male) citizens' well-being, while the doge liberally bestowed his paternal rewards on any privileged citizen who merited his benevolence. In Aretino's letter to the Marchese di Mantova (20 April 1530), he speaks of Doge Andrea Gritti as his own father, who looks out unselfishly for his personal welfare, "perché il mio padre è Principe di Venezia; e ben lo posso chiamare così perché opra per me paternalmente" (because the Prince of Venice is my father; and I may certainly call him thus because he acts paternally toward me).[70] And in the letter to Gritti, he refers to Venice as "la nutrice de l'altre città e la madre eletta da Dio per fare più famoso il mondo, per radolcire le consuetudini, per dare umanità a l'uomo e per umiliare i superbi, perdonando a gli erranti" (the nurse of all other cities and the mother chosen by God to bestow more glory upon the world, to soften our customs, to give man greater humanity, and to humble the proud, while pardoning those who err).[71] Thus, like a nurse who aids the sick or a mother who unwaveringly consoles her troubled child, so Venice embraces not only her own privileged citizens but all Italians in need:

> *Ella l'abbraccia s'altri la schifa, ella la regge s'altri l'abbatte; ella la pasce s'altri l'affama; ella la riceve s'altri la caccia, e nel rallegrarla ne le tribulazioni, la conserva in carità e in amore. (66)*

> Venice embraces Italy when others shun her and upholds her when others abase her; she feeds her when others starve her; she shelters her when others reject her, and comforting her in her tribulations, sustains her with charity and love.

Unlike the courtier's servile and unstable relationship with his prince, Aretino insists in a letter to Giovanni Agnello, echoing Sansovino's panegyric to Venice, that his status as Venetian allows him to remain the master of himself, the dictator of his own passions, the arbiter of his own taste:

> *E sì come non è passione che aggiunga a quello del cortigiano, che è stanco e non ha da sedere, che ha fame e non po mangiare, c'ha sonno e bisogna che vegghi, così non è consolazione che arrivi a la mia che siedo quando sono stracco, mangio quando ho fame, e dormo quando ho sonno, e tutte le ore son l'ore de le mie volontà. (318)*

> And just as there is no agony greater than that of the courtier who is tired and has no place to sit, is hungry and cannot eat, wants to sleep and must stay awake, so there is no contentment that can equal mine as I sit when I am tired, eat when I am hungry, go to sleep when I am sleepy, and every hour is mine to do as I wish.

The increasing numbers of upwardly mobile courtesans—honest courtesans—undoubtedly threatened Venetian male writers' "privilege," because the courtesans competed with the male writers for patrons' attention and support. Hence, male writers sought to expose courtesans' reputation-seeking techniques as fraudulent, claiming the courtesans' techniques to be alien to their own. The participants in Aretino's *Ragionamento delle corti*, a dialogue published in Venice in 1538, equate the courtesan's professional activities with the corruption of the Renaissance court where lies, they contend, are the expected currency of exchange.[72] In the court, madness reigns, and death provides the only escape from a depraved world out of control. Furthermore, mendacity is "donneata" (has become a woman) because it is courted by all, especially by those who have power as their principal goal. As Amedeo Quondam notes in his study of this dialogue:[73]

> *La bugia è donneata, corteggiata da tutti non soltanto perché è funzionale*
> *alla logica e alla strategia del potere . . . ma sopratutto perché costituisce*
> *il codice universale dei comportamenti sociali, e non consente deviazioni-*
> *infrazioni. . . . Soltanto chi sa mentire, assumere cioé il suo ruolo nel gioco*
> *teatrale delle parti che questa scena impone, sa regnare.*[74]

> Mendacity has become a woman, courted by everyone, not only be-
> cause it is instrumental in the exercise of logic and power strat-
> egy . . . but above all, since it constitutes the universal code of
> social behavior, it does not allow for any deviation-infraction. . . .
> Only the person who knows how to lie, that is, who performs his or
> her proper role in the theatrical play of parts as demanded by a
> given scene, knows how to rule.

All of the negative attributes of the court described in *Ragionamento delle*
corti are the ones Aretino had employed years earlier to portray the immoral
world of the Roman prelate and the Roman prostitute. When in this dialogue he exposes the deceptive, ruthless strategies of the courtier, he echoes
the description of his own fictional character, the prostitute, Nanna, of
I ragionamenti, published only a few years earlier in 1534. Embedded within
his writing is a contradiction, however; Aretino denounces a courtesan's
sexuality, but he revels in representing her in a perspective designed to appeal to the voyeuristic eroticism of male readers. Similarly, while denouncing the mercantile, competitive world at court, he betrays his fascination
with that world, portraying a courtier's ability to be cruel and to lie as if
these were virtues. The court, he says, is like a "mercatantessa" (a female
merchant) who displays her wares in the "gran mercato" (great marketplace) of the world.[75]

Careful neither to name specific courtesans nor to condemn individual
courts, throughout his years in Venice, Aretino succeeded repeatedly in
safeguarding himself from personal retribution. His satirical, pornographic dialogues paint in broad but vivid brush strokes, replete, however, with sharp, critical details, the overall designs of the courtesan's
anarchic world of mercenary love. As Raymond Rosenthal has noted in his
introduction to *Aretino's Dialogues,*

> His men are goaded to love-making by gross and vulgar lust; his
> women do not even have this excuse, but do it out of simple greed,
> for the money . . . lust and greed provide the basis for the decep-
> tive, entrapping machinery of the social world, in which money,

ambition, and cynical power rule. . . . Aretino, a nihilist before his time, defies his age by showing it its own miserable and distorted face in the mirror of its most degraded characters and their acts.[76]

Yet Aretino allows the prurient reader the opportunity to eavesdrop vicariously on two prostitutes and to spy on a mother's and a daughter's erotic conversations and obscene sexual acts. Forming a complicity with his reader, he exposes the commercial techniques the successful courtesan uses to win over her "victims": she exploits her clients in search of a financial reward, she swindles them through faked offers, she feigns illness to win their sympathy, and she assumes specific social roles (married woman, maiden, young man) in order to satisfy their desires.[77] Her erotic arts, as Nanna tells her daughter Pippa, are like those of a clever merchant who inflates the cost of his merchandise because he knows that his goods cannot be found anywhere else and thus can command high prices:

> *Fallo, Pippa, perché le carezze con le quali si fanno compire i giostranti son la rovina loro, il dargliene dolce gli ammazza; e poi una puttana che fa ben quel fatto è come un merciaro che vende care le sue robbe: e non si ponno simigliare se non a una bottega di merciarie le ciance, i giuochi e le feste che escano da una puttana scaltrita. . . . Ecco un merciaro ha stringhe, specchi, guanti, corone, nastri, ditali, spilletti, aghi, cinte, scuffioni, balzi, saponetti, olio odorifero, polver de Cipri, capelli e centomilia di ragion cose. Così una puttana ha nel suo magazzino parolette, risi, basci, sguardi; ma questo è nulla: ella ha ne le mani e ne la castagna i rubini, le perle, i diamanti, gli smeraldi e la melodia del mondo.*[78]

Do it well, Pippa, because the caresses that make cocksmen come quickly spell their ruin, and when you bestow them with especial sweetness you murder them. Besides, a whore who does that particular job well and neatly is like a dry goods dealer who sells his goods at a stiff price, and one can compare the lewd tricks, the sly twists, squeezes, and titillations of an adept and crafty whore to the goods that come out of a dry goods dealer's shop. . . . Well, look here, this is a dry good's dealer: he has gloves, looking glasses, laces, beads, ribbons, thimbles, needles, girdles, buttons, fringes, soaps, sweet-scented oils, Cyprus powder, wigs, and a hundred thousand different items. So in her shop a whore has sweet little words, laughs, kisses, and killing looks; but all this is nothing, for she has in her hands, cunt, and ass all the rubies, pearls, diamonds, and emeralds, the very melody of this world.

Aretino never praises the courtesan for her literary or artistic talents; instead his portraits stress the corrupt, materialist rewards that purportedly fuel her mercenary desires. Even in his famous letter to the Venetian courtesan Angela del Moro, or La Zaffetta, the daughter of a procuratore of San Marco, dated 15 December 1537, he praises her only ironically by claiming that she alone transcends the vulgar, commonplace courtesan by virtue of having "put a mask of decency on the face of lust." By describing what she is not, he succeeds in defining inversely what he believes the courtesan generally must do in order to be successful. Imbedded within this dispraise of courtesans is the praise he acquires from his fellow writers who also attack them. In this sense, the courtesan is an object through which male authors build their reputations. Indeed Aretino refers to his own female characters, Nanna and Pippa, when he points to la Zaffetta's powers:

> *Voi non essercitate l'astuzia, anima de l'arte cortigiana, col mezzo de i tradimenti ma con sì fatta destrezza che chi spende giura d'avanzare. . . . I vostri corrucci s'adirano a tempo, né vi curate d'esser chiamata maestra di lusinghe, né di tenere in lungo, avendo in odio quelle che studiano i punti de la Nanna e la Pippa. . . . La bugia, l'invidia e la maladicenza, quinto elemento de le cortigiane, non vi tengano in continuo moto l'animo e la lingua. Voi accarezzate le virtù e onorate i vertuosi: cosa fuor del costume e de la natura di coloro che compiacciono a i prezzi de l'altrui volontà. Perciò mi son dato a Vostra Signoria, parendomi che Quella ne sia degna.* [79]

You do not exercise cunning, the very soul of the courtesan's art, with treachery but with such skill that whoever pays you would swear he has gained. . . . Your bursts of anger are apposite and you do not mind being called a mistress of flattery or in taking your sweet time because you hate those women who study Nanna's and Pippa's points. . . . Mendacity, envy, slander, the quintessential qualities of a courtesan, do not keep your tongue and mind in perpetual motion. You embrace virtue and you honor virtuous men: both things alien to the habits and the nature of persons who indulge the whims of others for a price. Therefore I have given myself to your ladyship for I think you worthy of my doing so.

Not all Venetian authors were so charitable to Angela Zaffetta. About six years before Aretino's letter, his favorite "pupil," Lorenzo Venier, composed a scathing comic satire in ottava rima against her, characterizing her as a voracious devourer of male desire. [80] In *Il trentuno della Zaffetta* (The Thirty-One of the Zaffetta), a poem of more than nine hundred lines, Venier describes Angela's public humiliation when she is raped by no less than eighty men on the island of Chioggia. Led there by her scorned lover, who has organized this violent outing to seek revenge on her for recently refusing him entrance to her home, she is subject first to the squalid "whims" of a sodomite, and then to a host of lower-class characters—fishermen, gondoliers, priests, sacristans, servants, and porters. What concerns her most, the author tells us, is that this "private" abuse should not become public; but her pleas to her lover are to no avail. Upon returning to Venice, the band of men write on the wall that on 6 April, Angela Zaffetta has received a "thirty-one." Revealing that she has suffered the violence of eighty men, the male character (presumably Lorenzo Venier) tells the reader that after a few days she returned unabashedly to her "sordid" profession as though nothing had ever happened.[81]

Rape, although considered a crime of violence, was never severely punished by the Venetian Forty in the early modern period. Nobles often escaped severe penalty by bribing either the families of the victim or her servants with high sums. Women of all classes, often victimized by the aggression of bands of men, rarely were compensated by society for the physical abuse they endured:

> Rape prosecution was also most sensitive to a woman's age and status. The victimization of children (*puellae*) was treated with a stern hand. Wives, though much less important, were more valued than widows by the measure of penalties. Unmarried girls of marriageable age, however, found their rapists penalized with little more than a slap on the wrist. When rape struck down the social hierarchy, it could virtually disappear as a crime. . . . Rapes that crossed social boundaries upward, however, were quite another matter and entailed penalties of unique severity and the full richness of the Avogadori's rhetoric.[82]

The repercussions of gang rape were inevitably more damaging to a woman's honor and reputation than to a man's. Group rape was viewed as the most vicious and humiliating punishment that a courtesan could endure, while the worst risk a man ever ran, though it could be serious, was contracting a venereal disease. A "trentuno" (thirty-one), in fact, was intended not only to humiliate a courtesan publicly but indeed to increase her chances of becoming infected with syphilis so as to mark her permanently with a disfiguring disease. By deforming her physical appearance through private abuse, a courtesan's adversary would succeed in publicizing her alleged nefarious acts while protecting himself from ridicule.

Taking hold of a deeply disturbing element of Venetian society and then burlesquing it permitted the male satirist to gain some measure of control that he perhaps feared losing in other areas. Satire creates this fiction of power by allowing the satirist "for a time, (to) create a rhetorical stance which releases him and like-minded readers from the charms of the woman—and simultaneously absolves him and his readers from the responsibility for all that he finds reprehensible."[83] But as Felicity Nussbaum also demonstrates, "the satirist is not always fully in control of his persona, or he may not, especially in the lesser satires, understand or even wish to explore the complexities of his relation to the tradition, the conventions, and the myth."[84]

Lorenzo and Maffio Venier were never fully in control of their literary personae in this and in other compositions, even though their model, Aretino, had had a hand in "rhyming this woman dead."[85] In fact, Aretino refers to Lorenzo Venier in 1530, in a *capitolo* Aretino sent the Duke of Mantua, as "mio creato" (my creation). He also mentions in this poem Venier's "epic Rabelaisian fable," *La puttana errante* (The Wandering Whore), directed against another Venetian courtesan, Elena Ballerina:[86]

> *Ma perché io sento il presente all'odore*
> *un'operetta in quel cambio galante*
> *Vi mando ora in stil ladro e traditore*
> *Intitolata la Puttana Errante*
> *Dal Veniero composto mio creato*
> *che m'è in dir mal quattro giornate inanti.*
>
> But since I can sniff out a trend, I send you a small work which deals with that courtly exchange in a mischievous and perfidious style. It is entitled *The Wandering Whore,* and was written by Veniero, a creature of mine, who when it comes to a vicious tongue, runs four days ahead of me.

We find both courtesans listed in an anonymous satirical dialogue between a "gentiluomo" (gentleman) and a "forestiero" (foreigner), entitled *La tariffa delle puttane di Venegia* (The Price List of the Whores of Venice), probably first published in a clandestine edition in Venice in 1535.[87] Here, too, Lorenzo Venier and Aretino receive special mention. In the first case, the "gentiluomo" extols Venier's "ornato e terso / Stile . . . che quanto dir si puote / Di lor, cantando ha dimostrato il verso!" (adorned and terse / Style . . . who has proven how much can be said about them in verse!), and in the second case, the "forestiero," after hearing a few choice anecdotes teeming with lurid pornographic details, exclaims that only Aretino would be capable of outdoing his interlocutor's stories: "O gran sciagura! o odor di gentil vino! / Questo è un bel caso e non indegno forse / De la penna immortal de l'Aretino" (What a great mishap! What scent of fine wine! This is quite a case, not unworthy, perhaps, of Aretino's immortal pen!).[88] As a catalog, replete with prices and addresses, this list resembles the famous *Catalogo di tutte le principali et più honorate cortigiane di Venezia* (1565),[89] but this one is explicitly satirical in nature. Making fun of such moralistic texts as the Erasmus dialogue cited earlier, in which a Venetian gentleman attempts to convert a prostitute with eloquent, learned speeches worthy of the pulpit, the dialogue between a Venetian gentleman and a foreigner in the *Tariffa,* while denouncing the prostitute's deceptive allure, ends by recommending her seductive play: "Piene d'ogni malitia e falsitate / Son le puttane, e, come statue apunto, / Dentro hanno il fango, e son dii fuora ornate" (Whores are full of all kinds of malice and falsehoods, and exactly like statues, they have mud inside but are decorated on the outside). To these warnings the foreigner impatiently protests that such counsel should be left to the priest's moralizing sermons: "Deh! lasciate le prediche in buon punto / Ai Frati, che pur c'habbiano a gridarci" (Pray! leave these sermons / to the friars, who are wont to berate us anyhow).[90]

Although these catalogs identify real people, each piquant thumbnail sketch (those of *La tariffa* are especially vivid) enters the world of satiric commonplaces marshaled against prostitutes and thus departs considerably from reality.[91] Contrary to the suggestions often made by critics, *La tariffa* and the *Catalogo* did not, I believe, ever satisfy any practical purpose in the way that northern picture albums such as that of the Flemish Crispijn van de Passe, which included actual portraits of each prostitute, purportedly aided foreign clients in their selections.[92]

None of these vulgar verbal portraits would have recommended a courtesan to a male customer. Further, if they were meant to entice the reader into sexual encounters, they would have been counterproductive to say the least. Angela Zaffetta receives the singular honor of satisfying the lust of infinite numbers of males simultaneously (a reference to Lorenzo Venier's poem), even though she is said to be plagued with syphilis. While her name, "Angela," raises her above the vulgar hordes, the vile description she receives reminds the potential client, even if he is distracted by her physical presence, of her corruption. The author claims that because she is so haughty, she refuses to urinate in a simple chamber pot like other women but instead crouches down in the middle of the kitchen floor, for all to see and hear:[93]

> *La terza apunto è la Zaffetta e questa,*
> *Per aver nome d'Angela, a una foggia*
> *Vol venti, a l'altra trenta, se è richiesta;*
> *E pur il mal di Francia seco alloggia*
> *E la disgratia che vi sta in persona,*
> *Oltra il trent'un che le fu dato a Chioggia.*
> *Ma di lei così a fil scrive e ragiona*
> *Il mio Venier, nel suo sacrato Annale,*
> *Che l' nome suo per tutto ancho risuona.*
> *Però lasso di dir il suo reale*
> *Animo, e qual levando la mattina*
> *Non piscia per superbia in l'orinale,*
> *Ma a gambe aperte, in mezzo la cuccina,*
> *Con rumor qual se ne andasser le superne*
> *Cataratte del Ciel tutte a ruina.*

And the third one is la Zaffetta, who, since her name is Angela, demands twenty one way and thirty the other if that other way is requested; And she entertains the French pox and bad luck in person, besides the *trentuno* that she was dealt at Chioggia. But in his acclaimed catalog my Venier writes about her and discusses her in such detail that her name resounds everywhere. Yet he neglected to tell about her real character and how on rising in the morning she is too proud to pee into her urinal but does so with her legs spread wide apart in the middle of the kitchen floor with a roar greater than if all of heaven's floodgates came crashing open.

Elena Ballerina, on the other hand, reportedly less intelligent than Angela, is equally rapacious; what drives her sexual passion is jealousy. Like a stray dog, he says, she wanders the streets in search of "food" to satiate her ravenous appetite:[94]

> *Elena Ballarina è cara e bella,*
> *Ma la sconcia il cervel sciocco e leggero,*
> *E sempre gelosia l'urta e martella.*
> *Questa è quella gentile, per dir il vero,*
> *Puttana Errante, che di cazzi ingorda,*
> *Già spogliò questo e quell'altro hemispero.*
> *La pazzarella volentier s'accorda*

Per quattro scudi, et a chi di nascoso
Gliene da due, non tien l'orecchia sorda.

Elena Ballerina is pretty and dear, but her foolish featherweight brain is a great handicap, and jealousy forever wracks and pummels her. If truth be told, this is the gentle wandering whore, who having a voracious appetite for pricks, already has despoiled this hemisphere and the other one. The silly girl will gladly take four *scudi* to close a deal, and if anyone on the sly offers her two, she certainly does not turn a deaf ear.

Focusing on the venality and voraciousness of certain courtesans rather than the sexual appetites of her male clientele, these satirical dialogues underscore the mercenary values upon which these authors claim all courtesans' livelihoods depend. What informs their representations are precisely the polar extremes between angel and whore which characterized, as we have seen, male representations of the female in Venice in the early modern period, both in the civic myth and in literary traditions.

While the virginal female icon safeguarded Venetian male authors' "libertà," it also nurtured a hierarchical Petrarchan poetic that these authors challenged. In the place of the idealized female muse and the artificial, adulatory rhetoric that praises her, they elect the base and vulgar whore— the inverse of the female paragon of civic virtue—for their raucous, subversive verses.[95] In this sense their dispraise of courtesans belies a parasitical rapport with the object of their abuse. This hostile, unpaid use of the courtesan's body wins praise for the male writers who attack her. With Aretino, who as their iconoclastic master and leader invented generalized surrogate female figures "as expendable versions of himself," Lorenzo's and Maffio Venier's pornographic dialect verses parody literary conventions. They join together as writers against the courtesan, and they personalize Aretino's satirical denunciations.[96]

Aretino, however, was a "pimp" as much for himself as for the courtesan he denounced. He never speaks except through a surrogate (often female) character, such as Nanna, Pippa, or Antonia, whom he selects to do his dirty work for him. As the literary historian Michael Seidel claims in his study of the theoretical foundations of satire: "Satirists are ready to risk exposure to dirt and disorder for the power such a risk transfers to them."[97]

By choosing the low-level courtesan as the subject of their verses and the objects of their attacks, Pietro Aretino, Lorenzo and Maffio Venier, and others broke out of the generic bounds of the fashionable Petrarchan poetic idiom, which posited an adulating poet lover at one extreme and an idealized, immaculate female muse at the other. They adhered instead to the stylistic levels and formal guidelines that Francesco Sansovino had advocated, in imitation of Cicero, for prose or verse satire:

> *Ora la Satira vuol esser di stil umile e basso et imitante la natura, perciò che basta al satirico apertamente riprender gli errori altrui senz'altro artificio . . . la Satira richiede la verità nuda et aperta . . . si vede manifestamente ch'alla materia satirica non si convien l'ornamento né la grazia, né i fuchi, né la soavità del dire che vuol la materia eroica et alta, ma una schietta semplicità con una acerbità severa, mescolata talora con qualche sale e con qualche tratto gustevole et acuto.*[98]

> Now Satire requires a humble and down-to-earth style that imitates nature, and therefore it is enough for the satirist to reproduce another's mistakes without any artifice. . . . It calls for bare and unadorned truth. . . . Ornamentation and grace, embellished and urbane language do not suit satiric subjects but rather a terse simplicity and severe acerbity blended now and then with a pinch of salt and a few acute and tasty tidbits.

In so doing they were conscious of transgressing Bembo's rigid separation of stylistic levels according to subject matter and poetic decorum. Since he was the most influential literary theorist of the early sixteenth century, scores of poets and other theorists throughout Italy bowed to Bembo when making aesthetic and linguistic choices in their works. Bembo's treatise, the *Prose della volgar lingua,* mostly composed in 1512 but published in 1525, advocated a modern vernacular classicism, circumscribed by the canons of Ciceronian rhetoric and created from the complex discursive poetic style of Petrarch. The theories pronounced especially in book 2 became the standard manual for vernacular forms in the sixteenth century. Thus, when Aretino boasts that he follows nature rather than literary models while composing his verses, letting only Venice loosen his tongue: "La natura istessa de la cui semplicità son secretario mi detta ciò che io compongo, e la patria mi scioglie i nodi della lingua" (Nature herself, whose simplicity's secretary I am, dictates my compositions, and a love of my country unties my tongue), he deliberately repudiates Bembo's dictum, while at the same time paying him a sort of backhanded homage.[99] Maffio Venier later in the century argues that only Venetian dialect, and not Tuscan—the language of love poetry—is suitable for his verses, because it has more "sa[p]or" (flavor): "Questa è una lengua ch'è d'ogni savor, / dove che, se vorò scriver toscan, / bisogna per il più parlar d'Amor" (This is a language that is of many flavors, whereas if I wanted to write in Tuscan I would have to speak mostly of Love), thereby purposely disabusing Bembo's well-acclaimed recommendation that the Italian vernacular, that is, Tuscan, be used for the lyric. [100] Uncovering instead the "dirty" aspects of the courtesan's profession and equating her profession with the courtier's world they have willingly left behind, Venetian satirists furthered both the fictions of unparalleled Venetian "libertà" and their own uncorruptibility.

Thus, male representations of the courtesan in Venetian literary works draw their terms from both an anticourt arsenal and an immaculate civic myth already in place. When they elect the courtesan and prostitute as the objects of their attack, these Venetian authors find ready and waiting a wealth of ancient authors (Juvenal, Martial, Lucian) who would applaud such disparagement. For male satirists had always found in the courtesan both a lascivious potential and a means of eliminating through verbal warfare "whatever out there threatens [them]." [101]

What fueled Lorenzo and Maffio Venier's enormous venom against courtesans, whom they name in their personal invectives, has more to do, I believe, with personal envy, hatred, and fear than with a larger, corrective vision of a corrupt society. Maffio Venier deflects his anxieties about Franco's increasing stature in the literary marketplace by appropriating the threat she represented and using it as a foil for his own rebellious poetics. On the satiric level, he comically parodies the courtesan; at a deeper level, Maffio defends the privileges of his sex and class against Franco's literary ambitions. [102] Bolstered by a city that fostered anticourt discourses and championed Venice's unparalleled "libertà," Maffio Venier's satirical verses, disparaging the courtesan's "evil practices," would not have fallen on deaf or critical ears.

Ironically, Aretino had already described in his *Sei giornate* (or *Ragionamenti*) the potential damage done to a courtesan's reputation if she scorns a scholar-poet. Making comic reference to his own work but prefiguring the satirical invectives of Lorenzo and Maffio Venier, Aretino has Nanna, the older courtesan, warn Pippa, her neophyte daughter, never to give her scholar-client a reason to unleash his anger against her. To ward off retribution, she counsels her daughter to feign interest in her client's poems or at the very least, to pretend to value scholarly pursuits:

> Perché non ti mancarebbe altro se non che un tale ti facesse i libri contra, e che per tutto si bandisse di quelle ladre cose che sanno dir de le donne: e ti staria bene che fosse stampata la tua vita come non so chi scioperato ha stampata la mia, come ci mancassero puttane di peggior sorte di me: e se si

avesse a squinternare gli andamenti di chi vo' dir io, si oscurarebbe il sole.
E quanti abbai sono suti fatti sopra il fatto mio![103]

Why all you need is for someone to write a book against you and bandy about the dreadful things they say about us women; and it would serve you right if your life were published as some scoundrel published mine as if there were a lack of whores worse than myself: and if one brings into the open the doings of you know who, the sun would go into eclipse; but just look at the hue and uproar about my affairs!

And yet Pietro Aretino, unlike Sperone Speroni, shows in these dialogues a certain compassion for his women characters, whom he portrays as victims (as by inference he himself has been) of a society corrupted by mercantile concerns. As patricians, Lorenzo and Maffio Venier write invectives that smack instead of personal hatred and expose a malign vindictiveness. And whereas Aretino's *Sei giornate* can describe the "filth of commercial love without, itself, being filthy or vicious,"[104] Lorenzo's satirical verses against Angela Zaffetta and Elena Ballerina, and those of Maffio, his son, are obscene, even revolting—a lewd joke for Venetian men only.

III

When Maffio Venier returned to Venice in 1575, after his one-year service in the Medici court and his brief stay in Rome, the city that greeted him was far from the ideal, virginal portrait of the Serenissima championed in foreign tourists' accounts. The female paragon of virtue—the immaculate, virginal queen and secular Venus—had toppled from her royal, iconic heights into a mire of human contagion. Struck by the plague earlier that year, Venice, for both visitor and citizen, was now a tragic spectacle of misery, social chaos, moral dissolution, and severe poverty. A series of disasters (the flooding of 1559 and severe famine in 1569, the burning of the Arsenale in 1569, the war with the Ottoman forces from 1570 to 1573, and finally, the destruction of the Palazzo Ducale by fire in 1574) provoked Venetian citizens to view this plague (1575–77) as the culmination of God's wrath against Venetian *luxuria* and immoral practices. [105]

No longer an immaculate Virgin—the "vaga ninfa" (lovely nymph) situated miraculously on the waters—Venice appears to the grieving patriotic poet, Maffio Venier, as a disfigured "orrido mostro" (horrid monster). The defiled icon he describes testifies to the many layers of corruption that have transformed a once glorious and virginal city into a scene of spiritual ruin.

Gripped and chastened by the human misery he witnessed, Maffio composed a mournful canzone in which he prays for the city's deliverance. One of the most beautiful and moving poems on the subject, it attests to Venier's mastery as vernacular poet.[106]

The virginal Queen as emblem now contains the vanities and horrors of Venetian *luxuria*. What was the "del mar donna e reina" (queen and ruler of the sea) is now a scene of "immensa ruina" (immense downfall); what were her "pompe e i piacer" (delights and pomp) are now "volti in tormento" (turned to agony) owing to the "ciel contra di te" (heavens set against you). Her immaculate body, torn open by "piaghe aperte e voraci" (open and voracious wounds) and by the fury of hell's "foco e veleno" (fire and poison), exposes not the miraculous powers she once possessed but rather the disease and putrefaction that consume her body from within:

> *Col cor pien di pietade e di spavento*
> *miro e piango, o del mar donna e reina,*
> *la tua immensa ruina,*
> *e 'l mio grave cordoglio,*
> *le tue pompe e i piacer volti in tormento,*
> *e 'l ciel contra di te colmo d'orgoglio.*
>   *Quant'a ragion mi doglio*
> *di scoprir ne l'amato almo tuo seno*
> *piaghe aperte e voraci,*
> *e in te stessa nutrir foco e veleno!*
> *Come ti cangi e sfaci!*
> *Or le tue belle membra, e 'l crine adorno*
> *d'oro, di perle e d'ostro*
> *forman di vaga ninfa orrido mostro,*
> *mostro che geme e piange empio destino*
> *con mille insidie de la morte intorno,*
> *e col volto bagnato, oscuro e chino.*

O queen and ruler of the sea, my heart is filled with pity and with dread; As I weep and contemplate your immense downfall, I contemplate my dire loss; all your delights and pomp are turned to agony and the haughty heavens are set against you. I have good cause to grieve as I discern open and voracious wounds in your beloved breast and see you feed the fire and the poison within yourself. How you do change and are consumed! Now your comely limbs and tresses, adorned with gold, pearls, and crimson cloth, make a horrid monster of a lovely nymph, a monster that wails and weeps encircled by a thousand deadly traps, your face streaked with tears, somber and held low.

Her womb, once capable of miraculous birth, now annihilates human life rather than creating it anew. The diseased, pregnant "terra" (earth), swollen with its own infected "membra" (limbs), is heavy with the weight of thousands of dead bodies:

> *Cade ciascuno, i più gagliardi e forti,*
> *e già la terra gonfia il ventre e 'l fianco,*
> *inutilmente gravida de' morti.*

All of them fall, the most gallant and strong, while the womb and the sides of the earth swell in vain, pregnant with the dead.

When seeking to comprehend the cause of the enormity of this human destruction ("Deh perché, amata patria, in te discerno / cangiar la maestà di quell'aspetto / che fin qui mai turbò tempesta o verno?" [O beloved country, tell me why do I see such change in that majestic countenance that until now neither storm nor winter has perturbed?]), Venier refers to the natural and political disasters that Venice had endured over a ten-year period:

> *Pria la fame ti strinse, e 'l foco t'arse,*
> *ed a guerra crudel la strada aperse,*
> *l'acqua al fin ti coperse,*
> *né di mortal orrore*
> *l'alta presenza tua vidi mutarse*
> *da l'intrepido suo primo colore.*
> *Ma ben giusto dolore,*
> *o donzella del mar figliola e sposa,*
> *a lagrimar t'induce,*
> *or fatta di sì bella egra e leprosa.*

Famine besieged you and fire burned you, opening the path to cruel war, and finally the water submerged you, yet the original intrepid color of your lofty countenance remained unchanged by deadly horror. But most just grief makes you weep, o maiden, daughter, and bride of the sea, who once so beautiful, is now afflicted and marked by leprosy.

Astonished that the conjunction of God's wrath with the mass of dead bodies within the island's own leprous body has not brought about Venice's physical collapse, Venier exclaims that the heavens, not the waters, must still be supporting the city. For without this support, Venice would sink into the sea from the sheer weight of its shameful curse:

> *Deh come ha 'l cielo ogni ben tuo conteso!*
> *E pur il ciel ne l'aria ti sospende,*
> *ché non può l'acqua sostener tal peso.*

> Alas how heaven has fought to deprive you of all your wealth! And yet it still holds you suspended in midair, since the sea cannot support your weight.

Thus, turning to God to deliver Venice from the plague, he closes the canzone with an address to the virgin city. Like a phoenix it will rise from the ashes, he declares triumphantly, "quasi nova fenice, / questa Dea rinnovar vita felice" (like a new phoenix this goddess rises again to a happy life), to repossess the grandeur it has always enjoyed; one day Venice will rest proudly once again, he predicts patriotically, "on waves [that] turn to silver and sand [that turns] to gold":

> *Vedrai giungerle ognor gemme e tesoro,*
> *e farsi intorno al liquido paese*
> *l'onde d'argento e 'l lito arena d'oro.*

> You will see treasure and gems come to her, and all around this liquid land you will see the waves turn to silver and sand to gold.

Ironically, the literary attacks directed against Franco were issued from the very clan she had been trying to cultivate. Socially mobile and ambitiously determined to publish her works, Franco represented to Maffio Venier a disorderly force, a social hierarchy out of control, much like the plague that was devastating northern Italy in these years, or the mass of foreign immigrants advancing onto Venetian territory, who invaded ancient patrician enclaves. The men of the Venier family held onto their *nobiltà* and fantasized a connection between the political and social threats to the republic's hegemony and a feminine danger.

At the beginning of the outbreak of the plague, in 1575, Veronica Franco published her volume of poems, the *Terze rime*. [107] This volume, like others that Franco edited in this period, attests to her close associations with the patrician Venier clan. But such associations did not protect her from Venier attacks. The threat to social stability brought about by the plague, not to mention the constant fear of Turkish invasion which gripped Venetian society in those years, continued to play upon patrician anxieties about civic order. Such fears of disorder, represented as female, and political danger to the republic encouraged the kind of satires directed against courtesans that proliferated in the late sixteenth century. As Earl Miner has suggested, writing about English satires of the same period, satire arises from "a sense that things have gone wrong, that society or literature or morals are degenerating, and frequently the satirist shows an order ending or the very edifice of civilization crumbling into ruin." [108]

Indeed in the year 1575, and also shortly after Maffio Venier's return to Rome, his satirical verses scapegoating Veronica Franco began circulating in Venetian literary circles. Like the contagion which he represents as disfiguring the immaculate civic icon, so his venal courtesan, whose body he riddles with syphilitic sores, introduces anarchic and subversive forces into Venetian society, threatening the social cohesion and political stability of the island republic. [109] His satiric attack does not, however, offer any solution to the problem. Indeed it is ironic that it was not Franco who died from contagion but rather Maffio Venier, who reportedly contracted syphilis in Constantinople in 1580 and eventually succumbed to it in 1586, as would his brother, Alvise, years later, in 1618. [110]

The Venier family's relations with Franco vividly illustrate the privileges that a courtesan might hope for if connected to a potent patrician family and conversely, the public scandal they could create, owing precisely to the family's influence within Venetian society. All three male members of the Venier clan not only occupied prominent places in the political spheres and cultural elites of sixteenth-century Venice but in one form or another were central to Veronica Franco's life and career as honest courtesan. [111]

Just as Marco Venier's adulatory *capitoli* in praise of Veronica are the antitheses of Maffio's scathing satirical verses, so were their political profiles antitheses of each other. Maffio belonged to one of the most influential patrician families of Venice. And yet this son of Lorenzo Venier (Lorenzo died the year of Maffio's birth) and Maria Michiel was throughout his life an irresolute vagabond, nervously moving from court to court in search of patronage or a religious sinecure, perhaps in order to avoid the political responsibilities required of a Venetian patrician. [112] While serving the Medicean court of Grand Duke Francesco I and the pontifical courts of Gregorio XIII and Sixtus V, he repeatedly sought more prestigious appointments within the ecclesiastical infrastructures. He returned to Venice only for short periods, for example, when Sebastiano Venier was elected doge in 1577, when Bianca Cappello, adopted as a citizen of the Florentine government, married Francesco I in 1579, or when he accompanied the Venetian "bailo" (ambassador), Paolo Contarini, from Constantinople in 1580. [113] Although he received considerable support and protection from the much beloved Venetian citizen, Bianca Cappello, the Venetian government elected him only unwillingly to positions of political importance because, among other things, they suspected him of spying on the affairs of the republic for Florentine leaders. [114]

Thus, only after great difficulty and with much political maneuvering on his behalf was he elected Arcivescovo di Corfu in April 1583, a position that, as he soon realized with regret, placed him only further and deeper into financial debt. Once consecrated bishop in 1583, he sought unsuccessfully the more prestigious bishoprics of Massa and Brescia (holders of both positions had to be nominated by the Venetian senate).[115] When Gianfrancesco Morosini was elected bishop of Brescia, Maffio traveled back and forth to Rome in search of ecclesiastical support, and then to Florence in 1585, where he died shortly thereafter in Torrenieri, a small town outside of Florence, at the early age of thirty-six. A Roman *avviso* of "XV di Novembre 1586" solemnly reads, "Hieri con dolore universale di questa corte s'intese la morte di Monsignor Veniero Arcivescovo di Corfu su l'hosteria di Torrenieri di viaggio per Toscana a ritroversi convalescente dell'infirmità che prese questa etade in Tivoli, parendo ad ognuno, che habbia questo secolo perso un Prelato di valore singolare in molte cose" (Yesterday, with universal sorrow of this court, word was received of the death of Monsignor Veniero, Archbishop of Corfu, which took place at the inn of Torrenieri while he was on his way to Tuscany to recover from the illness that recently struck him at Tivoli, and everyone had the sense that our century has suffered the loss of a prelate of particular merit in many things).[116]

Divided between his conservative allegiance to the pope and his more oppositional, even radical, stance with regard to the political expectations imposed on Venetian patricians, Maffio embodied the contradictions of a late-sixteenth-century patrician. On the one hand he championed a singular Venetian "libertà," and, on the other, he "prostituted" himself to powerful patrons and courts in search of monetary and social rewards. But unlike Aretino or even his father, Lorenzo, Maffio Venier received few of the rewards of this much praised "libertà." Owing to the difficulties in his own life, during which his privileged status as patrician son could not guarantee him support or stable employment, he unleashed his frustration and anger against the upwardly mobile courtesan. Satire was in his case a way of righting such social imbalances through invective and verbal slurs. As a "servant" to papal and Florentine courts, Maffio affirmed the very rhetoric of power so abhorred by Aretino. And yet the subversive literary stance of his parodic dialect verses overturned the literary conventions that Aretino and Lorenzo poked fun at but never completely reversed themselves.

Marco Venier, on the other hand, who followed Domenico Venier's more conservative example, rose methodically and in an exemplary fashion through the ranks of Venetian politics.[117] Beginning as *savio agli ordini* (responsible for maritime affairs) at age twenty-five, an obligatory office for young patricians, Marco then went on to occupy such influential positions in the Venetian republic as *officiale alle cazude* (tax enforcer), *provedditore sopra la sanità* (commissioner of public health during the plague, a position which, once he was elected to it, a Venetian patrician could not legally refuse), *savio di terraferma* (responsible for military affairs on the mainland), *avogadore di commun* (chief state prosecutor), and *balio* to Constantinople (diplomatic envoy). Eventually he became a member of the more rebellious *giovani* faction, and finally he became the head of the Council of Ten, after it had undergone a radical redefinition of its powers. In addition to the council's executive overseeing of secret affairs and state security, it also assumed control over all financial questions. Having climbed from the bottom to the top of the political ladder, Marco Venier finally was elected *savio grande,* the highest-ranking member of the Collegio, the steering committee or cabinet of the Venetian Senate. [118]

Rivalries between male members for positions of power and influence, although not evidenced by primary documents, were undoubtedly present in this family. With the advent of the plague such tensions must have escalated; vicious squabbles over the rightful ownership of confiscated property suspected of infection were one consequence of the disease. [119] Suspicions and intrigues intensified among neighbors and family members; in the Venier family, these anxieties also were played out in literary arenas. Using the courtesan as either a foil or an object of attack, Marco and Maffio Venier vied with one another for authority. [120]

Once back in Rome during the Jubilee year, Maffio Venier composed the first of a series of satirical poems against Veronica Franco. Three poems in Venetian dialect ("Franca, credeme, che per San Maffio" [Believe me, Franca, that by San Maffio]; "An fia, cuomuodo? A che muodo zioghemo?" [Wouldn't you like that? What sort of game is this?]; "Veronica, ver unica puttana" [Veronica, veritably unique whore]), although undated and existing only in manuscript form, were most certainly written at the same time that he wrote two mock sonnets in Venetian dialect which he sent to Franco. One sonnet was designed to denounce the self-elevating motives for the engraved portrait of Veronica Franco that she planned to include as the frontispiece to her *Terze rime.* Since a laudatory sonnet, group of sonnets, or encomiastic letter traditionally accompanied an author's frontispiece medallion portrait, Maffio's sonnet both parodies the genre and at a more personal level discredits Franco's famed beauty and intellectual worth. Further, he mocks here her class pretensions, a subject he returns to in "An fia, cuomuodo? A che muodo zioghemo?" In the first two quatrains, he argues tongue in cheek that although one might doubt it, this engraved portrait unquestioningly represents Franco, because of its extreme ugliness. What is more, the Latin motto inscribed below the hand clasping a lighted torch—*agitataque crescit*—signals not only her pretensions to intellectual virtue, as she would have it, but also the flames of love, or better, lovemaking, that "move her" to earn the financial reward she so covets:

> *El retratto e la impresa è bona e bella,*
> > *L'un perché el te somegia in questo brutto,*
> > *L'altro, che in puttane Amor fa tutto*
> > *Per amor co' fael fuogo in la facella.*
>
> *Che l'arde solamente, quanto che ella*
> > *Dal mo(t)o e dal scorlar riceve agiuto,*
> > *Così chi vuol da vaca haver costrutto*
> > *Die strappazarla in questa parte e in quella.*

Both portrait and motto are a success, the one because it well reproduces your ugliness, the other because when it comes to whores, Love does for love what the flame does for the torch, which burns only as well as it is helped along by being waved and swung; hence whoever expects satisfaction from a whore must properly thrash her about.

The poem generally dethrones the courtesan, whom Venier also accuses of vanity for having falsified her age, while in the closing tercets he insists that she intended to deceive by having an incorrect age incised around her portrait. Her calculated deception feeds his joke about her decrepit physical appearance. He charges that although she hopes her portrait will persuade the reader of her beauty, youth, and intelligence, she is guilty of lying, deception, and vanity. Although she is trying to appear younger than she really is, the portrait, he argues, was executed not in this but in the previous Holy Year:[121]

> *Mi trovo in tel retratto un solo error*
> > *Che è de importantia assai tanto pì quanto,*
> > *Nol puol gnianche conzar el depentor.*
>
> *Che'l tempo è, se no' pì, do volte tanto*
> > *Pur ghe è via da' salvarla, e con sò honor,*
> > *da dir, che l'è stampà(l'altro anno santo.*

In this portrait I see but one error which is of great importance, since even the painter cannot set it straight: her age is at least twice that given, if not more; and yet there might be a way for him to save it without losing honor: declare that it was printed the Holy Year before this.

But in the final two capitoli directed against Franco—poems that had undoubtedly been circulating in Domenico Venier's salon at the same time as the others—what had been merely tame ventriloquizing of high literary traditions, using the courtesan as the satiric subject, become vicious, pointed attacks at the courtesan's expense. The difficulties in Maffio's own life appear to have motivated his hostility toward "upstart" courtesans, women who were rising to positions of eminence in spite of their lower-class origins. Satire for Maffio was a way of righting such social imbalances, if only through fantasy and verbal violence.

"Franca, credeme che per San Maffio" (Believe me, Franca, that by San Maffio) despite its comic moments, descends into a whirlpool of verbal ridicule, embellished with virtuoso vignettes of local Venetian life—an idiom for which Maffio was much heralded in his poem, *La Strazzosa*.[122] He achieves some of his most comic effects by exploiting his characters' self-elevating postures. Thus, in the opening tercets he makes a mockery of the selfless, distraught Petrarchan lover who pleads with his cruel beloved to reciprocate his love. The elevated statements of Petrarchan poetry are subverted by their transposition into Venetian dialect. The third tercet, however, discredits even this sophisticated love by repudiating the courtesan's insistence on receiving payment in return for her favors.[123] Although his "beloved" is a "carigolo boccon" (most expensive morsel), this courteous "valente servidor" (valiant servant), as he calls himself, refuses to commit himself to a woman who insists on earning a profit at his expense.

> *Perché el fotter no ha gusto né savor,*
> *I basi no xe basi, e spente spente,*
> *Senza quel certo che se chiama Amor.*[124]

Because screwing is neither pleasant nor tasty, kisses are not kisses, and thrusts no longer thrusts without that certain thing that one calls Love.

He condemns her for charging high fees for all of her sexual liaisons, as if she could boast, "balsamo o la mana su la figa" (balsam or manna on her cunt):

> *Intendo che, quand'un ve vuol basar,*
> *Vole cinque o sie scudi, e con fadiga*

Con i cinquanta ve lasse chiavar.

Pecca, alla fe, i parenti che no liga
Quei che ve fa ste paghe, co' avesse
El balsamo o la mana su la figa.

I mean that she asks for five or six scudi if you want to kiss her, and that for fifty she barely gives you a fuck. It truly is a shame that families do not tie up those who pay such prices, as though she had balsam or manna on her cunt.

Refusing to offer more than his "cuor" (heart) to his loved one, Maffio ridicules the desperate Petrarchan male lover who is willing to sell his soul to gain his lady's love:

No se trovarà mai testo ne glosa
Che vogia che l'amante diebba dar
Altro ch'el proprio cuor alla morosa.

Chi trove l'invention del bombadar,
Chi tradì Christo, xe dove è colu
Che con i soldi scomenze a chiavar

Farve de zorno e notte servitù,
E darve anche dozene e centenara
De scudi? Qualche can becco fottù.

No text or gloss will ever state that a lover must give his woman anything besides his heart. Whoever invented gunpowder, whoever betrayed Christ, keeps company with the one who first screwed for money. Wouldn't you like us to wait on you day and night and give you dozens and hundreds of scudi? Sure, go look for some damned cuckold of a cur.

Only "massare" (go-betweens), or "ruffiane" (pimps), or "sti prelati, / Che va drio d'ogni cosa desonesta" (these prelates who run after all sorts of dishonest things) should receive payment; his lovemaking he will reserve for "un vero amor fonda su santa fede / Un servir sviserao con tutto el cuor, / Xe d'ogni gran chiavar degna mercede" (a true love based on sacred trust, to serve with one's whole heart, are the proper rewards for a great fuck). The high priest of love, "San Maffio," disparages the courtesan's destruction of the sanctity of love, "fonda su santa fede" (based on sacred trust) through venality; while he recognizes her talents, he prefers to hold onto his "libertà" (freedom):

Co' de, per solfisar, la vose al ton
Che nasce dal ut, re, mi, fa, sol, la,

Vu fe mazzor miracol d'Anfion.
Val certo ste virtù, val la beltà,
Ma l'è più cara assai, più preciosa
De bellezza e virtù la libertà.

When getting your voice to match the tone produced by do re mi fa
sol la you perform a miracle greater than Amphion's. No doubt
such talents are worth a lot and so is beauty. But dearer and more
precious by far than beauty and talent is freedom.

In the second poem, "An fia, cuomuodo? A che muodo zioghemo?"
(Wouldn't you like that? What sort of game is this?) he attacks not only her
venality but also her beauty. He transforms the profane icon into a grotesque caricature of the first poem. With disparaging slurs he deflates the
courtesan's status. Indeed these Juvenalian verses present her attracting
lower-class customers by appearing on her balcony with breasts exposed:[125]

S'ti sta' con ste grandezze sul balcon,
Ti no sa mò, mecanica fallia,
Che ti no la fa a un orbo, né a un cogion?

Don't you know that when you stand on your balcony showing off
your grand attributes, it is a bankrupt strategem, since you could
not fool a blind man, or even a complete horse's ass?

Unabashedly stingy, she satisfies her voracious appetite with either the food
put out for animals or the "pomi o lesse" (apples and boiled chestnuts) that
the children throw:

Nemiga capital de cani e gatti,
Che se i rósega un osso, mariola,
Ti credi de cavàrghel dalle zatte.

Mo no hastu anca addesso levà mona
Che, se i putti ghe trazze pomi o lesse,
Ti fa metà con essa, poltronzona?

The deadly enemy of cats and dogs, for if they are gnawing at a
bone, you, scoundrel, try to grab it from between their paws. And
did you mean, slut, not to hoist your cunt just now so that you can
go halves if the boys from the street throw apples and boiled
chestnuts at it?

Although this is to be expected of a bastard child, an "infame nassua sotto
alla scala" (vile child born under the stairs) who poses as a "principessa"
(princess) in her "corte" (court), her house is, he says, merely "una stalla" (a

stable). Even her precious silver, which she complains was confiscated by the *Magistrato alle pompe,* is only "una scuella / stronza tutta in t'i óri, un bocaletto, / E mezza crepa d'una pignatella" (a bowl of completely shitty gold, a small goblet, and one-half of a cracked pot). [126]

The remainder of the poem consists of an antiblason in which Maffio dissects the infected body and engorged sexual parts of the vulgar courtesan, drawing on images of the plague as signs of her corruption. Her body, he charges, displays the stigmata of her vile profession; her head is marked with "un mar de brozze e de forfanteria" (a sea of pustules and larceny), signs of a diseased body; [127] her face head-on bears the signs of age, "de fronte tutto pien / De grespe" (a face that seen frontally is all covered with wrinkles) while her eyes bulge out of her head as if a priest were exorcising her of all her sins: "Ti ha' po quei occhi, che, s'ti vuol vardar, / Ti i stravolzi che el pàr che te sii sotto / El Prete che te vògia sconzurar" (Besides, you've got that kind of eyes that when you want to see something you pop and roll them as though you were in the hands of a priest and an exorcist). Her mouth is as foul as rotten mud, "La bocca è co' è un fango (marzo) corrotto" (Your mouth as well is [rotten] polluted slime); her body is so emaciated that her breasts hang low enough to use to row her boat on the canal: "Ti ha' po quelle tettazze maledette / Che ti va, intendo, a spasso in un albùol / Per canal, e (sì) ti voghi con le tette" (And you also have those damn ugly teats with which, I hear, you disport yourself in a boat and use those very teats as oars). Lest there be any doubt as to the person to whom Maffio addresses these virulent misogynist verses, he makes sure to name his victim very clearly:

> Se dis(s) e co' una in ossi xe reduta
> Che la somegia Veronica Franca,
> Che no ghe xe de ti la più destrutta.

They say that down to her bones she resembles Veronica Franca, and that no one is more destroyed than she.

Such an obscene portrait of unmitigated corruption was bound to arouse a cry of self-defense in a courtesan equipped to handle poetic contests. While Maffio Venier's diatribes against other Venetian courtesans went unanswered by his victims, Franco's poetic responses to Maffio's accusations not only oppose his portrait of her but ridicule the terms of his poetic discourse. [128] By transgressing the bounds of poetic decorum, she will argue, her detractor, not she, subscribes to a dissolute, chaotic world out of control. [129] Indeed she uses these poems, and most specifically the final one in the series, "Veronica, ver unica puttana" (Veronica, veritably unique whore) to enter into a poetic contest in which she defends herself and other courtesans against insults. The central poems in the *Terze rime* denounce the kind of man who delights in exalting women to the stature of virginal queen when it serves his legitimating purposes, but who when faced with social adversities, transforms women into vulgar whores whom he charges with the social and moral dissolution rampant in Venetian society. His outrageous slurs, and those of other Venetian poets before him, do not silence Veronica Franco but spur her on to poetic battle.

Two

FASHIONING THE
HONEST COURTESAN:
FRANCO'S PATRONS

Le donne son venute in eccellenza / di ciascun'arte ove hanno posto cura; / e qualunque all'istoria abbia avvertenza, / ne sente ancor la fama non oscura. / Se 'l mondo n'è gran tempo stato senza, / non però sempre il mal influsso dura; / e forse ascosi han lor debiti onori / l'invidia o il non saper degli scrittori.*
Ludovico Ariosto, *Orlando furioso* 20.2

La penna e 'l foglio in man prendete intanto, / e scrivete soavi e grate rime, / ch'ai poeti maggior tolgono il vanto. (1.76–78)†
Marco Venier to Veronica Franco, *Terze rime* (1575)

Veronica Franco advanced in Venetian society and literary circles despite patriarchal restrictions that confined Renaissance women to the private, domestic sphere and denied them the right to public speech.[1] Her participation in intellectual milieus thus called into question the efficacy of Renaissance humanists' and moralists' injunction against women's public status in Venetian society.[2] Courtesans were not subject to the strict social, familial, and class ideologies governing patrician women's lives and activities, and yet very few took advantage of this relative freedom. This is because courtesans who sought personal autonomy among the cultural elites—not to mention literary acclaim—faced considerable obstacles, although they were different in kind from those of patrician women.

Some explanation for the way Veronica Franco succeeded in publishing her works and in entering prestigious literary circles can be derived from an analysis of her family history, her involvement in social issues concerning

---

*Women have excelled in every art that they have tended, and whoever is informed of history hears yet of their fame. If the world has long been without it, this bad influence need not endure forever. And perhaps the envy or the ignorance of writers has obscured their rightful honors. (Cited and translated by Deanna Shemek in "Of Women, Knights, Arms, and Love: The *Querelle des Femmes* in Ariosto's Poem," *Modern Language Notes* 104, no. 1 (1989): 77 n. 18).

†Take pen and paper in hand in the meanwhile / and write delectable and gratious verses / which all poets will strip of superior fame.

women and marginalized groups in Venice, and her friendship with the poet and celebrated patron of letters, Domenico Venier. Through an examination of the material conditions of her life and her personal concerns—concerns most evident in the two wills she drafted in 1564 and 1570—we can begin to unravel the complex web of *mentalités* and the contradictory tensions surrounding the courtesan's profession as writer and public figure.[3] The strategies Franco employed to promote herself in literary circles and the defensive maneuvers she marshaled in legal arenas to defend herself from male detractors resemble the diverse roles she assumed in her epistolary poems and familiar letters: self-promoter, public debater, erotic lover, and self-justifier.

Veronica Franco in her occasional, patriotic compositions countered the negative image of the vulgar and venal courtesan promoted in male satirists' texts. She projected a view of her place and identity in Venetian society that directly opposed contemporaries' view of the courtesan's role in Venetian public life. Even though many of the laws passed in the first half of the sixteenth century were attempts to restrict Venetian courtesans' activities because of the civic misrule they created, Franco continued nonetheless to participate actively in intellectual and civic projects.

What most concerned governmental authorities was the blurring of social and class boundaries provoked by the courtesan's "unruly" presence in Venetian public life. On 21 February 1543, the senate asked that the magistracy of the Provveditori alle pompe (who oversaw the regulation of public expenditures) oversee this confusion.[4] Not only do Venetian citizens have difficulty distinguishing the "bone dalle triste" (good from the wicked) they argued, but foreigners to the city were unable to tell who was a noblewoman and who was a courtesan:

> *Sono accresciute in tanto excessivo numero le meretrice in questa città nostra, quale posposta ogni erubescentia et vergogna publicamente vanno per le stradde e chiesie et altrove sì ben ornate et vestite che molte volte le nobili et cittadine nostre per non esser differente dal vestir delle dette, solo non solum dalli forastieri ma dalli habitanti non conosciute le bone dalle triste, con cattivo et malissimo exempio di quelle che per mezo li stanno in stantia et che le vedono. (Senato Terra. Reg. 32, fol. 126)[5]*

The prostitutes in this city of ours have so excessively increased in number, and having cast aside all modesty and shame, they publicly frequent the streets, churches, and other places, adorned and dressed so handsomely that often our noblewomen and our citizens are dressed in much the same way, so that not only foreigners but local people as well are unable to tell the good from the bad, thus setting a bad and most pernicious example for those who cross their paths and see them, in view of the many advantages enjoyed by such persons of a low and abject standing.

The republic's legal efforts to reconstruct the eroding boundaries between social classes by enforcing sumptuary laws regulating a courtesan's dress and by proposing restrictions on her circulation in public were theoretically designed to protect patrician women's honor. But the laws were ultimately unsuccessful. Often courtesans transgressed the boundaries with little penalty. The sumptuary laws were rarely strictly enforced in Venice, perhaps because the *cortigiana onesta* satisfied her society's need for a refined yet sexualized version of the aristocratic woman.[6]

Despite the many attempts, then, to limit a courtesan's forays into Venetian public life, the occasional patriotic compositions Veronica Franco wrote and the poetic anthologies she composed and edited from 1570 to 1580 affirm her entrance into the intellectual life of the Venetian elite. They also set her apart from both the *cortigiana di lume* and the *meretrice* who depended solely on selling their bodies for financial support.[7] While her occasional compositions are on the whole highly conventional, Franco also manipulated civic encomiums for strategic purposes. This she did by adapting the language of courtly encomiums to the theme of civic pride and in the process rejecting Venetian male satirists' scorn. Further, she refused the subservient position assigned to her as an object of amorous exchange between male Petrarchan poets. By publicizing her connections with influential political leaders and intellectuals and associating herself in her lyric poems with the honorific image of Venice as sublime protectress, she placed herself, as honest courtesan and citizen poet, at center stage. She became both the subject of her works and the director of her literary career.

And yet a courtesan, like a male courtier, could not proceed unaided. In Franco's negotiations with patrons for intellectual support and textual commissions, she promoted herself as a writer and an editor in much the same manner as the sixteenth-century courtier projected a rhetorical persona in the interests of his political, cultural, and social advancement. Her search for male patronage resembles the strategies of the male courtier: verbal expertise and a sophisticated social demeanor were essential to courtesan and courtier alike. Unlike the male courtier, however, a courtesan found that it was not enough simply to acquire patronage and to master literary genres in order to advance in her literary career. She had to enlist the protection of male patrons willing to defend her reputation as founded not only on sexual labor but on "honest," that is, honorable, activities. Thus, the *cortigiana onesta* had first to overturn her community's manifold and multileveled prejudices against the common courtesan (already considered dishonorable) in order to fashion a literary career. The noblewoman, on the other hand, was instructed to safeguard her social standing within Venetian society by never incurring public rebuke. This was tantamount to renouncing a public voice and thus access to a literary vocation. The only exception to this unwritten rule was if a male patron or a father took it upon himself personally to foster a noblewoman's education or to assist her in literary projects.

Franco wrote her academic compositions and familiar letters within Domenico Venier's social milieu and literary *ridotto* (salon). The influence of Venier's circle is evident in the specific literary choices Franco made under his guidance. The poetics and literary theories advocated in the Venier *ridotto* also help to clarify the types of editorial commissions Franco succeeded in acquiring and the nature of the encomiastic poetic editions for which she composed verses upon request.[8]

As male patricians and upwardly mobile Venetian writers used the civic myth to improve their status, so the courtesan-poet would adopt it as an improving and enabling fiction.[9] Franco's self-portrait necessarily downplayed the sexual side of a courtesan's profession in favor of the intellectual activities she defended for all women. Without dismissing eroticism as one of the courtesan's allures, she was careful to dissociate it from the physical slavery of female prostitution. As Ann Rosalind Jones has aptly noted for both Franco and the Lyonnaise poet, Louise Labé, the courtesan's rhetoric is both "transgressive" and "contradictory":

> The public nature of their ambitions—the desire to rise socially, to be defined through and benefit from ties with powerful men—led both poets to a contradictory rhetoric. It is a transgressive rhetoric in two senses: they refuse injunctions to chastity and silence, and they speak to and for women in ways that shift the man-woman focus of love poetry to new concerns and positions. But theirs is also a rhetoric shaped and contained by the constant presence of men as the ultimate critics—of women's beauty, of their merit as poets, of their present and future reputations.[10]

Franco associated herself primarily with the liberty that Venice championed, as Aretino had done by his famous assertion in the familiar letters that in Venice "treachery has no place; here reigns neither the cruelty of harlots nor the insolence of the effeminate; here there is no theft, or violence or murder. . . . O universal homeland! Custodian of the liberties of man! Refuge of exiles!"[11] Franco also imitated her literary advisor's patriotism in his occasional vernacular poems. Like Venier, Franco praised her "immaculate" city as the Queen of the Adriatic. But unlike Venier, she took advantage of her sex to associate *herself* with the regal female attributes of the city, "dominatrice alta del mare, / regal vergine pura, inviolata" (royal virgin who dominates the sea, pure and inviolate: vv. 22–23). Further, in *capitolo* 22 of her *Terze rime*, she achieved a double strategy: exalting Venice as an earthly paradise—the locus of the miraculous union of divine, Christian, and profane pleasures—she praised herself indirectly as one of its most devoted citizens. She paid homage to the "maiden city's" physical beauty, opulence, and social cohesion. Just as the "Re del cielo" (King of the heavens) delights after the fact in his miraculous creation, his "eterno nido" (eternal nest), so this faithful citizen, far from Venice, returns there in her memory in *capitolo* 12 and marvels at the many wonders that have earned the Serenissima eternal acclaim:

> *In modo dal mondan tutto diviso,*
> *fabricata è Vinegia sopra l'acque,*
> *per sopranatural celeste aviso:*
> *   in questa il Re del cielo si compiacque*
> *di fondar il sicuro, eterno nido*
> *de la sua fé, ch'altrove oppressa giacque;*
> *   e pose a suo diletto in questo lido*
> *tutto quel bel, tutta quella dolcezza,*
> *che sia di maggior vanto e maggior grido. (12.37–45)*

> In a manner from the worldly set apart, Venice is built upon the water by celestial, supernatural decree: and the King of heaven was pleased to found in her the safe, eternal nest of his faith, which elsewhere lay oppressed; and for his own delight on this shore he placed all the most acclaimed and vaunted sweetness.

Even the sea, mesmerized by the city's extraordinary beauty, returns devotedly to contemplate her grandeur. Winding its way "per diverso e tortuoso calle" (by various and torturous channels) through the marble-constructed "Adria" perched miraculously on the waters, the sea, Franco claims in capitolo 22, pays homage to the regal, enthroned queen who majestically towers above the marble edifices:[12]

> *da quell'Adria tranquilla e vaga, a cui*
> *di ciò che in terra un paradiso adorni*

non si pareggi alcun diletto altrui:
da quei d'intagli e marmo aurei soggiorni,
sopra de l'acque edificati in guisa,
ch'a tal mirar beltà queto il mar torni:
e perciò l'onda dal furor divisa
quivi manda a irrigar l'alma cittade
del mar reina, in mezzo 'l mar assisa,
a' cui piè l'acqua giunta umile cade,
e per diverso e tortuoso calle
s'insinua a lei per infinite strade. (22.154–65)

from that tranquil and fair Adria, unequaled by any other in the things that adorn a paradise on earth: from those golden mansions of marble and carved stone built upon the waters in such a manner that the sea quietly returns to contemplate their exceeding beauty; and thus sends its waves, purged of their fury, to irrigate the noble city, queen of the seas, upon the seas ensconced, at whose feet the water humbly subsides, and by varied and torturous channels flows through her along countless paths.

But Franco's homage to her beloved city appears in a poem she addresses to an unfaithful lover from whom she has been forced to flee:

Poi ch'altrove il destino andar mi sforza
con quel duol di lasciarti, o mio bel nido,
ch'in me più sempre poggia e si rinforza.

Since fate forces me to go elsewhere,
the grief of leaving you, o beautiful nest,
continually grows within me and weighs me down.

By echoing the civic myth of the republic in a poem directed to a deceitful lover, she unites an encomium to Venice's liberty with a plaintive and sorrowful recognition of her own lack of freedom and that of all women when deceived in love:

E quanto avem di libertà più poco,
tanto 'l cieco desir, che ne desvia,
di penetrarne al cor ritrova loco:
si che ne muor la donna, o fuor di via
esce de la comun nostra strettezza,
e per picciolo error forte travia. (22.79–84)

And the less freedom we have,
the more our blind desire, which drives us off the path,

will find a way to penetrate our heart;
so that a woman either dies from this
or moves away from the restricted life that we all share
and owing to a small mistake is led far astray.

The poem closes with a tribute to her city's divine origins; her self-association with Venice's immaculate birth has allowed her to protect herself in part from the ravages of the human heart. Now far from Venice, she has distanced herself from the source of her pain and unhappiness, just as the impenetrable, unwalled city over the centuries has continually warded off attackers:

> Tutto 'l mondo concorre a contemplarla,
> come miracol unico in natura,
> più bella a chi si ferma più a mirarla;
> e senza circondata esser di mura,
> più d'ogni forte innaccessibil parte,
> senza munizion forte e sicura. (22.172–77)
>
> ad Adria col pensier devoto interno
> ritorno e, lagrimando, espressamente
> a prova del martir l'error mio scerno. (22.220–22)

The entire world comes to admire her
as a unique miracle in nature,
more beautiful for those who linger to gaze at her,
and, without encircling walls, a site more inaccessible
than a fortress, strong and safe though unarmed.

To Adria I return with my innermost and devoted thought,
and weeping, as proof of my grief,
I expressly denounce my mistake.

Here Franco aligned herself with the civic icon as both a patriotic gesture and a self-ennobling one. In so doing, she most certainly intended to attract the approval and support of specific patrons. For this reason, these patriotic verses abound in the praise required in the genre. Conversely, in her familiar letters, which may be read as glosses on her *capitoli* in terza rima, she proudly seized the role of social and moral critic. In this role she argued more aggressively that the Venetian civic icon aided only a limited and privileged segment of Venetian society. In so doing, Franco anticipated many of the complaints regarding Venetian women's inequality and subjugation raised by other, often more radical, sixteenth- and early-seventeenth-century Venetian protofeminists, such as Moderata Fonte, Arcangela Tarabotti, and Lucrezia Marinella. [13]

Ann Rosalind Jones contends that Franco participated in civic rhetoric and patriotic encomia in order to find "imaginative satisfactions" to compensate for the inequities that tyrannized the courtesan's life.[14] This, I believe, holds only in part. Rather, Franco invoked the civic myth of divine, immaculate origins in her works specifically in order to question for all women the extent of their participation in the values claimed by the Venetian civic myth, namely, personal justice and human liberty.

Franco was also well aware that to be a woman citizen in a city that characterized itself as an "donzella immaculata" (immaculate maiden) was problematic. Such a feminization of the city's myth of immaculate origins, and the exaltation of Venice as an icon of adoration, arguably restricted women's power by placing them under the control and definitions of an all-embracing patriarchal, patrician republic. Even in the civic Venetian ceremony of the "Sensa," or what is also called the "marriage of the sea" ritual, the doge sails from the heart of the city to the unprotected waters of the lagoon. There he pacifies the feminized sea ("la mar") by marrying her in a kind of hydromantic rite, as Edward Muir has described it. Much of the symbolism in this ritual was imbued with sexual images of male possession of an "unruly" female body.[15] Franco addresses this dilemma in her capitoli and familiar letters when she attempts to neutralize not only male authority but any class or social hierarchy that limits an individual's freedom. She insists on an equal and mutually enjoyable exchange between men and women.

In all of Franco's published works, and in critical moments in her life, she defines her involvement in Venetian society as inextricably tied to intellectual pursuits and social concerns. In this sense she claims the ameliorative epithet "honest," or "honored," as a necessary distinction between a courtesan whose only activity is to provide sexual favors to men in exchange for payment, and one whose principal means of social advancement parallels the artistry and the literary talents required of the male courtier.

II

Many courtesans provided the principal economic support for their families, a circumstance that runs counter to the popular representation of the courtesan as a greedy, self-serving individualist. Veronica Franco's wills demonstrate her commitment not only to her natal family's economic and social security but also to the future well-being of impoverished Venetian maidens, who, in the absence of a father or a strong father figure, had little hope of entering into the roles Venetian society had established for young women. Born in 1546 in Venice into a Venetian family about whom we know very little, Veronica Franco was fortunate to belong to the *cittadini originari* (citizens by birth).[16] This subpatriciate group constituted the salaried bureaucracy and professional order of Venice. Their names were recorded in the *Libro d'argento* (Silver book), while those of the nobility were registered in the *Libro d'oro* (Golden book). Denied high governmental positions or a vote in the Great Council (the Maggior Consiglio), this hereditarily defined caste nevertheless occupied positions in the *scuole grandi*, the Venetian confraternities, and in the chancery. The fact of Franco's birth thus disproves the theory proposed by Apostolo Zeno that the Franco family were of the lower classes, possibly merely poor fishermen. Giuseppe Tassini also discredited this theory by pointing to the existence of a Franco family shield at the entrance of the Calle dei Franchi in the *parocchia* of San Agnese in Venice.[17] Toderini's genealogy of the Franco family in the Venetian state archive has given us the names of Veronica's immediate family: her father, Francesco, the son of Teodoro and Luisa Federico, and her mother, Paola Fracassa, whose name appears together with Veronica's in the *Catalogo di tutte le principal et più honorate cortigiane di Venezia* in 1565.[18] In the year the catalog was printed, mother and daughter were said to be living in the parish of Santa Maria Formosa. Five years later, in Veronica's second will of 1570, we learn that Paola, her mother, was dead.[19] Four children are also listed on the genealogical tree: Veronica and her three brothers, Girolamo, Orazio, and Serafino. Married when she was still young, most probably in an arranged marriage, to a doctor, Paolo Panizza, Franco separated from him not long after.[20] She had six children (three died in infancy), although none of the children were, she claimed, by her husband, Paolo; according to what she reveals in her two wills, her children were all fathered by different men, including a nobleman, Andrea Tron, a member of one of the most powerful families in Venice.[21]

As becomes apparent from the laws that the Venetian senate legislated after 1542, a Venetian courtesan's reputation and social standing were made more secure if she were married, or more importantly, if she were protected by Venetian patricians.[22] Although Franco was married when still young, the union was not long lasting, and she never remarried. She did, as we shall see in her wills, profit from the support of certain Venetian patricians and well-placed citizens, but after 1570 we know very little about who actually assisted her in supporting her children and herself. The protection courtesans enjoyed from Venetian patricians worried authorities considerably, provoking them to pass a "parte" (ruling) in 1543 which cautioned noblemen against liaisons with courtesans. Indeed this ruling attempted to discourage noblemen from frequenting courtesans or any other "persona infame" (infamous person) at all and forbade them to support such people or defend them publicly in the Venetian courts:

> *Per li molti favori che hanno simil persona di mala et pessima conditione . . . alcun nobile nostro over altri di che conditione esser si voglia, non possi personalmente, né per polizza né per altri, pregar over intercieder per alcuna persona infame, la qual querelada al predetto Officio della Sanità, sotto pena de ducati cento . . . et esser bandito per anni doi dal nostro Maggior Consiglio essendo nobile; et non essendo nobile, di Venetia e del Destretto per li ditti anni doi.*[23]

> In view of the many advantages enjoyed by such persons of a low and abject order . . . none of our noblemen or anyone else of whatever order may personally or by proxy or at the behest of others plead or intercede on behalf of any infamous person, said person having been brought to court by the aforementioned Office of Public Health, under penalty of a fine of one hundred ducats and two years' banishment from our Supreme Council; if not a nobleman the same two years' banishment from Venice and from the district [will be enforced].

One of the obstacles authorities faced was how legally to distinguish a *meretrice* from a *cortigiana,* as well as an honest courtesan from a patrician woman. In the preceding year, 1542, they stated that a *meretrice* is a woman who either has not married at all and is sexually active with one or more men, or is married but does not live with her husband:

> *Quelle veramente se intendino esser meretrice quale non essendo maridate haveranno comercio et pratica con uno over più homeni. Se intendano etiam meretrice quelle che havendo marito non habitano con sui mariti, ma stanno separate et habbino commercio con uno over più homeni. (Senato terra, 21 Febuary 1542 m.v.)*[24]

> Prostitutes are to be considered those women who, while unmarried, have commerce and intercourse with one or more men. Furthermore, prostitutes are to be considered those women who while married do not live under one roof with their husbands but live apart from them and have intercourse with one or more men.

Defined, then, only by what she is not, the honest courtesan never received a precise legal definition of her own in the senate rulings of the sixteenth century.

As a result, difficulties in separating courtesans and prostitutes from "respectable" women continued to plague authorities. Unlike a patrician woman, whose life revolved exclusively around the private, domestic concerns of her family, the *cortigiana onesta* projected a highly sophisticated public image which she used to move beyond the domestic space of the family into the public spheres of Venetian life. Mimicking the graces and donning the costumes of the noblewoman, she was able to differentiate herself from the *cortigiana di lume* and the *meretrice*. Because courtesans' increasing wealth gave them access to extravagant costumes, they were visually indistinguishable from married women of the upper classes. Although the accumulated wealth of patrician women made them also increasingly powerful within the social and economic structures of the family (as Stanley Chojnacki has shown in his studies of patrician marriages of the fifteenth and sixteenth centuries), noblewomen's opportunities for constructive public or political interactions were virtually nonexistent.

In 1542, the Council of Ten proposed the election of three nobles for the sole purpose of overseeing public and social decorum. Their title was *Provveditori sopra l'honesto vivere et boni costumi della città:*

> *Sono tanto cressuti et multiplicati li vitii et mali costumi in questa città nostra, cum molto scandolo et peximo exemplo al ben vivere, che l'è necessario provederli a honor del Signor Dio, nella clementia del quale è da sperar che sì facendose l'habbi a placarse et esser propitio al Stato nostro . . . far si debba per scrutinio di questo Consiglio, elettione de tre primarii nobili nostri con titolo Proveditori sopra l'honesto vivere et boni costumi della città.*[25]

> Vice and disreputable practices have so increased and proliferated in our city, giving rise to such scandal and offering a most deplorable example where an honest way of life is concerned, that it has now become necessary to take adequate measures in honor of God our Lord in whose mercy we trust hoping that by our so doing he may be placated and propitious to our State . . . by decree of this council three of our primary noblemen given the title of *provveditori* will be elected to supervise the honest living and good morals of our city.

Further, the Council of Ten asked the *provveditori* to control courtesans' and prostitutes' public appearances, which they saw increasingly as socially disruptive. As Brian Pullan notes, "the decree of the Provveditori to save churches from desecration by prostitutes, originally formulated in 1539, was, if not the most consistently applied, at least the most repeatedly re-enforced of measures against prostitution: it reappeared in 1571, 1582 and 1613":

> *Né possino le soprascripte cortesane over meretrice andar in chiesia alcuna el zorno della festa et solenità principal di quella, a ciò non siano causa de mal exempio con motti atti parole et opere lascive a quelli over a quelle che vano a bonfine in ditte chiesie con vergogna de questa città et con dishonor et despregio delli luochi sacri et offesa della Maestà de Dio. Li altri giorni veramente andando le predicte in chiesia alcuna non possino star, ingenochiarsi over sentar sopra li banchi della detta chiesia ove si riducono le nobile et cittadine nostre de buona et honesta conditione, ma debbino star separate et lontane da quelle, essendo caute a non dare scandalo alle altre persone da bene.[26]*

Nor may the said courtesans or prostitutes enter a church on the day of its festival or during the principal celebration thereof so that they shall not in their several ways, by lascivious words and deeds, to the shame of this city, the dishonor and defilement of holy places, and offense to God's Majesty, set a bad example for the men and women who attend the above-mentioned churches to a good end. On other truly ordinary days the above mentioned are in no church whatever allowed to stand, kneel, or sit on the benches that in the church are occupied by noblewomen and by our female citizens of good and honest standing, but they must keep apart and at a distance from them, taking care not to give offense to other decent persons.

One way to call attention indirectly to the dangers of patrician women's extravagant tastes was to prevent courtesans from displaying themselves in the same sumptuous attire as the upper classes. Like courtesans, patrician women had also been subject to strict sumptuary laws, in part because of a prevalent concern with the enormous expense of sumptuous clothing, which was seen to be wasteful, and in part because such dress challenged male authority. As Chojnacki has written, "heavy spending on lavish dress could be viewed as doubly assertive, calling visual attention to individual identity and demonstrating the autonomous possession of wealth."[27] Sumptuary laws directed specifically against *meretrici,* many of whom obviously had the financial means to buy or rent luxurious costumes, reveal the pervasive and complicated nature of the problem. In 1562 a ruling stated that no *meretrice* may wear clothes of silk or put on any part of her person gold, silver, precious, or even fake jewels:

> *Le meretrici habitanti in questa città non possino vestir né in alcuna parte della persona portar oro, argento et seda, eccetto che le scuffie, qual siano di*

seda pura. Non possin portar cadenelle, anelli con pietra o senza, né meno alle orecchie alcuna cosa, tal che in tutto et per tutto sia proibito alle ditte meretrici l'oro, l'argento et seda et etiam l'uso delle zolie {gioie} di qualunque sorte, sì buone come false, sì in casa come fuori di casa, et anco fuori di questa nostra città. [28]

The prostitutes in this city are not allowed to wear gold, silver, or silk as part of their dress or any part of their body, exception being made for caps of pure silk. They are not allowed to wear chains, rings with or without gemstones, or any ornament in their ears, so that, in fact, they are under all circumstances forbidden the use of gold, silver, and silk, as well as that of jewels of any kind, genuine or false, inside and outside the house and even outside this city.

Cesare Vecellio's noted costume book of the period, when describing the courtesan's fashionable style, also illustrates how the visual codes identifying the married women, especially of the upper classes, had lost their clarity:

Di qui è che alle volte le Cortigiane e donne di partito rassembrano nell'Habito le maritate, portando anche gli anelli in deto, come le maritate fanno: e perciò chi non è più che prattico, ne rimane ingannato. . . . Lo strascico della vesta è molto lungo: anzi assai volte alcune di queste Cortigiane si lasciano vedere in Habito vedovile, molto simile alle Nobili Venetiane, appresso coloro, che non hanno la prattica della lor conditione. [29]

As a result, because of the way they dress, courtesans and *donne di partito* very much resemble married women; they wear rings on their fingers like married women and therefore anyone who is not more than aware can be deceived. . . . The train of their dress is very long; indeed at times some of these courtesans dress like widows and look very much like Venetian noblewomen to those who are not familiar with their condition.

But Vecellio's costume book was more than a guide to Venetian fashions; it served as a cautionary treatise directed to unsuspecting men, often foreigners, on the social mores of Venetian women. An example is his emphasis on appearance as one element in the courtesan's "devious" practices:

Courtesans stand at their windows making amorous signs to whoever interests them, displaying an astute haughtiness. After frequenting a Venetian patrician, they grab onto his family name, using it as their own and thus fooling many foreign men who come to the city and mistake them for Venetian ladies. Procuresses lend a helping hand. When a foreigner expresses the desire to enjoy the

favors of a highborn lady, a procuress dolls up some common prostitute. . . . Not knowing what Venetian noblewomen are like—
namely, that they care deeply about their respectability, the foreigners go around bragging that they have slept with them when
this is as far from the truth as one could get![30]

Not only was it difficult to distinguish a courtesan from a noblewoman
on visual grounds; the republic's repeated attempts to construct legal qualifications also went unheeded. Further, many of the sumptuary laws regulating public expenditure and decorum refer to *meretrice* and *cortigiana* in the
same sentence, applying the laws equally to each. As Rita Casagrande has
pointed out in her study of Venetian courtesans of the sixteenth century,
laws in the first half of the century did not clearly articulate the varying
levels of courtesanry, while senate decrees failed to separate the courtesan's
style of life (dress, residence, or social mores) from that of the aristocratic
woman:

> *Nel parlare di cortigiane si è creduto di esaminare la legislazione in genere
> contro il malcostume perché il Senato, sostanzialmente, non faceva dis-
> tinzione alcuna definendo le libere dispensatrici d'amore a volte "meretrici
> over cortesane," altre "cortesane over meretrici."*[31]

> In discussing the courtesans, we have meant to examine antivice
> legislation in general, since in substance, the senate made no dis-
> tinctions at all and referred to the free purveyors of love now as
> "prostitutes or courtesans" and now as "courtesans or prostitutes."

Following the plague in Venice in 1577, however, when the republic
appointed three additional officers to oversee the "sanitary" conditions of
the city and the sexual practices of its citizens, regulations directed at limiting courtesans' and prostitutes' circulation in public notably intensified.
Among the *provveditori alla sanità* elected in 1578 was Marco Venier,
Veronica's interlocutor in her *Terze rime,* published only three years
earlier.[32] Once again, a 1578 ruling addressed the difficulties in distinguishing courtesans from married women and widows. The *provedditori*
ruled to prevent courtesans not only from dressing as married women or
widows, but also from appearing at mass so dressed.

Not all courtesans accepted the Venetian senate's inability to differentiate courtesans from prostitutes. Their confounding of categories made certain courtesans, who saw themselves as superior to prostitutes, indignant.
To the rulings that limited courtesans' circulation in church (especially
during mass), one courtesan took vehement exception. A certain Madonna

Lucieta Padovana on 22 May 1543 was exonerated from the charges of being in church during "hore proibite per la lezze dello Excellentissimo Consiglio de Dieci" (hours forbidden by the law of the Most Excellent Council of Ten). Her contention was that "non reputandose meretrice" (she did not consider herself a prostitute) but rather a "cortesana" (courtesan), by implication a more distinguished profession. Further, she had "[suo] marito" ([her] husband) and therefore should not be subject to the laws regarding "meretrici."[33] Disregarding such protests as that of Lucieta Padovana, the senate decided to oversee the reconstruction of social divisions by returning again to the unresolved problem of differentiating courtesans from women of other classes and social rank:

> *Li Clarissimi messer Marin Gradenigo, messer Alvise Malipiero e messer Marco Venier honorabili Provveditori alla Sanità intendendo che nelle chiese di questa città a tempo che si celebrano li santi officii vano diverse meretrice e cortesane in esse chiese vestite da maridate e da vedove facendo atti disonesti con mal essempio e mormoratione de molti et da molti che non sono conosciute credeno che siano donne da bene e di bona fama e maridate . . . che sia aggionto alli capitoli che si è soliti publicarsi in tal materia, che le ditte cortesane e meretrice non possino andar vestite da donne maridate né da vedove sotto quelle istesse pene che sono contenute in essi capitoli, li quali capitoli siano publicati diman sopra le scalle e mandati per tutte le chiese di questa città acciò siano publicati in esse, et cussì hanno ordinato che sia notado. (20 December 1578)[34]*

The Most Illustrious Messers Marin Gradenigo, Alvise Malipiero, and Marco Venier, honorable health commissioners, having taken note that in the churches of this city, during the hours in which holy services are celebrated, a number of prostitutes and courtesans attend said churches attired as married women or widows performing lewd gestures, setting a bad example, and arousing the disapproval of many, and that many people who do not know them believe that they are honest women of good repute and married. . . . That to the notices normally made public on the subject be added the proviso that the mentioned courtesans and prostitutes cannot wear the garments of married women or widows subject to the same penalties contained in said notices, such notices to be published [posted] tomorrow at the top of the church steps and distributed to all churches in this city, there to be published [posted], and thus it is ordered and recorded.

For purposes of social promotion, however, it was not enough for the *cortigiana onesta* simply to be fashionably dressed. She had to offer herself, in the manner of the Japanese geisha, as an educated and skillful conversationalist and entertainer of men. Yet this very cultivation of the verbal arts, especially in conversation, prompted male writers and travelers to Venice to mistrust the courtesan's talents. They warned that a "public tongue" was tantamount to a dishonest woman. Thomas Coryat, echoing Montaigne's comments on the Venetian courtesan's art of conversation, declared that one had to be wary of the courtesan's many seductive musical and rhetorical powers:

> Moreover shee will endevour to enchaunt thee partly with her melodious notes that shee warbles out upon her lute, which shee fingers with as laudable a stroake as many men that are excellent professors in the noble science of Musicke; and partly with that heart-tempting harmony of her voice. Also thou wilt finde the Venetian Cortezan (if she be a selected woman indeede) a good Rhetorician, and a most elegant discourser, so that if shee cannot move thee with all these foresaid delights, shee will assay thy constancy with her Rhetoricall tongue.[35]

Perhaps because his own constancy had been "assayed," he insisted on cautioning others against her rhetorical powers. In any case, the honest courtesan's "Rhetoricall tongue" made her vulnerable to spiteful condemnation. It placed her at an ideological remove from the Venetian noblewoman, whose image and actions were confined by humanist notions of chastity and virtue that restricted her speech. Italian women humanist authors also suffered discrimination when they tried to publish their works. Whereas most noblewomen watched the goings-on of the public world from which they were excluded from the safe distance of their palazzo windows, the courtesan, like the male courtier, saw herself as actively involved in public affairs.

The courtesan attempted to elevate her social status by taking on the refinements of the patrician woman. During annual festivities and triumphal entries of powerful world leaders, her desire for elevation was shared by Venice. In these moments, the courtesan served the republic as a luxury object affirming the city's beauty and grandeur.[36] Sought after by certain foreign travelers to Venice for her cultivation and sensual elegance, she was one of the city's famous attractions. But when social pressures weighed upon authorities to oversee the city's moral conduct and to reduce excessive spending, as was often the case throughout the sixteenth century, the courtesans, along with other disenfranchised groups, such as Jews and homosexuals, were the first to be denounced for *luxuria*. During such a period of heightened moral and social tension, Franco herself was condemned by men who wanted to protect their reputations by denigrating hers, and by envious women who competed with her for social acclaim.

It is not surprising that certain noblewomen, perhaps out of frustration, felt bitterness toward courtesans. If one considers the extremely regimented lives they led in their private homes, not to mention the frequency with which noblemen continued to have liaisons with Venetian courtesans even after they were married, their reactions are understandable. Venetian women, especially of the upper classes, possessed few contractual rights in marriage; according to Venetian law, the woman was the subject and property of her husband. Although an unmarried Venetian woman owned her dowry, once she married, the dowry became her husband's property; he alone had the right to invest it for the family.[37] Stanley Chojnacki has argued, however, that patrician women in their testamentary practices "exercised a considerable influence in securing the internal stability of the Venetian patriciate by offering bequests that united natal and affinal kin." Because Venetian noblewomen were free either to dispose of their dowries in their wills or to use them to invest in business ventures, they increasingly gained psychological leverage on their male kin. Instead of offering bequests exclusively to the family lineage, patrician women also expressed personal attachments in their bequests.[38]

A reading of the two wills Franco composed during her first twenty-four years indicates the extent to which she shared many of the social and economic concerns of patrician women. Noblewomen's bequests, unlike those of their male counterparts, tended to be unconcerned with political maneuvering or rallying support among other influential *cittadino* or aristocratic families; rather these women were often intent on expressing their personal commitments and gratitude to other women who had shared their loneliness and forced seclusion or had assisted them in the labors of the household and palace complex—maidservants, tenants, and neighbors. Women's affections thus often moved beyond the family, incorporating people who shared strong personal bonds.[39]

Just as Venetian patriarchs controlled the lands of the *terraferma* (mainland), profiting annually from their investments, so most Venetian husbands continued to control the territory of their homes. They invested their wives' capital and commanded that they perform domestic tasks honorably, always with an eye to maintaining the family's dignity, and preserving by sensible household management the wealth accumulated over the generations. Rarely did noblewomen venture beyond domestic boundaries; in the earlier centuries, and to some extent in the sixteenth century, only the church and the parish feasts promoted by the *contrada* (parish) permitted them some access to the civic world, a world that delighted in the opulent display of prosperity, magnanimity, and piety.[40]

Franco's testaments reveal a woman devoted to the well-being of both her immediate family and her extended family, as well as to the future economic security of women friends and impoverished maidens. Although sections of her will conform to testamentary philanthropic and charitable concerns of the sixteenth century, these wills also point to Franco's particular interest in the future of other women. By aiding women in need, she both helped them and helped secure her own salvation. Perhaps because she had no female children of her own, Franco was intent on providing a young, unidentified woman with some economic support, thereby extending to her a measure of choice in selecting her future—a theme Franco returned to with unusual poignancy in letter 22 of her *Lettere familiari a diversi*.[41] This freedom of choice was precisely what she had lacked in her own childhood; her mother, Paola, was also a courtesan (albeit of a lower level), who needed the economic sustenance Franco's work provided once she became an older woman. It was most certainly Paola who introduced her daughter to the profession while Veronica was still quite young.

In her first will, composed on "10 agosto 1564" (10 August 1564) when she was only eighteen, Franco aimed to secure her children's financial well-being and provide for their education. (See appendix 2.1, no. 1, for a transcription of the will). As her dictation of the will reveals, Veronica was married, pregnant, and in fear of her life.[42] We see that Franco received support from certain influential patrician and *cittadino* families of Venice—families and individuals to whom she entrusted the management of the legacy of her family and children. That she herself belonged to a *cittadino* family undoubtedly helped raise her above the lower levels of courtesanry.[43]

Written in a lively mixture of Venetian dialect and Italian colloquial language, her wills bring to life many of Franco's most intimate concerns and her personal affections. In the first will, she names her parents as "Francesco Francho" and "Paola Fracassa." This is the sole document, in fact, that gives her mother's maiden name. She chooses two prominent Venetian *cittadini* as her executors, "Piero di Gozzi Rhaguseo" and "Messer Anzolo di Benedetti," who she prays will accept her request. Benedetti, Tassini notes, was from a distinguished Venetian *cittadino* family who owned an "altar" and "two tombs" in the church of Santi Giovanni e Paolo. "Jacomo Solian *quon-*

dam Agostin da Bersello" and "Fausto Bettani," the latter a "printer" at the Scotto publishing firm in Venice, are her two witnesses.[44] She states that she is living in the "contrà di San Marcilian" (parish of San Marcilian, also known as San Marziale in Italian) in the *sestiere* (quarter) of Cannaregio, but she requests burial in yet another quarter of the city, that is, in the church of San Francesco della Vigna (Castello), and the reciting of the masses of the Virgin and of Saint Gregory.[45] She would like to be placed in a simple coffin in keeping with the order of the Virgin, to be paid for by whatever resources her executors deem adequate.

Throughout this will, Franco displays a deep attachment to her brothers and to those who have taken active roles in their lives. Also scrupulous about rewarding fairly those women who served her or her family members well, Veronica leaves ten ducats to Agnesina, the daughter of her brother Orazio's wet nurse. She stipulates that this bequest is to be repeated any time Agnesina marries. She leaves another ten ducats for Zinevra, Magdalena's daughter, who remains unidentified, and once again, for each time the parish priest of San Marcilian declares her married. She emphatically requests that everything that she now owns or will come to own, whether immovable or movable, be given to either the son or the daughter to whom she is about to give birth. She qualifies this further by interjecting that she believes, though "only God knows," that the father of her child is Jacomo di Baballi, a noble merchant from Ragusa (Dubrovnik). For the love of God and the love that existed between her and Baballi, she asks that he assume responsibility for this child. Historical reports confirm that in 1558 a "Giocomo Bobali" came to Venice, where he stayed for almost twenty years, becoming one of the richest merchants active with the Orient and with Ragusa. He died in Venice in 1577, unmarried, and unfortunately intestate.[46] Franco stipulates that she wants her executors to draw up an inventory of all her possessions, and that all the money should be given to Baballi. Baballi is required, however, to match this capital every year, with 5 percent interest, for the benefit of her as-yet-unborn son or daughter until the child reaches legal age. If a boy, the child should be placed instead in the custody of the aforementioned executors, but when he reaches legal age, she asks that Baballi invest all of the remaining capital in goods or whatever he believes necessary to secure the child's future financial support. She is also concerned that her son be happy with this arrangement, as if to caution against any ill will from Baballi toward her son. If the child is instead a girl, she specifically requests that all the capital, with the interest accrued to that point, be given directly to her in the form of a dowry. Her daughter's decision to marry also must be approved by Baballi. The will goes on to state that if the child should die after having reached legal age, Franco's executors are to be allowed to do what they think best "of all of my case," but if the child should die before reaching legal age, all of the earnings, at 5 percent, that are in Baballi's possession should be given instead to Franco's mother. Her mother, however, is not authorized to use this capital, or to remove it from Baballi's possession. If Baballi should relinquish control of it because of choice, death, or leaving Venice, then Franco leaves the responsibility of overseeing her estate to Franco's executors. They are instructed to invest the capital and to provide her mother every year with the interest accrued until her mother dies. Finally she asks that when her mother dies, the interest be used by her three brothers Hieronimo, Oratio, and Seraphin. If, however, all of her immediate family and relatives are dead, and her brothers have no children, then after the death of her mother, all of the capital should be used for the "balloting system of the six guardians of the Scuole Grandi." The dowry balloting system for the marriage of poor maidens was one of the most popular forms of charity in the sixteenth century. These charitable institutions (the *scuole*) derived most of their revenue from personal endowments and trusts, which then provided dowries for their members' deserving daughters, as well as for the rich who had suffered unexpected reversals of fortune. Each year officers, who were appointed by the *scuole,* were responsible for identifying the young girls and reviewing their reputations in the neighborhood.[47]

Veronica's request that her entire capital be used for the dowry balloting system, allotting twenty-five ducats for each maiden, conforms exactly to the procedure that Brian Pullan has outlined. Those maidens who received the greatest number of "ballotte" (ballots) were to be awarded the allotments she allocated, according to the amount that remained of her capital.[48] But she stipulated that this charity should be put into effect only if she could first provide for her immediate family.

This interest in charitable concerns in the aid of Venetian women too poor to support themselves reemerges in letter 22, in which Franco advises a mother against allowing her daughter to become a courtesan. Since she was unequipped to enter the higher ranks of courtesanry because she was untalented and not sufficiently beautiful, Franco suggests that her addressee's daughter enter the Casa delle Zitelle instead. Founded in the sixteenth century, this home provided economic assistance to selected unmarried girls whose families were unable to support them; more importantly, as far as the republic was concerned, it was designed to safeguard their virginity as well as their reputation in the community.

This first will ends with a last, but very important and interesting request. She asks that her mother demand the restitution of Veronica's dowry from her husband, Paolo Panizza, and that her mother then be allowed to do with it what she pleases, "come quella che a me l'ha data" (like her who gave it to me). This addition suggests that Veronica's father never contributed to her dowry, but rather that she received a bequest from her mother, who provided her with the necessary assets to form an adequate dowry for a respectable marriage. What is interesting is that Veronica wants to repeat the same gesture in her own will by providing a young woman like herself with some money for her dowry. Finally, as a sign of her devotion and affection for Jacomo de Baballi, she concludes the will by leaving him her diamond. To the standard question as to whether she wants to leave any money to hospitals or other pious, charitable concerns, she answers no.[49]

Whereas Franco's incentive for composing her first will was the risk involved in childbirth, her second (and final) will, composed on 1 November 1570, when she was twenty-four years old, may be seen as a response to Venice's unstable political situation—the war in Cyprus—and the many dangerous environmental conditions that the Veneto endured over a ten-year period (see appendix 2.1, no. 2, for the transcription of the second will). During 1569, Venice and the Veneto region experienced heavy rains and flooding that severely damaged the annual grain harvests. The most serious consequences of these natural disasters were long periods of famine and a devastating typhus epidemic.[50] Moreover in 1570 a war against the Turks in Cyprus menaced Venice's maritime power. On 9 September 1570, the entire Christian force retreated and sailed back to Crete. Thus, the last Venetian stronghold, the city of Famagusta, surrendered to the Ottomans on 1 August 1571, after a siege of approximately eleven months.[51] Further, Franco's personal life had changed considerably, although only six years had passed since her last will; by 1570 her mother, Paola, was dead, and there is no mention of Jacomo de Baballi.

Thus this will returns to the question of the paternity of her child and to her children's future. She states in this will that she is the daughter of Francesco Francho, and that she is "sick in bed" in her home in the "parish of San Tomà." Having summoned Baldassare Fiume, notary of Venice, to write her will, and in the presence of her witnesses, she asks that her previous testament be discounted. She changes her executors to Lorenzo Moresini (a member of the Venetian Council of Ten), her brother Hieronimo, and Ludovico Ramberti.[52] Ramberti, a descendant of one of the most respected merchant families in Venice, was the owner of an apothecary shop at the Rialto bridge and was notorious in Venice for the scandal that had surrounded his brother, Pietro, many years before. By the time Franco met Ludovico, Pietro's crimes had long passed from Venetian citizens' memories. In 1540 Ludovico had attempted to save his brother from the hideous violence of capital punishment by giving him a deadly poison on the eve of his execution when he visited him in his prison cell. The nature of his act saved Ludovico from undergoing any severe punishment of his own. Regarded as a hero of fraternal devotion, Ludovico was sentenced only to a four-year banishment from the republic. When he met Veronica, thirty years later, he undoubtedly had reacquired the privileged status that his family had long enjoyed.[53]

In Ludovico Ramberti's will, written on 19 April 1570, he leaves "a farm estate with a house, haylofts, oven, and well" on the island Ca' Manzo near Chioggia to Veronica's son Achiletto.[54] He requests that Achiletto share the use and revenues of the property with Veronica until he reaches twenty-five years of age, after which time he may gain sole control of the property. If Veronica should die before her son, and if in her last will she leaves less to Achiletto than to her son Enea, then he (Achiletto) should in addition receive the usufruct payments that his mother has received over the years.

Whatever became of this bequest to Franco's son is unknown, because subsequent wills that might affirm Ramberti's kind gesture have not come to light. A paucity of documentation makes it difficult to understand the nature of their relationship and how long it might have lasted. Reconstructing Achiletto's and Enea's inheritance is also difficult because no other information regarding them survives. What is interesting is that only six years after Franco's first will, Ramberti took on the role of guarantor of affection and "paternal support," so to speak, that Baballi was assigned in the first testament; it is he who now stands as a father figure for Achiletto. There is no mention of support for Enea, Franco's second son.

By 1570, then, many of the men to whom Franco entrusted her children's future and the management of her monies were members of extremely prestigious Venetian patrician and merchant families. We find that Baballi is no longer authorized to protect and to take custody of her children; she assigns this responsibility to Zuan Battista Bernardo, a thirty-four-year-old military commander on the *terraferma* and a ducal counselor in the *savio del consiglio*. Further, she hopes that even though she has appointed him during his absence from Venice, he will not disappoint her request upon his return; indeed, she expresses the desire that if her children, as well as Andrea, the nephew of Ancilla her maid, should be ill-treated, "he should intervene and oversee their well-being as he sees fit."[55]

She now leaves everything she owns, and will come to own, to her sons, to whom she gives names drawn from classical epic, "Achille" and "Enea."[56] She asserts the first son is the child of Jacomo Baballi Raguseo ("il qual, quanto a me, credo sii suo fiolo e di messer Jacomo Baballi Raguseo"), that is, the child with whom she was pregnant at the time of the first will. She states that Enea is the son of Andrea Tron of Paolo Tron ("similimente mio fiol et fiol di messer Andrea Tron del Clarissimo Pollo").[57] As Giuseppe Tassini has indicated, Andrea Tron was married to the Venetian noblewoman Beatrice da Lezze in 1569 and was the son of Paolo Tron, an important Venetian senator, and Laura Priuli. This affair with Franco, if we accept her word, is evidence that Venetian patricians continued to frequent courtesans after marriage. Without Tron's wills, it is hard to know for certain whether he assumed any responsibility for Franco's sons as she requests in this will. Although we lack specific information about the government positions he held, we do know that he was "governatore di galea" (commander of a galley), and that at the age of twenty-six his name appeared in the list of forty nobles and deputies entrusted to organize Henri's entry into Venice and to accompany him in 1574.[58]

Franco stipulates that after her death her executors should sell all of her possessions and invest the sum acquired into a secure trust for her sons' benefit. What accrues from this investment should be used to support her children, as well as the son of Andrea, her maid, "whom I have accepted as an adopted son."[59] If the interest proves to be insufficient for both sustaining and educating them, she wants her executors "to cut into" her invested capital.[60] If her sons should want to become "friars," she continues, fifty ducats should be given to Marina (probably an adopted daughter, who lives in the home of "M. ni" [Morosini?] at Santa Maria della Fava) for her marriage.[61] If she is already married but has no wealth of her own, she should also receive this allotment of fifty ducats.

While there is little mention of Franco's father in these wills, she asks here that her executors provide her "carissimo padre" (dearest father) with fifty ducats, with the stipulation that they distribute this sum in three yearly installments. Despite her claim that he is her "carissimo padre," the way in which she allocates her money to him makes it appear that she does not trust him. Indeed she cautions that if by the time of his death he has not yet received all of this allotment, he must not be allowed to dispose of it in his own will. Instead, provided that both of her sons, Achille and Enea, are "friars," they should receive the "remainder" and interest of her capital and usufruct in two divided and equal parts. If they do not become "friars," both are nevertheless to be considered her heirs, and if one should die before the other, then his share should automatically pass to the surviving brother. She requires that they remain under the custody of her executors until they reach the age of fifteen; if they should die before her father, then he will be granted another fifty ducats a year in twelve-ducat allotments every three months with interest.

She bequeaths the balance of her capital to her brother Hieronimo's children. At this point, Veronica makes another unusual and striking request: if his wife should give birth to a daughter, this child should be granted the entire amount. Perhaps to assure some sense of continuity among her female heirs, and perhaps owing to the absence of any daughters of her own, she asks that "occorrendo che sua moglie facesse una fiola . . . con questo che gli sii messo nome Veronica al batesimo" (if her brother's wife should have a female child, she should be baptized with the name Veronica). If she has only male children, then Franco's capital should be divided among the sons in equal portions, and in the absence of any children, her brother Hieronimo should be the "patron" of the capital's usufruct. If her brother Serafin, "who is in the hands of the Turks" (she is doubtful whether he will ever return to Venice), needs money, he may be allowed to use a part of her fortune as ransom, namely two hundred ducats. If he does not need ransom money, all of the interest should be divided equally between the two brothers.[62]

In this will, then, unlike the first, Veronica carefully divides her capital among her natal heirs and extended family. She provides not only for her father and her children but also for her brother's family. Whereas in the first will she specifically indicated the dowry system of the *scuole grandi* as the recipient of her charity, here she leaves the "surplus" of her capital more generally for the marriages of "two worthy maidens." She qualifies this further by adding that in the event that "due meretrici" (two prostitutes) can be found who want to leave the wicked life and marry or enter a convent, they should be "embraced," rather than the two maidens.[63]

The remainder of Franco's will paints a vivid picture of her daily life, as she remembers, provides for, and repays outstanding debts to maids, servants, local merchants, and their families. This group portrait reveals a woman of considerable means who can afford the luxury of employing people in her home. It also reveals the hidden but much needed support of well-placed Venetian noblemen, men who apparently failed to acknowledge their involvement with her—a fact that will be used against her in the Inquisition hearings in 1580, when her children's tutor in consort with one of her maids denounces her to the Venetian tribunal.

To Agnese her cook she leaves four to six ducats for her salary; to Domisilla, "who is at present my maid," she bequeaths "all the things" that she had given to Caterina, her previous maidservant, and that must be recovered from her—items that have an estimated value of four or five ducats ("qual robba puol esser di valuta de ducati 4 o 5").[64]

To Suor Marina, a nun in the monastery of San Bernadin in Padua, she leaves ten ducats in one payment, which must be dispensed to her as soon as Franco's goods are sold—the same sum that Franco's maternal grandfather had left at one time to Veronica, to pay for prayers for her mother, Paola.

The final request to her executors reveals some of the luxuries that Franco enjoyed: for example, she requests that they repay in addition the following outstanding debts: to the heirs of Madonna Marieta, who is the wife of the "comb merchant of the Sol," she leaves three "ongari" and one scudo, "which he lent me"; to the "merchant of Salvadego," that which "he claims I owe him," as well as to the "druggists" and the "dressmakers" and any others who are real creditors. Finally she exonerates Jacomo Bozi from his "written debt of one hundred ducats" and asks that her commissaries "not ask him for anything, but that they let it be dropped." She concludes with a partial description of the items of her dowry that in her first will she had requested that her mother recover from her husband, Paolo Panizza. Some items, while not in Panizza's hands, are, she claims, still in Jacomo de Baballi's possession. He has, however, returned to her the money from her dowry that had been "given to him by her brother, that is ninety-three or ninety-seven ducats." The items that are still outstanding she lists as: "a string of fifty-one pearls with a value of one hundred ducats, a dress of pale yellow satin with silver and gold inlays, and a crimson bodice." Further, she contends that she received one hundred ducats approximately six months before from Don Donà, whom Tassini identifies as possibly from the monastery of Santo Spirito in Venice. She says that "he has taken for his security" the following silver items, all of which bear her "family crest": a "silver basin, six silver spoons, six silver forks, a salt dish that cost ten ongari," and "a silver candelabrum of the size of my candlesticks."[65] In response to whether she wants to leave anything to religious institutions, she answers no, but adds one final request. If her "adopted" son Andrea should become a monk, he is to receive during his lifetime five ducats yearly; if her two natural sons do not both become "friars," she asks that her "legacy" as she has defined it in this will be annulled.

These wills reveal Franco's allegiance to, and sense of responsibility for, young women who, owing either to lack of financial resources or lower social status, were denied the privileges of marriage or an education. Her bequests to young, undowered women underscore the precarious economic situation in which poor women, who lived on the margins of an affluent, patriarchal society, found themselves in early modern Venice. Despite the fact that Franco succeeded in educating herself and in attracting male patrons who supported her intellectual pursuits, she never forgot her commitment to women less fortunate than herself. In the late 1560s and early 1570s, as her wills reveal, she received little or no support from her father; she was, however, well connected to important *cittadino* and patrician families. Indeed Franco's two children, Achille, presumably Baballi's child, and Enea, the child of the nobleman Andrea Tron, were both from well-placed families; she was to have at least four more children by 1580, as we learn from her testimony in the Inquisition trial proceedings. The question of the paternity of Veronica's first child becomes even more vexed when we consider the testimony of Guido Antonio Pizzamano, brought before the Inquisition courts in 1572 on charges of living with an escaped nun. When asked if he has had any children, he responds that he has two children with his wife, Marina, who is still living, and also "a son" with Veronica Franco, "according to what she says," who is still living.[66] Although a few of the men she names in these wills were involved in literary enterprises, none was well known for his literary activities. While the social expectations of a *cittadina* and a noblewoman, not to mention a courtesan and an "honest" courtesan, were very different, one factor remains constant for all women who wanted to pursue a literary vocation, regardless of social standing or class: as already noted, without the financial and moral support of a father or a father figure who saw personally to a young woman's education, a Venetian woman had little hope of establishing a secure literary identity of her own.[67]

Since Venetian women, and Renaissance women in general, did not enjoy the systematic education required of the male courtier, they participated to a much lesser degree in intellectual discussions, or functioned in a literary capacity only to a very limited extent as readers of other women's writings. As readers they were mainly expected to turn their attention to religious texts, such as the *Fior di virtù*, a miscellany of religious materials from pious legends, the Ten Commandments, guides on how to make a good confession, and so on.[68] It was considered necessary, however, that a noblewoman receive some education to prepare her to raise her children honorably and wisely and to ward off the dangers of moral turpitude. In early modern Venice—a world in which literary success depended for the most part on one's social standing or on one's ability to rise socially through interpersonal connections and intellectual allegiances—women clearly were not allowed the kind of social mobility that more extensive education would have afforded. The only Venetian women who succeeded in publishing their literary compositions during the second half of the sixteenth century were members of either Venetian patrician families or noble families from the *terraferma*. Adult women lacked a public forum for exchanging views on intellectual matters, principally because they were kept in seclusion and because a woman's public voice was seen as lacking virtue. Not merely separated from men, they were isolated intellectually from each other.

As Paul F. Grendler recently has noted, while men might learn reading and writing at the hands of private tutors at home or in state-supported schools, noblewomen and *cittadine* were schooled primarily at home or in the convent. Their education consisted of elementary reading and writing in the vernacular, rudimentary arithmetic, and also handiwork, such as embroidery and weaving. Only in extremely rare cases did women benefit from a public, humanist education. Grendler explains that

> Social status and wealth, more than anything else, determined whether or not a girl received an education. Probably all noble and wealthy commoner girls learned to read and write. Middle-class girls had some opportunities to learn, and poor and working-class girls had few possibilities. Only a handful of girls of any class attended neighborhood independent schools.[69]

In Venice the number of women who attended formal schools was as low as 4 percent, compared to 26 percent for male children in 1587. As Grendler observes with respect to the upper classes, "the overall result is clear: it is very likely that all daughters of nobles and a good number of wealthy commoner girls received limited vernacular schooling, in the convent or by other means."[70] Whereas 30 percent of the male population in Venice possessed at least rudimentary literacy in 1587, only 10 to 12 percent of the female population was literate. Grendler argues, however, that maternal tutoring in families of higher social status increased female vernacular literacy when the prospect of tutors was financially prohibitive.[71]

Franco was not fortunate enough to have either a father who saw to her education, or a father figure who acted as her personal sponsor in literary undertakings, as was true, for example, of her contemporary, the *cittadina* writer, Moderata Fonte. Similarly, it is doubtful that her mother educated her. While certain mothers of upper-class families provided their children with a rudimentary education, it is most unlikely, as Grendler attests, that lower-class women would be able to do so: "Mothers in working-class and poor families . . . had to break the shackles of illiteracy in trying circumstances. An artisan mother probably had little free time to teach her daughter, and the daughter had few years in which to learn before being sent out to work as a servant girl."[72]

The Venetian writer Modesta da Pozzo (1555–92), alias Moderata Fonte, affords an interesting contrast with Veronica Franco. Having been orphaned at a very young age, she was placed by her grandparents in a convent where she received at age nine an adequate education. Once she returned to them, her grandfather tutored her privately and encouraged her to read and write poetry. Unlike her predecessors Isotta Nogarola and Cassandra Fedele, Modesta da Pozzo continued to write even after she was married to a well-placed Venetian *cittadino* and legal official, Filippo de' Zorzi, and gave birth to six children. In Franco's case, we have no explicit information on her education. Since she was the only daughter in a family of three sons, perhaps she was able to take indirect advantage of her brothers' schooling, especially if they received their lessons at home from a private tutor. But unlike da Pozzo, she had no one, so far as we know, who took a personal interest in fostering her education. That kind of sponsor she seems to have found only many years later, in Domenico Venier. As to the specifics of her brothers' education (not to mention her own), we can only conjecture. What is clear is that the private world of the salon gathering and the personal literary exchanges that were permissable there between courtesan and *letterato* was divorced from the public academic world of the university or formal academy. Moreover, distinguished courtesans such as Veronica Franco formed their own salons in which they too held informal soirees.

Another comparison between Modesta da Pozzo and Veronica Franco, this time of their tax reports, both drafted in 1582, reveals the financial rewards that da Pozzo reaped from a good marriage and paternal protection (her father had been well placed in Venetian government).[73] While tax reports do not reveal an individual's entire financial holdings (it was necessary to declare only income derived from real estate and agriculturally related holdings, or any interest income accrued from public debts, but not income related to one's profession or salary), they do provide a view into a sizable portion of an individual's wealth. Modesta da Pozzo had various rental properties and the security of a family home in which to live. Modesta reported that she was living comfortably in the home of her uncle "messer Zuan Nicolo Dogion, notary of Venice" (messer Zuan Nicolo Dogion, nodaro di Venezia). While Franco owned only two small properties outside of Venice, which reaped a meager rental income—perhaps they were the properties she received from Ramberti—and only part of her dowry intact, Modesta's property holdings provided her with a modest income. She owned a "casetta" (small house) in the "contrà de S. Hieremia" (parish of San Hieremia) from which she received a rental payment of eight ducats yearly, and nearby another "casa in soler" (upper-story house) for which she received twenty-four ducats annually in rent. Further, she owned two other houses from which she earned seven and twenty-four ducats yearly. She also reported joint ownership with her brother Lunardo of land on the *terraferma* that surrounded the "Villa de Borgoricco" (a small town northwest of Padua, near Camposampiero), which they rented out. For this she was paid yearly her share of eleven and one-half ducats. She also earned eighty-nine ducats yearly from the wine produced there and the animals sold (chickens, roosters, and pigs) from the land.

Franco's declaration reveals the precarious economic situation of a woman who lived outside marital and religious conventions (see appendix 2.2). As a courtesan she depended upon her youthful beauty and her capacity for self-promotion to sustain herself. Franco's reported property holdings were quite meager. As a result of the plague in 1575–77 and the thefts of precious items from her dowry in 1578–80, not to mention the added responsibilities she assumed when she inherited the care of her brother's children in addition to her own, Veronica Franco was impoverished by the early age of thirty-six. She lived in the region of Venice near the church of San Samuele, where many poor prostitutes congregated. The fact that she moved from house to house and from neighborhood to neighborhood in Venice many times during her life suggests that Franco might have had increasing financial difficulties.[74] Indeed, the ten-year period in which she had enjoyed household employees, sumptuous clothing, and elegant furnishings had, certainly by 1582, come to a crashing halt. Interestingly, this also was the year of Domenico Venier's death.

As we have seen, many factors contributed to the fragility of ties that bound courtesan to patron, especially the ambivalent feelings the courtesan engendered in contemporaries, who vied with her for public acclaim. Although the 1570s and 1580s marked an increase in the number of women who participated in literary milieus, only a small percentage of women published their works. Much remains to be learned about the salons women held; what we know comes from the occasional reference to social gatherings in women's familiar letters. In the absence of information on this important subject, or on the connections between women writers from different European countries who might have formed a literary subculture, it is hard to come to any other conclusion than that women had few intellectual networks that bound them together as a group. The silence that existed between Franco and Fonte (da Pozzo), for example, attests most vividly to the social boundaries that divided courtesan from *cittadina* writer—and this despite the fact that Franco was herself by birth a *cittadina*.

What set Veronica Franco apart from other courtesans, such as those listed in the *Catalogo,* was precisely her determination to educate herself and follow scholarly pursuits. She used her affiliation with the Venier circle to develop her talents and to publicize her literary endeavors. Indeed Franco's unparalleled success at self-promotion in the "teatro della pubblica concorrenza" (the theater of public competition), as she called it in letter 17, and her appeal to Venier's protection are remarkable. Her devotion to intellectual concerns emerges most forcefully in her familiar letters. In letter 17, addressed to an "idle and vain Venetian youth," she articulates both the conditions necessary for winning her love and the intellectual dedication she values, counseling her admirer to commit himself to the acquisition of "virtù" (virtue). His "wandering and vain exile" affirms his unwillingness to settle "not only in his beloved city but also near the woman he claims he loves so devotedly." She underscores her determination to participate in the public literary world so readily available to him but denied to most women. Charging him with the same vanity, idleness, and deception that satirists attributed to the courtesan, she suggests herself as an example for him to follow. She warns the youth to avoid the "ruin of the appetite more than the edification of reason,"[75] and, in a self-elevating gesture, she alludes to Cicero's question in his *Tusculan Disputationes:* "is anything in accordance with nature which is done in opposition to reason?"[76]

Recommending that her suitor live a "peaceful life in the tranquillity of study," and that he present *her* with "the fruit of his labors in honest doctrines," she places herself in the uncustomary position of reviewing his "exercises" and judging whether he deserves a reward from her. What this reward is she never says. Most importantly, he must prove to her that he is worthy of entrance into the "accademie degli uomini virtuosi" (academies of virtuous men):

> *Voi sapete benissimo che tra tutti coloro che pretendono di poter insinuarsi nel mio amore a me sono estremamente cari quei che s'affatican nell'essercizio delle discipline e dell'arti ingenue, delle quali (se ben donna di poco sapere, rispetto massimamente alla mia inclinazione e al mio desiderio) io sono tanto vaga e con tanto mio diletto converso con coloro che sanno, per aver occasione ancora d'imparare, che, se la mia fortuna il comportasse, io farei tutta la mia vita e spenderei tutto 'l mio tempo dolcemente nell'accademie degli uomini virtuosi.*

> You know full well that of all [those] who would expect to insinuate themselves into my love, most dear to me are those who labor in the practice of the liberal arts and disciplines of which (even though a woman with little knowledge) I am so fond. And it is with great delight that I converse with those who know so, that I might have further occasion to learn for, if my fate allowed, I would live my entire life and spend all my time with delight in the academies of virtuous men.

Far more than being a mere cultural curiosity or tantalizing anecdote (albeit one that reaches mythical proportions in most historical studies), Veronica Franco and the works she published remind us of the enormous obstacles faced by courtesans who attempted to acquire an education and an "honest" profession while hoping to maintain a measure of personal dignity. Before Franco articulated openly an erotic poetics of love, as she does in certain poems of her *Terze rime,* she secured public protection and literary acclaim from academic circles and influential patrons. This she did by redefining the courtesan's pursuits as "honest." Her entrance into a privileged male arena—the academy of virtuous men—required the pursuit of those "oneste dottrine" (honest [or honored] doctrines) so readily neglected by her male interlocutor and so hard won by most women, who were made to confine their activities to domestic concerns.

III

Fioriscono certo in quei tempi antichi, disse Lucretia, de rari, e maravigliosi ingegni; ma a giorni nostri, o che 'l mondo va invecchiando, o gli

huomini van peggiorando, non si trovan così fati ingegni: Come no, rispose
Corinna, perdonatemi voi errate; Ve ne sono de tali, che agguagliano quelli
del tempo passato. . . . Questo fu il Clarissimo Signor Domenico Veniero,
di cui la memoria chiarissima vivrà immortale nel mondo, e fin che vivo mi
starà sempre fissa nel cuore. (Moderata Fonte, *Il merito delle donne*
[1600])

Undoubtedly, Lucretia said, during those ancient times there flourished rare and marvelous minds; but nowadays either because the
world is getting old or because men are deteriorating, such minds
are not to be found. How so, rejoined Corinna, forgive me but you
are wrong. There are some minds that equal those of the past. . . .
One such was the most illustrious Domenico Veniero, whose shining memory will live on immortal in the world and will always remain firmly established in my heart.

The emotional, political, and intellectual support that Veronica Franco
received in the 1570s from Domenico Venier and other influential men in
Venetian society was crucial to her career as honest courtesan. However,
how she came to know Venier is not certain. She was counseled by him on
literary questions throughout the ten-year period in which she published
her literary works, and she also enjoyed, as did other courtesans and the
virtuosa Gaspara Stampa, the privilege of frequenting his literary salon in
Santa Maria Formosa. Ca' Venier was the most important gathering place in
Venice for intellectuals and writers during the mid-sixteenth century, with
the possible exception of the late 1550s, when the Accademia della Fama
flourished. But the Venier household survived the academy's demise in
1561.

Domenico Venier lent his protection and advice to a number of woman
poets and intellectuals. When the female character Lucretia, in Fonte's
treatise *Il merito delle donne,* claims that there are no modern "ingegni"
(minds) to equal the ancients, Corinna (Fonte's spokeswoman) vehemently
denies this assertion. She declares that the illustrious Domenico Venier,
"che era capo e sostegno de gli altri" (who was the leader and supporter of
others) surpassed all others in his intelligence and in the exemplary literary
gatherings held in his private home.[77] Indeed Moderata Fonte and many
other woman writers, including Irene di Spilimbergo, Gaspara Stampa,
Tullia d'Aragona, and Veronica Gambara, turned to Domenico for support.
Similarly, Franco's success in projects devoted to singing the praises of
Venice and its heroes undoubtedly owed much to Venier's influence in intellectual circles.[78]

Veronica Franco was both editor and collaborator for civic-oriented "academic" projects within the ten-year period 1570 to 1580 (the years in which all of her literary works were published). That she succeeded in realizing her projects, as she attests in letters 19, 32, 39, and 40 of her *Lettere familiari a diversi,* is confirmed by the presence of editions and manuscripts in the Biblioteca Nazionale Marciana in Venice. This kind of editorial work, while mentioned by earlier critics, has been underestimated in assessments of Franco's literary career. Although many of her occasional poems undoubtedly never were printed and are now lost, their rarity has as much to do with the informal nature of literary exchanges in Venice in the latter half of the sixteenth century as with the specific practices of her literary patron, Domenico Venier, who, as Francesco Erspamer has noted, never collected his own poems for publication during his lifetime.[79] Just as male literary reputations were often made by praising women, Franco collects praises written in honor of men in order to praise herself indirectly. She understood, as did Aretino before her, that records of prestigious literary connections facilitated political advancement and social mobility, and that the reverse was also true.

When away from Venice, or unable to attend Venier's salon, she records her absence in her poems and letters. Her attentiveness to the Venier salon, as crucial for creating a literary reputation, is most evident in *capitolo* 15 in her *Terze rime.* Franco points to the fragility of ties between male milieu and courtesan poet when she says that she is afraid ill-founded rumors will circulate regarding her absence from Venier's salon ("Io so pur troppo che da la brigata / far mal giudizio de le cose s'usa, / senza aver la ragion prima ascoltata" [I know too well that our circle is bound to pass adverse judgment on matters without having heard what the reason might be, vv. 16–18]). Hence, she provides Domenico with the real reason for her absence.

> *Signor, ha molti giorni, ch'io non fui*
> *(come doveva) a farvi riverenza:*
> *di che biasmata son forse d'altrui;*
> *   ma, se da far se n'ha giusta sentenza,*
> *le mie ragioni ascoltar pria si denno*
> *da me scritte, o formate a la presenza. (15.1–6)*

> Sir, for many days I have not (as I should have) come to pay you my respects: for which I may be blamed by some; but if just sentence is to be handed down, my reasons must first be heard, expressed in writing or in your presence.

She confesses that she has been absent owing to the unexpected departure "six days before" of her lover: "quest'è mia scusa, che l'amore, / ch'io porto ad uom gentile a maraviglia, / mi confonde la vita e toglie il core" (for this is my excuse: the love that I bear for a wonderfully noble man confounds my life and robs me of my heart [vv. 28–30]). How could she, she asks, come to his "celebre concorso" (illustrious gathering) in this miserable state, "meschina, inferma e mesta" (wretched, infirm and sad)? Witnessing her host's physical pain, her suffering would only increase, producing tears rather than learned conversation:

> *Come doveva over potea, con questa*
> *oppressa dal martir gravosa spoglia,*
> *venir da voi, meschina, inferma e mesta,*
> *   a crescer come la mia la vostra doglia*
> *e, in cambio di parlar con buon discorso,*
> *aver di pianger, più che d'altro, voglia?*
> *   In quel vostro sì celebre concorso*
> *d'uomini dotti e di giudicio eletto,*
> *da cui vien ragionato e ben discorso. (15.91–99)*

> How should or could I visit you with this dreary body wracked by pain; wretched, infirm, and sadly wanting, more than anything else, to weep? And [thus] I will increase your grief with mine instead of making intelligent conversation.

On the basis of allusions such as these, we can identify the physically infirm Domenico Venier as the recipient of this and other of Franco's letters and as the center of a salon whose opinions are critically important to her.

She identifies her lover as "mio colonello" (my colonel), "esperto in guerregiar" (expert in the arts of war), who has departed from Venice for Crete on a military assignment but has promised her a quick return. Although he is never explicitly named, it is probable that she refers to Francesco Martinengo, the brother of Estore, for whom she compiled a commemorative edition of poems in 1575.[80] Descendents of a noted Brescian family, Estore and Francesco Martinengo served the Venetian republic as military leaders in the war against the Turks. Estore's life appealed to the Venetians' love of melodrama and adventure. It combined military exploits with bravery: he was twice wounded while serving as an army artillery officer.[81] When the Turks invaded Famagusta, Estore escaped by hiding for five days in the house of Greek merchants. He then sold himself as a slave, escaping once again to Tripoli, where he first boarded a French boat sailing to Candia and then managed to hide on a Cypriot boat en route to Venice. Upon his arrival in Venice, he valiantly and quickly assembled new troops, raising sufficient money with which to return to continue the Venetians' struggle against the Turks. Well known not only for his heroic determination to defend Venice, he also left important historical reports on the attack of Famagusta and on other major battles of the period.[82]

Rime di diversi eccellentissimi auttori nella morte dell'illustre Signor Estor Martinengo Conte di Malpaga, honoring the Martinengo clan, includes Franco's dedicatory epistle to Estore's brother, Francesco. Here she asserts that she has taken the liberty of including and "interweaving" her own poetic compositions with those she has already solicited from "così divini intelletti" (such divine intellects):

> *La qual nella pretiosa Corona di così divini intelletti, pur mi sono inserita, et tessuta, componendo ancho io alquanti Sonetti sopra così degno, et importante soggetto, che insieme con gli altri le mando in picciol segno della mia devotione, et del senso, che io tengo commune con lei ne' suoi dolori.*
>
> I have included and interwoven myself in the precious crown of such divine intellects by also composing a number of sonnets on so deserving and important a subject; and I send them to you as a small token of my devotion and of the feelings that I share with you in the hour of your grief.

Hence, together with nine of her own sonnets, she completes the volume with seventeen sonnets by members of Venier's literary salon. This edition is without date, place, or name of publisher, but it is most likely that it was published in 1575, the same year as her *Terze rime.*[83] How this volume was produced, printed, and financed is not clear because we do not have any information regarding the circumstances of its preparation. But Franco writes to her fellow poets that rather than praise *her*—a subject she dismisses as unworthy in a pose of false modesty—they should direct their efforts to a worthier goal, the edition she is compiling; this is a goal nevertheless equally beneficial to her, because it associates Franco with an important public project honoring the republic.

Thanking a man, presumably Domenico Venier, who has kindly assisted her in the past, Franco reminds him in her letter 32 of his offer to assist her again. She provides him now with an opportunity to pay her a service by composing verses in Martinengo's honor:

> *Non ho parole bastevoli da ringraziar l'infinita cortesia di Vostra Signoria espressami in tante maniere . . . così vorrei aver modo di palesarvi la mia*

volontà desiderosa e obligata di servirvi . . . continuerò di manifestarvi la
mia intenzione con l'accettar la vostra cortesia, usandola in maniera che
pur un giorno vi venga voglia di prevalervi di me.

I do not have sufficient words to thank your lordship for the courtesy expressed to me in so many ways. . . . Therefore I would like
to have the opportunity to manifest to you my eager and dutiful
desire to serve you. . . . I shall continue to make my intentions
clear by accepting your courtesy and taking advantage of it, so that
one day you too may be enticed to make use of me.

Count Estore Martinengo, "gentiluomo di sangue illustre" (gentleman of
illustrious blood ties), she informs him, has died tragically (at the age of
thirty-two) in Corfu. Hence, she is planning an anthology in his memory
and would like to include Venier's works and those of his "academici" (academicians):

Questa è la somma breve dell'informazione, la qual io mando perché Vostra
Signoria scriva e faccia scrivere da quei suoi academici secondo le piacerà,
affermandole che le sue composizioni tra tutte l'altre mi saranno carissime,
sì come io sono certa che di bellezza e di dottrina saranno notabili tra tutte
l'altre.

This, in short, is the information I am sending you so that Your
Lordship may begin to write and request the academicians of your
choice to write, added to the assurance that among all others, your
compositions will be dearest to me, since I am certain that they will
be superior to all others in beauty and learning.

In another letter to Domenico Venier (39), Franco tells him why she has
not responded until now to his "cortesissime lettere" (most courteous letters); she has had to devote her full attention to her children, who have been
seriously ill:

Ho tralasciato lo scriverle non per mia elezzione, ma contra mia voglia per
impedimento fortunoso sovragiuntomi di malatia nella persona d'ambo i
miei figliuolini, che, l'un dopo l'altro, tutti questi giorni passati sono stati
aggravati di febbre con vaiuole e con altri accidenti che m'hanno tenuta
occupata e addolorata fuor di misura.

If I have neglected writing to you it is not by choice but against my
will, since I have unfortunately been prevented from doing so by
illness which has stricken me in the persons of both my small sons,
who, one after the other, have succumbed to fever and smallpox,
and also by other mishaps that have kept me occupied and have
aggrieved me beyond measure.

Pleased to be able to return to the Martinengo project, she hopes that Venier will compose as many sonnets as time will allow. She too has been asked by "chi può commandarmi" (one who can command me [presumably Francesco Martinengo]) to compose lyrics "sopra questa materia" (on this subject) and to commission others. She has succeeded already, she proudly informs him, in acquiring promises from "molti altri gentili spiriti" (many other gentle spirits) to compose verses:

> *mi basterà a farvi riverenza e a pregarvi ch'a mio compiacimento vi piaccia d'impiegar l'opra de' vostri delicatissimi studi, componendo quel numero di sonetti che vi concederà il tempo e la mia intercessione nella morte dell'illustre signor conte Estor Martinengo, da me grandemente osservato.*
>
> I can only salute you respectfully and beg you to indulge me by agreeing to apply your most refined skills to the composition of any number of sonnets that time and my entreaties will permit, on the occasion of the death of the illustrious Count Estor Martinengo, whom I hold in great respect.

Some have already written, on her urging; indeed, she plans to put the volume together quickly, though with care: "e molti sin qui hanno di già scritto sollecitati da me, che desidero di far presto e bene, s'io potrò" (and many persons have already written at my request because I want to work fast and well, if I am able). In her dedicatory letter to Francesco, which opens the volume, she insists that she is unequal to the task of praising his brother's "eccellente virtù" (excellent virtues) but also remarks that her efforts as an editor "have not been spent in vain."

Her anthology in fact includes some of the most distinguished poets of Ca' Venier. Domenico Venier's sonnet "Ahi che giace per man d'invida morte" (Alas, he lies stricken by the hand of invidious death), which follows the letter of dedication, solemnly invokes "death" (morte) and "life" (vita) in alternating lines; he juxtaposes the virtues of the present with the "better life" (miglior vita) awaiting the deserving in the "eternal life" (eterna vita) of the heavens. This is followed by two sonnets, "Di quei Vinetia antica invitti Heroi" (Of those unvanquished heroes of ancient Venice) and "Per te più d'ogni altrui felice vita" (To a life happier than anyone else's), by Domenico's nephew and Franco's lover, Marco Venier. Here the conceit centers on Martinengo's name and his military exploits; he likens him to "Marte" (Mars), who descends from the heavens to protect Venice and spends his all-too-brief life with "us here on earth."[84] In fact many of the verses, including Franco's, similarly rearrange the parts of Martinengo's name so as to compare his illustrious deeds with those of the ancient gods, thereby attributing to Venice a military grandeur paralleled only by the Roman Republic. Another conceit which runs throughout the edition centers on the illustrious members of the Martinengo family, who, although not of Venetian but of Brescian origins, continued throughout the century to defend the republic militarily.

The Paduan poet Bartolomeo Zacco, for whom Franco composed a number of poems to mourn the death of his daughter Daria in 1575, also contributed three sonnets to this anthology. In them, he lauds Estore's military deeds, claiming that Estore, like Nestor (the ancient Greek king of Pylos championed by Homer, Propertius, and Tibullus), who led his subjects to the Trojan War, embodied wisdom, justice, and eloquence. Unlike Nestor, however, this Estore attained such virtues while still a young man. Poems by Celio Magno, Orsato Giustinian, Andrea Menichin, Marco Stecchin, Horatio Thoscanella, Giovanni Scrittore, Valerio Sali, and Antonio Cavassico adopt one or the other of these themes, but only Giovanni Scrittore, a lesser-known poet, directs his praises to the volume's editor, Veronica Franco, while lauding Martinengo's many virtues:

> Qual gratia, o qual destin, che da la morte
>   Pianger del tuo fratel da noi partito;
>   Donna d'immortal pregio, e infinito
>   Ti frenasse Francesco invitto, e forte?
> Questa, onde vivo al Ciel con degna sorte
>   Sei tra le lodi del suo stil salito;
>   E sirena gentil, che d'Adria allito
>   Vien ch'alta gloria co' suoi doni apporte.
> Veronica celeste, unica, e vera
>   Dea tra noi di beltà, di cortesia,
>   Franca in valor, che indarno altri qui spera,
> Benché seguendo lei per dritta via;
>   Felicemente a la beata spera
>   Ogni nobile spirito s'invia.

Is it favor or fate that a woman of immortal and infinite worth should halt the tears that you shed over your departed brother's death, making you, Francesco, undefeated and strong? This woman, thanks to whom amid the praises of her verse you have risen to heavenly heights during your lifetime, is a gentle siren who hails from Adria's shore to bestow lofty fame with her gifts. The divine Veronica, unique and true goddess of beauty and courtliness in your midst, frank (enfranchised) by a valor to which all others

here aspire in vain, although they follow her along the correct path;
so felicitously all noble sentiments are sent to the blessed sphere.

He points to her many noble attributes by playing with the components of her name that signify valor, honesty, and singular, goddesslike beauty.

In her own sonnets, Franco moves from a solemn personification of death as the "blood-stained scythe" in the opening lines of the first sonnet ("La Morte ognihor ne l'opre rie più ardita / Con sanguinosa falce in atto vile, Al fratel vostro a voi caro, e simile / Tronco l'april de la sua età fiorita" [Forever boldest at its foulest deeds by a cowardly blow of its blood-stained scythe, Death struck the brother so dear to you and so alike, and cut short the April of his flowering days]) to a more jubilant note in the sixth sonnet—Estore's triumphant ascent to heaven:

> Poiché dal mondo al Ciel, suo proprio albergo,
> qual lampo a l'apparir tosto sparito,
> è il saggio, e valoroso Estor salito,
> quasi l'ali impennando al lieve tergo.

For from this world to heaven, which is his rightful abode, like a flash of lightning that vanishes as it appears, the wise and valiant Estor has ascended spreading behind him his feathery new wings.

The remaining sonnets in the volume are Franco's. They are all dedicated to the Martinengo family, in particular to Estore's brother, Francesco. Praising Francesco's military exploits, by extension she also praises Venice, the city he is intent on defending. Speaking to Venice personified, she reassures the city that Francesco will continue to fight in its defense:

> Morto è il grand'Estor, ma di lui maggiore
> vive Francesco, quel, ch'al empio Scita;
> combattendo mostrò l'invitto core.
> Questi con mano ti difese ardita,
> Vinetia bella, e con supremo onore
> l'opre sue degne a favorir t'invita.

The great Estor is dead, but greater than he still lives Francesco, who in battle showed the Scythian his undefeated heart: He defended you with a brave hand, O beautiful Venice, and now he invites you to celebrate his excellent deeds with supreme honors.

Indeed the last two sonnets champion Francesco and his other brother, Gherardo, who, owing to their extreme sorrow over the loss of their brother, are now pushed, she states, to defend Venice with increased vehemence from the ever-present threat of an Ottoman invasion:

Questi, ch'è anchor colonna ben fondata
  Contra l'Othoman impeto sì crudo,
  Di Marte con le man proprie innalzata;
Nel dolor del Fratel morto m'è scudo
  Con lieta gloria illustre, ondo abbagliata
  La vista d'ogni affetto abbasso, e chiudo.

This man who is also a firmly established column erected by Mars
with his own hands against the cruel assault of the Ottoman. While
grieving for his brother's death, he shields me with proud illustrious glory so that, bedazzled, I lower and close my eyes to all
distractions.

This edition attests to Franco's success in negotiating with the literary
world of sixteenth-century Venice, in which poetic anthologies advertised a
writer's social mobility, appearance of intellectual worth, and stylistic
achievement. Calling attention to her entrance into prestigious academic
milieus throughout her *Lettere familiari a diversi,* she explains to Domenico
Venier (as in letter 40) that she has not been to see him recently because she
has been under unusual pressure to finish quickly a certain "lugubrious
composition." This she must do in order to be able to give her composition
to an unidentified "gentiluomo" (gentleman) before his departure from
Venice. Her highly courteous and long-winded explanation builds up to
her final request; she reminds her interlocutor to complete his verses so that
she may add them to her own:

> *E questo è quello impedimento che mi tien ch'io non venga a farle la mia
> devuta riverenza, con la quale, accompagnata da caldissime preghiere,
> torno con queste poche righe a sollecitar instantemente e diligentemente la
> cortesia di Vostra Signoria, già per promessa da lei obligatami, che voglia
> scrivere in questa materia quel tanto ch'io le chiesi e ch'Ella mi promise
> . . . anch'io vengo spronata dalla brevità del tempo che s'avvicina della
> partenza di quel gentiluomo per cui faccio questa fattura.*

> And this is the impediment that prevents me from coming to pay
> my respects, which I offer accompanied by my warmest entreaties,
> as with these few lines I once again urgently and earnestly press
> Your Lordship for the already obligingly promised kindness of
> writing on this subject what I asked for and you promised. . . . I
> too am spurred on by the lack of time, since the departure of the
> gentleman for whom I am doing this work is approaching.

Further, he is to act as a mediator between her and "those gentlemen" who
have also promised to write for the edition by reminding them as well of the

approaching deadline. By taking the place of group choreographer for prestigious collections honoring the republic, Franco, in a gesture unprecedented for Venetian courtesans, built a reputation similar to the one that Aretino sought to project to posterity. In her works she established her public persona, as he did, by associating herself with powerful people.

Unlike Aretino, she rarely names her admirers in her letters or poems, but she often provides her readers with ample and well-pointed clues to the identity of men easily recognizable to Venetian cognoscenti. For example, she writes a letter (44) to a friend informing him that "she has gravely wounded her knee with a hairpin," rendering her unable to walk. While the stated purpose of the letter is to ask him to lend her his wheelchair, the request comes after a long introduction in which she praises him, and by implication herself; she claims that "fortune" has placed her in a position similar to that of her much-esteemed friend. Now she can participate in his suffering, because she too suffers from a "simil indisposizione di membra" (similar ailment of limb). Without naming him, we know, as did others, that it is Domenico Venier to whom she directs her letter:

> *La fortuna m'è favorevole a rendermi simil indisposizione di membra al nobilissimo capo di Vostra Signoria, avendomi quasi fatto perdere una gamba, sì come la natura e l'arte mi sono contrarie e scarse a far ch'io me le assomigli d'animo e d'ingegno. . . . Grata offesa, poiché, oltre all'imitare Vostra Signoria nella sua indisposizione per questa via, ancor goderò, secondo il mio bisogno, delle sue care spoglie, che sono, verbigrazia, una di quelle sue sedie da stroppiato.*

> Fortune favors me by regaling me with an ailment of the limbs similar to that of Your Most Noble Lordship, since it almost caused me to lose a leg, while by the same token both nature and art are most unwilling and ungenerous in helping me to resemble you in spirit and in mind. . . . A welcome injury because, besides imitating Your Lordship's ailment, I shall thus, as necessity demands, enjoy some dear belonging of Your Lordship, to wit, one of your wheelchairs.

Indeed many of Venier's contemporaries refer to his unfortunate physical condition, but all are quick to add that his superior intellect nonetheless keeps him alert and active in literary affairs.[85] Marco Valerio Marcellino described in *Il diamerone* (1561) the gravity of Venier's physical paralysis by contrasting Domenico's infirm body with the intellectual sublimity of his literary salon:[86]

Hora essendo questo gentil'huomo quasi del continuo tenuto in casa da tale infermità; tutti i belli ingegni, che in Venetia si trovano, a lui, quasi a prova, si riducono. Et quivi discorrendosi di diverse degne cose, hora si scuoprono le più secrete bellezze che sieno nella poesia; hor si rivelano i più occulti artificii, che habbia l'arte del dire; alcuna volta vi si parla della natura e proprietà delle lingue, specialmente della Toscana, altra volta vi si disputano alte e profonde questioni.

Now since this gentleman is nearly always confined to his house by said infirmity, all the best minds in Venice flock to him almost as if to prove [their allegiance]. And there, as various matters are discussed, now the most recondite beauties contained in poetry are laid bare, now the best hidden artifices inherent in the art of speech are revealed; sometimes there is talk about the nature and the properties of languages, of Tuscan in particular; at other times the loftiest and most profound questions are discussed.

Venice enjoyed for many years the position of an obligatory meeting point for writers of northern Italy because of its extensive publishing industry. In addition, informal literary salons such as Domenico Venier's offered poets, especially those from the *terraferma*, an intellectual forum in the absence of a centralized court. One of the poetic anthologies to which Franco submitted at least one sonnet includes for the most part local, lesser-known authors from the Veneto region—Brescia, Castelfranco, and Padua. The frontispiece indicates that Veronica Franco is the only Venetian author, strictly speaking, present in the edition. Although existing only in manuscript form, this slim fourteen-page volume, entitled *Canzoniere del Signor Bartolomeo Zacco Gentiluomo Padovano,* includes the compositions of "Bartolommeo Arnigio Bresciano, Girolamo Cantone da Castelfranco, Andrea Menichini da Castelfranco, Bernardo Tomitano da Padova, Veronica Franco Veneziana, and Bartolomeo Grana [?]."[87] Many of these names reappear in other poetic anthologies and in occasional texts of the period. Certain poems in the collection are by unidentified authors, or are simply attributed to an "incerto autore" (uncertain author). We might conjecture that Franco intended to edit this volume as well, since in her letter 19 she refers to a short edition of sonnets, in part of her own composition and in part commissioned by her:

E perché Vostra Signoria non rimanga senza quella sicurtà della mia servitù che 'l tempo e l'occasione mi promette di dare, vi mando, sì com'ancora sono stata essortata a fare dal signor N., una brieve opera di certa raccolta di sonetti da me fatta, e fatti fare, sopra 'l soggetto che dalla lettera del libro intenderete, usando con voi quella sicurtà e quella confidenza medesima ch'io faccio con i miei più cari e cordiali amici ad istanza de' quali n'ho fatto stampare alquanti volumi.

And so that your Lordship will not be left without assurance of my wish to serve, which time and opportunity promise to fulfill, and also at the behest of Signor N., I send you a small work containing a collection of poems compiled and commissioned by me on the subject that you will gather when reading the book. With this I offer you the same trust and confidence that I have for my dearest and most cordial friends, at whose instance I have had a number of copies printed.

A few of the sonnets were composed in like rhyme (2 and 4, 3 and 5, 6 and 7)—and thus were meant to be read together. Zacco answers the eleventh sonnet, a "proposta" by Franco, "D'alzarmi al ciel da questo stato indegno" (To raise myself to heaven from this unworthy state), in the ninth sonnet of the collection: "Posto duol tanto quanto egli è ben degno" (Given all the sorrow that he well deserves). Also a number of the sonnets mourn the death of Zacco's daughter, including the third, "Mentre la spoglia . . . rese a la terra" (While the body . . . was returned to the earth), sixth, "Deh non più tante lagrime spargete" (Pray, cease shedding so many tears), and the eighth, "Se la tua figlia è . . . bella e splendente" (If your daughter is beautiful and resplendent). Unlike the others, the sixth sonnet also praises "Veronica," who "con rima eccelsa e franca" (with noble and frank verse) has immortalized Daria's life in verse with "supremo e glorioso stile" (supreme and glorious style):

> *Deh non più tante lagrime spargete*
> *zacco gentil dai dolorosi lumi*
> *che sembran dui torrenti anzi dui fiumi*
> *tanto che Daria vostra vi affliggete.*
>
> *Ella pur vive ascesa a le più liete*
> *parti del ciel tra i fortunati numi*
> *et quivi ornata d'infiniti piumi*
> *di sue virtudi il pregio eterno. . . .*
>
> *Ne potrà il tempo ancor invido ed empio*
> *onde al fin di qua giuso ogni ben manca*
> *punto scemar del bel nome gentile.*
>
> *Poi che in supremo e glorioso stile*
> *Veronica con rima eccelsa e franca*
> *de l'immortalitate il sacra el tempio.*

Pray, gentle Zacco, cease shedding so many tears from mournful eyes which seem two torrents, nay two rivers, whereby you, yourself, your Daria afflict. She is living still and has ascended to heaven's most blissful parts amongst the lucky gods adorned by infinite plumes which are virtue's eternal prize. Nor will time, so envious and malign that here on earth everything good must finally come to an end, be able in the least to diminish her lovely gentle name. For with supreme and splendid style, with noble and frank verse, Veronica consecrates it to the temple of immortality.

In her familiar letters, Franco records the praise she receives from her interlocutors by pretending to be unable to match the skill with which they have praised her. When she thanks a man in letter 6 for "quei sonetti da voi fatti con obligo così stretto di rime" (the sonnets you have wrought with such strict *obbligato* rhymes), not to mention the "tanti onori e . . . tanti favori" (the many honors and . . . the many favors) received from him, she also informs him that even if she does not deserve such praise, she profits greatly from his example of how to laud others correctly: "perché ho bisogno d'essere aiutata dall'altrui benigne lodi, dove le mie proprie mi mancano" (because I need to be helped by the help of another's benign praise, for I have none for myself). As a sign of her gratitude, she sends him two more sonnets composed in like rhyme, to add to his four:

> *In segno della mia gratitudine, se ben con nota del mio giudizio, invio due sonetti fatti per l'istesse rime dei quattro vostri, e così n'avrò fatto quattro anch'io, che, se non valeranno per un solo di tutti i vostri versi, valeranno in farmi conoscere desiderosa d'imparare, poiché tanto in ciò m'affatico.*
>
> As a sign of my gratitude, albeit with a notation of my opinion, I send you two sonnets that I wrought by using the same rhymes as your four; and in the same manner I too will have made another four, which even though not of great value, when compared to even one of your verses, they will prove me desirous to learn, since I am putting such great effort into it.

It is clear that she is writing to a man outside of Venice, because she explains that if it were not for a "nuovo accidente" (new incident) she would couple her visit to see "una mia zia monaca" (an aunt of mine who is a nun) with a visit to her friend.[88] Instead she must content herself for the time being with remaining in Venice: "Sì che mio dispiacer convengo fermarmi in questa città per adesso" (so that to my regret, for the time being I must remain in this city).

In the same year, a collection of sonnets published on 12 May 1575, compiled by a Veronese gentleman, Giovanni Fratta, nicknamed the "animoso" (the Accademia degli Animosi was located in Padua), eulogized the "felice dottorato" (happy doctorate) of the "Illustre et eccellentissimo Signor Gioseppe Spinelli et Cavalier Splendida."[89] This edition, divided into two sections, was awarded a copyright (a *privilegio*); the second section contains Latin translations of many of the vernacular verses printed in the first half. Dedicating this *Panegirico* to the "Molto Magnifico Sig. Alberto Lavezola," Fratta opens the collection with a canzone which combines allusions to Spinelli's position among the pagan gods with allusions to his local grandeur, situating him along the river Brenta close to Venice. Indeed many of the thirty-one poets represented here are from the Venetian *terraferma*. Sonnets by two women poets, possibly Fratta's own wife "Signora Cintia da la Fratta" and Andromeda Felice, precede the sonnet composed by Franco "A la tua ceda ogni regale insegna" (All regal insignia must yield to yours), identified here as that of "la Virtuosissima Signora Veronica Franco" (the most virtuous Signora Franco).[90]

Venier's literary salon was not the only place in which Franco participated in learned discussions, negotiated literary commissions, or entertained friends, perhaps with musical concerts. But it was the principal venue in which she had the opportunity to be introduced to writers from all over Europe with whom she continued to correspond.

It was in her private home, however, that Franco had the unexpected privilege of welcoming the young, twenty-three-year-old king of Poland (he was on his way to France to assume the kingship), Henri III of Valois, during his ten-day visit to Venice (17–27 July) in 1574.[91] In order to avoid passing through Protestant Germany, Henri made his way to France by means of a circuitous route to Italy. In France he was to assume his reign after the death of his brother Charles IX. His triumphal entry occasioned the grandest, most extravagant preparations for the state reception of a foreign dignitary that Venice had ever witnessed.[92] Many contemporary chronicles carefully document the numerous events (balls, theatrical presentations, musical performances) scheduled by the Venetian republic and attended by Henri and his cousin, Alfonso II, Duke of Ferrara, during his sojourn. An exhaustive and lively journal has been assembled from the many contemporary manuscripts and *relazioni* written in Italian, French, and Latin. *Il viaggio in Italia di Enrico III Re di Francia e le Feste a Venezia, Ferrara, Mantova e Torino* (1890), by Pierre De Nolhac and Angelo Solerti, attempts to account as well for the "unofficial" evening outings in which Henri, it is reported, roamed the city incognito in search of Venice's much

acclaimed attractions. One evening after the theatrical and musical festivities and banquets at the *Fondaco dei Turchi* were over, Henri reportedly
did not return home:[93]

> *Enrico non rimase in casa quella sera, ma guidato dal Duca di Ferrara*
> *uscì segretamente, e saliti entrambi in una gondola, andarono a zonzo al-*
> *quanto e poi al Fondaco dei Turchi dove Alfonso gli aveva preparato una*
> *sontuossissima cena, con la più gradita sorpresa di una recita dei comici*
> *gelosi . . . così tra i lazzi dei buffoni, le musiche, e gli allegri progetti dei*
> *due principi per le notti future, il banchetto si protrasse a lungo; Enrico non*
> *tornò al palazzo che a giorno e andò a riposare.*
>
> Henri did not remain at home that evening, but led by the Duke of
> Ferrara, he secretly left, and both having stepped into a gondola,
> they rode around for a while, finally going to the *Fondaco dei Turchi,*
> where Alfonso had prepared a most sumptuous supper, for him the
> most pleasant surprise being a performance by the *Gelosi* (Jealous)
> comedians . . . and taken up by the jokes of the clowns, the mu-
> sic, and the two princes' merry plans for nights to come, the ban-
> quet lasted a long time. Henri did not return to the palace before
> daylight and he then went to rest.

On the following evening, none of the contemporary chronicles, De
Nolhac and Solerti report, could account for his actions.[94]

How Henri learned about Veronica Franco is not clear. Famous, however,
for his extravagance and bizarre sexual proclivities, he also reportedly indulged in all the pleasures that Venice offered such distinguished foreign
visitors. Thus it would not be surprising that Franco was singled out as the
kind of obligatory tourist feature that lured less-renowned foreign travelers
to Venice.

De Nolhac suggests that the famous *Catalogo* provided Henri and the
Duke of Ferrara (his cousin) with her name and whereabouts: "forse colla
scorta di un famoso *Catalogo* si perdevano insieme per i canali" (perhaps
with the aid of a famous *Catalogo* together they roamed through the ca-
nals).[95] But certainly this edition could not have included an accurate indication in 1574 (ten years after its publication) of where Franco lived. One
biographer discredits the *Catalogo* theory and points rather to her friendship with the politician and poet Marco Venier. Associated with the most
prominent literary academy in Venice, and a leading political figure during
the period in which Henri III was visiting Venice, Marco Venier was himself intimately involved with Franco, as we learn from her love poems in her
Terze rime. Still another theory has been advanced, deriving from an inves-

tigation of the list of noble *giovani* appointed to the king as his "addetto al servizio" (assigned to service). Here we find three orders of nobles, and in the "Primo Ordine" the eleventh man listed is "Il Magnifico Signor Andrea Tron del Clarissimo Signor Polo," the nobleman with whom Franco claimed to have had a child.[96]

It is precisely this unrecorded history, based on conjecture, that has led critics to transform Henri's encounter with Franco into merely an intriguing cultural anecdote. The information that has been pieced together is more the stuff of dramatic legend than precise detail. Nevertheless, the importance of this event in her life cannot be overestimated. The trials brought against her in 1580 reveal how the privileges and attention she enjoyed from patricians in these years engendered vindictive feelings of envy, spite, and rancor among her servants, neighbors, suitors, and friends.

Following Henri's visit, Franco composed two sonnets which appear together with a dedicatory letter to him as the opening pages of her *Lettere familiari a diversi,* published six years after his pageant in Venice. Whereas the sonnets to Henri never refer specifically to her plans to dedicate a given edition to him, the preceding letter of dedication to Cardinal Luigi d'Este makes specific mention of her "lettere giovenili" (youthful letters).[97] This earlier dedication leads me to believe that she had written the letter and the sonnets to Henri much earlier and that she possibly intended them as the dedication to her volume of poems, the *Terze rime,* published only a year after Henri's visit. That the poems were dedicated instead to Guglielmo Gonzaga, duke of Mantua and Monferrato, cannot be explained; however, it was quite unlikely that Franco would have received Henri's support in 1575. Her choice of the duke of Mantua as her dedicatee is not surprising, since Domenico Venier had attempted always to maintain friendly cultural relations with the Mantuan court.[98]

It is also probable that Franco had hoped to assemble a poetic edition honoring Henri, much like the other commemorative editions to which she contributed. The closing letter (50) of her *Lettere familiari a diversi* refers specifically to such an edition. She compares the fecundity of Henri's presence to the "campo sterile delle mie condizioni" (sterile field of my situation), from which her addressee has nonetheless succeeded in drawing such marvelous works:

> *Né mai fu ch'io desiderassi tanto di sapere, quanto in questa occasione, di rendere grazie ornate e accomodate a tanto onore da me ricevuto da così felice penna, la quale, se nel campo sterile delle mie condizioni ha prodotto tanto, che farà poi nel fecondissimo terreno delle divine parti dell'eccelso Enrigo?*

> Nor was I ever as desirous of knowledge as on the present occasion,
> to offer adorned and well-turned thanks for the great honor that I
> have received from so felicitous a pen, which having brought forth
> so much from the sterile field of my situation, may achieve we
> know not what greatness, in the very fertile grounds of the most
> excellent Henri.

She ends the letter first by offering to read what her interlocutor has already written on this subject; then, with a show of embarrassed false modesty, she requests that he kindly look over the compositions that she too has written. She states that she wants to learn from *his* verses how to praise someone else, "con mio dolce gusto e con nobile profitto nella volontà dell'imparare" (with my sweet pleasure and noble profit for my desire to learn).

In an earlier letter (46), she also had encouraged a man to publish the praises he had already assembled in Henri's honor: "mandar in luce l'eroiche lodi dell'invittisimo e cristianissimo Enrico, mostrando quanto, in così gran differenza di soggetti, Ella infinitamente vaglia" (bring to light the heroic praises of the most invincible and most Christian Henri, proving your infinite skill at such a great variety of subjects). Franco acknowledges that it is one thing for her interlocutor to have praised in the past such a "rosa imperfetta" (imperfect rose) with "essaltamenti di prose e di versi divini" (divine exaltations in prose and verse) and still another for him to employ his talents for a much higher and thus worthier goal—Henri's entry into Venice. Thus, she advises him to separate his desire to elevate her lowly condition through his improving verses from his wish to extol the "illustre reame" (illustrious kingdom).

While some critics believe that Franco's dedicatory letter to Henri was intended for her edition of familiar letters, I would argue, on the basis of these two letters, that she had hoped to collaborate with other poets on a commemorative edition in the future king's honor. One can imagine that if she indeed proposed this project to prospective publishers, she would have been forced to relinquish any association with it. Perhaps influential members of Venetian society thought it unsuitable that a courtesan, even one as talented as Veronica Franco, should organize or participate in such a distinguished and politically strategic edition.[99]

An edition commemorating Henri's entry, entitled *Compositioni volgari, e latine fatte da diversi, nella venuta in Venetia di Henrico III Re di Francia, e di Polonia,* was indeed published in Venice in 1575 and dedicated to Henri's ambassador, Sig. Arnaldo di Ferrier, by the publisher of the volume, Domenico Farri.[100] The publisher's letter to his readers indicates that the first half of the edition contains compositions that were performed, or were already in print, during Henri's stay in Venice, while the second half comprises works that had not yet been published. Finally, the third section includes compositions commissioned from "Poeti illustri" (Illustrious poets) expressly for this volume. The name of neither Domenico Venier nor Veronica Franco appears in any of the sections. Yet the first author, Andrea Menichini, submitted two sonnets to the Martinengo and Zacco editions that Franco assembled in the same year.

Franco placed the two sonnets to the king after her two dedicatory letters, "All'Illustrissimo e Reverendissimo Monsignor Luigi d'Este Cardinale" and "All'Invittissimo e Cristianissimo Re Enrico III di Francia e di Polonia," as the opening pages of her *Lettere familiari a diversi*. In these letters, she insists on her delight in bestowing rather than receiving gifts. Just as the republic's allegiance to the French leader was evident in its symbolic gesture of handing to him the keys of the city (and, it is implied, expecting his political support in return), so Franco received him in her home, exchanging gifts with him upon his departure. Indeed Henri reportedly took away with him two sonnets and a miniature enameled portrait of Franco. Always juxtaposing the smallness of her deeds and her modest literary talent with his enormous grandeur, Franco declares in her letter that the memory of his valor, inscribed forever as a "living image" on her heart, equals the immense challenge she now faces when championing his royal virtue. Comparing her smallness with his immensity, she timidly requests that he accept her mortal offer to praise "his divine benevolence":

> All'altissimo favor che la Vostra Maestà s'è degnata di farmi, venendo all'umile abitazione mia, di portarne seco il mio ritratto, in cambio di quella viva imagine, che nel mezo del mio cuore Ella ha lasciato delle sue virtù eroiche e del suo divino valore—cambio per me troppo aventuroso e felice,—io non sono bastevole di corrispondere, né pur col pensiero, né col desiderio: imperocché qual cosa può nascer da me che sia degna della suprema altezza dell'animo suo celeste e della sua beata fortuna? Né posso con alcuna maniera di ringraziamento supplire in parte all'infinito merito delle sue benigne e graziose offerte fattemi nel proposito del libro, ch'io sono per dedicarle, convenienti alla sua grandezza e al suo serenissimo splendor regale più che ad alcuna mia qualità.

> I am not equal to returning even in thought or desire the supreme favor that Your Majesty has deigned to bestow on me by visiting my humble house and taking away my portrait as an exchange for the lively image of heroic virtues and divine valor that you have left

at the center of my heart—an exchange only too fortunate and fe-
licitous for me—For what could be born from me worthy of your
celestial soul or your blessed fate? Nor can I by any form of
thankfulness make up for the infinite merits of the kind offers you
made to me with regard to the book that I am dedicating to you,
offers that are more attuned to your greatness and most serene regal
splendor than any quality of mine.

Although Henri was praised in the chronicles and poetic masques performed during his sojourn as the most valiant Christian leader fighting the
Protestant Hapsburg menace, as well as a loyal servant of the Roman
Catholic church, Franco begins instead by praising his more pagan attributes in her two sonnets, "Come talor dal ciel sotto umil tetto" (As sometimes from heaven to humble roofs) and "Prendi, re per virtù sommo e
perfetto" (Take, my king, paragon of virtue and perfection), which she presumably sent to him before the edition appeared. Franco represents herself
as Danae in the first poem; Danae, according to legend, was confined by
King Acrisius, her father, to a protected tower in order to prevent her impregnation and to preserve his reign after an oracle revealed to the king that
he would die at the hands of his grandson; and she transforms Henri into
the pagan "king," Jupiter. By so doing, Franco emphasizes both the unex-
pectedness of Henri's visit with her under her "umil tetto" (humble roof)
and his immensity enclosed within a small space. As the pagan god lowered
himself suddenly into Danae's chamber (according to Ovid's account in the
Ars amatoria, he was drawn by his immense desire for the forbidden) and
impregnated her in a shower of gold, so Henri descended without warning
from the heights of royalty to her "povero ricetto" (poor shelter). But
whereas Jupiter disguised his divinity in a stream of gold, Henri cast off any
"royal show," preferring to present to her a much humbler image. While
the Venetian republic was intent on displaying to Henri its many riches,
from the regilding of the Ducal Bucentaur to the silver and gold vessels that
the clergy paraded through the streets and the opulent decoration of private
patrician palaces he visited, Henri presented himself to this individual
citizen of Venice "senza pompa real ch'abbaglia e splende" (without the
shine and dazzle of royal pomp):

> *Come talor dal ciel sotto umil tetto*
> *Giove tra noi qua giù benigno scende,*
> *e perché occhio terren dall'alt'oggetto*
> *non resti vinto, umana forma prende;*
> *così venne al mio povero ricetto,*

senza pompa real ch'abbaglia e splende,
dal fato Enrico a tal dominio eletto,
ch'un sol mondo nol cape e nol comprende.
  Benché sì sconosciuto, anch'al mio core
tal raggio impresse del divin suo merto,
che 'n me s'estinse il natural vigore.
Di ch'ei di tant'affetto non incerto,
l'imagin mia di smalto e di colore
prese al partir con grato animo aperto.

As sometimes from heaven to humble roofs
Jupiter, benign, descends to us here below
And, to prevent earthly eyes from being blinded
By such a sublime sight, takes human form;
So to my modest dwelling
Without the shine and dazzle of royal pomp
Came Henri, called to so vast a kingdom
That one world alone cannot contain it.
Although he came disguised, he nonetheless
So imprinted upon my heart his heavenly merit
That my natural strength abandoned me.
So, being assured of my great affection,
With a gracious and open spirit, he took my portrait,
Worked in colored enamel, away with him.

Central to Franco's description of her meeting with Henri is an emphasis on
the exchange of gifts between sovereign and courtesan. Thus Franco transforms Jupiter's encounter with Danae from a story—one particularly suited
to a courtesan who was intent on reversing charges of venality, sexual wantonness, and avarice—that had traditionally emphasized Danae's venality
into one that focuses instead on a reciprocal and mutually profitable exchange of gifts. Indeed, the popular account of the myth tells of Jupiter's
immense desire to consummate his passion with the immured and chaste
maiden, and her sexual submission to his overpowering will. In Franco's
version their meeting is one of mutual consent; she is honored by his royal
presence and he is entertained without the fanfare prepared for him by the
republic.

Danae's impregnation by Jupiter was the subject of numerous paintings
during the sixteenth century, especially in Venice, where Titian in richly
layered strokes of color lavishly rendered the miraculous and dazzling spectacle of Jupiter's appearance to Danae in a shower of gold. [101] He attempted

to capture in paint the temporal as well as the emotional intensity of Danae's ecstasy when she was impregnated by a divinity whose ephemeral nature defied graphic representation. With an almost voyeuristic delight, Titian, and Correggio before him, focused explicitly on the erotic moment—the act of sexual intercourse between mortal and immortal— eternalizing Danae's sensual abandon. Combining luxury, spectacle, materiality, and the temporal, as opposed to the eternal, this story appealed to Venetian artists intent on capturing the sensuality of Venice in paint. [102]

Franco, too, captures the temporal nature of their encounter, but she de-emphasizes the erotic coupling of royalty and courtesan, accentuating instead her "immense desire" to celebrate Henri's valor beyond earthly limits. Playing with the solar associations in Henri III's royal motto, "D'un seul vient un sì grand'éclat" (from one man alone comes such a burst of light) or "ab uno tantus splendor" (from one so much splendor), Franco underscores the visual and literary homology between the divine Henri and the pagan Jupiter, who was also represented by early Renaissance commentators as the sun. [103] Following Ovid's lead rather than that of Boccaccio, who preferred to see the Danae myth as an allegory for the corruption of chastity by the power of the female sexual appetite or as a cautionary tale against venality, Franco emphasizes the virtuous exchange of gifts between French royalty and Venetian citizen. Thus, overturning Boccaccio's insistence on Danae's female cunning (he claimed that Danae made a deal with Jove to make love to her so as to free her from her prison), Franco directs the reader's attention away from the sexual act to the moment preceding Henri's departure: "di ch'ei di tant'affetto non incerto, / l'imagin mia di smalto e di colore / prese al partir con grato animo aperto." (So, being assured of my great affection, / With a gracious and open spirit, he took my portrait, worked in colored enamel, / Away with him." [104]

Well versed in Ovidian and Boccaccian sources, she asks her readers to "see" Danae as she too would like to be seen, rather than as men choose to view her. What is conspicuously missing in Franco's poetic version of the Danae story is precisely the act of sexual intercourse. Her reference to abandoning her "natural vigore" (natural strength), while certainly suggesting sensual abandonment, alludes to her amazement rather than to her sexual state. In the guise of Danae, Franco is "impregnated" only with Henri's valor, not with his sexuality, she claims, thereby undercutting associations between Danae and sexual rapaciousness. Rather than exchange her sexuality for his power or esteem, she gives him upon his departure two small gifts, one created by the artist's power of vision (her enameled portrait), and the other, her sonnet, also an artist's vision but inspired by *his* noble presence:

> *Prendi, re per virtù sommo e perfetto,*
> *quel che la mano a porgerti si stende:*
> *questo scolpito e colorato aspetto,*
> *in cui 'l mio vivo e natural s'intende.*
>
> *E, s'a essempio sì basso e sì imperfetto*
> *la tua vista beata non s'attende,*
> *risguarda a la cagion, non a l'effetto,*
> *Poca favilla ancor gran fiamma accende.*
>
> *E come 'l tuo immortal divin valore,*
> *in armi e in pace a mille prove esperto,*
> *m'empio l'alma di nobile stupore,*
>
> *così 'l desio, di donna in cor sofferto,*
> *d'alzarti sopra 'l ciel dal mondo fore,*
> *mira in quel mio sembiante espresso e certo.*

My king, paragon of virtue and perfection,
pray take what my extended hand holds out to you:
This carved and colored face
which is meant to present my true and living one.
And if your blessed gaze is unaccustomed to such lowly and
imperfect work, consider the cause and not the effect, for
even a small spark can kindle a great flame.
And, just as your valor, immortal and divine,
tried in a thousand tests in peace and war,
filled my soul with noble surprise,
so, now, observe a woman's heartfelt desire to raise you
above the world and to the skies
steadfastly expressed in this likeness of mine. [105]

Franco's presentation of her meeting with Henri has parallels to her interactions with other highly placed men who visited Venice. While the opportunity to praise him challenges Franco's literary talents, she is intent on dissociating this extraordinary privilege from a commercial transaction. Empowered by Henri's divine virtue, forever inscribed on her heart, she represents that which is in a sense beyond representation.

Extending his pagan attributes to include also his "most Christian" virtues, which have doubled her strength, Franco receives the inspiration necessary to compose verses in his honor. One of Henri's royal devices, which rearranged components of his Latinized name, Henricus tertius ("In Te Vere

Christus"), emphasized his Christianity. [106] On the leather bindings of the books of his wife, Louise de Lorraine, Henri appears as the sun whose rays illuminate a host of angels (one of whom is Louise) looking up at him admiringly. The inscription above their heads reads: "Ab uno tantus splendor." [107] Similarly, Franco, confronted with the task of praising the king in verse, depicts herself as looking into her own heart, where his "valor" has been implanted, and letting it speak for her. His grandeur ignites the small "spark" hidden there. Her sole reward, she claims in closing, is embodied within the poems that she has composed in his honor.

Overturning Venetian male writers' negative views that courtesans provoke civic misrule and sexual scandal, Franco constructs in her topical poems and commemorative editions an elegant self-portrait, unconcerned with sexual pleasure and financial profit. These compositions demonstrate her involvement in public literary projects as an honest courtesan committed to civic loyalties and intellectual coteries. Indeed Franco's occasional verse, when read together with her love lyrics and debate poems in her *Terze rime,* call into question the traditional division between private subjectivity and public identity for Renaissance writers.

Appendix: Two Testaments and a Tax Report

2.1 *Testaments* of Veronica Franco

The two testaments that Veronica Franco left, one in 1564, the other in 1570, are transcribed here to give readers of Italian a sense of the mixture of Venetian dialect and official Italian in the original document. Although much of the originals are in the translations, paraphrases, and capsule summaries presented in this book, the complete documents provide interesting samples of sixteenth-century Venetian testaments. The original orthography has been kept, but modern capitalization and punctuation have been used, abbreviations have been spelled out, and some accents have been added to facilitate understanding. Where a word was illegible or incomprehensible, this has been indicated by brackets or by a tentative suggestion followed by a question mark.

No. 1. Testament of Veronica Franco, Archivio Notarile, Testamenti, Atti Vincenti, Anton Maria di Vincenti, b. 1019, n. 806, 10 Agosto 1564.

In nomine Dei Eterni Amen, Anno Ab Incarnatione Domini nostri Jesu Cristi 1564 Indictione VII die vero X.mo mensis Augusti Rivoalti.

Considerando io Veronica Francha fiola di messer Francesco Francho, e de madonna Paula Fracassa li pericoli de questa nostra fragile vita retrovandomi maxime graveda ma sana di mente et intelletto et anche del corpo per grazia del Signor dio, volendo ordinar

[ordinar] li fatti mei ho fatto chiamar et venir a mi a casa in contra de S. Marcilian, Antonio Maria di Vincenti nodaro di Venetia, e quello ho pregato che scriva questo mio testamento; et prima raccomando l'anima mia a messer Jesu Cristo e alla sua madre sempre vergene madonna Santa Maria et a tutta la corte del cielo. Voglio per mei comissari messer Piero di Gozzi Rhaguseo, et messer Anzolo di Benedetti li quali prego vogliono accettar la mia Comissaria, e fedelmente adempir quanto qui sotto ordinerò. Voglio per l'anima mia sia fatta dir le messe dela madonna e de S. Gregorio, e sepulta a S. Francesco della Vigna e vestito del ordine dela madonna in cadaletto nudo con quella sorte di spesa che parerà alli mei comissarii; Lasso che sia dato diese ducati alla fia dela nena de mio fradel Horatio la qual nome Agnesina ogni volta che la farà fede de esser maridata, et altri diese a Zenevra fiola de donna Magdalena ogni volta ch'el piovan de S. Marcilian farà fede la sia maridata. Voglio che tutta quella che me ritrovo al mondo e tutto quello me potesse avegnir cossì mobel come stabel di dentro e di fuora sia de mio fio over fia che nasceranno de mi. Lasso a messer Iacomo de Baballi el figliolo over figliola che nasceranno de mi come a suo padre sia o non sia, il Signor Dio scia il tutto, che prima ad honor de Dio e per l'amorevoleza che son stata fra nui il debba governar come a lui piacerà. Io voglio che i mie comissarii formi uno aventario, et una memoria de tutto el mio e li dinari sia dati in man de messer Iacomo di Baballi a rason de 5 per cento. El ditto messer Iacomo debba far che ogni anno moltiplica el mio cavedal a beneficio de mio fio over fia che saranno, in fina che saranno ottimi. Io voglio sia sotto comissaria se sarà un mascolo. Io voglio quando el sarà ottimo che messer Iacomo li diebba investir tutto questo se ritroverà del mio cavedal in mercantia over in quello che a lui messer Iacomo parerà. Io voglio che mio fio sia contenta de tutto quello che a messer Iacomo piacerà, e se sarà una fia voglio che le sia dato tutto in dota il cavedal e il pro che se ritroveranno a quel tempo. Voglio non la se possa maridar senza licentia de messer Iacomo. A caso che mio fio over fia che nasceranno venisse a morte a tempo che i fusse ottimi, io voglio che i possa far quel tanto che a loro parerà de tutto el mio. E caso che i venisse a morte avanti che i fosse ottimi, io voglio che tutto el mio che si ritroverà in man de messer Iacomo sia de mia madre, cioé il guadagno a rason de cinque per cento e che mai la possa rimuover el cavedal, ne muoverlo mai de man de messer Iacomo. E caso che el ditto messer Iacomo de Baballi non li volesse più haver, over venisse a morte over andasse fuora, io lasso sto incargo alli mei comissarii che debbano investir e dar ogni anno a mia madre il pro che si caveranno de ditti danari per sustengo del suo viver in fin che la viverà, e che dapoi la sua morte la i possa lassar a chi li piacerà, cioé de mei fratelli Hieronimo, Horatio e Seraphin, e cossì vada da herede in herede; e caso che mia madre venisse a morte e etiam avanti morisse mei fratelli tutti tre non havendo fioli o havendo fioli vadino a loro, e si i non havesse fioli, io voglio che dapoi la morte de mia madre che tutto il mio cavedal sia ballotado per i sei guardiani dele Schuole Grande che sia maridade tante fie donzele per l'anima mia a vinticinque ducati per una, a quelle che haveranno più ballote in fin al numero che importerà el mio cavedal. La mia dote io voglio che mia madre se la possa far dare a mio marido messer Paolo Panizo e far quel tanto che a lei piacerà come quella che me l'ha data. Lasso a messer

Iacomo de Baballi el mio diamante per segno de amorevolezza. Interogata de hospedali e loci pii, respondo che non voio ordenar altro.

[Witnesses]: Io Iacomo Solian quondam Augustin da Bersello sensaro in Rialto fui testimonio pregado et zurado di questo testamento et cognoscho la ditta testatrize.

Io Fausto Bettani da i Orzinovi stampator in Vinetia alla di [stamperia] Scotti fui testimonio pregato et giurato di questo testamento.

No. 2. Testament of Veronica Franco, Archivio Notarile, Testamenti, Atti Fiume, Baldissera Fiume, b. 420, n. 870, 1 novembre 1570.

In Dei eterni nomine Amen: Anno ab Incarnatione domini nostri Jesu Cristi 1570. Indicatione quartadecima, die mercurii primo mensis novembris rivoalti.

Considerando io Veronica Francho fiola del messer Franco Francho, li pericoli di questa nostra fragil vita sana per la Iddio gratia dilla mente, senso, memoria et intelletto, benché alquanto dil corpo inferma in leto, ho voluto sin che la raggion reggi la mente, di beni miei disponer et ordinar; et cussì ho fatto venir et chiamar da me Baldissera Fiume nodaro di Venezia qui in casa mia posta nella contra di San Thoma; il qual anca con li testimoni sottoscriti ho pregato questo mio testmento et ultima volontà scrivesse. Et dappoi la morte mia lo compisse et roborasse sigondo li ordinii di Venezia per il qual prima l'anima mia raccomando al mio signor Iddio et alla Santissima Verzene Maria et a tutta la corte Celestial: Item casso revoco et annullo ogni mio testamento che io havessi fatto fin hora; item lasso miei comissarii et exequtori di questo mio testamento il magnifico messer Lorenzo Moresin fo del Clarissimo messer Barbon, mio fratello Hieronimo et messer Ludovico Ramberti quali prego siino contenti di eseguir quanto fa questo mio testamento sarà per me ordinato. In quando che il Clarissimo messer Zuan Battista Bernardo ritornerà di regimento, il prego quanto et posso che sii contento per amorevoleza haver per raccomendati mii fioli, et che lui possa farsi render conto alli comissari. Et occorendo che li mii fioli insieme con Andrea, nassudo di Ansilla mia cameriera, non fossero trattati bene, voglio che lui possi tuorli dove sarano et quelli far governar come a lui parerà, perché son certa che li farà tratar [ ] se fossero suoi fioli; item lasso tutti li miei beni mobelli et stabilli presenti et futuri caduchi inordinati et per proscritti a mi spetanti e che lui spetar mi potesse per qualunque modo et via, et Achille mio fiol et di messer Iacomo Baballi Raguseo il qual quanto a me credo sii mio fiolo, et a Enea similmente mio fiol e fiol di m. Andrea Tron del Clarissimo m. Pozzo [Pollo?], quali prego ghe siino raccomandati quali voglio siino miei heredi del tutto: Item voglio che li miei comissari dappoi la mia morte debbino vender tutti li miei beni di qualunque sorte, et il tratto di quelli sii investito in un fondo securo per benefitio di ditti miei fioli, et del tratto sive usufrutto che si caverà di detta investitura sii sustentado et alimentado miei figlioli et Andrea qual ho accetato per fio d'anima, et quello aricommando alli ditti miei comissarii quanto li altri due miei fioli. Et occorendo che detto usufrutto non fusse abastanza di poter sostantarli nutrir et dotar di tre ditti miei fioli, et Andrea, voglio che se possi intachar del cavedal, et chi detti miei fioli et Andrea volessino [andar?] frati, in quel caso, voglio che sii datto delli miei beni ducati cinquanta a Marina la qual sta in casa del [Mori o Morosini?] alla Madonna della Fava, quali sii per il suo maridar, et essendo maridata non habbi cosa alguna, et altri ducati cinquanta a mio carissimo padre, zoé ogni anno ducati xii in rate tre al anno; et ditto mio padre non possi testar di ditti ducati 50 se al tempo della sua morte non li havesse havuti. Et essendo miei fioli frati, voglio che il restante che sopravanzerà, così dil cavedal come del usufrutto, sii diviso in dui parti eguali tra ditti miei fioli, zoé una parte per uno, et non essendo monachi li lasso miei heredi tutti dui come ho detto di sopra, et morendo uno di loro vadi in quello chi sopraviverà [e di?] ditti dui miei fioli. Et debbino star sotto comessaria fino alla età di anni quindese, et occorrendo che ditti dui miei fioli manchassero avanti de mio padre, in questo caso voglio che ditto mio padre habbi detto miei beni altri ducati cinquanta a raggion de ducati xii all'anno in [paghe?] tre, zoé ogni tre mesi la sua portione, il restante veramente voglio vadi in li fioli di mio fratello Hieronimo et occorrendo che sua moglie facesse una fiola in questo caso tutta ditta restante vadi a ditta puta con questo che gli sii messo nome Veronica al batesimo. Et non facendo fiola femina, ma maschi, sii diviso fra loro a portioni, et caso che mio fratello non havesse fioli come [   ] ditto di sopra, voglio che mio fratello sii patron del usufrutto. Et occorendo che venisse in luce mio fratello Serafin qual è in man dei Turchi, voglio chel sii riscatado [   ] ducati dusento del mio cavedal. Et non havendo bisogno di rischatado tutto lo usufrutto sii diviso fra loro dui miei fratelli, e morendo uno de loro vadi in quello che sopra viverà; et occorendo che ditti miei fratelli al tempo della sua morte non havessero fioli, in questo caso voglio che il mio residuo sii dato a due donzelle da bon per il suo maridar. Che se si ritroverà due meretrici che volessero lassar la cattiva vita et maritarsi o monacharsi, in questo caso sii abrazado ditti dui meretrici et non le donzelle: Item lasso a Suor Marina monacha nel monastero di S. Bernardin in Padova ducati diese per una volta tantum, i qual ducati dissi ghè lasso per discargo del anima di mia madre perché suo padre gli li havea lassiati quanti gli siino dati subbito venduta la mia robba. In tutto che tutta la robba che era di Caterina mia massera sii data a Domisilla qua al presente è mia cameriera qual robba puol esser di valuta di ducati 4 o cinque. Item voglio che li miei comissarii debbino dar alli heredi di madonna Marieta che fu moglier del petener dal Sol [   ] ongari tre et scudo uno quanti mi imprestò. Item voglio che Agnese mia cuoga sii pagata dalla sua mercede qual po esser da ducati quattro cinque o sei incirca: Item voglio che sii pagato il marzer del Salvadeghi di quello el disse havea da mi, et sii pagato li spicieri et sartori et doveranno haver et altri che pretendessero esser veri creditori: Item voglio che li miei comissarii al mio funeral debbino dare [   ] due torzi di lira diese [   ] et farmi sepellir senza altra spesa, né pompa, né procession alguna et vestita dal habito della madonna et non altra pompa, et questo li cometto et li prego a non manchar di dar esecutione a questo mio voler: Item dichiaro che il scritto di ducati cento che è debitor Iacomo Bozi non voglio che nissuno li possino domandar cosa alguna ma quello voglio casso: item dichiaro haver havuto dal predetto messer Iacomo Baballi li danari che li fu dati da mio fratello, quali furno ducati 93 over 97 della mia dote et [   ] fin del mio nelle mani uno fillo di perli numero 51 ballote di valuta di ducati cento, et una vestura di raso pagierino intagliata di lama d'arzento et perfillata d'oro, et cremesina qual è solum il busto. Item dichiaro qualmente io ho habuto da Don Donà Avonio da Santo Spirito ducati cento cor. et lui ha per sua cautione, [primo?] un bacil d'arzento con la mia arma, e sei pironi d'arzento con la mia arma, et sei cuslieri et sei pironi d'arzento et una salliera costò ongari diese et mio candelier d'arzento della grandezza delli mei candelieri, et ho havuto ditti denari già mesi sei in circa. Interogata dal nodaro di luoghi pii giusta le lezi, ho risposto non voler ordinar altro: et occorendo che detto Andrea andasse frate, voglio che li sii dato ducati cinque all'anno in vita sua. Se perhò ancho li soprascritti miei fioli andassero anchor loro frati ma non andando frati tutti dui ditto legato resti nullo.

[Witnesses]:

Io fra' Giovanni Andrea Pizzamano di Lorenzo [   ] conventuale fui testimonio zurato e pregato sotto scrissi.

Io Zuanne di Gasparo filatoio fui testimonio zurado et pregado sotoscrissi.

2.2 *Tax Report* of Veronica Franco

Dieci Savi sopra le decime, Condizione del 1582, b. 157, 15 Febraio 1581 [m.v.,* = 1582]

Beni della signora Veronica franco fiole del quondam signor francesco franco relita del quondam signor Paulo Paniza medico. Abita a san samuello, dati in nota dell'offitio di Vostre signorie Clarissime Clarissimi signori Dieci Savi sora le decime in execution della parte ultimamente presa nel eccellentissimo conseio de pregai et prima.

Uno livello de stara diese venetiani di formento mi pagha messer Andrea fasiol quondam francesco. _____ stara 10

Un altro livello de ducati vinti quatro al'anno mi pagha messer Antonio Luisetti da Treviso val _____ ducati 24.

---

*M.v. stands for *more veneziano*. The Venetian year began on 1 March.

Three

ADDRESSING VENICE: FRANCO'S FAMILIAR LETTERS

Né mi sono curato in ciò di imitare i Ciceroni e i Demostheni, né usare arte alcuna di color rettorici, ma le ho scritte proprio nello stile che la natura la favella ne porge. Perché uno è scrivere lettere altro è scrivere novelle. *
Nicolo Martelli, *Il primo libro delle lettere* (1546)

Female habit carries with it a twofold idea—dress and ornament. By "dress" we mean what they call "womanly gracing": by "ornament," what is suitable should be called "womanly *dis*gracing." . . . Against the one we lay the charge of ambition, against the other prostitution.
Tertullian, "On the Apparel of Women"

With the arrival of distinguished literati in Venice, Veronica Franco seized the opportunity to publicize her literary endeavors. Thus on 4 November 1580, when the French essayist Michel Montaigne visited the city, Franco's servant delivered to him a copy of her recently published *Lettere familiari a diversi,* [1] which Montaigne recorded in his *Journal de voyage en Italie:*

> *Le lundy a souper, 6 de novembre, la signora Veronica Franca, gentifame venitienne, envoia vers lui pour lui presenter un petit livre de lettres qu'elle a composé; il fit donner deux escus audit home.*

> Monday at dinnertime, on the sixth of November, Signora Veronica Franco, a Venetian woman, sent a servant to his house to present him with a slim volume of letters written by her; he gave orders to pay the man two *scudi.*

Like Pietro Aretino before her, Veronica Franco used the familiar letter for self-promotion and to build a successful literary reputation dependent on the acknowledgment, approval, and support of influential male readers. Unlike her occasional verses, but like her *capitoli* in terza rima, Franco's

---

*Nor did I in this regard bother to imitate the Ciceros or the Demostheneses or use rhetorical colors, but rather I have written them in exactly the style that both nature and speech afford us. For writing letters is one thing, and writing stories is another.

letters assume an even bolder position with regard to generic conventions than did her contemporaries.[2] By focusing on the kinds of private concerns typically expressed in the vernacular familiar letter—concerns most often articulated by the upper classes or the socially mobile, intent on blending public and private personas—Veronica Franco presents a public version of a courtesan's private self that contests male authors' representations of the courtesan as base, duplicitous, and venal. Franco's letters thus blur the distinctions between a public and private voice; her private thoughts are formulated in a public genre, which she uses to represent both the shared principles of her class and the specific women's concerns of the period. In addition Franco disavows, as did Montaigne, the ceremonial flattery and the obsequious pose of much epistolary practice, thereby attempting to disentangle the courtesan from negative charges of calculated dissimulation.[3]

In Franco's occasional patriotic poems and commemorative editions, she adopts a position of literary authority not customary for Renaissance women. In her familiar letters, however, she elects a genre in which very few women had published, and she uses this genre to publicize her private thoughts and feelings in a public literary arena. Franco wrote these letters over a long period of time. Their content (they are undated) reveals that a number of them were written before certain of her lyric capitoli, while others gloss them retrospectively. Owing to the genre of the familiar letter, these epistles bring into clear relief the kinds of social courtship and independent critical voice at work in Franco's more lyrically inflected capitoli. Critics have consistently misread this personal voice in Franco's letters as implying nothing more than a courtesan's confessional autobiography, and in doing so they have failed to see how skillfully Franco redirects classical and Renaissance literary genres toward a literary epistolary voice capable of expressing views in favor of Renaissance women, unrelated to the affairs of the heart.[4] Critics have tended to use her letters to affirm a commonly held view that women record the concerns of the private self and never rework them for different ends.[5] What is most striking about Franco's epistolary texts (both her familiar letters and her epistolary capitoli in terza rima) is precisely the outward-directed artfulness with which she interweaves classical references into her discourse and plays with contemporary epistolary traditions.

That the letters of a "public" woman were published in the sixteenth century might not seem surprising in light of the equation often made in the early modern period between a woman's sexuality, her speech, and publication.[6] Franco's *Lettere familiari a diversi,* however, enjoyed neither the affirmation secured by a publisher's affiliation (on its frontispiece) nor a "privilegio" (copyright).[7] Both of these factors suggest that Franco either paid for the edition herself or received private support from influential friends to fund the printing of the volume. The absence of a copyright would also help to explain why the *Lettere familiari a diversi* was never reprinted in later years. And if it is true that Franco had to raise the funds to pay for publishing it, this would also help account for why the volume was issued in a small format.[8]

Veronica Franco uses the familiar letter to alter readers' expectations of a courtesan's private desires by dwelling little in her letters on her own amorous affairs. Rather the bulk of Franco's letters speak to the private affairs of others, most often those of her male interlocutors. She offers upper-class-male correspondents the kind of moral, social, and ethical advice appropriate to their social status. Thus she reminds her interlocutors that a courtesan is eminently capable of discerning another's intellectual merit and virtue. In so doing, Franco shuns the passive role of recipient of patriarchal advice, a part traditionally assigned women, who were denied access to civic and political arenas where important decisions were made for all Venetian citizens.

Although Montaigne cautioned in his *Essais* against an epistolary art intent on vainglory, he also used his criticism of the courtly letter writers of his day to defend his own literary choices: "The letters of this age consist more in embroideries and preambles than in substance," he complained.[9] In Montaigne's "Consideration Upon Cicero" (1:40), he charged Cicero and Pliny the Younger with wanting solely "to derive some great glory from mere babble and talk to the point of publishing their private letters to their friends," yet he conceded in the same breath that their desire transcended all "baseness of heart in persons of such rank," because it served to "recommend not their sayings but their doings." Similarly, he excused Seneca and Epicurus from his charges of using artifice for ambitious ends, because they were, he believed, concerned primarily with sharing their wisdom with others: their letters were "not mere empty and fleshless . . . holding together only by a delicate choice of words, but letters stuffed full of the fine arguments of wisdom . . . that teach us not to speak well but to do well."[10]

While Montaigne admitted somewhat ruefully that he would have written epistles if he had had "a certain relationship which attracted . . . and sustained and elevated" him, his own friends regarded him, he asserts, not only as an accomplished essayist but as an equally good letter writer: "Concerning letters, I want to say this word: that this is an area in which my friends claim that I have some talent. And I would have preferred that form for publishing my sallies, if I had had someone to whom I could speak."[11]

Montaigne, however, avowedly refused to use his friends to build his literary reputation, or to accommodate himself, as did Seneca and Epicurus, "to the vanity of others," and thus refrained from publishing his personal letters. He was nevertheless, as some critics have argued, just as guilty of pandering or of professional vanity as any of the epistolary authors he either admired or accused. But statements of his aversion to ceremonial flattery, or what he viewed generally as epistolary deceit, resurface many times in this and in other essays.[12]

Montaigne's dislike of epistolary pedantry and abstract moralizing was in conformity with the standard complaints leveled against sixteenth-century writers of familiar letters, who slavishly imitated ancient models rather than inventing epistles in their respective vernaculars. Likening rhetorical ornament and ceremonial address to meretricious servility, Montaigne abhorred the kind of epistolary artifice that signaled, in his mind, a selling out of the soul: "there never was so abject and servile a prostitution of complimentary addresses: life, soul, devotion, adoration, serf, all these words have such vulgar currency."[13] Yet despite these disavowals, Montaigne continued to be fascinated by the epistle's power simultaneously to communicate intense feelings, private thoughts, and public views on moral, political, and social matters. He was attracted not only to the ancient familiar epistolographers' "artless art of writing letters," from whom he borrowed so much to adorn his own essays, but also to certain Italian vernacular authors who published their familiar letters during the sixteenth century.[14]

In "A Consideration upon Cicero," Montaigne reported owning nearly one hundred printed volumes of Italian letters: "The Italians are great printers of letters. I think I have a hundred different volumes of them."[15] While one of the hundred volumes in Montaigne's possession was Veronica Franco's slim edition of fifty familiar letters, only Annibale Caro's letters received his positive endorsement: "those of Annibale Caro seem to me the best."[16] Not even Pietro Aretino's massive epistolary project elicited Montaigne's comment. And yet Aretino had been the first writer in Italian who used the familiar letter in the earlier part of the century not only for self-advertising and reputation building but also to inveigh against blind imitators of classical authors.

Aretino praised an epistolary method dictated by the impulses and inspirations of nature. [17] His argument is that nature should be the teacher of art and, hence, writers should follow the natural stimuli that only art may invoke. Boldly challenging the authority of classical models, Aretino opposed his hyperbolic, baroque use of the vernacular tongue to ancient authors' measured and controlled Latin, his sensuous delight in verbal flourish to their stoical restraint and meticulous attention to literary decorum. Francesco Sansovino took Aretino's theory of nature as the informer of art a step closer to rhetorical order (in keeping also with Ciceronian maxims) when he claimed that the body of the letter should reflect not only the order of nature but also the physical proportions of the ideal human form: "il corpo della lettera, come corpo dee aver le sue membra, onde di necessità bisogna che abbia regole e norme, poi ch'ogni corpo ha le membra proporzionate l'una all'altra" (Like any other body, that of a letter must have limbs. Hence the need for rules and norms because the limbs of all bodies are proportionate to each other). [18]

Aretino unabashedly used his letters as a platform to proclaim himself the inventor of the Italian familiar epistle:

> *Si è scoperto nelle orecchie dello intelletto un tuono di pistole che spaventerebbe i fulmini che cascono dal cielo de i concetti di Cicerone . . . io entro in questo discorso, perché le prime lettere, che in lingua nostra sieno state impresse, nascon da me.* [19]
>
> A rumble of e-pistols that could frighten the lightning bolts which fall from the heavens of Cicero's concepts has been discovered by the ears of intellect. . . . I bring this up because the first letters to be printed in our language come from me.

Many Italian contemporaries refused, however, to acknowledge him as their epistolary model, favoring instead an allegiance to classical authority. Even Aretino's friend, Bernardo Tasso (who also published his familiar letters), the father of Torquato Tasso—perhaps for competitive reasons—refused to champion Aretino as the inventor of this genre. In a noted exchange of letters between Bernardo Tasso and Annibale Caro on this subject, Tasso claimed Italian as the "figliuola ed erede della Latina" (daughter and heiress of Latin). Yet in Tasso's view, correct imitation must follow the riches ("delle sue ricchezze e della materia eredita" [of its riches and material inheritance]) that Latin, rather than Italian, offers, a claim distinct from Aretino's claim that art issues from the direct observation of nature and not from the imitation of learned references. [20] Aretino's answer to Tasso on the issue of imitation is instructive, since it anticipates what Montaigne will disparage years later—namely, artless mimicry and empty verbal flourish—and his repudiation of the adornments of rhetorical artifice:

> *Se nel divulgare in le stampe una così indiscreta arroganza, ne escludete me come imitabile; oltra il confrontarsi con l'opinione di chi sa; venivisi confermando anchora i modi del proceder vostro in le pistole, nel cui necessario essercizio supplite al mancamento del non mi potere contraffare in le sententie, né in le comparationi, (che in me nascano, e in voi moiano) co i lisci, e coi belletti.* [21]

> If by divulging such indiscreet arrogance in print you imply that I am inimitable, besides challenging the opinion of one who knows what he is talking about, we also see here the ways in which you go about writing letters, for in performing this necessary task you make up for your inability to imitate my sentences and comparisons (which in my case come to life and in yours keel over dead), with polish and cosmetics.

Aretino draws from a language of sensual experience and artistic method when he charges Bernardo Tasso with the vice of delighting in superficial pleasures while neglecting to savor instead the material of life and the fruits nature produces: "essendo il vostro gusto più inclinato all'odor dei fiori, che al sapor dei frutti" (since your taste prefers the scent of flowers to the flavor of fruits). Unlike Tasso, Aretino summons his almost godlike powers of invention to create an overall "relief" rather than dedicating his attention to what is only an artfully crafted "miniature" ("il rilievo della inventione, e non la miniatura dell'artificio" [the relief of full-bodied invention rather than the miniature of artifice]). Precisely the vacuous flattery and pompous ceremonial style denounced in Montaigne's essay are what had similarly fueled Aretino's biting tongue when he condemned Bernardo Tasso's epistolary style as merely ceremonial posturing: "con stil angelico, e non maniera d'harmonia celeste, risonate in gli epitalamai, e ne gli hinni, le cui soavità di dolcezze non si convengano in lettere" (with the style of angels rather than that of celestial harmony, you sound off in your epithalamiums and hymns whose sweet fulsomeness is inimitable in letters). [22]

In her familiar letters, Veronica Franco also responded, albeit more indirectly, to Aretino's commanding authorial presence. She could hardly have done otherwise: for among sixteenth-century Italian writers, his had been the most vociferous and eloquent denunciation of the rhetorical artifice of much epistolary prose—a denunciation made by equating rhetorical artifice with the calculated artfulness of the courtesan's facade. In Aretino's view this artfulness was constructed to allure a suitor's gaze through deceitful means, to seduce him and to manipulate his affections for the sheer delight of doing so. For Aretino, the courtesan, like the pedant or the servile courtier, sought public acclaim not through skillful invention but through slavish artistic mimicry.[23] However, by the time Franco published her letters, in 1580, Aretino's self-congratulatory claim to be the inventor of a vernacular genre, while certainly not forgotten, was greatly overshadowed by the sheer number of writers in Italian who had been admitted, in the second half of the century, into the privileged ranks of published epistolarians.[24] A quantity of single-authored editions overwhelmed the editorial market, pushing Aretino's bombastic claims further to the margins of literary fame.[25] But with the exception of a few aristocratic women, such as Lucrezia Gonzaga and Vittoria Colonna, who had published their letters in the earlier part of the century, epistolary authors were rarely women.[26]

Scores of letter editions by single authors and publishers' collections of multiauthored letter volumes constituted a literary vogue beginning in 1538 and ending in 1627 with Marino's edition of familiar letters. Further, many formula manuals, like Francesco Sansovino's *Il segretario* (first published in Venice in 1564 in four books, and then in 1578 in seven books), prescribing epistolary rules for courtiers who shared similar political perspectives and social codes, emphasized the correct moral and ethical practices of a privileged literary elite.[27] There were many reprintings of the same authors, such as Pietro Bembo, Annibale Caro, Girolamo Parabosco, Andrea Calmo, Claudio Tolomei, and Bernardo Tasso, throughout the century. Following market demand, publishers recycled the same names, while they began to print new epistolary authors from 1560 until the end of the century. They knew that they had an enormously profitable genre, rivaled only by single-authored editions of love poems or collaborative anthologies of sonnets.[28]

While the bulk of letter editions printed in Venice in the sixteenth century were by the same group of authors noted above, the letters of Diomede Borghesi, Giuseppe Pallavicino, and Veronica Franco marked a significant juncture:[29] not only were these authors the only ones to publish their familiar letters in Venice for many years, they were, most importantly, the only new writers in the familiar letter genre to publish since 1564.

Franco claims the textual persona of "segretario" (counselor) to a male elite gone astray. To achieve this persona, Franco dons with a feminine twist many of the public roles traditionally used by male humanist familiar letter writers. Her letters, like Montaigne's *Essais,* offer the reader an insight into the courtesan's multiple personalities as she experiments with, and retailors to her taste, the public, advisory discourses of the Venetian patriciate. Throughout her *Lettere familiari a diversi,* Franco is moral counselor, writer, and editor of collaborative literary projects, as well as devoted friend, mother uninterested in financial gain, affectionate companion, and partner in love.

The conversational tone in many of Franco's letters has supported critics' claims that her letters merely record the confessions of a fallen courtesan, one they transform into a repentant Mary Magdalene. Quite the contrary: Franco's conversational style adheres to the rhetorical strictures and social decorum of the familiar letter, which advocated the use of plain unadorned speech. She uses this rhetorical style to draw attention to her avoidance of rhetorical embellishments. To this end, the language of Franco's letters is impassioned yet restrained; she elects, as she states in letter 38, the concision of thought and "vero affetto" (honest feeling) that the familiar letter requires:[30]

> *E questa sia la risposta delle vostre ch'ho da voi ultimamente ricevute, alle quali non rispondo con più lunghezza, dovendosi attender nelle lettere familiari al vero affetto con che si scrive più che alle molte parole.*
>
> And let this be my reply to the letters that I have received recently from you, to which I do not answer at greater length, since in familiar letters one must devote more care to the true feeling with which they are written than to the production of a great many words.

While many of her letters provide consolation to troubled interlocutors, many others insist on giving back intact the advice she has previously received from correspondents. In letter 7, Franco not only reminds her correspondent of his earlier advice to her ("e non tanto per consolarvi quanto per mostrarvi ch'io tengo a memoria i termini della consolazione con la quale altre volte consolaste me" [and not so much to console you as to show that I well remember the words of consolation with which on other occasions you have consoled me]), she appeals to his religious conscience in emphasizing that just like him, she is a recipient of God's benevolence;

> *Considerate che tutte le cose di questo mondo sono possedute da noi per imprestito e non per dono, sì che, se 'l Sommo Datore, che in questo modo liberamente dispensa le sue grazie qua giuso, repetisce il beneficio, ringraziamolo di quel tempo ch'Egli ce l'ha lasciato godere, che pur poteva ancora non darnelo assolutamente.*

> Consider that all things in the world are held by us as loans, and not
> as gifts, so that if the Supreme Giver who freely bestows his bounty
> here on earth reclaims the benefice, let us thank him for all the time
> that he has allowed us to enjoy it for in fact he might not have be-
> stowed it at all.

Further, in many other letters she works at persuading her correspondents
of their wrongdoing or misguided opinions, perhaps in order to deflect
away from the courtesan what she calls in letter 18 "artificio dell'adu-
lazione" (artifice of adulation), or in another poem, the "iperbolica figura"
(hyperbolic figure). Rhetorical excess, she proclaims in letter 30, does not
signify female deceit or an artfully composed and seductive facade, but
rather male trickery:

> *Così essorto ancor voi nell'esser circospetto nel parlar di me; e, se alcuna
> volta, per abondanza di cuore o per usanza o per alcun altro accidente, vi
> vien fantasia di mettermi in favola nelle vostre scene d'ozio e di vani
> ragionamenti, ricordatevi di quel ch'avete fatto in casa mia . . . viviate
> ristretto nei vostri termini; e, se pur avete animo d'ampliarli, non vi preva-
> lete in ciò della calunnia né in altro modo della maldicenza, della re-
> tribuzion delle quali ne avete la esperienza con voi, ma usate il merito della
> virtù, se ne avete.*

> Thus I exhort you again to be circumspect when you speak about
> me, and if at one time or another, out of the kindness of your heart
> or habit or any other circumstance, you should be seized by the
> whim of writing about me and including me in one of your idle
> scenes and pointless discussions, remember what you did in my
> house—live according to the terms set by yourself, and should you
> wish to amplify them, do not turn to slander or malicious gossip in
> doing so, for you have experienced their retribution, but use the
> merit of virtue if you have any.

But not all of Franco's letters successfully avoid the dangers of rhetorical
artifice or courtly posturing. Some are strained, convoluted, and long-
winded; others suffer from an overcharge of flattery and self-deprecation.[31]
For the most part, however, Franco intelligently employs the epistolary
genre for corrective and friendly counsel as well as for imaginative self-
portraiture. Closer to the conversational mode of the Senecan epistle or to
the essay of Montaigne than to the humanist's occasional missive, which
was calculated primarily to document personal connections, Franco's letters do not identify her addressees. Only in the dedicatory letter to King
Henri III of France, which is the first letter of the volume (after her ded-

ication to Luigi d'Este), and in letter 21, in which she thanks "signor Tentoretto" for the portrait he has done of her, does she identify her recipients.[32] Although all letters necessarily provide the writers with an opportunity to align themselves with important people, the bulk of Franco's letters provide little specific information about her correspondents; she favors instead the projection of a more general image of the author, responding to and interacting with unidentified people in a variety of social contexts. Often we see Franco making a request on behalf of someone else.[33] Further, her letters do not provide the reader with either the date or the place of composition, and only two letters carry her signature.

The familiar epistle, inherited from the Ciceronian, Stoic, and Christian moral traditions, was widely imitated and discussed in Venetian literary academies and in particular in Domenico Venier's literary salon. Classical epistles translated into the vernacular were the source of many sixteenth-century commentaries on epistolary imitation and rhetorical practices by such theorists as Girolamo Ruscelli, Francesco Sansovino, Girolamo Garimberto, Giovanni Battista Guarini, Angelo Ingegneri, and Orazio Toscanella, who recognized that classical epistles designed for publication displayed an individual's knowledge of correct civic, moral, and social conventions.[34] Franco reveals in the body of her text her understanding of the "familiar" aspect of classical epistolography. In letter 22, she states that her letter is a "officio" (duty) borne out of the "obbligo dell'umanità" (obligations of humanity) in order to converse. More than that, hers is a discourse nourished primarily, she claims, by "familiarità" (familiarity).

A multiplicity of voices and rhetorical stances, unaligned with programmatic strictures on style and content, characterize Franco's *Lettere familiari a diversi*. The absence of any clearly defined rhetorical structure controlling the design of her edition explains why her letters have always resisted rigid classification. But Franco's familiar letters, written specifically for publication, recently have been characterized by Amedeo Quondam as "più prossime alla forma della lettera segmento di narrazione, la lettera 'novella' di cui parlava il Martelli" (closer to the letter form as narration, the "novella" letter to which Martelli referred). Here Quondam refers to Nicolo Martelli's self-congratulatory assertion that like his mentor Aretino, he follows not only the dictates of nature, free of any of the restrictions of codified formulas, but that he composes his letters expressly for real occasions and sends them to actual correspondents.[35]

While many of Franco's letters adhere to themes and rhetorical situations advocated in epistolary manuals of the period, still others elude interpretation altogether, owing precisely to a lack of concrete details that would help ground the reader in the specific contexts to which they allude. Both highly abstract and elusive, then, many of Franco's letters appear to have been written for the appreciation of a small group of friends rather than for a wide reading public. As social communications, much like the poetic proposta/risposta exchange in Franco's *Terze rime,* her familiar letters reflect the loosely organized social and literary exchanges characteristic of Venetian informal academies and private salons of the latter half of the sixteenth century. At certain points in Franco's text, the abstract references to specific recent events evoke the kind of local gossip that might have circulated among a small coterie of Venetian friends and Italian cognoscenti. She writes in letter 36, for example:

> *L'amor, che, provocato da giusto sdegno, si convertisce in disperazione, fa ch'io mi pento d'avervi amato infinitamente, sì come ho fatto, e pentita di lui a torto portatovi, spinta grandemente da quello che successe sabbato sera, parto da voi col corpo e rimango accompagnandovi con la memoria delle ricevute offese, la qual desidero che si convertisca in pietà del vostro pentimento, più tosto che in odio della vostra ingratitudine.*

> Love which provoked by just indignation turns into despair makes me regret having loved you as immensely as I did, and regretting the love I so mistakenly offered you, compelled to a large extent by what happened Saturday evening, I remove myself bodily from you while the memory of the insult I received remains to keep you company, and I hope this memory will change into the compassion of your repentance and not the hatred of your ingratitude.

For all of these reasons, Franco's *Lettere familiari a diversi* yield many different readings that are nevertheless intertwined. First, her letters may be read as separate essays, which by addressing a wide selection of topics, provide traces of a courtesan's interaction with her milieu. Second, Franco's letters, published only five years after her *Terze rime,* may be read as glosses on the material she presented in her epistolary poems, each text illuminating the other in a reciprocal fashion. And finally, her letters may be read along with her elegiac verse epistles or debate poems in the *Terze rime* as a continuous unfolding narrative that dramatizes Franco's discursive strategies and the ways that she managed her own life.

II

While Franco's occasional poems endorsed the social harmony, purity, and collective *virtù* championed by Venetian humanists in their eulogies of the serene republic, the patriotic praises in her familiar letters reveal instead a bitter double edge. At the center of the *Lettere familiari a diversi*, Franco vehemently denounces the hypocrisy of a political rhetoric and social practice that advocate individual restraint and collective self-discipline for the proposed common good, while simultaneously denying crucial personal freedoms to many Venetian citizens. In letter 22, Franco writes as a courtesan to another courtesan; she challenges these beliefs indirectly in exposing the difficulties that an impoverished Venetian woman faces when deciding the future for her young daughter. Implied in Franco's letter is that such a woman lacks the necessary freedom, economic means, and social status to be able to make correct choices. Social inequities, Franco suggests, are camouflaged by idealizing civic codes that are blind to an individual's needs. Owing either to class inferiority or to gender, Franco argues, many Venetian women are placed in morally precarious positions that compromise their human dignity, personal freedom, and individual beliefs. But the most enslaved human condition, in Franco's view, is to be not only subject to another's desires but also to be robbed of one's freedom of choice.

Critics have repeatedly interpreted Franco's letter 22 as proof of her desire to denounce the horrors of her profession and her need to announce her conversion to a life of repentance. Rather, I would argue, this epistle questions the ideological assumptions that have forced an innocent young woman and her mother into a morally compromising situation. What Franco condemns in the letter is the impossibility of freely choosing one's future—a situation in which she too must have found herself as a child. Franco paints a cruel and violent picture of female subjugation, inequality, and suffering. Her message is not repentance, I believe, but profound indignation. Using the example of life's "giuoco della fortuna" (game of fortune), when coupled with the vulnerability of a young girl's virginity, she argues that not all Venetian citizens are free, nor do they share equally in the prosperity touted by the Venetian state.

This ethically inspired "essai" exposes a serious social predicament that many young sixteenth-century Venetian women—especially if impoverished—faced. It also challenges literary judgments of the Venetian courtesan. Franco literalizes the ancient misogynist trope that had equated rhetorical excess and epistolary flattery with a dressed-up whore.[36] She follows the epistolary prescription for simplicity of style (honesty, brevity, plain speech) when she counsels a mother to strip her daughter of the corporeal embellishments and vulgar finery that might deceive a male suitor.[37] That is, Franco insists throughout the letter that her motivation to write her friend is dictated by "familiar concern," and that she has chosen to substitute an epistle only because her spoken words have proved insufficient. She calls attention simultaneously to the appropriate decorum of this familiar letter and to her willingness to offer her friend the useful, practical advice of an experienced courtesan. Moreover, she writes in a language relatively free from embellishment. Although she condemns the mother's unwillingness to accept Franco's earlier offer to assist her daughter to enter the Venetian Casa delle Zitelle (a home for young girls "at risk"), Franco intends her harsh words, not as a reproof, but rather as an attempt to "rimuoversi dalla vostra mala intenzione in quest'ultima prova" (remove oneself from bad intentions for this last test). By so doing, Franco points to the immediacy of the familiar letter; it serves as a warning signal to her addressee to prevent the young woman from falling from the "precipizio nascosto" (hidden precipice) for which she is dangerously headed.

In this letter Franco recasts the satiric portrait of Aretino's *Sei giornate*, in which a young woman is educated into the courtesan's profession.[38] Nanna, a former prostitute/courtesan, delights in training her neophyte daughter, Pippa, in the tricks and allurements of the trade. By contrast, Franco's impassioned epistle decries the horrors of a social context which constrains a young woman to choose such a precarious existence in the first place. The letter achieves unusual force by virtue of its location following a series of letters of counsel in which Franco ridicules the carelessness and moral negligence of male patricians. Here, by contrast, she points to the social needs of powerless or disadvantaged young women:

> *Voi sapete quante volte io v'abbia pregata e ammonita ad aver cura della sua virginità; e, poi che il mondo è così pericoloso e così fragile e che le case delle povere madri non sono punto sicure dall'insidie amorose dell'appetitosa gioventù, vi mostrai la via di liberarla dal pericolo e di giovarle nella buona instituzione della vita e nel modo da poterla onestamente maritare.*

> You know how many times I have begged and warned you to protect her virginity; and since this world is so dangerous and frail and the homes of poor mothers are not immune from the temptations of lusty youth, I showed you how you can shelter her from danger and assist her in settling her life decently and in such a way that you will be able to marry her honestly.

Franco vividly depicts the social injustices a poor young woman will endure in the future if forced now to enslave her body to the desires of another, solely to escape the horrors of poverty. Most importantly, Franco cautions the mother that if her daughter should follow such a dangerous path, she will be prevented forever from enjoying one of the few options available to young women who retain their chastity, that is, the right to "onestamente maritare" (marry honestly). In an impassioned plea to her friend's moral conscience, Franco vigorously denounces the greedy commercialization of female sexuality, made even more lamentable when a mother merchandises her own daughter's flesh. Implicit, however, in Franco's condemnation of the mother's conduct is her own painful awareness of the hypocrisy at the heart of Venetian social practices: owing to poverty and to the absence of a male protector, women end up being forced to do precisely those things they would otherwise choose to avoid.

While Franco's avowed purpose is to signal the many dangers lurking behind the seductive facades of courtesanry, she also provides religious advice when she alerts her woman friend to the "certezza di dannazione" (certainty of damnation) that she will bring not only upon her daughter but also upon herself ("la rovina di lei non può esser separata dalla vostra" [her ruin cannot be separated from yours]). She alone, rather than the customers who eventually will consume, will be considered guilty of "guastare e corrompere la fattura del vostro proprio sangue e delle vostre proprie carni" (spoiling and corrupting the creation of your own flesh and blood). Together with the sexual politics she is condemning, Franco offers spiritual counsel that is both helpful to her woman friend and exonerating for herself.

Franco's advice in this letter (her letters, although undated, would have been written in the 1570s) also provides an explanation, from the female's point of view, of a law passed in the Council of Ten in 1563. The ruling attempted to prevent mothers from prostituting their young daughters for the purpose of receiving economic support. On the last day in March ("die ultimo martii"), the senate legislated to punish any person involved in violating the chastity of an unwed girl, or anyone who received favors from young women, especially if minors:[39]

> *Le violationi delle povere verginelle sono state sempre et tuttavia sono giudicate per casi gravi et molto perniciosi, onde quelli che le commettono, giustamente deono esser castigati secondo la forma delle leggi nostre; ma se in genere questi sono flagitii enormi, senza dubbio sono di peggior qualità quando sono perpetrati con quelle che sono in età minore et immatura, le quali per non haver ancora l'uso della ragione, né cognitione del bene o male che se gli appresenta, non gli si può dire che consentano al peccato.*

> The rapes of unfortunate young virgins have always been, and still are, considered very wicked occurences; hence those who commit

them must be rightfully punished according to the letter of our laws. But even though they are in all instances enormous crimes, they doubtless are of a more grievous nature when they are perpetrated upon females who are immature and under age, who, as they do not yet have the ability to reason or any knowledge of the good or evil confronting them, cannot be said to be consenting to the sinful deed.

Rather than punish the young girl, whom the senate regarded as the innocent victim, the ruling prescribes that the offenders, often mothers, who "per cupidità di danari" (lust for money) prostitute their own daughters, or relatives, be severely penalized:

> *Si intende che in questa città grandemente moltiplica il vitio di violar le fanciulle che sono minori et in età molto tenera, prostituite spesse fiate et come vendute delle proprie matri overo da i suoi più congiunti di parentato per cupidità di danari.*
>
> It is noted in this city there has been a great increase in the vice of raping young girls who have not yet reached the age of consent and who often are prostituted and practically sold by their relatives owing to a lust for money.

The penalty, in fact, was by no means inconsequential. As a form of public humiliation, the mother was placed on a platform between two columns in Saint Mark's Square, with a crown of ignominy on her head and a herald proclaiming her specific crime.[40] Further, she was banished from Venice and the surrounding area for two years. Similarly, if a father or other male relative was accused, he was to wear a heraldic emblem across his breast publicizing his guilt and was to serve on the galley ships at the oars for two years; if such a man could not perform the latter task because he was physically unfit for strenuous activity, he was to be imprisoned for two years and then banned from the city for another two years.[41]

To appease discontented citizens and to control the ever-increasing problem of poverty, Venetian patricians found ways of protecting non-noble women by founding charitable institutions such as the Casa delle Zitelle for poor and unwed maidens.[42] Yet this kind of charitable institution was designed to prevent the social effects of the loss of a young woman's honor and reputation rather than to end the specific injustices suffered by underprivileged members of society. For if a young woman had already compromised her chastity, she ran the risk of being ineligible for an "honest" marriage. Marriage alone placed her within the restricted, but at least protected, province of patriarchal supervision offered to her by the state, as well as within the insular boundaries of the Venetian family.

Franco's concern for impoverished young women "at risk" took concrete form in 1577, three years before the publication of her letters, when she drafted a *supplica* (petition) to the Venetian government requesting the foundation of a home for women who, already married or having children, were thus ineligible for the existing Casa delle Zitelle or Convertite.[43] Although it appears from the Casa del Soccorso documents attesting to the actual administration of the home that Franco did not, in fact, have a part in administrating the home after it was founded in the late 1570s (these homes were administered by noblewomen), the original idea for the institution nevertheless remains Franco's.[44] Her petition, unlike the law cited above, directly addresses women's needs and takes into account the reasons why they might choose to continue in their present wayward life instead of accepting the severe restrictions imposed upon them when they entered into certain charitable institutions. In support of such women, she writes:[45]

> *Molte donne sono, le quali o per povertà o per senso o per altra causa, tenendo vita disonesta, componte alcune volte dal Spirito di sua Divina Maestà, e pensando al misero fine, al quale per tal via sogliono il più pervenire, respetto così al corpo, come all'anima loro si ritrarebbero facilmente dal mal fare, se avessero luoco onesto, dove potessero ripararsi e con sui figlioli sostentarsi, perché nelle Citelle non sarebbe lecito che entrassero, nemeno tra le Convertite, avendo elle o madre, o figlioli, o mariti, o altri suoi necessari rispetti, oltreche difficilmente si possino indurre a passare in un momento da una tanta licentia, ad una così stretta et austera sorte di vita, come è quella delle Convertite. Da questo mancamento di provisione in tal materia nasce la perseveranza loro nel . . . questa altra abominanda sceleratezza ancora, che le proprie madre ridutte in bisogno vendeno secretamente la verginità de le proprie innocenti figliole.*

There are many women who, having led a dishonest life because of poverty, sensuality, or other reasons, are sometimes touched by the Spirit of his Divine Majesty, and thinking of the miserable end to which this path most often leads them with regard to both body and soul, would easily change their wicked ways if they had some reputable place to repair to, and support themselves and their children, because it is impossible for them to join the *Citelle* or even the *Convertite,* since they have mothers or children or husbands, or other obligations. Furthermore, it would be difficult to induce them, from one moment to the next, to change from such great

licentiousness to a way of life as strict and austere as that of the
Convertite. From this lack of assistance derives their persis-
tance . . . the further abomination of mothers who, being desti-
tute, secretly sell the virginity of their innocent daughters.

The Casa del Soccorso, when it was first founded in Venice, consisted of a
small rented house attached to the church of San Nicolo da Tolentino. It
was administered by the same noblewomen who had been previously associated with the Zitelle and the Derelitti homes. Then, in 1591, a number
of houses were bought near the church of San Raffaele, which permitted
more women to be accommodated than in the previous location. This institution welcomed young women who, owing to a meager dowry, were
unable to marry but wanted nonetheless a safe place to live until they could
find the necessary means to reenter Venetian society by legitimate means. It
also accepted unhappy wives upon the consent of their husbands. Many of
these women, despite Franco's warnings in the petition, ended up involuntarily in the home of the Convertite, which required from them not only a
vow of chastity but an allegiance to a religious order.[46]

Franco's interest in founding the Casa del Soccorso, as her petition also
reveals, had much to do with her own increasing need for financial assistance in those years. When she requests five hundred ducats yearly for
herself and for her "eredi" (heirs), she is quick to add that this is not for
"alcun beneficio" (any benefit) of her own. She says that she has been severely impoverished by the plague—"che son dalla mia povertà astretta a
farlo, avendo io figlioli" (so that I am forced to do this because I have
children)—and has lost "la maggior parte della mia robba" (the bulk of
[her] possessions).[47] Further, her brother's death has meant that in addition
to the care of her own children, she has the unexpected responsibility of
both seeing to the marriage of "alcune mie Nezze ed alcuni Nepoti" (some
of my nieces and nephews) and "quali tutti convengo sostentare" (supporting them as well).

Thus, in letter 22 Franco exposes the reality not only of a lower-class
woman's economic peril but of the devastating conditions in which an impoverished courtesan might live when menaced as well by the threat of irrational and retributive male aggression. Her portrait of the life of a young
courtesan is totally different from that of Aretino, who charges Pippa and
Nanna with deception, guile, and venality. Much like the courtier's denunciation of a sycophantic court role that enslaves a man's soul, Franco's description of sexual tyranny both literalizes that complaint by stressing the
physical horrors of economic destitution and intensifies it by focusing on

the woman's fears of physical violence. This kind of slavery is far worse than that of the courtier; for it makes a woman's body, as well as her mind, subject to the will of another. Franco writes eloquently on the horrors of such spiritual and physical bondage:

> *Troppo infelice cosa e troppo contraria al senso umano è l'obligar il corpo e l'industria di una tal servitù che spaventa solamente a pensarne. Darsi in preda di tanti, con rischio d'esser dispogliata, d'esser rubbata, d'esser uccisa, ch'un solo un dì ti toglie quanto con molti in molto tempo hai acquistato, con tant'altri pericoli d'ingiuria e d'infermità contagiose e spaventose; mangiar con l'altrui bocca, dormir con gli occhi altrui, muoversi secondo l'altrui desiderio, correndo in manifesto naufragio sempre della facoltà e della vita; qual maggiore miseria? quai ricchezze, quai commodità, quai delizie posson acquistar un tanto peso? Credete a me: tra tutte le sciagure mondane questa è l'estrema; ma poi, se s'aggiungeranno ai rispetti del mondo quei dell'anima, che perdizione e che certezza di dannazione è questa?*

It is a most wretched thing, contrary to human reason, to subject one's body and industriousness to a servitude whose very thought is most frightful. To become the prey of so many, at the risk of being despoiled, robbed, killed, deprived in a single day of all that one has acquired from so many over such a long time, exposed to many other dangers of receiving injuries and dreadful contagious diseases; to eat with another's mouth, sleep with another's eyes, move according to another's will, obviously rushing toward the shipwreck of one's mental abilities and one's life and body; What greater misery? What riches, what comforts, what delights can possibly outweigh all this? Believe me, of all the world's misfortunes, this is the worst; but moreover, if to the concerns of this world you add those of the soul, could there be greater doom and certainty of damnation!

Hence, Franco urges her friend, while she still can, to protect her daughter's "virginity," because chastity and purity are the only female virtues negotiable in the Venetian marriage market. So as to allow her daughter to "onestamente maritare" (marry honestly) sometime in the future, Franco reminds her friend of her original offer: to assist her daughter in entering the Casa delle Zitelle.

Tied to Franco's denunciation of female subjugation is her insistence on upholding social propriety and artistic decorum. By using the "plain speech" of the familiar letter in letter 22, Franco emphasizes her own moral decorum. Indeed part of her rhetorical strategy, as I have already suggested, is to strip down the male trope of the "dressed-up whore" and to expose the grim social realities of prostitution, two issues carefully avoided in male authors' condemnations of the prostitute. In addition, she opposes the erotic *blasons* of courtesans' customers. Just as she urges the mother to forbid her daughter to wear the costumes that will render her marketable rather than chaste, so Franco clothes her own letter in the modest unadorned garments appropriate to the conversational familiar letter:[48]

> *Dove prima la facevate andar schietta d'abito e d'acconciamenti nella maniera che conviene ad onesta donzella, co' veli chiusi dinanzi al petto e con altre circostanze di modestia, a un tratto l'avete messa sulle vanità del biondeggiarsi e del lisciarsi, e d'improvviso l'avete fatta comparer co' capegli inanellati dintorno alla fronte e'l collo, col petto spalancato e ch'esce fuor dei panni, con la fronte alta e scoperta e con tutte quell'altre apparenze e con tutti quegli altri abbellimenti che s'usano di fare perché la mercanzia trovi concorrenza nello spedirsi.*

> Where once you had her go about and combed with simplicity in a manner befitting an honest maiden, with her breasts covered and other attributes of modesty, you now encourage her to be vain, to bleach her hair and paint her face, and all of a sudden you let her show up with curls dangling all around her brow and neck, her breasts exposed and popping out of her dress, her forehead high and without a veil, and all those other tricks and embellishments that people use to promote the sale of their merchandise.

In this section of the letter, Franco switches from a scolding condemnation of her friend's actions to a practical assessment of the daughter's situation. Consequently her language changes from the eloquent pronouncements of a moral counselor to the simple but wise popular sayings of a friendly advisor: "perché voi gettata in acqua la pietra, gran difficoltà vi sarà a volerne cavarla" (because once you have thrown the stone into the water, you will find it very difficult to retrieve). Franco claims that even if this mother were to force her daughter into the courtesans' ranks, she would not succeed, because the young woman is not sufficiently beautiful, graceful, sophisticated, or educated, all requirements necessary for the honest courtesan's advancement. Franco even interjects a note of humor and common good sense when she affirms that the mother would "romperete il collo" (break her neck) trying to make her daughter "beata nella professione de le cortegiane" (blessed in the profession of the courtesan):

> *Per considerar la cosa carnalmente ancora, è così poco bella, per non dir altro, perché gli occhi non m'ingannano, e ha così poca grazia e poco spirito*

nel conversar che le romperete il collo credendola far beata nella professione de le cortegiane, nella quale ha gran fatica di riuscir chi sia bella e abbia maniera e giudizio e conoscenza di molte virtù; nonché una giovane che sia priva di molte di queste cose e in alcune non ecceda la mediocrità.

And if we are to further consider this matter from a carnal point of view, she really is not very beautiful, to say the least, because my eyes do not deceive me, and her conversation is so lacking in grace and wit that you will break her neck if you think that she can do well in the profession of the courtesan, in which success is hard to come by, even for those who are beautiful, charming, and wise and are proficient in many skills; so just imagine a young woman who lacks many of these qualities and is no better than mediocre in others.

She closes by reminding her friend once again of her offers to assist her ("sarò prontissima a prestarvi ogni sorta di aiuto" [I will be very ready to lend you any form of help]). For not too much time will have to pass, she warns, before the woman's daughter will realize the horrible truth of her situation. Paradoxically, she will flee from her own mother, who she will come to see has "l'avrete oppressa e rovinata" (oppressed and ruined her). With this last warning, Franco asks her friend to turn to God for help and to take fate into her own hands.

This is one of the few letters written to an interlocutor clearly designated as female in which Franco provides moral as well as practical advice. She underscores her ability to see error and to follow correct judgment, reminding her addressee that practical considerations affirm the ability to make right moral choices. Franco emphasizes the extremely difficult emotional, spiritual, and economic demands that a courtesan's customer might inflict upon her.

While letter 22 addresses a woman of the lower classes, letter 16 speaks to an upper-class woman who can delight in the rewards and comforts of her social standing. In another letter also clearly addressed to a woman, Franco congratulates her interlocutor, a noblewoman who has just become a mother, on the successful birth of "un così bel bambino maschio" (such a beautiful male child), and for enduring "delle molestie della gravidanza" (the discomforts of pregnancy). The noblewoman's privileges are redoubled and mirrored in the growth of her beautiful male child:

L'allegrezza si va augumentando con la vita del fanciullo, il qual, sì come cresce in bellezze, non è dubio che insieme crescerà in bontà e in valore, e per esser pianta di tal radice che non può tralignar né produr se non ottimi frutti, e per esser nella custodia di persone tali che non mancheranno in un punto alla sua esquisita cultura . . . annunzian liete novelle della riuscita nel bene.

Happiness grows apace with the child, and as his beauty increases, so will his goodness and gallantry, and since he is a plant brought forth by such roots, he cannot turn wild, but will bear excellent fruits, since he is entrusted to persons who will in no way neglect his exquisite education . . . herald glad tidings of success in all good things.

Unlike the girl in the previous letter, who must struggle to preserve her reputation in the face of the dangers of poverty, this child enjoys the comforts and rewards of a "degna famiglia" (worthy family).[49] Opportunities will be his simply because he is born a male into the upper classes of Venetian society.

Franco further identifies these aristocratic masculine privileges in a number of letters to male patricians. In letters 4, 14, 18, she manipulates an economic discourse for her own designs by addressing the issue of what can happen to one's spiritual well-being if one is subjected to a sudden reversal of fortune, a theme often addressed in familiar letter collections of the period. But in her version, Franco uses the commonplace to emphasize not only the question of an individual's spiritual strength in facing adversity but also to call attention to her correspondent's unhealthy, even immoral, attachment to money and possessions. To overturn the standard accusation of a courtesan's venality, in these letters Franco insists on giving back her interlocutor's counsel precisely as she originally received it. Placing greater emphasis on the equal exchange of advice and on the reciprocal nurturing of friendship than on an unbalanced struggle of power or authority, Franco's only "debito" (debt) to her correspondent, she claims in letter 18, will emerge from a mutual exchange of "valor" (valor). She repays her "clients" solely with their "propria moneta" (own coin). This exchange, following a marketplace economics as Franco redefines it, radically differs from the sexual tyranny she so vehemently repudiates in letter 22. Franco reminds her correspondents that not only does she assimilate the teachings of her aristocratic friends, she lives in accordance with them. Indeed she presents herself as a courtesan counseling male patricians who have neglected to follow the advice that they have given to others; she redirects the terms of exchange away from the physical and venal toward what most people hold as virtuous and wise behavior.

In letter 4, by refusing to sacrifice her moral integrity for material possessions, she cautions her interlocutor to do the same. As if to demonstrate the virtuous behavior worthy of his social standing, she declares that she will repay his advice with the exact sum awarded to her—no more and no less:

> *E purché la memoria mi serva . . . vi discorrerò col vostro stesso discorso, e fate conto che, nel pagarvi il mio debito, io venga a restituirvi quella propria moneta a punto che voi m'avete dato: tal è ricambio della virtù, che m'attegna non pur in similitudine, ma in forma d'un medesimo modo.*
>
> And provided my memory serves me well, I will speak to you in your own words, and I want you to take into account that in repaying any debt, I am returning precisely the same coin that you gave me: the exchange of virtue is such that I must proceed not in a similar estimation but in exactly the same way.

This advice, she cautions, is motivated only by profound respect and reciprocity of feeling. He must follow the advice he gives others if he expects them to heed his counsel. If he does not, his words are meaningless ornamentation, divorced from reality, much like the "dressed-up whore" of rhetorical discourse:

> *Il discorrer in questa materia con voi forse è soverchio, ed è, come si dice, portar acqua al mare, mentre ch'io parlo con voi di quello che voi profondissimamente intendete e avete dato a me lume e precetti; ma nondimeno è officio che procede d'amore e gratitudine, il quale mi sforza inoltre a dirvi che la virtù è riposta nell'uso più che nell'abito: sì che in quelle cose che tante volte avete insegnate a me, mostrerete di non intenderle e di non possederle, se non le adopererete nei vostri bisogni.*
>
> Perhaps it is redundant for me to speak to you about this matter, and as they say, it is the same as carrying water to the sea, because I am talking about things that you understand perfectly well and about which you have in fact enlightened and advised me. Nevertheless a duty born of love and gratitude further compels me to say to you that virtue lies in practice and not in pretense: so when it comes to matters that you have so often taught me, you will show that you neither understand them nor own them unless you apply them when the need occurs.

Thus Franco entreats a male patrician to live up to the values of fairness, justice, moderation, and honesty that he merely professes to follow yet insists that others uphold. Her correspondent, she charges, has had the unique and enviable advantage of being born male rather than female, human rather than animal, and he resides in an immaculate city, free from barbarism and the servility of other beleaguered Italian cities:

> *Potendovi far nascer della più immonda e della più vil specie di tutte le*
> *bestie, v'abbia fatto nascer nella perfettissima umana, e di questa v'abbia*
> *attribuito il sesso del maschio e non, sì come a me, quel della femina, e tra*
> *gli uomini di diversi paesi v'abbia dato per patria una città non barbara,*
> *non serva, ma gentile, e non pur libera ma signora del mare e della più bella*
> *parte dell'Europa.*

> While he had the power to bring you forth from the most foul and vile species of all beasts, he drew you from the most perfect: the human, and of this species he made you a male rather than a female like myself, and among the men of many lands he gave you as your own country a city that is neither barbarous nor enslaved but gracious, and not only free but also mistress of the sea and of the most beautiful part of Europe.

Franco's patriotic eulogy here, in contrast to her commemorative poems, gives way to philosophical speculation on the negative effects of unbridled desires that have the effect of subjugating other people. The "ricchezze" (riches) most important to her correspondent should be those that already surround him and of which he should always be proud: he resides in Venice, a city that defies the powers of the human imagination. Further, he can boast of belonging not to the "feccia del popolo" (scum of the common people) but rather "nobiltà per continua descendenza [è] illustre e chiara" (to generations of illustrious nobility):

> *Città veramente donzella immaculata e inviolata, senza macchia d'in-*
> *giustizia . . . sì come sola per miracolo fondata nel mezo dell'acque, e con*
> *maravigliosa tranquillità stata in piedi e sempre augumentata per infinito*
> *spazio di tempo. Città piena di maraviglia e di stupore, e tale che, per*
> *descriversi senza vedersi, non si conosce né vien compresa da intelletto*
> *umano.*

> A truly maiden city, immaculate and untouched, untainted by injustice . . . built as only a miracle could be in the midst of the sea, standing aloft with admirable tranquility and forever expanding through endless time. A city full of marvels and surprise such that, if it is described but not seen, it cannot be known or understood by the human intellect.

Follow the noble dictates of your class, she warns, and subscribe to the principles embodied in the civic practices of this virtuous city, unsullied by foreign hands. Only by practicing what he has advised his friends to do will he come to realize the dangers he incurs in desiring or envying another's fortunes: "Vanità delle vanità e tutte le cose che sono, vanità" (Vanity of vanities; all is vanity) she reproves him, quoting Ecclesiastes.[50] To covet material wealth is to subscribe to a world already severely "corrotto dal soverchio uso" (corrupt by overuse). For if he were to lower his eyes for a moment to the spheres below him, he would see just how little most people actually possess:

> E se non vi par d'aver tanto che basti all'usanza del mondo corrotto dal soverchio uso, considerate quanto meno potreste avere e quanto potreste star peggio, abbassandovi con gli occhi agli essempi che sotto i piedi non vi mancano infiniti.

> And if it seems to you that you do not have enough to satisfy the needs of a world corrupted by excessive consumption, just consider how much less you might have and how much worse off you might be, by lowering your eyes and looking upon the many examples that abound under your feet.

Why compare his fate with that of the heavens? His quest for "virtù" (virtue) already sets him apart from life's more lowly pursuits. True wealth consists, she declares (alluding to Seneca's advice to Lucillius), in securing tranquility of mind and in pursuing the infinite rewards of learning and wisdom:[51]

> La vera ricchezza consiste nella tranquillità della mente e nel contentarsi, e il contentarsi dell'anima nostra non è altro che il possesso della virtù, la qual grandemente si conosce nelle sue operazioni, che hanno forza, contro ogni nemico sforzo di contraria fortuna, a render l'uomo felice.

> True wealth consists of peace and contentment, and the contentment of our soul is nothing else but the possession of virtue, easily recognized by its works, which in the face of all the hostile efforts of an adverse fate have the strength to give man happiness.

Franco returns in letter 30 to an earlier invective against a male living up to the virtuous example he has set for others. By refusing to acknowledge his professed "errore" (error) in his dealings with her, he betrays the tenets of friendly and courteous advice. Instead of simply mimicking his counsel, as she has done in response to other letters that she has received from him, and presumably from other men, she interjects here a differentiated response. As Stoic advisor, she proposes that he react to adversity with introspection, following peaceful meditation rather than the violence of confused emotions, which can inadvertently victimize innocent people:

Voi fate grandissimo torto alla mia cortesia a voler negar con tanta per-
tinacia quel vostro espresso errore, di che io non pur vi scuso, ma vel rimetto
liberamente. E se in ciò non volete bene usar la mia grazia col quetarvi,
poich'io soffrisco e taccio, almen non tentate di caricar del vostro peso l'altrui
spalle innocenti, sì che la mia umanità, diventata vostra insolenza, offenda
chi non ha colpa, mentre io tento di giovare a voi colpevole col celar e col non
vendicar il vostro fallo, il quale, perfin ch'è stato di danno a me, mi sono
contentata di sopportarlo, sì come non sopporterò che 'l mio scudo vi vaglia
per armi contra di chi non v'ha provocato.

You greatly abuse my courtesy when you deny your blatant error
with such persistence, even though I not only excuse you but freely
forgive you. And if in this regard you decide not to avail yourself of
my graciousness by holding your peace, while I suffer and say not a
word, at least do not try to saddle innocent shoulders with the burden of your mistake, for in that case my forebearance, having become your insolence, will offend someone who is not at fault.
While I try to help you who are guilty, by concealing and not
avenging your trespass, which I have agreed to suffer to the extent
that it has injured me, similarly I will not stand your using me as
your shield against a person who has not provoked you.

While Franco advises the interlocutor of letter 4 on how to endure in a stoical manner the unexpected disasters of economic ruin, she upbraids the
male interlocutor in letter 18 for his arrogance in believing that he can acquire love simply by buying it. Once again, a language of economic trans-
actions runs throughout this letter. While in letter 22 she emphasizes the
realistic mercenary dimensions of courtesanry and its psychic miseries
when she calls attention to her fear that "some man may steal all your acquired goods from you," here Franco ridicules in letter 18 the cost of buying and selling one's affections as if they were capital freely exchanged,
unattached to the weight of human emotion. Franco replies indignantly
that love is not a commodity; it cannot be purchased. Her love, as she has
disclosed to her correspondent many times before, is already committed
elsewhere:

Poich'io non posso ricambiarvi con l'egual corrispondenza di quell'amore che
voi fate professione di portarmi, avendo già collocato il mio pensiero al-
trove . . . vi sarò almeno grata e cortese nel cercar di giovarvi col discopri-
mento di quella verità.

Since I cannot reciprocate with equal intensity the love that you
profess to me, having already committed my thoughts else-

where . . . I shall at least be gracious and kind enough to try and help you discover the truth.

While a courtier might make it his profession to learn how to simulate love with an unequal and false exchange of "premii" (prizes), she prefers not to conceal her true feelings but rather to uncover them in an honest display of emotion. Although Franco acknowledges that she might have profited more from this man's literary artifice and fatuous adulation "tacendola con mio beneficio, potrei celarla" (by keeping silent I could conceal it and benefit), she refuses to take part in any form of calculated or commercialized deceit:

> Avrei potuto, usando l'artificio dell'adulazione, che non è impossibile né molto difficile, imprimervi nell'opinione del falso, per valermi secondo l'occasione di voi, che pur sete gentiluomo di gran qualità, dal quale potrei aspettare in molti modi aiuto e favore. . . . Non l'ho voluto fare per non ingannarvi, dove non posso riamarvi.

> By using the artifice of flattery, which is neither impossible nor difficult, I could have created a false impression in order to take advantage of you if that were needed, for after all, you are a gentleman of great quality from whom I could in many ways expect help and favors. . . . I decided not to do so because I did not want to deceive you since I am unable to return your love.

Unwilling to accept her explanations, preferring to adhere to his predefined notion of the venal courtesan, this interlocutor resorts to vicious accusations. He claims that she willfully withholds her love so as to incite him to love her more intensely:

> Avete mostrato di non creder che così fosse la verità come suonavano le mie parole, ma, credendo secondo quello dove vi tirava il vostro desiderio, avendo commentato il mio parlare in modo che mostravate d'intender che io facessi resistenza alle vostre domande per tanto più accendervi nella volontà e per spronarvi a ingagliardir l'offerta del dono, sì come avete di gran vantaggio fatto, non ho voluto mancare a quest'offizio di lealtà, nella quale io sono assuefatta per natura e per costume.

> You have made it clear that you thought the truth was different from the sound of my words, and believing what you wished, you have remarked on what I said to the effect that I resisted your entreaties in order to enflame your desire and goad you into increasing the gift you were offering. Since you have indeed lavishly done so, I have decided not to neglect this loyal obligation, to which I am accustomed by nature and habit.

It is he, she retorts, who vulgarizes love by insisting on "fa[cendo] mercato . . . della mia persona" (marketing [her]), especially by increasing the "value" of his offer with the hope of winning her affections, while accusing her of avarice.

By denouncing this man's unjust claims on her body and affections, Franco characterizes the aggressive, even dangerous, behavior men display toward women to which she earlier alluded in letter 22. A man who believes that he can acquire a woman's affection with money and false promises, or can subject her body to a "convenuto prezzo" (agreed-on price), deceives only himself:

> *E con queste righe torno ad accettarvi della medesima disposizione dell'animo mio, al quale voi fate espresso torto con l'imputarmi d'avarizia, mentre credete con premii poter comprar l'amor mio, il quale, benché sia amor di donna che non concorre di ricchezze né di certe altre circostanze con un par vostro, non è però di vil femina che per convenuto prezzo obligasse alcuna parte del suo corpo, nonché tutto l'animo, overo di altra femina, che, da voi falsamente riputata tale contra i suoi buoni portamenti, per la vostra buona opinione meritasse nel vostro giudizio d'esser aborita, benché, ciò non ostante, fosse amata da voi. E la cagion che m'acqueta nel dispiacer ch'io sento di vedermi così da voi richiesta con accrescimento di prezzo, quasi facendo mercato, se ben, a dir la verità, molt'ingordo della mia persona, che vale assai poco, è questa.*

> And with these lines I once again want to inform you of the inclination of my very soul, to which you clearly do an injustice, since you accuse me of avariciousness, while at the same time you think that by offering rewards you can buy my love. This love, even though it is that of a woman who in wealth and other privileges cannot compete with someone of your rank, is not the love of some lowly female who for an agreed-on price would engage any part of her body and her very soul. Nor is it the love of a woman who, despite her excellent demeanor, according to your best judgment and opinion, deserves to be scorned even while, despite it all, she is loved by you. And this is what tempers the displeasure that I feel at seeing you ask for me at a higher price, as though you were bidding in the marketplace, quite voraciously, I must say, for my person whose value is so small.

This is one of several letters in which Franco counters charges of a courtesan's calculated deception in love by exposing male deception instead. In letter 14, Franco alerts a scorned lover to the destructive effects of vindictively persecuting her solely because she has chosen not to exchange "amor vero" (true love) for his "amor finto" (feigned love). To force her to love him, a man whom she has never chosen mistakenly assumes that an unequal love is tantamount to a "verace amore" (true love):

> *Poi che 'l verace amore principalmente consiste nell'unione dell'animo e della volontà della persona ch'ama con quello della persona amata, e che l'obligo dell'amor finto non merita corrispondenza d'amor vero, siavi davantaggio ch'io vi manifesti la verità, ch'è pur effetto d'amorevolezza.*

> Since true love consists above all in the union of a lover's soul and will with those of the beloved, and since the commitment of feigned love cannot lay claim to the correspondence of true love, I advise you to profit from my telling you the truth, for this, too, is a mark of affection.

If he has not proven his love with "effetti" (effects), preferring to "oppugnar e violentar il mio cuore" (attack and violate my heart) with "assalti nemici" (enemy attacks), why should she in turn satisfy his desires? Whereas he interprets her witholding of love as her calculated unwillingness to reciprocate his passions, her real intentions, which he has misread, have always been quite different:

> *Or che vi sete messo su 'l contradirmi e su 'l voler oppugnar e violentar il mio cuore, v'interpreterò quel che vi dissi—ch'io non poteva sodisfarvi in questo sentimento—che il non potere significhi non volere.*

> Now that you have decided to contradict me and oppose and violate my heart, I will interpret for you what I said: that I cannot gratify you in this feeling. "Cannot" means "will not."

He constructs his love for her as a fiction: he intends his actions to convey true love. But her perception of them exposes his falsity:

> *E contentatevi, nella finzione del vostr'amore, ch'io v'attribuisca tanto che mi dispiaccia che voi non facciate stima di me e che liberamente vi scriva l'intenzion mia. . . . Tanto ho voluto scrivere; né sono per replicarvi altro in questo proposito se non che ut sementem facies, ita et metes.*

> And in your pretense of feigned love it should satisfy you that I have enough consideration for you to be saddened by your lack of esteem, and that I write to you frankly about my intentions. . . . This is all I wanted to say, and I will add no more on the subject except that *ut sementem facies, ita et metes.*

Franco extracts these concluding lines from Cicero's *De oratore* 2.261, a section devoted to the use of allegorical speech in oratory for the purposes of jesting. While the Ciceronian passage focuses specifically on a given word's double meanings, which can allow for an ironic and even comic effect, both Franco's citation of Cicero as source and her own letter emphasize the potential misinterpretation that figurative language and actions can elicit.[52] The first may produce a comic effect, the second deceit and mistrust. Rusca, Cicero tells us, when hoping to pass his Limit of Age Bill, responded in the following manner to the question of Marcus Servilius, an opponent of the measure: "Tell me, Marcus Pinarius, if I speak against you, are you going to revile me as you have done the others?" ("Dic mihi," inquit, "M. Pinari, num, si contra te dixero, mihi male dicturus es, ut ceteris fecisti?"):

> "Ut sementem feceris, ita metes," inquit.
> As you sow, so shall you reap," he replied.[53]

The force of Franco's injunction against male deception is further strengthened by the biblical overtones of these lines, namely Saint Paul's familiar utterance in Galatians 6:7:

> Quae enim seminaverit homo, haec et metet.
> God is not mocked, for whatever a man sows, that he will reap.[54]

Allusions to classical and Christian authors like these are frequent in these letters of counsel, yet Franco's references to ancient texts reveal a free hand. Indeed her imitation of the ancients is far from slavish or pedestrian; she avoids the servile imitation that Aretino and Montaigne so vehemently criticized in their contemporaries. In a way similar to Aretino's method of constructing his reputation for posterity by his pen, Franco claims discerning literary taste and cultural sophistication as the basis for social standing in the present. The classical authors she assembles in these letters support her observations; she makes them stand as admiring witnesses to her intellectual integrity and literary talent.

Also in letters 18, 23, 28, and 30, Franco cautions against the havoc that unbridled passions such as anger, jealousy, and obsessive love can play on a human being's power of reason. Too much love can destroy rather than intensify love, she declares in letter 23. If a lover persists in forcing her to reciprocate his love, he will end by losing any possibility of her love. Excess may lead to offense and rejection: "così avviene che l' troppo amore alcuna volta offenda" (thus it happens that too much love sometimes offends). Her reminders that her correspondent should follow the behavior appropriate to his social class issue, she insists, from the concerns of a loyal friend, a grateful colleague, and an affectionate companion, who conscientiously returns the advice offered to her in times of adversity in the manner and spirit with which she had originally received it. He is the one who lives, she warns, in dangerous accordance with the dictates of passion and immoderate pleasure. This is the same advice she offers another man in letter 28, when she argues that he must moderate his ruinous passions by adhering to the virtues and powers of human reason. If no remedy may be found for his particular misfortune at the present moment, his "affanno della mente" (mental distress) will only contaminate further his ability to alleviate the intensity of his suffering. If he "darsi in preda all'angoscia" (gives himself over to anxiety), unhappiness and irrationality will certainly follow; they will dominate and consume his noble "discorso" (discourse), rendering him unfit to participate in public and civic arenas. Thus, he must curb and discipline his warring internal conflicts through self-discipline and self-effacement, if necessary. Unruly passions tyrannize the soul rather than guide it toward the noble pursuit of virtue.[55]

To reverse the charges that the courtesan adopts deceitful strategies when trying to win a man's affections, Franco alludes to the warnings of Cicero and Seneca against the moral dangers and destructive effects of calumny and willful deception.[56] But she expands the boundaries of this classical theme, and others, such as the importance of friendship, proper ethical conduct, sudden reversals of fortune, illness, or adversity in political affairs, to include concerns that directly involve women. She focuses throughout her letters on the unjust victimization of innocent women by male aggression and feigned love.

In letters 13 and 14, Franco quotes directly from Cicero, but she alters his words to fit her designs.[57] In the first epistle, she extends a formal invitation to a man, "in terzo con l'amico vostro" (together with a third, your friend), to join her at home for an evening of "lieta conversazione" (pleasant conversation). Her house will provide him with warmth and refuge "'l tempo tutto volto alla pioggia" (from the rains), and in turn, his conversation will reward her as well as comfort her: "Tra quanti favori ch'io potessi ricever dalla vostra gentilezza a me sarà sopr'ogn' altro caro che mi facciate grazia di lasciarvi goder oggi in lieta conversazione" (Among all the favors that I might receive from your courtesy, the most cherished will be the kindness of your letting me enjoy you and your conversation today). She invites him to dine with her, and if he chooses, to bring along a bottle of his welcome "malvasia" wine:

> *Se vi degnerete di venir, potremo desinar caritevolmente insieme,* sine fuco et caerimoniis more maiorum, *di quella grazia che ci sarà. E se vorrete*

aggiungervi un fiaschino di quella vostra buona malvasia, di tanto mi con-
tento e di più non vi condanno.

If you will deign to come, we will be able to partake together *sine*
fuco et caeromoniis more maiorum [without pomp and ceremony in the
manner of our ancestors] of whatever food there will be. And
should you add to it a small flask of your excellent *malvasia*, I will
be quite happy and not ask for more.

This letter resonates with classical decorum at the same time that Franco
uses classical formulas to set the stage of a courtesan's boudoir. Franco
quotes Cicero's first letter to Atticus but replaces certain key words,
thereby radically transforming its original context. In Cicero's noted epistle he speaks about his prospects of candidacy for the consulship, informing
Atticus that fortunately only Galba is canvassing, but he has already been
turned down ("with a plain and simple, old-fashioned, no" according to the
custom of our ancestors").[58] He writes:

Petitionis nostrae, quam tibi summae curae esse scio, huiusmodi ratio est,
quod adhuc coniectura provideri possit. Prensat unus P. Galba: sine fuco
ac fallaciis more maiorum negatur.

With regard to my candidature, in which I know you take the
greatest interest, things stand as follows, so far as one can guess at
present. P. Galba is the only canvasser who is hard at work; and
meets with a plain and simple, old-fashioned, no.

Although Franco cites part of these opening lines, switching "fallaciis" for
"caerimoniis," she also excludes the two technical political words, "prensat" and "negatur," which identify Cicero's remarks as concerned chiefly
with political campaigning. In contrast to Cicero's stress on political
competition, Franco evokes an atmosphere of ease and pleasant conversation; she invites her addressee to dine with her without "pretense or
ceremony, in the custom of our ancestors." A repast in the comforts of her
home, together with dignified "conversation," replaces Ciceronian political affairs, the domain of men, with the private "ceremonies" of the courtesan's salon. Once again, moreover, she overturns the received notions of
courtesans' deceit, pretenses, and dishonesty by drawing the reader's attention instead to her alternative to the competitive maneuverings that dictate
the political actions of a realm strictly reserved for men.

Franco's defense of women under attack reoccurs throughout her *Terze*
rime. In *capitolo* 24, Franco speaks in defense of an innocent woman—a fellow
courtesan—who was unjustly accused by the unidentified man to whom

Franco addresses her poem. Not only did he insist in defaming this woman with "lingua acuta," but he threatened her with physical disfigurement: that is, he threatened to slash her face with a knife ("ma voi la minacciaste forte allora, / e giuraste voler tagliarle il viso" [but then you threatened her and swore that you would slash her face]), a common enough action against courtesans to have warranted the expression "dare la sfregia":

> Dunque a la mia presenza vi fu opposto
> ch'una donna innocente abbiate offesa
> con lingua acuta e con cor male disposto:
>   e che, moltiplicando ne l'offesa,
> quant'è colei più stata paziente,
> in voi l'ira si sia tanto più accesa,
>   sì che, spinto da sdegno, impaziente
> le man posto l'avreste adosso ancora,
> se nol vietava alcun, ch'era presente. (25–33)

So in my presence you were accused of having offended an innocent woman with a sharp tongue and an ill-tempered heart; and that, multiplying your offense, the more patiently she endured, the more your anger was inflamed, so that driven by your indignation, you would also have laid a hand on her unless someone prevented it who was present.

Franco's defense of an innocent woman echoes the counsel that she gives her correspondent in letter 30. As Ann Rosalind Jones has argued, Franco's courteous defense "exemplifies the diplomacy required under such circumstances by conceding that what she has heard about this man may not be true . . . [she] sets herself up as a model of proper behavior between the sexes." To do so, Franco emphasizes women's willingness to take on, as Jones calls it, a "voluntary 'vassalage' to men for the sake of keeping peace between the sexes and procreating the human race."[59] Indeed Franco's own subservient style in this poem is intended to point, by contrast, to this attacker's vulgar misbehavior and his lack of decorum, actions all the more alarming in a man who is, as Franco says, "diviso / dai fecciosi costumi del vil volgo" (apart from the debased habits of the vile populace).

Franco suggests what his model of proper behavior between the sexes might be in letter 8. She poses as moral counselor when she decries the negative effects that feigned and calculated emotions can have on one's spiritual well-being. She signals to a male patrician "la professione della nobiltà in che pur sete nato" (the nobility that you profess and to which you were indeed born) the danger of falling into the trap of falsely accusing the innocent: if he persists in doing so, he will condemn only himself, she cautions. Although Franco speaks, in a sense, in defense of all women who are subject to the irrational will of another person, here she condemns the injustice of his behavior specifically in relation to herself. Not only is she unworthy of such treatment, but this behavior is unbefitting to his class's most noble and allegedly peace-loving aspirations:

> *Non so a qual di noi due risulti maggior biasimo delle maledicenze che vanno intorno: o a me, che contra ogni dovere, vengo tassata da voi, o a voi, che, contra la professione della nobiltà in che pur sete nato, me andate infamando. Certa cosa è che dell'operazioni ingiustamente fatte, se ben il danno cade sopra di colui che riceve l'ingiustizia, la colpa nondimeno e 'l carico d'aver mal operato s'ascrive a colui che le fa. Ma io sono in più forti termini ancora, perché il peccato che condanna di calunnia me non offende, non essendo le cose divulgate tali che di me si debbano in alcun modo credere.*

> I do not know which of us deserves greater blame for the malicious rumors spread abroad; I, whom you tax so unduly, or you, who— despite the nobility you profess and to which you were indeed born—go about slandering me. There is no doubt that when injustice is done, the one on whom it is inflicted suffers the damage, while the one who inflicts it must bear the burden of a wicked deed. The sin of calumny taints me not, for the things divulged were such that no one would ever believe them about me.

Her motivation to write him, she says, is her desire to follow "la civiltà e per legge di natura" (the laws of nature and civilization). It is the style and critical acumen with which one applies one's talents that ultimately matters, Franco states, not having the accoutrements of nobility or the benevolent favors of the heavens. This is the position that Girolamo Muzio took in his discourse *Della nobiltà*.[60] True nobility must be earned by one's personal merit regardless of inherited social standing: "le proprietà del vero nobile sono quelle medesime che sono del buono e del virtuoso, poiché principalmente il nobile è nobile per la virtù" (the qualities of a truly noble man are the same as those of a good and virtuous one, because whoever is noble is noble mainly thanks to his virtue).[61] Echoing a Venetian humanist ethic that advocated the restraint of individual human passions in favor of the *unanimitas* produced by a collective harmonious will, Muzio adds that "il vero nobile è libero per la virtù, che è libera, non soggiace a passione di animo alcuna, anci domina a se stesso e a gli altri" (the true nobleman owes his freedom to virtue, which is free. He does not yield to the passions of the soul; indeed he dominates himself and others). In a similar vein, Franco advises her interlocutor in letter 17 to check the extremes of his "appetiti" (appetites) before ending in physical and moral ruin:

> Con le vostre ismanie e col vostro andar vagando e strepitando giorno e notte nell'importuno assedio della vostra servitù, vi fate tener da me giovane ozioso e vano, inclinato alla ruina dell'appetito più che alla edificazion della ragione.[62]

> With your frenzies, your wandering and ranting by day and night, intent on the inopportune siege of your services, you cause me to consider you an idle and vain young man with a greater propensity for ruinous appetites than for the edification of reason.

Franco reveals her own need for protection in a few of her letters to a male advisor. In letter 31, above all, she acknowledges in her opening the extent to which her correspondent's protection against insults directed at her has helped her emerge victorious from a painful experience:

> Non è stata così grande la mia grandissima disgrazia d'aver avuto occasione di rimaner mal sodisfatta di quel mio amico, che non sia stata molto maggior la buona fortuna d'aver avuto nella causa, che si trattò in mia assenza, la cortese protezzion vostra, la qual non pur m'è stato scudo di sicurissima diffesa contra quelli 'nsulti, ma, nel riparar all'impeto delle avverse accuse, in luogo di sostener le mie ragioni, ha ottenuto di rendermi vittoriosa nelle lodi . . . sono state confermate dall'opinione e della lingua di tutti gli circonstanti.

> My extreme misfortune of having been ill-served by that friend of mine was so great indeed, but greater yet was my good fortune in having had your kind protection during the trial (debate?) that was held in my absence, because it served me not only as a shield offering the most reliable defense against those insults, but by protecting me from the blows of hostile accusations instead of advocating my own case, it earned me victory amid praise . . . confirmed by the opinion and the words of all those who were present.

The courtesy that he has shown her in a moment of personal adversity elicits her courteous response. Indeed, throughout the *Lettere familiari a diversi* Franco responds to the kindness that an unidentified man has shown her in difficult moments. It is most certain that in letter 31 she writes to Domenico Venier.[63] In two letters that she sends to an unidentified literary advisor, she presents herself as engrossed in literary matters, and needing to confer with him about her collection of letters. In these letters she clearly states what she wants from her ally; she negotiates a profitable exchange for herself as a writer involved in publishing her works. In letter 41 she combines a request that her interlocutor, presumably Domenico Venier, look over her edition of letters with a declaration of her wish to see him in person as soon as possible. This letter, she concedes, is merely an imperfect substitute for "humana conversatione" (live face-to-face conversation), just as her edition of letters is an imperfect substitute for a public voice denied to her by Venetian society. In a teasing manner, she dismisses the importance of her "sciocchezze" (trifles) in favor of her desire "vedervi e di parlarvi alla presenza" (to see and to speak with him in person), only to return by the end of the letter to reiterate her initial request:

> *Le mando da leggere il presente volume di mie lettere raccolte il meglio ch'ho potuto, pregandovi che, supplendo col vostro giudizio alla mia imperfezzione, parte scusate e parte emendate gli errori, desiderando che toleriate non meno l'error ch'io faccio presumendo non pur di mandarvi da veder queste mie sciocchezze, ma ancora di desiderar di vedervi e di parlarvi alla presenza . . . vi priego quanto posso ad essermene grato di tal corrispondenza, qual si conviene all'umanità vostra.*

> I am sending you this volume of letters that I have collected as best I could so that you may read it, and with the entreaty that by making up for my imperfections with your wisdom you will in part excuse and in part correct my errors. I further hope that you will equally tolerate my trespass in not only taking the liberty of sending you these trifles of mine to look at but also of wanting to see you and talk to you in person. . . . I beg you to indulge me in this correspondence as your human kindness demands.

And in letter 49, Franco displays a light-hearted, playful tone when she characterizes herself as "tutto libera e lontana dal favor degli infiammati sensi" (completely free and far from the favor of inflamed senses) for his praise of the book that she has sent him for corrections. Obediently she sends him "il secondo quinterno" (the next quire), so that he may "strip it" of all errors, as he has already done for the first part. As he, too, "spogliato in giubbone" (strips down to his doublet) in the privacy of his home, so she imagines her letters undergoing the same disrobing in his care. So that he will not catch cold, she promises to continue to provide him with drafts of her other works, once she has copied them:

> *Mando il secondo quinterno per obedienza della vostra richiesta, perch'egli abbia da ricever quel favore d'esser da voi spogliato in giubbone ch'ha ricevuto il primo. Ben mi sarebbe caro ch'in quella libertà della vostra persona sciolta di vestimenti prendeste fatica di corregger l'opra, sì perché n'ha*

bisogno, come perché a star in quel modo senz'adoperarvi potreste raffreddarvi.

In compliance with your request, I send you the second quire, so that it, too, may receive from you the favor of being stripped down to its doublet as did the first. I would certainly be most happy if, being at your ease and having shed your garments, you would go to the trouble of correcting this work, both because if you were to just sit there thus disrobed and without keeping busy, you might catch cold.

Many of the compositions Franco sent to Domenico Venier for review, which she refers to in letters 19, 32, 39, 40, and 50, resulted in the commemorative editions (Martinengo, Zacco, and Spinelli) she either assembled or to which she contributed poems. In letters 5 and 6, she, not her male interlocutors, offers gifts to men from whom she has received important favors. In letter 5 she announces that she sends her addressee, "uomo pieno di vera e di rara sapienza" (a man of true and rare wisdom) who follows "cristiana dottrina" (Christian doctrine), a present of "una di quelle operine, che Vostra Signoria mi fece il favore ch'Ella sa" (One of those small works for which Your Lordship did me the favor that you know), to be followed by "alcuna delle cose mie da leggere" (some of my things to read). In letter 6 she exchanges her poems with another esteemed interlocutor, "alla quale, in segno della mia gratitudine . . . invio due sonetti fatti per l'istesse rime dei quattro vostri" (at which point, as a token of my gratitude . . . I send you two sonnets using the same rhymes as your four). Claiming that her verses are unequal to those by a man of his learning, she concedes that the sonnets she sends him will nonetheless reveal her eagerness to learn.

In 1580 Veronica Franco was the only woman to have published her familiar letters in many years. Franco reveals her venture into yet another literary territory (one virtually unexplored by sixteenth-century women authors) in her dedicatory epistle to "Monsignor Luigi d'Este Cardinale" that begins her edition of letters:

> *Forse che a tempo di maggior occasione e di più prospera fortuna e di più essercitato stile, ardirò con l'aiuto della vostra divina umanità tentar impresa di maggior espressione dell'animo e dell'obligo mio.*[64]

Perhaps at a time of greater consequence and more prosperous fortune, and when I will have further honed my style, I will, with the help of your divine kindness, attempt a work that more deeply expresses my spirit and my indebtedness.

It is unfortunate that the only letter publicly proclaiming the excellence of Franco's literary skills and attesting to this "impresa di maggior espressione dell'animo" (attempt at a work that more deeply expresses [my] spirit) appeared in print in 1606, fourteen years after her death. Writing to her from Nancy, France, Muzio Manfredi thanks Franco for her beautiful sonnet, "Ecco del tuo fallir degna mercede" (Here is the reward worthy of your failings) praising his newly printed epic tragedy, *La semiramis tragedia:*

> *Poi che in esso tanto mi honorate, e con tale spirito di sapere, e d'arte, che io ne sono rimasto non pure pieno di meraviglia, ma di stupore.*[65]
>
> For in it you honor me so greatly and with such spirit of knowledge and art that I was not only surprised but absolutely astonished.

He adds that he hopes to reward her soon for her kindness "in altro stile" (in another style) in order that she can give "l'ultima mano al Suo Poema Epico" (the finishing touches to your epic poem). The epic poem to which Manfredi refers, Franco, as far as I know, never wrote. However, the "impresa di maggior espression dell'animo" (the undertaking of greater expression of the soul) to which she alludes in her dedicatory epistle to Cardinal Luigi d'Este she had already achieved, I believe, in her powerful volume of poems, published in Venice five years earlier.

These familiar letters gloss the content of the poetic *tenzone,* and they highlight certain of the elegiac *capitoli* in the *Terze rime* in which Franco repudiates male deceit and treachery in love. In the *Lettere familiari a diversi,* Franco writes as a moral and social counselor to a male elite and as a critic of mercenary and cruel love; she writes to women as an ally in support of their freedom and to courtesans who are unjustly victimized by male aggression. In the guise of a courtesan secretary to male patricians who have been led astray, Franco's familiar letters reclaim for women an epistolary discourse that is critical of unequal relations between men and women. Like the poetic battle with the anonymous author in her *Terze rime,* these letters rework literary conventions to serve the concerns of women who have been silenced by male authority.

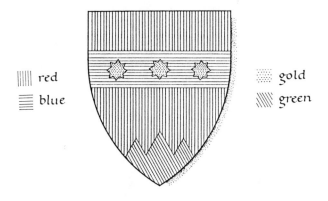

||||| red   ▦ gold

≡ blue   ⦀ green

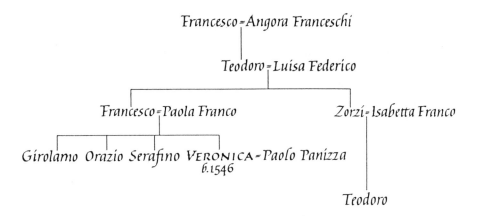

Francesco = Angora Franceschi

Teodoro = Luisa Federico

Francesco = Paola Franco   Zorzi = Isabetta Franco

Girolamo Orazio Serafino VERONICA = Paolo Panizza
                              b. 1546

                                            Teodoro

Tomaso, bishop of Venice, was a member of this family

The Franco coat of arms and family tree.
Description of the Franco arms: on a red shield, a blue horizontal bar with three eight-pointed
gold stars. At the bottom of the shield a three-peaked green mountain.

A Portrait of Veronica Franco by Jacopo Tintoretto? Oil on canvas, Sixteenth Century (1575?). Worcester Art Museum, Worcester, Massachusetts.

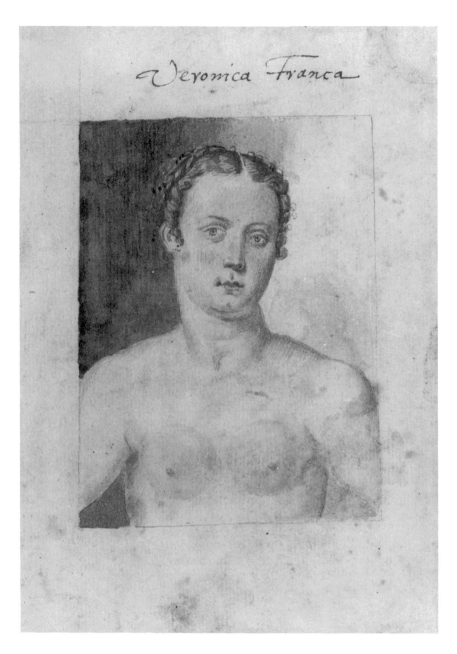

A portrait of Veronica Franco by an anonymous artist for an album of 105 watercolor drawings of Italian costumes and scenes of daily life, including two maps of Venice. Watercolor drawings mounted on paper, framed by narrow gold stripes. Venice, 1575. MS 457, "Mores Italiae," fol. 6. Beinecke Rare Book and Manuscript Library, Yale University, New Haven, Connecticut.

A Courtesan and a Visitor in Her Chamber. MS 457, "Mores Italiae," fol. 17.

A Prostitute Leaning from a Window and Two Gentlemen Below. MS 457, "Mores Italiae," fol. 72.

A Portrait of a Ragusan Woman in Venice (Il Ritratto Dela Ragusea in Venetia) with breasts exposed. A portrait of a Venetian courtesan, MS 457, "Mores Italiae," fol. 3.

Two Courtesans(?). Oil painting by Vittore Carpaccio, 1510–15, Museo Civico Correr, Venice.
Photo: Osvaldo Böhm.

Apotheosis of Venice, also known as *Venetian Peace*, by Paolo Veronese. Ceiling painting in the Sala del Maggior Consiglio in the Ducal Palace, Venice. Photo: Osvaldo Böhm.

A view of Venice in pen and ink. MS 457, "Mores Italiae," fol. 55.

La Sapienza (Wisdom), by Titian. Ceiling roundel in the main meeting hall for the Accademia della Fama in the Libreria Sansoviniana (J. Sansovino) begun 1537. Venice. Photo: Osvaldo Böhm.

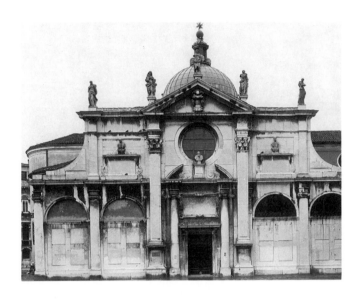

Church of Santa Maria Formosa in Venice rebuilt on a design by Mauro Coducci (1492). Veronica Franco's parish church at the time of her birth. Photo: Osvaldo Böhm.

Church of Santa Maria della Presentazione, or "Le Zitelle" (1579) by an anonymous architect on the island of the Giudecca. An institution for "endangered young women" was founded there in 1558. The architect placed the church between symmetrically arranged, flanking residential wings. Photo: Osvaldo Böhm.

Venice Prays to the Virgin to Intercede against the Plague by Domenico Tintoretto (1631) in the Church of San Francesco della Vigna, Venice. Photo: Osvaldo Böhm.

The Entry of Henri III of France into Venice (1574), by Andrea Michieli, il Vicentino, in the Sala delle Quattro Porte, Ducal Palace, Venice. Oil painting. Photo: Osvaldo Böhm.

Portrait of King Henri III of France, by Jacopo Tintoretto. Oil painting. Ducal Palace, Venice. Photo: Osvaldo Böhm.

The frontispiece to a commemorative anthology of poems dedicated to the triumphal entry into Venice of Henri III, king of France (1574), *Compositioni volgari, e latine fatte da diversi nella venuta in Venetia di Henrico III, Re di Francia, e di Polonia* (Venice: Domenico Farri, 1575–76). This frontispiece includes a watercolor medallion portrait of Henri III.

Portrait of Pietro Aretino by Titian in Florence, Palazzo Pitti (1537). Oil painting. Photo:
Alinari/Art Resource, New York.

Danae and Cupid by Titian (1546). Oil painting in Naples, Gallerie Nazionali di Capodimonte. Photo Alinari/Art Resource, New York.

Frontispiece *Portrait of Veronica Franco,* originally intended for her volume of poems, the *Terze rime* (1575). A detached engraving (anonymous) in the manuscript collection of the Biblioteca Nazionale Marciana, Venice. MSS it. IX 14 (=6988).

Sonnet by Maffio Venier (1575–80), "El retratto e la impresa è bona e bella," c. 254r, presumably regarding the engraved frontispiece portrait for Franco's *Terze rime*. In the manuscript collection of the Biblioteca Nazionale Marciana, Venice. MSS it. IX 173 (=6282).

First page of an obscene poem by Maffio Venier (1575–80), "Veronica, ver unica puttana," c. 56r in the manuscript collection of the Biblioteca Nazionale Marciana, Venice. MSS it. IX 217 (=7061).

An autograph canzone by Maffio Venier, "Sopra il Monte dell'Avernia ove San Francesco hebbe le stimate," ("Sacrati horrori, ove la folta chioma"), c. 81r in the manuscript collection of the Biblioteca Nazionale Marciana, Venice. MSS it. IX 271 (=6096).

LETTERE
FAMILIARI
A DIVERSI
DELLA S· VERONICA
FRANCA·
ALL·ILLVSTRISS· ET
REVERENDISS· MONSIG·
LVIGI D'ESTE
CARDINALE.

Frontispiece for Veronica Franco's *Lettere familiari a diversi* (1580), dedicated to Cardinal Luigi d'Este and Henri III, king of France. Biblioteca Nazionale Marciana, Venice. Rari V. 494.

RIME DI DIVERSI
ECCELLENTISSIMI
AVTTORI

Nella morte dell' Illustre Sign. ESTOR Martinengo Conte di Malpaga.

RACCOLTE, ET MANDATE
ALL'ILLVSTRE, ET VALOROSO
COLONNELLO IL S. FRANCESCO
MARTINENGO SVO FRATELLO,
CONTE DI MALPAGA.

DALLA SIGNORA
VERONICA FRANCO.

Frontispiece to commemorative anthology of poems assembled by Veronica Franco, *Rime di diversi eccellentissimi auttori nella morte dell'Illustre Signor Estor Martinengo Conte di Malpaga* (1580) in Biblioteca Nazionale Marciana, 390.d.159, Venice.

OME tal'hor dal Ciel sotto hu-
mil tetto
Gioue trà noi quà giù benigno
scende,
Et perche occhio terren dall'
alt'oggetto
Non resti uinto humana forma prende:

Così uenne al mio pouero ricetto
Senza pompa real, ch'abbaglia, e splende
Dal fato Henrico à tal dominio eletto ,
Ch'un sol mondo no'l cape, & nol comprende.

Benche si sconosciuto, anc'al mio core
Tal raggio impresse del diuin suo merto,
Che'n me s'estinse il natural uigore.

Di ch'ei di tant'affetto non incerto,
L'imagin mia di smalt', e di colore
Prese al partir con grat'animo aperto.

Rendi, Re per uirtù sommo,
& perfetto,
Quel che la mano à porger-
ti si stende:
Questo scolpito, & colorato
aspetto,
In cui'l mio uiuo, & natu-
rals'intende.

E,s'à essempio sì basso, & sì imperfetto
La tua uista beata non s'attende;
Risguarda à la cagion, non à l'effetto.
Poca fauilla ancor gran fiamma accende.

E come'l tuo immortal diuin ualore,
In armi, è in pace, à mille proue esperto
M'empio l'alma di nobile stupore,

Così'l desio di donna in cor sofferto
D'alzarti sopra'l Ciel dal mondo fore
Mira in quel mio sembiante espresso, & certo.

Two dedicatory sonnets by Veronica Franco, "Prendi, Re per virtù sommo e perfetto," for Henri III, king of France, after his entry into Venice in 1574, in Franco's *Lettere familiari a diversi* (1580), Biblioteca Nazionale Marciana, Venice. Rari V. 494.

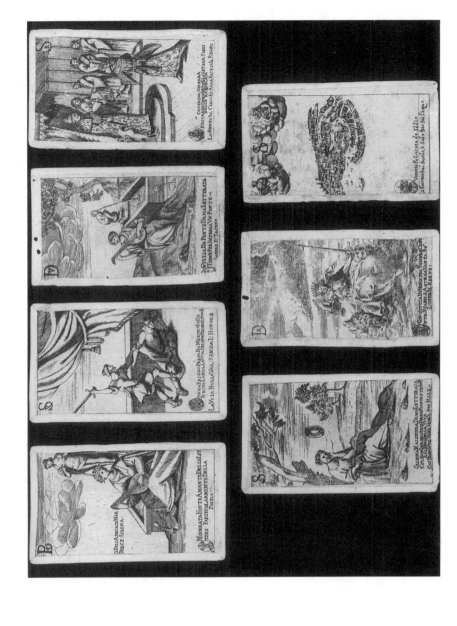

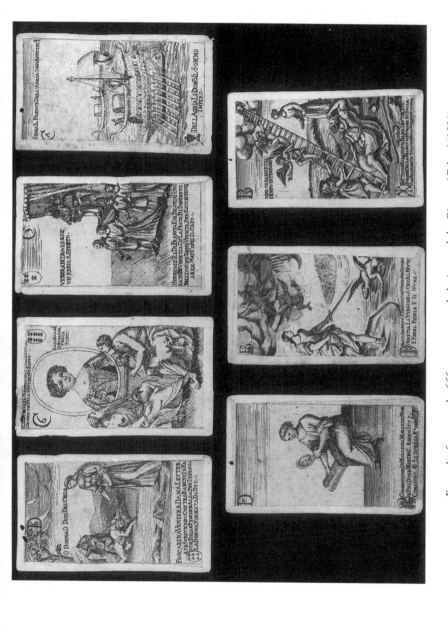

Examples from a pack of fifty-two engraved playing cards by Giovanni Palazzi (1681) representing famous aristocratic and citizen women writers and patrons of Venice and including various representations of the city. Biblioteca Civico Correr, Venice.

Coram D. Inquisitore vocato ad Dominam S. Veroni
de Pania, ibi paribus Rev.do eius Commissario
P. Vincentio Registari, et Achille Frasse cive
D. Veronis filio, ad instantiam eiusdem D. audivit
et dicte.....

Che per cosa de religion l'havevan fatto
dimandar per dirsi d'un certo Bortolo Bottaro
fratel del primer della censula, ser in cortil
de S. Piera, delle cose de ciò botteghera, che
l'havea voce, et fama e nominar fate in ciò
come le altre nan Donne Agnese, che la mal
a una man so socii portar a ca d'Stojan
tan le altre villanie la gha dicto, ne esser sta
a dir a mia della soi, e nol casa, (come me evise)
hora la dicta, ch' patteran, e te suspier ni che
via nan peti ne l'altesma. Er na Donna
Portola, che gle soi apprendisse Lisette parla
Examinar in casa de D. Antolo Vicentina
sotto de'Pioran de S. Julian, che cosa i de
spitana insieme nan ser, onor ho de spiriti
et dise la sopta d. Antolo che na disputana de
Pianti desi, et l'hor de ni. Vic. tien de ni
L'altro de si
Examinar Sepho el va nella med.ma usa, et
sense il tutto.

Il sopta Bortolo havevo tutti li di de Nadal
pross. passat et nan avio e nette d. gran
disse la sopta D. Antolo, et Laura sora
mia matera

Parlando con mi detto Bortolo, havevan
che'l negava il purgatorio, ma che'l
purgatorio fosse in qte mond.
Un altro a cinque altre eltecctte? qete all
pur sta intrapresa d parlar con in qe... a
nie, et adunn ma

Detta D. Antolo m'ha detto, che l'ha dine
tion, m la fregni, che la me ... esser
esser qualcheuna, la ne resppoa, che n
imposs ... ranta natra nulla Sepho, e Vic.
sopti gha ne havena homagio qe pure
penso la sera, ne mai l'ha ubligado has
...hera.

Parlando con mi alcun dini che .... e men
Dio, e mi suggiunsi, che ... a... a nan
bisignan nlutio, e de nette a nise, e ditt
cl ... se sa, che chi a me nan cosa, bespona
esedirla.
Si dise, che nan si confetti, et camunti.
Ha questa ... tutto mia sermon refugni da na
alq... su det qe qe più nolte nolte, et ha dormi
giu in qual sa ama pudsea, e sano sentio
da d. D. Antolo, e Laura mia matera piange.

Deposition of an oral denunciation made to Inquisition trial brought against Bortolo Bottoner (Bortolo, the button maker) on 12 May 1587, in which Veronica Franco appears as the chief witness in favor of the prosecution. The trial ends with Franco's signature. Venice, Archivio di Stato, Sant'Uffizio, Processi, b. 59, 1587.

303

Alla Signora Veronica Franca, à Venetia.

IL belliſſimo ſonetto, che V.S. mi hà mandato in laude della mia Semiramis Tragedia, moſtra con la ſua rarità, la diuinità dell'ingegno voſtro, e la forza dell'amore, che ſempre hò conoſciuto in voi verſo me, poi che in eſſo tanto mi honorate, e con tale ſpirito di ſapere, e d'arte, che io ne ſono rimaſo non pure pieno di marauiglia, ma di ſtupore. Poi l'hauere V.S. trouato modo di mandarlomi fin quà, mi hà chiarito, ch'ella in eſſere corteſe, hà pochi pari. La ringratio hora con queſta mia quanto più poſſo; ma fra poco le darò in altro ſtile, tal ſegno di gratitudine, che in tutto non rimarrò vinto di corteſia, e le priego ſanità, & otio da dar l'vltima mano al ſuo Poema Epico.

Di Nansì, à 30. di Ottobre 1591.

Letter from Muzio Manfredi to Veronica Franco dated 30 Ottobre 1591 in his collection of letters, *Lettere brevissime di Mutio Manfredi* (Venice: Roberto Meglietti, 1596).

Four

DENOUNCING THE COURTESAN: FRANCO'S INQUISITION TRIAL AND POETIC DEBATE

Io Redolfo Vannitelli per discarico della mia conscienza, et non per altro effetto do' in notitia al Santissimo Offitio dell'Inquisitione come una Veronica Franca pubblica meretrice havendo l'altro giorno perso alcune sue robbe in casa, et incolpando tutti quei che stavano nella sua casa . . . ricorse all'incanti delle donne superstitiose, et vane*.

(ASV, Sant'Uffizio, Processi, 1580)

Veronica, ver unica puttana
Franca, "idest" furba, fina, fiappa e frola,
E muffa e magra, e marza, e pì mariola,
Che si' tra Castel, Ghetto e la Doàna.†
Maffio Venier (1575–80)

When Veronica Franco was summoned by the Inquisition courts on 8 October 1580 to counter anonymous charges of performing heretical incantations in her house near San Giovanni Novo, she had already gained valuable experience in defending herself against vindictive opposition.[1] In 1575, just five years earlier, Franco had emerged triumphant from a poetic debate against a masked Venetian dialect poet who sought to belittle her success as a courtesan writer and to defame her with invective slurs intended to lower her from the heights of *cortigiana onesta* to *puttana pubblica*.[2] Three men represent in literary, social, and legal domains the many obstacles Veronica

---

*I, Redolfo Vannitelli, wishing to unburden my conscience and for no other reason, hereby inform the Most Holy Office of the Inquisition that Veronica Franca, a public prostitute, having the other day lost certain objects in her house and having accused all those who lived in her house . . . had recourse to the incantations used by superstitious and frivolous whores.

†Veronica, veritably unique whore, Franca, *id est* [i.e.] foxy, flighty, flimsy, flabby, smelly, scrawny, scrimpy, and the biggest scoundrel besides, who lives between Castello, the Ghetto, and the Customs. (Biblioteca Nazionale Marciana, MSS it. IX 217 (=7061])

Franco confronted in Venetian society: Maffio Venier, the anonymous misogynist poet with whom she does poetic battle in her *Terze rime*, Ri[e]dolfo Vannitelli, the disgruntled male tutor of her children who denounced her to the Inquisition tribunal, and the chastising inquisitor, to whom she was forced to submit during the trials.[3]

Vannitelli's rancorous charges against Veronica Franco, which he filed secretly with the Holy Office, and Maffio Venier's satirical invectives, which he composed anonymously, are evidence of two men resentful, for different reasons, of the political influence, social recognition, and literary patronage that Franco had succeeded in acquiring in the years 1575–80.[4] In both legal and literary cases, Franco's denouncers had recourse to powerful institutions that supported their attempts to reconstruct a crumbling social order based on patriarchal or patrician ideologies. Vannitelli's intention to file in secret a written *denuncia* against Franco, his employer, would have been endorsed by inquisitorial authorities, who had put into practice an increasingly anonymous method of identifying heretics. After 1550, Venetian church and state had joined forces against social disorder, as never before, by encouraging Venetians of all classes to support the republic in their fight against heresy, even if it meant pitting citizen against citizen, or servant against padrone.[5] And in the case of the rebellious Maffio Venier, he too would have had recourse to the important literary discussions held in Domenico Venier's salon on appropriate stylistic registers and linguistic choices when writing lyric poetry. Although there was a degree of animosity, fueled perhaps by competitive envy, between Maffio, his uncle Domenico, and his distant cousin Marco, Maffio's decision to transgress the rhetorical norms that Pietro Bembo had advocated in book 2 of his *Prose della volgar lingua*, published in 1525, would have won a measure of support, on stylistic grounds alone, among members of his uncle's coterie. Maffio's Venetian dialect poems against Veronica Franco carry Bembo's concept of *variazione* to an extreme. Rather than simply varying what Martha Feldman has referred to as the "compositional affects, sounds, word lengths, and accents in relation to Venetian poets' compositions of the sixteenth century," Maffio's poems descend into the bawdy, the lurid, or what might be called the profane underside of the Petrarchan lyric.[6]

For exactly what reasons Franco came to believe, incorrectly, that Maffio's verses (which he composed and circulated, presumably in Ca' Venier, while she was absent from Venice) were those of Marco Venier, Franco's interlocutor in her *Terze rime,* is not certain. This confusion is not surprising, however, if one considers that even Domenico Venier had experimented with composing verses in Venetian dialect.[7] That she wants to preserve the confusion of identities that Maffio's satirical verses generated as an operating poetic fiction in her *Terze rime* is important. A number of critics have advanced the theory that Franco intended to create the illusion of an actual poetic exchange. According to this view, Franco was the author of all sides of this three-way poetic debate. Although this theory is intriguing, because it would make Franco the only woman writer in the period to assume in print the male writer's voice as her own, it goes against the informality of poetic exchanges, as I understand it, in Venice during the latter half of the sixteenth century.[8] Even the poems of the patrician poet Domenico Venier rarely made their way into print. Unfortunately, with no manuscript sources for Franco's poems surviving, it is hard to prove any one theory conclusively. I believe that Veronica Franco did not construct a fictional poetic debate but actually exchanged poems with Marco Venier (most likely the author of all of the poems now labeled by the *incerto autore*) in Domenico Venier's literary salon, and that when she received poems by Maffio, she incorrectly believed them to be by Marco Venier. Domenico Venier, her literary "counselor," seized upon this confusion as an unusual opportunity for Franco to enter into an interesting and entertaining poetic debate with Domenico as her guide.[9]

Standing, then, as an invisible support behind male attacker, *incerto autore,* and courtesan writer is Franco's literary counselor and protector Domenico Venier. That his influence not only among literati but in Venetian society as a whole proved crucial in helping to secure a positive outcome in Franco's trials (the trial was suspended without calling in witnesses to testify against her) and in bolstering her courage to defend herself against vicious accusations in both legal and poetic arenas should not be underestimated. Because only one month after the second trial, Franco was once again actively engaged in literary endeavors. In November 1580, after the charges of heresy brought against her were dropped, Franco sent to Montaigne, while he was in Venice, a copy of her newly printed *Lettere familiari a diversi*. In this sense we cannot help but agree with the first part of Vannitelli's vindictive claim that Franco "ha ella troppo grande aiuto in questa città, et è favorita da molti, dai quali vorrebbe esser odiata" (she enjoys too much support in this city and is favored by many who should hate her).[10]

Both legal and poetic trials are exquisitely revealing of Franco's assertiveness and of her insistence on defending herself against sinister opponents. Regardless of Domenico Venier's support, once on trial, above all in the Venetian tribunal where no defense lawyers were present, Franco was on her own. Her courtroom speeches and poetic self-defense illuminate one another reciprocally as analogous linguistic occasions: Franco's interaction with the anonymous denouncer mirrors her poetic *tenzone* with a masked dialect poet; enforced submission to the inquisitor's questioning parallels her courteous self-restraint; and her calculated about-faces in the trial mirror the poses of innocent victim in her artful counterattack in the poetic debate. Whereas the poetic debate between male and female poets provided Franco with an imaginative scope in which to air and contest personal adversities and dramatize inequalities between the sexes to an ennobling advantage, the courtroom arena and the fear of public humiliation constrained her necessarily into a more submissive posture. Yet while on trial, Franco attempts to recover her domestic property and to regain her social standing as Venetian *cittadina*—economic and social equivalents to her personal honor and her public reputation as a courtesan writer, so denigrated by the vitriolic satiric poet. [11] We witness in the trial proceedings the intelligence of a woman who understood the legal procedures of the Inquisition courts sufficiently well to devise responses that strategically countered Vannitelli's charges against her. And in the poems, we similarly see Franco's competence at mounting a counterattack that challenges poetic authority, while facing down a misogynist adversary.

Why was Veronica Franco denounced by Redolfo Vannitelli and what were his charges against her? Although the specific charges would not have been disclosed to her until the moment of interrogation, Franco undoubtedly had already suspected Vannitelli, and her other servants and neighbors, of stealing precious objects from her and then conspiring against her to conceal their misdeeds. [12] For in May 1580, thieves had plundered her house, which resulted in tensions and suspicions circulating in the Franco household.

Franco's dual defense in verse and courtroom also suggest a series of parallels between the accusations she was facing. Maffio Venier attempted to dethrone her from *cortigiana onesta* with allusions to her class pretensions ("Ti vuol, ti, sfondraizza signoria" [What do you want, you, a broken-down woman]) and her infractions of the sumptuary laws. These laws were directed specifically against courtesans, prohibiting them from wearing or owning silver and gold, among other things:

> Te disi po d'aver ancor in pie,
> Dei to arzenti, alle pompe una quarela,
> Con un mar de to altre massarie.

Ma la to credenciera è po una scuella
stronza tutta in t'i ori, un bocaletto,
È meza crepa d'una pignatella.
(*Maffio Venier, "An, fia, cuomuodo? A che muodo zioghemo?")*[13]

You would like to boast of being highly placed, and in addition
you say that you still have a case in sumptuary court about your
silver and loads of other household objects. But in fact your
cupboard contains a bowl made of crappy gold, a small goblet,
and one half of a cracked pot.

Similarly, Redolfo Vannitelli's allegations filed with the Holy Office
pointed to Franco as a public nuisance who allegedly disregarded prescribed
social codes and class distinctions:

Dice di più esser maritata hora, hora essere vedova, hora volersi maritare,
et fingere tra l'altri un matrimonio falsamente fatto qui con uno Romano, et
ciò ha fatto solo per ricuperare li perli, le maniglie d'oro, et altre gioie,
ch'ella portava contro la dispositione della parte fatta del Serenissimo Prin-
cipe. (Vannitelli)[14]

Now she says she is married, now that she is a widow, now that she
plans to get married, and among other things, she pretends there
was a fake marriage here, with a certain man from Rome, and this
merely in order to recover the pearls, golden bracelets, and other
jewels that she used to wear, breaking the rules set by our Most
Serene Prince.

Just as Vannitelli claims that Franco deliberately blurs social and class distinctions to gain economic advantage by pretending in turn to want to
marry, or to be a widow, or at another moment, to have married a Roman
man, all for the sole purpose of reclaiming her precious silver and gold confiscated by the *Magistrato alle pompe* because of the sumptuary laws, Maffio's
verses too underscore Franco's manipulation of the truth for opportunistic
gain. Though she might boast owning expensive items that connote high
social standing, he retorts that all of her "mobili" (furniture) to be pawned
in the Jewish ghetto will not leave her even enough money to pay the
ferryman's fare:[15]

St'i porti quanti mobili ti ha in Ghetto
Cavame un occhio po' s'ti ha da poder,
Sora ogni cosa, da passar traghetto.

If you were to take all your furniture to the ghetto, I wager one of
my eyes that for the lot you would not get enough to take the ferry.

Many vindictive and petty squabbles of this kind between neighbors, spurned lovers, and disgruntled servants ended in the hands of the Inquisition tribunal. Recent research into inquisitorial practices in Venice indicates that of 150 trials regarding magical incantations, witchcraft, and sorcery (not including necromancy and diabolism) heard from 1552 to 1594, only a very few people brought to court (many of whom were courtesans) were actually sentenced; the majority of the cases were dropped in a few hearings.[16] Franco's case was in fact the only trial for magical incantations in the year 1580, although many such cases (98 percent against women) were presented to the courts during the sixteenth century. In the years 1581 to 1590, in fact, Venetian trials against popular witchcraft outnumbered those against Lutheranism.[17] Despite the increasing number of such cases, however, it is important to note that no person accused of witchcraft in Venice was either condemned to death or severely tortured, as was the case in the cities of other European countries during the same period.[18] Nevertheless, risking public humiliation and severe penalties if found guilty, as was the fate of many courtesans in those years, Franco faced legal as well as social and literary challenges with self-confidence.

The public humiliation that Emilia Catena, "meretrice pubblica" (public prostitute), and Isabella Bellocchio, "cortesana" (courtesan), were subjected to in 1586 and 1589, respectively, demonstrates how fortunate Franco was to be spared such degrading treatment. Accused of heretical incantations and witchcraft by similarly vengeful servants and neighbors, both women were condemned to a public whipping in Piazza San Marco, and then forced to wear a "mitria" (miter) for one hour with their accusations written on it in the public space of the Rialto bridge.[19] Bellocchio, despite the "favori" (favors) she enjoyed among Venetian patricians as a result of her higher status, was one of those few who did receive a sentence. She was banished from Venice for five years, during which time she was required "to repent her sins ever day kneeling in front of the picture of the Madonna, fast on Friday and on Saturday, recite the beads of the Most Holy Rosary" (ogni giorno . . . avanti l'imagine della Madona genuflessa, et il veneri digiunare, et il sabato dir la corona del santissimo rosario).[20]

The threat of public derision Franco faced, then, makes her composure during the trial proceedings all the more remarkable. Her answers, as we shall see, depended on her command of language, but also on an understanding of the nature and purpose of the inquisitor's line of questioning. To be sure, her friendship with Domenico and Marco Venier, not to mention other influential Venetian patricians, would have assisted her in summoning the necessary composure to combat the charges of such a serious opponent; but her expert handling of the inquisitor's questions also displays her independence and forthright manner.

Domenico Venier would have been useful to her in more ways than one. He was able to counsel Franco on certain legal procedures connected with the Inquisition tribunal, for he too had once been denounced to authorities on charges of heresy.[21] In 1576, only four years before Franco's trial, Domenico had found himself in need of the protection of his own friends, many of whom occupied important governmental positions. When Giacomo Gallo, a servant who worked in the home of the important Venetian Lippomano family near San Severo, reported a conversation to his confessor that he had had with Domenico Venier's servant, Gallo's confessor allegedly threatened to excommunicate him if he failed to denounce Domenico to ecclesiastical authorities. According to Gallo's testimony in court, Venier's servant, whose name he could not remember, had complained to him that Venier had prevented him from attending church during Lent because he was asked to work during these days in the Venier household. Because this servant normally did not live with Venier—"non stava in casa sua, ma . . . lo serviva fuor de casa" (I did not live in his house, but I did outside work for him)—he, unlike Venier's other servants, was otherwise able to attend church on a regular basis. During these holy days, however, he was prevented from attending mass, since, as Gallo reports, Venier needed the continuous assistance of his servants "portarlo in carega" (to carry him about on his chair). This last fact he uses to incriminate Domenico himself for not attending church.[22] Despite these accusations, Gallo's testimony appears not to have convinced the tribunal to pursue the matter any further; they did not request Venier's appearance in court, thereby virtually exonerating Domenico from any misdeeds and sparing him the humiliation of the Venetian tribunal and public exposure.[23] Veronica Franco was not as fortunate. Being required to appear in court and to present her case meant that she had to rely on many of the defensive strategies she had used years before to face down her abusive male attacker in the poetic debate.

The poetic *tenzone* in Franco's *Terze rime* sheds light on many of the poetic practices of the Venier literary salon in the latter half of the sixteenth century, while mirroring the dialogic exchange of the Inquisition trials. Composed either as alternating stanzas or as separate poems, the *tenzone* addressed a specific and preestablished theme. Not always a love poem, it also functioned as literary satire or poetic debate, sometimes serving as a platform for personal invective and vituperation.[24] An analysis of Franco's *tenzone* in relation to literary practice in late-sixteenth-century Venice reveals the extent to which she both reworked an existing amorous lyric tradition for her own purposes and appropriated a public rhetoric traditionally denied Renaissance women. The epistolary debate between male and female poets exposes literary inequalities; similarly, the vying for authority in the trial proceedings uncovers social tensions not articulated in sociopolitical domains.

The *Terze rime* includes eighteen capitoli in terza rima in the form of questions and answers, or "proposte" and "risposte," between Franco and an anonymous poet. The poet is referred to in one edition as the *incerto autore* and in others (now lost) as Marco Venier. Some of Franco's capitoli adhere to her interlocutor's rhyme scheme, others respond to a theme set by him.[25] Further, the *tenzone* in capitoli 1 and 2, 11 and 12, 13 and 14, and above all capitolo 16, which weaves together in one poem Franco's social and literary maneuvers, form the core of the *Terze rime*. The *sonetto caudato* "Veronica, ver unica puttana" (Veronica, veritably unique whore), the third poem in the series of three satirical verses against her, forms an integral but extratextual part of this *tenzone*.[26] Existing only in manuscript form, Maffio Venier's poems intrude into the exchange between Franco and the *incerto autore*, even though they are not included in the edition of Franco's *Terze rime*. It is important to read Maffio's verses in connection with the *tenzone*, because they not only malign her but also challenge (although in a way different from Franco's) the Petrarchan male lover poet Marco Venier. Maffio's obscene poems parody the adulatory rhetoric of Marco's love poems to Franco, and degrade her, as does her accuser, Vannitelli. What had been the *incerto autore*'s *blason*, written in the traditional Petrarchan language of love and praise, is inverted in Maffio's verses. As in the satirical texts we examined in chapter 1, Maffio deflates the sophisticated image of the courtesan and underlines the blunt facts of prostitution by means of double entendres that simultaneously praise and degrade her. A reading of these verses helps explain why many of Franco's poems to Marco Venier are defensive and foreshadow in interesting ways Vannitelli's secret, vindictive deposition to the ecclesiastical authorities.

Franco's choice of a genre traditionally associated with polemical debate is significant for a number of reasons. First, the *tenzone* is especially congenial to a courtesan poet, who by her very situation was frequently called upon, as in the case of the Inquisition, to defend herself against trumped-up accusations. Second, Franco uses this genre to perform a critical reading of her interlocutor's idolatrous praises of her by exposing the counterfeit nature of Petrarchan conceits. Thus, Franco's critical stance in many of the poems in the *tenzone* engages with the social and literary context in which the courtesan's texts were produced and embodies the power struggle intrinsic to the *tenzone* as a genre.

While Franco most likely anticipated Vannitelli's motive of ridiculing her publicly, her poems to Marco Venier suggest that she incorrectly supposed that the misogynist verses were composed by the *incerto autore,* perhaps as a kind of literary bravado. In both cases she felt unjustly accused and dishonored without cause. Her initial mistaken identification of the enemy poet generates vehement retorts, propelling Franco to challenge her "masked" antagonist to a duel of honor in capitolo 13: "Non più parole: ai fatti, in campo, a l'armi" (No more words: to action, to the battlefield, to arms).[27] Her innocent interlocutor unwittingly responds, "Non più guerra, ma pace: e gli odi, l'ire" (No more war, but peace: neither hate nor anger). It is not until capitolo 16, in the poetic fiction of the *Terze rime,* that true identities are revealed. In this defiant poem, Franco directly counters her now-unmasked adversary's rhetorical strategies—that is, Maffio's insulting wordplay in "Veronica, ver unica puttana" (Veronica, veritably unique whore).[28] In the poetic *tenzone* of the *Terze rime,* as in the trial proceedings, Veronica Franco, as both courtesan poet and solitary and independent woman, enters into a territory of rhetorical casuistry, public debate, and self-defense traditionally forbidden to Renaissance women.

II

Redolfo Vannitelli presented his written denunciation to the Inquisition authorities on 3 October 1580 (see appendix 4.2).[29] His deposition is most probably a response to the one that Franco had filed with the patriarch of Venice, Giovanni Trevisan, and Monsignor Thomasino Ascanio, his vicar, five months earlier (23 May 1580), reporting a theft at her house.[30] She hoped to retrieve certain precious items of her dowry—silver, jewels, and money—bequeathed to her by her mother, as well as unspecified "scritture" (writings).[31]

Many of these objects resemble those precious items of her dowry that in her first will (1564) she had requested that her mother, Paola, retrieve from her former husband, Paolo Panizza. They also resemble Maffio's list of Franco's possessions satirized in "An, fia, cuomuodo? A che muodo zioghemo?" And in her second will (1570), after listing and describing precious clothes and jewels, presumably also from her dowry, she claims that six months previously she had received from Don Donà Avonio of the monastery of Santo Spirito in Venice one hundred ducats "cor" in exchange for the following items, all of which, she adds, bear her family crest: "uno bacil d'arzenti" (a silver basin), "sei cuslieri" (six silver spoons), "sei pironi d'arzento" (six silver forks), "una saliera" (a salt dish) which cost ten "ongari" and, finally, "un mio candelier" (a silver candelabrum). This list, too, Maffio burlesques when he accuses Franco not only of securing a loan from a priest (Don Donà Avonio), to whom she had to lend her silver in exchange, but also of having amorous relations with him.[32]

As soon as Franco realized that she was missing these valuable objects, she most probably filed a complaint with the *Signori di notte al criminal* (Guardians of the night watch), made up of six officials who were elected to investigate any nocturnal disturbances, excessive ribaldry, or illegal possession of weapons. What is certain from the presence of a document dated 22 May 1580 in the Archivio Patriarcale in Venice is that she did appeal to ecclesiastical authorities. In this deposition, Veronica contends that she had hidden some of these valuables, and an unspecified amount of money, under her mattress, a practice common among women, as other trials reveal (see appendix 4.1).[33] She asks that if any person knows either the location of the stolen goods or the perpetrators of the thefts, he or she should contact the office of the *Cancelleria Patriarcha* within nine days after the public proclamation of the document. The penalty imposed after the termination of the nine-day period is excommunication ("tuti quelli et qualunque persona che non farà la debita restitution et revelation . . . per l'autorità di esso monsignor vicario, saranno excommunicati" [any and all persons who do not make restitution and revelation (confess) will be excommunicated by the authority of Monsignor the Vicar]). She requests that the local parish priest take the responsibility of publicly condemning the thief "a fuogo et aqua" (to fire and water), and with the "son di campanella" (ring of the bell); he must also contact the appropriate authorities if the thief should confess the crime in church, a practice carried out in the Inquisition case brought against Domenico Venier, as we saw earlier.[34]

This public injunction was never carried out, because the thief (or thieves) was never apprehended. It is possible that Franco's deposition refers, not to a recent theft, but to one that took place even earlier, perhaps during the plague years, 1575–77, when Franco was absent from Venice. It is likely she waited for more incriminating proof, since the charge was not made until 1579–80.[35] Leaving one's house unattended during the plague, and in the years directly following it, resulted in numerous thefts, eventually forcing the Council of Ten to elect six additional officers to the already-instituted night patrol.[36] Although most precious goods were automatically transferred on a temporary basis to local parishes, many household items were left in the custody of servants and maids, who remained in Venice in order to take care of the houses and children. Once the plague was unmistakably over in 1577, the government ordered that all goods be returned to the appropriate owners, which caused violent disagreements over the ownership of specific goods, often resuscitating hereditary squabbles among family members. Those servants or guardians who had remained behind, for example, demanded considerable sums, which were contested in the civic courts.[37]

Everyone in a sense was a potential "victim" during the plague, and certainly the anxieties that it elicited lingered on for many years. Even "la città immacolata" (the immaculate city) became the "sporca femena" (the dirty female) in the verses of Maffio Venier.[38] Accordingly, an atmosphere of heightened tension and fear of exposure and public humiliation permeated the lives of Venetian citizens who were called upon by the republic to purge their souls and to eradicate all evil habits and dissolute ways by constant prayer. The layers of corruption were so complex, however, filtering down from patricians to the lower classes, that to expose monks and nuns involved in sinful carnal acts, for example, meant directly to accuse and thus defame powerful noble families who had forced their daughters against their will, for financial and political reasons, to enter convents.[39] This secretive, corrupt environment certainly did not help protect courtesans from often-vindictive neighbors, jealous suitors, and fearful servants, who responded to authorities' attempts to cleanse the city of all "corrupting" influences. Social unrest, complicated by class rivalries, may have been a principal force behind Vannitelli's acrimonious charges against Veronica's alleged immoral and indecorous conduct.

The historian Richard Kieckhefer has observed that many witchcraft trials originated in petty squabbles, pointing often to tensions between social class or positions of authority: the "circumstances giving rise to accusations of witchcraft are not accidental. . . . Frequently it is possible to show prior animosity between the accuser and the accused—usually in the form of some specific quarrel. Most importantly, in many cases the suspected stands in a position of moral superiority in this quarrel, so that the accuser feels guilty, and reverses his guilt by projecting it on to the accused."[40] A similar dynamic between tutor and courtesan employer is apparent in the charges that Vannitelli brought against Franco.

What is clear is that Franco was a victim of theft on more than one occasion. Her deposition, however, was totally unsuccessful; she never retrieved her silver, jewels, books, or money, all items that would have distinguished her to some degree from the lower classes. Although she suspected her servants of committing the thefts, she lacked concrete proof. When she was robbed again in 1580, she threatened to cut or withold their salaries in order partially to recoup her losses. She claims during the first Inquisition hearing that only after her servants had plead with her at great length (the reversal of what Vannitelli claimed when he said that Franco "cominciò a far ditti incanti et invocationi di demoni . . . dando scandalo a tutti di credere a quelle cose, alli quali ella credeva fermamente" [began to perform the said incantations and to invoke the demons . . . with a scandalous display of her belief in these things, in which she firmly believed]), did she finally allow them to perform in her house a magical ritual, the "inghistera"—a popular hydromantic ritual designed specifically to disclose a thief's identity.[41]

Their attempt failed miserably, however, or so she claims. Suspicions circulated in the neighborhood and in the Franco household, for Franco immediately accused Bortola, her cook and maidservant, of stealing her "un paio di forbici con la guaina d'argento" (scissors with a silver chain), which in turn most likely made Vannitelli increasingly nervous that she might accuse him as well.[42] Possibly to cover himself, he quickly filed his epistolary deposition accusing Franco of performing heretical incantations in her home for the purpose of recovering her stolen goods (see appendix 4.2). Supported by two witnesses, "una donna dimandata Bortola" (a woman called Bortola), Franco's cook (who lives in "calle di Ca' Cocco," in the same parish of Santa Maria Formosa where Franco lived), and "Iuonne . . . Tedesco" (Giovanni, the German), Vannitelli claimed that Franco, "havendo l'altro giorno perso alcune sue robbe in casa" (having lost the other day some of her things in the house), accused everyone present (Vannitelli, Bortola, and Giovanni) of stealing the following items: "un paio di forbici con la guaina d'argento, et un'officiolo dorato" (a pair of scissors with a silver chain and a gilt prayer book), and "altre robbe" (other things).[43]

His most pointed accusation, prompted by his need for an "discarico della mia conscienza, et non per altro effetto" (unburdening of my [his] conscience and for no other reason), and the one most tailored for the audience of the Inquisition tribunal, was that Franco made use of "un'anello benedetto, l'oliva benedetta, l'acqua santa . . . cannele benedette, et una inghistera piena d'acqua" (a wedding ring, a blessed olive branch, holy water, blessed candles, and a basin filled with water) for incantations, and that with the assistance of "tre putti quattro putte" (three boys and four girls) who retrieved these holy items from the local parish church (San Giovanni Novo), she invoked "demoni, et altri nomi" (demons and other names).[44] Most important, "ella credeva fermamente" (she so firmly believed) in these heretical acts that she claimed that the children had actually seen "chi le havea havuti" (who had taken her things). Scandalized by her behavior and outraged by her accusations, Vannitelli declares that he took it upon himself to uncover the true thieves. In the following days, in fact, as he tells the court, he quite remarkably and perhaps all too conveniently found the gilt prayer book "in mano di un libraro in merzaria" (in the hands of a bookseller in the Merceria).[45]

But the specific grounds for his accusations—the heretical practice of invoking the devil and performing magical incantations—are quickly superseded by his personal denunciations of her as a "pubblica meretrice" (public prostitute), one of those "donne soperstitiosi, et vani" (superstitious and frivolous women), and "fattuchiara puttana pubblica" (a witch and public whore).[46] He exhorts the court to punish her severely, and "acciò vada in essempio di tutte l'altre persone" (to use her as an example for others who persist in wrongdoing). Indeed all of his remaining allegations are carefully fashioned to evoke a feeling of urgency in his audience. With this in mind, he designs his concluding statement to appeal to the authorities' moral and social consciences. He requests that they not be swayed by the influence of her powerful supporters when he pleads "et supplico che nonobstante detti suoi favori debbiate farla gastigare conforme al dovere, et subbito, subito" (and I implore you to have her punished immediately, despite her aforementioned favors [privileges, protectors]), so that "non infetti più questa Città" (she can no longer contaminate this city). This reference to infection, both moral and physical, a topos central to Maffio's satirical poems as well, constituted a standard charge brought against prostitutes, undoubtedly one that had special impact in the wake of the plague.[47] Indeed Maffio equated the infections provoked by the plague with "mal francese" (syphilis), a disease for which he says Franco, a courtesan/whore, is responsible:

> Quella che mantien guerra
> Contro la sanità. Mare del morbo,
> Quella che venne al mondo con el corbo.
> Quella che rende orbo
> Sto secolo presente, e che l'infetta,

Quella contra de chi no val recetta.
(*"Veronica, ver unica puttana"*)

She is the woman who is at war with good health. A sea swarming
with illness. The woman who came into this world with the crow.
The woman who makes our present century blind and contami-
nates it. The woman against whom no prescription can prevail.

The allegations Vannitelli lists expose the social and class tensions between servant and courtesan employer; and they echo the language used by
those bawdy satirical poets we examined in chapter 1, who delighted in
using women as a target for moral condemnation by reducing them to the
level of vulgar whores.[48] Vannitelli warns:

> *Non gastigandosi questa fattuchiara puttana pubblica barra, molti si met-*
> *teriano a far simili cose contra la santa, et catholica fede.*
>
> If this witch, this public, masked, and cheating prostitute is not
> punished, many others will begin to do the same things against the
> holy Catholic faith.

In a sense, however, Vannitelli no longer presents a case worthy of an Inquisition tribunal whose primary concern was to discern and eradicate heretical beliefs. Rather his accusations become increasingly spiteful; he
switches from a self-righteous tone to a venomous tone. His complaints,
more in keeping with the kind of trials held in the state courts (the *Avogaria
di Comun*), could nonetheless easily have impelled the Inquisition tribunal
to convene.[49]

He accuses Franco of playing "giuochi prohibiti cio è di carte" (prohibited games, such as cards) and "tutti sorti di giuochi (all other kinds of
games); once "ha vinciuto i danari" (she wins her money), she bribes her
guests with "la buona mano" (tips), so that they will not publicly disclose
these "furfanterie" (illegal pastimes). This accusation resembles the section
of the dialogue between Nanna and Antonia, two mature courtesans, in
Aretino's *Sei giornate,* in which Nanna brags about her art at swindling her
male guests at gambling:[50]

> *Quanti denari ho io guadagnati con mettere in mezzo questo o quello! In*
> *casa mia cenava spesso gente, e dopo cena, venute le carte in tavola, "Orsu"*
> *diceva io, "giochiamo duo giuli di confetti, e a chi viene, poniamo caso, il re*
> *di coppe, paghi"; e così, perduti e comperati i confetti, le persone che, viste le*
> *carte, tanto si ponno tener di non ci fare quanto una puttana di non farne,*
> *cavati fuora denari, cominciavano a far da dovero.*

Oh, how much money I have earned by swindling this man or that! Many men often used to dine in my house, and after dinner the cards would appear on the table. "Come on," I would say, "let's play two julios' worth of candy. The man who gets the King of Cups will have to pay." When the candies were lost and paid for, those who had cards in their hands could no more stop playing than a whore can stop screwing. So they pulled out their money and began gambling in earnest.

Vannitelli's list of stereotypical offenses continues. He says that Franco "mai andata a . . . messa" (has not once been to mass) "due mesi in qua et mezo" (during the two and one-half months) that he has been living in her house, as the "parrocchiano di detta Chiesa" (parishioner of this church) and "tutta la contrada" (whole parish) would attest.[51] She is constantly involved in these "giuochi" (games) and other "negotii dishonesti et illiciti" (dishonest and illicit dealings) with "con gli huomini, et suoi inamorati" (her lovers and other men). And she wears "le perle" (pearls), specifically prohibited to courtesans by the Venetian sumptuary laws.[52] What is more, Vannitelli argues, she takes advantage of her ambiguous social position by changing her costume and guise to suit her purpose at a given moment.[53]

His last charges, appended at the end of his written deposition, bring us back to Franco's purported heretical practices. He urges the court to punish her for having devised invocations that "per fare inamorare di lei alcuni Tedeschi, che praticavano in sua casa" (make certain Germans who have been frequenting her house fall in love with her), a fact that he claims a certain "Bozzo," an artisan who makes "tabernacoli a oro" (golden taberna-cles) in the area, would support. He uses this allusion to German mer-chants—who resided in Venice in a permanent colony in the *Fondaco dei Tedeschi* and were known as self-proclaimed Lutherans—to point to Franco's exposure to heretical ideas.[54] Furthermore, she eats meat on Friday, which her cook, Bortola, he adds, served to her in bed during a feigned illness. All of these charges he can also support by testimony from Franco's neighbors, "Costantino . . . et Lucretia Greghetta," of whom the latter lives "dirim-petto a detta Veronica" (right in front of Veronica).[55] Although Vannitelli is careful to name important potential witnesses in his defense, such as "Pre Vicenzo primo prete di San Giovanni Novo" and "Checco luganegher," who would corroborate his allegations that Franco "habbia fatte le invoca-tioni di demonii, et cercati i putti per farle" (has invoked demons and went looking for children to assist her), the tribunal curiously never follows up on his incriminating evidence.

Vannitelli's denunciation of Veronica Franco was successful insofar as she received a "mandata di comparizione" (order to appear), presented to her by the *minister s. officii,* to appear at the Inquisition courts on Saturday, 8 October 1580, for the first hearing.[56] Although the reason for her summons would not have been explained to her at that time, Veronica undoubtedly already knew (see appendix 4.3). In the presence of Girolamo Foscarini, elected eight times to the position of *savio sopra eresia,* Domenico Priuli, who served as *savio* three times between 1570 and 1580, Alberto Bolognetti, the papal legate to Venice, and the Venetian patriarch, Giovanni Trevisan, Veronica defended herself not merely against Vannitelli's vindictive accusations attesting to her "dishonest" behavior but also against charges of performing magical incantations in her house "per saper qualche secretto o ritrovar qualche cosa" (with the intent of learning some secret or retrieving some object).[57]

The presence of Alberto Bolognetti, the bishop of Massa, in these trial proceedings sheds further light on why her trials ended positively and why her defense takes on the tone of a "public abjuration."[58] Bolognetti's *relazione,* published in 1590 while he was nuncio to Poland, and in particular, chapter 9, explains the procedure, limits, and types of trials he officiated at while apostolic legate to the Holy Office ("Del Santo Offitio dell'Inquisitione") in Venice from 1578 to 1581.[59] The trials against Veronica Franco conform to the bulk of the trials described by him in which sorcery and invocations are components:

> *Con tutto ciò, il Tribunale di Venezia è stato in continuo essercitio in varie materie d'heresia fra le quali le più frequenti, o almeno quelle che l'hanno tenuto più occupato, sono state due: cioé superstitioni d'incantesimi et infedeltà di christiani giudaizanti. Gl'incantesimi, se bene per la maggior parte haveano quelle circostanze che gli faceano esser materia d'Inquisitione cioé adoratione di demoni, oratloni et suffumigi di storace d'incenso, di zolfo, d'assa fetida et altri così buoni come tristi odori, nondimeno si vedeva che non venivano da inclinatione che si havesse all'heresia, ma tendevano a quei suoi fini, cioé d'amore e di guadagni, che tanto possono negl'huomeni vani. . . . Lascio molt'altre superstitioni, come di far veder i furti dentro l'ampolle et nelle pietre d'anella i successi delle cose future, con farvi anco comparer dentro le Sibille.*[60]

Despite all this the Venice Tribunal has been ceaselessly active with regard to various cases involving heresy. Among these the most frequent, or at least those which have kept it the most busy, are two: that is, superstitious incantations and acts against the faith on the part of Christians with Jewish connections. . . Even though for the

greater part they were surrounded by circumstances that made
them a matter for the Inquisition, that is to say: the worship of
demons, prayer and burning of incense, sulphur, asafetida and
other sundry as well as foul odors, one could see that these incantations did not come from an inclination toward heresy, but were
aimed at those goals, i.e., love and profit, which have such great
power over vain mankind. . . . I omit many other superstitions
such as the seeing of thefts in an ampoule or the outcome of future
events in the stones of rings by causing the Sybils to appear in
them.

Through the exploitation of religious objects placed in everyday contexts,
these popular incantations and acts of sorcery went against established rituals of the Catholic liturgy. One of the questions that we might pose in
connection with these trials, one that equally preoccupied ecclesiastical authorities, is: Did the Venetian Inquisition distinguish between popular superstition such as magical incantations (and love potions), understood as
generally unharmful, and diabolism, whose primary purpose was to harm
people or things by deliberately and heretically invoking the devil?[61] Further, how did officials understand the participation of the devil? Was the
devil simply an agent through whom a "witch" performed incantations? As
Richard Kieckhefer observes:

The most fundamental distinction between the popular and
learned notions of sorcery . . . is that in learned tradition the devil
had a necessary role in all bewitchment. In short, learned ideas
were not merely added to popular beliefs, but were thoroughly in-
termingled with them, and altered them. . . .

In the European witch trials, Kieckhefer says, diabolism was most often
not the original charge brought against the accused but was rather "super-
imposed in the courtroom on some prior accusation, usually sorcery."[62]
Further, by introducing diabolism into the trials, the inquisitors, or what
he calls the "literate élite," were attempting "to make sense of the notion of
sorcery."[63]

Marisa Milani provides useful information about the practice of invoking the devil in the superstitious beliefs of Venetian prostitutes and courtesans. Often to regain the affections of an unfaithful lover, they performed
various types of "martelli" (love magic), which were incantations that involved burning inscribed pieces of broken glass said to provoke intense
feeling of affliction so that the "Grand Diavolo . . . andasse al cuore
dell'infedele e gli desse tanto *martello* da costringerlo a tornare" (Great

Devil . . . would attack the heart of the unfaithful man and so *hammer* away at him that he would be compelled to return). One such ritual made use of the tarot cards, especially the one that portrayed the devil, which they would place next to a light until a certain time of day when prayers were addressed to it and formulas were recited. Franco's disavowal of invoking the devil was not only designed to exonerate her of heretical beliefs but must also have been calculated to set her apart from the popular practices of other less sophisticated courtesans. Did Franco see herself as a witch by contemporary standards? Did others see her as such? Or were her inquisitors simply determined to make sense of, and have her explain, the exact practice of this very popular "inghistara" ritual, an explanation that might help identify heretical intention and thus be useful to the inquisitors in subsequent and perhaps more severe cases? Franco's testimony, as we shall see, neither sanctions devil worship nor provides the inquisitors with any important information regarding other people guilty of these crimes. But what she does offer is a clear, educated description of the ritual that would have undoubtedly proven useful to authorities in subsequent cases of this type. Indeed her answers reveal that unlike many other women tried on similar charges, she understood the important difference, from the court's point of view, between the simple act of performing a superstitious magic ritual and holding heretical beliefs.[64] That she understood this distinction is evident if we look at how she manipulated the evidence during her testimony. At crucial moments she directed the inquisitor's attention away from her own specific beliefs to those of her servants and neighbors.

We see her emerge in the hearings as an actress in full control of her role, prompted to alternate, as if on cue, between a childlike tone of humble obedience and proud and almost indignant retorts. When she claims that she performed the rituals "in effetto" (effect), but not with "affetto" (affect), she echoes not only the subtle wordplay she had already adopted in her poetic debate but also the tribunal's tendentious separation between, on the one hand, carrying out superstitious rituals with no evil intent and, on the other hand, promulgating potentially dangerous heretical beliefs.

III

In the first hearing, Franco is asked whether for the purpose of finding her lost things she has had "virginal children" (putti vergene) chant "some prayers" (alcune orationi) and look into a "basin full of water" (inghistara piena d'aqua).[65] She answers obediently but in colorful Venetian dialect (a language she never uses in her literary works) that this is only partly true. It was Redolfo who had initially begged her; he even "fell to his knees with his hands joined" (si ghettò in genochioni con le man giunte), praying her to allow the mother and children to continue the incantations when she declared that these practices were merely "frivolities" (bagatelle). There were "two little boys and one little girl" (do putini maschi et una puttina femena) present with their mother, who lives, she adds, "in a house behind me" (sta arente de mi a S. Zuanne Nuovo), "whose name I do not know" (el nome de la qual non ve so dir); the mother is "wife of a tailor who has boys and girls in school" (è moglie de un sartor et tien putti a schuola et puttine). It was "the mother who fetched the basin full of water" (et la madre di questi putini predetta tolse una inghistera piena di aqua) and put into it "a little holy water" (un puocho de aqua santa). Franco says that this woman placed "her wedding ring under the basin" (ghe messe sotto la sua vera benedeta, con la qual era stata sposata), above it "two leaves of olive branch" (doi foglie o rame dell'oliva benedetta) braided in the "shape of a cross" (per tresso), and had her children kneel down in front, "each one with a lighted blessed candle in hand" (candella benedetta apiciata per uno in man). In the presence of Redolfo, "my son's teacher" (maistro del mio puto) and "my German servant" (mio servitor Thodesco), the mother taught the children, Veronica reports, the following chant: "Holy Angel, White Angel, by your sanctity and my virginity, show me the true one and the truth. Who took that thing" (Anzolo santo, Anzolo biancho, per la tua santità et per la mia verzinità mostrame il vero et la verità chi ha tolto la tal cosa).[66]

When the children had finished the incantation (despite Franco's protests), they were "unable to disclose what they had seen" (non sapevano dir quel che havevano visto), "one saying one thing, one another" (chi diceva una cosa chi un'altra). Thus, she impatiently gave them something to eat and "sent them away" (et li mandai via). It was at this point, she argues, and on account of her refusal to believe the incantations, "that everyone present, and [it is implied] in the neighborhood, turned against me" (tutti comenzorno a esser contra de mi). They said she was "crazy not to believe in such things" (matta a non creder queste cose).

Marisa Milani has suggested persuasively that perhaps Franco was impatient with the mother and children only because they had not marshaled sufficient evidence to incriminate the two people Franco had suspected from the very beginning—Vannitelli and Bortola[67]—despite Franco's claim that her impatience stemmed rather from her intolerance of superstitious practices. Yet a mystifying anecdote that she offers without solicitation to the court at this point, one oddly chosen because potentially very damaging, strangely undermines this claim. She informs the inquisitor that as a child, she too had performed this ritual with positive results (a fact that the court will reiterate in the second hearing)—a claim that suggests that she had indeed believed at one time in the efficacy of such an incantation. She reports that her mother had instructed her to recite "that same prayer and three paternosters and three Ave Marias" (quella medesima oratione et tre paternostri et 3 ave marie) while looking into a basin. Not only did the incantation work, she reports, but she even discovered that it was her father who had stolen "a coat" (una cappa) from her mother, a crime, she says, "to which he later confessed" (che lo confessò dapoi). But if we read this assertion from within the context of the trial's development, the curious aside permits Franco to discredit the ritual, because, as she tells the court, it is not always successful. By following this twisted logic, she aims to dissociate herself from any heretical beliefs and to distinguish herself from her employed help. The inquisitor, not satisfied, will return to this point at a later moment in the proceedings.

Having discredited the superstitious practices, Franco incurs the court's favor at precisely the moment when the inquisitor is intent on proving heretical belief. By redirecting his focus away from present misdeeds to those she innocently performed as a child, an event that she can now in hindsight disavow, she controls the evidence in her favor. Or at least she seems to think so. When the inquisitor informs her that having consented to the "aforementioned things" (sopradette cose), especially having allowed them to take place in her own house, constitutes a "kind of heresy" (specie di heresia) and does not excuse her from wrongdoing, she proclaims, as noted above, that if she has indeed sinned, it was only with "effect" (l'effetto) and not "affect" (l'affetto), because ultimately, "I did not believe in it" (non ci ho creduto).[68] This kind of linguistic sophistry is impressive in poetic contests, but it does not satisfy the inquisitor. He forces her to confess her error. He insists, furthermore, that she provide the court with an adequate explanation, or at least an interpretation of what she believes is the significance of the incantation. Once again, Franco provides a strange answer: "I think [thought] that that White Angel meant the devil because even here in Venetia one calls a Saracen white" (Io credo che quel Anzolo Biancho volesse dir el diavolo, perché anco qua a Venetia si chiama biancho el sarasino).[69] In other words, Franco is saying that Saracens who are black are called white in Venice. Thus, when you say "white angel" you can also mean "black angel."

Just when he thinks that he is able to determine heretical belief by the very examples she offers him, she does an about-face and obediently confesses her error. To the question of whether she had ever devised "other invocations to the devil, or made men, particularly Germans, fall in love with her" (altra invocation de demonii o fatto fare per far inamorar de se alcuni et particularmente thodeschi), she hurriedly switches from confession to calculated alarm:

> *Signor no, Dio me ne guardi et la Madona. Son la più timida dona del mondo de demonii et di morti.*
>
> Sir, no, and may God and the Madonna protect me. I am the most timid woman in the world when it comes to demons and the dead.

In response to the inquisitor's repeated warning that she has sinned and can only be absolved if she openly recognizes "her error" (il suo error), she answers with appropriate resignation:

> *Io fui presente per la causa che ho ditto de sopra et cognosco haver errato et voi domando perdono.*
>
> I was present for the reason I have mentioned above, and I recognize that I have erred, and I ask to be pardoned for it.

This first trial concludes with Vannitelli's allegation that Franco had eaten meat on "Friday or Saturday or during similar vigils" (venere e sabbado et altre vigilie), to which she firmly responds, "Never, neither on Fridays nor on Saturdays or vigils, nor on prohibited days have I eaten such things" (Mai né de Venere né de sabbado né de vigilie né in zorni prohibiti ho manzato simil cose). [70]

This answer is further qualified in the second hearing on 13 October, when she explains that if she had ever eaten any such foods, including cheese and eggs, on prohibited days it was because of a specific need for nourishment—serious illness or pregnancy. We learn that she has given birth six times, and "always, in fact, I have given birth on a Friday" (sempre ho partorido de venere). She adds that in this year alone she has been ill many times, "I have been confined to bed four times this year" (son stata 4 volte amalada che mai me ho movesto de letto). [71]

In this first trial, Franco's pose as innocent victim draws the inquisitor's sympathy toward her, but her frank, about-face confessions of having participated in such rituals as a child also disarm him. Whereas she attempts to place herself above suspicion by discounting the popular superstitious beliefs performed in her house, in the second trial she will provide such a careful and detailed description of the nature and practice of this incantation ritual that the inquisitor becomes suspicious of her intentions once again. As she attempts to exonerate herself from any association with heretical practices, she shifts the blame to others, especially to those people who, she believes, were intent on maligning her in the first place. Here we again hear the strains of poetic debate both motivated by mistrust of another's intentions and a rebuttal of another's vindictive charges. Also, as in the poetic debate, Franco's insistence on retrieving the domestic property stolen from her in the trial hearings mirrors her determination to redeem her personal reputation, denigrated by Maffio Venier, who uses both the *incerto autore* and Franco as victims of satirical abuse.

The shift of blame to Vannitelli and to others becomes more acute as Franco feels the pressure of the inquisitor's questioning. And yet she never loses her composure; she responds to all of his questions with an air of neutral detachment. Much as in her debate with the *incerto autore,* which intensifies with the advent of Maffio's satirical poem, "Veronica, ver unica puttana" (Veronica, veritably unique whore), Franco's need to retaliate increases with each new piece of incriminating information aired in court. But whereas in the poetic debate she will call her interlocutor to battle, in these trial proceedings she must contain her anger toward Vannitelli and respond obediently to the inquisitor's queries.

The inquisitor returns in the second hearing to Veronica's mystifying anecdote about her childhood and asks whether she told the court the whole truth during the first hearing. He claims that she cannot reject entirely the efficacy of the incantation, because not only had she performed the same one as a child, she had obtained the desired results; by looking into the basin of water, she had been able to discern the thief's identity. He demands that she tell the court the truth. Franco obstinately affirms that it is in fact virtually impossible to believe in this ritual, because "for every time the devil tells the truth, there are a hundred times he tells a lie" (el diavolo per una volta che dica la verità per cento volte dice la busia). Either her candor disarms the inquisitor, causing him to ask her to repeat her account of what happened, or he hopes to catch her in the act of contradicting herself.[72] Perhaps in contrast to what her accusers have alleged, she reiterates that it was Redolfo Vannitelli who begged her to let the children look into the basin, because he claimed she had lied about the thefts so as to avoid paying him his expected salary. She in turn refused to take part in the incantation and "went into my room" (andì in camera) and "let them do what they wished" (a lassar far quel che i volse). She insists that she was not even "present in the room during the incantations" (né io fui presente quando si fece la experientia). What is more, she reports that she threatened Vannitelli by telling him that only "the cord of the Night Patrol, without so many candles, will find the truth" (la corda de Signori di Notte senza tante candelle troverà la verità).[73] At this point insults were exchanged back and forth between neighbors. The mother charged Franco with having ruined the efficacy of the ritual because she gave the children something to eat when they were supposed to be fasting, and Veronica retorted that they had in fact consumed the bread the day before.[74] The inquisitor insists that although her servants and neighbors were wrong to conduct the rituals, she was equally guilty for allowing them to perform them in her house.

She never responds directly to the scolding but rather changes the subject completely. She says that when the mother insisted that the ritual was indeed effective, she exposed her ignorance by pointing to the fact that "the only image the children were able to see was their own reflection" (quel chi i vedeva era loro medesimi), because they were "on top of one other" (erano l'un per mezo dell'altro)!

Always concerned with redirecting the court's attention away from her own "evil" practices to those she considers worse, Veronica relates another curious anecdote, this time concerning "the Greek woman" (la greca) whose husband she reports is in prison owing to the Inquisition courts. This woman, Franco contends, keeps a dead man's severed head in a basin and annoints it daily with holy water while chanting prayers presumably to the devil. Told almost in the manner of a Boccaccian tale, Franco's anecdote remains open-ended. She provides no further details about "la greca," and the inquisitor does not follow up her lead.[75] Although she does not denounce her own accusers or mount trumped-up accusations against them, she does, as I suggested at the beginning of this discussion, cover herself at crucial moments in her testimony by insinuating that there are other people in Venice much more dangerous than she and more worthy of the tribunal's attention.

The hearing concludes with the pro forma question of whether she can name any of her enemies.[76] To this she responds that "Redolpho" and a woman Borthola, "a pregnant maid who, as I had already convinced the court, took my scissors," (una dona borthola massera gravia la qual ho fatto convinzer dala iusticia che me ha tolto quelle forfette), are her "greatest enemies" (maggiori inimici), and possibly "Checho, the sausage maker" (Checho luganigher), who lives below her and "serves me sometimes at the table" (me serve qualche volta in tavola), although she does not believe that Checho is her enemy.[77]

Throughout this second hearing, Franco's account of what happened in her house holds the inquisitor's attention. The strength of her testimony seems to persuade the authorities that although she is guilty of having allowed the illegal practices to be performed in her house, she is innocent of Vannitelli's allegations of heretical belief. Of course it is difficult in the end to know if it is the nature of the evidence she presents that sways the court in her favor, or her skill at constructing a plausible fiction that manipulates the inquisitors' thinking, or finally, Domenico Venier's invisible support and protection. What is evident is how well Franco performs her role. That she had learned a great deal from the poetic debate in earlier years, most specifically about how to fashion answers to elicit the desired reactions in her listeners (or readers), is evident in this self-defense.

There is no official sentence for the trials, although many such trials were suspended after only a few hearings. As far as we know, Franco was spared the humiliation of a formal abjuration in which she would have been exposed to public derision.[78] The inquisitor's moralizing stance and his insistence on Franco's confession of her sins during the hearings suggests that he viewed his role during the trials as that of a spiritual guide rather than just a legal opponent. But just as she was not spared the petty gossip of neighbors or the public humiliation of private abuse that the poetic debate created, so she suffered the ignominy connected with having been called to the tribunal. And yet, as she confesses in a letter (31) she writes to Domenico Venier, she thanks him for his "cortese protezzion" (courteous protection) in the poetic debate that has, paradoxically, given her much self-esteem. She tells Venier that his protection both justified her subsequent call to poetic battle and, she implies, afforded her the important opportunity to prove her skills as poetic debater: "di quella controversia il mio avversario aveva perduto assai e io avanzato molto (in that controversy my opponent lost a great deal, and I made much progress).[79]

It is doubtful that Veronica Franco ever retrieved her stolen goods or fully recovered financially from her losses. Given the thefts, coupled with the economic devastation resulting from the plague, it is no wonder that her tax report of 1582 reveals impoverishment.[80] Further, in 1582 she lost her most faithful supporter and friend, Domenico Venier. Indeed with the death of Venier, many Venetian poets mourned the end of an age, symbolized by the loss of an especially helpful and skillful patron. But what Franco had gained, as did many other Venetian poets who frequented his informal academy, was the confidence to defend herself against incrimination. The specific nature of Franco's literary interaction with members of Ca' Venier is the subject to which I will now turn.

IV

The Accademia Veneziana, also known as the Accademia della Fama, was founded in 1557 by the Venetian nobleman Federico Badoer, a powerful politician, diplomat, and literary scholar.[81] Many years earlier, Domenico Venier had formed his own informal academy out of a close coterie of Venetian friends when he relinquished his duties as senator in 1546. Some of the writers, artists, musicians, and patrician scholars who participated in Venier's meetings in his private palazzo in Santa Maria Formosa frequented as well the formal academy meetings in Jacopo Sansovino's newly designed Library of San Marco, also known as the Libreria Sansoviniana. This library housed Cardinal Bessarion's magnificent collection of Greek and Latin manuscripts (bequeathed to the republic in 1468) and memorialized the city's combination of wealth, splendor, and humanist learning. Together with the Doge's Palace and the Loggetta, also by Sansovino, the library completed Piazza San Marco's regal entranceway to the city. While the iconographic program of the Doge's Palace extolled the victories and virtues of the republic, the learned allegories *all'antica* that adorned the staircase leading to the vestibule were conceived to remind Venetian nobles who met in the reading room at the top of the staircase of the rewards to be gained by a commitment to the *studia humanitatis*. Titian's female allegory of Wisdom looked down from on high on those Venetian patricians who assembled in the vestibule for learned discussions.[82] Thus, Badoer's academy fostered the education of the republic's noble youth; it also served the public image of Venice as a city founded on liberty, justice, and honorable deeds, functioning as a self-contained body dedicated to civic, cultural, and literary projects.

The academy was at first extremely well received by the Venetian government. In 1557 Badoer was at the height of his political career, having returned to Venice from an important diplomatic mission to the Imperial Court. Riding on this success, Badoer's overly ambitious designs for the Accademia della Fama eventually led to its downfall and his own economic ruin in 1561.[83] Although his friendship with Domenico had begun years earlier when he devotedly frequented Venier's salon gatherings, Venier's membership or continued involvement in the academy cannot be proven from any of the available documents.

Veronica Franco's participation in Venier's informal gatherings in the 1570s—a group of poets who were interested in the use of Greek, Latin, and Provençal poetic forms for the Venetian love lyric—helps to explain why her poems in the *Terze rime* do not adhere to traditional models of Italian Petrarchism. One of the foremost Venetian poets of the period, Domenico Venier experimented with complex rearrangements of the Petrarchan sonnet. He was also interested during this period in retrieving pre-Petrarchan poetic forms. Domenico exerted, as we noted previously, considerable influence and power over the group of poets (Fortunio Spira, Girolamo Molino, Girolamo Parabosco, Girolamo Muzio, Bernardo and Torquato Tasso, and many others) who frequented his private literary salon in Venice.[84]

The poems that make up Franco's *tenzone* are all composed as capitoli in terza rima, a form that was not widely used among women poets of the period (Gaspara Stampa, Veronica Gambara, Tullia d'Aragona, and Vittoria Colonna). During the first half of the sixteenth century, the capitolo was the preferred form for academic, satiric, and comic compositions; it was inherited from a complex poetic tradition that extended back to the Provençal *tenso*, Petrarca's *I trionfi*, and the love lyrics of the quattrocento court poets. In the hands of early-sixteenth-century Florentine poets—Francesco Berni, G. B. Gelli, Il Lasca, and others—the capitolo became the foremost polemical weapon against literary pedantry. Given its triadic rhyme scheme and the difficulty it imposed upon developing a lengthy poetic conceit, the capitolo signaled poetic virtuosity. Veronica Franco's *Terze rime* represents, so far as I can discern, the only text by a woman written exclusively in the capitolo form during the latter half of the sixteenth century.[85] In contrast, the sonnet or group of sonnets (and other Petrarchan verse forms) assembled in one edition as a Petrarchan *canzoniere*, or a collection of *rime sparse*, sometimes taking the form of a dialogue between the sexes or a debate on a given and preestablished topic, was the dominant form for poetic correspondence, love poetry, and encomiums during the sixteenth century.

Girolamo Ruscelli, one of the members of the Accademia della Fama and an active participant in Ca' Venier, clarifies how the *tenzone* was reinterpreted in Venetian sixteenth-century poetic practice as a "proposta/riposta" exchange. To respond in "terzetti" (tercets), he claims, underscores a poet's ability to manage complex rhyme schemes:[86]

> *All' Ottave Rime, e alle Terze sieno stati alcuni arditi, e valorosi ingegni,*
> *che hanno risposto. In esse, perché sarebbe troppo duro l'obbligarsi a tante*

Rime, basta di serbar la Testura di quelle della proposta, cioé, di risponder
con Ottave ad Ottave, con Terze a Terze. . . . E chi ancor volesse obbligarsi
a rispondere con tanto numero di stanze, e di Terzetti, o di Versi, sarebbe
tanto più vagamente fatto.

Some bold and valiant spirits have indeed responded in ottava rima
and terza rima. However, as it would be too arduous to commit
oneself to produce so many rhymes, it is enough to maintain the
scheme of the *proposta,* that is, to respond to octaves with octaves
and to tercets with tercets. . . . Should anyone nevertheless undertake to answer with so great a number of stanzas, tercets, or verses,
the accomplishment would accordingly gain in distinction.

He identifies various methods for this exchange. One is to "rispondere per
le rime" (answer in like rhyme), another "per le desinenze" (by the endings).
In addition, he lists four other forms that a "risposta" (reply) might take.
For example, the second poet can answer by adopting the proposed rhymes
but by varying their order, or he can use the same end words (a practice akin
to the *sestina*) but change the order in which they occur in the first text.
Third, he can alternate forms by having one verse conform to the same
rhyme and one to the same word in the "proposta." The stylistic norms that
Ruscelli dictates for the "proposta/risposta" exchange clarify the genre and
the high level of virtuosity it demands.[87]

Although Domenico Venier never assumes an active presence as interlocutor in Veronica Franco's *Terze rime,* his role as literary and moral counselor is often evoked in her verses. Capitoli 15, 18, 23, and 24 address an
unnamed "signor," and in them she refers to a gathering of friends in a literary salon for the purposes of conversation and literary exchange. In capitolo
23 she appeals to a man, presumably Domenico Venier, "a cui son note /
le forme del duello e de l'onore, / per cui s'uccide il mondo e si percuote" (one
who knows the codes of dueling and honor by which one strikes and slays
the world), for both counsel and protection. In a self-deprecatory rhetorical
move, she asks for advice on how to carry out a counterattack against a man
who seeks to defame her.[88] Adopting a language of military combat, she
discloses the nature of the attack directed against her while she was absent
from Venice in order to make it clear to her addressee and her social circle
why, until now, she has resisted entering into a direct confrontation with
her accuser. As his anger grew, she explains, she comforted herself with
"pensieri migliori" (better thoughts). But given the fear of the effects of the
"peggior stile" (worse style), she asks him whether she should have armed
herself as a female warrior, in a self-ennobling allusion to such warriors of

epic romance as Ariosto's Bradamante and Marfisa, to counter each blow with a counterattack.[89]

What follows is a detailed description of the kind of "singular battaglia" (singular battle) she would wage if permitted. Paradoxically, she couches her assertions in a humble request for moral counsel while she demonstrates her verbal mastery of the situation: she appeals to her counselor's wisdom and decries her adversary's viciousness. She writes that she fears the effects of silence but is wary of entering into battle with one who is "di malizia e di viltate infetto" (with malice and knavery contaminated):

> Ma s'io sto queta, e, come avien ch'accada
> un giorno, che passar quindi gli avenga,
> incontra armata a ucciderlo gli vada? (23.166–68)
>
> Dunque commetterò sì gran diffetto
> di bruttar di quel sangue queste mani,
> ch'è di malizia e di viltate infetto? (172–79)

But what if I held my peace, and when, as might perchance occur, one day he happened to cross my path, I went to meet him armed to kill? . . . Shall I indeed commit the grievous error of soiling these hands with that blood contaminated by malice and knavery?

The hypothetical condition posed at the conclusion of this *capitolo* sets the stage for the poetic *tenzone*, conceived as a poetic debate in which word-play is her weapon in the struggle for dominance over her accuser. In the concluding verses of capitolo 23, the woman speaker identifies herself, nonetheless, as a frail and inexperienced warrior whose every action must be reviewed and approved by a male counterpart:

> Cessin da me pensieri così strani.
> Ma che farò? S'io taccio, mal; e poi
> s'io faccio, peggio. Oh miei discorsi vani!
> Datemi, signor mio, consiglio voi. (175–78)

Enough of such outlandish thoughts. But what am I to do? Silence is unwise, action worse. O mindless talk! Kind sir, for advice I turn to you.

Articulated as a battle of wits, the *tenzone* through which the speaker challenges the *incerto autore* proclaims her poetic mastery: she seeks to outdo the male poet in a play of sexual dominance and flirtatious coquetry. Through witty banter and verbal proficiency the courtesan emphasizes her expertise in both amorous and textual "relazioni" (relations).

It is necessary to reconstruct how Franco might have read this exchange of poems in order to appreciate the cumulative effect they had on her before her final call to battle in *capitolo* 16. Just as Franco brings to the inquisitional tribunal any evidence that she believes will help counter the charges that Vannitelli might have listed in his *denuncia,* so she lets the evidence mount against the *incerto autore* in this poetic debate. Thus, the "proposta/ risposta" exchange between Franco, as woman speaker, and the *incerto autore* in capitoli 1 and 2 stands as a kind of prologue to the entire *Terze rime.* It is here that she first questions the function of an amorous discourse that repeats depersonalized poetic conceits in order to praise a female "oggetto" (object). Franco proposes that her interlocutor redefine the abstract "affetti" (affects) of his professed love as "effetti" (effects), or as publicly defined, tangible "fatti" (deeds). Her "risposta" argues that poetic abstraction and the courtier poet's ability to move in and out of various amorous postures emphasize his unwillingness to include the female correspondent in an active collaboration. The woman, she points out, serves simply as the pretext for musings on love rather than as a fellow debater of love's fortunes:

> *S'esser del vostro amor potessi certa*
> *per quel che mostran le parole e 'l volto,*
> *che spesso tengon varia alma coperta;*
> *   se quel che tien la mente in sé raccolto*
> *mostrasson le vestigie esterne in guisa*
> *ch'altri non fosse spesso in frode colto,*
> *   quella tema da me fòra divisa,*
> *di cui quando perciò m'assicurassi,*
> *semplice e sciocca, ne sarei derisa.* (2.1–9)

If I could be made certain by what your words and countenance display, which often conceal a changing soul; if external signs displayed what the mind holds gathered within and others were not too often ensnared by deceit; if I should cast from me such fear and be reassured, like a simpleton and a fool I should therefore be mocked.

Traditional Provençal and medieval *tenzoni* on courtly love are transformed in her response into a Ciceronian dialogue in which the two parties are given the opportunity to argue different ideals.

In capitolo 1 the male speaker invokes the Petrarchan topos of the "donna crudel" (cruel woman), asking for a release from the suffering that she inflicts upon him. He implores her, in a language of courtly subservience interlaced with erotic innuendoes, to appease his "mal" (pain) by a more desirable "maggior mal" (greater pain). He warns her that if she persists in disregarding his first "mal" (pain) by refusing to reciprocate his love, she will risk losing the beauty she possesses, which has transformed her into an "opra" (artifact) of his adoration:

> S'io v'amo al par de la mia propria vita,
> donna crudel, e voi perché non date
> in tanto amor al mio tormento aita?
> E, se invano mercé chieggio e pietate,
> perch'almen con la morte quelle pene,
> ch'io soffro per amarvi, non troncate? (1.1–6)
> La gran bellezza a voi data di sopra
> spender in morte di chi v'ama e in doglia,
> qual potete peggior far di quest'opra? (19–21)

O cruel woman, I love you as dearly as my own life, so why amid such great love will you not relieve me from my agony? And if my pleas for mercy and pity are in vain, why will you not give me death to end the pains I suffer because of my love for you? . . . To lavish the beauty you were given on the death of one who loves you and on sorrow: how could you use worse that artifact?

Allusions to an exchange of commodities run throughout each author's poems. Whereas he alludes to a physical and sexual reunion of lovers in the "letto" (bed) that first witnessed their passion, she argues that "quello de la certezza è destro calle" (that of certainty is the only sure path). She introduces active verbs in the place of the paratactic "se" (if) series with which her interlocutor constructs his poem. She wants assurance that his professed love for her is not duplicitous: "falsi detti e finta sembianza" (false sayings and feigned demeanor). Whereas he praises her "opre" (artifacts) as informed by the nine muses, and moreover by her particular muse, "la beltà" (beauty), she regards the arts of love and poetry, both of which she has mastered, as separate and distinct achievements.

She counters her interlocutor's elevated praise with a methodical argument that culminates in a witty and ironic wordplay on the "favole" (fables), or the imaginings of love, rather than lived experience. She teasingly warns him that he will have to continue to wait for her disclosure of the arts and pleasures of love. In an intricate struggling and positioning of real versus feigned love, noun against adjective, she pits the false "favole" of his love against the genuinely "favoloso accetto" (fabulous welcome) of her own sensuality:

> Dagli effetti, signor, fate stimarvi:
> con questi in prova venite, s'anch'io

il mio amor con effetti ho da mostrarvi;
  ma, s'avete di favole desio,
mentre anderete voi favoleggiando,
favoloso sarà l'accetto mio;
  e, di favole stanco e sazio, quando
l'amor mi mostrerete con effetto,
non men del mio v'andrò certificando. (2.37–45)

Ask to be judged by your deeds, sir, let them be your test, if I too am to prove my love by deeds. But if you wish for fables, while you spin tales, my welcome will be fabulous, and when weary of fables and once having satisfied your appetite for them, you will prove your love for me with facts, I shall vouchsafe no lesser proof of mine.

In his first capitolo, the male poet returns to the notion of female cruelty by reminding her that her beauty will be rendered "eterna" (eternal) only on the condition that she release him from his bondage and pain. This argument culminates in a struggle for erotic supremacy whereby the "donna di vera ed unica beltade" (woman of true and unique beauty) is assaulted and tamed in the male lover's imagination; any desire that she may have to imitate Apollo alone is defeated by the lover's celebration of her beauty. For it is solely her beauty, according to the amorous language of Petrarchan idolatry, that informs her "opra" (work/artifact). The male poet imagines an erotic scene worthy of Giulio Romano's *I modi* in which the carnal woman reciprocates the male lover's declared love in a sacred and profane union with him:[90]

Oh che dolce mirar le membra ignude,
e più dolce languir in grembo a loro,
ch'or a torto mi son sì scarse e crude!
  Prenderei con le mani il forbito oro
de le trecce, tirando de l'offesa
pian piano, in mia vendetta il fin tesoro.
  Quando giacete ne le piume stesa,
che soave assalirvi! e in quella guisa
levarvi ogni riparo, ogni difesa! (1.118–26)

How sweet it is to gaze upon those naked limbs and sweeter yet to lie languidly in the lap which is now so unyielding and cruel. I would like to take the burnished gold of those tresses in my hands and pull that fine treasure ever so gently to avenge my hurt. When you upon the feathers lie stretched out, what tender delight it is to seize you and thus strip you of refuge and defense.

Franco, intent on subverting the image of the courtesan as vulgar trick-ster, responds by reversing the blame, firmly assigning to the male poet the ability to feign and to deceive a lover. She repudiates the "beffa" (trick) of verbal courtesy: "Signor l'esser beffato è cosa dura, massime ne l'amor" (To be mocked is harsh, kind sir, especially in love). Her caution, she explains, arises from her refusal to reciprocate his love as he defines it rather than from the female avarice of which he accuses her:

> Ben per quanto or da me vi si risponde,
> avara non vorrei che mi stimaste,
> che tal vizio nel sen non mi s'asconde;
> ma piaceriami che di me pensaste
> che ne l'amar le mie voglie cortesi
> si studian d'esser caute, se non caste. (2.82–87)[91]

Despite what I now must answer you, I should not like you to con-sider me miserly, because my breast does not conceal this vice. I would instead like you to think that in love my tender desires are studiedly cautious, if not chaste.

Denying any monetary reward ("di mia profession non è tal atto") which she claims is "unsuited to my profession," she asks that he reimburse her sim-ply with his "amor in fatto" (love in deed{s}):

> E però quel, che da voi cerco adesso,
> non è che con argento over con oro
> il vostro amor voi mi facciate espresso;
> perché si disconvien troppo al decoro
> di chi non sia più che venal, far patto
> con uom gentil per trarne anco un tesoro.
> Di mia profession, non è tal atto;
> ma ben fuor di parole, io 'l dico chiaro,
> voglio veder il vostro amor in fatto.
> Voi ben sapete quel che m'è più caro:
> seguite in ciò com'io v'ho detto ancora,
> che mi sarete amante unico e raro. (2.94–105)

And so I do not ask you now to express your love with gold or silver; for to have an understanding with a noble man in order to extract from him a treasure is most unsuited to the decorum of any but an utterly venal soul. Such behavior does not befit my profession; but leaving words aside, I clearly state that facts must prove your love. You know quite well what I like best: perservere in this as I already told you before and you shall be my unique and only lover.

The meaning of that "altro" (other) of male praise is made explicit: she requests that he compose verses not for her alone, but in collaboration with her, in praise of someone else.

Once she has submitted this definition of the courtesan's profession as intellectual collaborator rather than sexual partner, she discloses in her closing verses what would constitute the "opra" (artifact) of reciprocal love if all her demands were to be met:

> *Così dolce e gustevole divento,*
> *quando mi trovo con persona in letto,*
> *da cui amata e gradita mi sento,*
>   *che quel mio piacer vince ogni diletto,*
> *sì che quel, che strettissimo parea,*
> *nodo de l'altrui amor divien più stretto.* (2.154–59)
>   *ond'io instrutta a questi so dar opra*
> *sì ben nel letto, che d'Apollo a l'arte*
> *questa ne va d'assai spazio di sopra,*
>   *e 'l mio cantar e 'l mio scriver in carte*
> *s'oblia da chi mi prova in quella guisa,*
> *ch'a suoi seguaci Venere comparte.* (166–71)

> Whenever I am in bed with one who, as I sense, loves and enjoys me, I become so delectable and tender that my pleasure surpasses all other delights, and what appeared to be a very tight knot of love grows even tighter. . . . Thus, when requested, I perform so well in bed that this form of art proves vastly superior to the art of Apollo, and all my singing and writing are forgotten by the one who assays me in the manner accorded by Venus to her followers.

Implicitly correcting the male poet's language of sexual conquest, she switches into a courtly idiom marked by calculated restraint, interwoven, however, with sexual allusions to the "tenace nodo" (tight knot) and "fermo legno chiodo" (firm wooden nail) that eroticize her final request. In the conclusion to *capitolo* 2, all of the strands of discourse deployed earlier—erotic and courtly—are woven together:

> *Fate che sian da me di lei vedute*
> *quell'opre ch'io desio, che poi saranno*
> *le mie dolcezze a pien da voi godute:*
>   *e le vostre da me si goderanno*
> *per quello ch'un amor mutuo comporte,*
> *dove i diletti senza noia s'hanno.*
>   *Aver cagion d'amarvi io bramo forte:*

prendete quel partito che vi piace,
poi che in vostro voler tutta è la sorte.
   Altro non voglio dir: restate in pace. (2.181–90)

Show me all the works that I ask to see, for then you will fully enjoy
my tender gifts, and I will enjoy yours as mutual love affords, in
which without conflict one takes delight. I strongly wish for sound
reason to love you: Decide as you think best, fate lies completely in
your hands. I wish to say no more: Go in peace.

By redefining the Petrarchan muse as poetic collaborator rather than disembodied and silent addressee, Franco decenters the lyrical love tradition
which commonly uses the woman simply as literary currency. However, she
also manipulates the courtly and erotic elements of the poetic system represented in the *incerto autore*'s verses in order to promote herself as intellectual
and erotic *virtuosa*.

The next series of "proposte/risposte" places the woman far from both
her native city and her beloved. Within the text's fiction the woman has
been forced to flee her "patria" (homeland) for two reasons: in order to direct
her interlocutor's obsessive love away from her, and to escape the "repulse"
(repulses) leveled against her. It is clear from the later capitoli that Franco
has begun to receive, or hear about, the defamatory verses that are circulating within the Venier salon. Thus, the debate about the nature of love poetry versus real love in capitolo 1 and capitolo 2 turns in these capitoli into a
defense of Franco's position as a woman and a woman poet.

Convinced that the *incerto autore* and the satirical dialect poet are the
same person, she continues to mistrust her interlocutor's insistence (in
capitoli 4, 7, 9, and 11) that his declarations of love are founded on virtue
and devotion. In light of the vituperative attacks on her, she interprets her
interlocutor's verses as still another linguistic trick or "beffa" characteristic
of feigned discourse on love.

Franco and the *incerto autore* operate as innocents; he is unaware of the
dialect poet's presence, and she is blinded to the satirical poet's true identity. Maffio Venier's verses, which exuberantly deploy an anti-Petrarchan
rhetoric, parody topoi in the woman speaker's and the *incerto autore*'s
capitoli. Although the masked dialect poet's verses are directed at both the
woman poet and the male poet, only she is specifically named in such verses
as "Franca, credeme che per San Maffio" (Believe me, Franca, that by San
Maffio), and "Veronica, ver unica puttana" (Veronica, veritably unique
whore). Maffio exploits the *incerto autore*'s capitoli by burlesquing his language, thereby reducing it to the bathos of Petrarchan courtly conceits.

Further, he subverts the courtesan's "virtù" (virtue) by decrying her corruption, and he transforms the male poet's *blason*—his "opra"—into an image of perversity, disease, and degradation.

In "Veronica, ver unica puttana" (Veronica, veritably unique whore), for example, he offers a hyperbolic description of the courtesan's toilette, which he claims she uses to conceal her diseases. In this description he also parodies the *incerto autore*'s insistence in capitolo 7 on praising her singular beauty "vera, unica al mondo eccelsa dea" (the world's veritably, unique, supreme goddess) by insisting on the corruption that forms his icon. The *incerto autore* repeats this paronomastic play on her name, Veronica, "vera" and "unica," in capitolo 11 by extending it to Verona, "vera" and "una," which he uses to emphasize her divine nature.[92] Here he pleads with his beloved to return to Venice by sending his praises of her to Verona, the city to which she has presumably escaped:

> *Invero una tu sei, Verona bella,*
> *poi che la mia Veronica gentile*
> *con l'unica bellezza sua t'abbella.* (11.1–3)
>
> O beautiful Verona, you are veritably only one, because my gentle Veronica adorns you with her unique beauty.

But Franco rejects the *incerto autore*'s association between her and Verona; her rejoinder in capitolo 12 undercuts his terms of praise by reprimanding his use of Verona to exalt her virtues. He should have elected a referent that was truly divine: Venice, a city that clearly merited his celebration. Franco's critique emphasizes that misrepresentation in the form of an "iperbolica figura" (the mendacious hyperboles) underwrites a departure from the "vero" (true) of lived experience and genuine worship. The ill-chosen direction of the *incerto autore*'s appeal exposes the falsity of his premises. To try to win her favor by extolling Verona's virtues is added proof that his discourse is misguided:

> *Senza discorrer poeticamente,*
> *senza usar l'iperbolica figura,*
> *ch'è pur troppo bugiarda apertamente,*
> *si poteva impiegar la vostra cura*
> *in lodando Vinegia, singolare*
> *meraviglia e stupor de la natura.* (12.16–21)
>
> Dispensing with poetic discourse and too patently mendacious hyperboles, you might have turned your attention to praising Venice, singular marvel and wonder of nature.

Franco's condemnation of a deceptive discourse that misrepresents the "vero" (true) ironically prefigures the intrusion of Maffio's obscene poem, "Veronica, ver unica puttana" (Veronica, veritably unique whore), into this private amorous exchange. Under Venier's attack, the *incerto autore*'s icon dissolves into an array of puns and sordid topoi that insist upon the courtesan's petty venality. The masked dialect poet's verses answer two claims, by two different poets, at the same time. Franco's mistrust of disembodied poetic symbols that praise worldly objects he answers by transfiguring the holy into the "mondano" (mundane). To the *incerto autore*'s appeal for his beloved's return to her native city, he comically opposes the squalid environment in which this vulgar temptress actually lives.

Maffio appropriates the courtesan, denigrated into the figure of the lowly prostitute, as a means of attacking his main target—the Petrarchan and Bembist love lyric of his contemporaries. By subverting the *incerto autore*'s elevated praise in his rewriting of the "vera" and "unica" topos, Maffio also refutes the woman poet's eulogistic identification with Venice's immaculate origins. His portrait is instead formed by the deformed laughter of the moral satirist, and he draws his details from all that is crude, plebeian, and depraved. His "Veronica" is motivated solely by sexual desire and monetary reward but suffers from the tyranny of sex and its most lurid aspects. She bears on her body the boils and fetid marks of syphilis, contracted presumably in the practice of her profession, which he reduces to that of corrupt prostitute:

> Veronica, ver unica puttana,
> > Franca, "idest" furba, fina, fiappa e frola,
> > E muffa e magra e marza e pì mariola,
> > Che si' tra Castel, Ghetto e la Doàna.
> Donna reduta mostro in carne umana,
> Stucco, zesso, carton, curàme, e tòla,
> Fantasma lodesana, orca varuola,
> > Cocodrilo, hippogriffo, Struzzo, Alfana.
> Ghe vorria centenara de concetti,
> > E miara de penne, e caramali,
> > E un numero infinito de Poeti,
> Chi volesse cantar tutti i to mali,
> > Tutte le to Caie, tutti i difetti,
> > Spettativa de ponti, e de hospedali.[93]

Veronica, veritably unique whore. Franca, *id est* [i.e.] foxy, flighty, flimsy, flabby, smelly, scrawny, scrimpy, and the biggest scoundrel besides, who lives between Castello, Ghetto, and the Customs. A woman reduced to a monster made of human flesh: plaster, chalk, cardboard, leather, and wooden board, a grisly spook, a scabby [poxy] ogre, a crocodile, a hippogriff, an ostrich, a knock-kneed mare. To sing of all that is wrong with you, your flaws, your faults, would take a hundred concepts, thousands of pens and inkwells, and countless poets, the prospect of bridges and hospitals.

Not surprisingly, given Maffio's ferocious attack, the language of love and sexual conquest that intersects in male and female capitoli in this three-way poetic *tenzone* reaches a climax in capitoli 13 and 14. The woman speaker calls her adversary to battle, and he innocently responds "Non più guerra, ma pace: e gli odi, l'ire" (No more war but peace: neither hate nor anger) that he prefers to wage, if he must, a courtly and peaceful war. She counters his deceptive strategies by summoning him to the battlefield:[94]

> *Non più parole: ai fatti, in campo, a l'armi,*
> *ch'io voglio, risoluta di morire,*
> *da sì grave molestia liberarmi.*
>   *Non so se 'l mio "cartel" si debba dire,*
> *in quanto do risposta provocata:*
> *ma perché in rissa de' nomi venire?*
>   *Se vuoi, da te mi chiamo disfidata;*
> *e, se non, ti disfido; o in ogni via*
> *la prendo, ed ogni occasion m'è grata.* (13.1–9)

No more words: to action, to the battlefield, to arms, for I want to free myself of such grievous abuse and am prepared to die. I know not whether my challenge ought to be spelled out, since I respond to provocation: but why quarrel over names? If you so wish I shall consider myself challenged; if you do not, I will challenge you; I will take any route, any opportunity suits me well.

Unaware of the satirical verses directed against his beloved, the *incerto autore* contests her accusations of him and tries to find the cause for her anger. For the first time, he proposes that perhaps someone is deliberately trying to keep them apart:

> *Non so, ma forse ch'a taluno increbbe*
> *del viver nostro insieme; che 'l suo tosco,*
> *nel nostro dolce a spargerlo, pronto ebbe.* (14.64–66)

I do not know, but perhaps someone resented our living together,

and having his poison ready, promptly poured his bitter venom
onto our sweetness.

The woman speaker is unimpressed. Her invitation to a duel draws a
further poetic tradition, informed by the virtuous "atti" (acts) described in
epic romance (typified, for example, in the language of battle between male
and female warriors in canto 45 of the *Orlando furioso*) into the poetic *tenzone*
as a contest of verbal strategies.

Both her evocations of technical prowess and his declared passivity belie,
however, the ambiguities of physical desire. Just as Ruggiero yearns to
"morir" (die) by Bradamante's hand ("Pensa talor di fingersi men forte /
e porger nudo alla donzella il fianco; / che non fu mai la più beata
morte / che se per man di lei venisse manco" [At times he decides to pretend that he is less strong and to offer to the lady his flank, for there could
never be more blissful death than that inflicted by her hand]), so the woman
speaker in capitolo 13 wants to die with her lover/opponent, a battle in
which she assumes complete erotic authority as she silences her victim and
climbs on top:

> *Per soverchiar la tua sì indegna offesa*
> *ti verrei sopra, e nel contrasto ardita,*
> *scaldandoti ancor tu ne la difesa,*
> *teco morrei d'egual colpo ferita.* (13.82–85)

> To avenge your unjust abuse, I should fall upon you and in bold
> contact, while you, too, bent upon your defense are set afire, die
> with you pierced by the same thrust.

Using, but refocusing, the elevated language of the chivalric epic, Franco
exploits the sensually charged "duello" (duel) in Ariosto's poem by making
sexual desire graphically explicit.

But the *tenzone* with the *incerto autore* comes to a close once Franco discovers the masked dialect poet's true identity. In capitolo 16 she unmasks
and then denounces her adversary's poetic and linguistic strategies. In this
capitolo the battle between the sexes no longer nostalgically refers to erotic
dueling informed by epic romance; here the battle is defined as a verbal
sparring match in which the woman performs a critical reading of her adversary's vituperative poem. Supported by the "vero"—the revelation of
mistaken identities—Franco's address switches from the first person to
alternating between an abstract and collective "noi" (we, referring to
"donne," that is, women as a group) and a personalized "io" (I), who now
stands in defense of all women. Franco first adopts an ironic posture. She

pleads helplessness in the opening verses in order to emphasize her male adversary's cowardice (he directed his verses at her while she was absent and therefore unable to defend herself), as well as his physical aggression. The presumed fragility of the female constitution, which draws upon Aristotelian dogma about women's physical and moral inferiority, is pitted against the ideal of the allegedly "ardito cavaliere" (brave knight):[95]

> D'ardito cavalier non è prodezza
> (concedami che 'l vero a questa volta
> io possa dir, la vostra gentilezza),
>   da cavalier non è, ch'abbia raccolta
> ne l'animo suo invitto alta virtute,
> e che a l'onor la mente abbia rivolta,
>   con armi insidiose e non vedute,
> a chi più disarmato men sospetta,
> dar gravi colpi di mortal ferute. (16.1–9)

It is not a brave knight's gallant deed (if by your leave, I may here speak the truth); it is not the deed of a knight who has taken sublime virtue into his undefeated heart and turned his mind to honor to inflict harsh blows upon, and mortally wound, with insidious and concealed weapons, one who stands unarmed and unsuspecting.

This capitolo lacks the seductive grammar and switches of tone in earlier capitoli of the *tenzone*. Here the sexual act of deflowering, "fuor del lato mi traeste / l'armi vostre del sangue asperse e rosse" (out of my side you drew your arms wet and red with blood), is equated with textual violence: the image of the sword that penetrates the women's "lato" (side), precisely when she is unable and unwilling to defend herself, performs the same kind of violence as do the verses that defame her:

> Spogliata e sola e incauta mi coglieste,
> debil d'animo, e in armi non esperta,
> e robusto ed armato m'offendeste;
>   tanto ch'io stei per lungo spazio incerta
> di mia salute; e fu da me tra tanto
> passion infinita al cor sofferta. (22–27)

You came upon me when I was alone, defenseless and off guard, fainthearted and inexperienced in combat, and powerful and armed, you wounded me so that for a while I doubted that I would survive, even though all along my heart burst with boundless passion.

She bolsters her position as female "guerriera" (warrior) by warning her interlocutor that he runs a great risk:

> *Non so se voi stimiate lieve risco*
> *entrar con una donna in campo armato;*
> *ma io, benché ingannata, v'avvertisco*
> > *che 'l mettersi con donne è da l'un lato*
> > *biasmo ad uom forte, ma da l'altro è poi*
> > *caso d'alta importanza riputato.* (58–63)

I do not know whether you consider it a trifling risk to enter the field against a woman; but though I might be deceived, I warn you that if on the one hand it is unseemly for a strong man to joust with a woman, on the other it is considered a highly important event.

If he accepts her challenge to meet in the textual arena, he may well prove her poetic mastery and technical skills.

Posing as an Amazon warrior who fearlessly leads her tribe into combat, Franco adopts a double strategy: she urges women to take up arms, but she also emphasizes her own gender propriety. She alternates between indignant demands for the bellicose example she wants other women to follow and praise for a distinctly womanly trait, "la feminil bellezza" (feminine beauty), provided "dal ciel . . . perch'ella sia felicitate in terra / di qualunque uom conosce gentilezza" (granted by heaven . . . so that it may be turned into happiness on earth for all kind men):

> *Quando armate ed esperte ancor siam noi,*
> *render buon conto a ciascun uom potemo,*
> *che mani e piedi e core avem qual voi;*
> > *e, se ben molli e delicate semo,*
> > *ancor tal uom, ch'è delicato, è forte;*
> > *e tal, ruvido ed aspro, è d'ardir scemo.*
> > *Di ciò non se ne son le donne accorte;*
> > *che, se si risolvessero di farlo,*
> > *con voi pugnar porian fino a la morte.*
> > *E per farvi veder che 'l vero parlo,*
> > *tra tante donne incominciar voglio io,*
> > *porgendo essempio a lor di seguitarlo.*
> > *A voi, che contra tutte sete rio,*
> > *con qual'armi volete in man mi volgo,*
> > *con speme d'atterrarvi e con desio;*
> > *e le donne a difender tutte tolgo*
> > *contra di voi, che di lor sete schivo,*
> > *sì ch'a ragion io sola non mi dolgo.* (64–81)

When we too are armed and trained, we can convince men that we have hands, feet, and a heart like yours; and although we may be delicate and soft, some men who are delicate are also strong; and others, coarse and harsh, are cowards. Women have not yet realized this, for if they should decide to do so, they would be able to fight you until death; and to prove that I speak the truth, amongst so many women, I will be the first to act, setting an example for them to follow; and on you who have sinned against them all, I turn with whichever weapon you may choose, with the wish and hope of throwing you to the ground.

Following the etiquette of the "cartello di sfida" (the call to duel), she indirectly identifies her adversary in the opening lines of her poem. She then dissects Maffio's poem. She disputes the grammatical correctness, for example, of "unica" as an adjective not intended to praise its object. The defamatory poet's use of "unica" coupled with the epithet "ver" is nonsense; it subverts the proper use of both terms as praise:

> *"Ver unica" e 'l restante mi chiamaste,*
> *alludendo a Veronica mio nome,*
> *ed al vostro discorso mi biasmaste;*
> > *ma al mio dizzionario io non so come*
> *"unica" alcuna cosa propriamente*
> *in mala parte ed in biasmar si nome.* (139–44)

> You called me *ver unica*, veritably unique, and all the rest, alluding to my name Veronica; but while you meant it as abuse, according to my dictionary, I fail to see how one can properly call a thing "unique" in order to offend or blame.

Franco's analysis not only uncovers a misdirected poetics; she also focuses on the enemy poet's stylistic errors. Franco points out that her adversary's literary indecorum reveals his social indecorum: his abasement of the traditional vocabulary of love poetry parallels his misogynistic misrepresentation of proper relations between the sexes. Her appeal to social and literary decorum flaunts both her learnedness and her attention to poetic practice:

> *Quella di cui la fama è gloriosa,*
> *e che 'n bellezza od in valor eccelle.*
> *senza par di gran lunga virtuosa.*
> > *"unica" a gran ragion vien che s'appelle;*
> *e l'arte, a l'ironia non sottoposto,*
> *scelto tra gli altri, un tal vocabol dielle.*
> > *L'"unico" in lode e in pregio vien esposto*
> *da chi s'intende; e chi parla altrimenti*
> *dal senso del parlar sen va discosto.* (148–56)

One who enjoys a shining reputation, excels in beauty or valor, and by far surpasses all others in virtue is most properly called "unique." And art chooses to bestow on her that attribute amongst all others, untainted by irony. Those who understand the meaning of "unique" express by it praise and esteem. Whoever says otherwise strays from the meaning of the spoken word.

A further criticism of her adversary is implicit in her ironically polite gesture of gratitude when she addresses the question of how he chose to name her:

> Questo non è, signor, fallo d'accenti,
> quello, in che s'inveisce, nominare
> col titol de le cose più eccellenti.
>   O voi non mi voleste biasimare,
> o in questo dir menzogna non sapeste.
> Non parlo del dir bene e del lodare,
>   ché questo so che far non intendeste:
> ma senz'esser offeso da me stato,
> quel che vi corse a l'animo scriveste,
>   altrui volendo in ciò forse esser grato;
> benché me non ingiuria, ma se stesso,
> s'altri mi dice mal, non provocato. (157–68)

It is not, kind sir, a matter of erroneous accents when, in hurling abuse, an address is made by employing the title due to most excellent things. Either you did not mean to defame me or you did not lie when you said what you did. I do not refer to good words or praise, for I know you intended none; but without my having offended you, you wrote what rushed into your mind, wishing perhaps thereby to please somebody else. However, one who unprovoked speaks injuriously, injures himself, not me.

To denounce her, as will Vannitelli, by identifying her as a "meretrice"— one of the lowest classes of prostitutes—in a poem based on reverse adulation, she maintains, actually exalts both the prostitutes' clan and Veronica Franco as their most celebrated member:

> E se ben "meretrice" mi chiamate,
> o volete inferir ch'io non vi sono,
> o che ve n'en tra tali di lodate.
>   Quanto le meretrici hanno di buono,
> quanto di grazioso e di gentile,
> esprime in me del parlar vostro il suono.

Se questo intese il vostro arguto stile,
di non farne romor io son contenta,
e d'inchinarmi a voi devota, umile. (178–86)

Although you call me *meretrix* (venal whore), you imply that I am
not one of them or that among them some are to be praised. The
tone of your words extols all that is good, gracious, and noble about
these meretricious whores. If this is what your clever style intended, I shall be glad not to complain and bow to you, humble
and devoted.

But if his intent was rather to ridicule her by assigning to her attributes
connoting corruption, then she is ready to arm herself with pen in hand and
to elect whichever "armi" (weapons) or "idioma" (idiom) he prefers:

Apparecchiate pur l'inchiostro e 'l foglio,
e fatemi saper senz'altro indugio
quali armi per combatter in man toglio.
　　Voi non avrete incontro a me rifugio,
ch'a tutte prove sono apparecchiata,
e impazientemente a l'opra indugio:
　　o la favella giornalmente usata,
o qual vi piace idioma prendete,
ché 'n tutti quanti sono essercitata. (193–201)

So now ready paper and ink and tell me without further delay
which weapons I must wield in combat. You have nowhere to run
from me, because I am prepared for any test and impatiently wait to
begin. You may choose everyday parlance or whichever idiom you
please, for I am skilled in all.

By the close of capitolo 16, the woman speaker reproposes that they exercise their respective literary skills in a public *tenzone,* informed this time
by revealed identities and equal linguistic weapons:

La spada, che 'n man vostra rade e fora,
de la lingua volgar veneziana,
s'a voi piace d'usar, piace a me ancora:
　　e, se volete entrar ne la toscana,
scegliete voi la seria o la burlesca,
ché l'una e l'altra è a me facile e piana. (112–17)

Should you wish to use common Venetian, the sword that in your
hand abrades and pierces, I shall be content as well. Should you
wish to delve into Tuscan, I leave it to you to choose between the

serious and the comic strains, for the one is just as easy and plain for me as the other.

She proudly declares that she can master any poetic idiom or language her adversary should propose, and she unmasks him by indirectly referring to his poem in "lingua selvaghesca" (combined poetic styles), presumably that of Maffio Venier in *La Strazzosa*:[96]

> *Io ho veduto in lingua selvaghesca*
> *certa fattura vostra molto bella,*
> *simile a la maniera pedantesca:*
> *se voi volete usar o questa o quella,*
> *ed aventar, come ne l'altre fate,*
> *di queste in biasmo nostro le quadrella,*
> *qual di lor più vi piace, e voi pigliate,*
> *ché di tutte ad un modo io mi contento,*
> *avendole perciò tutte imparate.* (118–26)

I've seen a very handsome work of yours in *selvaghesca* somewhat akin to the pedantic manner; if you wish to use this or that manner to loose at me your arrows of abuse, as you do in other idioms, choose whichever you prefer, for I am equally happy with them all, since I have learned each one.

By the concluding tercets of capitolo 16, then, we have come full circle. We have witnessed the unfolding of a poetic *tenzone* performed as a battle of wits, and as a comic struggle deformed by mistaken identities. Sometimes Franco's rejoinders read like a textbook manual of literary theory marshaled to counter her satirical adversary's claims while simultaneously underscoring her erudition. At other times her responses undercut her idealizing interlocutor's elevated discourse of love. While in the trials Franco finally submitted to the inquisitor's patriarchal authority and even confessed a small measure of evil conduct, in this poetic debate she concedes that she will agree to a peaceful resolution to their "battaglia" (battle) only if and when her adversary proves himself to her:

> *E, se voi poi non mi risponderete,*
> *di me dirò che gran paura abbiate,*
> *se ben così valente vi tenete.*
> *Ma, perché alquanto manco dubitiate,*
> *son contenta di far con voi la pace,*
> *pur ch'una volta meco vi proviate:*
> *fate voi quel, che più vi giova e piace.* (202–8)

Should you not answer me, I will say that you are in great fear of me
even though you consider yourself so brave. But since I do not want
you to entertain any doubt, I will gladly make peace with you provided that you joust with me one time. Do what best suits and
pleases you.

In this *tenzone,* courtesan and courtesanry are united in a poetic perfor-
mance aimed at various audiences: the *incerto autore,* the satiric defamer, and
the audience of Venetian readers outside their specific poetic exchange. In
Franco's dialogue with the *incerto autore,* she acts as literary and social critic
simultaneously. She rejects an idolatrous poetic discourse that insists on
exalting the woman as a disembodied object of male praise, and she also
deploys a public, polemical mode commonly denied women to expose her
satirical detractor and to reverse his misogynistic portrait of the courtesan.
While her control of language in the poetic debate is certainly greater than
that which she displayed in the inquisitorial tribunal, it is similar in kind.
In both cases, Franco defends herself expertly against opposing forces that
seek to denigrate her as courtesan and writer. Both inquisitorial trial and
poetic debate reveal the courtesan's struggles and her strategies for survival
in the social, literary, and legal worlds, of sixteenth-century Venice. To enter into these discourses of opposition with her fellow Venetians, Veronica
Franco manipulates existing poetic traditions to suit her own designs, and
she crosses the restrictive boundaries of private domesticity and public silence traditionally set for Renaissance women.

Appendix: DOCUMENTS OF THE INQUISITION

Documents included in this appendix include the text of a lawsuit presented by
Veronica Franco to the patriarch of Venice requesting the excommunication of unidentified thieves (4. 1); Redolfo Vanitelli's written denunciation of Veronica to the Inquisition's tribunal in Venice (4.2); and a transcript of her trial (4.3).

4.1 Request for Excommunication

**Archivio Patriarcale di Venezia, Registri Actorum et Mandatorum
1579 et 1580, n. 16, 22 May 1580, cc. 83–84**

Per Domina Veronica Franco
    De comission del Reverendo Monsignor Ascanio Thomasino, Dottor dell'una et l'al-
tra legge, et vicario dell'Illustrissimo Patriarcha de Venetia, et ad instantia di Madonna
Veronica Francha da Venetia, si comanda, sotto pena di excommunicazione, a qualun-

que persona, di qualunque grado, stato, et condition si sia, che glie havessono rubbato robbe, danari, argenti, et particolarmente danari donatagli da madonna Paula sua madre, quali danari erando in vari stramazzi, et che havesse tolti anneli d'oro, argenti di varie sorti, mentre che detta Madonna Veronica era maritata; ac etiam a ciascuno che sapesse sopra di ciò cosa alcuna; et chi sapesse anco de le scritture appartenenti a essa madonna Veronica, che in termine di giorni 9 prossimi futuri—li quali se li assegna 3 per il [primo], 3 per il [secondo], et li altri 3 giorni per [terzo] ultimo et perentorio termine—da essere computati doppo la pubblication de le presenti. Et doppo che li sarà venuto a notitia tal publication, quelli che havessero tolto le robbe, danari, anneli et argenti—tutti o veramente parte de essi—debbano restituirle alla predetta madonna Veronica; ac etiam ciascuno che sopra di ciò ne sapesse cosa alcuna, et che sapesse anco de le scritture soradette, in ditto termine debbono palesar et manifestar alla detta madonna Veronica, o veramente a qualche altra persona fedele, mediante la qual si venga alla consegna, restitution et manifestation sopra ditte; o veramente, haver riposto nell'officio de la cancelleria patriarchale tuto quello che sano, per descargo de le conscientie loro. Altramente, passati li ditti nove giorni, tuti quelli et qualunque persona che non farà la debita restitution et revelation, come di sopra è detto, per l'autorità di esso monsignor vicario, saranno excommunicati; et per tali si dechiareno et publicheranno al populo nelle chiese di questa inclita città di Venetia, a fuogo et aqua et son di campanella, per li Reverendi piovani, cappellani, et curati a chi sarano presentati le presenti.

   In quorum fidem datum Venetiis in aedibus habitationis predicti reverendi Vicari, ex opposito eclesia Sancti Bartholomei de Rialto, die veneris XX mensis mai 1580. [Signed by: Joannes Trivisanus, Patriarcha Venetirum Dalmatiaeque, and Ascanius Thomasinus, iudex diligatus ab Illustrissimo Domine Patriarcha]

4.2   Written Denunciation by Redolfo Vannitelli

Archivio di Stato di Venezia, Sant'Uffizio, Processi, b. 46, 1580

Die 3° mensis Octobris contra Veronicam Francham*

Io Ridolfo Vannitelli per discarico della mia conscienza, et non per altro effetto do' in notitia al Santissimo Officio dell'Inquisitione come una Veronica Franca pubblica meretrice havendo l'altro giorno perso alcune sue robbe in casa, et incolpando tutti quei che stavano nella sua casa, tra i quali eri io Ridolfo sudetto, Giovanni Tedesco, sta col secretario . . . Frumenti, et una donna dimandata Bortola sta' in calle di Ca' Cocco nella contrada di Santa Maria Formosa, et non havendo testimonii a proposito di ritrovare un paio di forbici con la guaina d'argento, et un' officiolo dorato, et altre

---

*This note appears on the verso of the last page of the document, and indicates the day on which the denunciation appeared in the Inquisition tribunal. The denunciation occupies three separate pages which have writing only on the recto. The verbal testimony that follows Vanitelli's denunciation occupies eight unnumbered pages.

robbe, le quali havea perso, ricorse all'incanti delle donne soperstitiosi, et vani, et fece chiamare una che sta ivi vicino con tre putti quattro putte, et pigliò un'anello benedetto, l'oliva benedetta, l'acqua santa in ditta chiesa di S. Giovanni, et cannele benedette, et una inghistera piena d'acqua, et cominciò a far ditti incanti et invocationi di demoni, et altri nomi, dando scandalo a tutti di credere a quelle cose, alli quali ella credeva fermamente, dicendo che li putti, e putte dicevano vedere chi le havea havuti: di là ad certi giorni, io non potendo sopportare tale cose con'oppostimi, andai fuora, et ritrovai detto officiolo in mano di un libraro in merzaria, per questo prego le Signorie Vostre Illustrissime debbano gastigare, et far gastigare detta Veronica Franca, e gli altri, che sono intravenuti a far detti incanti, et invocationi dei demonii, secondo comandano le sacre e divine leggi sopra di ciò fatte, acciò vada in essempio di tutte l'altre persone: perché non gastigandosi questa fattuchiara puttana pubblica barra, molti si metteriano a far simili cose contra la santa, et catholica fede. Di più fa lei ridutti di giuochi prohibiti cio è di carte, et vi usa la maggior diligenza che sia possibile, e sa fare molte vigliaccherie in tutti sorti di giuochi, et quando ha vinciuto i danari ne dona la buona mano a chi vi è presente, acciò non publichi dette sue furfanterie.

Ella non va mai a messa, come si può provare per tutta la contrada, et per il parrochiano di detti Chiesa, il quale non può affirmare, che da due mesi in qua et mezo che io sono stato in casa sua sia mai andata ad ascoltare messa, ma sempre attende a detti giuochi, et altri negotii dishonesti et illiciti con gli huomini, et suoi inamorati, ma invero ha ella troppo grande aiuto in questa città, et è favorita da molti, dai quali vorrebbe esser odiata, però io vi scongiuro, et supplico che nonobstante detti suoi favori debbiate farla gastigare conforme al dovere, et subbito, subito acciò non infetti più questa Città, la quale per sua causa mi dubito, che non habbia da incorrere in qualche grandissimo pericolo, et quel che merita lei, non faccia venirlo sopra li innocenti.

Dice di più esser maritata hora, hora essere vedova, hora volersi maritare, et fingere tra l'altri un matrimonio falsamente fatto qui con uno Romano, et ciò ha fatto solo per ricuperare li perli, le maniglie d'oro, et altre gioie, ch'ella portava contro la dispositione della parte fatta del Serenissimo Principe.

[Witness]: Io Iuonne Wendelino Todesco, affermo quanto de supra secuntiene sic. Si come più appieno depunerò quando serò chiamato.

[On two separate sheets, written only on the recto side, with the same handwriting as the Vannitelli denunciation, is the following]:

C. 1: Vi si aggiunge all'informatione contra Veronica Franca, che ha fatto alcune altre invocationi di demonii per fare inamorare di lei alcuni Tedeschi, che praticavano in sua casa, sicome apparerà per testimonianza del Bozzo, che fa tabernacoli a oro: sta in calle delle acque sopra la spetiaria in detta contrada. Che mangiava carne, e il venere, e il sabato, et altre vigilie lo sa Costantino . . . et Lucretia Greghetta sta dirimpetto a detta Veronica.

Che habbia fatte le invocationi di demonii, et cercati i putti per farle lo sa Pre Vicenzo primo prete di S. Giovanni Novo. Et l'acqua benedetta, et cannela benedetta, et palma benedetta la portò Acchille suo figliuolo, et quello ancora sa Checco luganegher.

C. 3: Aggiungo di più come detta Veronica Franca il giorno di Venere, tra'l dì et la notte, giocando con due giovani a carte mangiò la carne, et Checco luganegaro ghe la tagliò, e portò in tavola.

E molte altre volte di detto dì si metteva a letto, e fingendo d'essere malata si faceva comprare i pollastri, et si faceva apparecchiarse da Bortola coca e poi si li mangiava.

4.3   Inquisition Trial against Veronica Franco

Sant'Uffizio Processi, b. 46, 1580

Die Sabbati 8 mensis Octobris {Saturday, 8 October} 1580, assistentibus Clarissimis Dominis Jacopo Fuscareno Doctore et Dominico de Priolis Coram Illustrissimis et Reverendissimis Dominis Alberto Bologneto Legato Apostolico et Joanne Trivisano Patriarcha Venetiarum.

Constituta Veronica Francha, filia quondam Franchi, et eidem delato iuramento de veritate dicenda, et primo.

INTERROGATA: se sei alcuna volta per saper qualche secretto o ritrovar qualche cosa ha fatto far alcune orationi a putti vergine et guardar nella inghistara piena d'aqua e in che modo et quando era alla presentia di chi et per che causa.

RESPONDIT: Signor sì l'altro giorno per ritrovar un paio de forfette et la vazina d'arzento et il mio officio, alla presentia dila madre de quelli tre puttini do putini maschi et una puttina femena el nome de la qual non ve so dir ma è moglie de un sartor et tien putti a schuola et puttine et sta arente de mi a S[an] Zuanne Nuovo et anche alla presentia de Redolfo maistro del mio puto il qual Redolfo, vedendo ch'io non volevo farlo perché diceva che quelle cose erano bagatelle, si ghettò in genochioni con le man giunte pregandome di ch'io dovesse far veder aciò si potesse ritrovar i ladri, et alla presentia di un mio servitor Thodesco che non mi recordo el suo nome ma adesso sta col secretario Formento. Dicens postea: me ricordo che ha nome Joanne et la madre di questi putini predetta tolse una inghistera piena di aqua et ghe messe un puocho de aqua santa dentro et la messe in un basil questa inghistera et ghe messe sotto la sua vera benedeta, con la qual era stata sposata. Et de sopra dela inghistera ci messe doi foglie o rame dell'oliva benedetta per tresso et fece inzenochiar questi puttini con una candella benedetta apiciata per uno in man, et a queste pute quella dona ghe insegnò che dovessero dir et gli fece dir: "Anzolo santo Anzolo biancho, per la tua santità et per la mia verzinità mostrame il vero et la verità chi ha tolto la tal cosa cioé le forfette et l'officio." Et così intravenni che quei puti vene fuora et non sapevano dir quel che havevano visto chi diceva una cosa chi un'altra et io ghe dette una merenda et li mandai via. Et tutti comenzorno a esser contra de me, cioé messer Redolfo et li altri che io era matta a non creder queste cose. Subdicens: quando io ero puttina piccola con quella medesima oratione et tre paternostri et 3 ave marie di più guardando in una ingistera vidi che mio padre robbava una cappa a mia madre et è vero che mio padre l'haveva robbà che lo confessò dapoi.

EI DICTUM: che havendo lei aconsentito a li sopradette cose non si può scusare che non habia partecipato in questo peccato et errore poi che, intravendoci l'acqua benedetta oliva benedetta candele benedette, l'uso de quali non deve esser in cose simile ma solo in honor de Dio. Però questo peccato è specie di heresia né si può remetter o perdonare se il peccator non ricognosce il suo errore essendo fatto maxime con oratione. Però dica quello intende.

RESPONDIT: Io credo che quel anzolo biancho volesse dir il diavolo perché anco qua a Venezia si chiama biancho il sarasino et ne son pentida et ne dimando perdono alle Vostre Signorie Illustrissime. Et se bene ho peccato con l'effetto non ho peccato con l'affetto per che non ci ho creduto.

EI DICTUM: che sapendo lei o almeno dovendo saper che le dette cose benedette non se dovevano adoperare in simil cose, et sapendo che se intendeva per l'angelo biancho il diavolo lei se non ci credeva non doveva intervenirci né permetter che altri lo facesse in casa sua.

RESPONDIT: Io fui presente per la causa che ho ditto de sopra et cognosco haver errato et voi domando perdono.

EI DICTUM: se essa ha fatto alcuna altra invocatione di demoni e fatto fare per far inamorar di sé alcuni et particularmente thodeschi.

RESPONDIT: Signor no, Dio me ne guardi et la Madona; sono la più timida dona del mondo di demonii et di morti.

EI DICTUM: se de venere e sabbado et altre vigilie ha magnato carne.

RESPONDIT: Mai né de Venere né de sabbado ne de vigilie né in zorni prohibiti ho manzato simil cose.

Die Jovis mensis Octobris {Thursday, 13 October} 1580, assistente Clarissimo Domino Jacopo Fuscareno.

Coram multum Reverendo Patre Inquisitore constituta supradicta Veronica Francha, et delato sibi iuramento de veritate dicenda.

EI DICTUM: se ha pensato dire el vero compitamente.

RESPONDIT: l'ho detto il primo giorno.

EI DICTUM: che adverta che consta a questo Santo Tribunale che lei ha magnato carne de venere, de sabbato et altri giorni prohibiti, et per ciò vogli confessarlo, pentirsene et per l'advenire non incorrer più in simil error.

RESPONDIT: caro Signor, ve zuro per queste lettere de Dio, et chiamo per testimonio la maestà de Dio et la so benedetta Mare che non ho mai magnato né formazo né ovi, non che carne in questi giorni prohibiti, se però non sono sta amalada o de parto. Et tra le altre ho partorido 6 volte et sempre ho partorido de venere et quest'anno me ho amalada assai volte et a mo un anno sono stata 4 volte amalada che mai me ho moveste de letto.

EI DICTUM ET EXORTATA: a confessar la verità per che consta in processo che lei una sera di venere alle due hore de notte in circa doppo haver giochato alle carte con doi giovani mangiò carne et ve sono testimoni che la portò in tavola et che la tagliò et che dal puto istesso se vide che a quel tempo lei non era amalata.

RESPONDIT: non saver mai d'haverne magnata ne zuogato et se pur ghene havessi magnato chi mi nol so me si dia el tempo che proverò che haveva necessità di magnarla, è grande anche che, se la non fosse sta grande non havaria magnata.

EI DICTUM: che dale cose confessate da lei di sopra nell'altro examine in materia d'haver fatto far l'incanto dell'inghistara lei non si può schusare che non credesse in quel punto, poi che confessà che mentre era putta lei stessa fece tal cosa et che dala sua vista si trovò che veramente era fatto sì come lei haveva visto. Et che alli giorni passati essendo lei patrona di casa ha fatto far el medesimo experimento ne la schusa la importunità dei *servitori* essendo lei patrona et quella che haveva perso le robbe del cui interesse si trattava. Però si exorta a dir la verità.

RESPONDIT: io non ghe credeva perché el diavolo per una volta che dica la verità per cento volte dice la busia et quel che ho fatto l'ho fatto da sdegno dele parole che diceva la mia servitù cioé che io non voleva far guardar nella ingistara perché non haveva perso cosa alcua ma che fenzeva per non ghe dar el suo salario. Et di più Redolpho precettor di mio figliol qual mi ha querelada me se ghettò in zinochioni pregandomi ch'io dovesse lassar guardar aciò se vedesse che era triste in casa mia. Io ghe risposi che queste bagatelle non farà veder questa verità ma la corda de *Signori* di notte senza tante candelle troverà la verità et così me partì et andì in camera a lassar far quel che i volse, né io fui presente quando si fece la experientia. È ben vero che alle volte mi chiamavano et io ghe andava perché mi dicevano "Aldì signora, i putti han ditto così." Et perché li putti dissero che non havevan visto quella che è mia vicina disse che questo avveniva perché un dei putti haveva magnato quella matina un pocho de panne, ma che la cosa se feria l'altra matina. Et io li mandai in malhora. È ben vero che io a questa dona ghe diede l'inghistara l'aqua benedetta, l'olivo benedetto ch'io haveva in camera mia le candelle io li mandai a comprare per un ragazzo.

EI DICTUM: che le cose *presente* non la excusa poi ché essa perché se facesse tal experientia in casa sua et per suo interesse ha subministrato alla ditta donna aqua benedetta, olivo benedetto sapendo che non s'havevano a adoperare in mal uso e nella invocatione del demonio et perciò sola questa partecipatione et subministratione quantunque fosse vera la importunità della sua servitù non la schusa che non sia colpevole et rea.

RESPONDIT: quando che la madre dei putti me diceva "I putti vede non so chi," per farla capace dela sua ignorantia la menai dove erano i putti et ghe fece vedere che quel che i vedeva era loro medesimi perché i erano l'un per mezo dell'altro.

EI DICTUM: de novo che le dette cose non la schusano havendo lei confessato dele cose benedette come di sopra.

RESPONDIT: io ho errato, ne domando perdono et son parecchiata a farmi far ogni peni-
tentia.

EI DICTUM: chi fosse presente quando el detto Redolpho se inzenochiò a farve la detta
instantia.

RESPONDIT: Zuanne Thodesco che hora sta col Formento et la madre de questi putti et
tuti i putti.

SUBDENS EX SE: una dona che è qua di fuora che è vincentina che trema di mano la qual
è moglie di uno che è in priggion per questo santo officio mi ha detto che in questa
città è una donna chiamata la greca che ha una testa di morto in un bacile la qual la
bagna con l'aqua santa et che gli fa alcuni orationi et che fa venir un udro di aqua in
camera et che versa tanta aqua che le persone non puol star in camera che bisogna
che si tirano a largo.

INTERROGATA: se ha alcuno malevolo o inimico et chi et per che causa.

RESPONDIT: non cognosco li maggior inimici et massara di casa che me robbano, et
specialmente Redolpho e una dona borthola massera gravia la qual ho fatto convinzer dala iusticia che me ha tolto quelle forfette che erano tanto politte che va-
levano 4 o 5 schudi. Et io non so de altri inimici. Ho un sotto di me, che ha nome
Checo luganigher, el qual me serve qualche volta in tavola el qual non me è inimico
ch'io sappia.

Five

THE COURTESAN IN EXILE: AN ELEGIAC FUTURE

The lover is oft aware of his own ruin yet clings to it, pursuing that which
sustains his own fault. I also find pleasure in my books though they have
injured me, and I love the very weapon which made my wounds.
Ovid, *Tristia* 4.1.11

You may ask why my verses alternate, when I am better suited to the lyric
mode. I must weep, for my love—and elegy is the weeping strain; no lyre
is suited to my tears.
Ovid, *Heroides,* Sappho to Phaon, 15:5–8

Not all of Veronica Franco's capitoli summon male detractors to poetic
battle. Many of her epistolary poems, composed while in exile from Venice,
meditate on love's afflictions in a lyrical elegiac mode. Claiming that she
has been driven into exile by a vindictive male lover, Franco's elegiac epistles alternate between accusatory outbursts directed to him and inward
meditations in which she addresses her own heart. She asks it how she will
endure the pain of unreciprocated love. In these introspective moments,
Franco's capitoli share a plaintive rhetoric characteristic of Ovid's *Heroides,*
in which the woman speaker switches from direct address to interior monologue and back again within the same epistle. [1] The past often represents
nostalgic yearning, the present, uncertainty and disillusionment, while
the future proposes to the woman lover's tortured mind the prospect of a
release from suffering. Franco effects a similar compression of time and psychological confusion; individual poems comment upon one another from
different points within the poetic narrative. Just as Franco used the familiar
letter to reverse definitions of the honest courtesan's profession, and the poetic epistolary *tenzone* to assume a critical polemical stance for women, so
too in her amorous verses she manipulates ancient elegy to redeem the courtesan's reputation. Bolstered by the authority of classical conventions,
while at the same time undercutting an ancient tradition in which female

desire had been used in the service of male erotic fantasies, Franco reclaims for women an amorous voice that is at once passionate, plaintive, erotic, and also accusatory.[2]

Unwillingly exiled from his country, but most importantly, deprived of personal solace, friendly protection, and female companionship, Ovid decried in his elegiac texts the psychologically destructive effects of separation from both beloved city and lover, blending the two into one indistinguishable figure.[3] Similarly, but with a crucial difference, Franco finds herself unjustly accused in involuntary exile, not because of verses she has composed that have elicited her patron's anger but rather because of irrational male love, deception, and maliciousness.

And yet Franco's amorous verse epistles do not simply record private experiences in love, as some scholars, preferring to read her poems as mere autobiographical confession, have contended. The highly eclectic form, the capitolo in terza rima, provided her, along with other Venetian poets, with a private forum for musings on unreciprocated love. Further, within late-sixteenth-century Venetian literary circles, poets often used the capitolo to translate classical elegy into the vernacular and to express feelings about deceit in love, personal loss, separation, and abandonment. The elegiac verse epistle inherited from antiquity, combining the prose letter with the amorous verse complaint, registered a poet's contradictory feelings and dramatic changes of mood when confronted with an unfaithful lover.[4] Adopting this poetic vehicle to express both plaintive and accusatory complaints, Franco's epistolary poems, like her familiar letters, constitute fictional models—dialogue, poetic exchange, debate, verse epistle, elegiac lament—that point to, act out, and contain the tensions present in Franco's ongoing polemical dialogue with a misogynistic society.

Whereas her familiar letters comment and reflect upon love's adversities with philosophical detachment, several of Franco's elegiac verse epistles dramatize scenes of betrayal between male and female lovers to denounce duplicity in love. In the elegiac love poems we will consider here, Franco appropriates classical tradition for her own ends. She refashions both the denunciatory female voices in Ovid's *Heroides,* and the forthright amorous stance of Cynthia and Corinna, two Roman courtesans, in Propertius's *Elegies* and Ovid's *Amores,* respectively. Franco rejects contemporaries' accusations of a courtesan's calculated deception in love; conversely, she asserts with indignation her own amorous fidelity.[5] By so doing, she transfers the position of moral superiority from the male lover to the lamenting female, and she questions the textual stereotype of the deceitful whore. In these elegiac epistles in the *Terze rime,* distinctions between author and narrator are collapsed; the "Franca" persona emerges as the actress in her own story.

Franco's choice of the amorous voice drawn from classical elegy invokes what was for Ovid and Propertius an already transgressive dynamic. Classical male elegists adopted a woman's voice to oppose traditional conventions of genre and to assert a poetic identity of their own fashioning. Refusing to write in the noble genre of heroic epic, Ovid ventriloquized a female voice in order to articulate his dissatisfaction with martial exploits.[6] He favored instead the vicissitudes of private love battles. Throughout their elegies, Propertius and Ovid looked critically upon Roman vainglory and blind national pride. Rejecting the public, political, and military domains required of them as male citizens in Augustan Rome, they endorsed the private, romantic, and intellectual expression of their amorous attachments. Propertius admitted to his patron, Maecenas, that he preferred to write in the "exiguum flumen" of love poetry rather than in the lofty epic.[7] Indeed he opposed throughout his love poems the "tumidum mare" of epic poetry, yielding to pressure only in book 4 of his *Elegies,* where (for a single time) with patriotic fervor he exalted the grandeur of Rome.[8] Propertius and Ovid thus transferred vocabularies of politics, finance, and martial exploits to the amorous arena in order to portray their steadfast service to love. Further, in certain of their elegiac texts Ovid and Propertius reversed traditional sexual expectations when they cast their female lovers into the active, dominant positions customarily played by men, placing themselves instead in the position of the passively faithful lover. They endowed their courtesan lovers with such uncustomary characteristics as independence, sexual forthrightness, and masterful action, characteristics normally denied women (especially of the upper classes) by Roman society.[9]

Thus, Roman elegists saw in amorous lyrical poetry both a vehicle for publicly refusing the military ethos of Augustan Rome and a polemical forum for expressing their disenchantment with the sexual restrictions imposed on Roman women. And it is in this sense that Franco found congenial allies in ancient Roman elegists, although the reasons for their common dissatisfaction with prescribed social and gender norms had very different origins. For a classical male poet to reverse gender norms is one thing; for a Venetian courtesan intent on improving her social position to do so is necessarily a very different gesture. Indeed it has recently been argued that Ovid in the *Heroides* prevented his female subject, the female poet Sappho, from articulating her own passions by ventriloquizing her amorous discourse as his own. [10] Franco takes back this male rhetoric of female passion and fashions from it a female rhetoric of female passion.

Whereas Roman elegists inverted the sexual dynamic proposed in Alexandrian erotic poetry by placing men in the position of the enslaved and women as the *domina,* the enslaver (a reversal of the real conditions imposed on women by the laws and customs surrounding Roman marriage), Franco sought to establish a social equality between men and women. Expecting the same kind of faithfulness and intellectual merit in men as she required of herself, Franco defines in capitolo 2 of her *Terze rime* the nature of the affection she both deserves and requires from a male lover. It is for her an "amor mutuo," that is, a mutually satisfying and equally shared love. [11]

A courtesan was often associated with an insatiable sexual appetite. But the amorous epistolary voice purloined from classical elegy aided Franco in dissociating sensual desire from notions of vulgar lust. If Ovid was an "unruly son" who was unwilling to carry on the literary tradition of his forefathers and who dramatically altered the nature of elegiac poetry, Franco was an "unruly daughter" who refused to assume the voice and position solely of an abandoned and passive woman lover. [12] She adopted the subversive dynamic of the ancient elegists for her own designs; she used the criticisms of traditional gender and genre roles made by Propertius and Ovid to overturn commonly held notions that a courtesan is guilty of sexual promiscuity, dishonesty, and treachery.

The elegiac verse epistles in Franco's *Terze rime* may be divided into two groups that are nevertheless interconnected through internal allusions and an interlocking linear narrative. In the first group (capitoli 3, 9, 11, 17, 20), the poems are composed in the fictional present—during the moment of exile—while in the second group (capitoli 21, 22), the poet relies on her power of memory to reconstruct the initial scenes of betrayal, deception, or cruelty which forced her to flee from Venice in the first place and to seek solace in a pastoral landscape. While the first group invokes the quattrocento poetic tradition of the *dipartita,* the second echoes the *rimembranza.* Memory becomes a structural component in the *Terze rime.* The first group of poems builds a bond with an external reality, while the second group emphasizes the internal meditations of a beleaguered soul, afflicted by illusions and distorted thoughts. [13] When both parts are read together, they constitute a continuous fictional narrative which has led some critics to regard Franco's poems, together with certain familiar letters that gloss the capitoli, as forming an epistolary novel *avant la lettre.* [14] Read in such a way as to allow past reflections to illuminate present confusions, Franco's amorous epistles eloquently depict an individual's experiences in love as a struggle for self-discovery and self-knowledge.

In this sense Franco's amorous elegies share a bond with Tibullus's more introspective and philosophical musings on the nature of love. He yearned for a lost golden age, in which civic concord, mutual love, and social harmony once existed for all Roman citizens; his nostalgia is, however, highly pessimistic.[15] By contrast, Franco's capitolo 25—the final poem in the *Terze rime*—is pessimistically nostalgic when she longs for a happier present, yet optimistic as well. Inspired by the noble and spiritual presence of her host, Della Torre, the canon at the cathedral in Verona whom the poem honors, Franco envisages a utopian world where love and friendship are complimentary. Here men and women of all classes and races live in harmony with one another. Appropriately placed as the conclusion to her edition, this long pastoral idyll, which recalls the sociopolitical poetics of the country-house lyric, is an exquisite homage to the joys of mutual love and sensual pleasures.

This final capitolo joins together many of the lyrical strands Franco uses in her self-presentation as honest courtesan that I discussed in earlier chapters. In her praise of her host in Fumane she counters the negative male voices which satirize her profession as courtesan. Further, when she praises him, she praises by extension all who come into his service, not to mention herself. Just as poets used the pretext of the country-house poem to extol their patrons' many virtues in order to call attention to their own abilities, so Franco aligns herself with a noble elite for self-elevating purposes, as she did in her editorial activities on commemorative poetic anthologies.[16] Far from the destructive forces that she deplored in earlier elegiac capitoli, this final encomium to Della Torre's country villa at Fumane in the Veronese valley rejoices in the comingling of beauty, calm, plenitude, and sensuous delights with the excellence of artistic human creations. As an arbiter of taste conjoined with fellow artists, Franco calls attention to her ability to discern beauty both in nature and in art as she compliments her noble host's artistic choices in the decoration of his classical Roman–style villa and in the beautiful gardens surrounding it.

Franco's capitolo 25 recalls Boccaccio's description of the elegant country villa and gardens of the Tuscan countryside in his *Decameron;* a country setting where the Florentine *brigata* sought pastoral refuge from the horrors of the fourteenth-century Black Death. By alluding to the Boccaccian text in her description of the natural surroundings in Fumane, she indirectly invokes the now-distant (because she is geographically removed from Venice) plague-infested city. [17] In Boccaccio's text, an aristocratic group of friends succeeds in reestablishing through the social bond of storytelling a cohesive "community," one that it had lost in Florence during the deadly epidemic. In a like way, Franco discovers in Fumane a world where decorum reigns together with sensual pleasures. In this world, men and women enjoy the experience of friendship when in love. Although the plague is never explicitly invoked in Franco's verses, the pastoral mode with which she depicts this idyllic world and her insistence on liberating herself from male treachery allude indirectly and abstractly to the irrational violence of the epidemic that ravaged Venice in 1575–77. [18] One can read Franco's musings on artistic creativity, human ingenuity, and reciprocal love as a longing for a world governed by neither irrationality nor aggression. Celebrating the comforting presence of Della Torre and his fellow prelates, whose portraits adorn the gallery of his villa, Franco composed her most inspired eulogy to the sensual pleasures of earthly life aroused by abundance and order, and of physical pleasure which is joined with moral and spiritual virtues. This is a world, Franco believed, where the human imagination lives in consonance with the bonding of the flesh and the spirit.

II

Veronica Franco's elegiac epistolary poems bring us back to the meeting rooms of the Accademia della Fama and to the literary discussions held in Ca' Venier. In both academy and salon settings, Venetian poets actively debated the stylistic requirements for the love lyric that had a direct bearing on many of Franco's poetic choices. [19] Franco's passionate repudiation of male duplicity and her amorous laments in her elegiac verse epistles in the *Terze rime* are akin to the kind of amorous complaint found in classical elegy. But until her *capitoli,* no female poet had used the form to give voice to the point of view of a woman betrayed in love. Although many of the conventional themes of classical elegy are present in her verses, as is the rhetorical form of Ovid's verse epistles, Franco pushed the flexibility of the capitolo in terza rima to highlight the woman's voice.

Always struggling to give prominence to modern vernacular forms, while recognizing the authority of ancient poetic forms, Venetian poets of the latter half of the sixteenth century expanded the perimeters of the love lyric by reinstituting poetic forms ousted in Bembo's *Prose della volgar lingua* (1525) in the earlier part of the century. [20] Indeed, the Accademia della Fama's *Somma delle opere* (printed in 1557)—the list of scholarly and philological projects that academy members intended to study, translate, and publish—reveals the widening of the perimeters of inquiry into various poetic styles. Perhaps more ambitious than realistic, this encyclopedic agenda covered all aspects of human thought.[21] It sought to join a pagan and a Christian orientation to the world. While the academy officially declared that their intention was "to return the world to a golden age," their motto announced their specifically Christian designs: "Io volo al cielo per riposarmi in Dio" (I fly to heaven to find rest in God). In wedding Christian morality to classical culture, academy members planned to exalt Venice as a new Rome.[22]

Owing to an interest in reclaiming texts from antiquity, Venetian literati of the latter half of the sixteenth century prepared scholarly commentaries to accompany classical texts. Indeed Ovid's works, and those of other Roman elegists, occupy a prominent position in the section of the *Somma* devoted to poetry.[23] Academy members intended to examine Ovid's uses of rhetorical and artificial devices, and more generally, the expressive and emotional nature of the elegiac love lament. A study of Catullus concentrates specifically on his use of the hendecasyllable,[24] while an analysis of the works of Propertius and Tibullus examines more generally the nature of elegy as a poetic form and its power to express sentiment and to give voice to conflicting states of being.[25] For Propertius they proposed a complete edition of his elegies, coupled with "una breve, e vera interpretazione, dalla qual saranno fatti facili tutti i luoghi difficili di questo poeta" (a brief and accurate interpretation by which all the difficult passages of this poet will be made easy).[26] The entry on Ovid declares an interest in studying not solely his *Heroides* but all of his elegiac texts, especially with a view toward preparing translations in the vernacular.[27]

While Domenico Venier, Lodovico Dolce, and others did try their hand at translating Ovid's *Metamorphoses* (Venier never completed this project), the *Heroides* in the end was not translated by academy members but rather by writers outside of Venice. But these writers nevertheless maintained close connections with the academy, Venier's salon, and Venetian publishers. Remigio Nannini (Fiorentino), a Florentine writer and a Dominican monk, first offered a translation in 1555, followed by the Aretine Camillo Camilli, in 1587. Both translations were printed by Venetian presses.[28] Only Camilli's vernacular translation of Ovid's *Heroides* is in capitoli in terza rima. Although this translation appeared in print many years after Franco's *Terze rime,* theoretical discussions concerning the use of the *capitolo* in terza rima to express an elegiac lament in epistolary form occupied the interests of many members of Ca' Venier in the 1570s. This resurgence in interest in the elegies of Ovid and Propertius must have suggested rich and powerful rhetorical models to a courtesan poet.

While always upholding Bembo's intention to elect Italian over Latin for lyric poetry, academy members also promoted studies on the ancient origins of the Italian lyric.[29] They hoped to prepare the ground for critical editions of classical texts, as well as for studies of early-sixteenth-century Italian authors. Intent on differentiating their theoretical and literary projects from those already undertaken by Bembo, and prompted by Domenico Venier's interest in retrieving poetic models from a romance vernacular tradition, these poets turned to the ode, eclogue, madrigal, *tenso,* and elegy in the vernacular, which they drew from even earlier roots—not only classical elegiac poets but also the Provençal troubadours.[30]

With very close ties to the publishing industry in Venice—ties that had already been formed in part by fifteenth and early-sixteenth-century Venetian humanists and *poligrafi*—many of the academy's projects were printed with astonishing speed and in extremely elegant editions. This of course was linked to Venice's position as the European center of printing. As Dionisotti has persuasively argued, Venice occupied a central geographical role in all literary undertakings in Italy, a privilege it maintained throughout the century:

> *Quando finalmente si tenga conto che Venezia sola era in grado con la sua industria tipografica di produrre più libri di quanti se ne producessero in tutto il resto d'Italia, bene anche s'intende come e perché durante la prima metà del Cinquecento la letteratura italiana si svilupasse su di una base generalmente settentrionale e specificatamente veneziana.*[31]

> And finally, if we take into account that with the printing industry Venice alone was able to produce more books than were produced in all the rest of Italy, we can well understand how and why, during the first half of the sixteenth century, Italian literature developed on a generally northern and specifically Venetian basis.

The strength of Venice's publishing industry is one of the principal factors which lured Bernardo Tasso to Venice in 1559 to become the academy's *cancelliere.* When Girolamo Molino, Venier's close friend and fellow poet, tried to persuade Tasso to accept the position in a letter written from Venice to him in Pesaro in 1558, he stressed the academy's public dimension. He argued that they had rented a workshop for doing their own publishing in a highly visible, because centrally located, quarter of the city—the Mercerie ("hanno tolto ed affitto la più bella bottega e nella più bella posta che sia in tutta la . . . Merceria" [they have found and rented the best shop in the best position in all of the Merceria]). He assured Tasso that if he were to come to Venice he would be able to publish his *Amadigi* immediately upon his arrival, "nella più bella stampa, e carta che si sia ancor veduta . . . una rara e vaga stampa sopra ogni altra" (with the most beautiful paper and in the most elegant fashion ever imaginable).[32] The intellectual vitality that Venice offered intellectuals was precisely the kind of environment for which Bernardo Tasso, not to mention many other Renaissance courtiers, continually yearned.

When Bernardo Tasso accepted the position in the following year, he explained his decision in a letter to Giovanni Michiel; he said it was related to his immense desire to escape the tyranny of princes and the servility enforced upon him by court life:

> {*Sono*} *stanco ormai dell'insopportabili fatiche che l'azioni del mondo portano, e desideroso di sottrarre il collo al difficile, noioso e duro gioco della servitù de' Prencipi, al quale son stato legato quarant'anni.*[33]
>
> [I am] tired by now of the miserable efforts demanded by the ways of the world, and I want to free my neck from the difficult, irksome, and heavy yoke of being at the resource of princes—a yoke to which I have been harnessed for forty years.

Not long thereafter, however, on 3 March 1560, less than two years after his arrival in Venice, he wrote to Sperone Speroni of his intention to divorce himself completely from any associations with the academy; in addition he reported that he had decided to relinquish the house he had received as *cancelliere*:

> *Io mi sono licenziato dall'Accademia, e mi voglio licenziare anche da questa casa, perché la vicinità causa che'l Clarissimo mi da alcuna volta più fastidio, che io non vorrei.*[34]
>
> I have left the Accademia, and I also want to leave this house because of proximity to the Illustrious [Badoer], which sometimes causes me greater inconvenience than I would like.

The specific reasons for his disenchantment with the academy are not certain, although his decision to leave his post was probably linked to Badoer's expropriating funds for private rather than public use, a fact which finally brought about the Accademia della Fama's downfall in 1561. Although the academy was short-lived, its editorial interests strongly influenced the Venetian literary community, the publishing industry in Venice, and Venier's coterie until the end of the sixteenth century.[35]

Having as members the most esteemed Venetian writers, theorists, and politicians of the period, the Accademia della Fama worked in close collaboration with the Venetian patrician and publisher Paolo Manuzio and later with Gabriel Giolito de' Ferrari. Giolito de' Ferrari agreed to publish individual members' works and those editions recommended by the academy even after the academy disbanded. In 1560, just one year before the academy folded, the Council of Ten had authorized it to take on the unprecedented privilege of printing all of the republic's official political acts without concern for expense and on the best paper available: "habbia cura di comprar la carta, la quale però senza haver rispetto in spesa, sia de la miglior che si trovi" (see to the purchase of the paper which, without any consideration for its cost, must be the best that can be found).[36]

Theorists in Venice who participated in the salon meetings in Ca' Venier, such as Lodovico Dolce, Sebastiano Erizzo, Giovan Battista Pigna, Girolamo Molino, Girolamo Ruscelli, Bernardo Tasso, and Girolamo Muzio, warned against the slavish imitation of classical authors. They turned to Domenico Venier for his approval in this matter. Italian poets often traveled great distances to consult with Domenico about their literary projects. In the 1560s Bernardo Tasso's son, Torquato, turned to Venier for advice on his *Rinaldo* (which he published in 1562 with a dedication to Cardinal Luigi d'Este). In canto 9. 30 there is a direct reference to Venier, in which Torquato associates Domenico's intellectual excellence with Venice's miraculous beauty:

> *Tai cose ancor, ma con più dolce canto,*
> *ho già, Veniero, a te spiegar sentito,*
> *e visto uscir del salso fondo in tanto*
> *i marin pesci ad ingombrar il lito;*
>   *e quasi astretti da ben forte incanto*
> *i varii augei, per appagar l'udito,*
> *ne l'impeto maggior frenare il volo*
> *e fermarsi intorno a stuolo a stuolo.*

> I already heard you, Veniero, explain such things with a much sweeter voice, and I saw the fishes of the sea rise from the salty depths to crowd the shore; and I also saw birds of all kinds halt in the midst of their swiftest flight as if to indulge their ears and gather round you flock after flock.

Later, in 1575, he once again turned to Venier for revisions of his *Gerusalemme liberata*.[37]

In the view of academy members, the vernacular, especially as used for elegiac compositions, contained within it the same flexibility as did classical Latin; it was capable of expressing a wide range of human feelings in many forms and meters. While they deemed a study of the ancient lyricists crucial for an appreciation of poetic excellence, like most Italians, they rejected the view that vernacular forms should recreate classical meters. They regarded the vernacular's powers as unique, to be enriched by the inspiration of classical texts, but not restricted by them. Lodovico Dolce wrote his *I quattro libri delle osservationi* (1550) perhaps partly as a polemical response to Claudio Tolomei's *Versi et regole de la nuova poesia toscana* (1539).[38] In it he proposed the use of a modern vernacular form for amorous elegy—the tercet composed in hendecasyllables—to take the place of the ancient hexameter and pentameter:

> *Alcuni altri non meno dotati d'ingegno, che di dottrina, perdettero gl'inchiostri in apportare in questa lingua gli Hessametri, i Pentametri, e la maggior parte de' versi, che posero in tanta riputatione la Lingua Greca e la Latina; e non s'avidero, che nella nostra non tengono punto di gratia, né di harmonia. . . . Percioche possiamo dire, che invece dell'Hessametro e Pentametro, con che essi formavano le loro Elegie, noi habbiamo quella sorte di versi, detta Terzetti.*[39]

> Some others no less endowed with intelligence and knowledge have wasted much ink in applying to this tongue hexameters, pentameters, and a great number of verses that earned such a great reputation for Greek and Latin, and they do not realize that in our language these forms are neither graceful nor harmonious. . . . Therefore we can say that instead of the hexameters and pentameters that they used to compose their elegies, we have a type of verse called tercets.

Girolamo Muzio, in a more humorous vein, in his *Dell'arte poetica* (1551) poked fun at contemporaries who insisted on overlooking vernacular verse forms such as the sonnet, *canzone,* and madrigal in favor of classical meters and forms:

> *Alcuni son, che forse troppo amanti*
> *D'ogni cosa d'altrui, lor rime nove*
> *Chiamar con gli stranieri antichi nomi*
> *Ode, Epigrammi, e Hinni e Elegie.*
> *Io più che la virtù Latina, e Greca*
> *Viva nel mio legnaggio, non mi curo*
> *Che vestendo si vada de i lor panni.*[40]

> There are those who perhaps being too fond of what belongs to oth-
> ers give their new rhymes ancient foreign names such as epigrams,
> hymns and elegies. Aside from the Latin and Greek virtue that is a
> living part of my heritage, I take no pains for it to don their garb.

The vernacular, although sharing with Latin many of the same rules, grammatical forms, and rhetorical devices, also contains much, he reminded his
contemporaries, that is distinctive to it alone. Hence, the issue for Muzio,
and others, was to distinguish clearly the exact grammatical, rhetorical,
and formal differences between the two languages.[41]

Giovan Battista Pigna's study of Ariosto's poetry, *I Romanzi,* published
in Venice in 1554, reinforced Dolce's suggestion that elegy can best be rendered in the vernacular *terzetto.* This was because, as he argued, unlike other
forms it permitted an expression of flux and confusion. Pigna believed that
by linking tercets together in a forward-moving chain of interlocking
rhymes, an author was able to create a suspended, yet controlled, sense of
uncertainty, motivated by intensely subjective and conflicting emotions.[42]
In addition Dolce claimed that whereas many Italian poets, including
Dante, Boccaccio, Petrarch, Sannazaro, Ariosto, Bentivoglio, Tasso,
Mauro, and Berni, had already adopted *terzetti* for their verses, only in the
sixteenth century had authors given the name elegy to their amorous verses:

> *Noi habbiamo quella sorte di versi, detta Terzetti, perché per lo più di tre
> versi in tre versi lo scrittore va chiudendo la sua sentenza. Onde in questa
> età alcuni descrivendo in sì fatti Terzetti le loro amorose passioni, quelli
> Elegie nominarono.*[43]
>
> We have a type of verse called tercets because the writer almost al-
> ways closes a sentence every three lines. Hence, during this time, a
> number of those who describe their amorous passions in these
> tercets called them elegies.

Celio Magno, a poet steeped in the elegiac tradition, was appointed the
academy's official translator on 10 December 1557. In his *Prefatione sopra il
Petrarca,* most probably commissioned by the academy, he argued that the
lyric genre surpassed both the tragedy and the epic because of its divinely
inspired origins and its representation of the most ancient expressions of
humanity.[44] Similarly Sebastiano Erizzo, a Venetian senator in the Council
of Ten and a scholar of antiquity, included a history of the ancient origins of
the lyric in his commentary to three of Petrarch's *canzoni.* Associating the
themes, rhetoric, and tone of the Petrarchan lyric with the poetics of clas-

sical elegy, Erizzo argued in his *Espositione* (1561) that although elegy was originally conceived for "la funebre lamentatione" (funereal lamentation), it was also perfectly suited to amorous lament. An intensely musical and passionate verse form, elegy expressed, he believed, the most intimate and contradictory poles of human desire:

> *Il verso Elegiaco inchinò a cose più lievi, havendo i Poeti datisi a gli amori, et alle delitie, fatta la Elegia Amatoria, quando ne i loro amorosi versi si dolevano, et si lamentavano, mescolando ne i poemi sospiri, pene et tormenti, overo mostravano il lieto stato loro, o che pregavano di mercede, ammonivano, accusavano di crudeltà, over lodavano la donna sua, o che si scusavano, dimandavano perdono.*[45]

The elegiac verse turned to lighter themes when the poets who devoted themselves to loves and the delights of love invented the amatory elegy, as in their amorous verses they moaned and wept mixing sighs, sorrows, and torments, or they displayed a state of happiness, or pleaded for mercy, reproached their woman, accused her of cruelty or praised her, or apologized and begged for forgiveness.

Ovid, he argued, best understood how bereavement over the mortal loss of one's beloved parallels a lover's experience of deprivation when deceived, betrayed, abandoned, or unreciprocated in love:

> *Conciosia cosa, che essendo lo stato de gli amanti di sua natura lamentevole, ragionevolmente questa sorte di Poesia si hanno eletto, la qual scorgevano propria de i tristi et lagrimosi lamenti, come noi vediamo in Ovidio, che tante et sì diverse cose in questa maniera di versi scrisse.*[46]

In view of the fact that the condition of lovers is by its very nature lamentable, it stands to reason that they would choose this sort of poetry, which they recognized as their own because of its sad and tearful laments, as we can see in the case of Ovid, who wrote so many different works in this manner of verse.

And Girolamo Ruscelli, an active member of the academy and Domenico Venier's close friend and colleague, defined in his *Del modo di comporre in versi nella lingua italiana* (1558) the manner by which *terzetti,* when grouped together as capitoli (as we find in Franco's case), often function as *epistole:*

> *I Terzetti nostri {non} sieno per servire in niun modo convenevolmente a soggetto Eroico, et grave, essendo la natura loro obligatissima, et difforme dalla maestà Eroica, et non atta a ricever altezza di stile, ma solo da Elegie, o Epistole, o altri sì fatte cose, che possano ricevere o fine, o altissimo*

posamento col numero di non molti versi, onde degnamente gli hanno
chiamati Capitoli.[47]

Our tercets can under [no] circumstances be properly used for a heroic and grave subject, because their form is extremely restrictive
and unlike heroic majesty. It is not suitable to convey a lofty style
but only that of elegies or epistles or other similar compositions
which can convey subtle or very grand elegance with a small
number of verses, so that they have quite deservedly been called
Capitoli.

Ruscelli's conflation of the "elegia" (elegy) and the "epistola" (epistle) form
refers not only to the ancient elegiac poets who used the elegy to encompass
both forms but perhaps also to Ariosto, a poet whom Venetians defended
energetically against Tuscan detractors. Among the many editions that
Ruscelli was responsible for overseeing and editing was a study, included in
the academy's *Somma*, of Ariosto's *Satire*. Ruscelli writes:

Onde l'Ariosto, veramente divino in ogni sua cosa, volendo nelle Satire sue
alzar lo stile delle dette Terze Rime, oltra quello, che elle sogliono haver
nelle Epistole, o Elegie, o sì fatte compositioni, pare che a niuna cosa atten-
desse con più cura, che a questo spezzar de versi.[48]

Hence Ariosto, who truly excelled in everything he undertook, in
his *Satire* want[ed] to elevate the style of the already-mentioned
terze rime beyond and above that which they usually present in
epistles or elegies, or such constructed compositions; it seems that
he paid more care to dividing these verses than any others.

Responding to the pressures of an ever-widening readership, Venetian
publishers promoted academy members' projects by flooding the literary
market with *volgarizzamenti* of classical texts, a fact only possible after
Bembo's death in 1547. In so doing, they opened up to outsiders a classical
canon that had been well fortified by fifteenth- and early-sixteenth-century
humanists. This expansion of the linguistic terrain in midcentury permitted such "avventurieri della penna" (adventurers of the pen) as Pietro
Aretino and champions of the "nuova lingua" (new language) untrained in
the *studia humanitatis* to publish their works. Similarly, as Dionisotti first
demonstrated, it afforded women access to a language previously available
only to a privileged elite:

Il fenomeno della rigogliosa letteratura femminile italiana a metà del Cin-
quecento anzitutto si spiega con l'improvvisa, larghissima apertura lin-

guistica di quegli anni. Si erano spalancate le porte di una società letteraria
ristretta e gerarchicamente ben differenziata . . . l'accesso e afflusso delle
donne nei ranghi ufficiali della nuova società letteraria italiana si spiega
dopo il 1530 per le condizioni stesse che ormai consentivano e stimolavano
l'afflusso di uomini prima diseredati e reietti come Pietro Aretino.[49]

The phenomenon of a thriving Italian women's literature halfway
through the sixteenth century can be explained above all by the
sudden, very broad opening up of the language during those years.
The doors of a restricted and hierarchically well differentiated literary society had been thrown wide open. . . . The access and influx
of women into the official ranks of the new Italian literary society
can, after 1530, be attributed to the same conditions that at the
same time permitted and encouraged the influx of formerly disin-
herited and rejected men like Pietro Aretino.

Often with little concern for the integrity of the original texts, however,
sixteenth-century publishers put increasing pressure on translators to turn
out translations as fast as market demands called for them. Indeed translations multiplied just as quickly as new writers joined in literary projects.

Thus, Veronica Franco's move away from the sonnet to the capitolo in
terza rima is closely linked to Venetian poets' and theorists' widening of
poetic choices in the latter half of the sixteenth century. That she chose the
capitolo in terza rima for her amorous epistolary verse constitutes an important departure from the Petrarchan tradition, in which the sonnet was
the principal poetic vehicle for amorous lyrics. Indeed the eclecticism of
Franco's *Terze rime* and the polyphonic array of poetic voices assembled there
(facilitated, as we have seen, by the wide range of genres that the capitolo in
terza rima embraced) remained a rarity in Renaissance women's amorous
lyrics.

III

Whereas Franco's familiar letters address a variety of topics, her amorous
verse epistles, especially capitoli 3, 17, and 20, center on the effects of duplicitous and obsessive love. What further distinguishes these *capitoli* from
the other poems in the *Terze rime* that include elegiac laments on the pain of
unrequited love is their precise function as love letters in verse; it is in
these poems that we see most clearly the influence of Ovid's *Heroides*. Each
capitolo opens with a tercet addressed to an unnamed "sir" and identifies
the speaker as either "Veronica" or "Franca." This three-line exordium introduces the woman speaker's psychological state and the attributes of the

male recipient. While the familiar letter genre permitted Franco to posit a definition of the courtesan's profession as "honest," that is, honored and virtuous, the poetic elegiac mode allowed her to align herself with truthfulness and honesty in love relationships, as her own name, "Franca," suggests. At times, the exordium defines and prefigures the letter's dramatic turn of events; often the relationship between the two people establishes the thematic content of the entire poem.[50] Indeed the direct addresses in Franco's capitoli 3, 17, and 20 are formally very similar to the exordiums in *Heroides* 1, 2, and 4, as they appear in Camilli's translation:[51]

> *Questa la tua fedel Franca ti scrive,*
> *dolce, gentil, suo valoroso amante;*
> *la qual, lunge da te, misera vive.* (3.1–3)

> Your faithful Franca, who, when far from you,
> lives in misery, writes this letter to you who are her
> sweet, gentle, and gallant lover.

> *Questa la tua Veronica ti scrive,*
> *signor ingrato e disleale amante,*
> *di cui sempre in sospetto ella ne vive.* (17.1–3)

> Veronica writes this letter to you,
> thankless lord and disloyal lover,
> whom, while she lives, she will suspect.

> *Questa quella Veronica vi scrive*
> *che per voi, non qual già libera e franca*
> *or d'infelice amor soggetta vive.* (20.1–3)

> This letter is written to you by that Veronica
> who lives now neither free nor frank
> but as a slave of unrequited love.

Franco further evokes the epistolary exchange of the second book of the *Heroides* by including in her *Terze rime* a few male responses to the woman's accusations. While in book 1 of the *Heroides*, the woman's narrative airs only her side of the story of betrayal, in the double letters in book 2, both sides of the love dialectic are presented.[52] The male hero finally has the chance to tell his story. His account often vies for authority with his beloved's narrative. The reader is left to judge which version is not only more pitiful but also more persuasive. Similarly, through the inclusion of the male-authored poems in her volume, the male speaker (as in capitolo 4) insists that his love for her is not duplicitous.[53]

In the *Heroides*, the women speakers recount their drama of betrayal retrospectively, assigning blame to specific figures drawn from myth or ancient history. By contrast, the male interlocutor in Franco's verse epistles remains anonymous. The classical epistles produce an ironic effect, because the reader already knows that the woman's lament is in vain; the outcome of her story predates her narrative. Thus, the reader's attention is drawn not to the narrative's resolution but rather to the pathos of the woman's lament as it unfolds, and to the expressive tension created between a need to fulfill desire and a need to resolve the conflicts of unrequited love. The words of the elegiac lament, most particularly their sounds and textures, lure the reader into a realm of verbalized sorrow.[54] This language of lament is closely connected to Franco's passionate disparagement of male duplicity in capitoli 3, 17, and 20.

There are no preexisting narratives, however, that inform or determine the fiction of capitoli 3, 17, or 20, nor are there any that recount episodes drawn from the stories of heroes or heroines of antiquity. In Franco's amorous verse epistles no authorial ventriloquist speaks through the woman; here the letter writer and the author are the same subject. She is the suppliant, and her lover the object of her plea. Moreover, it is she, as both writer and narrator, who acts (rather than is acted upon) and who therefore has a role in determining her own fate; she leaves her beloved in capitolo 3 and intercepts him, upon her return to Venice, in capitolo 17, at the moment when he publicly discloses his unfaithfulness to her.

Many of the rhetorical devices in Ovid's *Heroides* are used in her text. Abrupt changes in emotion disrupt the speaker's narrative. Franco also draws from Boccaccio's *Elegia di Madonna Fiammetta* and the amorous complaints in Ariosto's love poems, in which exchanges of voices within the lover's tormented fantasy create an imaginary dialogue with a cruel beloved; her woman speaker is continually distraught by warring emotions that cloud her ability to reason.[55] Unlike the abandoned heroine of Boccaccio's work, Franco's woman speaker is the one who flees from her lover, and it is he who begs for her return. Sometimes a poem that begins as an accusation condemning Franco's beloved on the grounds of infidelity ends conversely; for example, capitolo 20 ends in a plea for his mercy, pity, and compassion. The speaker always hopes to change her present situation through the powers of persuasion.

If we view capitoli 3, 17, and 20 as an epistolary narrative, we may read the first capitolo as an introduction to a love story that culminates in capitolo 20. What begins in capitolo 3 as an intimate, personal confession of love and desire ends in capitolo 20 with a proclamation against male cruelty, deceit, and infidelity. Capitolo 17 stands as the mediator between the two. In a melodramatic scene worthy of Renaissance comedy, the woman apprehends her beloved as he is textually, though not physically, unfaithful to her. In classical elegy the event that often followed a lover's quarrel and accusations of infidelity was the male lover's forced exile from the woman's home. This, in turn, prompted him to compose a song or a poetic address to his beloved's door. In Franco's version it is the woman lover who denounces her beloved and charges him with cruelty, deceit, and betrayal in love. She reworks the *exclusus amator* and *paraclausithyron* traditions of classical elegy in capitolo 20 by having the woman lover wander the Venetian streets at night, unable to sleep because of the relentless pain of unreciprocated love. Pulled to her lover's home by her desire, accompanied by a faithful male companion, she is barred entrance by the doorkeeper; her lover is not at home, he tells her, but sleeps in the bed of a woman more fortunate than she. This drives the woman speaker to address the door, mediated by the doorkeeper; Propertius's *paraclausithyron* of book 1.16, in which the door is the sole speaker throughout, and Ovid's *Amores* 1.6 function as intertexts.[56] In these poets' texts it was the woman who prevented the man from entering, because, it was implied, she entertained another lover. Her sexual rejection unleashed the male lover's invectives against his courtesan lover's dissolute ways. Made popular by Roman comedy, above all in the plays of Plautus and Terence, this theme was also widely used in Renaissance comedies by such playwrights as Bernardo Pino da Cagli, Lodovico Dolce, and Girolamo Parabosco.[57]

Franco reconstructs these roles by rearranging the referents in Ovid to point to male infidelity and men's corrupt sexual mores. But her antagonistic stance reverts at the close of capitolo 20 to an appeal for the man's pity and for his recognition of her intrinsic virtue and merit. Praise and blame, the rhetorical paradoxes of both Ovidian elegy and the Petrarchan love lyric, inform her speech.[58]

The male lover adopts the same rhymes proposed by the woman in his response in capitolo 4 to her capitolo 3. This exchange, the only one between male and female speakers in the three elegiac epistles, evokes the alternating discourses of book 2 of the *Heroides*.[59] The woman claims that she has been forced to leave her city, and he retorts in an ironic rejoinder, playing with verbal ambiguities, that her departure was unnecessary, probably motivated not by his cruelty but by another man. Her accusations of infidelity prompt his denial of her suspicions. Both her accusations and his denials are eroticized in a play of absence and presence in which she invokes

Petrarch's sonnet no. 265 ("Aspro core et selvaggio, et cruda voglia"). In Franco's version, physical pleasure is celebrated in both poems as a natural resolution of love's passions. The woman speaker, full of longing, reminds her interlocutor of the sensual pleasures that they once shared by dramatizing an imagined physical reunion. She takes on the traditional rhetorical stance of the wounded lover and then appeals to her lover's virtue by comparing him to Apollo:

> Subito giunta a la bramata stanza,
> m'inchinerò con le ginocchia in terra
> al mio Apollo, in scienzia ed in sembianza;
>   e, da lui vinta in amorosa guerra,
> seguirol di timor con alma cassa,
> per la via del valor, ond'ei non erra. (3.61–66)

> The moment I will enter that coveted room, my knees will touch the ground and I will bow to the one who is my Apollo in knowledge and mien. Then vanquished by him in amorous war, my soul shattered by fear, I will follow him on the path of valor whence he does not stray.

He responds as a courtly love poet who pleads with his cruel beloved to diminish his anguish by recognizing the extent of his suffering.

Once driven from her adored virginal city, "la donzella d'Adria" (the maiden of Adria), by the pain of unrequited love, and exiled in a pastoral setting, she laments the effects of separation that serves only to intensify the anguish she now experiences. Proceeding from a praise of her beloved to extolling the virginal city, Franco identifies herself as a courtesan with her city's pure and unviolated origins.

In capitolo 3, the woman speaker acknowledges her error: "Oh quanto maledico la partita, / ch'io feci, oimé, da voi, anima mia / bench'a la mente ognor mi sete unita" (Alas how I curse my parting from you, dear soul, though in my thoughts you are still joined to me). She has left her lover—and by extension her beloved city—and has mistakenly believed that she could find refuge from love's travails in nature's landscape. Her words are mirrored and transformed into "afflitti lai" (sorrowful cries):

> E, di languir lo spirito costretto,
> de lo sparger gravosi afflitti lai,
> e del pianger sol trassi alto diletto.
>   Oimé, ch'io 'l dico e 'l dirò sempre mai,
> che 'l viver senza voi m'è crudel morte,
> e i piaceri mi son tormenti e guai. (3.10–15)

So that only from uttering grieved, sorrowful cries and weeping do
I draw supreme delight. Alas, I say, and shall always say, that life
without you is cruel death and my pleasures but torments and ills.

Nature responds to the woman's lament by echoing and duplicating her
internal passions. Not an alien force, but rather a consoling one, nature
evokes, however, the power that human sentiment has to distort reason
into jealousy:

> ma poi congiunta con la gelosia,
> che, da voi lontan, m'arde a poco a poco
> con la gelida sua fiamma atra e ria! (3.55–57)

but possessed by jealousy, which, when I am far from you, slowly
consumes me with its ice-cold gloomy and vicious flame.

It is this irrational emotion that ultimately transfigures the mental landscape into an unyielding narcissistic mirror in which all of nature reproduces and intensifies her lament as it sings in unison with her. Her sorrow is
metonymically answered by two female mythological victims of deceit,
Echo and Philomel.[60] Echo, whose voice had been taken away from her
because of Juno's vindictive anger and jealousy, responds to her lament with
"voci tronche" (truncated calls), and Philomel's sorrowful song accompanies her as she wanders in search of pastoral comfort.

> Spesso, chiamando il caro nome forte,
> Eco, mossa a pietà del mio lamento,
> con voci tronche mi rispose e corte;
>   talor fermossi a mezzo corso intento
> il sole e 'l cielo, e s'è la terra ancora
> piegata al mio sì flebile concento;
>   da le loro spelunche uscite fuora,
> piansero fin le tigri del mio pianto
> e del martir, che m'ancide e m'accora;
>   e Progne e Filomela il tristo canto
> accompagnaron de le mie parole,
> facendomi tenor dì e notte intanto. (3.16–27)

Often when crying aloud the dear name, Echo was stirred to pity by
my lament and answered it with brief truncated calls. At times the
sun and sky did halt intent on listening in midcourse and even
the earth bowed to my plangent tones. Emerging from their lairs
the tigers yet would weep to see the torments and the tears that
pierce my heart and take my life away. Procne and Philomel accompany my words and their sad melody, and they provide a tenor for
my song through day and night.

Her tears, the simulated words of love that stain the page on which she records the anguish of her soul (a topos ubiquitous in classical elegy),[61] cathartically extinguish her pain:

> Le lagrime, ch'io verso, in parte il foco
> spengono; e vivo sol de la speranza
> di tosto rivedervi al dolce loco. (3.58–60)
>
> The tears I shed quench the fire, in part, and only the hope of seeing you soon in that sweet site again keeps me alive.

In Ovid, Briseis's tears substitute similarly for words, forming traces of her sorrow, which, were he to follow them, would lead her beloved, Achilles, back to her:

> Quascumque adscipicies, lacrimae fecere lituras; sed tamen et lacrimae pondera vocia habent. (3.3–4)[62]

If Franco loses her beloved to another woman, as her suspicions of infidelity keep warning her she will, paradoxically, she may also forfeit the pretext for composing her verses. Penelope, in the first letter of the *Heroides,* also realizes the futility of her lament if her beloved Ulysses has already chosen another woman: "Haec ego dum stulte metuo, quae vestra libido est, / esse peregrino captus amore potes."[63] If the strength of her plea does not effectively convince Franco's beloved of her pathetic condition, she asks that "il picciolo dio, bendato arciero" (the small god, the blindfolded archer), who initially wounded her, intercede on her behalf.[64]

In the closing verses of capitolo 3, she evokes the original scene of their love and their intimate encounters in the "bramata stanza" (coveted room) enclosed within the boundaries of the protected and virginal city: "mio nido" (my nest) and "dolce loco" (sweet site). Franco eulogizes her city as the locus of natural "piaceri" (pleasures); in her revery, she unites a terrestrial and profane Venus with her divine Apollo, who in "scienzia ed in sembianza" (knowledge and in mien) excels all other lovers. Or is this the reunion of lovers in the "stanza" of love poetry—a love that exists solely in the lover's imagination and on the written page?

The setting moves from the country back to the city in capitolo 17. A reunion of lovers constitutes the dramatic focus of this poem. The woman speaker's jealously switches into passionate anger which precipitates a quarrel that has as its backdrop the literary salon, presumably in her lover's own home. It is here that she catches him unawares, as he holds (or possibly discusses with friends) his new edition of poems in praise of another woman.

> *Ma pur furono ingrate l'opre tue,*
> *poi che pensar ad altra donna osasti,*
> *e limar versi de le lodi sue:*
>   *farlo celatamente ti pensasti,*
> *ma io ti sopragiunsi a l'improviso,*
> *quando manco di me tu dubitasti.* (17.31–36)

> But also your endeavors were unkind, for of another woman you dared think and you limned verses offering her praise; you hoped to do this on the sly, but suddenly I came upon you when you least suspected that I might.

Her courtly evocation of the "bramata stanza" (coveted room) that closed capitolo 3 transforms into *stanze* that betray her affections. In his praise of another woman, her beloved has externalized and made public his exaltation and celebration of another muse:

> *Quel libro d'altrui lodi in sen si mise*
> *questo importuno, acciò ch'io nol vedessi:*
> *ahi contrarie in amor voglie divise!* (17.64–66)

> The book praising another against his breast the scoundrel hid from me. Ah, divided and at odds are the desires of love!

This rejection conceived in textual terms, much more severe than a sexual betrayal, radically reworks a scene of male betrayal in Propertius's *Elegies*. In elegy 8 in book 4, Cynthia, overwhelmed by suspicions of her beloved's infidelity and by anger, catches her lover unaware and physically assaults him as he entertains and makes love to two courtesans.

> It was the creaking of the door hinges I heard first,
> and the hum of voices in the entrance hall,
> but it wasn't long before Cynthia burst
> in, flattening the doors against the wall,
> with her hair unkempt, but beautiful
> in the wildness of her fury; and the cup slipped
> from my paralysed fingers, my jaw dropped
> and my wine-stained lips grew pale. [65]

In Propertius's view, male infidelity provokes female passion, the ultimate sign and manifestation of female love and desire. Cynthia's fury, he believes, attests to her sexual desire. [66]

Franco alters this scene in order to emphasize, not the woman's physical passion, but her lack of faith and her impatience with her lover's repeated proclamations of fidelity. She denounces the deceptive power of his language, which has falsely convinced her of the validity of his professed love. She cries: "Ben son di vezzi e di lusinghe pieni / i tuoi detti eloquenti" [vv. 52–53] (Your eloquent discourse is full of endearments and affectations). Here the elegiac laments of Ovid's heroines inform the pathos of the woman speaker's lament. The amorous love epistle composed by Phyllis and addressed to her beloved Demophoon, who is away at sea, might have suggested to Franco the means by which such radical shifts in emotion and tone may be expressed by a deceived woman.

Hence in the exordium to capitolo 17 the man's attributes have changed radically from the "valoroso amante" (valorous lover) of capitolo 3 to the now "disleale amante" (disloyal lover):

> *Questa la tua Veronica ti scrive,*
> *signor ingrato e disleale amante,*
> *di cui sempre in sospetto ella ne vive.*
> *A te, perfido, noto è bene in quante*
> *maniere del mio amore ti feci certo,*
> *da me non mai espresse altrui davante.* (17.1–6)

> Veronica writes this letter to you, thankless Lord and disloyal lover, whom, while she lives, she will suspect. Perfidious as you are, you know quite well the many things I did to assure you of my love and never had expressed before to another.

What began as an accusation of male infidelity is replaced by a courteous reminder of the appropriate form that his love for her should assume in an epistolary relationship with a woman:

> *Tu non m'avresti in tanti giorni scritto,*
> *che star t'avvenne di parlarmi privo,*
> *mostrando esser di ciò mesto ed afflitto,*
> *com'io cortesemente ora ti scrivo.* (17.22–25)

> You did not speak to me for many days and claimed you were sad and dejected because of it, but you would not write to me, as I so courteously am writing to you now.

One must, she dogmatically asserts, follow the correct mode of prescribed behavior dictated by society's code for a public amorous discourse. At the very least this behavior can substitute an appropriate courtly demeanor for true feeling. In a reversal of received notions about the unfaithful, uneducated, and vulgar courtesan, she criticizes her lover's chivalric posture by assuming the kind of moral and even superior tone that she later uses in her *Lettere familiari a diversi*.

An ambiguously seductive allusion to, and deliberate polysemy of, the many "maniere" in which her love had expressed itself to him quickly changes into a *captatio benevolentiae* in which she champions and praises her beloved's virtues.

> *Non niego già che 'n te non sia gran merto*
> *di senno, di valor, di gentilezza,*
> *e d'arti ingenue, onde sei tanto esperto.* (17.7–9)
>
> I certainly would not deny that you possess great merits of wisdom, valor, gentleness, and in the liberal arts in which you are most proficient.

She coyly reminds him that there are many others who appreciate and take delight in her grace and beauty:

> *Ma la mia grazia ancor, la mia bellezza,*
> *quello che 'n se medesma ella si sia,*
> *da molti spirti nobili s'apprezza.* (17.10–12)
>
> But my charm, too, my beauty—whatever it might be in itself— is prized by many noble souls.

To continue to show him her love, she knows, is to prolong her error. Nonetheless, she proceeds "contra ragione" (against reason) to explain to him why other "nobili" (nobles) deem her worthy of their admiration.

Her scolding alternates between erotic double entendres ("teco legata in dolce nodo vivo" [tied to you in a double knot]), tongue-in-cheek coyness, and respectful submission to her beloved's mastery of a chivalric poetic code. Altering the erotic nature of the classical elegists' scene of betrayal, the scene of infidelity in capitolo 17, replete with vibrant detail, assumes comic proportions. We watch the struggle between male and female lovers unfolding in the woman speaker's narrative as we might watch the unraveling of a love-intrigue plot.[67] The courtesan snatches from her disloyal lover the volume of poems that praise another woman.

> *e 'l libro stretto in mano,*
> *altrove il piè da te fuggendo volsi,*
> > *bench'ir non ti potei tanto lontano,*
> *ch'al lato non mi fosti, e non facesti*
> *tue scuse, e 'l libro mi chiedesti invano.* (17.71–75)

> The book clasped in my hand, I turned from you in flight but you
> were not even outdistanced, when at my side, once again, you pre-
> sented your excuses and begged in vain that I should yield the
> book.

She publicly exposes, as a means of retaliation, the nature of their amorous relationship. She responds to her beloved's public betrayal by uncovering their private commitment in love. Whereas the laments of Ovid's
heroines in the *Heroides* are confined to a one-way trajectory of inaction,
never able to exceed the letter's insular boundaries, Franco's accusations, in
the tradition of satire, refer and appeal to a recognizable and tight-knit Venetian society. Both the opinions of his "buoni vicini" (good neighbors) and
the prompting of Ovid's *Amore* have convinced her to assume the benevolent rhetorical stance of the courteous lover who permits her beloved another chance to redeem himself:

> *La buonasera in nome suo ti manda*
> *per me 'l buono e cortese Lomellini,*
> *e ti saluta e ti si raccomanda.*
> *Tu hai, non so perché, buoni vicini,*
> *che ti lodano e impetranoti il bene,*
> *se ben per torta strada tu camini.* (17.97–102)

> On his behalf the good and courteous Lomellini bids you a good
> night and greets you and commends himself to you. You have, I
> cannot see why, good neighbors who praise you and plead all the
> best for you, even though you walk a crooked path.

But by the third and final verse epistle in the group, capitolo 20, "Veronica" no longer feels any intimacy with her beloved, nor is she convinced
that the persuasive power of her verses will succeed in changing his cruelty
into love. In the exordium to capitolo 20, she calls herself "that one," and
she further estranges herself from her lover by using the formal and courteous "voi" in her address. Here the opening extends beyond the third line
to the end of the next tercet:

> *Questa quella Veronica vi scrive,*
> *che per voi, non qual già libera e franca,*
> *or d'infelice amor soggetta vive;*
> *per voi rivolta da via dritta a manca,*
> *uom ingrato, crudel, misera corre*
> *dove 'l duol cresce e la speranza manca.* (20.1–6)

> This letter is written to you by that Veronica who lives now neither
> free nor frank but as a slave of unrequited love; turned for your sake

from the righteous onto the wrongful path, oh thankless cruel man, in misery she hastens where sorrow thrives and hope does not abide.

She posits one definition of the act of loving, "libera e franca" (free and frank), against its converse, "soggetta" (enslaved), by referring to the multivalent interpretations of her name. By playing with verbal resonances, she creates a tension between society's traditional notion of the free and unfaithful courtesan who loves more than one man, and her own self-identification as a faithful and devoted lover.[68]

To call further attention to the role reversal, Franco adopts the *exclusus amator* scene from classical elegy; there the male lover is refused access to the woman's home. He stands at its threshold and sings to the unyielding door that divides her from him.[69] Franco's rendition enfolds three scenes into one. The Propertian rejected and drunken lover's lament is mirrored in an ironic reversal in the swooning woman's reaction to the doorkeeper's report that her beloved sleeps with another woman. Instead of swooning under the effects of inebriation, as was common practice among scorned male lovers of classical elegy, she falls into the arms of her faithful companion, overcome by grief rather than wine.[70] But the faithful companion accompanies her, she suggests, not only out of devotion but because he loves her. She asks, why can she not love him who loves her?

> *Dure disagguaglianze in aspro amore,*
> *poi ch'a chi m'odia corro dietro, e fuggo*
> *da chi de l'amor mio languisce e more!*
>
> Fierce, inequities of cruel love; for I chase after him who detests me
> and I shun the one who pines and dies of love for me. (20.58–60)

The Ovidian confrontation and dialogue between the excluded lover and the doorkeeper occupy a central position in her address. In Ovid's text the male lover's address is no longer directed solely to an inanimate object (the door), but to a real person, a situation that increases the potential for dramatic action. In a series of *captatio benevolentiae*, the lover tries various tactics in order to convince the doorkeeper of the urgency of his request. Ovid's parody of both Propertius's self-absorbed lover's lament and the role of the door (he introduces a servile doorkeeper) stand at the least serious extreme of the *paraclausithyron* tradition in classical elegiac poetry.[71]

As in capitolo 17, the characters presented in Franco's verse epistle are placed within an intimate and identifiable Venetian stage set. The woman's wandering the street at night in an attempt to consummate her desire alludes not only to the classical elegists' *exclusus amator* but also perhaps to the restless wanderings of the foreigner Julio in the popular and sensually charged Venetian dialect play, the anonymous *La venexiana*. Julio comes to Venice in search of female companions and ends up moving through the streets at night between one woman and another.[72] In a switch of roles in capitolo 20, the courtesan, rather than the foreign male visitor, goes to her lover's home in an effort to quell her desire, but is barred entrance by the doorkeeper. She becomes the *exclusus amator* and thus condemns her lover's cruelty and infidelity. And rather than the courtesan entertaining many lovers, it is the male who betrays her trust by making love to another woman. His refusal to reciprocate her love only reinforces and intensifies the bond, now conceived as an imprisoning force, that pulls her to him. He is the one who tyrannizes, and she, by contrast, the one who pleads for his love. Not only is she chained by Amor's playful and irresponsible will, she is also "a slave" to a merciless lover.

In Propertius's 1.16, the door is the speaker throughout. As Catullus had done before him in *carmen* 67, the door attests to the woman's lack of fidelity:[73]

> My mistress doesn't seem to care
> though she's the loosest girl in Rome,
> and you know what modern Romans are.
> And I can't stop her doing wrong.
> Alas that I should come to this:
> the subject of a dirty song.
> And then, what makes it even worse,
> there's always someone left outside
> who tries to woo me with his verse.

The lover is chained to his beloved like the door, which, contrary to its wishes, is forced to listen to frustrated lovers' "dirty songs."[74] The stern moralistic door exploits the situation to unburden itself and comments upon the hundreds of drunken male lovers' erotic laments that it has endured and recorded over the years. In a reciprocal dialogue with the rejected male lover—silent throughout the monologue—the door confirms the corrupt ways of the woman of the house.

While the male lover's lament in Propertius 1.16 does not succeed in softening the door's rigidity:

> O cruel, cruel door, more heartless than my mistress,
>   will you never open up and let me in?

> Will nothing ever move you to break your stubborn silence
>   and smuggle in a message to my love?

Franco's lament in capitolo 20 is more successful. The unhinging and
groaning bolts, as the woman lover's lament forces the door to yield, call to
mind Dante's description of the majestic opening of the gates of purgatory,
sealed from human access for hundreds of years.[75]

Unlike in Propertius's 1.16, in Ovid's *Amores* 1.6 and Franco's capitolo
20, each of the roles—the *exclusus amator,* the door, and the doorkeeper—
has a distinct and separate voice. No longer is the door the sole focus.
Thus, in Franco's version the exchange among the lover, the door, and the
beloved's doorkeeper oscillates from one voice to another in an operatic trio:

> —*Deh siatemi in amor benigne scorte;*
> *apritemi 'l sentier del mio ben chiuso,*
> *del notturno mio error per uso accorte.*
>   *Di letal sonno e tu, custode, infuso,*
> *desto al latrar de' tuoi vigili cani,*
> *non far il prego mio vano e deluso:*
>   *deh, pietoso ad aprirmi usa le mani,*
> *così i ceppi servili aspri dal piede,*
> *che continuo ti stian sciolti e lontani!*—
>   *Ma ch'è quel, che da me, lassa, si chiede?*
> —*Vattene in pace*—*il portinaio dice,*—
> *che le notti il signor qui non risiede;*
>   *ma, del suo amor a far lieta e felice*
> *un'altra donna, con lei dorme e giace,*
> *e tu invan qui ti consumi, infelice.*
>   *Vattene, sconsolata; e, s'aver pace*
> *non puoi, pur con saldo animo sopporta*
> *quel ch'al destino irrevocabil piace.* —(20.31–48)

Ah, would that in love you were my benign guides
who, accustomed to my nightly errand,
might cut for me a path to locked-in joy,
and you, doorkeeper, steeped in mortal sleep,
aroused by the bark of your watchful dogs,
do not reject and disappoint my plea;
ah, lift your hand and mercifully unlock;
your servile shackles then will fall away
forever gone and loosened from your feet.
    But what do you demand, alas, of this poor soul?
"Be gone in peace." the watchman says

"My master does not reside here at night:
but with another woman lies and sleeps,
to make her gay and happy with his love,
while you, disconsolate, stand here despairing in vain.
    So leave, poor wretch; and though you cannot
find peace, you must endure with steadfast heart
what pleases irrevocable destiny."

Franco's doorkeeper does not refuse her access to his master's home; he simply warns her that his master sleeps with another woman. Even though there is no extended development of the concept of the doorkeeper's servility, as in Ovid's transformation of the Propertian servile lover, there is a reference to servility when she exhorts the custodian to unlock "i ceppi servili aspri dal piede" (the servile shackles from his feet).[76]

The *paraclausithyron* in capitolo 20 introduces, in the manner of a theatrical prologue, the rest of the poem, in which the woman speaker nearly loses herself in repeated and lengthy laments on her misfortunes in love. Denials of love spur her amorous expressions, intended "indurvi a pietà con le preghiere" (to induce you to pity with prayers). Her piteous laments are crossed, however, with moments of rational detachment in which she ponders the futility of amorous disorder, a theme Franco treated with delightful, even comic, objectivity in capitolo 8. But in capitolo 20 she focuses instead on the tragic absurdity of her personal dilemma: she pursues a lover who despises her, rejects a man who devotes himself faithfully to her, and by intensely suffering from her lover's betrayal, she paradoxically consoles another woman who continues to enjoy the company of her unfaithful lover:

> E così ad un me stessa ed altrui struggo,
> e 'l sangue de le mie e l'altrui vene
> col mio grave dolor consumo e suggo:
>   benché da l'altro canto le mie pene
> forse consolan altra donna, e 'l pianto
> con piacer del mio amante al cor perviene. (20.61–66)

And thus I destroy myself and another at the same time, and with my deep grief, I consume and drain the blood from my own and from another's veins: although my sorrows will perhaps console another woman and my tears reach and please my lover's heart.

She switches back and forth from controlled explanations for her plight, insisting that her lover treat her with the kind of respect and courteous behavior she deserves ("Ma né con questo voglio acquistarvi io: / solo a l'alta pietà del mio martire / farvi per cortesia benigno e pio" [But neither do I intend to conquer you by this: I only wish that out of courtesy you should kindly and with benevolence look upon the piteous depths of my travail]), to irrational swirls of jealous delusion, in which she requests an early death to mitigate her torments, invoking thereby the *carpe diem* motifs of classical elegy. Unlike Labé's elegies addressed to "ladies of Lyons," Franco's elegiac verses speak directly and passionately to a male lover.[77] Yet while addressing this verse epistle to him who persists in wrongdoing, she also alerts women not suspecting male treachery.

> *Nè così vola fuor d'arco saetta,*
> *com'al mio essempio mosse fuggiranno*
> *d'amarvi a gara l'altre donne in fretta;*
> *e, quanto del mio mal pietate avranno,*
> *tanto, dal vostro orgoglio empio a schivarsi,*
> *caute a l'esperienzia mia saranno.* (20.247–52)
>
> The arrow does not so swiftly flash from the bow as other women
> moved by my example will flee in hasty contest from loving you;
> and to the extent that they will pity my grief, made cautious by my
> experience, they will eschew your wicked pride.

Her condemnations of male deception are interlaced nonetheless with erotic longings; she yearns to have the man before her desire is spent in vain, thus dramatizing the illogical extremes of sexual desire:

> *Prima che 'l duol di me si sazi e sbrame,*
> *e mi riduca in cenere quest'ossa,*
> *date ristoro a le mie ardenti brame.* (20.133–35)
>
> Before grief sates its hunger and lust for me and these bones are
> reduced to ashes, pray quench my ardent yearnings.

However, an increasing solidarity with women betrayed in love resurfaces in capitoli 21, 22, and especially in capitolo 24, when Franco examines her reasons for banishing herself voluntarily from her beloved *patria*. The passing of time and the power of memory assist her in reconstructing the "commesso errore" (committed error) and in eradicating her grief. Like Philomel, who weaves her story of sexual violence and physical mutilation into a tapestry for others to read, Franco first addresses her own heart in capitolo 21 in an interior monologue, and then in capitolo 22, she exposes her personal situation for another's profit. Finally in capitolo 24 she addresses a male interlocutor who has threatened a woman with physical aggression and verbal slurs. Thus, she moves from the passive solipsistic laments in capitoli 21 and 22, in which she uncovers her own self-delusions in love, to, in capitolo 24, the active position as defender of another woman's rights.

Franco chastises herself in capitolo 21 for having believed that "la lontananza" (the distance) can heal love's afflictions. If "le armi mie proprie" ([her] own weapons) have brought her such misery, she asks, what will cruel fortune inflict on her already pitiable state? Just as Philomel and Procne mirror her amorous grief, Echo responds to her desperate laments, which have left her devoid of strength.[78] Probing her psychological vulnerabilities, Franco attempts to uncover not only her own personal weaknesses but those common to any woman lover, especially when faced with male treachery.

> *Io dicea:—Mio cor, se ciò mi fanno*
> *l'armi mie proprie, quelle, onde mi punge*
> *la fortuna crudel, che mi faranno?—*
> *S'io stessa, col fuggir dal mio ben lunge,*
> *sento che 'l duol via più mi s'avvicina,*
> *che la partenza mia mel ricongiunge;*
> *al mio languir contraria medicina*
> *certo avrò preso al vaneggiar del core,*
> *che per misera strada m'incamina.* (21.1–9)

I said: "Dear heart, if my own weapons do this to me, what will those do with which cruel fate stabs me?" If I myself feel that, as I flee from my beloved, my departure brings him closer to my side: I must certainly have taken a medicine contrary to my languid state and to the ravings of my heart, which lead me down a wretched path.

Her exile, she declares in the next poem, was spurred involuntarily by "l'odio di colui" (the rancor of him) who has wrongly accused her of deception. The memory of his disdain elicits a restaging of the initial scene of departure. Having already identified herself in capitolo 3 with her inviolate city, Franco defines her grief in this poem as the pain of a divided self: she is far from her homeland and by extension, herself, and far from her lover's "raggio" (ray).[79]

> *Oh com'è privo d'intelletto, e quanto*
> *colui s'inganna, che nel patrio nido*
> *viver può lieto col suo bene a canto,*
> *e va cercando or l'uno or l'altro lido,*

pensando forse che la lontananza
ai colpi sia d'Amor rifugio fido! (21.52–57)

O, how self-deceiving and bereft of intellect is anyone who can live
happily in his homeland with his beloved at his side, exploring this
shore and that, thinking perhaps that distancing oneself offers a
safe refuge from the pangs of Love!

Unlike in capitolo 21, in the next capitolo she remembers both what was a
denial of love and what now is an absence of passion. Indignation replaces
self-pity. No longer do her verses seek to move her interlocutor to feel compassion. Rhetorical questions interrupt her laments, which now are self-
directed. Her description of the pastoral "locus amoenus" to which she is
unjustly confined is highly charged with lusty vitality, thus anticipating
the pastoral portrayal of her sojourn in Della Torre's villa in Fumane in
capitolo 25. While she is in involuntary exile, every natural spectacle, from
wild animals roaming the valleys to birds perched together on a tree, adds
to her torment rather than extinguishing it. Unlike Petrarch, who in sonnet 35 ("Solo et pensoso i più deserti campi") also lamented the sensuality of
nature, from which he felt alienated by his unhappy love, Franco's feeling of
dissatisfaction extends beyond her individual misery to include a meditation on the unfortunate situation in which all women in love find themselves.[80] Female nature, "molle, ed imbecilla" (weak and foolish), makes it
more difficult, she argues, for women to resist the uncontrollable force of
love's passion:

> *Far non può de le donne resistenza*
> *la natura sì molle ed imbecilla,*
> *di Venere del figlio a la potenza;*
>   *picciol'aura conturba la tranquilla*
> *feminil mente, e di tepido foco*
> *l'alma semplice nostra arde e sfavilla.* (22.73–78)
>
> Women's weak and foolish nature cannot offer any resistance to the
> power of Venus's son; the softest breeze disturbs the female mind,
> and a tepid fire sends our simple souls up in flames and sparks.

Even though man is provided with reason and intelligence with which to
govern the world, he chooses paradoxically an "abominosa guerra" (detest-
able war) in love, rather than the peaceful "desir dolci d'amor" (sweet
desires of love). And women, "weaker" than men when struck by the force
of love, do not "oppugnar o assaglia" (oppose or assail) them, but passively
resist their aggressions.

L'uom, che, se non vuol, rado o mai non erra,
fa, nei desir d'amor dolci, a se stesso
così continua abominosa guerra,
  sì ch'a lui poi d'amar non è concesso,
senza trovar di repugnanti voglie
de la persona amata il core impresso. (22.64–69)

Man, who if he so wishes rarely or never errs, wages such continuous and abominable war against himself in his desire for sweet
loves that in the end it is impossible for him to love without finding
the beloved's heart marked by repugnant lust.

Rather than contesting irrational male anger directly, women relinquish
control by assuming the position of "vassalla" (vassal). Franco, too, has
gone against her own desires by willfully absenting herself from a city that
she loves in order to quell the force of her lover's anger. She reflects on the
self-destructiveness of her own selflessness and on the error of believing that
she might gain her lover's commitment by providing him, through her absence, with the freedom to choose.

Per darti luogo, venni in queste parti,
ed al tuo arbitrio di te cassa vivo,
sperando in tal maniera d'acquistarti.
  Qui, dov'è 'l prato verde e chiaro il rivo,
venni, e de le dolci onde al roco suono,
e degli uccelli al canto e parlo e scrivo. (22.97–102)

To give you room I have come to these parts, and by your whim, I
live without you hoping thus to conquer you. Here, where the
meadow is green and the brook is clear, I have come, and surrounded by the raucous sound of sweet waves and the song of birds,
I speak and write.

Per far la voglia altrui paga e contenta
io diparti, sperando alfin quell'ira,
se non estinguer, far tepida e lenta. (22.199–201)

To satisfy and please another's wish I left, hoping at last, if not to
extinguish, at least to cool and slow that anger down.

By the poem's close, however, the woman speaker dissociates herself from
her cursed love. Resolved to leave her pastoral refuge, a place that only
mimics her pain, she now directs her address to "Adria," asking devotedly
for forgiveness, while announcing her intention to return there as quickly
as possible:

> *Ad Adria col pensier devoto interno*
> *ritorno e, lagrimando, espressamente*
> *a prova del martir l'error mio scerno.* (22.220–22)

To Adria I return with my inner and devoted thought, and weeping, to offer a proof of my grief, I expressly denounce my mistake.

Hence, once restored to her beloved city, Franco speaks in capitolo 24 on behalf of a woman unable to defend herself from the aggressions of an irrational lover. Extending what was an abstract theory of women's physical weakness in capitolo 22, Franco now offers reasons why a woman, when opposed physically or denounced with injurious verbal assaults, chooses to succumb rather than to counter male vindictiveness with an equal display of force.

Having regained the strength that she had temporarily lost in the torment of unrequited love, Franco provides an astute analysis of the power struggle between men and women. Foreshadowing the language and tone of her *Lettere familiari a diversi,* Franco advises a young noble, "un uomo diviso, / dai fecciosi costumi del vil volgo" (a man set apart from the base customs of the rabble), to control the force of his emotions before committing a crime of passion—the disfiguring of his beloved's face—that reports say he has threatened. She tells him that she knows only too well the extremes to which irrational anger can push an unhappy lover, and she therefore implores him to make amends and to admit to the immorality of his behavior:

> *Da l'altra parte so quanto è molesto*
> *lo spron de l'ira, e come spesso ei mena*
> *a quel ch'è vergognoso ed inonesto:*
> > *né sempre la ragion, che i sensi affrena,*
> *a stringer pronto in man si trova il morso,*
> *e 'l gran soverchio rompe ogni catena.* (24.43–48)

On the other hand I know how vexing the spur of anger is, and how often it leads to what is dishonest and shameful: nor does reason, which governs the senses, always hold the bit, ready to pull it in, and excessive force will break any chain.

Though lacking the freedom of choice that men enjoy in their amorous relationships, and physically weaker than men, women nevertheless possess, she reminds him, equal intelligence and virtue:

> *Povero sesso, con fortuna ria*
> *sempre prodotto, perch'ognor soggetto*
> *e senza libertà sempre si stia!*
> * Né però di noi fu certo il diffetto,*
> *che, se ben come l'uom non sem forzute,*
> *come l'uom mente avemo ed intelletto.* (24.55–60)

> Pitiable sex, always brought forth with a cruel fate, so that it will
> forever be deprived of freedom and enslaved! But surely it was not
> our fault, for even if we are not as strong as men, we nonetheless,
> like men, have a mind and intellect.

Further, women tend to be wiser than men, because they adhere to the dictates of reason, patience, and modesty rather than the "insolenze" (insolent
acts) indicative of a "pazzo" (crazy man). Virtue, she emphasizes, resides
not in corporeal strength but in the "vigor de l'alma" (vigor of the soul):

> *Né in forza corporal sta la virtute,*
> *ma nel vigor de l'alma e de l'ingegno,*
> *da cui tutte le cose son sapute.* (24.61–63)

> Nor does virtue reside in bodily strength, but in the vigor of the
> soul and in the mind, through which all things are known.

As if to underscore the worldly wisdom she herself has acquired, the language of the observations that follows is increasingly colloquial and prover-
bial, replete with utilitarian maxims and homespun aphorisms drawn from
the habits of daily life:

> *Del pazzo è proprio l'esser insolente,*
> *ma quel sasso del pozzo il savio tragge,*
> *ch'altri a gettarlo fu vano e imprudente.* (24.73–75)

> It is typical for a madman to be insolent, but a wise man retrieves
> from the well the stone that another, who is foolish and impudent,
> has cast into it.

Importantly, while offering the reasons for controlling unleashed anger,
Franco also reflects on the origins of female passivity. This woman's patience had blinded this man from seeing that her unwillingness to respond
is not a sign of weakness or an admission of guilt, but rather a conscious
decision not to destroy the world, "which is so beautiful." This explanation
of female submissiveness takes into account what Franco had in previous
capitoli attributed only to their physical "natura." She argues in this poem
that a woman assumes an enslaved position only because she is intent on

rejecting unwise actions or subscribing to physical aggression. Thus partly from a learned social response and partly from innate desire to "preserve" the world, a woman submits to male power, relinquishing her equal right to rule.

> *Per non guastar il mondo, ch'è sì bello*
> *per la specie di noi, la donna tace,*
> *e si sommette a l'uom tiranno e fello,*
> *   che poi del regnar tanto si compiace,*
> *sì come fanno 'l più quei che non sanno*
> *(ché 'l mondan peso a chi più sa più spiace),*
> *   che gli uomini perciò grand'onor fanno*
> *a le donne, perché cessero a loro*
> *l'imperio, e sempre a lor serbato l'hanno.* (24.88–96)

So as not to spoil the world, which thanks to our species is so beautiful, a woman keeps silent and submits to a villainous and tyrannical man, who is then so very pleased at ruling over everything, as are all those who do not know (for mundane burdens most vex those who know most), that men honor women so highly because they (women) relinquished power to them and always preserved it for them.

What is more, even the "uom tiranno e fello" (the male tyrant and traitor) honors women who obediently cede the power to rule to them. Men bow reverently to the "alto tesoro" (esteemed treasure) that women represent when embellished with silks, embroideries, and precious jewels. In their worshipping of women as idols, men adhere as well to the courteous dictates of sixteenth-century society:[81]

> *Quinci sete, ricami, argento ed oro,*
> *gemme, porpora, e qual è di più pregio*
> *si pon in adornarne alto tesoro;*
> *   e, qual conviensi al nostro senno egregio,*
> *non sol son ricchi i nostri adornamenti*
> *d'ogni pomposo e più prezzato fregio,*
> *   ma gli uomini a noi vengon riverenti,*
> *e ne cedono 'l luogo in casa e in strada,*
> *in ciò non punto tardi o negligenti.* (24.97–105)

Hence silks, embroideries, silver and gold, gems, crimson cloth, and all that is most valuable is used to adorn their great treasure; and as behooves our distinguished wisdom, not only are our adornments enriched with every stately and precious frill, but men

> approach us with reverence and make way for us at home and in
> the street, being not a bit remiss or slow in this.

Franco's stance here is more that of moral and social counselor on questions of etiquette than of a repudiator of male deceit; a corrective and advisory voice runs throughout her amorous elegiac verses. In these verse epistles, unlike in her familiar letters, however, Franco restores a language of desire to Renaissance women poets by furnishing a female-authored voice for the "truncated calls" of Ovidian heroines. This she does by aligning herself with women's denunciatory complaints in the Ovidian epistle and by reappropriating a classical, female ventriloquized lament as her own.

IV

While Franco's elegiac verses exhibit the illogical extremes to which unrequited love and deception conventionally push a lover poet, in capitolo 25 the woman speaker's measured verses and sensuous details demonstrate her renewed sense of inner peace and self-control.[82] Drawing from a rich panoply of descriptive languages—landscape and pastoral poetry, and poetic ecphrasis—Franco praises Della Torre's country villa in Fumane where she has had the pleasure of being his guest. She paints, with close attention to aesthetic composition, an elegant, decorous portrait of the life of the leisured classes in the Venetian *terraferma*.[83] The poem extols her host's moral and spiritual excellence, coupled with his worldly connoisseurship. Rejoicing in the reciprocal union of sensual pleasures with spiritual excellence, Franco's tone throughout this lengthy capitolo (561 verses) is exuberant.

The poem was composed upon her return to Venice, possibly in 1575. In it Franco calls upon her artistic, spiritual, and sensual powers to help her to reconstruct from her memory the visual and spiritual impact of her pastoral sojourn:

> *E pur, formando un pensier dolce amaro,*
> *con la memoria a quei diletti torno,*
> *che infiniti a me quivi si mostraro:*
>   *sempre davanti gli occhi ho 'l bel soggiorno,*
> *da cui lontan col corpo, con la mente,*
> *senza da me partirlo unqua, soggiorno:*
>   *ricrear tutta in me l'alma si sente,*
> *mentre qua giù sì lieto paradiso*
> *da dover contemplar le sta presente.* (25.16–24)

And yet, forming a bittersweet thought, with my memory I return to the infinite delights that appeared to me there: I always have

before my eyes that fair site where, absent in body, I still dwell with
my mind without ever leaving it: the soul in me feels completely
reborn when such a cheerful paradise on earth lies in front of her for
her to contemplate.

While complimenting Della Torre's aesthetic sensibilities, she also calls attention throughout the poem to her own ability to perceive beauty in art
and nature. Indeed, this strategy of double praise recalls Franco's involvement in collaborative poetic projects where the praise of one is tantamount
to the praise of many.

Franco sets up a series of contrasts in the opening tercets: on the one
hand, she contrasts the pain of having had to leave such a glorious haven
with the "soverchio piacer" (abundant pleasure) she has obtained; on the
other, she compares the power of the human imagination with the rewards
of heavenly favor. Her imagination guides and assists her in reassembling
"le vestigie espresse" (the external signs) to form an integrated aesthetic
whole.

> *Non vorrei da l'un canto esser mai stata*
> *a quel bel loco, per dover partire,*
> *come fei, non ben quivi anco arrivata.*
> * Così gravoso il ben suol divenire,*
> *che, quant'egli è maggior, via maggior duolo*
> *col dilungarsi in noi suol partorire:*
> *   tosto ne va 'l piacer trascorso a volo;*
> *né ponendo in ragion l'util passato,*
> *a la perdita mesti attendem solo.*
> * E non vorrei però da l'altro lato*
> *sì vago nido non aver veduto,*
> *a la tranquillità soave e grato.* (25.1–12)

On the one hand I would prefer never to have been in that beautiful
place only to leave, as I did, even before I had properly arrived. A
good thing often becomes so burdensome that the greater it is, the
greater is the grief it breeds in us by lingering on; the pleasure we
enjoyed quickly flies off, and giving no thought to past benefit, we
sadly remember only our loss. On the other hand, though, I would
rather not have missed seeing such a serene nest, gracious and dear
to tranquillity.

Her memory aids her as she "rereads" the landscape; she rediscovers in her
meditative musings the natural geometric precision of the terrain and

gardens, delighting in the hidden and unexpected variations of the natural spectacle.[84]

She returns in her memory to the villa's "verron del marmo bianco" (white marble balcony), where she first trained her eye to distinguish nature's art from human ingenuity. Emphasizing the "impresa alta" of her *fictional* undertaking, she stresses two things simultaneously: the power of art to correct nature's imperfections, a view lent authority by Aristotle, Horace, and Seneca, and the poet's skill—by implication her own—to perfect the aesthetic beauty she beholds:

> *In questo piglio in man pronta lo stile;*
> *e, per gradir al sentimento, fingo*
> *quel loco quanto possi al ver simile:*
>   *e, se ben so ch'a impresa alta m'accingo,*
> *tirata da la mia propria vaghezza,*
> *senz'arte quel ch'io so disegno e pingo.*
>   *Oh che fiorita e gioconda bellezza*
> *quivi mostra e dispiega la natura,*
> *raro altrove o non mai mostrarla avezza!* (25.34–42)

> For this I readily pick up my pen, and to gratify my emotions I recreate that place as close to the truth as I can: and though I know that I am undertaking an arduous task, urged on by my affection, I artlessly paint and draw that which I know. O what flowering and joyful beauty nature displays there, such as she rarely or never is accustomed to show elsewhere!

Her painterly evocation of the "bellezze eterne" (eternal beauties) in Fumane associates nature with artifice, forming yet a third term, *natura artificialis*.[85] Alluding to Boccaccio's description of the naturally ordered configuration of the *Valle delle Donne* in the conclusion to the sixth day of the *Decameron*—a place removed from the evils and excesses of urban life—Franco's description of Fumane's "rotonda valle" (round valley) similarly celebrates a landscape ruled by "natural" reason.[86] In each case, the valley constitutes a perfect rational shape—a circle:

> *Il piano che nella valle era, così era ritondo come se a sesta fosse stato fatto, quantunque artificio della natura e non manual paresse.* (Boccaccio 6.20)

> The floor of the valley was perfectly circular in shape, for all the world as if it had been made with compasses, though it seemed the work of nature rather than of man.

Di lieti colli adorno cerchio serra
l'infinita beltà del vago piano,
dove Flora e Pomona alberga ed erra.
    Quasi per gradi su di mano in mano
di fuor s'ascende 'l poggio da le spalle
sempre al salir più facile e più piano;
        quinci in giù per soave e destro calle
s'arriva a la pianura in pochi passi,
ch'è posta in forma di rotonda valle. (25.64–72)

The adorned circle of merry hills encloses the infinite beauty of the
fair plain where Flora and Pomona abide and roam. Outside, almost by degrees, a step at a time you climb up the slope from the
back, and it becomes easier and less steep as you ascend; from there,
downward along a smooth and gentle path, in a few steps you reach
the plain, which is set in the shape of a round valley.

The ladies' refuge in day 6 of the *Decameron,* a place seemingly free from
disturbance and molestation, provides them with a false sense of security.
But as they undress and bathe in the transparent pool, they reflect on the
effect that this "unruly" action would have on the male companions they
left behind.[87] Recognizing the extent to which they have willfully undermined the *brigata*'s newfound stability, Pampinea, the group's leader, concedes to the men upon their return that "oggi vi pure abbiam noi
ingannati" (we have stolen a march upon you today), to which Dioneo responds, "E come? Cominciate voi prima a far de' fatti che a dir delle parole?" (What? . . . Do you mean to say that you have begun to do these
things even before you talk about them?). To this Pampinea answers, "Signor nostro, sì" (Yes, Your Majesty). While the ladies' overstepping of the
boundaries constructed by the *brigata* to neutralize the morally reprehensible aspects of the tales they narrate temporarily threatens their newfound
order, Franco, by contrast, fearlessly participates in the secluded valley's
wonders as an unthreatened spectator.[88]

Populated by female divinities, the goddesses of flowers and the spring
(Flora and Pomona) and lovers driven by the forces of earthly desire (Apollo
and Daphne), this fragrant landscape unfolds in Franco's imagination as a
mythological narrative—a bucolic tapestry of erotic and sensual love.

De la ninfa la sorte così acerba
pietoso Apollo ai grati rami tira,
ed a quivi posar vago tra l'erba:

l'aria d'intorno ancor dolce sospira
di Dafne al caso, e spirto d'odor pieno,
le vaghe foglie ventilando, spira. (88–93)

Full of compassion, Apollo is drawn by the nymph's bitter fate to
the grateful branches and to rest tenderly on the grass: all around
the air still sighs softly over Daphne's bitter destiny, and a scented
breath stirs, breathing, through the enchanted leaves.

The cool waters forming a clear pool at the base of the valley are continually
replenished by nymphs:

Quivi con l'urne non mai stanche o vuote
a portar l'acque son le ninfe pronte,
tai che 'l cristal sì chiaro esser non puote. (25.97–99)

There, with their amphorae never empty or listless, the nymphs
swiftly carry water so that not even a piece of crystal could be so
clear.

They in turn provide temporary physical relief to Diana, the chaste hunt-
ress:

Ed a l'altre compagne cacciatrici,
che, dietro i cervi stanche, a rinfrescarsi
vanno le fronti angeliche beatrici,
  co' bei liquidi argenti intorno sparsi
porgon dolce liquor da trar la sete,
e le candide membra da lavarsi. (25.103–8)

And to their other companions who went to hunt and, exhausted
by their pursuit of the deer, come to freshen their angelic virginal
brows with the delightful silvery water scattered all around, they
offer sweet liquids to quench their thirst and bathe their snow
white limbs.

Following the roaming of her eye back to the waters, now leading from the
natural terrain to the "fiorito amenissimo giardino" (most delightful
flowered garden), Franco's gaze rests on the joining of nature with artifice,
first in the form of a garden planned by human beings and then in the figure
of the palace "giardiniere" (gardener), who controls the waters' natural flow
to form a desired visual aesthetic. Finally her eye settles on the villa whence
she first began her visual survey of her surroundings. Her eye scrutinizes
Della Torre's classicizing "palagio" (palace), situated on the summit of a hill
that dominates the bucolic landscape below. Once again her description of
the palace site echoes Boccaccio's depiction of the geographical location of

the Tuscan country villa (which in turn alluded to Dante's description of the mount of *Purgatorio*), to which the *brigata* have fled from plague-ridden Florence:

> *Era il detto luogo sopra una piccola montagnetta, da ogni parte lontano alquanto alle nostre strade, di vari albuscelli e piante tutte di verdi fronde ripiene piacevole a riguardare; in sul colmo delle quali era un palagio con bello e gran cortile nel mezzo, e con loggie e con sale e con camere, tutte ciascuna verso di se bellissima e di liete dipinture ragguardevole e ornata.*
> (Boccaccio, *Il decamerone*)

Perched on its summit was a palace, built round a fine, spacious courtyard, and containing loggias, halls, and sleeping apartments, which were not only excellently proportioned but richly embellished with paintings depicting scenes of gaiety.

> *Non cede l'arte a la natura il vanto*
> *ne l'artificio del giardin, ornato*
> *d'alberi colti e di sempre verde manto;*
> *   sovra 'l qual porge, alquanto rilevato,*
> *d'architettura un bel palagio tale,*
> *qual fu di quel del Sol già poetato.* (25.127–32)[89]

Art to nature will not yield the crown in the creation of a garden always adorned with rare trees and a green mantle; above this, set on higher ground, architecture offers us a palace as handsome as poets have versified about, that of the Sun.

Like Boccaccio's escape from the bondage of love to rational freedom, so the narrators ascend to an earthly paradise of fertility and order. In this pastoral refuge, moderation and *onestà* prevail.

In the following verses, Franco moves from the balcony inside to the palace's exquisitely decorated rooms: there art outdoes nature, modern talents surpass the ancients, and the visual arts, inspired by both the senses and the intellect, attest to the limitless powers of the human imagination:

> *Infinito tesor ben questo vale*
> *per l'edificio proprio, e gli ornamenti,*
> *che 'n ricchezza e in beltà non hanno eguale.*
> *   I fini marmi e i porfidi lucenti,*
> *cornici, archi, colonne, intagli e fregi,*
> *figure, prospettive, ori ed argenti*
> *   quivi son di tal sorte e di tai pregi,*
> *ch'a tal grado non giungono i palagi,*
> *che fer gli antichi imperadori e regi.* (25.133–41)

This palace is an unlimited treasure for the building itself and also for the many ornaments that are housed there, in opulence and beauty equal to none. The fine marbles and polished porphyries, cornices, arches, columns, carvings, and friezes, the figures, perspectives, the silver and gold are here of such kind and fine quality that it is unmatched by the palaces built by ancient emperors and kings.

While her praise of Della Torre unfolds within a pastoral frame that dramatizes her involvement in her natural surroundings, this Arcadian refuge is far from a celebration of rural innocence. Rather Della Torre's palace represents not a turning away from the urban sophistication of academic coteries—a complaint traditional with pastoral poets—but rather an embracing of the arts as situated within a country setting. His world is not presented as an alternative to the everyday experience of most people but rather as a compelling version of what the world might be. His classical villa attests to the power of human civilization where learning, culture, and spiritual guidance intermingle with the pleasurable simplicity of a pastoral retreat.[90] Indeed the bucolic scene Franco witnesses in Fumane mirrors the artistic decorations that line the palace walls: in many rooms natural human love finds its artistic counterpart in the luxurious tapestries depicting Jupiter's amorous conquests.[91]

> *I dei scender dal cielo innamorati*
> *dietro le ninfe qui si veggon finti,*
> *in diverse figure trasformati;*
> *   e d'amoroso affetto in vista tinti,*
> *seguitar ansiosi il lor desio,*
> *dove dal caldo incendio son sospinti.*
> *   Qui trasformata in vacca si vede Io,*
> *e cent'occhi serrar il suo custode,*
> *al suon di quel, che poi l'uccise, dio.*
> *   Da l'altra parte Danae in sen si gode*
> *vedersi piover Giove in nembo d'oro,*
> *dov'altri più la chiude e la custode;*
> *   il quale altrove, trasformato in toro,*
> *porta Europa; ed altrove, aquila, piglia*
> *Ganimede e 'l rapisce al sommo coro.* (25.157–71)

We see represented the enamoured gods descending from on high in pursuit of nymphs who are transformed into various figures; and they are represented visibly flushed with amorous sentiments, following their lust wherever the hot fire chases them. Here we see Io transformed into a cow, and her warden close by blinks his hundred eyes at the sound of the god by whom he was later slain. In another place Danae is overcome with delight at seeing Jupiter pour into her lap a shower of gold, precisely in the chamber where she is kept under lock and key; Jupiter, who elsewhere is transformed into a bull, carries off Europa and elsewhere, when changed into an eagle, seizes Ganymede and abducts him from the supreme choir.

In these representations, Jupiter's exploits with mortal women take on positive connotations whereby physical love is exalted to an ethereal, even spiritual, level. Much like Franco's positive self-identification with Danae in her depiction of Henri III's visit with her in Venice, discussed in chapter 2, these artistic scenes of Jupiter's passion underscore not an unequal desire between pursuer and love object but an amorous reciprocity between people of different ranks and genders.

Allying herself with Venetian artists who repeatedly challenged ancient authority in their painting and sculpture, Franco attempts to compete with previous poetic ecphrasis in referring to another villa, "quel del Sol già poetato" (v. 132), already the subject of poetic description. She had already compared two Neapolitan villas to Fumane in lines 556–58, but Fumane's architectural excellence surpassed both of them.[92] What is also implied is that her ability to evoke Fumane has outdone her unnamed predecessor. Just as ancient culture posed a formidable challenge for Renaissance artists and writers, so earlier-sixteenth-century poetic descriptions present her with an equally demanding intellectual task.

The battle between the ancients and moderns, so crucial to Venetian poets in the latter half of the sixteenth century, is especially central to art theory in the same period. Franco echoed this debate in a letter she wrote to the Venetian painter Tintoretto (no. 21), published in her *Lettere familiari a diversi,* when she thanked him for the portrait he had done of her. As Ann Rosalind Jones has argued, Franco's "elegant compliments to the painter position her as the subject of a literary portrait she herself composes."[93] Just as she uses ancient culture to laud Della Torre's unparalleled aesthetic excellence, she compliments Tintoretto for outdoing Apelles, Zeuxis, or Praxiteles. Indeed his portrait of her has the magical, even diabolical power, she says, to conjure up a vision. Yet unlike Narcissus, she is capable of resisting the image's illusionistic force. Other viewers, she suggests playfully, might not be so able and will succumb eventually to the painter's mimetic power.

Io non posso, signor Tentoretto, sentire certi, li quali alle volte lodano tanto
gli antichi tempi e biasimano i nostri, che vogliono che la natura agli
uomini della vecchia età fosse tenerissima madre e a quei della nostra sia
crudelissima matrigna. . . . Le quali, infra le altre cose per cui mettono
gli antichi in cielo, fanno che sia la vaghissima e nobilissima arte del di-
pingere e dello scolpire e formar di rilievo, affermando non trovarsi oggidì in
niuna parte del mondo chi arrivi all'eccellenza di Apelle, di Zeusi, di
Apollodoro, di Fidia, di Prasitele e altri nobili e famosi pittori e scultori di
que' tempi, e non so con che fondamento. . . . Vi prometto che, quando ho
veduto il mio ritratto, opera della vostra divina mano, io sono stata un
pezzo in forse se ei fosse pittura o pur fantasima innanzi a me comparita per
diabolico inganno, non mica per farmi innamorare di me stessa, come av-
venne a Narciso, perché, Iddio grazia, non mi tengo sì bella che io tema di
avere a smaniare delle proprie bellezze, ma per alcun altro fine, che so io?

Signor Tintoretto, I cannot bear to listen to certain people who on
occasion will praise ancient times so overhighly and find fault with
our own. People who would claim that the rule of old nature was a
most tender mother, while to our contemporaries she is a very cruel
stepmother indeed. . . . Among the other things that cause them
to praise the ancients to the skies, they include painting, sculptur-
ing, and working in relief, and based on I do not know what, they
declare that nowhere in the world is there to be found anyone who
attains the excellence of Apelles, Zeuxis, Phydias, Praxiteles, and
other noble and famous painters of those days. . . . I promise you
that when I saw my portrait, the work of your divine hand, I won-
dered for quite some time whether it was a painting or a ghost that
had appeared before me because of some diabolical trick. It was certainly not in order for me to fall in love with myself, as happened to
Narcissus, because, thank God, I do not consider myself so beautiful that I should be afraid of going raving mad over my own
charms; but it was for some other reason that I do not know.

Similarly, in her praise of the artistic decorations in Della Torre's villa,
Franco insists on the futility of disparaging contemporary artists by reducing their artistic excellence in comparison to classical models. She marvels
at the countless examples of "il nostro umano ingegno" (our human skill)
she has found in Fumane and delights particularly in the "varie lane tinte"
(different tinted wools) which create an illusion of life simply by "forze di
colori e di disegno" (means of color and design); the Fumane tapestries
bring to life a fictional world of sensual love:

Quanto è possente il nostro umano ingegno,
che vive fa parer le cose finte
per forza di colori e di disegno!
  Di seta e d'oro e varie lane tinte,
nei tapeti, ch'adornan quelle stanze,
da l'imitar le cose vere en vinte. (178–83)

Ah, how mighty is our human skill, that through the power of
color and design gives life to artifice! In the tapestries that adorned
those rooms, made of silk and gold and multicolored wools, imitation surpassed true things.

Witness to these erotic scenes of pagan love are a host of God's vicars who
have been placed on earth to oversee human affairs. Portraits of prelates,
popes, cardinals, and bishops adorn the palace walls, thus reordering by
spiritual and moral example the disorders of pagan love.[94] Their presence,
however, does not reprove earthly desire but lives together with it in reciprocal harmony:

Questi, ancor morti, insegnar ponno ai vivi,
anzi in ciel vivon sì, che 'l loro nome
in terra sempre glorioso arrivi. (25.211–13)

These, even though dead, can still teach the living; indeed, in
heaven they live so that their names, forever glorious, resound on
earth.

Le costor fronti a mirar riverenti,
così pinte, ne fanno, e in noi pensieri
destano de le cose più eccellenti. (217–19)

Thus portrayed, their brows inspire us to admire them with rever-
ence and awaken in us thoughts of the most lofty things.

When Franco moves outside onto the balcony once again, she takes part
as a spectator in a pastoral scene replete with shepherds and their flocks, and
emerald pools teeming with fish ("di smeraldi in fresca riva adorna / di liq-
uido cristal" [vv. 406–7] [a cool bank of emeralds adorned with liquid
crystal]); she reenters a prelapsarian world of plenty and prosperity. She discovers a wood so thick that it conceals many species of wild animals. But
this rustic sight, where nature's abundance protects itself from man's pil-
laging, is suddenly interrupted by the arrival of a group of the palace's gentlemen who dash furiously across the fields intent on the hunt. Rather than
rudely disrupting the idyllic calm with excited calls to the hunt and the

barking of dogs, their human activity jolts Franco's eye to follow eagerly the hunt's course, which in turn uncovers still further scenes of human sport—bird catching and fishing (vv. 307–441). Not even the forced disentangling of shepherds' and shepherdesses' half-naked bodies at the sound of the hunt's "corno roco" (raucous horn) produces a feeling of discord between shepherd and noble:

> Talor la pastorella ivi, ch'egli ama,
> de la fistola al suon mossa ne viene,
> in modo che di lui cresce la brama:
>
> fisse le luci avidamente ei tiene
> ne le braccia e nel sen nudi, e nel viso,
> e d'abbracciarla a pena si ritiene.
>
> Ma poi quindi a guardar l'occhio diviso
> tira l'udito suon d'un corno roco,
> quando più in quei pastori egli era fiso;
>
> ed ecco, da color lontano un poco,
> cani co' cacciator disposti in caccia,
> ciascuno intento al suo ufficio e 'l suo loco. (25.364–75)

Sometimes the shepherdess he loves comes there stirred by the sound of his panpipe, and thus his desire is increased: he keeps his gaze fixed avidly on her naked arms and breasts and face and can barely refrain from embracing her. But then, at the sound of a raucous horn, the more it was absorbed, the more abruptly the shepherd's gaze turns away; and look, not far from them, hounds and hunters are deployed for the chase, each intent on his task and place.

Never tiring from this animated spectacle, Franco leaves what she considers her most difficult task to the poem's end: that is, the specific praise of her host, Marcantonio Della Torre. To rise to the heights required to honor him, she has needed the entire poem to convince herself and, it is implied, her readers of her ability:

> Vorrei, ma in parte non so alcuna, dire
> le lodi del signor, che ti possiede,
> né stil uman poria tant'alto gire. (25.457–59)

Of the master who owns you, I would sing the praise, but I know not how to begin, nor can such heights be attained by human pen.

Her naive stance here recalls the deliberate naïveté Franco enlists at appropriate instances during the Inquisition trial proceedings when seeking to invoke the sympathy of her inquisitor. In a similar gesture, Franco bends humbly to her host, Della Torre, reminding him that she was guided by his "chiaro e dolce lume" (clear and sweet light), which safely conducted her to the "dolce spettacolo" (sweet spectacle) of Fumane. His noble "lume" (light) permitted her to leave behind a world of "torbidi e gravi pensieri" (disturbing and serious thoughts). The abundance of earthly pleasures, coupled with his noble presence, console and comfort her. His is a world where even servants delight in attending to his needs; indeed all races and ages live together as one well-integrated community:

> *E intorno a lui con ordine ridutta,*
> *di varia età, di vario pelo mista,*
> *vestita a un modo, corrisponde tutta.* (547–49)
>
> Gathered round him in good order, of various ages and various shades of hair, all dressed in the same way, they answer to him as one.

This insistence on friendship in love permits Franco the opportunity to counter the moralistic reproaches against a courtesan's infidelity and lasciviousness by suggesting an alternative model for love between a man and a woman. Just as in her familiar letters, Franco envisages a society that permits intellectual exchanges, based on mutual respect and equality, between male patrician and honest courtesan, so in her depiction of an Arcadian world Franco imagines a love relationship as a joining of desire with friendship—an ideal she had posited in an earlier poem, capitolo 19. In this poem, she addresses a distinguished man of the cloth who has returned to Venice after a long absence.[95] His physical presence rekindles within her the feelings of desire that she had once felt so intensely but had been forced to conceal from others and from him. Just as Danae's chastity was protected by her father when he sequestered the beautiful maiden in a fortified tower, so Franco, as she confesses, buried the desire she felt so intensely for this man of religion by imprisoning it necessarily within the chambers of her heart:

> *Tanta a me intorno guardia si facea,*
> *che d'assai men dal cielo a Danae Giove*
> *in pioggia d'oro in grembo non cadea.*
> *Ma l'ali, che 'l pensier dispiega e move,*
> *chi troncar mi poteo, se mi fu chiuso*
> *al mio arbitrio l'andar co' piedi altrove?* (37–42)
>
> I was kept under such close guard all around that less guard would

have prevented Jupiter from pouring into Danae's lap in the guise of golden rain. But who could deprive me of the wings that thought spreads and moves, even if my will was precluded from going elsewhere?

Now spurred to reveal to him her secret of many years, she confesses the enormity and profundity of the desire she once nurtured in secrecy:

> *Quel che ascoso nel cor tenni gran tempo*
> *con doglia tal, ch'a la lingua contese*
> *narrar le mie ragioni a miglior tempo;*
>   *quelle dolci d'amor amare offese*
> *che di scovrirle tanto altri val meno,*
> *quanto ha più di far ciò le voglie accese;*
>   *or, che la piaga s'è saldata al seno*
> *col rivoltar degli anni, onde le cose*
> *mutan di qua giù stato e vengon meno,*
>   *vengo a narrar, poi che, se ben noiose*
> *a sentir furo, ne la rimembranza*
> *or mi si volgon liete e dilettose.* (19.1–12)

That which I kept hidden in my heart for so long with a pain so great that it prevented my tongue from telling my reasons at a better time; those bittersweet injuries of love that one is most anxious to reveal as one less ought to; now that the wound in my breast has mended with the passing of the years whereby the things of this earth change and fade, I am going to tell you now, since though they were certainly irksome to feel, when remembered, they become cheerful and delectable.

Although his absence and the passing of time have succeeded in quelling the force of her passion ("il vostro andar in region lontana / saldò 'l colpo, benché la cicatrice / render non si potesse in tutto vana" [vv. 67–69] [your leaving for a distant land was the last blow, although the scar could never be erased]), the memory of his fervent preaching is still vividly present to her.

> *Or sicura ho 'l pericolo a la mente,*
> *quando da' be' vostr'occhi e dal bel volto*
> *contra me spinse Amor la face ardente:*
>   *ed a piagarmi in mille guise volto,*
> *dal fiume ancor de la vostra eloquenza*
> *il foco del mio incendio avea raccolto.* (16–21)

Safe now, I remember the danger of when, through your eyes and handsome face, Love held out to me its burning torch, and intent

on wounding me in a thousand ways, he had gathered the flames of
my fire even from the river of your eloquence.

But just as she has grown older, so has he. With the careful and loving
attention to detail that a portraitist displays to a favored sitter, Franco
paints a portrait of a youthful love; she portrays the passing of time from his
youth to the "viril robusta etate" (the virile robust age) in a single but powerful detail—the transformation of his golden hair into a mass of silvery
strands:

> E, se ben in viril robusta etate,
> l'oro de la lanugine in argento
> rivolto, quasi vecchio vi mostrate;
>   benché punto nel viso non s'è spento
> quel lume di beltà chiara e serena,
> ch'abbaglia chi mirarvi ardisce intento. (19.121–26)

And although of a robust and virile age, as the gold of your hair
turns to silver, you almost look old; while in your face the light of
clear and serene beauty which bedazzles all who dare to gaze at you
is not at all extinguished.

But while her physical attraction to him was never fulfilled, she now understands her present passion for the "lume di beltà chiara e serena" (light of
clear and serene beauty) albeit "più temperat[e] e di minor fervenza" (tem-
pered and of less fervor) rather as "voglie caste" (chaste desires):

> In amicizia il folle amor trasformo,
> e, pensando a le vostre immense doti,
> per imitarvi l'animo riformo;
>   e, se 'n ciò i miei pensieri vi fosser noti,
> i moderati onesti miei desiri
> non lascereste andar d'effetto vuoti. (19.148–53)

I transform my mad love into friendship, and thinking of your immense gifts, I reshape my soul to emulate you; and if my thoughts
on this were known to you, you would not let my honest and tem-
perate desires go unfulfilled.

Franco insists here, and throughout capitolo 25, on the positive power of a
courtesan's love. Drawing from a Platonic vocabulary to portray the superior sensitivities she embodies, she also concedes that Della Torre's wisdom
and courtesy were the principal motivations that spurred her to undertake
the "arduous" journey from Venice to the Veronese countryside. Although

his example mitigated the difficulties of her voyage, she also admits that her "gran desio" (great desire) made the road to him seem all the longer:

> *Andai, dal gran desìo tirata, un giorno:*
> *non per error di via, né ch'io passassi*
> *quindi avante d'altronde al mio ritorno;*
> *ma d'Adria mossi a quest'effetto i passi,*
> *né interromper giamai volsi il viaggio,*
> *perch'a l'andar via pessima trovassi.*
> *Di questo mio signor cortese e saggio,*
> *nel sentier aspro, mi fu grata scorta,*
> *de la virtute il sempiterno raggio:*
> *da così chiaro e dolce lume scorta,*
> *la strada, ch'al desio lunga sembrava,*
> *al disagio parea commoda e corta.* (25.517–28)

I went one day drawn by a strong desire: not because I took the wrong road or passed nearby returning from another place; but I left Adria precisely for this, and I never thought of interrupting the journey just because I found that the road to get there was the worst. The eternal beacon of your virtue, my courteous and dear Sir, was welcome company during the rough trip: seen under that bright and sweet light, the road, which to my yearning seemed so long, to my discomfort appeared smooth and short.

Once securely in Fumane, Franco finally enjoys the kind of harmonious balance between the sexes that she had only imagined was possible in other capitoli in her *Terze rime*. Fumane, "unica, amata terra, ov'albergan le delizie" (unique, beloved land where all delights dwell) is a world where earthly pleasures, aesthetic beauty, superhuman virtue, and sensual delights live together in a nurturing union. The verbal echoes ("unica, amata terra") of Maffio Venier's misogynist dissection of her name in his poem "Veronica, ver unica puttana" (Veronica, veritably unique whore) point to the distance Franco has traveled from victimization to masterful action. Indeed such a verbal allusion underscoring male aggression renders by contrast the social harmony she has found in Fumane all the more compelling. This pastoral exile has had the power to heal an "infected" soul and to join a Venetian courtesan with a noble, religious man. Together they live in peace, in friendship, and in mutual contentment. It is with this restored sense of inner peace, coupled nonetheless with a restless desire to return to Fumane, that Veronica Franco concludes her edition of the *Terze rime*, flying with her thoughts, her tongue in knots:

E, perch'al loco internamente io pensi,
quanto più di lui parlo, e manco il lodo,
e i miei desir di lui si fan più intensi,
   Volando col pensier, la lingua annodo. (25.562–65)

And because inside of me I think of that place, the more I speak
about it, the less I praise it, and my yearning for it grows more
intense. As I fly with my imagination, I twist my tongue into
knots.

In this concluding idyll, Veronica Franco joins together many of the
poetic stances and literary self-representations she has used in her self-
construction as honest courtesan. Leaving behind the frustrating love tri-
angles of earlier elegiac capitoli (3, 17, 20) and the tortured inner confusions of her meditative poems, she ends her volume with a sense of renewed
vigor. In her movement from the city to a pastoral landscape and back
again, she has called attention to her flight from victimization and to her
return to a wiser love uncontaminated by negative forces. Indeed all traces
of male aggression, subjugation, and alienation have been replaced in this
concluding poem with what may be called a restorative moment of postero-
tic serenity. In a language that is, as one critic has noted, "dense with Petrarchan echoes," Franco undoes her male precursor's tortured rejection of
"quel che piace."[96] She openly delights in the sensual pleasures that Petrarch so anxiously abhorred. Rather than turning to the Virgin for liberation from the torments of unfulfilled desire and for salvation, as Petrarch
does in his final, yet unsuccessful, appeal for spiritual transcendence in the
Canzoniere, Franco writes as an honest courtesan from a position of secular
fulfillment. Her corrective vision rejects hierarchical differences that promote divisiveness; she recuperates a world where nature and reason coexist
and where individuals come together freely in mutual friendship and in
love. The social harmony she proposes depends upon the equal participation of all men and women.

Notes

INTRODUCTION

1. Ann Rosalind Jones, *The Currency of Eros: Women's Love Lyric in Europe, 1540–1620* (Bloomington and Indianapolis: Indiana University Press, 1990), 4.

2. Ibid., 9.

3. Giuseppe Tassini, *Veronica Franco: Celebre poetessa e cortigiana del secolo XVI* (Venice: Fontana, 1874; reprint, Venice: Alfieri, 1969); Arturo Graf, "Una cortigiana fra mille: Veronica Franco," in his *Attraverso il Cinquecento* (Turin: Loescher, 1888); Benedetto Croce, "Veronica Franco," in his *Poeti e scrittori del pieno e tardo rinascimento* (Bari: Laterza, 1970); idem, *Lettere dall'unica edizione del MDLXXX con proemio e nota iconografica* (Naples: Ricciardi, 1949).

4. Benedetto Croce, *Lettere*.

5. Riccardo Scrivano, "La poetessa Veronica Franco," in his *Cultura e letteratura nel Cinquecento* (Rome: Ateneo, 1966), 197–228.

6. Sara Maria Adler, "Veronica Franco's Petrarchan *Terze Rime:* Subverting the Master's Plan," *Italica* 65 (1988): 213–33; Fiora A. Bassanese, "Private Lives and Public Lies: Texts by Courtesans of the Italian Renaissance," *Texas Studies in Language and Literature* 30, no. 3 (1988): 295–319; Francesco Erspamer, "Petrarchismo e manierismo nella lirica del secondo Cinquecento," in *Storia della cultura veneta,* ed. G. Arnaldi and M. Pastore Stocchi (Vicenza: Neri Pozza, 1983), 4:189–222.

7. Alvise Zorzi, *Cortigiana veneziana: Veronica Franco e i suoi poeti* (Milan: Camunia, 1986); Marcella Diberti Leigh, *Veronica Franco: Donna, poetessa e cortigiana del Rinascimento* (Ivrea: Priuli and Verlucca, 1988). Both studies appeared after I completed the research for the present book. These two books contain some of the same conclusions at which I have independently arrived.

8. This is a reference to Veronica Franco's letter 17 in her *Lettere familiari a diversi,* 28, as reproduced in Benedetto Croce, *Lettere dall'unica edizione del MDLXXX con proemio e nota iconografica.*

CHAPTER ONE: SATIRIZING THE COURTESAN

1. Thomas Coryat (1577–1617) remained in Europe for five months, and one-third of his journey he spent in Venice. For this and other quotations, see *Coryat's Crudities,* ed. James Maclehose (1611; reprint, Glasgow: University of Glasgow Press, 1905), vol. 1 (New York: 1905), 264; this is hereafter cited as *Coryat's Crudities.* There are many references throughout his work to Venetian courtesans: their costumes, manners, social outings, religious works, and "sinful" practices. He offers the following interesting etymology for the term "courtesan" (264): "The woman that professeth this trade is called in the Italian tongue *Cortezana,* which word is

derived from the Italian word *cortesia* that signifieth *courtesie*. Because these kinde of women are said to receive courtesies of their favourites. Which word hath some kinde of *affinitie* with the Greek word ἑταῖρα, which signifieth properly a sociable woman, and is by Demosthenes, Athenaeus, and divers other prose writers often taken for a woman of a dissolute conversation."

2. Marin Sanuto, *I diarii,* ed. Rinaldo Fulin et al. (Venice, 1879−1902), 8:414. On the city's population in these years, see Karl Julius Beloch, *Bevölkerungsgeschichte Italiens* (Berlin: De Bruyter, 1937−61), 3:17; he claims that in the beginning of the sixteenth century the population totaled 105,000. Daniele Beltrami (*Storia della popolazione di Venezia dalla fine del secolo XVI alla caduta della Repubblica* [Padua: Cedam, 1954], 59) argues that the figure was 115,000, while in 1563, the population was already 168,627. He estimates that it rose to 175,000 before the plague of 1575−77. I agree with Guido Ruggiero's suggestion (*The Boundaries of Eros* [Oxford: Oxford University Press, 1985], 152−53) that the numbers of courtesans are exaggerated in tourist reports. For other views on the question of numbers of prostitutes, see Donald E. Queller, *The Venetian Patriciate: Reality versus Myth* (Urbana: University of Illinois Press, 1987), 14−37.

3. *Coryat's Crudities,* 265. For this and other English travelers' accounts of Venice in the early modern period, see Antonio Barzaghi, *Donne o cortigiane? La prostituzione a Venezia: Documenti di costume dal XVI al XVIII secolo* (Verona: Bertani, 1980), 57−64; Boies Panrose, *Urbane Travelers, 1591−1635* (Philadelphia: University of Pennsylvania Press, 1942); Edward Muir, *Civic Ritual in Renaissance Venice* (Princeton: Princeton University Press, 1980), 52−55, and with particular reference to Coryat, 58−108; Jonathan Goldberg, *James I and the Politics of Literature: Jonson, Shakespeare, Donne, and their Contemporaries* (Baltimore: Johns Hopkins University Press, 1983), especially 74−81, 255 nn. 23, 29.

4. For a general discussion of the Venetian civic myth of the republic, see Franco Gaeta, "Alcune considerazioni sul mito di Venezia," *Bibliothèque d'Humanisme et Renaissance* 23 (1961): 58−75; Gina Fasoli, "Nascita di un mito," in *Studi storici in onore di Gioacchino Volpe per il suo 80 compleanno* (Florence: Sansoni, 1958), 1:445−79; William J. Bouwsma, *Venice and the Defense of Republican Liberty: Renaissance Values in the Age of the Counter Reformation* (Berkeley: University of California Press, 1968); Myron P. Gilmore, "Myth and Reality in Venetian Political Theory," in *Renaissance Venice,* ed. J. R. Hale (London: Faber and Faber, 1974), 431−43. For a recent and comprehensive discussion of this myth and for extensive bibliography, see Margaret L. King, *Venetian Humanism in an Age of Patrician Dominance* (Princeton: Princeton University Press, 1986), 174−78. She argues that Venetian humanists advocated the restraint of passions, which were regarded as disruptive to a community, for the benefit of the society as a whole. Only the nobly born were considered suitable for guiding a society made up of "the irrational and passion-ridden" (174−78). For the connections between Venice's perceived "libertà" and the intellectual context of the sixteenth century, see Gino Benzoni, *Gli affanni della cultura: Intellettuali e potere nell'Italia della controriforma e barocca* (Milan: Feltrinelli, 1978), especially 28−143. A study that challenges the myth's idealism is Queller, *Venetian Patriciate.* See also the comprehensive review of the primary and secondary sources on the subject by James S. Grubb, "When Myths Lose Power: Four Decades of Venetian Historiography," *Journal of Modern History* 58 (1986): 43−94. This review also explicates the methodologies of Venetian historians over the last few centuries. For a review of sixteenth-century Venetian sources that extol the civic myth, see Maria Luisa Doglio, "La letteratura ufficiale e l'oratorio celebrativa," in *Storia della cultura veneta: Il Seicento,*

ed. G. Arnaldi and M. Pastore Stocchi (Vicenza: Neri Pozza, 1982), 4:163–87; and Franco Gaeta, "L'idea di Venezia," 4:605–10.

5. For a ground-breaking discussion of the civic myth as an indicator of the self-serving nature of public rituals sponsored by the Venetian patriciate, see Muir, *Civic Ritual,* 147–56. For useful descriptions and information on Venetian daily life in Venice in the Renaissance, see Pompeo G. Molmenti, *La storia di Venezia nella vita privata,* 7th ed. (Bergamo: Istituto italiano d'arti grafiche, 1928). For Piazza San Marco as a scene of "disorderly display," see Queller, *Venetian Patriciate,* 19.

6. This powerful female symbol contrasts sharply with humanists' injunctions against the reality of women's public status and speech. See Margaret L. King, "Caldiera and the Barbaros on Marriage and the Family: Humanist Reflections of Venetian Realities," *The Journal of Medieval and Renaissance Studies* 6 (1976): 19–50; idem, "Book-lined Cells: Women and Humanism in the Early Italian Renaissance," in *Beyond their Sex: Learned Women of the European Past,* ed. Patricia H. Labalme (New York: New York University Press, 1980), 66–90; Margaret L. King and Albert Rabil, Jr., eds., *Her Immaculate Hand: Selected Works by and about the Women Humanists of Quattrocento Italy* (Binghamton, N.Y.: Center for Medieval and Early Renaissance Studies, 1983), especially the introduction; Anthony Grafton and Lisa Jardine, *From Humanism to the Humanities: Education and the Liberal Arts in Fifteenth- and Sixteenth-Century Europe* (Cambridge: Harvard University Press, 1986), 29–57; Ann Rosalind Jones, "Surprising Fame: Renaissance Gender Ideologies and Women's Lyric," in *The Poetics of Gender,* ed. Nancy K. Miller (New York: Columbia University Press, 1986), pp. 74–95; Ann Rosalind Jones, "Nets and Bridles: Early Modern Conduct Books and Sixteenth-Century Women's Lyrics," in *Essays on Literature and the History of Sexuality,* ed. Nancy Armstrong and Leonard Tennenhouse (London: Methuen, 1987), 39–72; Patricia H. Labalme, "Venetian Women on Women: Three Early Modern Feminists," *Archivio veneto,* 5th ser., 117 (1981): 82–83; Merry E. Weisner, "Women's Defense of Their Public Role," in *Women in the Middle Ages and the Renaissance: Literary and Historical Perspectives,* ed. Mary Beth Rose (Syracuse: Syracuse University Press, 1985), 1–27. See also the introduction to a ground-breaking anthology of essays devoted to a revisionist reworking of Renaissance studies: *Rewriting the Renaissance: The Discourses of Sexual Difference in Early Modern Europe,* ed. Margaret W. Ferguson, Maureen Quilligan, and Nancy J. Vickers (Chicago: University of Chicago Press, 1986). In particular, see Constance Jordan, "Feminism and the Humanists: The Case of Sir Thomas Elyot's *Defense of Good Women,*" 242–58, 376–83, for a comprehensive bibliography. See also idem, *Renaissance Feminism: Literary Texts and Political Models* (Ithaca: Cornell University Press, 1990). On humanist treatises that speak of the virtue of female chastity, among other things, and the necessity of the woman's position as the protector of the moral welfare of her family, see the anthology and translations of representative humanist writers of the Renaissance edited by Benjamin G. Kohl and Ronald G. Witt, *The Earthly Republic: Italian Humanists on Government and Society* (Philadelphia: University of Pennsylvania Press, 1978).

7. See, for example, *Coryat's Crudities,* 278: "It is a matter very worth the consideration, to thinke how this noble citie hath like a pure Virgin and incontaminated mayde in which sense I called her a mayden citie in the front of my description of her . . . Jerusalem was [also] called a Virgin . . . kept her virginity untouched these thousand two hundred and twelve years . . . though Emperours, Kings, Princes, and mighty Potentates, being allured with her glorious beauty, have attempted to deflowre her, every one receiving the repulse: a thing most wonderfull and strange." Samuel Y. Edgerton (*Pictures and Punishment: Art and Criminal Prosecution during the*

Florentine Renaissance [Ithaca: Cornell University Press, 1985]) provides a useful definition of pictorial icon that I follow here: an "artificial image in which the subject matter is arranged in standard compositions already familiar to the viewer, to whom an expected, didactic message is then communicated. Icons must be located in such prepared settings as Churches or law courts where the audience will be able to recognize by association the picture's meaning." On the use of popular icons in civic settings, see Edward Muir, "The Virgin on the Street Corner: The Place of the Sacred in Italian Cities," *Religion and Culture in the Renaissance and Reformation*, ed. Steven Ozment (Kirksville, Mo.: Sixteenth Century Studies Publishers, 1987): 25–40.

8. For the visual iconography of the civic myth in Venetian public buildings and paintings, see David Rosand, "Venetia Figurata: The Iconography of a Myth," in *Interpretazioni veneziane: Studi di storia dell'arte in onore di Michelangelo Muraro*, ed. David Rosand (Venice: Arsenale Editore, 1984), 177–96; Rona Goffen, *Piety and Patronage in Renaissance Venice: Bellini, Titian, and the Franciscans* (New Haven: Yale University Press, 1987), especially with reference to "Venezia Vergine," 139–54, and 239 n. 2, 240 nn. 6, 9. For references to the civic myth in literary works of the period, see Antonio Medin, *La storia della Repubblica di Venezia nella poesia* (Milan: Ulrico Hoepli, 1904). The connection between the Virgin and the city's foundation myth, the *Origo Venetiarum*, is made clear in one of the sculptural reliefs adorning the facade of the Basilica of San Marco. For iconographic studies of the Virgin, see Victor Lasareff, "Studies in the Iconography of the Virgin," *Art Bulletin* 20 (1938): 26–65; and for the decorations of the Basilica, see Otto Demus, *The Church of San Marco in Venice: History, Architecture, Sculpture*, vol. 6 (Washington: Dumbarton Oaks Studies, 1960), and for an analysis of the icon of the Virgin, see 125–35.

On the myth of Venice's origins as a personification of the Virgin and as a vehicle in a distinctly Venetian humanist rhetoric, respectively, see Ellen Rosand, "Music in the Myth of Venice," *Renaissance Quarterly* 30 (1977): 511–37; and King, *Venetian Humanism*, 174–76. On the divine origin of Venice in relation to the Virgin, see Staale Sinding-Larsen, *Christ in the Council Hall: Studies in the Religious Iconography of the Venetian Republic* (Rome: Institutum Romanum Norvegiae, 1974), 142–44 and passim; David Rosand, "Titian's Presentation to the Virgin in the Temple and the Scuola della Carità," *Art Bulletin* 58 (1976): 55–84, especially, 76–81. On the complex and ambiguous nature of the image of the Virgin Mary in art and literature, especially in medieval France, see Penny Schine Gold, *The Lady and the Virgin* (Chicago: University of Chicago Press, 1985).

9. On the connections between the representation of Venice and ancient Rome, see Rosand, "Venetia Figurata," 180–87; Deborah Howard, *Jacopo Sansovino: Architecture and Patronage in Renaissance Venice* (New Haven: Yale University Press, 1975), 2–7. On the historical consciousness implicit in this political association, see Eco O. G. Haitsma Mulier, *The Myth of Venice and Dutch Republican Thought in the Seventeenth Century*, trans. Gerard T. Moran (Assen: Van Gorcum, 1980), 1–25 and passim. For depictions of the goddess Roma in ancient Rome, see Cornelius C. Vermeule, *The Goddess Roma in the Art of the Roman Empire* (Cambridge: Harvard University Press, 1959).

10. Dennis Romano (*Patricians and Popolani: The Social Foundations of the Venetian Renaissance State* [Baltimore: Johns Hopkins University Press, 1987], 157–58), discusses the Ducal Palace as a symbol of change in the social, political, and religious organization of Venice from the fifteenth to the sixteenth century. See also Edward Muir, "Images of Power: Art and Pageantry in Renaissance Venice," *American Historical Review* 84, no. 1 (1979): 16–52, for an analysis of the interaction between the Venetian government and the public rituals they sponsored in Venetian urban spaces to affirm their power. As David Rosand points out in "Venetia Figurata," the Vir-

gin, together with Saint Mark, became enshrined in the early modern period as a symbol of Venice. For an excellent discussion of the function and significance of Piazza San Marco and its adjacent buildings as a "male center" of Venetian culture and civic activities, see Dennis Romano, "Gender and the Urban Geography of Renaissance Venice," *Journal of Social History* 23, no. 2 (1989): 339–53. For useful bibliography on the transformation of the cityscape during processions, see 349–50. For an illuminating examination of urban institutions and patterns of sociability in civic spaces, or what the authors call the "social geography" and "symbolic geography of a city," see Edward Muir and Ronald F. E. Weissman, "Social and Symbolic Places in Renaissance Venice and Florence," in *The Power of Place: Integrating Geographical and Sociological Imaginations,* ed. John Agnew and James Duncan (Boston: Unwin Hyman, 1989), 81–103. An important early essay linking religious practices and civic urban spaces is Natalie Zemon Davis, "The Sacred and the Body Social in Sixteenth-Century Lyon," *Past and Present* 90 (1981): 40–70.

11. According to David Rosand ("Venetia Figurata," 189–93, especially 188), Venice was also represented as a Venus Anadyomene. For a sixteenth-century source, see Giovanni Nicolo Doglioni, *Venetia trionfante et sempre libera* (Venice: 1613), which also makes the connection between Venice and Venus. Rona Goffen, in *Piety and Patronage,* 138–54, examines the associations between the female personification of Venice and artistic representations of the female in Venice.

12. On the iconographic program for the decoration of the Ducal Palace after the second fire in 1574, including Veronese's *Apotheosis of Venice,* see Girolamo Bardi, *Dichiaratione di tutte le historie che si contengono ne' quadri posti novamente nelle Sale del Scrutinio, e del Gran Consiglio del Palagio Ducale della Republica di Vinegia* (Venice: 1587, 1607); and for a contemporary reference, see Francesco Sansovino, *Venetia città nobilissima et singolare* (1581), especially 122–24. See also Terisio Pignatti, *Veronese,* 2 vols. (Venice: Alfieri, 1976); Stefania Mason Rinaldi, "Storia e mito nei cicli pittorici di Palazzo Ducale," in *Architettura e utopia nella Venezia del Cinquecento,* ed. Lionello Puppi (Milan: Electa Editrice, 1980), 80–88 for analyses of the decorations for the Ducal Palace; Juergen Schultz, *Venetian Painted Ceilings of the Renaissance* (Berkeley: University of California Press, 1968), 97–99. And see Michelangelo Muraro, "Venezia: Interpretazione del Palazzo Ducale," *Studi urbinati di storia, filosofia e letteratura* 45 (1971): 1160–75, especially 1166, where he speaks about the identification of Venice with Justice. See also David Rosand, "Venezia e gli dei," in *"Renovatio urbis": Venezia nell'età di Andrea Gritti (1523–1538),* ed. Manfredo Tafuri (Rome: Officina Edizioni, 1984), 201–15; idem, *Painting in Cinquecento Venice: Titian, Veronese, Tintoretto* (New Haven: Yale University Press, 1982), 127–30, 239–41, 276–77. Norbert Huse and Wolfgang Wolters (*The Art of Renaissance Venice: Architecture, Sculpture, and Painting 1460–1590* [Chicago: University of Chicago Press, 1990], and especially 321–22) discuss Veronese's painting in the Ducal Palace for which they provide the title, "Venetian Peace." They argue (320) that the painting was "supposed to show the general renown of Venetian rule in a final apotheosis, after its foundation and growth." The figure of Venetia is placed over cities, much as Roma had towered over its dominions on ancient coins. Flying Victories crown her with laurel, and figures representing "peace, abundance, happiness, and honor surround her." Although jubilant crowds of unidentified figures attend to her, Huse and Wolters advance the theory that the figure representing the "Allegory of Honor," who is placed above the other virtues and "almost on the same level as Venetia," has the "features of Henri III of France, whom the republic had received with utmost ceremony in 1574 in the hope of a lasting alliance" (322).

Linda Carroll offers an intriguing way to interpret this and other paintings of the period which she places within the larger sociopolitical and military climate of the latter half of the sixteenth century. She associates the depiction of virile, strong males with Italy's return to political stability and social normality after the Peace of Bologna. The return of the male virile figure in specifically Venetian painting she links with the "stabilization of the city's economic fortune" after the triumph at Lepanto. See her "Who's on Top? Gender as Societal Power Configuration in Italian Renaissance Drama," *Sixteenth Century Journal* 20, no. 4 (1989): 531–38. For the darker aspects of the Veronese painting, in which the "applauding multitudes" reveal a defeated version of the same theme ("discarded armor recalls war and defeat," and the "lion of St. Mark above looks angry rather than benevolent"), see Huse and Wolters, *Art of Renaissance Venice,* 322. The importance of Henri III's meeting with Veronica Franco is discussed at length in chapter 2.

13. For these terms, see Muir, *Civic Ritual,* 14. For a particularly useful discussion, see chapter 1, "The Myth of Venice," 13–61.

14. *Coryat's Crudities,* 264. Coryat adds on 271, "As for mine owne part I would have thee consider that even as the river Rhodanus . . . doth passe through the lake Losanna, and yet mingleth not his waters therewith; and as the Fountaine Arethusa runneth through the Sea, and confoundeth not her fresh water with the salt liquor of the sea; and as the beames of the Sunne doe penetrate into many uncleane places, and yet are nothing polluted with the impuritie thereof: so did I visite the Palace of a noble Cortezan, view her own amorus person, heare her talke, observe her fashion of life, and yet was nothing contaminated therewith, nor corrupted in manner."

15. Ibid., 290.

16. As cited in Muir, *Civic Ritual,* 53–54.

17. For a contemporary account of the restrictions imposed on Venetian women by their husbands, see *Coryat's Crudities,* 1:403; in 1608 he wrote "For the Gentleman do even coope up their wives alwaies within the Walles of their houses." Two studies argue that fifteenth- and sixteenth-century aristocratic and lower-class Venetian women found refuge from patriarchal ideological strictures by gaining increased economic independence. The wives of artisans, both Catholic and non-Catholic, were involved in a variety of religious devotions and heretical practices outside the home that afforded them a measure of autonomy. See John Martin, "Out of the Shadow: Heretical and Catholic Women in Renaissance Venice," *Journal of Family History* (1985): 21–33; and Dennis Romano, "Charity and Community in Early Renaissance Venice," *Journal of Urban History* 2 (1984): 63–82. For interesting discussions of partician Venetian women's wills and dowries, albeit of an earlier period, as evidence of female bonding and an increase in the status and economic power of aristocratic women, see Stanley Chojnacki, "Patrician Women in Early Renaissance Venice," *Studies in the Renaissance* 21 (1974): 176–203; idem, "Dowries and Kinsmen in Early Renaissance Venice," *Journal of Interdisciplinary History* 5 (1975): 571–600; idem, "Kinship Ties and Young Patricians in Fifteenth-Century Venice," *Renaissance Quarterly* 38 (1985): 240–70; idem, "'The Most Serious Duty': Motherhood, Gender, and Patrician Culture in Renaissance Venice," in *Refiguring Woman: Perspectives on Gender and the Italian Renaissance,* ed. Marilyn Migiel and Juliana Schiesari (Ithaca: Cornell University Press, 1991), 133–54. For a fascinating examination of the emotional bonds of marriage among Venetian patrician families, and with special reference to women's increasing economic leverage and social maneuverings in the allotment of a family's legacy, see Stanley Chojnacki, "The Power of Love: Wives and Husbands in Late Medieval Venice," in *Women and Power in the Middle Ages,* ed. Mary Erler and Maryanne Kowaleski (Athens: University of Georgia Press, 1988), 126–48. On the question of the tension between the allotment of one's legacy to either natal kin or marital families, see Diane Owen Hughes, "From Brideplace to Dowry in Mediterranean Europe," *Journal of Family*

History 3 (1978): 262–96, and "Representing the Family: Portraits and Purposes in Early Modern Italy," *Journal of Interdisciplinary History* 17 (1986): 7–38, especially 10–11. With respect to the economic maneuverings of women in their testament practices, see James C. Davis, *A Venetian Family and Its Fortune* (Philadelphia: American Philosophical Society, 1975).

18. For a discussion of the laws passed against sexual crimes, prostitution, and immoral and disruptive behavior in early-Renaissance Venice, see Guido Ruggiero, *Violence in Early Renaissance Venice* (New Brunswick: Rutgers University Press, 1980), and idem, *Boundaries of Eros*. For the connections between patriarchal humanist ideologies that attempted to regulate upper-class women's activities in Venetian civic life, see Margaret L. King, "Personal, Domestic, and Republican Values in the Moral Philosophy of Giovanni Caldiera," *Renaissance Quarterly* 28 (1975): 535–74; idem, "Caldiera and the Barbaros on Marriage and the Family: Humanist Reflections of Venetian Realities," *Journal of Medieval and Renaissance Studies* 6 (1976): 19–50. One way to control externally the crossing over of social boundaries was to monitor a courtesan's dress. On the sumptuary laws passed by Venetian officials aimed at limiting courtesans' mimicry of aristocratic women's styles of dress, see Stanley Chojnacki, "La posizione della donna a Venezia nel Cinquecento," in *Tiziano e Venezia: Convegno Internazionale di Studi* (Vicenza: Neri Pozza, 1980), 65–70; Diane Owen Hughes, "Sumptuary Laws and Social Relations in Renaissance Italy," in *Disputes and Settlements: Law and Human Relations in the West,* ed. John Bossy (Cambridge: Cambridge University Press, 1983), 69–99. See also chapter 2 below for further discussion of this issue.

19. With specific regard to the sexual relations between men and women, the issue of late marriage, inflated dowries, and poverty, see Ruggiero, *Boundaries of Eros,* 9–11, 41–42, 64–65, 118–21, 146–47, 161. See also 170 nn. 4, 5, where he discusses the problem of late marriage and expensive dowries for young maidens. For more on the dowry system in Renaissance Italy and in Venice, see chapter 2 nn. 37, 38, and 48. For the role of the courtesan with respect to the repressed sexual desires of young men, see Achillo Olivieri, "Erotisme et groupes sociaux a Venise au XVIe siècle: La Courtisane," *Communications* 35 (1982): 85–91. On the practice of Venetian officials who periodically punished offenders of public decorum and prostitutes, see Renzo Derosas, "Moralità e giustizia a Venezia nel '500–'600: Gli esecutori contro la bestemmia," in *Stato, società e giustizia nella Repubblica Veneta,* ed. Gaetano Cozzi (Rome: Jouvence, 1980), 431–528, especially 444–46. See also Giovanni Scarabello, "Devianza sessuale ed interventi di giustizia a Venezia nella prima metà del XVI secolo," in *Tiziano e Venezia,* 75–84; Elizabeth Pavan, "Police del moeurs, societé et politique à Venise à la fin du Moyen Age," *Révue Historique* 264 (1980): 244–66.

For a similar development in early modern Spain, and as evidence of Spanish government's toleration of prostitution as a necessary evil, see the fascinating discussion of the "picara" tradition in Spanish literature of the early modern period in Anne J. Cruz, "Sexual Enclosure, Textual Escape: The *Picara* as Prostitute in the Spanish Female Picaresque Novel," in *Seeking the Woman in Late Medieval and Renaissance Writings,* ed. Sheila Fisher and Janet E. Halley (Knoxville: University of Tennessee Press, 1989), 135–59. For historical case studies of prostitution in early modern Seville that have been particularly useful for this study, see Mary Elizabeth Perry, "'Lost Women' in Early Modern Seville: The Politics of Prostitution," *Feminist Studies* 4, no. 1 (1978): 195–214; idem, "Deviant Insiders: Legalized Prostitutes and a Consciousness of Women in Early Modern Seville," *Comparative Studies in Society and History* 27 (1985): 138–58; idem, *Gender and Disorder in Early Modern Seville* (Princeton: Princeton University Press, 1990). Within the northern European context of the same period, see the useful discussions of the need for female prostitution in German cities in Merry E. Weisner, "Paternalism in Practice: The Control of Servants and Prostitutes in Early Modern German Cities," in *The Process of Change in Early Modern Europe: Essays in Honor of Miriam Usher Chrisman,* ed. Phillip N. Bebb and Sherrin Marshall (Athens: Ohio University Press, 1988), 179–200, especially 186–200, and Merry E. Weisner, *Working Women in Renaissance Germany* (New Brunswick: Rutgers University Press, 1987).

20. James S. Grubb argues in "When Myths Lose Power" (45) that the Venetian civic myth is more useful as an "ideological indicator" than as a "vehicle for historical analysis." He articulates the important difference between myth as a guide for political action and as an interpretive scheme for people's actions in the ideal sense. He advocates, as do Edward Muir and others, the "affective force" of such myths. Gino Benzoni (*Gli affanni della cultura: Intellettuali e potere nell'Italia della controriforma e barocca* [Milan: Feltrinelli, 1978], 73–77) associates quite correctly the civic myth of "libertà" with the unruly presence of courtesans in the city as an indication of the republic's need for a sexual outlet.

21. For a definition of what constitutes the "cittadino" class in Venice, see Beltrami, *Storia della popolazione,* 65; Brian Pullan, *Rich and Poor in Renaissance Venice: The Social Institutions of a Catholic State, 1580 to 1620* (Cambridge: Harvard University Press, 1971), 100–105; Robert Finlay, *Politics in Renaissance Venice* (New Brunswick: Rutgers University Press, 1980), 45–47; Muir, *Civic Ritual,* 38–44. Brian Pullan writes that "citizenship, in sixteenth-century Venice, was a legal status conferring specific social and economic rights. In theory at least, it was granted to persons who, though they might be of non-Venetian origin, had chosen to throw in their lot with Venice and to identify themselves complicitly with the Venetians. The term included persons of merchant rank, and men who followed the liberal professions, as civil servants, advocates, notaries or physicians. During the sixteenth century, the government granted two forms of citizenship by privilege: citizenship *de intus,* and citizenship *de intus et extra.*" In addition, citizens were never to have been involved in manual labor. According to J. R. Hale ("Venice and Its Empire," in *The Genius of Venice, 1500–1600,* ed. Jane Martineau and Charles Hope [New York: H. N. Abrams, 1984], 11–15, "the rich *cittadini* . . . comprised some seven to ten percent of the population . . . from accountants and code-breakers to secretaries of the Senate and the Ten and the head of the service, the Chancellor himself . . . those *cittadini* who did not devote themselves to commerce and banking became identified with the values and purposes of the patricians they served and advised" (413). Patricia F. Brown describes the "cittadini" as an order (estates or caste) rather than a class (*Venetian Narrative Painting in the Age of Carpaccio* [New Haven: Yale University Press, 1988], 10–27 and passim). On the Chancery positions held by *cittadini,* see Mary Frances Neff, "Chancellery Secretaries in Venetian Politics and Society, 1480–1533," (Ph.D. diss., UCLA, 1985) 1:9–30.

Dennis Romano argues (*Patricians and Popolani*) that by the fifteenth century, "patricians were not the only ones exhibiting a greater sense of exclusivity . . . the trend was most apparent among the *cittadini,* who came increasingly to see themselves as a separate, distinct, and privileged group" (156). A sixteenth-century source confirms this theory. Girolamo Muzio, a Venetian theorist and writer, commented in his treatise *Il gentiluomo* (Venice: Giovanni Andrea Valvassori, 1571) that there are three levels in Venetian society: "Et civilmente parlando, diremo, che nella città sono per ordinario i gentiluomini, i Cittadini, et la Plebe . . . i cittadini . . . son tra i nobili, et i vili, saranno essi i non vili" (23). Francesco Sansovino also wrote a dialogue on what constitutes a Venetian gentleman (*Dialogo del gentilhuomo vinitiano* [Venice: 1566]).

22. On the uses of self-fashioning in Renaissance literature for political and social aims, see

Stephen Greenblatt, *Renaissance Self-Fashioning from More to Shakespeare* (Chicago: University of Chicago Press, 1969). Kenneth Burke (*A Rhetoric of Motives* [1950; reprint, Berkeley and Los Angeles: University of California Press, 1969], 285–86) first argued for the sense of abjection that the courtier experienced in relation to his patron. See also Daniel Javitch, *Poetry and Courtliness in Renaissance England* (Princeton: Princeton University Press, 1978); idem, "The Impure Motives of Elizabethan Poetry," in *The Power of Forms in the English Renaissance,* ed. Stephen Greenblatt (Norman, Okla.: Pilgrim Books, 1983), 225–38; Frank Whigham, "Interpretation at Court: Courtesy and the Performer-Audience Dialectic," *New Literary History* 14 (1983): 623–41; idem, *Ambition and Privilege: The Social Tropes of Elizabethan Courtesy Theory* (Berkeley and Los Angeles: University of California Press, 1984); Ann Rosalind Jones and Peter Stallybrass, "The Politics of Astrophil and Stella," *Studies in English Literature* 24, no. 1 (1984): 53–68.

23. On the republic's concern to preserve the social order in Venice by controlling any potential social disturbances brought on by illicit sexuality, poverty, natural disasters, beggars, and disease, especially in the latter half of the sixteenth century, see Pullan, *Rich and Poor*. Patricia H. Labalme argues ("Sodomy and Venetian Justice in the Renaissance," *Legal History Review* 52 (1984): 217–54, especially 211) that by the mid to late sixteenth century the concern with illicit sexuality was replaced by an attempt to regulate blasphemy, insolent behavior, corruption in the nunneries, gambling and gaming. On this subject, see also Ruggiero, *Boundaries of Eros,* 109–45.

24. For interesting parallels with the satirical, misogynist literature in England, especially in the eighteenth century, see Ellen Pollak, *The Poetics of Sexual Myth* (Chicago: University of Chicago Press, 1985), especially 4–19, 54–66. For an earlier period in England (the late sixteenth century), see Mary Beth Rose, *The Expense of Spirit: Love and Sexuality in English Renaissance Drama* (Ithaca: Cornell University Press, 1988), 21 and passim. She argues that "sexual desire, even when conceived as leading to a consciousness of the divine, was never considered beneficial or good in itself. Loved women were better left exalted, remote, and untouched. It is therefore not surprising to discover that where idealization of women occurred, misogyny was rarely far behind . . . in the English Renaissance . . . this dualizing, polarizing consciousness begins to break down, to lose its authority, as the predominant, or at least as the only, articulate view of women and sexuality." On misogyny in the early modern period, see Katharine M. Rogers, *The Troublesome Helpmate* (Seattle: University of Washington Press, 1966), especially 132. She claims that "a more common sign of fear of women in the Renaissance was the repeated attack on the whore, which often attributed enormous powers to her, more than she could possibly in fact have." See also R. Howard Bloch, "Medieval Misogyny," *Representations* 20 (1987): 1–24; R. Howard Bloch and Frances Ferguson, eds., *Misogyny, Misandry, and Misanthropy* (Berkeley: University of California Press, 1988).

25. How Franco gained Venier's favor and how she came to be involved with his nephews, Maffio and Marco in a three-way friendship is unknown. For details about Domenico's political activities, see Zorzi, *Cortigiana veneziana,* 83–90; and on the members of this salon, such as Girolamo Molino, Federico Badoer, Girolamo Parabosco, Sperone Speroni, Celio Magno, Jacopo Zane, Bernardo Tasso, and Girolamo Ruscelli, among many others, see 69–83. I discuss in greater detail Domenico Venier's position as the leading exponent of Venetian Petrarchism in chapters 4 and 5. For Domenico Venier's biography, the only comprehensive work is outdated: Pierantonio Serassi, *Rime di Domenico Veniero senatore viniziano raccolte ora per la prima volta ed illustrate* (Bergamo: Pietro Lancellotto, 1751). A recent dissertation further clarifies the connections

of the Venier salon to the literary activities of the Accademia della Fama. See Martha Feldman, "Venice and the Madrigal in the Mid-Sixteenth Century," Ph.D. diss., University of Pennsylvania, 1987, 1:442–55. Feldman argues that "there is no convincing evidence to support the claim often voiced in recent scholarship that Badoer's Accademia Veneziana was born directly from Venier's circle, or that a precise equation can be made between the two." (452). Although, as Feldman reports, Domenico signs a letter to Camillo Vezzato inviting him to participate in Badoer's academy, his name never appears on any of the academy's bylaws. Once the academy folds, however, in 1561, the members move back to Venier's salon. See also Martha Feldman, "The Academy of Domenico Venier, Music's Literary Muse in Mid-*Cinquecento* Venice," *Renaissance Quarterly* 44, no. 3 (1991): 475–510. The most recent discussion of Domenico Venier's literary salon and his relationship with Veronica Franco is that of Alvise Zorzi. See his *Cortigiana veneziana,* 57–65, 69–90, and 163–64, for further bibliography.

26. See chapter 4 below for notes on this subject.

27. Alvin Kernan, "Aggression and Satire: Art Considered as a Form of Biological Adaptation," in *Literary Theory and Structure: Essays in Honor of William K. Wimsatt,* ed. F. Brady, J. Palmer, and M. Price (New Haven: Yale University Press, 1973), 115–29.

28. See Felicity Nussbaum, *The Brink of All We Hate: English Satires on Women 1660–1750* (Lexington: University Press of Kentucky, 1984), 19. Especially useful for this study are 1–23, 159–67.

29. On a similar dynamic in English theater of the early modern period, see Lisa Jardine, *Still Harping on Daughters: Women and Drama in the Age of Shakespeare* (Totowa: Barnes and Noble, 1983), 93. On sumptuary laws that attempt to regulate not only excessive spending but the crossing of class and sexual boundaries, see n. 18 above and chapter 2 nn. 4, 6, 27, 28, 29, 32.

30. I refer throughout to two modern editions of Franco's works, which also discuss their textual history and Franco's activities as editor. For the poems (*Terze rime,* 1575), see Abdelkader Salza, *Rime: Gaspara Stampa e Veronica Franco* (Bari: Laterza, 1913); and for the letters (*Lettere familiari a diversi,* 1580), see Benedetto Croce, *Lettere dall'unica edizione del MDLXXX con proemio e nota iconografica* (Naples: Ricciardi, 1949). All translations of Franco's works, and other non-English texts, are my own unless otherwise indicated. For an earlier discussion of Franco's transformations and uses of the civic myth in her civic poems and editions, see my "Veronica Franco: The Courtesan as Poet in Sixteenth-Century Venice" (Ph.D diss., Yale University, 1985), 23–27, 57–66.

On the subversive nature of parody, see Mikhail M. Bakhtin, *Rabelais and His World,* trans. Helene Iswolsky (Cambridge: Harvard University Press, 1968); idem, *The Dialogic Imagination: Four Essays by M. M. Bakhtin,* ed. and trans. Michael Holquist (Austin: University of Texas Press, 1981), especially 3–83. On the uses of parody in Italian Renaissance literature, see *Réécritures 1–3: Commentaires, Parodies, Variations dans la littérature italienne de la Renaissance* (Paris: Université de la Sorbonne Nouvelle, 1983–87).

For many interesting insights into Aretino's pornographic text, I am indebted to an unpublished graduate seminar paper by Laura Walvoord, "'A Whore's Vices are Really Virtues': Prostitution and Feminine Identity in Sixteenth-Century Venice," (University of California, Berkeley, Department of History). She argues that Aretino's construction of the prostitute is not man or woman, but an ambiguous third "category."

31. *Canon Pietro Casola's Pilgrimage to Jerusalem in the Year 1494,* ed. M. Margaret Newett (Manchester: University Press of Manchester, 1907), 145; this is a translation of Casola's *Viaggio di Pietro Casola a Gerusalemme* (Milan: 1855).

32. For an account of Sir Henry Wotton's trip to Venice, see *The Life and Letters of Sir Henry Wotton*, ed. Logan Pearsall Smith (Oxford: Oxford University Press, 1907); for this quote, see page 18.

33. Michel Montaigne, *Journal de voyage en Italie*, ed. Maurice Rat (Paris: Editions Garnier, 1955), 72.

34. Ibid., 73.

35. Ibid., 73. On courtesan's lavish costumes in the Renaissance, see Rosita Levi Pizetsky, *Storia del costume in Italia* (Turin: Einaudi, 1964−69). For the sixteenth century, see vol. 3. For Venice, see Doretta D. Poli, "La moda nella Venezia del Palladio, 1550−1580," in Lionello Puppi, ed., *Architettura e utopia nella Venezia del Cinquecento* (Milan: Electa, 1980), 219−22. For a fascinating examination of an inventory of one sixteenth-century Venetian courtesan's belongings, see Cathy Santore, "Julia Lombardo, 'Somtuosa Meretrize': A Portrait by Property," *Renaissance Quarterly* 41, no. 1 (1988): 44−83.

36. *Coryat's Crudities*, 267. Coryat also warns against the courtesan's power of language: "Also thou wilt finde the Venetian Cortezan . . . a good Rhetorician, and a most elegant discourser, so that if shee cannot move thee with all these foresaid delights, shee will assay thy constancy with her Rhetoricall tongue"; Jones argues in "City Women and Their Audiences: Louise Labé and Veronica Franco," in *Rewriting the Renaissance*, 304, that "Coryat's remark as ideology, provides a useful entry into the poems of Labé and Franco. They are indeed rhetoricians: they use their femininity as a basis for claims to doubly public reputations . . . the public nature of their ambitions—the desire to rise socially, to be defined through and benefit from ties with powerful men—led both poets to a contradictory rhetoric."

37. On the connections between the courtesan and the plague and the alleged sinful practices of the Venetian people, see Paolo Preto, *Peste e società a Venezia, 1576* (Vicenza: Neri Pozza, 1978), 66−79, 78−87, and passim. Paolo Preto locates this collective feeling of guilt, more specifically, primarily in the ruling classes. He states that "la convinzione che l'eccesso dei peccati abbia mosso la mano di Dio contro Venezia riappare decisa in tutta la classe dirigente con un'insistenza ed una capacità di spinta operativa che ricorda senz'altro i giorni della Lega di Cambrai" (the conviction that many sins were committed, moving God's hand against Venice, reappears definitely in all of the ruling class and with such an insistence and with the ability to move people to action that it recalls without doubt the days of the League of Cambrai). Francesco Sansovino (*Venetia città nobilissima et singolare* [Venice: D. Giustinian Martinioni, 1581], 233) writes: "sul far della sera si sentiva una harmonia mirabile di diverse voci di coloro, che al suono dell'Ave Maria lodavano Dio, cantando, chi le litanie e chi salmi" (as evening falls one can always hear a wonderful harmony of different voices including they who, at the sound of the Ave Maria, praised God with song, some with litanies, others with psalms). On the relation of these acts of repentance to the reforms instituted by Cardinal Borromeo, see Preto, *Peste e società*, 81−83. For a comprehensive bibliography on the subject, see Paul F. Grendler, *The Roman Inquisition and the Venetian Press, 1540−1605* (Princeton: Princeton University Press, 1977), 326−48.

Also extremely useful is Giovanni Scarabello, "Paure, Superstizioni, Infamie," in *Storia della cultura veneta* 4:343−76, especially 364−76; Fabio Mutinelli, *Annali urbani di Venezia dall'anno 810 al 12 maggio 1797* (Venice: G. B. Merlo, 1841). See also Cheryl Lynn Ross, "The Plague and the Figures of Power" (Ph.D. diss., Stanford University, 1985); *Venezia e la peste, 1348−1797* (Venice: Marsilio Editore, 1979).

38. *Coryat's Crudities*, 264.

39. Ibid., 270.

40. Marvin B. Becker (*Civility and Society in Western Europe 1300–1600* [Bloomington and Indianapolis: Indiana University Press, 1988]), describes Fynes Moryson (1566–1630) as "that sober, factual, reliable and rather unimaginative recorder of European mores, habits and customs (mind-bogglingly detailed), who provides us with a less literary, more concrete version of these times of change" (37). See *Shakespeare's Europe: A Survey of the Condition of Europe at the end of the Sixteenth Century*, ed. Charles Hughes. 2d ed. (New York: Benjamin Blom, 1903; reprint, 1967), especially 130, 411–12, 441–42, 453–54, 462, 467, and passim. See also Panrose, *Urbane Travelers*, 4–39.

41. Hughes, *Shakespeare's Europe*, 409–10.

42. *Coryat's Crudities*, 265.

43. Ibid., 264.

44. Ibid., 265. In 1514, Marin Sanuto recorded in his diaries that the taxes collected from Venetian prostitutes and courtesans had helped to pay for the construction of the Arsenale: "Noto come in questi xorni zoe domenega adì 22 fo proposto per ser Hironimo Contarini proveditor al Arsenal come l'arsenal se amuniva et evia necessario a farlo cavar et per non esser denari si havia pensa tansar tutte le putane" (I note how in these days, that is, Sunday the 22nd, it was proposed by Ser Hieronimo Contarini the *provveditor* to the Arsenale that in order to fortify the Arsenale, it is necessary to excavate; and lacking the necessary funds to do so, it has been proposed that all prostitutes be taxed). Referring to prostitution in southern France in the fifteenth century, Jacques Rossiaud argues (*Medieval Prostitution*, trans. Lydia G. Cochrane [London: Basil Blackwell, 1988], 43) that "not only did prostitutes have a social responsibility; they had a moral responsibility as well, since they contributed to the defense of collective order . . . (they) helped to defend the honour of women 'of estate' and protect them from unruliness."

45. On the Italian courtesan as a commercial asset, see Georgina Masson, *The Courtesans of the Italian Renaissance* (London: Secker and Warburg, 1975), 10–11. On the subject of young men repressing their sexual needs owing to societal, economic, and political pressures, and in turn looking for outlets in prostitutes, in Venice and also in other European cities of the fifteenth and sixteenth century, see Pietro Costa, *Courtisanes et la police des moeurs à Venise* (Sauveterre: Imprimerie Chollet, 1886). Rossiaud argues ("Prostitution, jeunesse et société dans les villes du sud-est au XVe siécle," *Annales, E.S.C.* 31 (1976): 289–325) that the legal brothel in southern France before the sixteenth century integrated young men into the social order. Richard C. Trexler ("La prostitution florentine au XVe siécle: Patronage et clienteles," *Annales, E.S.C.* 36 (1981): 983–1015) suggests that fifteenth-century Florence legalized prostitution as a way of dealing with the rise in male homosexuality and the declining rate of legitimate births.

46. On the question of licit and illicit sexuality within the Venetian context of the fifteenth and sixteenth century, see Ruggiero, *Boundaries of Eros*, especially chap. 1, "The Sexual Environment of Renaissance Venice: An Introduction," 3–15, and chap. 7, "Perspectives on Normal Sexuality: An Essay," 146–68.

47. Ibid., 161.

48. Leah Lydia Otis, *Prostitution in Medieval Society: The History of an Institution in Languedoc* (Chicago: University of Chicago Press, 1985), 2–3. Mary Perry in "Deviant Insiders," 146–47, describes a polar separation of women in Seville into angel (Holy Virgin) and whore (prostitute) similar to the separation I have defined for male representations of Venetian women in early modern Venice. She believes that because there was more popular interest in the Virgin in the mid-sixteenth century as the doctrine of the Immaculate Conception became widespread

throughout Western Europe, so a woman's strength was perceived as a potential threat to "displace males from their position of power over females unless it was counterbalanced by rituals that emphasized the depravity of female sexuality."

49. Ruggiero, *Boundaries of Eros*, 153. He claims that for women who lacked an adequate dowry, or were considered ineligible for the charitable dowry system that Brian Pullan has described in detail (see chapter 2 nn. 47, 48), prostitution offered a kind of outlet, one which he is careful to concede "may have [made women feel] more victimized than aided by such placement."

50. Ibid., 9.

51. Labalme, "Sodomy and Venetian Justice." On the quasi-familial relationships caused by adultery and fornication, see Ruggiero, *Violence in Early Renaissance Venice*, 101, where he states that at all social levels except the highest, "rape was not a serious crime, and it was surely underreported among workers. Equally important, a rapist sometimes could marry his victim, reducing the prosecution levels as a result. Such cases sometimes reached the courts where the judges permitted the rapist to pay his debt to society either by marrying his victim or by serving a jail sentence or paying a fine" (101). As Ruggiero also notes (*Boundaries of Eros*), by the fifteenth century, the courts' rulings against adultery and fornication were "leaner" than they had been, especially for women, in the earlier centuries and were more focused on "more mundane concerns with property, status, affection, and occasional violence as well as a concern with protecting marriage as an institution" (49 and passim).

52. Ruggiero, *Boundaries of Eros*, 109–45.

53. Otis, *Prostitution in Medieval Society*, 72. On the commercialization for profit of a woman's body within early modern England, especially as figured within Ben Jonson's play *Epicoene*, see Karen Newman, "City Talk: Women and Commodification in Jonson's *Epicoene*," *English Literary History* 56, no. 3 (1989): 503–18.

54. For an examination of the positive and negative connotations of the Virgin Mary, see Marina Warner, *Alone of All Her Sex: The Myth and Cult of the Virgin Mary* (New York: Vintage Books, 1983). See also the interesting analysis of the representation of the Virgin and the Mary Magdalene in fourteenth-century Tuscan art as both negative and positive symbols for early-Renaissance women in Margaret R. Miles, *Image As Insight: Visual Understanding in Western Christianity and Secular Culture* (Boston: Beacon Press, 1985), especially 75–93; Ian Maclean, *The Renaissance Notion of Woman: A Study in the Fortunes of Scholasticism and Medical Science in European Intellectual Life* (New York: Cambridge University Press, 1980). For a marked increase in women writers in the cinquecento as linked to a general rise in the use of the vernacular, see Carlo Dionisotti, *Geografia e storia della letteratura italiana* (Turin: Einaudi, 1967), 237–54. See Rose, *Expense of Spirit,* especially for her discussion of sexuality and social mobility in Jacobean comedy (47–58).

55. Francesco Sansovino, *Ragionamento di M. Francesco Sansovino nel quale brevemente s'insegna a giovani huomini la bella arte d'amore* (Venice: 1545), 19.

56. The complete edition of Speroni's works is the *Opere di M. Sperone Speroni degli Alvarotti: Tratte de' Mss. Originali,* ed. Natal dalle Leste and Marco Forcellini (Venice: Domenico Occhi, 1740). For a more modern but partial edition of Speroni's *Dialoghi,* see Mario Pozzi, *Trattatisti del Cinquecento* (Milan: Ricciardi, 1978), 25:471–850, and for documentation, 1178–94. I refer throughout to the sixteenth-century edition of this *Orazione contra le cortegiane,* together with others in Sperone Speroni, *Orationi del Signor Speron Speroni Dottor et Cavalier Padovano* (Venice: Ruberto Meietti, 1596), 168–213. For an early study of Speroni's dialogues, see Riccardo

Scrivano, "Cultura e letteratura in Sperone Speroni," in his *Cultura e letteratura nel Cinquecento* (Rome: Ateneo, 1966), 117–41. And for an excellent recent study of the theories of dialogue in the late Italian Renaissance which includes a consideration of Speroni, see Jon R. Snyder, *Writing the Scene of Speaking: Theories of Dialogue in Late Italian Renaissance* (Stanford: Stanford University Press, 1989). For the text of the *Orazione contra le cortegiane*, dedicated to Jacopo Cornaro, Capitano di Padova, see also Speroni, *Opere di M. Sperone Speroni degli Alvarotti*, 3:170–244. For the oration as a response to Antonio Brocardo's oration *In lode delle cortegiane*, see Santore, "Julia Lombardo," 50 n. 17. Jonathan Shiff ("'Lingua zerga' in the Grimani Banquet Plays," *Italica* 66, no. 4 (1989): 399–411, especially 400) speaks of Brocardo as the author of the immensely popular sixteenth-century handbook on Venetian argot (lingua zerga), the *Nuovo modo de intendere la lingua zerga*. An Italian scholar first proposed Brocardo as the author and reproduces a letter Brocardo wrote in *lingua zerga* from Padua in 1531 to a courtesan friend in Venice, Marietta Mirtilli, in which he refers to this volume as one that he is about to publish. See Franca Ageno, "A proposito del *Nuovo modo de intendere la lingua zerga*," *Giornale storico della letteratura italiana* 135 (1958): 370–91. For a discussion of the antagonistic love relationship between the Roman *cortigiana onesta* Tullia d'Aragona and Sperone Speroni, see Lynne Lawner, *Lives of the Courtesans* (Milan: Rizzoli, 1987), 46–47. For an excellent analysis and interpretation of Tullia d'Aragona's collection of poems, which also included many male authors' poems, I am indebted to Ann Rosalind Jones for many valuable suggestions. See "Surprising Fame," 87–93, and "The Poetics of Group Identity: Self-Commemoration Through Dialogue in Pernette du Guillet and Tullia d'Aragona," in her *Currency of Eros: Women's Love Lyric in Europe, 1540–1620* (Bloomington and Indianapolis: Indiana University Press, 1990), 79–117. She sees Tullia's collection of poems (*Rime*) as an "improving fiction for the realities of a courtesan's life and the rivalry among her clients. In the *Rime*, potential rivals are transformed into flattering mirrors for each other. Tullia is a channel through which her interlocutors emerge as members of a masculine elite constructed within the group text" in *The Currency of Eros*, 91.

57. For an interesting discussion of Boccaccio's views on exemplary women, see Constance Jordan, "Boccaccio's In-Famous Women: Gender and Civic Virtue in the *De mulieribus claris*," in *Ambiguous Realities: Women in the Middle Ages and Renaissance*, ed. Carole Levin and Jeanie Wilson (Detroit: Wayne State University Press, 1987), 26,

58. Speroni, *Orationi*, 186–87. Hereafter all page numbers will be included within the text.

59. Jon R. Snyder (*Writing the Scene of Speaking*, 90–91) discusses how Speroni rewrote the *Oration* because of pressure from the Counter-Reformation censors in Rome.

60. On Venetian convents, see Pio Paschini, "I monasteri femminili in Italia nel 1500," in his *Problemi di vita religiosa in Italia nel Cinquecento* (Padua: Antenore, 1960); Aldo Stella, *Chiesa e stato nelle relazioni dei nunzi pontifici a Venezia: Ricerche sul giurisdizionalismo veneziano dal XVI al XVIII secolo* (Vatican City: 1964), 32–33 n. 46 and passim. On women's forced entry into convents as an economic and social constraint imposed upon them by their fathers, see Patricia H. Labalme, "Women's Roles in Early Modern Venice: An Exceptional Case," in *Beyond Their Sex: Learned Women of the European Past*, ed. Patricia H. Labalme (New York: New York University Press, 1980), 137–44; and King and Rabil, *Her Immaculate Hand*.

61. Desiderius Erasmus, *I Ragionamenti, overo colloqui famigliari di Desiderio Erasmo*, trans. Pietro Lauro (Venice: Vincenzo Valgrisi, 1549), 175–79. This is the second of two editions. The first was published with the title *Colloqui familiari* by the same publisher in 1545. On Erasmus's Venetian dialogues, see Manlio Dazzi, *Aldo Manuzio e il dialogo veneziano di Erasmo*, vol. 26 (Vicenza: Neri Pozza Editore, 1969), especially 78, 126, where Dazzi speaks of his literary debt

to Lucian's *Dialogues*. For an Italian translation of Lucian's dialogues, see *Dialoghi di dei e di cortigiane*, trans. and ed. Alessandro Lami and Franco Maltomini (Milan: Rizzoli, 1986). On Erasmus's period in Italy, see the definitive study by Silvana Seidel-Menchi, *Erasmo in Italia, 1520–80* (Turin: Bollati Borenghieri, 1987).

62. Nussbaum, *Brink of All We Hate*, 6.

63. Erasmus, *I Ragionamenti*, 179.

64. For an interesting survey of the anticourtier discourse in French and Italian literature of the Renaissance and antiquity, see Pauline M. Smith, *The Anti-Courtier Trend in Sixteenth-Century French Literature* (Geneva: Droz, 1966). She sees this discourse as stemming from "political, social, economic unrest" (10).

65. Aretino's literary activities in relation to the literary context of Venice in the sixteenth century are discussed in Giovanni Aquilecchia, "Pietro Aretino e altri poligrafi a Venezia," in *Storia della cultura veneta*, ed. G. Arnaldi and M. Pastore Stocchi (Vicenza: Neri Pozza, 1982), 4:61–98; Christopher Cairns, *Pietro Aretino and the Republic of Venice: Researches on Aretino and His Circle in Venice, 1527–1556* (Florence: Leo Olschki, 1985), especially 251–60; this work includes an extensive bibliography. And see Patricia H. Labalme, "Personality and Politics in Venice: Pietro Aretino," in *Titian, His World and His Legacy*, ed. David Rosand (New York: Columbia University Press, 1982), 119–32. Peter Stallybrass speaks of the attacks on women and the court in the context of Jacobean theater as the result of one oppressed group denouncing another ("Patriarchal Territories: The Body Enclosed," in *Rewriting the Renaissance*, ed. Margaret W. Ferguson, Maureen Quilligan, and Nancy J. Vickers [Chicago: University of Chicago Press, 1986], 123–42).

66. On this point, see Murtha Baca, "Aretino in Venice 1527–1537 and 'La Professione Del Far' Lettere" (Ph.D. diss., University of California, Los Angeles, 1978); Lora Palladino, "Pietro Aretino. Orator and Art Theorist" (Ph.D. diss., Yale University, 1984).

67. All references to Aretino's letters (in Italian) are to *Lettere, il primo e il secondo libro*, in *Tutte le opere*, ed. F. Flora and A. Del Vita (Milan: Mondadori, 1960), hereafter cited as Aretino, *Lettere*. For this letter, see 29. All translations, unless otherwise indicated, are my own.

68. Tomaso Garzoni, *La Piazza universale di tutte le professioni del mondo* (Venice: Giovanni Battista Somasco, 1585). All references are to this edition, and all page numbers will be noted hereafter in the text. There was also an earlier edition in 1584 published in Venice by Ziletti. By 1675, the book had been published in twenty-five editions. On this monk from Bagnocavallo, see Benedetto Croce, "Pagine di Tommaso Garzoni," in his *Poeti e scrittori del pieno e tardo rinascimento* (Bari: Laterza, 1970), 2:208–20; Giuseppe Cocchiara, *Popolo e letteratura in Italia* (Turin: Einaudi, 1959), 54–56; Paul F. Grendler, *Critics of the Italian World, 1530–1560: Anton Francesco Doni, Nicolò Franco and Ortensio Lando* (Madison: University of Wisconsin Press, 1969), 191–93, 207. For a discussion of the various editions, sources, and literary traditions surrounding *La Piazza*, including Alessandro Citolini's *La tipocosmia* (Venice: Vincenzo Valgrisi, 1561), see Paolo Cherchi, *Enciclopedismo e politica della riscrittura: Tomaso Garzoni* (Pisa: Pacini Editore, 1980); Paolo Cherchi and Beatrice Collina, "Esplorazioni preparatorie per un'edizione della 'Piazza Universale' di Tomaso Garzoni," *Lettere Italiane*, no. 2 (1991): 250–66.

69. Jonas Barish, *The Antitheatrical Prejudice* (Berkeley: University of California Press, 1981); Frank Whigham, "Interpretation at Court: Courtesy and the Performer-Audience Dialectic," *New Literary History* 143 (1983): 623–41. For interesting connections between courtier and courtesan, and the "donna di palazzo," as Castiglione defines this role, and "cortigiana," see Adriana Chemello, "Donna di palazzo, moglie, cortigiana: Ruoli e funzioni sociali della donna

in alcuni trattati del Cinquecento," in *La corte e il Cortegiano,* ed. Amedeo Quondam (Rome: Bulzoni, 1980), 113–33. On attitudes toward women in the text of Castiglione's *Cortegiano,* see Dain A. Trafton, "Politics and the Praise of Women: Political Doctrine in the *Courtier's Third Book,"* in *Castiglione: The Ideal and the Real in Renaissance Culture,* ed. Robert Hanning and David Rosand (New Haven: Yale University Press, 1983), 17–44; J. R. Woodhouse, *Baldesar Castiglione: A Reassessment of "The Courtier"* (Edinburgh: Edinburgh University Press, 1978).

Laura Walvoord argues that "Prostitutes' strategies for confounding their clients are almost entirely based on an appropriation of *sprezzatura* in order to forward their destructive agenda. Their creation of a transparent self-representation mirrors the self-fashioning which occurs at court, and it is this new system of representation which destabilizes the normative order" ("A Whore's Vices are Really Virtues," 17–18). Nanna, in Aretino's *I Ragionamenti,* associates the courtier with the courtesan when she says, "Indeed, Master Andrea used to say that whores and courtiers can be put in the same scales; in fact you see most of them looking like defaced silver coins rather than bright gold pieces" (as cited in Walvoord, "A Whore's Vices are Really Virtues," 17).

70. As cited by Giovanni Aquilecchia in his introduction to *Aretino: Sei giornate* (Bari: Laterza, 1975), xi.

71. Aretino, *Lettere,* 29–30.

72. Pietro Aretino, *Ragionamento nel quale M. Pietro Aretino figura quattro suoi amici che favellano delle corti del mondo, e di quella del cielo* (Venice: Marcolini, 1539), first published in Novara in 1538. On this work, see Amedeo Quondam, "La scena della menzogna: Corte e cortigiano nel 'Ragionamento' di Pietro Aretino," *Psicon* nos. 8–9 (1976): 4–23; he also discusses connections to Aretino's comedy *La cortigiana,* composed in the 1520s during his sojourn in Rome. See also Paul Larivaille, *Pietro Aretino: Fra rinascimento e manierismo,* trans. Mariella Di Maio and Maria Luisa Rispoli (Rome: Bulzoni, 1980), 123–37; and see 98–104 for his first years in Venice and his affiliation with the Venier family. Paolo Procaccioli ("Per una lettura del 'Ragionamento,'" *La Rassegna della letteratura italiana* 91 [1987]) discusses Aretino's work in light of Lucian's dialogues on courtesans. In addition see Giovanni Aquilecchia, "Pietro Aretino," 61–98, and idem, "Pietro Aretino e la lingua zerga," in Aquilecchia, *Schede di italianistica* (Turin: Einaudi, 1976), 153–69. For Aretino's connections with the publisher Francesco Marcolini, see Amedeo Quondam, in "Nel giardino del Marcolini: Un editore veneziano tra Aretino e Doni," *Giornale storico della letteratura italiana* 157 (1980): 75–116.

73. One of the principal reasons that the courtier and courtesan's "art" is so profoundly threatening is that it has the power to deceive the "other" through misrepresentation. The courtesan overturns the male symbolic system to her own advantage by obfuscating the semiotic system of social hierarchies.

74. Aretino, *Ragionamento delle corti* in Quondam, "La scena della menzogna," 8.

75. For more on the connections between these two worlds, see ibid., 14 and passim.

76. For these comments, see the English translation of the modern Italian edition, *Aretino: Sei giornate,* ed. Giovanni Aquilecchia (Bari: Laterza, 1975), and the introduction by Raymond Rosenthal in Pietro Aretino, *Aretino's Dialogues* (New York: Stein and Day, 1971), 7. For a study of Aretino's "pornographic" texts, see Larivaille, *Pietro Aretino,* 139–227. Larivaille discusses Aretino's autocensoring strategies in an interesting article on the anonymous play *La Venexiana* in his *"La Venexiana* ou les ressources du langage honnête: Censure et théâtre à Venise," in *Le pouvoir et la plume: incitation, contrôle, et répression dans l'Italie du XVIème siècle* (Paris: CRRI, 1982), 159–76;

Pietro Aretino, 98–100 and 442. For interesting connections between "l'arte puttanesca" and "cortigianeria," see Quondam, "La scena della menzogna," especially 15–19 n. 21.

77. Recent feminist theorists on pornography provide useful ways of understanding the cultural representations of women as commodities that affirm "male supremacy" over the female object. Catherine A. MacKinnon, for example, argues (*Feminism Unmodified: Discourses on Life and Law* [Cambridge: Harvard University Press, 1987]) that "pornography is not harmless fantasy or a corrupt and confused misinterpretation of an otherwise natural and healthy sexuality. Along with the rape and prostitution in which it participates, pornography institutionalizes the sexuality of male supremacy, which fuses the erotization of dominance and submission with the social construction of male and female" (148–49).

78. Aretino, *Aretino*, 156, and *Aretino's Dialogues*, 173.

79. Aretino, *Lettere*, 366–67. On the importance, however, of protecting a young girl's virginity in order for her to be able to marry honorably, see Ruggiero, *Boundaries of Eros*, 17–18, 23–24, 36–39, 42–44, 152–54, 162–63; idem, "'Più che la vita caro': onore, matrimonio e reputazione femminile nel tardo rinascimento," *Quaderni storici* 66 (1987): 753–75. See also Lucia Ferrante, "L'Onore ritrovato: Donne nella Casa del Soccorso di S. Paolo a Bologna," *Quaderni storici* 53 (1983): 499–527; Sherrill Cohen, "Convertite e Malmaritate: Donne 'irregolari' e ordini religiosi nella Firenze rinascimentale," *Memoria: Rivista di storia delle donne* 5 (1982): 46–65.

80. Giovanni Aquilecchia discusses the relationship between Aretino and Lorenzo Venier as that of teacher and disciple: "poteva essere considerato suo discepolo, se non per altro per la composizione, entro i primi quattro anni del soggiorno aretiniano a Venezia, dei due poemetti satirici contro due cortegiane veneziane. . . . La collaborazione dell'Aretino sembra molto probabile, sopratutto nella redazione finale di queste composizioni, come risulta da una lettera di Alessandro Zanco del 26 marzo del 1536" (he could have been considered his disciple, if not for anything else than for the composition, during the first four years of Aretino's sojourn in Venice, of two short satirical poems against two Venetian courtesans. . . . That Aretino collaborated on them seems most probable, above all in the final version of these compositions, as is evident in a letter of Alessandro Zanco of 26 March 1536) ("Pietro Aretino," 85–86). Aquilecchia also suggests that Aretino most certainly had a hand in this and in other Venier compositions of a satirical nature. Christopher Cairns speaks of Aretino's affiliation with the Venier family in his early years in Venice (*Pietro Aretino*, 30 and passim).

81. Jacques Rossiaud (*Medieval Prostitution*, 12–13) notes the frequency with which rape, and gang rapes, occurred in southern France in the early modern period. He adds that this violence committed against women of all classes was "always accompanied by degrading insults, humiliation of the victim, and blows. Well before they passed to the act itself, the aggressors exculpated themselves, and from the outset the woman they chose was treated as guilty and viewed as a mere object and as obliged to submit" (21–22). He speculates that the frequency of such rapes indicates that they might have been considered a "rite of passage to manhood and of admission to neighborhood gangs" (22). The woman's status was severely affected in the cases reported in southern France, because it opened her to public scandal and reprobation, which discouraged women from filing a complaint with authorities. The status of a raped woman, he notes, "was brought singularly closer to that of a common prostitute. Rendered vulnerable, psychologically and physically, she had little hope of regaining her honor as long as she remained in the city. This violence was often a prelude to forced prostitution or procuration" (29–30).

82. Ruggiero, *Boundaries of Eros,* 96.

83. See Michael Seidel, *Satiric Inheritance: Rabelais to Sterne* (Princeton: Princeton University Press, 1979), 3–25, for theoretical considerations about the "satiric impulse," which have been especially useful for this discussion.

84. Nussbaum, *Brink of All We Hate,* 4–5.

85. This expression "rhyming the woman dead" is borrowed from Nussbaum, *Brink of All We Hate,* 4. She discusses an English satire, Oldham's "A Satyr Upon a Woman" (1678), in reference to the ancient tradition of misogynist works: "In some instances the antifeminist satiric theme seems to be used to exorcize one female individual from the mortal world, as in the case of Oldham, who rhymes a woman dead and curses her with an eternity of tortures in the seventeenth-century tradition of the *satyr.*"

86. Aretino refers in a letter (6 December 1537) to Gianiacopo Lionardi, ambassador to the Duke of Urbino in Venice, to "alcuni giovani" (some young men) who are already his followers. Among those he lists are Francesco and Federico Badoaro, Girolamo Lioni, and Domenico and Lorenzo Venier. See Aretino, *Lettere,* 351. For this relationship, see Aquilecchia, "Pietro Aretino," 85–87.

87. The catalog, *La tariffa delle puttane di Vinegia* (Price-List of the Whores of Venice), has been reprinted in Barzaghi, *Donne e cortigiane?* 168–91. Hereafter I refer only to this reprinted version. This catalog lists 110 courtesans and 25 procuresses by name. It was printed without the name of an author, and it did not include the publisher's name. For an interesting discussion of *La tariffa delle puttane* in relation to the Venetian courtesan Julia Lombardo, mentioned earlier, see Santore, "Julia Lombardo," 48–51. It has also been suggested that Antonio Cavallino, and not Lorenzo Venier, is the author of this catalog. On this, see Larivaille, *"La venexiana,"* 164 n. 16; idem, *Pietro Aretino,* 98–100, 442.

88. *La puttana errante* (The wandering whore; Venice: 1531; reprint, Paris: 1883). For a discussion of this text, see Lawner, *Lives of the Courtesans,* 77.

89. Many of the courtesans listed in the catalog—a kind of sixteenth-century telephone book—are associated with their mother's trade insofar as prospective clients are requested to pay the required fee directly to the mother, who acts as a go-between for her daughter. This was the case, as well, for Veronica Franco, and it suggests that she was not yet married at the time of the conception of the catalog, as she is recorded as living in her mother's house. A rare edition of the *Catalogo* (1575) exists in the Museo Civico Correr in Venice. For a modern "edition" of the catalog, see Rita Casagrande di Villaviera, *Le cortigiane veneziane del Cinquecento* (Milan: Longanesi, 1968). She reproduces the catalog in her volume. On the publishing history of the catalog, see Tassini, *Veronica Franco,* 9 n. 1, and 56 n. 2. He argues that this list of courtesans, first reprinted in 1870–72 by the editor G. Batta De Lorenzi for Lord Orford (*Leggi e Memorie Venete sulla prostituzione fino alla caduta della Repubblica* [Venice: 1870–72]), was not originally commissioned by the Venetian government, but rather by Hieronimo Calepino, a publisher who was eventually tried by the Inquisition courts on 23 July 1566 for heresy. About this trial, Paul Grendler notes that in "1566 the Esecutori had fined Girolamo (or Troian) Calepin for printing a *Tariffa delle puttane.* . . . In March 1568, the Esecutori ordered Zio [a former printer] to visit Calepin's store. He found the *Tariffa* . . . as well as a number of prohibited books." After the questioning of his neighbors, Grendler reports, it was revealed that Calepin had sold many of Aretino's books for Aretino's publisher, Marcolini—books that had also been prohibited by authorities. Calepin had already escaped by the time the authorities arrived at his home. See Grendler, *Roman Inquisition and the Venetian Press,* 160–61, 161 n. 79, for archival source. See

also Zorzi, *Cortigiana veneziana,* 20; he discusses the clandestine nature of the catalog. It is also possible that the catalog, much like *La tariffa della puttane,* was conceived as a satire, which would help explain why Veronica's fee is indicated as only 2 scudi. Paola Franco, her mother, is listed as a "pieza," or go-between. For a definition of this term, see Giuseppe Boerio, *Dizionario del dialetto veneziano,* 2d ed. (Venice: Giovanni Cecchini, 1856), 509.

90. For this quote, see Barzaghi, *Donne o cortigiane? La tariffa delle puttane,* 171.

91. For satiric commonplaces about courtesans in English literature, especially for theatrical texts, see Anne Haselkorn, *Prostitution in Elizabethan and Jacobean Comedy* (Troy, N.Y.: Whitson, 1983).

92. See the Flemish Crispijn van de Passe, *Le miroir des plus belles courtisannes de ce temps* (1631), which is an album of forty engraved portraits of international courtesans in appropriate costumes with brief vitae in verse form in three different languages that accompany the portraits.

93. Barzaghi, *Donne o cortigiane?,* 172.

94. Ibid., 177.

95. The polarization of the woman's body into angel and whore, or "good" and "bad," is discussed by anthropologist Mary Douglas in her *Purity and Danger: An Analysis of Concepts of Pollution and Taboo* (London: Routledge and Kegan Paul, 1969). See also Stallybrass, "Patriarchal Territories," 123–42, 344–47; and Peter Stallybrass and Allon White, *The Politics and Poetics of Transgression* (Ithaca: Cornell University Press, 1987).

96. For a fascinating, although outdated, biography of Maffio Venier, see Nicola Ruggieri, *Maffio Venier: Arcivescovo e letterato veneziano del cinquecento* (Udine: Tipografia Bosetti, 1909). See also Zorzi, *Cortigiana veneziana,* 93–111, and for further bibliography, 164–65. Recently all of Maffio Venier's dialect verses have been critically attributed and cataloged by Tiziana Agostini Nordio, in "Rime dialettali attribuite a Maffio Venier. Primo regesto," *Quaderni veneti,* no. 2 (1985): 7–23; Tiziana Agostini Nordio and Valerio Vianello, "'La Strazzosa,' Canzone di Maffio Venier: Edizione Critica," in their *Contributi Rinascimentali: Venezia e Firenze* (Padua: Francisci Editore, 1982), 9–131. See also Antonio Pilot, *Canzoni inediti di Maffio Venier* (Capodistria: 1906) and Armando Balduino, "Restauri e ricuperi per Maffio Venier," in *Medioevo e rinascimento veneto con altri studi in onore di Lino Lazzarini* (Padua: Editrice Antenore, 1979), 2: 231–63. For an extremely informative and interesting reading, textual study, and translation into Italian of three of Venier's dialect poems, see Giorgio Padoan, "Maffio Venier. Tre liriche: I. Do donne me sè drio quasi ogni dì II. Amor, son co' xe un can da scoassera III. M'ho consumà aspettandote, ben mio," *Quaderni veneti,* no. 2 (1985): 7–30. Padoan claims that Maffio openly challenged Bembist dictates and thus attached himself to a long-standing Venetian dialect literature that includes works by Leonardo Giustinian and Giorgio Baffo. For an extensive selection of Maffio Venier's verses compiled by Venier's friend Anzolo Ingegneri, together with works by other Venetian dialect poets, see Ingegneri, *Versi alla vinitiana, zoé canzon, satire, lettere amorose, matinae, canzonette . . .* (Vicenza: Salvadori, 1617), 58–141. On Maffio's relation to his father, Lorenzo, and to the other members of his family, see Bodo L. O. Richter, "Petrarchism and Anti-Petrarchism among the Veniers," *Forum Italicum* 3 (1969): 20–42. For the most important recent essay that treats Venetian Petrarchism and Mannerism in the lyric of the second half of the sixteenth century, including an excellent discussion of Franco's poetry, see Erspamer, "Petrarchismo e manierismo nella lirica del secondo Cinquecento," 4:189–222.

97. Michael Seidel, *Satiric Inheritance,* 16.

98. Francesco Sansovino, *Sette libri di satire* (Venice: Iacomo Vidali, 1573) as quoted in *Trattati di poetica e retorica del Cinquecento,* ed. Bernard Weinberg (Bari: Laterza, 1970–74), 2: 517–18.

For the sixteenth-century edition that I consulted, see *Satire di cinque poeti illustri*, ed. Paterno (Venice: G. A. Valvassori, 1565), which includes satires by Ariosto, Sansovino, Alamanni, Bentivoglio, and Paterno. For the tradition of the satirical *capitolo* in Italy, see the extremely informative study by Silvia Longhi, *Lusus: Il capitolo burlesco nel Cinquecento* (Padua: Antenore, 1983).

99. On Aretino's transgression of Bembo's stylistic mandates, see Giovanni Aquilecchia, "Pietro Aretino e la lingua zerga," G. Arnaldi and M. Pastore Stocchi, *Storia della cultura veneta* (Vicenza: Neri Pozza, 1982), 4:153–69. For this, see Aretino, *Lettere* (book 1, 156 to Lodovico Dolce), 194. On Bembo's literary and political career and on the influential *Prose della volgar lingua*, see Pasquale Sabbatino, *La "scienza" della scrittura: Dal progetto del Bembo al manuale* (Florence: Leo S. Olschki, 1988).

100. These lines come from Maffio Venier's dialect poem, "No ve maravegié, sia chi se vogia" (Do not be surprised, whoever should care), as cited in Zorzi, *Cortigiana veneziana*, 94 (manuscript collection of the Biblioteca Nazionale Marciana, MSS. it. IX 217 (=7061), c. 1r). The slight variations were suggested to me by Tiziana Agostini Nordio, who has transcribed many of Maffio Venier's dialect verses from the Venetian collections. On linguistic and literary uses of Venetian dialect in Ruzzante and in Goldoni, see Linda Carroll, *Language and Dialect in Ruzzante and Goldoni* (Ravenna: Longo Editore, 1981); see also her discussions of the origins of Venetian dialect and other Italian dialects in Italian literature (9–31 and passim).

101. I borrow these terms from Nussbaum, *Brink of All We Hate*, 4.

102. Michael Seidel speaks about the satirist's defensive strategies in *Satiric Inheritance*, where he argues, following Freud, that satirists generate "their own insecurities and then elaborate a fable in which they attempt to displace themselves from what they have generated . . . the satirist tries to sustain the impression that the monstrous is different from him" (11–12). Lisa Jardine (*Still Harping on Daughters*, 93) also argues that "moralists and satirists were quick to convert an uneasy sense that women (like younger sons, the low born, and traditional servant groups) were acting with greater freedom, into a potent symbol of general disorder."

103. Aretino, *Aretino*, 164, (Aretino, *Aretino's Dialogues*, 181) with minor modifications in the translation.

104. Raymond Rosenthal in the preface to Aretino, *Aretino's Dialogues*, 9.

105. On the plague in Venice in 1575–77, see Paolo Preto, *Peste e società a Venezia, 1576* (Vicenza: Neri Pozza, 1978), and idem, "La società veneta e le grandi epidemie di peste," in G. Arnaldi and M. Pastore Stocchi, *Storia della cultura veneta* (Vicenza: Neri Pozza, 1982), 4:377–406; it has an extensive bibliography. See also the extremely informative case study of the interaction between one of the cities of the Venetian *terraferma* and the Venetian republic by James S. Grubb: *Firstborn of Venice: Vicenza in the Early Renaissance State* (Baltimore: Johns Hopkins University Press, 1988), ix–xxii and passim. For interesting connections between the increasing prejudice toward Jews and a fear of pollution in Renaissance Italy, in a work that also includes references to the fear of women's power over men, see Diane Owen Hughes, "Earrings for Circumcision: Distinction and Purification in the Italian Renaissance City," in *Persons in Groups: Social Behavior as Identity Formation in Medieval and Renaissance Europe*, ed. Richard C. Trexler (Binghamton, N.Y.: Medieval and Renaissance Texts and Studies, 1985), 155–77. Leah Lydia Otis also makes the connection in her *Prostitution in Medieval Society*, 69–70; she states, "the social group which prostitutes most resembled was that of the Jews. Like the Jews, prostitutes defied the teaching of the Church, yet were tolerated because of the importance of their services in an urban society. . . . Prostitutes' commerce was the antinomy of Christian mores, yet a

town without prostitutes was as inconceivable as one without usurers." She gives examples of laws that were directed at both groups (70−71).

106. On Maffio Venier's vernacular poems, see Armando Balduino, "Restauri e ricuperi per Maffio Venier," in *Medioevo e rinascimento veneto con altri studi in onore di Lino Lazzarini,* (Padua: Editrice Antenore, 1979), 2:231–63; and Valnea Rudmann, "Lettura della canzone per la peste di Venezia di Maffio Venier," *Atti dell'Istituto Veneto di Scienze, Lettere, ed Arti* 121 (1963): 599–641; and Antonio Pilot, "Di alcuni versi inediti sulla peste del 1575," *Ateneo veneto* 26 (1903): 350–58.

107. Why the edition of the *Terze rime* was changed at some uncertain stage in its production has not been determined. A detached frontispiece, housed in the manuscript collection of the Biblioteca Nazionale Marciana in Venice, bears an engraved medallion portrait of Veronica Franco, and a circular inscription, "Veronica Franco/Ann./xxiii/MDLXXVI," surrounds the frame. Recent archival evidence supports the theory that Veronica Franco traveled to Rome as a pilgrim in order to celebrate the Jubilee Year of 1575. Two documents housed in the Archivio di Stato in Rome (ASR, Not. Cap. Uff. 30, Atti Romauli, vol. 31, 17 April 1556 and 27 August 1576, fols. 753r–755r and 304r–305v, respectively) attest to the fact that Franco was living in the Palazzo Medici in Campo Marzio and in the Palazzo San Marco in Piazza Venezia; the latter was owned by the Cardinal Luigi Cornaro. The documents concerns a "debito di 220 scudi nei confronti dell'ebreo Iacob di Mursia" (a debt of 220 scudi to the Jew Iacob di Mursia), for the furnishings of what must have been a rather sumptuous dwelling: "c'erano i corami per tre stanze, sei sedie, o forse meglio seggioloni, per la sala, con cinque sgabelli, una credenza, ed altrettanto tavolini, tutto un complesso di materiale pregiato e di colori e disegni vivaci. Ne mancavano una lettiera di noce 'alla franzese' e due letti per i domestici" (there were leather-embossed furnishings in three rooms, six chairs, or rather large armchairs, for the living room with five footstools, a cupboard, and as many little tables, all of the furnishings made of precious materials with bright colors and designs. Nor was there lacking a bed made of walnut "in the French style" and two small beds for the maids). On these documents, see Gian Ludovico Masetti Zannini, "Veronica Franco a Roma: Una pellegrina 'tra mille,'" *Strenna dei romanisti* 1982: 322–31. I would like to thank Patricia H. Labalme for bringing this article to my attention. According to the second document, it seems that Veronica not only was protected by Cardinal Luigi Cornaro and other Venetian patricians, but that they took charge of relieving her from any financial indebtedness by making payments for her. Zannini claims that it is possible that Franco stayed in Rome as long as one year, or until February 27, which would have been the last date for the repayment of her debt.

Manlio Dazzi (*Il fiore della lirica veneziana: Il libro segreto (chiuso)* [Vicenza: Neri Pozza, 1956]) argues that the *Terze rime* was printed in the first months of 1576 *more italico,* while the Venetian year would have been 1575 (12 n. 2). The Venetian calendar year began in March.

108. As cited in Nussbaum, *Brink of All We Hate,* 9.

109. Aretino (*I ragionamenti*) refers to the pathology of the courtesan's demeanor, which he connects to the viciousness of disease when he says, "the envy of a whore is so avid that it devours itself, like the French disease consumes those who have it in their bones." On the proposed intersection of Maffio Venier's verses, see Dazzi, *Il fiore della lirica veneziana,* 9–57. See also Margaret F. Rosenthal, "Veronica Franco's *Terze Rime:* The Venetian Courtesan's Defense," *Renaissance Quarterly* 42, no. 2 (1989): 227–57. The belief that her true adversary is someone other than Marco Venier is expressed, not in the *Terze rime,* but in letter 48, 64–65, of her *Lettere familiari.* Here she admits to her addressee (presumably Marco Venier) that she had incorrectly

believed that "quella satira fusse fattura di Vostra Signoria" (that satire was of Your Lordship's making), and she reveals how she came to realize her mistake. She states that she composed a poem in response to her male attacker that was sent to Marco by mistake: ("il capitolo del quale . . . sia stato mandato a lei per errore"). She excuses herself for having thought that Marco Venier was capable of writing a poem so full of imperfections and so unworthy of his intelligence: "avendo risguardato all'imperfezzione dell'opera piena d'errori e per altra causa non degno parto del nobile intelletto suo" (having looked at the imperfections in a work so full of errors and certainly unworthy of your noble intellect).

Prostitution had always been conceived as a threat to public health, and Venetian prostitutes were traditionally accused of transmitting syphilis to members of the community through their contact with sailors, who some believed to be the source of the spread of the epidemic. For a similar perception in early modern Seville, see Perry, "Deviant Insiders," 147–49; and for southern France, see Rossiaud, *Medieval Prostitution,* 50 and 156. For the connections between perceptions of women, specifically prostitutes, during plague epidemics, see Rossiaud, *Medieval Prostitution,* chapter 7, "Nature Besieged by War and Pestilence: Visions of the Parousia," 86–103. See also Otis, *Prostitution in Medieval Society,* 40–42. Marin Sanuto records in *I diarii* in July 1496 the first sign of syphilis in Venice, which he attributes to the French—the "mal franzoso": "Nota che, per influxi celesti, da anni doi in qua dapoi la venuta de' francesi in Italia, si ha scoperto una nuova egritudine in li corpi humani dicta mal franzosa" (it is noted that owing to heavenly influences, in the last two years since the arrival of the French in Italy, one has discovered a new disease in the human body which is called the French pox) (20–21). An informative discussion of the public charitable institutions founded to combat syphilis in Venice and throughout Italy in the early modern period is in Pullan, *Rich and Poor,* 222–23, 232–36.

110. Ruggieri (*Maffio Venier*) gives a full account of the political positions that Venier held throughout his lifetime. See also Zorzi, *Cortigiana veneziana,* 93–111. While Maffio was in Constantinople, he wrote *Descrizione dell'impero turchesco* (Venice: 1580). When Maffio died in 1586, Bianca Cappello wrote to Maffio's brother Luigi, who was then *reggitore* (a governor) of Bergamo, leaving him all the things that Maffio had left to her. On this, see Ruggieri, *Maffio Venier,* 39. Most of the primary material Ruggieri uses for this biography is taken from the Medici archives in the Archivio di Stato in Florence.

111. Abdelkader Salza, (*Rime: Gaspara Stampa e Veronica Franco* [Bari: Laterza, 1913]) in his modern edition of the *Terze rime,* includes a discussion of the three editions that Emmanuele Antonio Cicogna recorded in his *Delle inscrizioni veneziane* (Venice: Giuseppe Orlandelli, 1824–63), vol. 5, 421; two of them (now lost) registered Marco Venier as the author of the first *capitolo.* For some hypothetical suggestions regarding the removal of Marco Venier's name from the edition, see Salza, *Rime,* 116–19, 125–26; for his relationship to the Venier family, see 115–33.

112. On these requirements, see Stanley Chojnacki, "Political Adulthood in Fifteenth-Century Venice," *American Historical Review* 91 (1986): 791–810.

113. Nicola Ruggieri speaks at some length about the friendship between Maffio Venier and Bianca Cappello (*Maffio Venier,* 13–20 and passim). The daughter of an old Venetian family, Bianca eloped in 1563, at the age of fifteen, with a Florentine bank clerk, Pietro Bonaventuri. Although safe in Florence from the attempts made by her father and the Avogadori di Comun (state prosecutors) to arrest her, she quickly sought to liberate herself from her marriage to Bonaventuri. The mistress of the reprobate son of Grand Duke Cosimo de' Medici, she married him in 1578 (after his wife, Joanna, died in childbirth), and they notified the doge a year later.

Similar matters are discussed in a recent biography by M. L. Mariotti Masi: *Bianca Cappello: Una veneziana alla corte dei Medici* (Milan: Mursia, 1986).

114. Ruggieri, *Maffio Venier,* 34–35.

115. On the resistance of the popes, especially Sixtus V, to giving Maffio Venier ecclesiastical positions of authority, see ibid., 30–39.

116. Maffio Venier's death is recorded in the *avvisi* of the Biblioteca Apostolica in Rome. Other *avvisi* that I consulted record his appointment as arcivescovo of Corfu (bishop of Corfu): "Il Clarissimo Maffio Veniero Nobile Veneto gran letterato et poeta è stato fatto Arcivescovo di Corfu" (9 aprile 1583, *Urb. lat.* 1051, fol. 159v.); and on the same day, "Dopo l'avviso della morte del nuovo Arcivescovo di Corfu si è sparso voce, che quella chiesa si darà al Signore Maffio Veniero gentilhuomo Venetiano qua di spirito elegantissimo et gratiossissimo" (fol. 160v). In the same volume, on 22 January 1583, there is an entry that records that Marco Venier has returned to Venice from Dalmatia, where he has been to investigate matters pertaining to the republic: "Ritornò martedì sera da Dalmatia il Clarissimo Avogadore Marco Veniero, dove è stato a formare processo sopra varii casi occorsi li mesi passati in alcuni di quei luoghi, et città marittime" (the illustrious prosecutor Marco Veniero returned Tuesday evening from Dalmatia, where he had been to bring to trial certain cases that had occurred in the past months in some of these places and in the seacoast cities [fol. 33v]). *Avvisi* are manuscript newsletters which record the most important events of early modern Italy. On the use of *avvisi* as historical sources, see Jean Delumeau, *Vie économique et sociale de Rome dans la seconde moitié du XVIe siècle* (Paris: De Boccard, 1957–59), 1:25–36.

117. On Domenico's conservatism and for a general account of Domenico Venier's condition, see Pompeo G. Molmenti, *La storia di Venezia nella vita privata,* 7th ed. (Bergamo: Istituto italiano d'arte grafica, 1928), 2:303–4. Domenico was forced to relinquish his duties as senator owing to severe gout, which confined him to bed for the remainder of his life. Many important literary editions of the period praise his critical and scholarly acumen and his inestimable value as patron, advisor, and citizen serving his city. In Verdizotti's sixteenth-century biography of the Venetian poet and contemporary of Venier, Girolamo Molino, he (Verdizotti) asserts the importance of Venier's salon to Molino and other Venetian writers and intellectuals of the period: "Ma di tutte queste honorate conversationi niuna egli più frequentava, che quella del Clarissimo Domenico Veniero gentilhuomo di valor singolare; la casa del quale nel la città di Venetia è un continuo ridutto di persone virtuose cosi di nobili della città, come di qual si voglia altra sorte d'huomini per professione di lettere, & d'altro rari, & eccellenti" (But of all those honored conversations none did he frequent more than that of the illustrious Domenico Veniero, a gentleman of singular valor; his house in Venice is the meeting place of learned people and of noblemen of Venice, and that of many other types of men in the profession of letters, both rare and excellent). Paolo Manutio dedicated the third book of his letters to Domenico Venier; in it he wrote, "ma vive soggetta da molti anni in qua, come a tiranno, ad un crudelissimo catarro, il quale, nonche di uscire di casa, ma di movere i piedi non le permette e nondimeno ella, non lasciandosi sottomettere al male in quella parte . . . con invitto animo resiste alla violenza del nemico, e trapassa . . . l'hore del giorno . . . dilettandosi hora co' libri . . . hora con gli amici, i quali tratti da desiderio di gustare la dolcezza de' suoi dottissimi ragionamenti, ne vanno volentieri quasi ogni giorno a visitarlo" (but he lives subject for many years, as if to a tyrant, to a very cruel gout, which prevents him not only from going out of the house but just from moving his feet; but he does not give himself over to his illness . . . with invincible will he resists the violence of the enemy, spending . . . hours of the day . . . amusing himself now with books . . . now

with friends, who, because gripped with the desire to taste the sweetness of his very learned discussions, go willingly almost every day to see him). See Paolo Manutio, *Lettere volgari di Paolo Manutio* (Venice: Aldus, 1560), 94. Francesco Sansovino (*Delle cose notabili della città di Venetia* [Venice: Comin da Trino da Monferrato, 1561]) says of Domenico Venier: "se chiedete letterati, il numero è grande ma i più conosciuti sono, messer Domenico Veniero spirito illustre, il qual sarebbe gran Senatore, se la malignità del suo influsso non lo havesse tenuto in letto tant'anni stroppiato delle gambe con dolor di ciascun ch'il conosce" (31) (if you are speaking of literary men, the number is great, but the most well known are Domenico Veniero, an illustrious spirit, who would have been a great senator if the malice of the heavens had not confined him to bed for many years, crippled in the legs, giving pain to all who knew him).

118. On the position of *savio grande,* see Finlay, *Politics,* xvi, 40, 187–88, 193, 229, 243, 250, 254, 272; and Zorzi, *Cortigiana veneziana,* 132. Marco was elected to the position four times. On the *giovani* as younger activist senators and revivors of Venetian republicanism, see Bouwsma, *Venice and the Defense of Republican Liberty,* 162–292, 417–82; Muir, *Civic Ritual,* 35–38; Martin Lowry, "The Reform of the Council of Ten, 1582–83: An Unsettled Problem?" *Studi veneziana* 13 (1971): 275–310; Finlay, *Politics,* 126–27, 136–37, 174–75, 182–83, 206–7. With specific reference to Marco Venier's interaction with the *giovani* faction of the Senate, see Zorzi, *Cortigiana veneziana,* 120–33. For interesting observations on the effect of the plague on the increase in political action among the *giovani,* see Preto, "La società veneta," 396. On the Council of Ten and other important governing bodies in Venice, see Giuseppe Maranini, *La costituzione di Venezia* (Florence: La Nuova Italia, 1974). As Margaret L. King (*Venetian Humanism,* 278) states, "The Council of Ten—infamous for its silent and thorough investigations—was charged to protect Venice against political and moral crime." See also 279–89 for a discussion of the political and religious offices held by Venetian patricians and citizens in the fifteenth and sixteenth centuries.

119. On the tensions that increased in families owing to the plague, and for useful information on the confiscation and correct redistribution of property, see Pullan, *Rich and Poor,* 319–324 and passim; Bartolomeo Cecchetti, "Testamenti fatti in tempo di peste," *Archivio veneto* 32 (1886): 188–89. For an interesting interpretation of the effects of the plague in Florence on the psychology of the people during the fifteenth century, see Richard C. Trexler, *Public Life in Renaissance Florence* (New York: Academic Press, 1980), 362–64. See also Carlo M. Cipolla, *Public Health and the Medical Profession in the Renaissance* (Cambridge: Cambridge University Press, 1976), especially 12–29; idem, *Fighting the Plague in Seventeenth-Century Italy* (Madison: University of Wisconsin Press, 1981), especially 3–18.

120. On using a woman, or more specifically a prostitute, in order to speak across her to other men in early modern literature, see Cruz, "Sexual Enclosure, Textual Escape." For an account of the use of women within certain sociopolitical structures, see Gayle Rubin, "The Traffic in Women: Notes on the 'Political Economy' of Sex," in *Toward an Anthropology of Women,* ed. Rayna Reiter (New York: Monthly Review Press, 1975).

121. On Franco's participation in the Jubilee year in Rome, see n. 105 above. Maffio Venier's satirical sonnet, "El retratto e l'impresa è buona e bella," on the Franco portrait is housed in the Biblioteca Apostolica Vaticana (Vatican Library) in Rome. See Vaticano Ottoboniano 1960, c. 27v. In the Biblioteca Marciana in Venice, this sonnet is followed by another one on the same theme, "Gli è pi' fadiga a meter, che a cavar." See MSS it. IX 173 (=6282), c. 254r.

122. On the *Strazzosa* (1588), see Richter, "Petrarchism and Anti-Petrarchism," 20–41;

Ruggieri, *Maffio Venier,* 61. For a critical edition of the poem which lists all the available manuscript sources, see Nordio and Vianello, "'La Strazzosa,'" 9–131. The poem was never published during Venier's lifetime. As Giorgio Padoan notes in the preface to this book, "La fortuna, davvero enorme, di questa canzone . . . è tuttavia attestata dal gran numero di trascrizioni cinque-settecentesche e dalle stampe cinquecentesche, che documentano la sua diffusione in ambito veneto e in ambito toscano" (the enormous fortune of this canzone . . . is nevertheless attested to by the great number of sixteenth- to eighteenth-century transcriptions and of the sixteenth-century editions which document its circulation in the Veneto and in Tuscany [9]).

123. On the economics of the *blason* in lyric poetry, see Patricia Parker, *Literary Fat Ladies* (London: Methuen, 1987), 126ff. The vogue for the Petrarchan lyric in late Renaissance Italy and in England during the reign of Elizabeth I was inseparable from a political dynamic in which political and erotic codes interrelated, especially in the English case, considerably. The male poet was "subject," as Petrarch was to his cruel mistress, in both a political and a lyrical sense. Although this "rule" of the woman was not the case in the Venetian context, the myth of Venice posited a woman—the Virgin—at its center. The subject status of the male lover is described in Nancy J. Vickers's penetrating analysis of the Petrarchan lyric structure: "Diana Described: Scattered Women and Scattered Rhyme," in *Writing and Sexual Difference,* ed. Elizabeth Abel (Chicago: University of Chicago Press, 1982), 95–109.

124. For the manuscript source of "Franca, credeme, che per San Maffio," see Biblioteca Nazionale Marciana (Venice), MSS it. IX 217 (=7061), cc. 45r–48r.; see Dazzi, *Il fiore della lirica,* 24, for a modern transcription.

125. For the manuscript source of this poem, see Biblioteca Nazionale Marciana (Venice), MSS it. IX 217 (=7061), cc. 59v–62v; and for a modern transcription see Dazzi, *Il fiore della lirica,* 28. Juvenal's sixth satire was translated by Lodovico Dolce; see his *Paraphrasi nella sesta satira di Giuvenale* (Venice: 1538). For uses of Juvenal in Venetian literature, especially in Pietro Aretino's pornographic texts, see David O. Frantz, *Festum Voluptatis: A Study of Renaissance Erotica* (Columbus: Ohio State University Press, 1989), 61 and passim. For a fascinating study of the uses of obscenity in ancient Roman literature, see Amy Richlin, *The Garden of Priapus: Sexuality and Aggression in Roman Humor* (New Haven: Yale University Press, 1983). And for illuminating connections between pornography, prostitution, and ancient Roman satire, see Richlin, *Garden of Priapus,* 78–80 and passim.

126. On this accusation, see chapter 2.

127. An anonymous dialect poet described the plague of Venice as a woman's diseased body, "Ah povera Venetia! . . . / Za tempo intata e verzene / Per costumi laconichi . . . / Adesso sporca femena" (Ah poor Venice! . . . For a long time intact and a virgin / laconic in its customs . . . / Now a dirty woman); this was cited in Molmenti, *La storia di Venezia,* 219; which in turn is taken from Pilot, "Di alcuni versi inediti sulla peste del 1575." Francesco Berni also made the connection between the plague and sexual diseases transmitted by women in his *Rime,* "Non ti maravigliar, maestro Piero" (21); "Ancor non ho io detto della peste" (22); Giovanni della Casa also did in his *Rime:* "Tutte le infermità d'uno spedale" (1530). For an analysis of these poets' relationships to their patrons, and for interesting parallels to the Venetian literary and social context, see Antonio Santosuosso, *Vita di Giovanni Della Casa* (Rome: Bulzoni, 1978), especially chapter 4, "'Le speranze sono debolissime, ed i tempi asciutti e secchi,'" 31–51.

128. There are other poems of Maffio Venier in which Veronica Franco's name appears. See, for example, the *capitolo* "Daspuò che son intrà in pensier sì vario" (MSS it. IX 217 (=7061),

cc. 83v–86r), where, among his lists of famous Venetian courtesans, he accuses Franco of "frequenting" Germans:

> *Veronica la Franca dal Proemio*
> *che col so rasonar, che è tanto affabile*
> *svoda la borsa speso a qualche Boemio*

> Veronica the Franca of the Proem
> who with her reasoning, which is so affable,
> often empties the purses of the Germans.

Later, as we shall see in chapter 4, she will be accused of entertaining Germans in her private home.

129. Dazzi (*Il fiore della lirica veneziana,* 46) refers to the exchange of poems (in *capitoli* 13 and 14) in Franco's *Terze rime* as a "duello rusticano" (a rustic duel), but with *capitolo* 16 he calls it a "duello nei modi cavallereschi" (duel in the chivalric style).

CHAPTER TWO: FASHIONING THE HONEST COURTESAN

1. The principal sources for Veronica Franco's biography are Giovanni degli Agostini, *Notizie istorico-critiche intorno la vita e le opere degli scrittori veneziani* (Venice: S. Occhi, 1752–54), 2:615–22; Emmanuele Antonio Cicogna, *Delle inscrizioni veneziane* (Venice: G. Orlandelli, 1824–1853), 5:421; Giuseppe Tassini, *Veronica Franco: Celebre poetessa e cortigiana del secolo XVI* (reprint, Venice: Alfieri, 1969); Rita Casagrande di Villaviera, *Le cortigiane veneziane del Cinquecento* (Milan: Longanesi, 1968), 235–72; Georgina Masson, *The Courtesans of the Italian Renaissance* (London: Secker and Warburg, 1975), 145–68; Alessandra Schiavon, "Per la biografia di Veronica Franco: Nuovi documenti," *Atti dell'Istituto Veneto di Scienze, Lettere, ed Arti* 137 (1978–79): 243–56; and Alvise Zorzi, *Cortigiana veneziana: Veronica Franco e i suoi poeti* (Milan: Camunia, 1986).

2. For a useful distinction between public and private realms for women as applied to northern European cities, see Martha C. Howell, "Citizenship and Gender: Women's Political Status in Northern Medieval Cities," in *Women and Power in the Middle Ages,* ed. Mary Erler and Maryanne Kowaleski (Athens: University of Georgia Press, 1988). Howell defines the public realm as "the realm in which issues not of direct concern to and not under the control of the domestic unit were located. The public realm, in contrast to the private, or domestic, realm, can be further defined as the sphere in which community concerns predominated—the locus . . . of the production of goods and services to be shared outside the domestic unit or the sources of laws, mores, and morals applicable throughout the community" (54–55 n. 1). While female silence was prescribed (especially for women of the upper classes) as a necessary indicator of female chastity, the courtesan, already "unchaste," had to reestablish a new sort of chastity for herself by redefining the concept as based on "virtù," namely, intellectual pursuits rather than sexual ones. In this sense, she assumed the manly requirements of the courtier's "virtù" as her own. In keeping with this theory, Adrianna Chemello has recently argued that the courtesan was most closely associated with the "donna di palazzo," as described in Castiglione's *Il cortegiano,* as discussed in *La corte e il "cortegiano,"* ed. Carlo Ossola and Adriano Prosperi (Rome: Bulzoni, 1980). On the problem of chastity as aligned with female speech in the early modern period, see Margaret W. Ferguson, "A Room Not Their Own: Renaissance Women as Readers and Writers," in *The Comparative Perspective on Literature: Approaches to Theory and Practice,* ed. Clayton Koelb

and Susan Noakes (Ithaca: Cornell University Press, 1988), 93–116, especially 97–104; Peter Stallybrass, "Patriarchal Territories: The Body Enclosed," in *Rewriting the Renaissance,* ed. Margaret W. Ferguson et al. (Chicago: University of Chicago Press, 1986), 123–42. For more extensive documentation, see chapter 1, n. 6.

3. The works in the *histoire de la mentalité* that have been most useful for this study are Carlo Ginzburg, *Il formaggio e i vermi: Il cosmo di un mugnaio del '500* (Turin: Einaudi, 1976); English translation, *The Cheese and the Worms,* trans. John Tedeschi and Anne C. Tedeschi (Baltimore: Johns Hopkins University Press, 1980); Carlo Ginzburg, "Morelli, Freud and Sherlock Holmes: Clues and Scientific Method," *History Workshop* 9 (1980): 5–36; Natalie Zemon Davis, *The Return of Martin Guerre* (Cambridge: Harvard University Press, 1983); idem, *Society and Culture in Early Modern France* (Stanford: Stanford University Press, 1975); idem, *Fiction in the Archives: Pardon Tales and Their Tellers in Sixteenth-Century France* (Stanford: Stanford University Press, 1987). On the rulings passed against prostitution from the fifteenth to the sixteenth century, see *Leggi e Memorie Venete sulla prostituzione fino alla caduta della Repubblica,* ed. G. Batta De Lorenzi (privately published for Lord Orford, Venice, 1870–72); Carlo Calza, *Documenti inediti sulla prostituzione tratti dagli archivi della repubblica veneta* (Milan: Tipografia della Società Cooperativa, 1869), 3–42.

Both of Veronica Franco's wills are located in the Archivio di Stato, Venice (hereafter cited as ASV), Notarile Testamenti, (hereafter cited as NT), notary Anton Maria di Vincenti, 10 agosto 1564, busta 1019, fol. 806; notary Baldissera Fiume, 1 novembre 1570, busta 420, fol. 870. See appendix 2.1 for transcriptions of both wills. As Stanley Chojnacki states ("The Power of Love: Wives and Husbands in Late Medieval Venice," in *Women and Power in the Middle Ages,* ed. Mary Erler and Maryanne Kowaleski [Athens: University of Georgia Press, 1988], 126–48), the study of wills is especially useful because they allow us "to observe women, and men as well, confronting the last things, taking careful stock of the contents of their lives, and expressing their ultimate preferences and hopes" (128). For an earlier transcription of Franco's wills, one that differs in places from my own, see Tassini, *Veronica Franco,* 107–18; and Schiavon, "Per la biografia," 243 no. 1.

4. The Magistrato alle pompe was another name for the Provveditori alle pompe. Courtesans were by no means the only people to suffer from prejudice. On other marginal groups in Venetian society, especially Jews, who were ill-treated, see Brian Pullan, *The Jews of Europe and the Inquisition of Venice, 1550–1670* (Oxford: Basil Blackwell, 1983); and chapter 4 below. For a study of the republic's attempt through philanthropic institutions to "draw the outcast into the social structure" (16) and to direct the individual toward "the road to virtue and salvation" (18), see idem, "The Old Catholicism, and New Catholicism, and the Poor," in *Timore e carità: I poveri nell'Italia Moderna,* ed. Giorgio Politi et al. (Cremona: Annali della Biblioteca Statale e Libreria Civica di Cremona, 1982), 13–25. Diane Owen Hughes draws a parallel between the fear of Jews in Renaissance Italy and a larger perceived threat of "pollution," which she links to the association between Jews and prostitution, in her "Earrings for Circumcision: Distinction and Purification in the Italian Renaissance City," in *Persons in Groups: Social Behavior as Identity Formation in Medieval and Renaissance Europe,* ed. Richard C. Trexler (Binghamton, N.Y.: Medieval and Renaissance Texts and Studies, 1985), 155–77. Linda Carroll has demonstrated that certain playwrights in Venice and the Veneto (notably Angelo Beolco-Ruzzante) were the victims of the "restriction of personal and political expression" owing to the "increased . . . domination of Italian city-states by national powers" (488–89). See her "Carnival Rites as Vehicles of Protest in Renaissance Venice," *Sixteenth Century Journal* 16, no. 4 (1985): 487–502.

5. As cited in Antonio Barzaghi, *Donne o cortigiane? La prostituzione a Venezia. Documenti di costume dal XVI al XVIII secolo* (Verona: Bertani, 1980), 138–39; he publishes the entire ruling.

6. The most penetrating study of Italian sumptuary laws, especially for northern Italy of the Renaissance period, is Diane Owen Hughes, "Sumptuary Laws and Social Relations in Renaissance Italy," in *Disputes and Settlements: Laws and Human Relations in the West*, ed. John Bossy (Cambridge: Cambridge University Press, 1983), 69–99. Hughes argues that in Venice the laws were seen in the sixteenth century as a means to restrain "feminine license" (71), which in turn reflected an antifeminist stance. Earlier laws appear to have been intended to curb "the upstart rather than to fetter the aristocrat" (74), in the name of republican virtue. Hughes claims that "public morality, not money, was the magistrate's concern" (79). With an increasing fear of the power of women, especially since husbands' livelihoods often depended on their wives' dowry, it is little wonder, as Hughes argues, that many restrictions were passed to restrict women from squandering the paternal wealth they had inherited and which their husbands sought to keep within the new family. For laws specifically passed in Venice, see the by now classic study by Margaret Newett: "The Sumptuary Laws of Venice in the Fourteenth and Fifteenth Centuries," in *Historical Essays by Members of the Owens College, Manchester*, ed. T. F. Tout and James Tait (Manchester: Manchester University Press, 1907). For the laws passed by Venetian authorities in the sixteenth century, and Venetians' defiance of them, see Giulio Bistort, *Il Magistrato alle Pompe nella Repubblica di Venezia* (Venice: Emiliana, 1912; reprint, Bologna: Forni Editore, 1969).

Lisa Jardine argues cogently ("'Make the Doublet of Changeable Taffeta': Dress Codes, Sumptuary Law and 'Natural' Order," in her *Still Harping on Daughters: Women and Drama in the Age of Shakespeare* [Totowa, N. J.: Barnes and Noble, 1983], 141–68) that sumptuary laws in Shakespearean England were used as a means of regulating class differences, public morality, and private extravagance, especially when applied to women.

7. The legal distinctions between "meretrice" and "cortesana" in Venetian legal practices of the Renaissance were not well drawn. Most of the rulings that were passed refer to "prostitute" and "courtesan" in the same sentence. For a discussion of the paradoxical term "cortigiana onesta," see Casagrande, *Le cortigiane veneziane*, 19–43; Benedetto Croce, *Poeti e scrittori del pieno e tardo rinascimento* (Bari: Laterza, 1970), 318–19; Eugenio Musatti, *La donna in Venezia* (Padua: Arnaldo Forni, 1892), 120; Masson, *Courtesans of the Italian Renaissance*, 9–12, 152; Paul Larivaille, *La vie quotidienne des courtisanes en Italie au temps de la Renaissance* (Paris: Hachette, 1975), 32–40. Each author speaks of the differences between the Venetian "cortigiana onesta" and the lower-class "cortigiana di lume"; the latter term designated those courtesans who lived in inns, most often in the region near the Rialto bridge called the Castelletto (in the fifteenth century, prostitutes' and courtesans' activities and housing were restricted). A further distinction is made for the lowest class of prostitutes, or "meretrici," who earned their living solely by selling sexual favors to men. Fiora A. Bassanese ("Private Lives and Public Lies: Texts by Courtesans of the Italian Renaissance," *Texas Studies in Language and Literature* 30, no. 3 [1988]: 295–319) offers further qualifications.

The Roman *avvisi* also never clearly distinguish between "meretrice" and "cortigiana." On this point, I have profited greatly from Elizabeth and Thomas Cohen's study of prostitutes in early modern Roman neighborhoods. They conclude from the records of the criminal courts of the governor of Rome that despite society's attempts to marginalize the prostitute and the courtesan, they lived as integral members of a local community irrespective of their particular social standing, wealth, and cultivation. I refer to Elizabeth S. Cohen, "Courtesans and Whores:

Words and Behavior in Roman Streets," *Women's Studies* 19 (1991): 201–8. John Brackett also argues ("Bureaucracy and Female Marginality: The Florentine Onestà and the Control of Prostitution, 1403–1746," paper delivered at the Sixteenth-Century Studies Conference, Tempe, Arizona) that the Florentine institution, while designed to deal with female prostitution and its legalization with the hope of integrating prostitutes into society, "actually contributed to their progressive emargination." I thank him for sharing with me this paper. For a similar view, see Richard C. Trexler, "La prostitution florentine an XVe siécle: Patronage et clientèles," *Annales, E.S.C.* 36, no. 6 (1981): 1003–6.

8. Domenico Venier had also composed civic panegyrics praising Venice that were then set to music. See Ellen Rosand, "Music in the Myth of Venice," *Renaissance Quarterly* 30 (1977): 511–37; she discusses three madrigals by Baldassare Donato, published in 1550, that set to music sonnets by the Venetian poet Domenico Venier that "actually give expression to the myth of Venice" (528). See also her discussion of Venier's three texts, "Viva sempre in ogni etade," "Gloriosa felic'alma Vineggia," and "Quattro dee che'l mondo onora," in relation to the joint celebration of Ascension Day and the Marriage of Venice to the Sea. Martha Feldman states ("Venice and the Madrigal in the Mid-Sixteenth Century," [Ph.D. diss., University of Pennsylvania, 1987], 1:365–66) that "the madrigals were composed for outdoor performances. The octave, 'Gloriosa, felic'alma Vineggia,' describes the Marian virtues of Venice—eternal purity, justice, love, and peace—in a poem that celebrates the association of the Virgin with the mythology of the birth of Venice." The settings were published in *Baldissara Donato musico e cantor in santo Marco, le napolitane, et alcuni madrigali a quattro voci da lui novamente composte, corrette, & misse in luce* (Venice: 1550). For a transcription of the music, see 2:677–83, and for a translation of the poems, 2:534. Venier's text is also given in Domenico Venier, *Rime di Domenico Venier senatore viniziano*, ed. Pierantonio Serassi (Bergamo: Pietro Lancelotto, 1751), 40. Baldassare Donato also set poems by Giovanni Battista Amalteo, Fortunio Spira, and Lodovico Dolce, all members of Venier's literary circle. See Feldman, "Venice and the Madrigal," 1:366–67.

On the Venetian literary context and the poetic anthologies prepared by members of Domenico Venier's circle, see Edoardo Taddeo, *Il manierismo letterario e i lirici veneziani del cinquecento* (Rome: Bulzoni, 1974); W. Theodor Elwert, *Studi di letteratura veneziana* (Venice: Istituto per la Collaborazione Culturale, 1958); Benedetto Croce, "Letterati poeti del Veneto e dell'Italia meridionale sulla fine del cinquecento" in his *Poeti e scrittori*, 298–312; Giorgio Padoan, ed., *Petrarca, Venezia e il Veneto* (Florence: Leo Olschki, 1976); Carlo Dionisotti, *Geografia e storia della letteratura italiana* (Turin: Einaudi, 1967), 233–54; Riccardo Scrivano, *La norma e lo scarto: Proposte per il cinquecento letterario italiano* (Rome: Bonacci, 1980); Giancarlo Mazzacurati, *Misure del classicismo rinascimentale* (Naples: Liguori, 1977); Gino Benzoni, *Gli affanni della cultura: Intellettuali e potere nell'Italia della controriforma e barocca* (Milan: Feltrinelli, 1978), 7–77; and Giulio Ferroni, *Poesia italiana: Il cinquecento* (Milan: Garzanti, 1978), especially the introduction.

9. For the most important critical literature on Franco's poems and letters, see Arturo Graf, "Una Cortigiana fra mille," in his *Attraverso il Cinquecento* (Turin: Chiantore, 1888), 174–284; Riccardo Scrivano, "La poetessa Veronica Franco," in his *Cultura e letteratura del Cinquecento* (Rome: Edizioni dell'Ateneo, 1966), 195–228; Benedetto Croce, "Veronica Franco," in his *Poeti e scrittori*, 218–34; Francesco Flora, *Storia della letteratura italiana* (Milan: Mondadori, 1965), 2:517; A. Giovanni Frugoni, "I capitoli della cortigiana Veronica Franco," *Belfagor* 3 (1948): 44–59. Three recent essays discuss Franco's poems and letters and her position as *cortigiana onesta*. An excellent essay by Sara Maria Adler ("Veronica Franco's Petrarchan *Terze rime*: Subverting the Master's Plan," *Italica* 65, no. 3 (1988): 213–33) sheds new and interesting light on

Franco's uses and subversions of Petrarchan models. See also Bassanese, "Public Lives and Public Lies"; Elvira Favretti, "Rime e Lettere di Veronica Franco," *Giornale storico della letteratura italiana* 163, no. 523 (1986): 355–82.

10. For the concept of an "improving fiction," see Ann Rosalind Jones, "City Women and Their Audiences: Louise Labé and Veronica Franco," in Margaret W. Ferguson, Maureen Quilligan, and Nancy J. Vickers, eds., *Rewriting the Renaissance: The Discourses of Sexual Difference in Early Modern Europe* (Chicago: University of Chicago Press, 1986), 316. She also makes the important claim, "however clearly Franco points out the injustice of men's power and women's dependence on them, she frames her defense, as she must, within the discursive possibilities generated by such gender relations" (314). Jones sees the collected *Rime* (Venice: 1547) of another courtesan, Tullia d'Aragona, as substituting "an improving fiction for the realities of a courtesan's life and the rivalry among her clients" ("Surprising Fame: Renaissance Gender Ideologies and Women's Lyric," in *The Poetics of Gender,* ed. Nancy K. Miller [New York: Columbia University Press, 1986], 74–95, and for this quote, 91). On Venetian women's use of civic rhetoric, see also Patricia H. Labalme, "Venetian Women on Women: Three Early Modern Feminists," *Archivo veneto* 5th ser., 117 (1981): 81–109, especially 105–9. On a different kind of rhetorical strategy for women's lyrics in early modern France, see François Rigolot, "Gender vs. Sex Difference in Louise Labé's Grammar of Love," in Ferguson et al., *Rewriting the Renaissance,* 287–98; and see the ground-breaking essay by Ann Rosalind Jones: "Assimilation with a Difference: Renaissance Women Poets and Literary Influence," *Yale French Studies* 62 (1981): 135–53.

11. I am quoting from Aretino's famous letter to Doge Andrea Gritti: Aretino, *Lettere,* 30.

12. On the Virgin as queen, see Marina Warner, *Alone of All Her Sex: The Myth and the Cult of the Virgin Mary* (New York: Vintage Books, 1983), 81–117; Margaret M. Miles, *Image as Insight: Visual Understanding in Western Christianity and Secular Culture* (Boston: Beacon Press, 1985), especially chapter 4 ("Images of Women in Fourteenth-Century Tuscan Painting"), and see 76–80 for a discussion pertaining specifically to the Virgin.

13. On Moderata Fonte (Modesta da Pozzo), see Patricia H. Labalme, "Venetian Women on Women," 84–91; Adrianna Chemello, "La donna, il modello, l'immaginario: Moderata Fonte e Lucrezia Marinella," in *Nel cerchio della luna: Figure di donna in alcuni testi del XVI secolo,* ed. Marina Zancan (Venice: Marsilio, 1983), 95–170; Margaret F. Rosenthal, "Venetian Women Writers and Their Discontents," in *Sexuality and Gender in Early Modern Europe: Institutions, Texts, Images,* ed. James Grantham Turner (Cambridge: Cambridge University Press, 1992), and see this for full bibliography on Fonte. Discussions that also include consideration of the published works of Lucrezia Marinella and Arcangela Tarabotti, as well as Fonte's treatise on the defense of women, are, in addition to the studies already cited: Ginevra Conti Odorisio, *Donna e società nel Seicento* (Rome: Bulzoni, 1979); Constance Jordan, *Renaissance Feminism: Literary Texts and Political Models* (Ithaca: Cornell University Press, 1990). For an extremely informative modern critical edition of Fonte's *Il merito delle donne,* including a fine introductory essay, see Adrianna Chemello, *Il merito delle donne* (Mirano: Eidos, 1988). On other learned women of the Renaissance in Italy, see Margaret L. King, "Thwarted Ambitions: Six Learned Women of the Early Italian Renaissance," *Soundings* 76 (1976): 280–300; Patricia H. Labalme, "Women's Roles in Early Modern Venice," in her *Beyond Their Sex* (New York: New York University Press, 1980), 137–44. In her dialogue (*Il merito delle donne,* ed. Adrianna Chemello [Mirano: Eidos, 1988]) Moderata Fonte attacks the Venetian marital institution which, as her spokeswoman Corinna says, unjustly isolates women from the public world; by relinquishing her own right to

independence in favor of her husband's desires, the married woman renounces any claim to free-dom of movement and participation in the public world.

14. Ann Rosalind Jones argues that Franco's patriotism "presents deep contradictions and important imaginative satisfactions" through the "identification with an ideal of feminine pu-rity, safety and privilege," in "City Women and Their Audiences," in Ferguson et al., *Rewriting the Renaissance*, 299–316.

15. On the marriage of the sea ritual on Ascension Day as the republic's most "carefully orchestrated apogee of the state liturgy," and the most explicit acting out of the requirements of female subservience, especially in marriage, see Edward Muir, *Civic Ritual in Renaissance Venice* (Princeton: Princeton University Press, 1981), 119–34 and passim. The complex and ambig-uous nature of the image of the Virgin Mary in French medieval art and literature is examined in Penny Schine Gold, *The Lady and the Virgin* (Chicago: University of Chicago Press, 1985). For the Italian and more specifically Tuscan context in the fourteenth century, see the positive and negative assessments of images of the Virgin and Mary Magdalene in Margaret R. Miles, *Image as Insight*, 79. In some cases Italian women received positive messages from religious images. They saw the symbol of the Virgin as liberating them from "the potentially overwhelming biological contingencies of childbearing and the physical and environmental necessities of household, farm, or business, or nursing infants" (88). See also idem, "The Virgin's One Bare Breast: Female Nudity and Religious Meaning in Tuscan Early Renaissance Culture," in *The Female Body in Western Culture*, ed. Susan Rubin Suleiman (Cambridge: Harvard University Press, 1986), 193–208.

On the philanthropic alternatives for religious women in Venice in the sixteenth century, see the interesting essay by Marion L. Kuntz: "The Virgin of Venice and Concepts of the Millenium in Venice," *The Politics of Gender in Early Modern Europe*, ed. Jean R. Brink, Allison P. Coudert, and Maryanne C. Horowitz (Kirksville, Mo.: Sixteenth Century Journal Publishers, 1989) 12: 111–30. For the iconography of the Virgin as the Bride of Christ and Queen of Heaven in con-nection with a Marian cult in fifteenth- and sixteenth-century Venice, see Rona Goffen, *Piety and Patronage in Renaissance Venice: Bellini, Titian, and the Franciscans* (New Haven: Yale University Press, 1987), 139–54; and in relation to a Counter-Reformation rhetoric, see Maurice E. Cope, *The Venetian Chapels of the Sacrament in the Sixteenth Century* (New York: Garland, 1979).

16. The coat of arms of the Franco family consists of an orange field with a blue band in the upper portion decorated with three yellow stars. The charge in the lower portion of the shield has a green mountain with three peaks. On the privileges associated with *cittadini* and for defini-tions of Venetian citizenship, which Brian Pullan argues is psychologically definable as middle class, see Pullan, *Rich and Poor in Renaissance Venice* (Cambridge: Harvard University Press, 1971), 100; Dennis Romano, *Patricians and Popolani: The Social Foundations of the Venetian Renais-sance State* (Baltimore: Johns Hopkins University Press, 1987), 29; Mary Neff, "A Citizen in the Service of the Patrician State: The Career of Zaccaria de' Freschi," *Studi veneziani* 5 (1981): 33–61. Neff underscores Venetian citizens' monopoly of positions in the chancery. And see Robert Finlay, *Politics in Renaissance Venice* (New Brunswick: Rutgers University Press, 1980), 45–47; Muir, *Civic Ritual*, 38–44; Margaret L. King, *Venetian Humanism in an Age of Patrician Domi-nance* (Princeton: Princeton University Press, 1986), 289–91. As Brian Pullan has suggested (in *Rich and Poor*), the *scuole grandi* (confraternities) provided an outlet for the political ambitions of *cittadini*. For the restrictions imposed in the fourteenth century on admitting Venetian citizens to the Venetian patriciate with the closing of the Serrata in 1297, see Frederick Lane, "Enlarge-ment of the Great Council Hall of Venice," in *Florilegium Historiale: Essays Presented to Wallace K.*

Ferguson, ed. J. G. Rowe and W. H. Stockdale (Toronto: University of Toronto Press, 1971), 236–74; Stanley Chojnacki, "In Search of the Venetian Patriciate: Families and Factions in the Fourteenth Century," in *Renaissance Venice*, ed. J. R. Hale (London: Faber and Faber, 1974), 47–90; Guido Ruggiero, "Modernization and the Mythic State in Early Renaissance Venice: The Serrata Revisited," *Viator* 10 (1979): 245–56. For a discussion of the distinctions between the *cittadini originarii* (ancestral origins) and the *cittadini de intus* or *de intus et extra*, which were grants of citizenship, often to foreign merchants who had taken up residence in the city and paid taxes, see chapter 1, n. 22.

17. Tassini, *Veronica Franco*, 81 n. 1.

18. See Teodoro Toderini, *Genealogie delle famiglie Venete ascritte alla cittadinanza originaria*, Miscellanea codici, I, 2:6. The same coat of arms appears as the frontispiece to Veronica Franco's *Terze rime* which is reproduced in Masson, *Courtesans of the Italian Renaissance*, 87. In a manuscript housed in the Biblioteca Civico Correr, Cod. Gradenigo 192, fol. 18 (*Cronaca delle antiche famiglie dei cittadini veneziane, 1536*), the "Franco" family is reported to have a "Zorzi Franco fo' Secretario Ducale" (Zorzi Franco was ducal secretary), and "altro Zorzi secretario del 1524, [et è] sepolto in S. Zaccaria" (another Zorzi was secretary in 1524 and is buried in San Zaccaria). This helps clarify the mention of a Zorzi *deputato* on the family shield mentioned above.

19. We know that Paola Franco was a courtesan because of the existence of the famed *Catalogo di tutte le principal et più honorate cortigiane di Venezia*. Many of the courtesans listed in this catalog—a kind of sixteenth-century telephone book—were associated with their mother's trade, insofar as prospective clients were requested to pay the required fee directly to the mother, who acted as a go-between for her daughter. This was also the case for Veronica Franco, and it suggests that she was not yet married at the time of the conception of the catalog, since she is recorded as living in her mother's house. A rare edition of the *Catalogo* exists in the Museo Civico Correr in Venice. For a discussion of the publishing history of the catalog, see Tassini, *Veronica Franco*, 9 n. 1 and 56 n. 2. Zorzi (*Cortigiana veneziana*, 20) discusses the clandestine nature of the catalog. It is also possible that the book was conceived as a satire, which would help to explain why Veronica's fee is indicated as only two scudi. Paola Franco is listed as a "pieza," or go-between. For a definition of this and other Venetian dialect words, see Giuseppe Boerio, *Dizionario del dialetto veneziano*, 2d ed. (Venice: Giovanni Cecchini, 1856), 509.

20. We know almost nothing about the identity of Paolo Panizza. What is certain is that the marriage could not have lasted very long, because Franco asks in this will that her mother request the restitution of her dowry from her husband. I follow Tassini's suggestion (*Veronica Franco*, 84 n. 5) that he was a doctor: "potrebbe essere ch'egli fosse quel Paolo, fratello di Antonio Panizza, speziale in parocchia di San Moisé all'insegna del Carro, e testatore nel 1558 in atti di Filippo de Cavaneis" (it is possible that he was that Paolo, brother of Antonio Panizza, druggist in the parish of San Moisé at the sign of the chariot, and testator in 1558 with the notary Filippo de Cavaneis). The will to which Tassini refers was drafted in 1558 (ASV, NT, notary Filippo de Cavaneis, 1 luglio 1553, b. 250, fol. 74); in it Antonio Panizza refers to a "Paulo," whom he identifies together with "Lunardo" as "miei fratelli" (my brothers) and as the "commissari" (executors) of his inheritance, which he stipulates is to be divided equally among them (he also includes "Alessandro mio fiol natural," Alessandro my natural son). He identifies his father as "m. Lodovico spiciar al Carro" (m. Lodovico, druggist at the chariot).

21. In letter 39 of her *Lettere familiari a diversi*, Franco refers to her maternal obligations. Excusing herself to her addressee (presumably a fellow writer, and possibly a patron) for not having written to him for a long time, she explains that she has had to put aside her editorial

work and her own compositions temporarily (she is editing and commissioning verses for a commemorative anthology for the naval officer, Estore Martinengo, who fought heroically against the Turks), because her children have been very ill with fever and chicken pox in 1575. On this see chapter 3 below. Andrea Tron married a patrician, Beatrice da Lezze, in 1569. His father was Paolo Tron, a famous Venetian senator, and his mother was a member of the patrician Priuli family. Antonio Manuzio, the brother of Paolo Manuzio, in 1544 dedicated a second volume of *Lettere volgari* to Paolo Tron. Andrea Tron occupied several important political positions in Venice, including *governatore di galea* and *savio grande*. His brothers Girolamo and Santo were both in the Venetian navy and died in 1571. Another brother, Vincenzo, became a member of the Collegio as *savio di terraferma* and ambassador to the emperor Rudolph I, as discussed in Zorzi, *Cortigiana veneziana,* 42.

22. On patrician marriages in Venice as evidence of an increase in affinal ties and the emotional bonds between husband and wife, as well as the strengthening of political and economic contracts, see Stanley Chojnacki, "The Power of Love: Wives and Husbands in Late Medieval Venice," in Mary Erler and Maryanne Kowaleski, eds., *Women and Power in the Middle Ages* (Athens: University of Georgia Press, 1988); idem, "'The Most Serious Duty': Motherhood, Gender, and Patrician Culture in Renaissance Venice," in *Refiguring Woman: Perspectives on Gender and the Italian Renaissance,* ed. Marilyn Migiel and Juliana Schiesari (Ithaca: Cornell University Press, 1991), 133–54. See also Lucia Ferrante, "L'onore ritrovato: Donne nella Casa del Soccorso di San Paolo a Bologna" (sec. 16–17), *Quaderni storici* 53, no. 2 (1983): 499–527. On the importance of marriage as one of the limited options available to women in the early modern period, and in relation to the Council of Trent's attempt to "improve and sacralize the ways that marriages were arranged and experienced," see the important research by Sherrill Cohen on alternative public institutions designed to deal with the severe economic and social disadvantages in which women found themselves in the period of the Counter-Reformation: "Asylums for Women in Counter-Reformation Italy," in *Woman in Reformation and Counter-Reformation Europe: Private and Public Worlds,* ed. Sherrin Marshall (Bloomington and Indianapolis: Indiana University Press, 1989), 166–88.

For the 1542 ruling, see Casagrande, *Le cortigiane veneziane,* 87–88. Cesare Vecellio refers to the overlapping of courtesan's and married woman's costumes in his *Degli habiti antichi et moderni di diverse parti del mondo* (Venice: D. Zenaro, 1590), 137. He refers to the courtesan's appropriation of her male protector's status when he says, "After frequenting a Venetian patrician, they grab onto his family name, using it as their own and thus fooling many foreign men who come to the city and mistake them for Venetian ladies. Procuresses lend a helping hand. When a foreigner expresses the desire to enjoy the favors of a highborn lady, a procuress dolls up some common prostitute . . . he is taken in and believes she's a noblewoman"; quoted in Lynne Lawner, *Lives of the Courtesans: Portraits of the Renaissance* (New York: Rizzoli, 1987).

23. Casagrande, *Le cortigiane veneziane,* 88–89. This *parte* was supposed to be hung on the entrance to the Tribunal of the *provveditori* so that when either a patrician or a citizen went to this office to voice a request for pardon, the notary was obliged by law to read to him the aforementioned ruling. If he did not immediately desist, the notary was authorized to denounce him to the Council of Ten. On the 1543 ruling, see Fiora A. Bassanese, *Gaspara Stampa* (Boston: Twayne, 1982), 77 n. 176.

24. Casagrande, *Le cortigiane veneziane,* 87–88. In theory, then, after 1542 all unmarried courtesans were punishable by law if they violated the specific laws directed against them. In practice, though, as Casagrande suggests with reference to the ruling cited above, "quasi sempre

la mancata applicazione delle sanzioni nei loro confronti è da ricercarsi nel fatto che general-
mente avevano accanto uno di quei patrizi che per diritto di nascita formavano il governo della
Serenissima e che erano sempre pronti a difenderle nei confronti dell'autorità" (almost always the
failure to apply the sanctions against them can be explained by the fact that generally courtesans
had one of those patricians protecting them, patricians who by birthright took part in the governing of the Serenissima and were always ready to defend them against authority) (88). How
this applies to Franco's Inquisition court case will be discussed in greater detail in chapter 4.
Cathy Santore argues ("Julia Lombardo, 'Somtuosa Meretrize': A Portrait by Property," *Renaissance Quarterly* 41, no. 1 (1988): 44–83) that it was only in 1524, as Sanudo records in his
famous diaries, that "the first official acknowledgment of hierarchical distinctions within the
profession is recorded in a document (ASV, Provveditori Sopra la Sanità, Capitolare, I.C.33) in
which the phrase 'le cortesane e altra sorte de putane over meretrice' is used" (45 n. 4). Santore
carefully documents the ways in which, as she says, Lombardo made use of her "ingegno sottile"
(quick-witted talent) when recording her possessions, because "she managed to avoid stating her
exact worth. The whole is a play for sympathy; the ploy is feminine ignorance of the masculine
matter of finance" (51ff.).

25. On the formation of this subgroup and its failure to make any changes, see Casagrande,
Le cortigiane veneziane, 117–20. For the administration of the public health organization—the
Provveditori alla Sanità—of which the above-mentioned subgroup was to be a smaller part, see
Pullan, *Rich and Poor*, 262–63, 296–99, 301–2, 316–17, 319-22, 366–67 and passim. As
Pullan demonstrates, the Venetian government "possessed a permanent magistracy in charge of
public health—the Provveditori alla Sanità" (219). He states that in 1539, the Council of Ten
"extended the competence of the Provveditori . . . to include the control of prostitution. . . .
It aimed, not at eliminating, but at curbing prostitution, by attaching a stigma to it and by
formally separating prostitutes from reputable society" (380). On similar attempts to control
prostitution and civic misrule in Lyons, see Natalie Zemon Davis, "Scandale à l'Hotel-Dieu de
Lyon (1537–1543)," *La France d'Ancien Régime: Etudes réunies en l'honneur de Pierre Goubert*, ed.
Pierre Goubert (Toulouse: Société de Démographie Historique Privat, 1984), 1:175–87.

26. Pullan, *Rich and Poor*, 381. For the Italian text of the earlier ruling prohibiting courtesans and prostitutes from attending church, see Carlo Calza, *Documenti inediti sulla prostituzione
tratti dagli archivi della repubblica veneta* (Milan: Tipografia della Società Cooperativa, 1869), 34.

27. Chojnacki, "Power of Love," 131. On renting the appropriate costumes for the desired
role as a means of self-assertion, see the cases cited in Casagrande, *Le cortigiane veneziane*, 120–
26. On dressing as *gentildonne* or other "respectable" women, see Barzaghi, *Donne o cortigiane*, 23,
and Santore, "Julia Lombardo," 61 n. 65. An extremely useful glossary of terms (80–83) relating to a courtesan's costume and other possessions appears at the end of Santore's article. Cesare
Vecellio describes "donzella venetiane" (in *Degli habiti*) as "guardate et custodite nelle case pa-
terne, che bene spesso no anche i più stretti parenti le veggono . . . quando escono fuori di casa,
il che accade derado, portano in testa un velo di seta bianca, ch'esse chiamano fazzuolo, d'assai
ampia larghezza et con esso si coprono il viso, e 'l petto . . . le sopraveste di queste sono la
maggior parte di color rovano o nere, di lana leggiera . . . o altra materia di poca valuta" (so
well guarded and looked after in their paternal homes that often not even the closest of relatives
sees them . . . when they go out of their houses, which happens rarely, they wear a veil of white
silk on their heads, which they call a handkerchief, one so large that it covers their entire face and
breast . . . the dress they wear is most often black or rust colored and is made of a lightweight
wool or of another inexpensive fabric) (95). See also Giacomo Franco, *Habiti delle donne venetiane*

intagliate in rame nouvamente di Giacomo Franco (Venice: Ferdinando Ongania, 1610), 43, 70, 71–73, 76–77. Diane Owen Hughes claims ("Sumptuary Laws," 92) that "the difference between *meretrix* and *matrona* stands at the heart of sumptuary distinction." Prostitutes, she argues, were allowed rich dress as a means of "shaming the virtuous into simplicity," and noblewomen's dress was periodically restricted as a way of signaling the kind of "virtuous" practices that the courtesan and prostitute should uphold and emulate.

28. For laws against "perle" (pearls) and other jewels prohibited to courtesans, see Casagrande, *Le cortigiane veneziane,* 64ff. For this law, see Hughes, "Sumptuary Laws," 64–65. For other sumptuary laws directed specifically to them, see 47–83. See also Newett, "Sumptuary Laws," 245–78.

29. (See n. 22 above) Vecellio, *Deglio habiti,* 1:137. The only clothes that the courtesan wore that were not a part of the *gentildonna*'s wardrobe were the masculine "camise de dona alla mascolina" (a woman's blouse in the masculine style) and "le braghesse" (breeches). See also Pietro Bertelli, *Diversarum Nationum Habitus Centum* (Padua: Alciatum Alcia, 1589); he illustrates a courtesan's skirt that has been lifted to reveal male breeches underneath. Casagrande (*Le cortigiane veneziane,* 130–31) suggests that this cross dressing worried the republic, because courtesans appealed to the "apetiti" (appetites) of the "gioveni" (young men) by attracting them through the use of male costumes. The law that Casagrande cites is directed not only to courtesans but also to the "barcaioli" (boatmen) (130).

30. Lawner, *Lives of the Courtesans,* 19, in Vecellio's description of "Courtesans Outside of Their Houses."

31. Casagrande, *Le cortigiane veneziane,* 87.

32. For notice of this election, see Zorzi, *Cortigiana veneziana,* 127. On the exaggerated tendency of Venetian officials periodically to punish offenders of public decorum, and especially prostitutes, see Renzo Derosas, "Moralità e giustizia a Venezia nel '500–'600: Gli esecutori contro la bestemmia," in *Stato, società e giustizia nella repubblica veneta,* ed. Gaetano Cozzi (Rome: Jouvence, 1980), 431–528, especially 444–46. He claims that the civil police became an instrument of moral cleansing, and that the problem of public decorum was an overriding concern in this period. Laws were directed primarily to the lower levels of the population and to marginal groups, such as prostitutes. See also Giovanni Scarabello, "Devianza sessuale ed interventi di giustizia a Venezia nella prima metà del XVI secolo," in *Tiziano e Venezia: Convegno Internazionale di Studi* (Vicenza: Neri Pozza, 1980), 75–84.

33. For the reaction of M. Lucieta Padovana, see Santore, "Julia Lombardo," 45 n. 5. The document (Notatorio 5, Provveditori alla Sanità, 1542–1554, 22 Maggio 1543, fol. 30v, Absolution de M. Lucieta Padovana) states that she was "in giesia alle hore prohibite per la lezze dello Excellentissimo Consiglio de Dieci" (in church during prohibited hours by law of the most excellent Council of Ten).

34. As cited in Casagrande, *Le cortigiane veneziane,* 132.

35. *Coryat's Crudities,* 267. On the "rhetorical" aspect of the courtesan's profession, see Ann Rosalind Jones, "City Women," 304ff. Also, for an incisive analysis of the uses that women in the early modern period made of conduct manuals and treatises, including Guazzo's mentioned above, see idem, "Nets and Bridles: Early Modern Conduct Books and Sixteenth-Century Women's Lyrics," in *Essays on Literature and the History of Sexuality,* ed. Nancy Armstrong and Leonard Tennenhouse (London: Methuen, 1987), 39–72, especially 42–48.

36. On the civic display of courtesans for important rituals such as the Sensa, see Lina Padoan Urban, "La festa della Sensa nelle arti e nell'iconografia," *Studi veneziani* 10 (1968): 291–

353; and for the sequestering of Venetian noblewomen, see James C. Davis, *A Venetian Family and Its Fortune* (Philadelphia: American Philosophical Society, 1975), 110 and passim.

37. On the inflation of the dowry and its importance with regard to the transmission and circulation of patrimonal property of the ruling class, see Julius Kirshner and Anthony Molho, "The Dowry Fund and the Marriage Market in Early *Quattrocento* Florence," *Journal of Modern History* 50 (1978): 403–16; Julius Kirshner, "Pursuing Honor While Avoiding Sin: The Monte delle Doti of Florence," *Quaderni di "Studi senesi"* 41 (1978): 1–82; Christiane Klapisch-Zuber, "The Griselda Complex: Dowry and Marriage Gifts in the Quattrocento," in her *Women, Family, and Ritual in Renaissance Italy*, trans. Eric Cochrane and Lydia Cochrane (Chicago: University of Chicago Press, 1985), 213–46; Luisa Ciammitti, "Quanto costa essere normali: La dote nel Conservatorio femminile di Santa Maria del Baraccano (1630–1680)," *Quaderni storici* 53 (1983): 469–97. In an informative review essay, Barbara B. Diefendorf ("Family Culture, Renaissance Culture," *Renaissance Quarterly* 40 [1987]: 661–81) untangles the many different approaches to the dowry issue and sorts out the places of divergence in the authors cited above. Diane Owen Hughes has argued ("Sumptuary Laws," 97 and passim) that the dowry "was the single most important transfer of personal assets" in a period when the size of the dowry had increased so much that men were forced to marry later because women's families were loaded with an incredibly difficult financial burden.

38. Stanley Chojnacki has provided important information on dowry accumulation among patrician Venetian women, although from a period earlier than the one discussed here: "Patrician Women in Early Renaissance Venice," *Studies in the Renaissance* 21 (1974): 18–84; idem, "Dowries and Kinsmen in Early Renaissance Venice," *Journal of Interdisciplinary History* 4 (1975): 571–600; idem, "Kinship Ties and Young Patricians in Fifteenth-Century Venice," *Renaissance Quarterly* 38 (1986): 240–70; idem, "Power of Love." I quote from Romano, *Patricians and Popolani*, 134; he refers, in turn, to Chojnacki's study of noblewomen's dowries in Venice in "Dowries and Kinsmen." Romano states that female patronage "was oriented toward the delivery of tangible benefits such as dowries and clothing. Women were seen (and saw themselves) as intercessors in this world in much the same way that the Virgin Mary was seen as an intercessor in the next" (140). Romano also suggests that the actual formation of the palace complex in Venice contributed to the frequent contact between women of different classes and occupations.

39. On the "sprawling edifices with courtyards and covered passageways" as an "extended household," see Romano, *Patricians and Popolani*, 131–39. On the "geopolitics" of Venetian architecture and the types of housing available in sixteenth-century Venice, see James Ackerman, "Geopolitics of Venetian Architecture," in *Titian: His World and His Legacy*, ed. David Rosand (New York: Columbia University Press, 1982), 41–71; and for a useful explanation of terms relating to the construction and divisions of a typical Venetian house of the cinquecento, see Juergen Schulz, "The Houses of Titian, Aretino, and Sansovino," in Rosand, *Titian*, 73–118. On Venetian domestic architecture and more specifically for a description of middle- and lower-class houses, see Paola Pavanini, "Abitazioni popolari e borghesi nella Venezia cinquecentesca," *Studi veneziani* 5 (1981): 63–126; Giorgio Gianghian and Paola Pavanini, *Dietro i palazzi: Tre secoli di architettura minore a Venezia, 1492–1803* (Venice: Arsenale, 1984). For information on typical salary ranges for Venetian citizen workers in the Arsenale or in the woolen industry, see Pavanini, "Abitazioni popolari," 68–73; Frederick Lane, *Storia di Venezia* (Turin: Einaudi, 1978), 385–87 and passim. See also Isabella Palumbo-Fossati, "L'interno della casa dell'artigiano e dell'artista nella Venezia del Cinquecento," *Studi veneziani* 8 (1984): 109–53. For excellent overviews of the economic history of Venice in the sixteenth century, see Brian Pullan's introduction to *Crisis and*

Change in the Venetian Economy in the Sixteenth and Seventeenth Centuries, ed. Brian Pullan (London: Methuen, 1968), 1–21; idem, "The Occupations and Investments of the Venetian Nobility in the Middle and Late Sixteenth Century," in *Renaissance Venice,* ed. J. R. Hale (London: Faber and Faber, 1974), 379–408; Ferdinand Braudel, "La vita economica di Venezia nel secolo XVI," in *Storia della civiltà veneziana,* ed. Vittore Branca (Florence: Sansoni, 1979), 2:259–80.

40. The Festival of the Marys serves as an example of women's symbolic participation in the civic world of Venice. See Muir, *Civic Ritual in Renaissance Venice,* 135–56.

41. For further discussion of this letter in relation to Franco's interest in charitable institutions in support of young women at risk, see chapter 3 below.

42. Many women composed their testaments when they were pregnant, while men had "generally testated after their families were already born" (579). See Chojnacki, "Dowries and Kinsmen," 584–86. Natalie Zemon Davis points out that women wrote multiple wills in sixteenth-century Lyons when they feared dying, especially in childbirth; see "City Women and Religious Change," in her *Society and Culture,* 68–69.

43. This point was first made by Giuseppe Tassini in *Veronica Franco,* but he never fully developed its implications in Franco's life and profession as courtesan.

44. For a discussion of the identity of Fausto Bettani as a "stampatore in Venezia alla d[itta] Scotti," and of his involvement in the Scotto publishing family, see Paul F. Grendler, *The Roman Inquisition and the Venetian Press, 1540–1605* (Princeton: Princeton University Press, 1977), 5 and 227. Tassini identifies Anzolo Benedetti as perhaps belonging to the "famiglia cittadinesca Benedetti . . . che aveva due tombe ed un altare di sua proprietà in chiesa di Santi Giovanni e Paolo" (the citizen family Benedetti who had two tombs and an altar in the church of Santi Giovanni and Paolo) (*Veronica Franco,* 107 n. 1).

45. On the church of San Francesco della Vigna, see Manfredo Tafuri, *L'armonia e i conflitti: La chiesa di San Francesco della Vigna nella Venezia del cinquecento* (Turin: Einaudi, 1983). As Santore points out in relation to Lombardo, many courtesans were entombed within the walls of a church, ("Julia Lombardo," 53 n. 25). Franco was buried in San Moisé, according to Tassini (*Veronica Franco,* 260–61), but her tomb was removed with subsequent changes to the church over the centuries. See Casagrande, *Le cortigiane veneziane,* 272.

46. No biographer has provided any information on Baballi. However, in the ASV library holdings (op. 7801), there is a sheet summarizing the findings of P. Kolendic in 1961 (based on research conducted in the State Archives in Dubrovnik), entitled "Giacomo Bobali (Bobaljevic): Uno degli amanti di Veronica Franco" (one of the lovers of Veronica Franco) (43), in which he states that Bobali was a "nobile . . . figlio di Andrea Bobali e di Anna Giorgi (Durdevic), che nacque verso il 1536 e che rimase orfano di padre nel 1543. Nel '58 passò a Venezia dove, per una ventina di anni, fu uno dei più ricchi commercianti fra Venezia e l'Oriente pur essendo sempre in vivissimi rapporti commerciali anche con la sua Ragusa. Morì nella primavera del 1577 celibe, e senza lasciare testamento . . . non sappiamo neppure in quale chiesa di Venezia il Nostro Bobali sia stato sepolto," (a nobleman . . . son of Andrea Bobali and Anna Giorgi (Durdevic) and born around 1536 and left without a father in 1543. In '58 he went to Venice, where, for around twenty years, he was one of the richest merchants between Venice and the Orient, while all the while maintaining active commercial relations with his native city, Ragusa. He died in the spring of 1577, a bachelor and without a will . . . we do not know in which church he was buried). On commercial relations between Ragusa and Venice in the sixteenth century, see Branislava Tenenti, "Venezia e il commercio Raguseo delle carisee (1550c.–1620c.)," *Studi veneziani* 17–18 (1975–76): 240–41. Tenenti speaks of a Marino Bobali in Venice in 1584 (240–41

n. 17). See also her "Noli ragusei per Venezia nella seconda metà del cinquecento," *Studi veneziani* 16 (1974): 229–30, for another mention of a Bobali "noleggiatore" (freighter) in the years 1567–1574 in Venice; this would corroborate the findings recorded above.

47. As religious societies designed to encourage piety and charitable aid among the members of the Venetian republic, the *scuole*, unlike the guild systems in other parts of Italy, were not necessarily tied to, or supported by, a particular craft or trade. As Brian Pullan has shown in *Rich and Poor*, during the sixteenth century, two distinct groups of rich and poor had formed within these institutions. No longer were the *scuole* merely confraternities of rich members dispensing charity to outsiders; they now provided an institutional framework by which most of the relief (economic, political, religious, and fiscal) was publicly administered. On the history of the guardians in the different *scuole*, see 67–72; and on the practice of raising funds for religious institutions by the systematic collection of alms for "luochi pii," see 135–38, 268, 299. See also Reinhold C. Mueller, "Procurators of San Marco," *Studi veneziani* 13 (1971): 190–220; Manfredo Tafuri, "Scuole Grandi" in his *Venezia e il Rinascimento* (Turin: Einaudi, 1985), 125–31; Giovanni Scarabello, "Strutture assistenziali a Venezia nella prima metà del '500 e avvii europei della riforma dell'assistenza," in *"Renovatio urbis": Venezia nell'età di Andrea Gritti (1523–1538)*, ed. Manfredo Tafuri (Rome: Officina Edizioni, 1984), 119–33; Ruggero Maschio, "Le Scuole Grandi a Venezia," in *Storia della cultura veneta: Dal primo Quattrocento al Concilio di Trento*, ed. Girolamo Arnaldi and Manlio Pastore Stocchi (Vicenza: Neri Pozza, 1981), 3:193–206. Patricia F. Brown ("Honor and Necessity: The Dynamics of Patronage in the Confraternities of Renaissance Venice," *Studi veneziani* 14 [1987]: 179–212) identifies the specific forms of the patronage of art and architecture in the Venetian *scuole grandi* as members' expression of religious devotion and piety within a competitive civic context. See also idem, *Venetian Narrative Painting in the Age of Carpaccio* (New Haven: Yale University Press, 1988).

48. On the dowry balloting system, see Pullan, *Rich and Poor*, 85; for the specific task of choosing eligible maidens for those dowries allotted annually, see 169, 184–86, 189–92. The average dowry for the period 1550–1560 (157 and 189) was about eighteen ducats.

49. A contemporary source stresses Venetians' enormously generous acts of charity to help "women at risk." See Giovanni Nicolò Doglioni (Moderata Fonte's protector), *Venetia trionfante, et sempre libera* (Venice: Andrea Muschio, 1613); he discusses the function and administration of charitable homes for young women. That Franco was interested in supporting charitable homes for young women is attested by her involvement in the Venetian Casa del Soccorso. This home was most probably founded in 1577, but unfortunately, none of the original founding documents have survived which might help to clarify its early foundation history. (A Casa del Soccorso was first founded in Rome in 1543). The Casa del Soccorso was designed to provide temporary refuge for young women tempted by prostitution and for women adulterers who already lived separated from their husbands. Unlike the already-existing Zitelle or Convertite homes, the Casa del Soccorso provided a place for women who were responsible for the care of parents, children, or husbands. To be eligible for acceptance, the women had to repent their sins, and they could not be ugly, old, sick, or pregnant. They had also to take an oath that they would leave the home only if they were reunited with their husbands or if they intended to marry or were about to enter the Convertite.

A tradition that dates back to 1761 links Franco's name with the foundation of the Casa del Soccorso. See Angelo Malipiero, *Notizie istoriche della Pia Casa di Santa Maria del Soccorso*. Emmanuele Antonio Cicogna followed this tradition (*Delle inscrizioni veneziane*, 5:414–15). He provided as evidence the transcription of three petitions, including a *supplica* of Veronica Franco which she intended to present to the Venetian Senate but never did. In addition, he claimed that an altar painting executed by Benedetto Caliari for the Casa attested to Franco's participation, because the central figure resembled her. The Casa del Soccorso first occupied a rented house next to the Church of San Nicolò da Tolentino, run by Theatine fathers in 1580. Giuseppe Tassini (*Veronica Franco,* 93–97) also corroborates this theory, as does Rita Casagrande (*Le cortigiane veneziane,* 268–69). In recent years, however, Alessandra Schiavon has challenged this tradition ("Per la biografia," 249). After investigating the contents of a two-year contract for the home (19 October 1580) and the legislative rules ("Capitular della Casa del Soccorso," Tomo Primo), she reports no mention of Franco or any document (other than the first petition) with her signature. Further, on the register recording the bequests to the home during the years 1587–89, Franco's name does not appear among the lists of "nobili" and "cittadini." Benedetto Croce (*Lettere,* xiii) recognized the lack of evidence supporting the theory of Franco's so-called conversion. However, a new publication sponsored by Giuseppe Ellero, the head archivist of the *Istituto di Ricovero e di Educazione* archive, which houses the Casa del Soccorso documents, takes issue with Schiavon's thesis. With the discovery of Franco's *supplica,* which has her signature (although never formally presented), and in which she describes the purpose of the home, it once again seems very likely that Franco was actively involved in the early years of the Casa del Soccorso. For the new evidence and for the most exhaustive treatment of the question, see the work of Giuseppe Ellero. He published his and others' archival findings in *Archivio I.R.E.: Inventari di fondi antichi degli ospedali e luoghi pii di Venezia: Istituzioni di Ricovero e di Educazione* (Venice: 1984–87), 225–26; and see *Nel regno dei poveri,* ed. B. Aikema and D. Meijers (Istituto di Ricovero e di Educazione, 1989), 225–41, for the Casa delle Zitelle, and 241–42 and 247 nn. 1 and 3.

On the history of the I.R.E. archive, which is the same one that houses the documents pertaining to Julia Lombardo, see Santore, "Julia Lombardo," 44 n. 1. And for further discussion of Franco's interest in charitable institutions for women, see chapter 3 below. On the practice of raising funds for religious institutions by the systematic collection of alms for "luochi pii," see Pullan, *Rich and Poor,* 135–38, 268, 299; Reinhold C. Mueller, "Procurators of San Marco," *Studi veneziani* 13 (1971): 190–220.

50. The disastrous chain of events over a ten-year period, both prior to and during the outbreak of the plague in 1575, are discussed in Grendler, *Roman Inquisition,* 25–29; and Fabio Mutinelli, *Annali urbani di Venezia dall'anno 810 al 12 maggio 1797* (Venice: G. B. Merlo, 1841), 167–68. On the problem of famine in Venice in this period as a direct result of natural and environmental disasters, see Pullan, *Rich and Poor,* 288–89, 290, 373; and see 632 for the typhus epidemic.

51. In the year 1571, Venice experienced both a military defeat, in the fall of Cyprus, despite the efforts of the Venetian military hero, Marcantonio Bragadin, and in the following months, its greatest maritime victory, in the battle of Lepanto on 7 October 1571. See Gino Benzoni, *Venezia nell'età della controriforma* (Turin: Mursia, 1973), 27. As Ferdinand Braudel claims (*The Mediterranean and Mediterranean World in the Age of Phillip II* [London: Collins, 1973]), Venice was in a sense unprepared for the defeat at Famagusta, because it "had been at peace for thirty years . . . and was extremely short of manpower and totally lacking in food supplies" (2:1084–85). On the economic consequences of the war with Ottoman Turkey and on Venetian investments in Cyprus, see Pullan, "Occupations and Investments," 381–83 and passim.

52. On the Council of Ten as one of the most powerful magistracies and governing bodies in Venice, see Giuseppe Maranini, *La costituzione di Venezia dopo la serrata del Maggior Consiglio,* 2d

ed. (Florence: La Nuova Italia, 1974). As Margaret L. King (*Venetian Humanism*) states, "The Council of Ten—infamous for its silent and thorough investigations—was charged to protect Venice against political and moral crime" (278). See also 279–89 for a discussion of the offices (political and religious) held by Venetian patricians and citizens in the fifteenth and sixteenth centuries. For the connections between this magistracy and the *scuole grandi,* see William B. Wurthmann, "The Council of Ten and the *Scuole Grandi* in Early Renaissance Venice," *Studi veneziani* 18 (1989): 15–66. On the identities of Ramberti and Morosini, see Tassini, *Veronica Franco,* 82–83; and for the Morosini family, see Finlay, *Politics,* 84 and 107.

53. Ramberti's will raises more questions, however, than it answers. Why, for example, is he intent on providing support for her child if he is not the father? Some biographers have claimed that Ramberti was the father of one of her children, possibly Achiletto. But this would directly contradict Franco's claims, as evidenced in her two wills. Although she admits that she cannot be completely sure of the paternity of her first child ("Achille mio fiol è di m. Jacomo Baballi Raguseo, il qual, quanto a me, credo sii il suo fiolo"), she nevertheless assumes that it is Baballi's. Rather than a true father, therefore, Ramberti was most probably a father figure to Achiletto in the absence of any real father. It is very possible that Ramberti remained Veronica's close friend throughout these years; in fact in her second will she appoints as executor (Lorenzo Moresini) and the protector of her children (Gian Battista Bernardo) the same two men whom Ramberti had designated as commissaries in his own will, composed only seven months before. In one of Maffio Venier's satiric poems (Veronica, ver unica puttana) directed against Franco, he mentions the name Bernardo when he accuses her of sleeping with priests but of claiming that patricians like Bernardo and Tron are the fathers of her children. Since Ramberti's will was drafted before Franco's second will, it is likely that Ramberti wanted to ensure her son Achiletto's inheritance against any claims made by Ramberti's nephew Giangiacomo.

54. What further complicates an understanding of the nature of their relationship is a second will (although not a legal document) of Ramberti's, clearly satirical in spirit, dated 7 January 1573. Written in Venetian dialect and sent to his friend Zuane Bragadin, Ramberti's second will made a parody of the contents of his first will. In it he declares that he is sound in mind but not in body, owing to his age and the many "disorders" committed with his most delectable friend "Madonna Veronica Franco." To her he bequeaths his feather bed with the stipulation that she cannot sell it, use it, or give it to the Jews ("nol possa né render, né impegnare, né dar a Zudii"). Whether they are married or not ("sposata o non sposata che sia di mi"), he leaves to her his income of four blocks of caviar and four sausages. In a codicil, he asks that the residue of his estate be spent for constructing a deposit of baked pears ("pieracotta"), on top of which a large "piera viva" (pear) should bear an epitaph in verse composed by Franco. He also refers to the threat of physical dismemberment directed against his brother. See Giuseppe Tassini, *Alcune delle più clamorose condanne capitali eseguite in Venezia sotto la repubblica* (Venice: Filippi Editore, 1966), 146–51. Giuseppe Tassini discusses both wills in *Veronica Franco,* 115–23. He reports that Cicogna incorrectly gave the date of "7 gennaio" instead of its actual date of "5 Zener." The second will was found among the miscellaneous papers of the Codice Malvezzi 153 in the Biblioteca Civico Correr entitled *Essercizi accademici, traduzioni, discorsi et altre cose istruttive e piacevoli* (Academic exercises, translations, discourses, and other instructive and pleasing things [my translation]). This confirms the satirical intention of this will, which was perhaps composed extemporaneously in the company of friends. See also Masson, *Courtesans of the Italian Renaissance,* 155. Certainly much of the will alludes to contemporary events; Ramberti's reference to her "feather bed" is probably a joke on a law passed in Venice on 5 November 1570, prohibiting

the confiscation of debtor's beds. On laws for this purpose in the period, see Pullan, *Jews of Europe*, 146–53 and passim.

55. Giuseppe Tassini reports (*Veronica Franco*, 207–8 n. 3) that Bernardo was born of another G. Battista and Laura Morosini on 25 February 1536 (*more veneto*) and was married to Cristina Badoer. He was military commander on the *terraferma* and held the offices of *savio del consiglio* and *consigliere*. He died, according to the Barbaro genealogy, on 3 January 1601 (*more veneto*). The office of *savio* (*grande*) *del consiglio* was one of the most important positions in the Venetian government. It had a regular term, unlike the office of *provveditore*, and was supposed to oversee and help guide policy. See King, *Venetian Humanism*, 278–84; and Felix Gilbert, *The Pope, His Banker, and Venice* (Cambridge: Harvard University Press, 1980), 4–13. For the Morosini clan, especially in the early fourteenth century, and their wives' wills, see Chojnacki, "Dowries and Kinsmen," 577–600.

56. On Franco's learned choices of names, all drawn from classical epic, for her sons, and for a similar trend among Renaissance schoolteachers, see Paul F. Grendler, "The Organization of Primary and Secondary Education in the Italian Renaissance," *Catholic Historical Review* 71, no. 2 (1985): 197 n. 37. For an earlier period in Tuscany, see David Herlihy, "Tuscan Names, 1200–1530," *Renaissance Quarterly* 41, no. 4 (1988): 561–82.

57. Giuseppe Tassini (*Veronica Franco*, 112 n. 12) incorrectly identifies Andrea Tron as a descendant of the "Pollo" family. But on closer inspection of Franco's will, in which she claims him as the father of her son, I conclude that "Pollo" is the Venetian dialect form for "Paolo," referring instead to his father, Paolo Tron. I would like to thank Dennis Romano for his assistance and suggestions in the reading of Franco's wills.

58. On Andrea Tron, see also Pierre De Nolhac and Angelo Solerti, *Il viaggio in Italia di Enrico III Re di Francia e le feste a Venezia, Ferrara, Mantova e Torino* (Turin: 1890), 58 n. 2; they reproduce the list of nobles as recorded in the contemporary source by Pietro Buccio, in *Le coronationi di Polonia et di Francia del Christianissimo Re Henrico III* (Padua: Lorenzo Pasquati, 1576), 177–79.

59. On the system of adopting children ("fiol d'anima") in Venice, see Ruggiero, *Boundaries of Eros*, 41, 150–51, and 197–98 n. 7.

60. On the education of children in early modern Venice, see the important study by Paul F. Grendler, *Schooling in Renaissance Italy: Literacy and Learning, 1300–1600* (Baltimore: Johns Hopkins University Press, 1989), 42–70, 87–110 and passim.

61. Perhaps he or she was a member of the same Morosini family that Franco designates as one of her commissaries to this will.

62. From the Casa del Soccorso petition noted above (n. 49), we learn that her brother was ultimately killed in the war and that in the 1580s Franco took on the responsibility and added financial burden of caring for his children.

63. Ruggiero (*Boundaries of Eros*) discusses the reasons for the choices between the convent, marriage, and prostitution; see 152–54, 162–63.

64. I disagree with Tassini's transcription of Franco's bequest to her maidservant when he says that she leaves her objects with a value of "405 ducats." I believe she has rather left the more reasonable amount of "4 *o* 5 ducats," which is more in keeping with her other bequests to servants and maids to whom she feels a certain loyalty. See Santore, "Julia Lombardo," 44–83, for an example of a wealthy Venetian courtesan. Two valuable contemporary sources list the various merchant professions in this period: Tomaso Garzoni, *La Piazza universale di tutte le professioni del mondo* (Venice: Giovanni Battista Somasco, 1585); and Francesco Sansovino, *Venetia città no-*

bilissima et singolare (Venice: I. Sansovino, 1581). The tax reports usually report immovable rather than movable wealth. They refer most commonly to houses and land. See B. Canal, "Il collegio, l'ufficio e l'archivio dei Dieci Savi alle Decime in Rialto," *Nuovo archivio veneto* 16 (1908).

65. It is interesting to note that both "perle" (pearls) and her dress, "di raso pagierino intagliata di lama d'arzento et perfiliata d'oro" (of yellow satin embroidered with silver and gold threads), were precisely the part of the courtesan's wardrobe that was subject to sumptuary laws. See Hughes, "Sumptuary Laws." A sixteenth-century Venetian manual for fabric dyers claims that the dye used for the bodice of the dress that Franco mentions here ("cremisin") was the most expensive of all the dyes available in the period. See Giovanventura Rossetti, *Plichto de l'arthe de tentori che insegna tenger pani telle bambasi et sede* (Venice: Augustino Bindoni, 1548).

66. Tassini (*Veronica Franco,* 83–85 n. 8) reports that Antonio Pizzamano held the position of "Ragionato degli Avogadori Fiscali." Pizzamano was apprehended for living with the nun, Camilla Rota, who had fled from the convent of Santo Spirito in Venice to live with him as his "concubina." On this scandal, and for others that presumably occurred in this convent, which had a long history of illicit practices among the Venetian nobility, see Tassini, *Curiosità veneziane,* 8th ed. (Venice: Filippi Editore, 1970), 624–25. The tax report of a Marina Pizzamano of "21 agosto 1582" refers to an "Antonio Pizzamano dotor" as her husband, dead at the time of the report. See ASV, *Dieci Savi sopra le Decime,* Condizione del 1582, b. 736. She owns "una porcion de casa posta in contrà di San Polo," for which she receives six and one-half ducats yearly because the house is "vecchia et ruinosa" (old and in ruins) and "in contrà di San Moisé una casetta vecchia et malissimo condicion . . . la qual sta sempre quasi disafitada" (in the region of San Moisé a small, old house and in very poor condition . . . which is almost always unrented). While her husband was alive they rented the house yearly for five and one-half ducats. She states that she is now living in "corte di G. Zorzi in campo Ansolo in le case delli fratti di G. Zorzi" (the courtyard of G. Zorzi in campo Ansolo in the homes of the brothers of G. Zorzi).

67. On the educational possibilities available to women in sixteenth-century Italy, see Gian Ludovico Masetti Zannini, *Motivi storici della educazione femminile: Scienza, lavoro, giouchi* (Naples: M. D'Aurio, 1982); Maria Ludovica Lenzi, *Donne e madonne: L'educazione femminile nel primo rinascimento italiano* (Turin: Loescher, 1982). A number of recent studies discuss the importance of a father or father figure for a woman's success in receiving some form of an education in the early modern period in Italy. Among them are Grendler, *Schooling in Renaissance Italy,* 87–102; he reviews the opportunities that certain aristocratic Italian women humanists and early feminists of the citizen rank, such as Moderata Fonte, Lucrezia Marinella, and Arcangela Tarabotti, received owing to patriarchal support. See also Labalme, "Venetian Women on Women," 81–109; idem, "Women's Roles in Early Modern Venice"; Chemello, "La donna, il modello, l'immaginario"; King, "Thwarted Ambitions"; Joan M. Ferrante, "The Education of Women in the Middle Ages in Theory, Fact, and Fantasy," in Labalme, *Beyond Their Sex,* 9–42. See also Anne Jacobson Schutte, "Teaching Adults to Read in Sixteenth-Century Venice: Giovanni Antonio Tagliente's *Libro maistrevole,*" *Sixteenth Century Journal* 17, no. 2 (1986): 3–16; Paul F. Grendler, "What Zuanne Read in School: Vernacular Texts in Sixteenth-Century Venetian Schools," *Sixteenth Century Journal* 13, no. 1 (1982): 41–53; idem, *Schooling in Renaissance Italy,* 87–102. On the education of women in convents, see Elissa Weaver, "Spiritual Fun: A Study of Sixteenth-Century Tuscan Convent Theater," in *Women in the Middle Ages and the Renaissance and Historical Perspectives,* ed. Mary Beth Rose (Syracuse: Syracuse University Press, 1985), 173–205. For a fascinating discussion of the books most popular among Venetian cour-

tesans, even those who were illiterate, see Marisa Milani, "La verità *ovvero* il processo contro Isabella Bellocchio" (Venezia, 12 gennaio–14 ottobre 1589)" (Padua: Centrostampa, 1985), 2:150 n. 59; and Santore, "Julia Lombardo"; Santore, after an examination of Lombardo's inventory, states that she owned a number of literary works.

68. Paul F. Grendler discusses the use of this text in women's education (*Schooling in Renaissance Italy,* 278–81 and passim). On the issue of female literacy in the early modern period and on the issue of literacy in general in this period as a source of tension between oral and written cultures, see Peter Burke, *The Historical Anthropology of Early Modern Italy: Essays on Perception and Communication* (Cambridge: Cambridge University Press, 1987). At least one book published in the sixteenth century regarded learned conversation among women as dangerous. See *Libro di Marco Aurelio con l'Horologio de' Principi* (Venice: Francesco Portonaris, 1556). For example, in chap. 9 of book 2, fol. 15r., the title reads "Qual danno, overo utile segue alle prencipesse, e gran signore dall'andare a visitare le altre, o di starsi in casa" (What ill or usefulness follows princesses or gentlemen from going to visit others or being in the house). There are a number of editions of this work; the next was in 1575.

69. Ibid., 101–2.

70. Ibid., 99–100.

71. Ibid., 100.

72. Ibid., 101.

73. On Fonte's father and the paternal protection of Giovanni Nicolò Doglioni, see Chemello, "La donna, il modello, l'immaginario," 106–7 n. 15; Labalme, "Venetian Women." I thank Patricia H. Labalme for generously sharing with me her findings and notes on Moderata Fonte. For Fonte's and Franco's tax reports, see ASV, Dieci Savi sopra le decime, Condizione 1581–82. For Fonte, see busta 157, n. 751, 24 agosto; and for Franco, see busta 157, n. 92, 15 febbraio. For a transcription of Franco's tax report, see appendix 2.2. A "livello" was a personal loan at interest, which replaced bonds in this period. "Livelli" were disguised as leases of real property whereby the renters could circumvent the laws against usury. For concrete examples of how the "livello" system functioned, see Pullan, "Occupations and Investments," 380–89. A general explanation of these legal terms can be found in Marco Ferro, *Dizionario del diritto comune e veneto* (Venice: 1778–81), and for the "livello," 7:40–41.

74. Franco lived, as far as I can determine, in at least six different houses in Venice, in the regions of S. Maria Formosa, S. Marcilian, S. Tomà, S. Giovanni Novo, S. Samuele, and S. Moise.

75. "Inclinato alla ruina dell'appetito più che alla edificazion della ragione," in Franco, *Lettere familiari a diversi,* 26–28.

76. Cicero, *Tusculan Disputationes,* 4.79.

77. The most recent discussions of Domenico Venier's literary salon and his relationship with Veronica Franco are those of Alvise Zorzi (*Cortigiana veneziana,* 57–65, 69–90, and 163–64 for further bibliography); Francesco Erspamer, "Petrarchismo e manierismo nella lirica del secondo cinquecento," in *Storia della cultura veneta,* ed. G. Arnaldi and M. Pastore Stocchi (Vicenza: Neri Pozza, 1983), 4:189–222, especially 192–97. Elena Bassi (*Ville della Provincia di Venezia* [Venice: Rusconi, 1987]), discussing Palazzo Trevisan in Murano, claims that Camillo Trevisan, a descendant of an ancient citizen family in Venice, was one of the founding members, together with Badoer, of the Accademia della Fama. Bassi reports that the signing of the academy's founding documents took place in Domenico Venier's home (41).

78. For Venier's relationship with Gaspara Stampa, see Abdelkader Salza, "Madonna

Gasparina Stampa, secondo nuove indagini," *Giornale storico della letteratura italiana* 62 (1913): 1–101; and Erspamer, "Petrarchismo e manierismo," 191–92. Erspamer states that Stampa was "ben inserita nel circolo di letterati che si riuniva in casa di Domenico Venier" (well inserted into the circle of literary types who met in Domenico Venier's home). Venier's interest (and that of many other Venetian poets of the period) in the Friulian poet, Irene di Spilimbergo, is evident in the collection of poems, *Rime di diversi nobilissimi et eccellentissimi autori in morte della signora Irene delle signore di Spilimbergo* [. . .] (Venice: Domenico and Giovanni B. Guerra, 1561), edited by Dionigi Atanagi composed in her memory. On this collection, see Elvira Favretti, "Una raccolta di Rime del Cinquecento," *Giornale storico della letteratura italiana* 158 (1981): 543–72; Anne Jacobson Schutte, "Irene di Spilimbergo: The Image of a Creative Woman in Late Renaissance Italy," *Renaissance Quarterly* 44, no. 1 (1991): 42–61.

In the manuscript *Lettere inedite di Pietro Gradenigo: Patrizio veneto,* housed in the Biblioteca Nazionale Marciana, one of the members of Venier's circle writes to a certain Signora Lucia Albana Avogadra a Brescia" on "l'ultimo di settembre del '55" (the last day of September of '55) and praises her for her "epistola." In another letter to a certain "Signora Theodora Visconta," he provides a thorough analysis of her sonnets (fol. 59). I would like to thank Martha Feldman for pointing out to me the importance of this manuscript.

79. Erspamer, "Petrarchismo e manierismo," 193 and 207. Erspamer claims that there were three kinds of poetic volumes published in the second half of the sixteenth century in Venice, many under Venier's guidance: those that followed the Petrarchan model, as a "biografia esemplare"; anthologies of "rime diversi"; and *"Templi"* in praise of, or commemorating the death of, a specific person. There were also unpublished poems, informally brought together for discussions in the salon. On the Venier salon, and for clarifications of the salon's connections with the Accademia della Fama, see Feldman, "Venice and the Madrigal," 1:442–55 and passim.

80. On this edition, but without any analysis of the poetic conventions or literary context from which it comes, see Abdelkader Salza, *Rime* (Bari: Laterza, 1913), 380–86.

81. On the history of the illustrious Martinengo family, see Francesco Sansovino, *Della origine et de' fatti delle famiglie illustri d'Italia* (Venice: Altobello Salicato, 1582), 296–305. For a description of the specific "ramo" of this family (Ramo Terzo: Da Barco) from which Estore descends, see Paolo Guerrini, *Una celebre famiglia lombarda, I Conti di Martinengo: Studi e ricerche genealogiche* (Brescia: Geroldi, 1930), 239–43. Francesco, his brother, and possibly Franco's lover, was married to Beatrice, who was the daughter of Count Tomaso Langosco di Stroppiana, grand cancelliere of the duke of Savoy. After two husbands, she married Francesco in 1580. Estore in 1570 had married a Roman noblewoman, Livia degli Amici, and had seven sons as well as one daughter who was a Benedictine nun in San Giulia. A Roman *avviso* dated 22 October 1580 reports that "giunse giovedì in questa città, il conte Giovanni Francesco Martinengo detto il Malpaga Cavaliere dell'Ordine dell'Annunciata mandato ambasciatore dal Duca di Savoia" (the count G. F. Martinengo called Malpaga chevalier of the order of the Annunciata was sent as ambassador to the duke of Savoy). See BAV, Urb. lat. 1048, fol. 370v.

It is interesting to note that there were many cases of heresy brought against the Martinengo Da Barco family in the sixteenth century. As Christopher Cairns notes, "the Martinengo family possessed vast feudatory holdings in the areas south and south west of Brescia and their tolerance and support of deviant sects and later, Jews, was to be a considerable hindrance to the Catholic efforts to eradicate heresy in that area." See Christopher Cairns, *Domenico Bollani, Bishop of*

Brescia: Devotion to Church and State in the Republic of Venice in the Sixteenth Century (Nieuwkoop: De Graaf, 1976), 152–53.

82. See Francesco Martinengo, *Relatione di tutto il successo di Famagosta* (Venice: Giorgio Angelieri, 1572). Francesco Martinengo composed a number of volumes on the battle of Famagusta that are in the Biblioteca Nazionale Marciana in Venice. The loss of Cyprus also meant that certain Venetian families who for generations had owned land there were suddenly deprived of an important source of salt, sugar, cotton, and grain and "an important, if not indispensable base for navigation to Syria." See Pullan, "Occupations," 382. A number of Ca' Venier poets were involved in cultural projects that were politically motivated. Luigi Groto and Ferrante Carafa put together an anthology celebrating the victory at Lepanto. See, for example, their *Trofeo della vittoria sacra* (1573). Francesco Erspamer ("Petrarchismo e manierismo," 207) argues that this political engagement constituted a move away from the "sperimentalismo" (experimentalism) of midcentury.

83. There has been a problem, however, among critics in establishing the exact date for this edition. See Graf, *Attraverso,* 328; and Cicogna, *Delle inscrizioni veneziane,* 245 n. 1. Cicogna states that "non essendovi data, conghetturo che Estore [è] già morto dopo il 1572 in cui era Capitano di fanti della repubblica . . . e prima del 1580" (having no date, I conjecture that Estore was already dead after 1572, when he was captain of the republic's infantrymen, and sometime before 1580). For further discussion of this group, see chapter 4 below. See also Zorzi, *Cortigiana veneziana,* 59–65, 80–82.

84. On the artifice of Venier's sonnets, written in a style often characterized as "freddo" (cold), see Erspamer, "Petrarchismo e manierismo," 193–97. Erspamer asserts that Venier's experimental poems set him apart from most Petrarchists of his day. See also Damaso Alonso, *Pluralità e correlazione in poesia,* trans. M. Rosataing and V. Minervini (Bari: Adriatica, 1971), 156–65; and Taddeo, *Il manierismo,* 56–70. Taddeo discusses Venier's use of the correlative sonnet. On the play with proper names and the use of acrostics as the beginning words for each sonnet as an extension of a Petrarchan conceit, see W. Theodor Elwert, "Pietro Bembo e la vita letteraria del suo tempo," *La civiltà veneziana del rinascimento* (Florence: Sansoni, 1958), 125–76. Taddeo sees Venier's interest in technical virtuosity as connected to the "rime di corrispondenza" (rhymes of correspondence) between Venier and Orsatto Giustinian. He defines Venier's sonnets as a "letteratura di scambio, vincolata al costume sociale . . . costituite in maggioranza di sonetti di risposta" (a literature of exchange constrained by social customs . . . constituting mainly sonnets of reply) (45). In six sonnets the rhymes are the same, and they adopt "lo stesso acrostico delle lettere iniziali di verso" (the same acrostic that is formed by the first letters of each verse) (45).

85. For a general account of Venier's condition, see Pompeo Molmenti, *La storia di Venezia nella vita privata dalle origini alla aoduta della repubblica,* 7th ed. (Bergamo: Istituto italiano d'arti grafiche, 1928), 2:303–4.

86. Marco Valerio Marcellino, *Il diamerone* (Venice: Gabriel Giolito de' Ferrari, 1965), 3–4.

87. Poetic anthologies also reflected Venice's mainland expansion in the sixteenth century into northern Italy, from Cremona and Bergamo in the west to Friuli in the east and to Ravenna in the south. The Zacco edition is housed in the manuscript collection of the Biblioteca Nazionale Marciana, MSS it. IX 14 (=6988), fols. 77–82. On Zacco, see the entry in G. Vedova, *Biografie degli scrittori padovani* (Bologna: 1836), 440–41; this states that according to ab. Gennari, the Zacco "*Canzoniere* . . . alla chiarezza del sangue unisce con raro esempio la più

squisita letteratura" (*Canzoniere* brings together a purity of blood with a rare example of the most exquisite literature). An epitaph to Zacco appears in the church of the Carmine in Venice; it reads, "Bartholomaeo Zacco / Laurentii Doctoris et Equitis Filio / Poesis Eloquentiae Caeterumque Bonarum Artium / Studiis Valde Claro / Hieronymoque Eius Filio Patavinae Ecclesiae / Cathedralis Archipresbytero / S. T. Magist. Artium et Medicinae Doctori / Obiere ille an. MDLXXXV. Aetatis Suae LXIII / Hic Anno MDCIX Aetatis LX. P. P. A. MDXV."

It is clear that Zacco was a close friend not only of Domenico Venier but of many members of Ca' Venier, especially Sperone Speroni. Speroni addressed many of his personal letters to Zacco, as has been revealed in a recent survey of Speroni's correspondence in the manuscript collection of the Biblioteca Capitolare in Padua. See Maria Rosa Loi and Mario Pozzi, "Le Lettere familiari di Sperone Speroni," *Giornale storico della letteratura italiana* 163, no. 523 (1987): 383–413. Zacco also wrote a history of Padua, *Storia di Padova sino alla estinzione dei principi Carraresi*, referred to in Vedova, *Biografie*, 2:440–41. In an edition celebrating the king of Poland, Moderata Fonte, editor, *Del giardino de' poeti in lode del Serenissimo Re di Polonia* (Venice: Guerra fratelli, 1583), Zacco appears as one of the contributing poets. On fol. 17, following Fonte's sonnet, "Sparge quando rimena Apollo il giorno," Zacco writes "D'oltra le care e patrie selve." There are over forty poets, but Fonte is the only woman poet.

88. Perhaps her "zia monaca" is "Suor Marina," to whom Franco referred in her first will.

89. The exact title of this edition is *Panegirico nel felice dottorato dell'Illustre, et Eccellentissimo Signor Gioseppe Spinelli, Dignissimo Rettor de legisti, et cavalier splendidissimo* (Padua: Lorenzo Pasquati, 1575). This edition contains in the same volume a Latin translation of all of the verses (there are thirty-one poets, including two women), presumably executed by the poets themselves. On the history of the "Accademia degli Animosi" in Padua, see Michele Maylender, *Storia delle accademie d'Italia* (Bologna: 1926–30), 1:197–200. In the list of members he records, we find a "Giovanni Fratta Veronese." Author of a volume of eclogues and a pastoral poem, *Nigella* (1582), Fratta also published a "poema eroico" entitled *Maltheide* that is introduced with a preface by Torquato Tasso.

90. By midcentury, women writers began to contribute on a fairly regular basis to poetic anthologies. In 1545 Ludovico Domenichi edited an anthology including ninety-one poets (a number of them women), *Rime diverse di molti eccellentissimi autori* (Venice: Gabriel Giolito de Ferrari, 1545), which became the first in a series, initiating a vogue for such collections throughout the century. In 1559 Domenichi edited a volume containing only women poets: *Rime diverse d'alcune nobilissime e virtuosissime donne* (Lucca: Vincenzo Busdragho, 1559); there are fifty-three poets. On this edition, see Marie-Françoise Piejus, "La première anthologie de poèmes féminins: L'écriture filtrée et orientée," in *Le pouvoir et la plume* (Paris: Université de la Sorbonne Nouvelle, 1982), 193–213. Piejus argues that this edition underwent changes according to the control exercised between editor and publisher.

91. For Henri III's entry into Venice in 1574, the principal sources are Charles Yriarte, *La vie d'un patricien de Venise au seizième siècle* (Paris: E. Plon, 1874), 46–51; Pierre De Nolhac and Angelo Solerti, *Il viaggio in Italia di Enrico III Re di Francia e le feste a Venezia, Ferrara, Mantova e Torino* (Turin: 1890). A complete record of the contemporary literary texts and manuscripts composed to commemorate his entry are included in this volume, 3–27. One of the most important of these contemporary sources is Pietro Buccio, *Le coronationi di Polonia et di Francia del Christianissimo Re Henrico III* (Padua: 1576), 177–79.

92. On triumphal entries of a monarch into a principal city as an important phenomenon of the Renaissance, see Werner Weisbach, *Trionfi* (Berlin: G. Grote, 1919); Josephe Chartrou, *Les*

entrées solennelles et triomphales à la Renaissance (1448–1551) (Paris: Presses universitaires de France, 1928); Jean Jacquot, *Les fêtes de la Renaissance* (Paris: Editions du centre nationale de la récherche scientifique, 1956), vol. 1; Roy Strong, *Art and Power: Renaissance Festivals, 1450–1650* (Berkeley: University of California Press, 1984), and for a discussion of Henri III's entry, see especially 115–16. And see Bonner Mitchell, *The Majesty of the State: Triumphal Progresses of Foreign Sovereigns in Renaissance Italy, 1494–1600* (Florence: Leo S. Olschki, 1986), 112–26, for full documentation. Mitchell offers an interesting explanation for how triumphal entries provided an "emotional catharsis" for the citizens; he says, "the emotion purged was not pity or fear but a political one, the possession of civic devotion and loyalty. The local spectator saw his own city or state and the visiting sovereign in an ideal light" (212). For an interesting discussion of the musical and theatrical performances prepared for the king's sojourn, see David Nutter, "A Tragedy for Henry III of France, Venice, 1574," in *Essays in Honor of Craig Hugh Smyth,* ed. Andrew Morrogh et al. (Florence: Giunti Barbera, 1985), 2:591–611. For the artistic decorations, see Lina Padoan Urban, "Gli spettacoli urbani e l'utopia," in Lionello Puppi, ed., *Architettura e utopia nella Venezia del Cinquecento,* (Milan: Electa, 1980), 144–66.

93. De Nolhac and Solerti, *Il viaggio,* 110–12.

94. Ibid., 118.

95. Ibid., 119 n. 2. On this visit with Franco, see Tassini, *Veronica Franco,* 89; and Masson, *Courtesans of the Italian Renaissance,* 156.

96. Masson, *Courtesans of the Italian Renaissance,* 156; Zorzi, *Cortigiana veneziana,* 115–40. Pierre De Nolhac and Angelo Solerti (*Il viaggio,* 58 n. 2) reproduce the list of nobles as recorded in the contemporary source by Pietro Buccio: *Le coronationi di Polonia et di Francia del Christianissimo Re Henrico III* (Padua: Lorenzo Pasquati, 1576), 177–79. A Roman *avviso* also offers the names of the men who were assigned to Henri during his stay. See BAV, Urb. lat. 1044, 3 luglio 1574, fol. 150v–151r.

97. Cardinal Luigi d'Este (1538–86) was the son of Ercole II and Renata of France, who urged Luigi, against his will, to enter into the religious life. He escaped Ferrara as a young man and went to France, where he secretly entered into marriage agreements with the countess of Saint Paul. In 1561 he was forced to return to Italy. Though he intended to abandon his religious post and to marry in order to leave heirs to the throne, this never happened. He was known for his unruly behavior and his violent temper. With a certain interest in art and literature, he was the patron to the young Torquato Tasso, and he completed during his lifetime the building of Villa d'Este in Tivoli and the Palazzo dei Diamanti in Ferrara. According to an *avviso,* Luigi d'Este would occasionally enter Venice incognito. He was reported to have done so on "6 agosto 1580," according to the document in BAV, Urb. lat. 1048, fol. 231r.

98. Like the duke, Domenico Venier had an interest in music that often brought him into contact with musicians and composers. Guglielmo Gonzaga (1550–87) was an important musical patron of the period, having employed such composers as Wert, Gastoldi, and Pallavicino. Richard Sherr discusses his musical interests in "Guglielmo Gonzaga and the Castrati," *Renaissance Quarterly* 33, no. 1 (1980): 33–56, especially 33–34 nn. 2–3. See Iain Fenlon, *Music and Patronage in Sixteenth-Century Mantua* (New York: Cambridge University Press, 1980), especially 1:82–95. He discusses Duke Guglielmo's musical patronage and refers to Henri's entry into Mantua. On Venier's involvement with musicians and composers, see Feldman, "Venice and the Madrigal," 1:472–86; idem, "The Academy of Domenico Venier, Music's Literary Muse in Mid-Cinquecento Venice." *Renaissance Quarterly* 44, no. 3 (1991), 475–510.

99. When Henri was unexpectedly asked to return to France to assume the royal crown be-

cause of the premature death of his older brother, the Venetian republic saw that they had an unusual political opportunity to win his allegiance to the republic. Despite a recent maritime victory against the Turks in the Battle of Lepanto in 1571, the republic still faced the threat of Spain and the power it wielded on the mainland. The triumphal arch erected for the occasion at the Lido was designed by Palladio and decorated by Veronese and Tintoretto. The canvases depict the king against the Hugenots, with Faith triumphing over Heresy. In the summer of 1575 literary and publishing activities were brought to a standstill, owing to the spread of the plague in Venice and the Veneto region. As Paul F. Grendler has noted, the press had declined quantitatively since the peak of 1560–74, and even more when Venice suffered the plague during 1575–77. He states in *Roman Inquisition,* 226–27, that "death, the flight to the countryside, and the spasmodic efforts of the government to halt the plague by suspending commercial activity combined to depress the entire economy, including the press." Also on this subject, see Pullan, *Rich and Poor,* 315–19, 325. Not only were certain publishers not printing, but many of them disappeared completely from Venice in these years.

100. On the basis of evidence provided by Apostolo Zeno, Tassini has suggested that in 1575 Franco was planning, after Henri III's departure, to compile an anthology of *Rime* commemorating his triumphal entry into Venice in 1574 (Tassini, *Veronica Franco,* 89 n. 19, and 91). See also Benedetto Croce, *Lettere,* 68 (for the letter itself). Croce points out the importance of Franco's letter in which she discusses her plans for such an edition, 70–71. The *Compositioni volgari . . . ,* in fact, was printed in 1575 and 1576 as an anthology commemorating Henri's visit to the republic. This volume, edited by Domenico Farri and dedicated to the French ambassador, Du Ferrier, is divided into "componimenti volgari" and "latine." Each poet represented in this anthology subsequently published separate and individual editions of his poems. I consider it possible that Franco had begun to prepare the volume in dedication to Henri III, but with the sudden impact of the plague, was forced to abandon the project. One added fact might also shed further light on this issue. In her charge of theft presented in 1579–80 to Ascanio Thomasino, the vicario of the patriarch of Venice, she claims that among other items (which she lists) that were stolen from her, there were her "scritture." Could these writings be, in fact, the proposed edition of poems? See chapter 4 below. Among those authors who composed poems in Latin are Cesare Spinelli, Paolo Ramusio, Francesco Morandi, Ottaviano Menino, and Bernardo Tomitano. For a description of this projected edition, see Salza, *Rime,* 384.

101. For an extensive and comprehensive review and analysis of the Danae myth in the classical and Renaissance literary sources and in the paintings of the Renaissance, see the fascinating and informative article by Madilyn Millner Kahr, "Danae: Virtuous, Voluptuous, Venal Woman," *Art Bulletin* 58 (1978): 43–55. See also Leonard Barkan, *The Gods Made Flesh: Metamorphosis and the Pursuit of Paganism* (New Haven: Yale University Press, 1986), especially 184–94 and 196–98. Barkan discusses the Danae myth in relation to the paintings (*poesie*) of Titian, as well as to the varying uses of the myth in selected poems. For Titian's depictions of Danae, see Corrado Cagli and Francesco Valcanover, *L'opera completa di Tiziano* (Milan: Rizzoli, 1969), 116, 123. See also Charles Hope, *Titian* (London: Jupiter Books, 1980), 117–18, 127–28, and 189–90, for a discussion of Titian's two Danae paintings in the Capodimonte Museum in Naples and in the Prado Museum in Madrid.

102. For Venier's interest in Ovid's *Metamorphoses* and his partial translation of the text into the vernacular, see chapter 5 below. On the erotic nature of sixteenth-century Venetian painting as influenced by Venetian "volgarizzamenti" (writings in the vernacular) by such writers as Ludovico Dolce and Francesco Sansovino, see Carlo Ginzburg, "Tiziano, Ovidio, e i codici della

figurazione erotica del Cinquecento," *Paragone* 339, no. 29 (1978): 3–24; Hope, *Titian,* 135, 142 n. 18; Rona Goffen, "Renaissance Dreams," *Renaissance Quarterly* 40 (1987): 682–706, especially 691–97. For examples of a woman artist reinterpreting the theme of sexual coercion from the female point of view, see Mary D. Garrard, *Artemisia Gentileschi: The Image of the Female Hero in Italian Baroque Art* (Princeton: Princeton University Press, 1990).

103. A recent study looks at Henri's intellectual formation, especially his interest in Italian culture. See Jacqueline Boucher, *La cour de Henri III* (Rennes: Ouest-France, 1986). On his motto, see 143–44. Boucher states (143) that one of his medals was engraved with a sun that hovered above another solar group of admiring spectators (presumably his wife and his sister, Marguerite de Navarre). They too were represented as the sun, with the device "Aspice et Aspicar" (look at me and you will see me). For Henri's solar images, see Strong, *Art and Power,* 118 and p. 206 n. 26. Boucher reports (27) that Henri III was trained in Italian humanist studies by Jacopo Corbanelli, a Florentine, especially in reading Latin and in speaking and reading in Italian. She also reports that he spoke Italian (Tuscan) extremely well, and that 16 percent of his books were in Italian. In the early years of his reign, in 1576, he organized regular salon gatherings of intellectuals in his royal residence, but in later years, Boucher continues, he indulged in other, "less than honorable, pastimes, such as gambling, illicit sexual activities," and so forth.

104. Boccaccio's rendition of the Danae story is analogous to that of Appollodorus as cited in Kahr, "Danae," 43 n. 4, 44 n. 13. In his *La Genealogia de gli dei de gentili . . .* (Venice: 1581), Boccaccio states, "Jove's being transformed into a shower of gold and falling through the roof into Danae's lap . . . must have meant: the chastity of the virgin had been corrupted with gold . . . [she] made a bargain with Jove at the price of intercourse with him."

105. For a stimulating discussion of these dedicatory sonnets, see Ann Rosalind Jones, *The Currency of Eros: Women's Love Lyric in Europe, 1540–1620* (Bloomington and Indianapolis: Indiana University Press, 1990), 170–71. See also Croce, *Poeti e scrittori,* 226. A poem, "Ecco Vinegia bella," composed for Henri's entry and set to music by Andrea Gabrieli, depicts both France and Venice as offspring of Jupiter. I thank Martha Feldman for this reference.

106. Boucher, *La Cour,* 143.

107. Ibid., 143–44. Louise de Lorraine was the cousin of the duke Charles III. On her inability to have children, perhaps, as Boucher suggests, because of Henri's sterility caused by veneral disease, see ibid., 27 and passim.

CHAPTER THREE: ADDRESSING VENICE

1. Only one copy of Franco's *Lettere familiari a diversi,* most probably published in Venice, survives in the Biblioteca Nazionale Marciana in Venice, which suggests that only a limited number were originally printed. The name of the publisher is not recorded, and there is no "privilegio" (copyright). For a modern edition of her letters that includes a critical essay, a consideration of its textual history, and a note on the iconography representing Veronica Franco, see Benedetto Croce, *Lettere dall'unica edizione del MDLXXX con proemio e nota iconografica* (Naples: Ricciardi, 1949). Before Croce, some of Franco's letters were anthologized by Bartolomeo Gamba in *Lettere di donne italiane del secolo XVI* (Venice: Alvisopoli, 1832). Franco's gift of her familiar letters to Montaigne is recorded in his *Journal de voyage en Italie,* ed. Maurice Rat (Paris: Editions Garnier, 1955), 72.

2. Amedeo Quondam (*Le "carte messaggiere": Retorica e modelli di communicazione epistolare per un indice dei libri di lettere del Cinquecento* [Rome: Bulzoni, 1981], 57) argues that by the time of the publication of Franco's letters, two distinct types of letter collections were published in Italy—

one designed to demonstrate a circuit of personal relations with influential people attesting to one's social status, and one that exhibited a rhetorical and linguistic mastery of the form, adhering to correct situations according to appropriately chosen rhetorical guidelines. Quondam places Franco's letters into the second category.

3. For a similar phenomenon for the familiar letter in France, see Elizabeth Goldsmith, *"Exclusive Conversations": The Art of Interaction in Seventeenth-Century France* (Philadelphia: University of Pennsylvania Press, 1988), 28–40. Also useful on the social functions of epistolography is a recent collection of essays on women's letters: *Writing the Female Voice: Essays on Epistolary Literature,* ed. Elizabeth C. Goldsmith (Boston: Northeastern University Press, 1989). In letters 37 (55–56), and 40 (57–58) of Franco's *Lettere familiari a diversi,* she refers to the conflicting rhetorical theories of the practice of composing the familiar letter that echo Erasmian principles as he outlines them in *Opus de conscribendis epistolis* (1.2.209–27), 353. In letter 38, for example, she speaks about the need to compose brief, well-constructed letters that evoke real conversation between absent friends about their own affairs; and in letter 37, she advocates matching correct rhetorical style to the type of letter one wishes to write. Erasmus had claimed that the ancients "argued the relative merits of the Attic, Rhodian, and Asiaic styles, but Quintilian rightly said that the best style was that most suitable to the subject, time, place, and audience" (353). I quote here from the excellent study of Erasmus's treatise and his influence on Italian theorists in the fifteenth and sixteenth centuries: Judith Rice Henderson, "Erasmus on the Art of Letter-Writing," in *Renaissance Eloquence: Studies in the Theory and Practice of Renaissance Rhetoric,* ed. James J. Murphy (Berkeley: University of California Press, 1983), 331–55. Franco also refers to the required brevity of the familiar letter as an indication of true feeling, when she says in letter 37 that her praise is in "forma laconica" (laconic form), and not "asiatica" (Asiatic). Crucial also for an appreciation of Erasmus's impact on epistolary theory in the Renaissance is Marc Fumaroli, *L'age de l'éloquence: Rhetorique et "res literaria" de la Renaissance au seuil de l'époque classique* (Geneva: Droz, 1980), 92–108 and passim.

4. For considerations of Veronica Franco's letters and poems that rely on this point of view, see Arturo Graf, "Una cortigiana fra mille," *Attraverso il Cinquecento* (Turin: Chiantore, 1888), 215–351; Giuseppe Tassini, *Veronica Franco: Celebre poetessa e cortigiana del secolo XVI* (1874; reprint, Venice: Alfieri, 1969), especially 99–105; Croce, *Lettere;* Riccardo Scrivano, "Veronica Franco," in his *Cultura e letteratura* (Rome: Ateneo, 1966), especially 204–6; and A. Giovanni Frugoni, "I capitoli della cortigiana Veronica Franco," *Belfagor* 3 (1948): 44–59.

5. This critical stance characterizes many evaluations of women's subjective poetry and autobiographical writings. See Peter Dronke, *Women Writers of the Middle Ages* (Cambridge: Cambridge University Press, 1984), 84–143; Helisenne de Crenne, *Renaissance Woman: Helisenne's Personal and Invective Letters,* trans. Marianna M. Mustacchi and Paul J. Archambault (Syracuse: Syracuse University Press, 1986), 8–33. The epistolary collection of Helisenne de Crenne, *Les Epistres familières et invectives* (1539) is a remarkable work which reveals a Ciceronian influence, combined with concerns that are crucial to women, such as marriage, children, education, and domestic seclusion. The work is divided into thirteen personal letters and five invectives directed to her husband. This volume merits careful study and comparison with Franco's own volume of letters. Recently, but for a later period and for English women's autobiographical literature, Felicity A. Nussbaum (*The Autobiographical Subject: Gender and Ideology in Eighteenth-Century England* [Baltimore: Johns Hopkins University Press, 1989]) has challenged the view that women's "personal" writings do not rework preexisting first-person narratives. She sees

these private literary genres instead as a place where women experimented and revised and resisted contemporary generic conventions.

On the uses of humanist rhetoric and classical models in the Renaissance school curricula from the fifteenth through the sixteenth centuries, where Cicero's letters formed an important part, see Paul F. Grendler, *Schooling in Renaissance Italy: Literacy and Learning, 1300–1600* (Baltimore: Johns Hopkins University Press, 1989), especially chapter 8, "Rhetoric," 203–34, in which he also refers to the debate between Ciceronians and followers of Quintilian (214–17). Many of the authors of letter manuals in the sixteenth century listed above participated in designing school syllabi, including Battista Guarini, who, according to Grendler, "gave pride of place to Cicero's epistles and Vergil's poetry." By 1546 in Lucca, and later, in 1567, in Venice, the generic pedagogic instructions to teach standard subjects became more specific. Grendler lists all of the Latin classics taught by Venetian teachers in 1587–88 (206).

6. Karen Newman ("City Talk: Women and Commodification in Jonson's *Epicoene,*" *English Literary History* 56, no. 3 (1989): 503–18) has written on this problem in relation to early modern England and in relation to the connection between women (commodification) and the growth of the urban city.

7. The frontispiece to the edition bears only the title to the work. There is no other indication as to who the publisher is or where it was printed. The laws regarding securing a copyright in Venice acted as a form of censorship, but by the middle of the sixteenth century they had begun to lose their hold on publishers' activities. See Paul F. Grendler, *Critics of the Italian World, 1530-1560: Anton Francesco Doni, Nicolò Franco, and Ortensio Lando* (Madison: University of Wisconsin Press, 1969), 4–5. There were other editions of letters printed in Italy in 1580: the four volumes by Andrea Calmo, *Lettere* (Venice: Domenico Farri, 1580); Cesare Rao, *L'argute et facete lettere di M. Cesare Rao* (Pavia: G. Bartoli, 1580); *Lettere amorose et sonetti familiari in diversi propositi: Confrontati alle lettere per poter scriver a casi occorrenti* (Venice: Frezzaria al Segno della Regina, 1580); the seven volumes by Francesco Sansovino, *Del secretario* (Venice: Valgrisi, 1580); and the two volumes by Bernardo Tasso, *Le lettere* (Venice: Cavalcalupo, 1580).

8. On the format of this volume and the other two editions printed in the same year, see Quondam, *Le "carte messaggiere,"* 54–58.

9. For the English translation of Montaigne's essay "A Consideration upon Cicero," I refer to Michel de Montaigne, *The Complete Essays of Montaigne,* trans. Donald M. Frame (Stanford: Stanford University Press, 1965), 183–87. For this quote, see 186–87. For the French, I refer to *Essais: Livre I,* ed. Alexandre Micha (Paris: Garnier-Flammarion, 1969), 300–306. My understanding of Montaigne's interest in classical epistolography in relation to his own use of the "essai" has been aided by the following: Richard L. Regosin, *The Matter of My Book: Montaigne's "Essais" as the Book of the Self* (Berkeley: University of California Press, 1977); Lawrence Kritzman, *Destruction/Découverte: La fonctionnement de la rhétorique dans les Essais de Montaigne* (Lexington: University Press of Kentucky, 1980); Terence Cave, *The Cornucopian Text: Problems of Writing in the French Renaissance* (Oxford: Oxford University Press, 1979); Michel Beaujour, *Miroirs d'ancre: Rhétorique de l'auto-portrait* (Paris: Seuil, 1980). Especially insightful are the essays in *Montaigne: Essays in Reading,* in *Yale French Studies* 64 (1983). For a useful overview of many of the critical positions represented in this volume, see the review article by Richard L. Regosin: "Recent Trends in Montaigne Scholarship: A Post-Structuralist Perspective," *Renaissance Quarterly* 37, no. 1 (1984): 34–54.

10. These comments appear in the French version (301 and 303–4). A stimulating Lacanian

interpretation of Montaigne's relationship to his deceased friend, La Boétie, and to epistolography in general is presented by François Rigolot in relation to Montaigne's essay "A Consideration on Cicero," in "Montaigne's Purloined Letters," *Yale French Studies* 64 (1983): 145–66. Rigolot argues that "the letter, both as literary genre and humanistic study, seems to function as a symbolic substitute for an original, inaugural loss. To counterbalance this loss . . . Montaigne will quote and refer to Cicero's, Pliny's, and Seneca's letters, establishing the priority of the epistolary form as a signifier, prolonging it and directing it from its path throughout the Essays" (149). The sixteenth-century Venetian poet and theorist Luigi Groto defines the familiar letter (*Lettere famigliari* [Venice: Giovacchino Brugnolo, 1601, 13–14) as evoking an absent friend. On the concept of writing as a dialogue with an absent friend, especially as Montaigne describes it in his essay, "De l'amitié," see Cave, *Cornucopian Text,* 328–30.

It is intriguing to speculate that Veronica Franco learned about Montaigne's writing through Henri III of France, whom she had met in Venice five years earlier. Henri received a copy of Montaigne's *Essais,* newly published by Simon Millanges (books 1 and 2) in Bordeaux, which Montaigne himself delivered in person to the king. On Montaigne's service in the court of Henri III in 1580 and on Henri's interest in his *Essais,* see Donald M. Frame, *Montaigne's Discovery of Man: The Humanization of a Humanist* (Westport, Conn.: Greenwood Press, 1983), 111, 120–25. See also Luigi Groto's letter to Scipio Costanzo (22 December 1582), in which he discusses preparing another edition commemorating Henri's visit to Venice (137); in another letter he refers to Nasello's 1567 translation of Montaigne's essays (50). See his posthumous edition, *Lettere famigliari di Luigi Groto* (Venice: Giovacchino Brugnolo, 1601).

Montaigne's *Essais* were not translated into Italian until 1590. Then they appeared as *Discorsi morali, politici et militari del molto illustre Signor Michiel di Montagna Cavaliere dell'Ordine del Re Christianissimo . . . ,* trans. Girolamo Naselli (Ferrara: Benedetto Mamarello, 1590). Another translation in Italian appeared in 1633 as *Saggi di Michel Signor di Montagna overo Discorsi naturali, politici, e morali,* trans. Marco Ginammi (Venice: Marco Ginammi, 1633); this was most likely based on the 1588 version of the *Essais.*

11. "Sur ce suject de lettres, je veux dire ce mot, que c'est un ouvrage auquel mes amys tiennent que je puis quelque chose. Et eusse prins plus volontiers ceste forme a publier mes verves, si j'eusse eu a qui a parler" (304). The classic works on translations of Cicero, Seneca, and other classical authors in relation to sixteenth-century rhetorical practices remain Fumaroli, *L'age de l'éloquence;* and R. R. Bolgar, *The Classical Heritage and Its Beneficiaries* (London: Cambridge University Press, 1954), 508–41. With specific reference to the Italian tradition, see Carlo Dionisotti, *Geografia e storia della letteratura italiana* (Turin: Einaudi, 1967), 125–78; and Quondam, *Le "carte messaggiere,"* 59–80; and for the acquisition of correct modes of behavior from the study of classical epistles, see 120–49, 177–97.

Orazio Toscanella, a teacher, theorist, and pedagogical writer, who settled in Venice around 1566, where he wrote (Grendler [223] claims he wrote "more than twenty books between 1559–79") the *Discorsi cinque* (Venice: Pietro de' Franceschi, 1575), emphasizes the importance of following Cicero's letters as a rhetorical model. In his *I modi più communi con che ha scritto Cicerone le sue epistole* (1559; Venice: Bolognino Zaltieri, 1575) he states that "lettere famigliari sono quelle, che trattano le cose, che fanno gli huomini tutto dì. Queste cose sono o utili e necessari ad ognuno communi. Vogliono essere scritte in stil basso, et con tanta facilità, che a ciascuno quantunque ignorante paia di poter fare il somigliante . . . una epistola famigliare vuole essere come un bel sereno cielo, ciò è da ogni parte chiara et aperta" (familiar letters are those that treat things that men do every day. These things are useful or necessary to everyone.

They should be written in a low style and with great facility so that all people, even those igno-
rant of such things, will feel that they can write them . . . A familiar letter should be like a
beautiful and clear sky . . . that is, in all parts clear and open) (56). On Orazio Toscanella's life
and works, and for extensive bibliography on his commentaries on Cicero, see Grendler, *Schooling in Renaissance Italy,* 222–29 and 222 n. 51.

12. See Rigolot, "Montaigne's Purloined Letters," 162–66; and Marc Fumaroli, "Genèse de
l'épistolographie classique: Rhétorique humaniste de la lettre, de Petrarque à Juste Lipse," *Révue
d'Histoire Litteraire de la France* 78, no. 4 (1978): 888. Fumaroli speaks of Petrarch's reactions to
Cicero's motivations for writing his *Familiares* as similar to the self-righteous stance of Montaigne that we see here.

13. "Il ne fut jamais sì abjecte et servile prostitution de presentations; la vie, l'ame, devotion, adoration, serf, ésclave, tous ces mots y courent si vulgairement" (304).

14. I borrow the term "artless art of writing letters" from Rigolot, ("Montaigne's Purloined
Letters, 158), who connects this rhetorical style not only with Seneca, an author whom
Montaigne admired, but to "a discussion of his [Montaigne's] unforgettable friendship with La
Boétie." On other essays of Montaigne that refer to Seneca, see Rigolot, "Montaigne's Purloined
Letters," 156–60.

15. "Ce sont grands imprimeurs de lettres que les Italiens. J'en ay, ce crois-je, cent divers
volumes" (Montaigne, *Journal de voyage,* 305). For a comprehensive list of the many editions of
familiar letters published in Venice and in Italy in general during the sixteenth century and
a discussion of the translations of ancient epistolographers into the Italian vernacular, see
Quondam, *Le "carte messaggiere,"* 13–150, 177–98. See also Cecil H. Clough, "The Cult of
Antiquity: Letters and Letter Collections," in *Cultural Aspects of the Italian Renaissance: Essays in
Honor of Paul Oskar Kristeller,* ed. C. H. Clough (Manchester: University of Manchester Press,
1976), 33–68. On the vernacular epistolary tradition in Italy and France in the Renaissance, see
Henderson, "Erasmus on the Art of Letter-Writing," 331-55; Ann Jacobson Schutte, "The *Let-
tere Volgari* and the Crisis of Evangelism in Italy," *Renaissance Quarterly* 28 (1975): 639–85;
Gigliola Fragnito, "Per lo studio dell'epistolografia volgare del Cinquecento: Le lettere di
Ludovico Beccadelli," *Bibliothèque d'Humanisme et Renaissance* 43, no. 1 (1981): 61–87, and
idem, "*L'Epistolario* di Ludovico Beccadelli: Autoritratto e manuale epistolografico," in *La correspondance,* Actes du Colloque International (Aix-en-Provence: 1984), 185–203. For an informative overview of Renaissance letter editions in Italy, see Aulo Greco, "Tradizione e vita negli
epistolari del Rinascimento," in *Civiltà dell'umanesimo,* ed. Giovannangiola Tarugi (Florence:
Leo Olschki, 1982), 105–16. And for a discussion of the textual problem of defining a genre, see
Mario Marti, "L'epistolario come 'genere' è un problema editoriale," in *Studi e problemi di critica
testuale,* Convegno di Studi di Filologia italiana nel Centenario della Commissione per i testi di
lingua, 7–9 aprile 1960 (Bologna: 1961), 203–8.

16. "Celles de Annibale Caro me semblent les meilleures" (305). On the letters of Caro, see
Andrea Gareffi, " 'La lettera uccide, ma lo spirito vivifica' (Paolo, II, *Corinzi* 3:7): L'epistolario di
Annibal Caro: Lettere, letteratura, letteralità," in Quondam, *Le "carte messaggiere,"* 237–53.
Gareffi accounts for the enormous popularity of *poligrafi* authors, such as Aretino and Caro, who
were directly connected to, and depended on for support, their publishers. See Paul F. Grendler,
"Venetian Presses and *poligrafi,*" in his *Critics of the Italian World,* 3–19. Caro's letters first appeared in Paolo Manuzio's important anthology, originally printed in 1542, *Lettere volgari di
diversi nobilissimi huomini et eccellentissimi ingegni scritte in diverse materie,* and was reprinted every
year after that until the seventeenth century. On Aretino's close relationship with the Venetian

printer Francesco Marcolini, see Scipione Casali, *Gli annali della tipografia veneziana di Francesco Marcolini,* no. 26 (Forli: Matteo Casali, 1861). Aretino's first volume of letters was reprinted ten times in 1537, and subsequent editions were printed in 1542, 1546, 1550, and 1557. All references to Aretino's letters in books 1 and 2 are taken from *Lettere: il primo e il secondo libro,* ed. Francesco Flora and Alessandro Del Vita (Milan: Mondadori, 1960). Only these first two volumes of Aretino's letters have received systematic scholarly attention. For the other four volumes, we must still rely on the seventeenth-century edition, *Lettere* (Paris: Matteo il Maestro, 1609).

17. In letter 1, 156 (Venice, 25 June 1537), Aretino writes to Lodovico Dolce denouncing pedantic imitation as mindless and artless "furto" (theft). He repudiates, as did Montaigne, the empty rhetoric of his contemporaries who mine authors such as Petrarch and Boccaccio, not for "concetti" (conceits), but for, as he says, "'quinci' dei 'quindi' e dei 'soventi' e degli 'snelli,' ma dei versi interi" (not for 'hences' and 'thences' and 'oftimes' and 'graciles,' but for whole verses [102]). The "cacar sangue de i pedanti che vogliano poetare rimoreggia de l'imitazione" (our pedantic poetasters turn imitation into bombast) (102), he contrasts with his own view of poetry as a "ghiribizzo de la natura ne le sue allegrezze" (nature's joyful flights of fancy) (102). He closes his letter with this infamous statement: "La natura istessa de la cui semplicità son secretario mi detta ciò che io compongo, e la patria mi scioglie i nodi della lingua. . . . E certo ch'io imito me stesso, perché la natura è una compagna badiale che ci si sbraca, e l'arte una piattola che bisogna che si apicchi: sì che attendete a esser scultor di sensi e non miniator di vocaboli," (Nature herself [to whose simplicity I act but as secretary] tells me what to compose, and my native land unties the knots in my tongue whenever it gets entangled by any highflown foreign lingo. . . . And certainly I imitate myself, because Nature is a boon companion who lavishes her inspiration on us, whereas literary contrivance is a louse that has to feed on others: so you must strive to be a sculptor of the true meaning of things and not a miniaturist of mere words) (Aretino, *Lettere,* 193–94). Paul Larivaille has uncovered eight unpublished letters by Aretino in the Archivio di Stato in Lucca. On these, and also on letters already published, see Paul Larivaille, *Lettere di, a, su Aretino nel fondo Bongi dell'Archivio di Stato di Lucca* (Nanterre: Centre de Récherches de Langue et Litterature Italiennes, 1980). A useful discussion of the different volumes of letters printed by Aretino's publisher, Marcolini, and of these in relation to other letter editions by Venetian printers in the sixteenth century, appears in Schutte, *"Lettere Volgari,"* 650–55.

Two recent dissertations examine Aretino's letters, the first within the context of Italian literature of the sixteenth century, and the second as evidence of Aretino's use of the letter form for artistic description and as documentation of his relation as connoisseur and advisor to Venetian painters of the period. See Murtha Baca, "Aretino in Venice 1527–1537 and 'La Professione Del Far' Lettere" (Ph.D. diss., University of California, Los Angeles, 1978); and Lora Palladino, "Pietro Aretino: Orator and Art Theorist" (Ph.D. diss., Yale University, 1984). Christopher Cairns reads Aretino's letters (especially letters addressed to Venetian patricians) as evidence of "a network of contacts based on the Gritti, Zeno, Corner, Venier, Molin, Querini, Da Lezze" (*Pietro Aretino and the Republic of Venice* [Florence: Leo Olschki, 1985], 25). Also useful are Paul Larivaille, *Pietro Aretino: Fra rinascimento e manierismo* (Rome: Bulzoni, 1980), 297–330; Giovanni Aquilecchia, "Pietro Aretino e altri poligrafi a Venezia," in *Storia della cultura veneta,* ed. G. Arnaldi and M. Pastore Stocchi (Vicenza: Neri Pozza, 1982), 3:61–63, 66–72, 74–80. For Aretino's letters as part of a comic epistolary tradition, see Adrianna De Nichilo, "La lettera e il comico," in Quondam, *Le "carte messaggiere,"* especially 213–22.

18. Francesco Sansovino, *Del secretario di M. Francesco Sansovino: Libri quattro* (Venice: Francesco Rampazetto, 1565). The most important essay on the connections between letter writing, rhetoric, and oratory in sixteenth-century Italian letter editions, and with specific reference to the Venetian context, is Nicola Longo, "De epistola condenda: L'arte di 'componer lettere' nel Cinquecento," in Quondam, *Le "carte messaggiere,"* 177–201. For a complete and extremely useful appendix listing all of the formula books and advice manuals for *segretari* in the sixteenth century, see 198–201. For this reference to Sansovino's description of the rhetorical form of the epistle as also adhering to principles of ancient oratory, see Longo, "De epistola condenda," 193–95; Schutte, "Le *Lettere Volgari*," 655–60.

19. This is taken from a letter to Nicolo Martelli (book 3, 22 August 1542), 28–29. Martelli (1498–1555), a Florentine merchant, met Aretino in Rome while Martelli was very young. He was one of the founders of the Accademia degli Umidi. In France he met the Italian poet Luigi Alamanni, and he later dedicated his *Il primo libro delle lettere* (Florence: Anton Francesco Doni, 1546) to Alamanni's wife, Maddalena Buonaiuta delli Alamanni. His *Opere poetiche* were published in Florence in 1548. See Mario Pelaez, "Nicolo Martelli," *Enciclopedia Italiana,* vol. 22 (Rome: Istituto della Enciclopedia Italiana, 1934), 431.

20. On Bernardo Tasso's letters to Annibal Caro on this subject, see Baca, "Aretino in Venice," 18; she cites Tasso's and Caro's exchange of letters on imitation. Tasso's letters were printed in Venice for the first time in 1549 (first volume) and thereafter in 1551 (Valgrisi), 1553, 1557, and 1559, and in many years following, owing to their enormous success. The second volume was republished in 1560 (Giolito), 1562, and 1574–75. I cite from the 1570 edition by Jacopo Sansovino: *Le lettere di M. Bernardo Tasso utili non solamente alle persone private, ma anco a Secretarii di Prencipi, per le materie che vi si trattono, e per la maniera dello scrivere le quali per giuditio de gli intendenti sono le più belle e correnti dell'altre.* This edition follows the earlier Giolito edition's *Prima parte* (1562). An important study of Bernardo Tasso's life and works is Edward Williamson, *Bernardo Tasso* (Rome: Edizioni di storia e di letteratura, 1951), especially 15–17, 90–99, on Bernardo Tasso's two volumes of letters. On the practices of imitation in the Renaissance, and especially for the concept of nature being usurped by human language, see Cave, *Cornucopian Text,* 324–34 and passim.

21. Aretino's letter to Bernardo Tasso is dated October 1549. I refer to *Il terzo {quarto, quinto, sestol} libro delle lettere di M. Pietro Aretino* (Paris: Matteo il Maestro, 1608–9), 4:242. Bernard Williamson (*Bernardo Tasso,* 91–92), discusses this exchange of letters between Aretino and Tasso and argues that although Aretino was angered by Tasso because Tasso refused to acknowledge Aretino as the inventor of a vernacular genre, they nonetheless remained friends.

22. On Aretino's massive impact on Venetian literature until 1556, the year of his death, see Dionisotti, *Geografia e storia,* 240–41.

23. Much of the debate on women as embodying dissimulation, especially with relation to epistolarity, for example, in Ovid's *Heroides,* is recounted in Linda S. Kauffman, *Discourses of Desire: Gender, Genre, and Epistolary Fictions* (Ithaca: Cornell University Press, 1986), 50–61. Joan DeJean (*Fictions of Sappho: 1546–1937* [Chicago: University of Chicago Press, 1989]) reviews the recent literature on the subject (43–48, 60–84). See also chapter 5, n. 10 below.

24. On the numbers of newly admitted letter writers in the sixteenth century, see Quondam, *Le "carte messaggiere,"* 13–19, 29–38, 48–59 and passim. Quondam argues that before 1564, letter collections were still not an "autonomous" genre, but were written for authors according to the stylistic constraints of the *segretario* formula (21).

25. According to Quondam (*Le "carte messaggiere"*), from 1538 to 1627 there were 130

single-author letter editions, 27 anthologies, and 540 volumes of letters (including reprinted editions and anthologies). The bulk (three-fifths) of the reprinted editions were by the following authors: Andrea Calmo, Girolamo Parabosco, Pietro Bembo, Bernardo Tasso, Francesco Sansovino, Pietro Aretino, Cesare Rao, Annibale Caro, Torquato Tasso, Giovanbattista Guarini, Madonna Celia Romana, and Alvise Pasqualigo. The first authors to publish their letters in 1538–42, after Aretino, were Vittoria Colonna, Francesco Sansovino, Nicolò Franco, and Anton Francesco Doni. From 1546 to 1588 there were many new authors, including the evangelical letter collections discussed in Schutte, "Le Lettere Volgari," 663–67. For letters as a literary phenomenon with social dimensions, see Dionisotti, *Geografia e storia,* 236–37.

26. Between 1568 and 1580, only three editions of familiar letters were printed in Venice (those of Giuseppe Pallavicino, Diomede Borghese, and Vernoica Franco). For a comprehensive list of Italian sixteenth-century women epistolographers from Vittoria Colonna (1544) to Isabella Andreini (1607), see Quondam, *Le "carte messaggiere,"* 255–76, 279–316. But all of the letter editions by women who were not members of the aristocracy, such as Isabella Andreini and Arcangela Tarabotti, appeared after Franco's edition in 1580. A careful distinction must be drawn between real letters not intended for publication and letters written with the thought of eventually publishing them. The letters of Alessandra Macinghi Strozzi fall into the first category. For a recent analysis of the fifteenth-century personal letters of Alessandra Macinghi Strozzi, see Maria Luisa Doglio, "Scrivere come donna: Fenomenologia delle 'Lettere familiari' di Alessandra Macinghi Strozzi," *Lettere Italiane,* 36, no. 4 (1984): 484–97. On the distinction between letters designed for publication, letters dispatched, and letters that adhere to formulated "conceits," see the excellent study by Janet Gurkin Altman, "The Letter Book as a Literary Institution 1539–1789: Toward a Cultural History of Published Correspondences in France," *Yale French Studies* 71 (1986): 17–62, especially 17–31; idem, *Epistolarity: Approaches to a Form* (Columbus: Ohio State University Press, 1982).

27. On this point, see n. 11 above. Angelo Ingegneri, a close friend of Maffio Venier, wrote (*Del buon segretario: Libri tre* [Rome: Guglielmo Faciotto, 1594]) that the profession of the *segretario* is "lo scrivere delle lettere . . . d'un padrone, posto ch'egli non s'intrometta in altri maneggi, ne sappia verun'altro segreto" (the writing of letters of his patron, provided that he does not interfere in his other dealings nor knows any other secrets) (34–35). The most important authors of manuals for a *segretario* in Italy in the sixteenth and seventeenth centuries were Francesco Sansovino, Torquato Tasso, Giulio Cesare Capaccio, Battista Guarini, and Angelo Ingegneri.

28. For the classic and indispensable study on the vogue of poetic anthologies in the cinquecento, see Dionisotti, *Geografia e storia,* 237–54. Also useful are Gino Benzoni, *Gli affanni della cultura: Intellettuali e potere nell'Italia della Controriforma e barocca* (Milan: Feltrinelli, 1978); Amedeo Quondam, *Il petrarchismo mediato* (Rome: Bulzoni, 1974); idem, *La parola nel labirinto: Società e scrittura del manierismo a Napoli* (Bari: Laterza, 1975).

29. Diomede Borghesi, a Sienese courtier and member of the Accademia Intronato, worked in the courts of Mantua, Padua, and Turin, publishing many commemorative occasional verses which were commissioned for poetic anthologies, as well as his own *Rime* (Padua: L. Pasquati, 1566–67) and *Lettere del S. Diomede Borghesi Gentiluomo senese et Accademico Intronato* (Padua: L. Pasquati, 1574–1603). He was in Venice from 1564 to 1574, and in Padua from 1585 until 1596; there he met Sperone Speroni, Francesco Piccolomini, and others. On Borghesi's activities as courtier, see Giovan Mario Crescimbeni, *L'istoria della volgar poesia* (Venice: L. Basegio, 1730–31), 3: 112–13. On his stay in Padua, see the entry in the *Dizionario biografico degli italiani,*

vol. 12, 643–46. Amedeo Quondam comments on the fact that Borghesi's and Franco's volumes were printed in smaller formats consisting of only fifty letters. Borghesi's letters include letters to two of Franco's important collaborators. One letter, addressed to Muzio Manfredi (written from Reggio in 1577), praises his literary merits (101), while another is addressed to Maffio Venier (written from Bologna in 1577), welcoming him back to the Venetian republic: "nel suo felice ritorno alla patria" (88). On Muzio Manfredi's friendship with Veronica Franco, see n. 67 below. Giuseppe Pallavicino's letters (200) (*Delle lettere del Signor Gioseppe Pallavicino da Varrano. Libri Tre*. [Venice: Francesco Rampazetto, 1566]), especially the dedication to Francesco Sansovino, are interesting, because unlike most epistolary authors, he was a doctor. Quondam argues that Pallavicino's edition (1579) permitted other writers, such as Franco, to publish their letters without adhering to the epistolary models of "famous authors" that preceded them.

30. This letter challenges the true feelings of the man to whom Franco writes by advocating various rhetorical rules for writing familiar letters. She speaks of her letter as a "visitazione di mente e di pensiero," (visitation of the mind and thought).

31. I would agree in general terms with Elvira Favretti ("Rime e Lettere di Veronica Franco," *Giornale storico della letteratura italiana* 163, no. 523 (1986): 355–82, especially 375–82), who argues that when Franco writes to distinguished people, her letters are often fraught with complicated syntax. In Favretti's view, letter 16, which she writes to a noblewoman who has recently given birth, is needlessly exaggerated. Although I do not agree with this last estimation, I would submit that letters 2 (9) and 20 (33–34) are so convoluted that they obscure the subjects addressed in the letters.

32. Luigi Groto also wrote a letter to Tintoretto thanking him for his portrait, which is included in his *Lettere famigliari*. In it he alludes, as does Franco, to the ancient vs. modern question, when he praises Tintoretto as surpassing any ancient artist in his powers to evoke the real. He concludes the letter by asking to have his portrait hung in his own home, so that when his life comes to an end, "Death" will be uncertain which to take, Groto himself or the portrait, (137). Domenico Venier, in an exchange of *proposta/risposta* sonnets with Celio Magno, refers to a portrait of Magno executed by a unidentified painter. In it he rehearses the same debate, about which is more verisimilar, the artist's hand or nature. See their *Rime di Celio Magno et Orsatto Giustinian* (Venice: Andrea Muschio, 1600), 143. A *risposta* sonnet by Marco Venier (155) appears in this volume; it is a reply to a sonnet by Magno on a painting he has received from Venier "in dono" (a gift). Finally Magno writes a sonnet to Domenico Tintoretto to praise him for the portrait he has done of him (162). For further discussion of the content of Franco's letter, see chapter 5 below.

33. For these types of letters, see letters 3, 15, and 24.

34. A number of ancient letters were translated into the vernacular by academy members. See, among others, *Epistole di G. Plinio, di M. Francesco Petrarca e del S. Pico della Mirandola . . .* (Venice: Gabriel Giolito de' Ferrari, 1548), translated by Lodovico Dolce. Anton Francesco Doni had translated Seneca's epistles in 1549 as *L'epistole di Seneca ridotte nella lingua* (Venice: 1549). On the role that Seneca's letters played in the Renaissance and on the confusion between the older and younger Seneca until 1587, see Fumaroli, *L'age de l'éloquence*, 57–63.

35. This epigraph comes from Martelli's edition of familiar letters cited above (n. 19). On the relationship between Martelli and Aretino, see Quondam, *Le "carte messaggiere,"* 43–44, 53–59. For the specific reference to the connection between Martelli's pronouncement and that of Franco, see 57.

36. For my definition of "essai" as a trial—a trying out of judgments—or as a way to "make

the text the means for displacing what is exterior and alien and the medium for articulating what is personae as a 'self,'" see Lawrence Kritzman on Montaigne (*Destruction/Découverte* [Lexington: University Press of Kentucky, 1980]) 14. See also John O'Neill, *Essaying Montaigne: The Study of the Renaissance Institution of Writing and Reading* (Boston: Routledge and Kegan Paul, 1982). For the equating of rhetorical excess, effeminacy, misogyny, and the "dressed-up whore" with "correct" rhetorical styles and the avoidance of unnecessary embellishment, see R. Howard Bloch, "Medieval Misogyny," *Representations* 20 (1987): 1–24. Bloch reviews the question of "woman . . . conceived as ornament" in early patristic, misogynist writings; he argues that "to decorate oneself is to be guilty of 'meretricious allurement,' since embellishment of the body, a prideful attempt 'to show to advantage,' recreates an original act of pride that is the source of potential concupiscence. This is why Tertullian is able to move so quickly and naturally from the idea of dress to a whole range of seemingly unapparent associations . . . between transvestism and the monstrous; or between the toga and lust, adultery, cannibalism, intemperance, and greed. It is as if in each and every act of clothing an original nakedness associated with the sanctity of the body, and not the weakness of the flesh, were a corrupting recapitulation of the Fall entailing all other perversions" (12). Bloch notices an interesting conjunction between the rhetorical ornament of misogynist discourse and "the extent to which it denounces woman as ornament" (22 n. 29).

A fascinating discussion of the discourse on or against femininity in the seventeenth century, especially in France, raises the connection between the fear of masculine effeminacy and Quintilian's question of ornament in rhetoric as emasculating and making effeminate an orator, whom he calls a "dressed-up whore." See Jacqueline Lichtenstein, "Making Up Representation: The Risks of Femininity," *Representations* 20 (1987): 77–87, especially 79–80. She writes: "The innumerable critics of rhetoric, in fact, have generally condemned such Asiatic stylistic figures in a vocabulary borrowed from the lexicon of the prostituted body, from the indecent attire and the profligate sexuality of women, as if every manifestation of an excessive taste for images could only be thought of through the aesthetic-moral category of perversity, of a culpable seduction that originates in a certain femininity" (79). This question of excessive ornamentation, interestingly, is precisely what later Venetian feminists of the early seventeenth century, such as Lucrezia Marinella and Arcangela Tarabotti, among others, challenged in their treatises and familiar letters.

37. See Quintilian's *Institutio oratoria* 2.5, 5.12, and 8.3, where these connections are raised. This work was translated in the sixteenth century, as *L'Institutioni oratorie di Marco Fabio Quintiliano* . . . (Venice: Gabriel Giolito de' Ferrari, 1566), by Orazio Toscanella. He dedicated it to Domenico Venier and Celio Magno, claiming that they had urged him to translate "this exceedingly difficult and long work." He lauds Venier as "uno de' più dotti e valorosi gentilhuomini, che s'habbia Vinegia, e forse tutta Italia" (one of the most learned and valorous gentlemen in Venice and perhaps in all of Italy). For the passages from Tertullian, see "On the Apparel," in *The Anti-Nicene Fathers: Translations of the Writings of the Fathers Down to* A.D. *325,* ed. Alexander Roberts and James Donaldson (Grand Rapids, Mich.: Eerdmans, 1971–86), 4:17–20. For the references to Quintilian in Montaigne's essays, and Quintilian's charges against an effeminate style, see Antoine Compagnon, "A Long Short Story: Montaigne's Brevity," in *Montaigne: Essays in Reading,* in *Yale French Studies* 64 (1983): 24–50.

38. For a discussion of Aretino's *Sei giornate* and for secondary bibliography on Aretino's work, see chapter 1 above.

39. The text of this ruling appears in Carlo Calza, *Documenti inediti sulla prostituzione* (Milan: Tipografia della società cooperativa, 1869), 39. There is also a reference to this law (Comuni del Consiglio dei Dieci, Registro 26, 1563–1654, fol. 10) in *Storia del malcostume a Venezia nei secoli XVI e XVII*, ed. L. Menetto and G. Zennaro (Abano Terme: Piovan Editore, 1987); for the punishments if a person were found guilty of violating the chastity of an unwed girl, see 52–53, 57, 61–62.

40. On the increasing theatricality (after 1565) of the punishments enforced by the Venetian Inquisition, which were intended to make public anyone's conviction of heresy, see John Martin, "L'Inquisizione romana e la criminalizzazione del dissenso religioso a Venezia all'inizio dell'età moderna," *Quaderni storici* 66, no. 3 (1987): 777–802; on this issue specifically, see 789–91. See also *Nunziature di Venezia,* ed. Aldo Stella (Rome: Istituto storico italiano, 1958–77), 8:227, for examples of public spectacles designed as public humiliations. This kind of social surveillance and public humiliation, in which an institution such as the Inquisition contains religious dissent within certain political confines, is what Michel Foucault describes in another context in his *Discipline and Punish: The Birth of the Prison,* trans. Alan Sheridan (New York: Vintage Books, 1979). See also Petrus Cornelis Spierenburg, *The Spectacle of Suffering: Execution and the Evolution of Repression from a Preindustrial Metropolis to the European Experience* (New York: Cambridge University Press, 1984).

41. The law reads (62): "Siano coronati col breve sopra il petto ut sopra, et poi siano posti a servir al remo in ferri nelle galee nostre di condannati per anni due, et non essendo sufficienti a tal servitio, debbano esser posti in prigione, ove habbiano a star serrati per lo tempo di anni due, et poi siano banditi di questa Città, et suo distretto per altrettanto tempo." Brian Pullan discusses this law and the punishment, which was enforced in Venice after 1565 (*The Jews of Europe and the Inquisition of Venice, 1550–1670* [Oxford: Basil Blackwell, 1983], 67). He claims that being sent to serve on the galley ships was essentially a death sentence.

42. Sherrill Cohen ("Asylums for Women in Counter-Reformation Italy," in *Women in Reformation and Counter-Reformation Europe: Private and Public Worlds,* ed. Sherrin Marshall [Bloomington and Indianapolis: Indiana University Press, 1989], 166–88) has argued that the charitable institutions promoted during the Catholic Reformation also had the impact of "enlarg[ing] women's horizons" (166). As she demonstrates, there were many types of institutions, which she calls "custodial asylums," that attempted to deal with the ever-growing social ills of poverty, public health, and public order. These institutions housed orphans, poor girls, widows, and women with marital problems. Essentially they were "refuges." Others attempted to convert prostitutes from a sinful life (the Convertite) and were more related to the problem of "women's limited options." As Cohen argues, the first type of institution was in many cases "innovative," providing an important "prototype" for social welfare in Western societies. When considering the home that Franco proposed to Venetian authorities, Cohen asks the important question: "We must ask whether there was a point of intersection between the perspectives of early modern women and of societal authorities" (171). She provides the case of the institution of the *Malmaritate* (founded in 1579) as evidence of a refuge that proposed an "economic cure" for women by recycling them to the world as "trained laborers, capable of earning their upkeep and benefiting the body social" (174). For extensive bibliography on this subject, see 169 and 184 n. 12.

43. On the *supplica* (petition) that Franco drafted, see Pullan, *Rich and Poor in Renaissance Venice* (Cambridge: Harvard University Press, 1971), 391–92.

44. On these new documents, see chapter 2 n. 49.

45. Pullan, *Rich and Poor*, 391; Alessandra Schiavon, "Per la biografia di Veronica Franco: Nuovi documenti," *Atti dell'Istituto Veneto di Scienze, Lettere, ed Arti* 137 (1978–79): 243–56.

46. On the problem of women being forced to enter the Convertite against their will, see Cohen, "Asylums for Women in Counter-Reformation Italy," 169.

47. On the disastrous economic effects of the plague, especially on the lower classes in Venice, see chapter 1 n. 37 and chapter 5 below for more extensive bibliography.

48. Cesare Vecellio, *Degli habiti antichi et moderni di diverse parti del mondo* (Venice: D. Zenaro, 1590) ("Habiti usati dalle donne di Venetia del 1550"): L'instabilità, et l'amore della varietà, che regna nelle donne introdusse poco da poi i ricci sopra la fronte, cominciando dall'orecchie, et seguendo con ordine diritto fino in cima della fronte, coprendo poi d'alcune scuffiette quella parte de' capelli, che s'intrecciava. Parve loro, che tale acconciatura rendesse il viso molto bello" (The instability and the love of variety which rules women has lately introduced curls above the forehead, starting at the ears and following across to the top of the forehead, with hairnets covering that part of the hair that used to be braided. It seems to them that this hairstyle makes their face very beautiful).

49. One of the stock themes referred to in manuals on letter writing in the cinquecento is congratulating a woman on having given birth. Many manuals were printed offering thematic models, such as Girolamo Garimberto's extremely popular *Concetti*, which was published almost every year from 1551 to 1609, most often in Venice. I refer to the 1553 edition (Venice: Vincenzo Valgrisi) of the *Concetti*, which lists under the heading "Allegrarsi," the subject "Di parto" (on childbirth) (13).

50. Eccles. 1:2, Revised Standard Version.

51. Anton Francesco Doni translated Seneca's epistles: *L'epistole di Seneca ridotte nella lingua toscana* (Venice: A. Pincio, 1549). Some of the epistle headings correspond to the subjects treated in Franco's letters, such as "sulle ricchezze, de gl'affetti dell'animo, la presenza de buoni amici giova molto a ricuperar la sanità, remedi contro ai casi di fortuna, servi come si debbano trattare" (on riches, the affections of the soul, the presence of good friends helps to recover one's health, remedies against cases of fortune, how servants should be treated).

52. Cicero, *De oratore* 2.65.261–62. I thank Martha Malamud for useful suggestions regarding the context of this quotation. On the use of this and other Ciceronian texts in Venetian humanist school curricula, see Grendler, *Schooling in Renaissance Italy*, 214–17. Orazio Toscanella argued that Cicero's *De oratore*, as Grendler notes (214 n. 29), "imparted wisdom to the learned . . . [and] became inspiration and authority for the civic and cultural conception of Renaissance rhetoric."

53. Circero, *De oratore* 2.65.261. Directly before the passage that Franco extracts, Cicero writes that "jests dependent upon language further include such as are derived from allegory, from the figurative use of a single word, or from the ironical inversion of verbal meanings. Allegory as a source was illustrated by Rusca long ago, in moving his Limit of Age Bill, when Marcus Servilius, an opponent of the measure, said to him . . . ."

54. Revised Standard Version.

55. On restraining an individual's passions in order to preserve social harmony according to the tenets of Venetian humanism, see King, *Venetian Humanism*, 175–79. She provides as well extensive bibliography on this subject. In 1563, Cicero's *De officiis* was translated into the vernacular by M. Federico Vendramino, with the assistance of Ludovico Dolce, as *Opere morali di Marco Tullio Cicerone: Cioé tre libri de gli uffici* (Venice: Gabriele Giolito de' Ferrari, 1563). When

describing the differences between man and beast, the central characteristic Cicero mentioned is "man's use of reason." (1.8–9). King (*Venetian Humanism*) argues that Venetian humanists advocated the restraint of passions, which were regarded as disruptive to a community, for the benefit of the society as a whole. Only the nobly born were considered suitable for guiding a society made up of "the irrational and passion-ridden" (175). She also points out that "verbal assaults" on individuals or against the state itself received heavy penalties (176 n. 239). Paolo Manuzio in his *Tre libri di lettere volgari* (Venice: Aldus, 1556) refers to this need to control one's passions when he writes to Domenico Venier that he hopes to follow his (Venier's) illustrious example: "cercherò di disporre la mente a più sani consigli, lascierò i desideri delle cose caduche; fuggirò le passioni; ingegnerommi d'imitare, s'io potrò, Vostra Magnificenza" (I will try to lend my mind to saner advice; I will leave behind the desire for transitory things; I will flee passions; I will do my best to imitate, if I will be able, Your Magnificence" [95]).

56. Cicero, *Letters to Atticus* 1.1., trans. E. D. Winstedt, Loeb Classical Library (Cambridge: Harvard University Press, 1928), 1:2–3.

57. Other readers of Franco's poems have noted these allusions to Cicero but have not attempted to use them as a way of reading Franco's intertextual reworking of the source. See, for example, Favretti, "Rime e lettere," 378 n. 53.

58. Franco introduced friends into her own home as well, for learned conversations and musical concerts. In letter 45, she invited her correspondent to her home "domani alla musica per tempo" (early tomorrow for some music), so that she might "avanti il cominciar del suono musicale" (before beginning to play music) have the opportunity to "godere della dolcissima armonia de' soavi ragionamenti di Vostra Signoria" (enjoy the very sweet harmony of Your Lordship's gentle discussions) (63). Moreover, in letter 9 Franco alludes to her own abilities as a musician when she asks to borrow from her correspondent "del suo stromento da penna . . . in occasione ch'io faccio musica" (of your plucked instrument . . . for the occasion of my playing some music). Here she refers to a harpsichord. I thank James Tyler for informing me that a "stromento da penna" is a stringed keyboard instrument whose sound is generated by the plucking of quills. On courtesans as skillful musicians, as is evident from engravings of the period, and on the possession of musical instruments in wealthy courtesans' homes, see Cathy Santore, "Julia Lombardo, 'Somtuosa Meretrize,'" *Renaissance Quarterly* 41, no. 1 (1988): 58–60. Also very informative is Anthony Newcomb, "Courtesans, Muses, or Musicians? Professional Women Musicians in Sixteenth-Century Italy," in *Women Making Music: The Western Art Tradition, 1150–1950*, ed. Jane Bowers and Judith Tick (Urbana and Chicago: University of Illinois Press, 1986), 90–115. This edition includes several interesting essays on the subject of women and music in Italy from the fifteenth through the seventeenth centuries. See in particular the essay by Ellen Rosand ("The Voice of Barbara Strozzi" [168–90]) on the Venetian *virtuosa* Barbara Strozzi, an author of eight volumes of vocal works published in Venice between 1644 and 1664. In Maffio Venier's "Franca, credeme che per San Maffio," he refers to Franco's singing, which he uses as an example of her artistic pretensions. See Alvise Zorzi, *Cortigiana veneziana* (Milan: Camunia, 1986), 82; and Manlio Dazzi, *Il fiore della lirica veneziana: Il libro segreto (chiuso)* (Vicenza: Neri Pozza, 1956), 2:23–27, and for these verses, 2:26.

59. Ann Rosalind Jones, *The Currency of Eros: Women's Love Lyric in Europe, 1540–1620* (Bloomington and Indianapolis: Indiana University Press, 1990), 186.

60. The discourse *Della nobiltà* is included in Girolamo Muzio, *Due discorsi* (Padua: Paolo Meietti, 1590), 69; this was originally published in 1564 as *Il gentiluomo*. The importance of "onore" (honor) in Italian literature of the late sixteenth century as supplanting the theme of

"amore" is discussed by Carlo Dionisotti in the conclusion to his classic essay, "La letteratura italiana nell'età del Concilio di Trento," in his *Geografia e storia*, 253–54.

61. Girolamo Muzio, *Due discorsi*, 69.

62. Ibid., 69.

63. Domenico Venier provided many authors with similar literary council and protection. Among many others, Luigi Groto wrote to Venier for help with correcting his verses. See, for example, his *Lettere famigliari (di Luigi Groto Cieco d'Adria)* (Venice: Giovacchino Brugnolo, 1601), 99. It is also interesting to note that in one of the formula manuals by Bartolomeo Zucchi (*L'Idea del segretario* [Venice: Compagnia Minima, 1606]), many of the letters that serve as rhetorical and conceptual models are addressed to Domenico Venier from various writers, politicians, and intellectuals throughout Italy. For these letters, see 32–33, 110–111, 274.

64. For this letter of dedication, see Croce, *Lettere dall'unica edizione*, 3–5.

65. Muzio Manfredi's name appears in many letter collections of the sixteenth century. Among others are Torquato Tasso's *Lettere familiari* (Venice: Lucio Spineda, 1605), in which Giacomo Vincenti, who dedicated this work to Antonio Costantini, claims that he met Tasso "in compagnia del Signor Mutio Manfredi" (in the company of Signor Mutio Manfredi), whom he describes as "da costumi preclarissimi, e da bellissima letteratura" (of illustrious customs and of a most beautiful literature) (3). Manfredi was originally from Cesena and was a member of the noble Manfredi family of Faenza. He was employed in the French court at Nancy as secretary to the duchess of Brunswick. See his *La semiramis boscareccia* (Bergamo: Comino Ventura, 1593), dedicated to Cardinale Farnese, the duke of Parma.

In Diomede Borghesi's *Lettere*, there is a letter to Manfredi in which Borghesi refers to Manfredi's "nobiltà, l'ingegno e la virtù" (nobility, talent and virtue) (101). On the frontispiece of Manfredi's volume of letters, he claims that they have been written "tutte in un Anno, cioé una per giorno, et ad ogni condition di persona, et in ogni usitata materia" (all in one year, that is one a day to all types of person and in every usual topic). See *Lettere brevissime di Mutio Manfredi* (Venice: Francesco Rondinelli, 1606). The letter to Franco, 303 ("Alla Signora Veronica Franca a Venetia"), written from Nancy, appears on 249. In this letter he praises Franco's sonnet "Ecco del tuo fallir degna mercede" (Here is the reward worthy of your failings), which he includes in his edition, along with other sonnets by various poets praising Manfredi's play *La Semiramis*. On this edition, see Emmanuele Antonio Cicogna, *Delle inscrizioni veneziane* (Venice: Giuseppe Orlandelli, 1824–53), 5:423–24.

Manfredi's other edition (this is only a partial list) include poetic editions composed for well-placed noblewomen: *Cento madrigali* (Mantua: Francesco Osanna, 1587), dedicated to "Donna Vittoria Principessa di Molfetta," a volume which also includes two madrigals by Torquato Tasso (107–8); *Cento sonetti . . . in lode di cento donne di Pavia,* dedicated to the "Illustrissima et eccellentissima Principessa della Mirandola (Pavia: Girolamo Bartoli, 1601); *Cento donne cantate* (Mantua: Stamperia d'Erasmo, 1580), dedicated to Vincenzo Gonzaga; *Per donne romane: Rime di diversi* (Bologna: Alessandro Benacci, 1575), dedicated to Giacomo Buoncompagni. For a discussion of Manfredi's works, see Antonio Bertolotti, *Muzio Manfredi e Passi Giuseppe letterati in relazione col duca di Mantova* (Rome: Tipografia delle scienze matematiche e fisiche, 1888).

CHAPTER FOUR: DENOUNCING THE COURTESAN

1. For a general history of the Inquisition courts in Venice, and for a discussion of trials held for crimes of heresy, see Ludwig von Pastor, *The History of the Popes from the Close of the Middle Ages* (Wilmington, N. C.: Consortium Books, 1978), 12:504, 14:267–68, 16:310–16, 334; Paul

F. Grendler, *The Roman Inquisition and the Venetian Press, 1540–1605* (Princeton: Princeton University Press, 1977), 35–42.

On the procedure of the Inquisition tribunal in Venice and throughout Italy, see Aldo Stella, *Chiesa e stato nelle relazioni dei nunzi pontifici a Venezia: Ricerche sul giurisdizionalismo veneziano dal XVI al XVIII secolo* (Vatican City: Biblioteca Apostolica, 1964); Grendler, *Roman Inquisition,* 51ff. He explains that lay deputies assisted the inquisitor by representing the authority of the Council of Ten; they authorized the warrants for arrest and also assisted in the trials (46). The three ecclesiastics were the only ones who could pronounce a final sentence. During the trials, only the inquisitor asked questions; the patriarch and the nuncio assisted him, although they spoke infrequently (the deputies almost never). See also John Tedeschi, "Preliminary Observations on Writing a History of the Roman Inquisition," in *Continuity and Discontinuity in Church History,* ed. F. Forrester Church and Timothy George (Leiden: E. J. Brill, 1979), 232–49. For the composition of the inquisitional tribunal in Venice, see Brian Pullan, *The Jews of Europe and the Inquisition of Venice, 1550–1670* (Oxford: Basil Blackwell, 1983), especially part 1, "The Recording Institution," 3–117. John Martin has written a detailed study of the institution of the tribunal in Venice as an attempt by governmental authorities to suppress social disorder, which they saw as directly connected to religious dissent and popular disobedience: "L'Inquisizione romana e la criminalizzazione del dissenso religioso a Venezia all'inizio dell'età moderna," *Quaderni storici* 66, no. 3 (1987): 777–802. See also Silvana Seidel-Menchi, "L'Inquisizione come repressione o inquisizione come mediazione?" *Annuario dell'Istituto Storico Italiano per l'Età Moderna e Contemporanea* 35–36 (1983–1984): 56–61.

The use of Inquisition trial documents has raised interesting interdisciplinary debates in recent years on the respective methods of social and literary historians, on the one hand, and anthropologists on the other. See Carlo Ginzburg, "The Inquisitor as Anthropologist," in *Clues, Myths, and the Historical Method,* trans. John Tedeschi and Anne C. Tedeschi (Baltimore: Johns Hopkins University Press, 1989), 156–64; Carlo Ginzburg, "Prove e possibilità," postface to the Italian translation of Natalie Z. Davis, *The Return of Martin Guerre: Il ritorno di Martin Guerre* (Turin: Einaudi, 1984), 131ff.; Thomas Kuehn, "Reading Microhistory: The Example of *Giovanni and Lusanna," Journal of Modern History* 61 (1989): 512–34; this is a review of the theoretical implications of a recent microhistorical study by Gene Brucker: *Giovanni and Lusanna: Love and Marriage in Renaissance Florence* (Berkeley: University of California Press, 1986). For further debate, see Dominique LaCapra, *History and Criticism* (Ithaca: Cornell University Press, 1985), 11, 36–38, 53, 62–63 and passim; Rudolph M. Bell and Judith C. Brown, "Renaissance Sexuality and the Florentine Archives: An Exchange," *Renaissance Quarterly* 40 (1987): 96–100; this refers to Brown's provocative study, *Immodest Acts: The Life of a Lesbian Nun in Renaissance Italy* (New York: Oxford University Press, 1986).

2. All references to Franco's poetic debate in the *Terze rime* are to the modern edition by Abdelkader Salza, *Rime: Gaspara Stampa e Veronica Franco* (Bari: Laterza, 1913). I first discussed Franco's involvement in this salon and her departure from Petrarchan forms in "Veronica Franco: The Courtesan as Poet in Sixteenth-Century Venice" (Ph.D. diss., Yale University, 1985), 92–235. For a more recent study of Franco's poetic debate in her *Terze rime,* see idem, "Veronica Franco's *Terze Rime:* The Venetian Courtesan's Defense," *Renaissance Quarterly* 42, no. 2 (1989): 227–57.

3. On the function of *denuncie* (denunciations) in the inquisitorial process and within the Venetian civic courts, see Pullan, *Jews of Europe,* 92–97. Pullan claims that denunciation "was the commonest method by which trials or inquiries were set in motion, although some serious

crimes were referred to the Inquisition by secular magistracies which, in the course of their own investigations of other crimes, had happened on evidence which might interest the Holy Office. Denunciations fell into four broad categories. They might arrive in writing, in the form of anonymous, or at any rate consigned delations. Or they might be signed and presented by persons who had a close acquaintance, or business dealings, or a relationship as debtor or creditor, or even some tie of blood with the person they named. Or again, a report might be put in by a person not closely acquainted with the offender . . . but reporting a general scandal which had been caused in a neighborhood or parish, in a church, or in some public place such as a prison" (93). For the insistence on the secrecy of *denuncie,* see Martin, "L'Inquisizione romana," 787–88, 791, 801 n. 48. See also Renzo Derosas, "Moralità e giustizia a Venezia nel '500–'600: Gli esecutori contro la bestemmia," in *Stato, società e giustizia nella Repubblica Veneta (sec. XV–XVIII),* ed. Gaetano Cozzi (Rome: Jouvence, 1980), 431–528; and Marisa Milani, "Il caso di Emilia Catena, meretrice, 'striga et herbera,'" *Museum Patavinum* 4 (1985): 76 n. 4.

Giuseppe Tassini (*Veronica Franco* (reprint, Venice: Alfieri, 1969), 91–93 nn. 2 and 22) was the first to publish the text of the *denuncia* against Veronica Franco, filed by her employee, Ridolfo Vannitelli. Because the trials had not come to light at the time Tassini wrote these observations, he was led to believe, incorrectly, that "il processo venne sospeso, e nulla poterono ottenere gli accusatori" (the trial was suspended and the accusers were not able to obtain anything). With Alessandra Schiavon's improtant article ("Per la biografia di Veronica Franco: Nuovi documenti," *Atti dell'Istituto Veneto di Scienze, Lettere, ed Arti* 137 (1978–79): 243–56), we now have both the transcribed denunciation that Vannitelli filed and the denunciation of theft (or lawsuit) filed by Franco that is located in the Archivio Patriarcale di Venezia (Registri Actorum et Mandatorum 1579 et 1580, n. 16). The denunciation of theft was written by a scribe in the house of the patriarch's vicar on "22 maggio 1580." Further, Schiavon provides a transcription of the Inquisition trial proceedings that resulted from Franco's complaint. The trial hearing documents are preceded by a one-page written denunciation filed by Redolfo Vannitelli, followed by two detached pages, written only on the recto. The denunciation provides the names of possible witnesses to testify against Franco in the trial proceedings. For my transcriptions of these documents (to which I have added modern punctuation, when needed, and capitalization, which differ in certain points from the Schiavon and Milani transcriptions), see appendixes 4.1–3. For the location of the Inquisition trials, see Venetian State Archives: Archivio di Stato di Venezia (hereafter ASV), Sant'Uffizio, 1580, busta 46, fascicolo "Veronica Franco." For the most recent article on Veronica Franco's trials, seen from within a larger context of trials brought against women in Venice during the latter half of the sixteenth century, see Marisa Milani, "L'"Incanto' di Veronica Franco," *Giornale storico della letteratura italiana* 262: no. 518 (1985): 250–63. And for an account of the trials in relation to Franco's ties with the Venier family, see Alvise Zorzi, *Cortigiana veneziana: Veronica Franco e i suoi poeti* (Milan: Camunia Editrice, 1986), 145–53. Zorzi takes issue with the transcriptions of the trials of both Schiavon and Milani and provides his own version. On the practice of revealing the claims of the denunciation only at the moment of trial, see Marisa Milani, "Il caso di Emilia Catena, meretrice, 'striga et herbera, '" *Museum Patavinum* 4 (1985): 75–97, especially 76 n. 4.

4. For the relationship between Maffio Venier and Veronica Franco, and her relationship with other members of the Venier "clan," see Zorzi, *Cortigiana veneziana,* 59–90, 93–111, 137–40, 164. Manlio Dazzi was the first to propose the intersection of Maffio Venier's verses with those of Veronica Franco and the *incerto autore;* see his *Il fiore della lirica veneziana: Il libro segreto (chiuso)* (Vicenza: Neri Pozza, 1956), 1:9–57. We have no further information on Ridolfo (the Milani

transcription cites his name as "Redolfo," and her text refers to him as "Rodolfo"). I will refer to him as "Redolfo." Milani argues that he is of Umbrian origin, owing to his use of that dialect in his *denuncia*. See her "L''Incanto' di Veronica Franco," 258 n. 5.

5. John Martin argues in an interesting article ("A Journeymen's Feast of Fools," *Journal of Medieval and Renaissance Studies* 17, no. 2 [1987]: 149–74) that heresy "was the dominant concern of the Venetian Inquisition until the early 1580s, when the emphasis began to shift to such matters as necromancy, witchcraft, cunning women, and the practice of amorous and therapeutic magic" (150 n. 4). Franco's testimony reveals an understanding of the importance of disproving heretical beliefs. On the exaggerated tendency of Venetian officials periodically to punish offenders of public decorum, especially prostitutes, see Derosas, "Moralità e giustizia," 444–46; Guido Ruggiero, *The Boundaries of Eros: Sex Crime and Sexuality in Renaissance Venice* (New York: Oxford University Press, 1985), 118–21, 146–47 and passim.

6. Martha Feldman has studied the connections between Venetian music and poetic practices in Domenico Venier's literary salon; she emphasizes his reinterpretation of Bembo's poetics for the Venetian context. See her "Venice and the Madrigal in the Mid-Sixteenth Century" (Ph.D. diss., University of Pennsylvania, 1987), 442–55; idem, "The Composer as Exegete: Interpretations of Petrarchan Syntax in the Venetian Madrigal," *Studi musicali* 18, no. 2 (1989): 203–38; idem, "The Academy of Domenico Venier, Music's Literary Muse in Mid-*Cinquecento* Venice," *Renaissance Quarterly* 44, no. 3 (1991): 475–510.

7. The suggestion that Domenico Venier was composing verses in Venetian dialect in these years was first advanced by Manlio Dazzi (*Il fiore della lirica veneziana,* 1:368–69), but he unfortunately provides no manuscript sources to support his theories. Martha Feldman has recently pointed out to me the existence of an unstudied manuscript in Venetian dialect in London— composed as a lewd exchange between Domenico Venier and Benedetto Corner—concerning a woman "Helena" that both boast they have "chiavà" (screwed). The author's identity is most certainly Domenico, because the manuscript contains allusions to Domenico Venier's crippling disease. See British Library, Ms. Ad. 12.197. Tiziana Agostini Nordio has shown me a similar Venetian dialect exchange MSS it. IX 173 (=6282) in the Biblioteca Nazionale Marciana.

Recently all of Maffio Venier's dialect verses have been attributed and cataloged in a critical index by Tiziana Agostini Nordio: "Rime dialettali attribuite a Maffio Venier: Primo regesto," *Quaderni veneti,* no. 2 (1985): 7–23; idem, "'La Strazzosa,' Canzone di Maffio Venier: Edizione critica," in Tiziana Agostini Nordio and Valerio Vianello, *Contributi rinascimentali: Venezia e Firenze* (Padua: Francisci Editore, 1982), 9–131.

8. Many of Franco's letters in her *Lettere familiari a diversi,* published five years after her poems, comment retrospectively upon the content of the *capitoli,* which the letter writer now understands more clearly. In letter 47, she refers to this poetic debate with the *incerto autore* and to the satirical poetic attacks that were directed against her, and she excuses herself for mistakenly thinking that her addressee was "chi ha scritto que' versi contro di me" (he who wrote those verses against me) (64–66). She thanks him for his offer to protect her from her vicious attacker, and although she decides to discontinue her poetic duel with the man, she expresses an interest in continuing to exchange poems with him in order to exercise her poetic skills in literary debate. For a modern edition of her letters, together with a critical essay and a consideration of its textual history, see Benedetto Croce, *Veronica Franco: Lettere dall'unica edizione del MDLXXX con Proemio e Nota Iconografica* (Naples: Ricciardi, 1949). For this quotation, see letter 17, 28. I will refer only to this edition throughout this chapter.

9. For Domenico Venier's biography, which includes the unique edition of his poetic works,

see Pierantonio Serassi, *Rime di Domenico Veniero senatore viniziano raccolte ora per la prima volta ed illustrate* (Bergamo: Lancillotto, 1751). The crippled brother of the scurrilous dialect poet Lorenzo (author of the *Trentuno de la Zaffetta*), Domenico was also the leading exponent of Venetian Petrarchism. See Marco Valerio Marcellino, *Il diamerone* (Venice: Gabriel Giolito de' Ferrari, 1564), for a discussion of Venier's salon. In addition, the connection between Venier and Badoer is alluded to in a letter by Anton Francesco Doni in his *I Marmi* (1552-53), in which Venier is exalted, together with Girolamo Molino and Federigo Badoer, as the principal figure responsible for establishing a distinctly Venetian grandeur, in contrast to an already much heralded Florentine magnificence. For the full citation of these letters and quotations, see Lina Bolzoni, "L'Accademia Veneziana: Splendore e decadenza di una utopia enciclopedica," in her *Università, accademie e società scientifiche in Italia e in Germania dal Cinquecento al Settecento* (Bologna: Il Mulino, 1982), 119.

10. On Domenico Venier's varied and influential political career in Venetian government, in which he held many important governmental offices before he was confined to a wheelchair owing to gout, see Zorzi, *Cortigiana veneziana*, 69-90. It is also interesting to speculate that Marco Venier might have had some influence in securing a positive outcome for the trial. In 1580 he was an *avogadore* (state attorney)—an office that was authorized to suspend and to call sentences of different magistracies, including the the Council of Ten. Also in 1580, Marco opposed Michiel, the archbishop of Spalato, for appropriating an inheritance not lawfully his own and had him prosecuted in the courts of the Consiglio del Quarantia (a supreme appeals court with forty judges who were empowered to review criminal and civil cases).

11. The importance of maintaining a woman's honor in Italian Renaissance society is discussed in Guido Ruggiero, "'Più che la vita caro': Onore, matrimonio, e reputazione femminile nel tardo rinascimento," *Quaderni storici* 66, no. 3 (1987): 753-75. See also Luisa Ciammitti, "Quanto costa essere normali: La dote nel conservatorio femminile di Santa Maria del Baraccano (1630-1680)," *Quaderni storici* 53 (1983): 469-97; Lucia Ferrante, "L'onore ritrovato: Donne nella Casa del Soccorso di San Paolo a Bologna," *Quaderni storici* 53 (1983): 499-527; Sherrill Cohen, "Convertite e Malmaritate: Donne 'irregolari' e ordini religiosi nella Firenze rinascimentale," *Memoria: Rivista di storia delle donne* 5 (1982): 23-33, 46-65. For the concept of honor and shame in Italian society, see Peter Burke, *The Historical Anthropology of Early Modern Italy: Essays on Perception and Communication* (Cambridge: Cambridge University Press, 1987), 13-14, 95-109, 134.

12. See n. 4 above for the location of the document. Alessandra Schiavon was the first to publish the document, in "Per la biografia di Veronica Franco," 255-56. I remain indebted to this transcription. On withholding the reason for arrest from the "accused" until the moment of the trial proceedings, see Martin "L'Inquisizione romana," 789-90.

13. On the foundation of the Magistrato alle Pompe, see Giulio Bistort, *Il magistrato alle pompe nella repubblica di Venezia: Studio storico* (Venice: 1912; reprint, Bologna: Forni Editore, 1969). For the text of this poem, see Dazzi, *Il fiore della lirica veneziana*, 28-33. The manuscript source is Biblioteca Nazionale Marciana, MSS it. IX 217 (=7061), cc. 59v-62v.

14. On the sumptuary laws directed against courtesans, see chapter 2 above.

15. On the Venetian Ghetto in this period, see Pullan, *Jews of Europe*; Cecil Roth, *History of the Jews in Venice* (New York: Schocken Books, 1975).

16. Milani, "L''Incanto' di Veronica Franco," 251-52 n. 5; "Il caso di Emilia Catena," 76 and passim.

17. See Mary R. O'Neil, "*Sacerdote ovvero strione:* Ecclesiastical and Superstitious Remedies in

Sixteenth Century Italy," in *Understanding Popular Culture*, ed. Steve Kaplan (New York: Mouton, 1984), 53–83. O'Neil remarks that the "regional offices of the Roman Inquisition increased prosecutions of superstitious offenses in the period after 1570, leading to a marked increase in trials against lay persons involved in magical healing, divination, and love magic" (55). On the preponderance of Italian witchcraft trials dealing with harmful spells brought against women, see William Monter, "Women and the Italian Inquisitions," in *Women in the Middle Ages and the Renaissance and Historical Perspectives*, ed. Mary Beth Rose (Syracuse: Syracuse University Press, 1985), 73–87, especially 79–85. A very informative study of magical practices and the Inquisition in Venice concentrates on the role women played in popular witchcraft and superstitious incantations. That study appeared after this book was written. See Ruth Martin, *Witchcraft and the Inquisition in Venice, 1550–1650* (New York: Basil Blackwell, 1989), especially 167–68, for references to Franco's Inquisition hearing.

18. Torture was practiced very little in Venetian witchcraft trials in this period. See Milani, "L'Incanto' di Veronica Franco," 252 n. 5. On the practice of keeping men and women in separate prisons rather than executing them, see Milani, "Il caso di Emilia Catena," 76 n. 5 and 79 n. 13. See also Umberto Franzoi, *Le prigioni della repubblica di Venezia* (Venice: Stamperia di Venezia, 1966). One of the tribunal's prisons was located at San Giovanni Nuovo, near where Franco was living at the time of her trials. On this prison, see Milani, "Il caso di Emilia Catena," 76 n. 5. Milani also discusses the prison guardian Girolamo Vetriario, who lived in the prison with his family and who was one of the ministers of the Inquisition tribunal.

19. See Milani, "Il caso di Emilia Catena," 75 and passim. See Milani, "La verità *ovvero* il processo contro Isabella Bellocchio (Venezia, 12 gennaio–14 ottobre 1589)" (Padua: Centro-stampa, 1985), 1:4, for a transcription and commentary of the trials against this Venetian courtesan. Catena is listed in the *Catalogo di tutte le principali et più honorate cortigiane di Venezia* as no. 127, "a S. Caterina."

20. On "bando" (banishment) as a punishment in the case of the courtesan Emilia Catena, see Milani, "Il caso di Emilia Catena," 75.

21. For a transcription of the trial against Domenico Venier, and for some discussion of its content, see Zorzi, *Cortigiana veneziana*, 155–57, 85–89, respectively. See ASV, Sant'Uffizio, 1576, busta 40, no. 2, fascicolo "Domenico Venier." On the use of the clergy and religious practices to redirect popular superstition into orthodox channels, see O'Neil, "*Sacerdote ovvero strione*," 53–85. O'Neill points out that "absolution in confession was made contingent on denunciation not just of one's own failings . . . but on the observed lapses of neighbors and relatives as well" (55, 78 n. 11).

22. On Venier's infirmity, see chapters 2 and 3 above.

23. Zorzi (*Cortigiana veneziana*, pp. 86–89) postulates that Venier's possible friendship with the two inquisitors, who were the *savi all'eresia* (sages against heresy)—Tommaso Contarini and Jacopo Foscarini—and the fact that Venier might have been holding an office as *procuratore*, as did Contarini, might have helped secure a dismissal of the accusations. He also reads this trial in connection to the charges of heresy brought against Paolo Veronese two years earlier, where the same inquisitors prevailed.

24. The poetic *tenzone*, derived mainly from the Provençal tradition, was incorporated into Italian poetic practice in the thirteenth century. Beginning with Giacomo da Lentini and Jacopo Mostacci, Italian poets elected the *tenzone* for personal poetic exchanges. The first author proposed the theme and established the rhyme scheme, and the second author, in a second poem, responded in like rhyme or theme. This tradition continued with Dante and then with

Petrarch. For a definition of the term "tenzone" as derived from "tenso," see W. Theodor Elwert, *Versificazione italiana: Dalle origini ai giorni nostri* (Paris: Le Monnier, 1973), 133. In early Sicilian poetry, the "contrasto" was a "tenzone" in "canzone" form. On the specifically Italian "tenzone," there are very few critical studies. For the most notable, see Giovan Mario Crescimbeni, *L'istoria della volgar poesia* (Venice: L. Basegio, 1730–31), 1:178–82; Salvatore Santangelo, *Le tenzoni poetiche nella letteratura italiana dalle origini* (Geneva: Leo Olschki, 1928); and Carlo Previtera, *La poesia giocosa e l'umorismo,* (Milan: Francesco Vallardi, 1939), 178–80. For further bibliography on the "tenzone" as a popular form during the duecento and trecento, see *La poesia giocosa e l'umorismo,* 183–84 nn. 1–24. On the influence of the Provençal "tenso" in Italian literature, see Santorre Debenedetti, *Gli studi provenzali in Italia nel Cinquecento* (Turin: Loescher, 1911).

25. On the active political career of Marco Venier (1532–1602) in Venetian government and the polemical positions he assumed in relation to papal authority, as well as an examination of his relationship to the Venier family, see Zorzi, *Cortigiana veneziana,* 115–33. Marco belonged to the *giovani* faction of the Venetian government, which acquired more decision-making power in the senate in the 1580s. On the ideological divisions between this young activist group and the *vecchi,* see Gaetano Cozzi, *Il doge Nicolo Contarini: Ricerche sul patriziato veneziano agli inizi del Seicento* (Venice: Istituto per la Collaborazione Culturale, 1958), 24–25, 32 and passim; and Martin Lowry, "The Reform of the Council of Ten—1582–83, An Unsettled Problem?" *Studi veneziani* 13 (1971): 275–310. For some hypothetical suggestions regarding the removal of Marco Venier's name from the edition, see 116–19, 125–26. His name appears in a number of manuscript collections in the Biblioteca Nazionale Marciana in Venice. See MSS it. IX 162 (=6310), and see MSS it. IX 272 (6645), which is entitled "Rime di diversi in lode di Cinthia Braccioduro Garzadori . . . Vicentine." It includes six sonnets of Marco Venier and other sonnets by Pietro Gradenigo, Celio Magno, Iacopo Mocenigo, and other poets.

No comprehensive study exists on the capitolo in terza rima in Italian poetic practice. There is a brief discussion, however, in W. Theodor Elwert, *Versificazione italiana: Dalle origini ai giorni nostri* (Paris: Le Monnier, 1973), 143–44; and see Previtera, *La poesia giocosa e l'umorismo.* See also Silvia Longhi, *Lusus: Il capitolo burlesco nel Cinquecento* (Padua: Antenore, 1983). *Capitoli* 5 and 6, and 9 and 10, conform to specific rhymes to which the *incerto autore* responds in like rhyme. In the first exchange, not all of the rhyme endings are repeated; but in the next exchange, not only are the rhymes repeated but also key words in the "proposta." Similarly, *capitoli* 3 and 4 conform not only to the same rhymes but also to the same words, such as "sole, giri, poco and desio" in lines 30, 31, 56, and 73, respectively. For an interesting example of how "parole rime" is used in a Renaissance literary *tenzone,* see the exchange between Annibale Caro and Giovanni Mario Barbieri, "Il Treperuno," reproduced in Gino Bertoni, *Le Rime di Giovanni M. Barbieri* (Modena: 1907), 3–23. For examples of the uses of "rime al mezzo" (rhymes in the middle) in the sonnets of both Petrarch and Domenico Venier, see Edoardo Taddeo, *Il manierismo letterario e i lirici veneziani del Cinquecento* (Rome: Bulzoni, 1974), 52–55.

26. A "sonetto caudato" is a sonnet that has lines added on to the standard fourteen. These lines usually have one seven-syllable and two hendecasyllabic lines. Benedetto Croce (*Poeti e scrittori del pieno e tardo rinascimento* [Bari: Laterza, 1970], 223) recognized the significance of Veronica Franco's departure from a traditional Petrarchan discourse on love, signaled by her use of the *capitolo* in terza rima; but he never connected this to her involvement in the poetic activities of the Venier academy and salon. On this involvement, see Margaret F. Rosenthal, "A Courtesan's Voice: Epistolary Self-Portraiture in Veronica Franco's *Terze Rime* (1575)," in *Writing the Female Voice: Essays on Epistolary Literature,* ed. Elizabeth Goldsmith (Boston: Northeastern

University Press, 1989). On Franco's reworking of the Renaissance love lyric to suit her own designs, see Ann Rosalind Jones, "City Women and Their Audiences: Louise Labé and Veronica Franco," in Margaret W. Ferguson et al., eds., *The Discourses of Sexual Difference in Early Modern Europe* (Chicago: University of Chicago Press, 1986), 299–316.

27. On poetic duels during the cinquecento, see the recent study by Francesco Erspamer, *La biblioteca di Don Ferrante: Duello e onore nella cultura del Cinquecento* (Rome: Bulzoni, 1983).

28. This play on Franco's name "Veronica" also burlesques the reference to the "vera eicon" or "vera immagine" on the cloth that Veronica used to wipe Christ's brow on the road to Calvary as related in Matt. 9:20 and Luke 8:43.

29. Marisa Milani ("L''Incanto' di Veronica Franco," 252) argues that Vannitelli waited until the end of September to see what happened as the result of the incantations performed in Franco's home. I agree with her when she argues that when the incantations were unsuccessful, Franco brought charges against Bortola for stealing a pair of scissors with a silver chain. In order to cover for himself, Milani says, Vannitelli quickly presented the *denuncia* against Franco in October.

30. On Giovanni Trevisan, see Brian Pullan, *Rich and Poor in Renaissance Venice: The Social Institutions of a Catholic State, 1580 to 1620* (Cambridge: Harvard University Press, 1971), 343–44. Trevisan was patriarch of Venice from 1560 to 1590, and abbot of San Cipriano in Murano. Carlo Borromeo condemned Trevisan for his failure to guide the Venetian people.

31. She never qualifies what these "scritture" (writings) are in her trial testimonies or in this document.

32. A detailed account of the contents of her will appears in chapter 2 above; for a transcription, see appendix 2.1.

33. Marisa Milani ("L''Incanto' di Veronica Franco," 250; and "La verità," 183 n. 255) notes that this practice was very common among courtesans.

34. On the use of the confessor to identify possible heretics, see Martin, "L'Inquisizione romana," 788. On the punishments for thieves during the fourteenth century, see Guido Ruggiero, *Violence in Early Renaissance Venice* (New Brunswick: Rutgers University Press, 1980), 41–42. The most common penalties were imprisonment, fines, "gratie," (irrevocable sentences) and corporeal punishment. Capital punishment was reserved only for the most serious crimes. See Giuseppe Tassini, *Alcune delle più clamorose condanne capitali eseguite in Venezia sotto la repubblica* (Venice: Filippi Editore, 1966), especially v–184.

35. Paolo Preto, *Peste e società a Venezia, 1576* (Vicenza: Neri Pozza, 1978), 101; and Pullan, *Rich and Poor in Renaissance Venice, 319*.

36. Preto, *Peste e società a Venezia 1576, 99–100*. The *signori di notte* (police posts) were responsible for organizing and overseeing the police patrols in the city and for administering the investigation of certain crimes, such as murder and robbery. See Ruggiero, *Violence in Early Renaissance Venice, 26–27*. See also Giovanni Scarabello, "Devianza sessuale ed interventi di giustizia a Venezia nella prima metà del XVI secolo," in *Tiziano e Venezia: Convegno Internazionale di Studi* (Vicenza: Neri Pozza, 1980), 75–86.

37. On relative salaries in late cinquecento Venice, see Paola Pavanini, "Abitazioni popolari e borghesi nella Venezia cinquecentesca," *Studi veneziani* 5 (1981): 63–126. On the differences between the various courts and court systems in Venice during the sixteenth century, see Robert Finlay, *Politics in Renaissance Venice* (New Brunswick: Rutgers University Press, 1980), 68–69; and on the specific role of the "Avogaria di Comun," see Ruggiero, *Violence in Early Renaissance Venice, 19–26*. On sexual patterns as influenced by the effects of the plague on the city's economy and mores, see Guido Ruggiero, *The Boundaries of Eros: Sex Crime and Sexuality in Renaissance*

Venice (New York: Oxford University Press, 1985), 148, 178 n. 32. With specific reference to the pervasive sexual corruption among nuns, often from patrician families, see 76–84; and see Dennis Romano, *Patricians and Popolani* (Baltimore: Johns Hopkins University Press, 1987), 54–55.

38. For this metaphorical transformation of the city, see Valnea Rudmann, "Lettura della canzone per la peste di Venezia di Maffio Venier," *Atti dell'Istituto Veneto di Scienze, Lettere ed Arti* 121 (1963): 599–641.

39. See Pio Paschini, "I monasteri femminili in Italia nel 1500," in his *Problemi di vita religiosa in Italia nel Cinquecento* (Padua: Antenore, 1960), 31–60. For this problem in Venice during the apostolic legate's term, see Stella, *Chiesa e stato nelle relazioni dei nunzi pontifici a Venezia,* 32–33 n. 46. See also Brian Pullan, "The Old Catholicism, the New Catholicism, and the Poor," in *Timore e carità: I poveri nell'Italia moderna,* ed. Giorgio Politi et al. (Cremona: Annali della Biblioteca Statale e Libreria Civica di Cremona, 1982), 13–27; Ruggiero, *Boundaries of Eros,* 71–81, 163–64, 178 n. 32. On the parochial clergy as "social intermediaries" in Venetian society, albeit for an earlier period (fourteenth and fifteenth centuries), see Romano, *Patricians and Popolani,* 91–118.

40. Richard Kieckhefer, *European Witch Trials: Their Foundations in Popular and Learned Culture, 1300–1500* (Berkeley: University of California Press, 1976), 79.

41. On the practice in popular culture of looking into a basin of water (the "inghistara") in order to perform magical incantations, and its treatment in the literature of the period, see Mario N. Pavia, *Drama of the Sigla de Oro: A Study of Magic, Witchcraft and Other Occult Beliefs* (New York: Hispanic Institute in the United States, 1959), 103ff. For this specific experiment, Pullan, *Jews of Europe,* 89–90. He writes: "The ritual . . . had been practiced among the Venetian people for many years, and had been noticed with disapproval by the Inquisition since the 1580s. It commonly called for a glass bowl filled with water; for the presence of innocent children, virgins, or even pregnant women with innocence alive in their wombs; and for the use of mildly sacred properties such as candles or holy water."

42. For a reference to a "Bortola," see Milani, "Il caso di Emilia Catena," 78 n. 10; Milani states that this was an abbreviated form for a common Venetian name for women, Bortolomea.

43. For a reference to Ca' Coco, see Giuseppe Tassini, *Curiosità veneziane,* 8th ed. (Venice: Filippi Editore, 1970), 169–70. Vannitelli adds that Giovanni Tedesco also worked for the "secretario Formenti," who, according to Tassini (250–51), was elected *cancellier grande* (directly responsible to the doge) in 1580. He died in 1585.

44. On neighborhood quarrels, partly as a function of the close proximity in which families of all classes lived to one another, see Romano, *Patricians and Popolani,* 131–40.

45. The Merceria (named after the mercers) was one of the main commercial centers of the city and principal routes (*vias magistras*) leading from San Marco to Rialto. See Romano, *Patricians and Popolani,* 119–20; idem, "Gender and the Urban Geography of Renaissance Venice," *Journal of Social History* 23, no. 2 (1989): 339–53, especially 341; Martin, "Journeymen's Feast of Fools," 157–58 and passim.

46. This language echoes the satirical defamation of the courtesan in Maffio Venier's verses. On the "grotesque body" and its relation to women, see Peter Stallybrass and Allon White, *The Politics and Poetics of Transgression* (Ithaca: Cornell University Press, 1987), 21–25, 64–66, and in relation to satire in early modern England, 100–118.

47. For an interesting interpretation of the effects of the plague in Florence on the psychology of the people during the fifteenth century, and as viewed within a sociological context, see

Richard C. Trexler, *Public Life in Renaissance Florence* (New York: Academic Press, 1980), 362–64; Ann G. Carmichael, *Plague and the Poor in Renaissance Florence* (Cambridge: Cambridge University Press, 1986); Carlo M. Cipolla, *Fighting the Plague in Seventeenth-Century Italy* (Madison: University of Wisconsin Press, 1981). A recent examination of the metaphorical associations between leprosy and syphilis links the fear of the disease with the discovery of the New World and the threat of the "other." See Anna Foa, "The New and the Old: The Spread of Syphilis (1494–1530)," trans. Carole C. Gallucci, in *Sex and Gender in Historical Perspective*, ed. Edward Muir and Guido Ruggiero (Baltimore: Johns Hopkins University Press, 1990), 26–45.

48. On sexual relations between servants and masters in Venice, see Ruggiero, *Boundaries of Eros*, 40–41, 107–8, 152–53; and on the mixing of classes in the patrician household, see Romano, *Patricians and Popolani*, 134–38.

49. These courts were equally active in Venice in the sixteenth century. See Ruggiero, *Boundaries of Eros*, 199–201.

50. On laws against "giochi d'azzardo" (gambling) for its alleged corruption of social patrimony, see Derosas, "Moralità e giustizia," 448–49. For the Aretino passage, see the edition of Giovanni Aquilecchia (Bari: Laterza, 1975), 109. For the English translation, see Pietro Aretino, *Aretino's Dialogues*, trans. Raymond Rosenthal (New York: Stein and Day, 1971), 123–24. See also G. Dolcetti, *Le bische e il giucco d'azzardo a Venezia, 1172–1807* (Venice: Manuzio, 1903).

51. This constitutes a standard charge that appears over and over again in trials against courtesans.

52. For laws against the "perle" and other jewels prohibited to courtesans during these years, see Rita Casagrande di Villaviera, *Le cortigiane veneziane del Cinquecento* (Milan: Longanesi, 1968), 47–83.

53. One way that courtesans allegedly changed their costumes to suit their specific designs was to dress as men. On female transvestism as an allure for male homosexuals—a cross-dressing promoted by the Venetian state—see Casagrande, *Le cortigiane veneziane del Cinquecento*, 130, and specifically with regard to courtesans, 120–22, 130–32. See also Nicholas S. Davidson, "Il Sant'Uffizio e la tutela del culto a Venezia nel Cinquecento," *Studi veneziani* 6 (1982): 87–103; he cites a law of "14 luglio 1578" of the Council of Ten (Consiglio de' Dieci, *Comune*, reg. 33, fol. 167) that prohibits courtesans from wearing male clothes to attract men. See also Patricia H. Labalme, "Sodomy and Venetian Justice in the Renaissance," *Legal History Review* 52 (1984): 217–54, especially 249–50.

54. It is possible that Vannitelli was making an indirect reference to the large community of German Jews who lived in Venice, both in the Fondaco dei Tedeschi, the residence and warehouse of German merchants for which Giorgione was commissioned to paint the frescoes (only fragments of which now remain), and in the region of Santa Maria Formosa. On this community, see Pullan, *Jews of Europe*, 155–56; Henry Simonsfeld, *Der Fondaco dei Tedeschi in Venedig und die deutsch-venetianischen Handelsbeziehungen* (Stuttgart: Cotta, 1887), 2:269–75.

55. Franco claims later in her testimony that she was indeed ill for a total of four months in 1580. See n. 75 below.

56. For an explanation of what constitutes a "mandata di comparizione" (summons), see Milani, "L''Incanto' di Veronica Franco," 253.

57. For an account of Bolognetti's position as nuncio to Venice (1578–81), see Stella, *Chiesa e stato nelle relazioni dei nunzi pontifici a Venezia*, especially chap. 2, 17–40.

58. Alberto Bolognetti was elected papal nuncio to Venice by Pope Gregorio XIII on 10

September 1578. On this appointment, see the *avviso* in the Biblioteca Apostolica Vaticana (hereafter BAV), Urb. lat. 1046 (25 October 1578), fol. 371r. Bolognetti immediately found himself caught, on the one hand, between the jurisdictional positions of the Venetian republic in general and those of the papacy and, on the other, between the conflicting positions held by the two ruling factions in the Signoria: the "vecchi," who represented the conservative oligarchical and propapal stronghold in the Council of Ten, and the "giovani," the youthful reformists, the antipapal and expansionist ideological presence in the senate. For Marco Venier's participation in the "giovani" faction, as *avogador di comun* (state attorney), and his controversial role in arresting and banishing the bishop of Spalato, see Zorzi, *Cortigiana veneziana,* 120–33. For a history of the ideological divisions between the "giovani" and the "vecchi" factions in Venetian government, see Cozzi, *Il doge Nicolo Contarini,* 24–25, 32 and passim; Stella, *Chiesa e stato nelle relazioni dei nunzi pontifici a Venezia,* 3–16, 21–28, 33–36; Martin Lowry, "The Reform of the Council of Ten, 1582–83: An Unsettled Problem?" *Studi veneziani* 13 (1971): 275–310.

59. For the text of this *relazione,* see Aldo Stella, *Chiesa e stato nelle relazioni dei nunzi pontifici a Venezia,* 105–295, especially 277–95.

60. Ibid., 286.

61. On the distinction between popular and religious superstition in Counter-Reformation Italy as it affected the clergy who were enlisted to fight heresy on the local level, see O'Neil, "*Sacerdote ovvero strione,*" 56–57 and passim. A treatise, *Tractatus de superstitionibus* (reprinted in Venice, 1581), by Martino de Arles, attempted to clarify this distinction. See Martin, "Journeymen's Feast of Fools," 150 n. 4.

62. Kieckhefer, *European Witch Trials,* 78–79.

63. Ibid., 79 and passim.

64. On the importance of proving heretical intent, see Milani, "La verità," 2:110: "Se l'*effetto* delle *stregherie* veneziane era ben poca cosa, l'*affetto,* cioé l'intenzione, veniva dai giudici esaltato al massimo, in modo da dar loro materia per una condanna esemplare" (if the *effect* of Venetian sorcery was of very little account, the *affect,* that is, the intention, was raised by the judges to the highest [offense], so that they could have grounds with which to pass a sentence").

65. It seems that the only person missing from this first trial is the *inquisitore* himself. In these years, it was Giovan Battista da Milano, a Dominican. On his absence, see Milani, "L'Incanto' di Veronica Franco," 259–60 n. 10. On the practice of using virgins for chants, together with "una donna gravida" (a pregnant woman), who (as in this case) holds a "virgin" in her womb, see ibid., 255 n. 9. See also Gene Brucker, "Sorcery in Early Renaissance Florence," *Studies in the Renaissance* 10–11 (1963–64): 7–25.

66. For this precise chant, adopted by agrarian cults in the Friuli region in Italy, see Carlo Ginzburg, *Witchcraft and Agrarian Cults in the Sixteenth and Seventeenth Centuries,* trans. John Tedeschi and Anne C. Tedeschi (New York: Penguin Books, 1985), 49, 56, 89–90. And for other trials in which this chant occurs, see Milani, "L'Incanto' di Veronica Franco," 257.

67. Milani, "L'Incanto' di Veronica Franco," 252.

68. This same wordplay appears in the *Terze rime,* when she insists that her male interlocutor must turn his attention away from proving his love for her to involving her in intellectual and literary exchanges.

69. This assertion is very odd, and I do not know how to explain it. If we read it as another veiled allusion to foreign immigrants in Venice and tensions Venetians might have felt by their presence, it would be useful to look at Agostino Sagredo and F. Berchet, *Il Fondaco dei Turchi in Venezia* (Milan: 1860).

70. The allegation of eating meat on prohibited days is a standard complaint aired in the Inquisition tribunal. See Milani, "La verità," 2.

71. In July of that year, Venice was subject to a deadly "fever" which closed the Inquisition tribunal until October 1580. For the typhus epidemic in Venice in that period, Pullan, *Rich and Poor in Renaissance Venice*, 290, 373, 632. A Roman *avviso* in the BAV reports the seriousness of the illness in Venice. See MSS Urb. lat. 1048 (October 1580), fol. 343r.

72. The inquisitor often repeated questions in order to confuse the defendant, or to find the defendant in the act of contradiction. This curious assertion is the only time that Franco explains her understanding of the participation of the devil in the incantations. Her response reveals an almost offhand manner in speaking about an issue that was of great concern to the court. On the danger of devil worship and exorcism, see O'Neil, "*Sacerdote ovvero strione,*" 53–83; and for contemporary treatises used by the Inquisition courts on this subject, see 54–56, 58–60 and passim.

73. She is referring here to the Renaissance instrument of torture. On the "Signori di Notte," see Ruggiero, *Violence in Early Renaissance Venice*, 26–27.

74. It was common practice, as other such trials reveal, for the person performing the ritual to have fasted on that day.

75. A "Virginia Greca" who lived in campo Santa Margherita in Venice was denounced and then tried in the Inquisition courts in 1592 on charges of heresy. For the contents of the trial, see ASV, *Sant'Uffizio*, 1592, busta 69, as cited in Milani, "Il caso di Emilia Catena." It is possible that this is the same woman to whom Franco refers in this trial. In the BAV, an interesting *avviso* reports that a "donna greca" (a Greek woman) is in prison for stealing children and subsequently selling them. See Urb. lat. 1046 (21 June 1578), fol. 250r. John Martin has noted ("L'Inquisizione romana") that the lower classes in Venice were becoming increasingly intolerant of religious dissenters and practicers of superstitious incantations, and thus used as their scapegoats the many foreigners who lived in Venice in the sixteenth century (793). For another interesting discussion of the sociology of heretical groups in Venice, see idem, "Salvation and Society in Sixteenth-Century Venice: Popular Evangelism in a Renaissance City," *Journal of Modern History* 60, no. 2 (1988): 205–33. On Greeks in Venice, see G. Fedalto, *Richerche storiche sulla posizione giuridica ed ecclesiastica dei greci a Venezia nei secoli XV e XVI* (Florence: Leo S. Olschki, 1967).

76. All the trials that I have examined end with this question, which allowed the inquisitors to call those people in for testimony or to verify the denouncers' claims.

77. On this man, see Milani, "L'"Incanto' di Veronica Franco," 259.

78. For an interesting example of a sentence brought against a Venetian merchant, see Rossato, "Religione e moralità," 245ff.

79. Franco, *Lettere,* 49–50.

80. ASV, *Dieci Savi sopra le decime*, busta 157, 1581. For a transcription of this tax report, see appendix 2.2.

81. For an overview of this academy and others during the Renaissance and throughout Italy, see Michele Maylender, *Storia delle accademie d'Italia* (Bologna: 1926–30); and for this academy in particular, see 5:36–43. Also important for a discussion of the Venetian academy are Pompeo G. Molmenti, *La storia di Venezia nella vita privata dalle origini alla caduta della repubblica,* 7th ed. (Bergamo: Istituto d'arti grafiche, 1928), especially chap. 9, 308–10; Domen Maria Pellegrini, "Breve dissertazione previa al Sommario dell'Accademia Veneta della Fama," *Giornale della italiana letteratura* 22–23 (1808): 3–32, 113–38; Cicogna, *Delle inscrizioni veneziane,*

3:50–55; A. A. Renouard, *Annales de l'imprimerie des Aldes, ou histoire des trois Manuce,* 3d ed. (Paris: 1843), 267–79, 434–42. For more recent contributions, see Gino Benzoni, "Aspetti della cultura urbana nella società veneta del Cinquecento e Seicento: Le accademie," *Archivio veneto* 108 (1977): 87–159; Paola Ulvioni, "Accademie e cultura in Italia dalla Controriforma all'Arcadia: Il caso Veneziano" in *Libri e documenti: Archivio storico civico e Biblioteca Trivulziana* (Milan: Archivio Storico Civico e Biblioteca Trivulziana, 1979), 21–75; Martin Lowry, *The World of Aldus Manutius: Business and Scholarship in Renaissance Venice* (Ithaca: Cornell University Press, 1979), 180–216. The most recent discussions of the history and function of the Venetian academy are Pietro Pagan, "Sulla Accademia 'Venetiana' o della 'Fama,'" *Atti dell'Istituto Veneto di Scienze, Lettere ed Arti* 132 (1973–74): 359–92; Paul Lawrence Rose, "The *Accademia Venetiana:* Science and Culture in Renaisance Venice," *Studi veneziani* 11 (1969): 191–242; Lina Bolzoni, "Il 'Badoardo' di Francesco Patrizi e l'Accademia Veneziana della Fama," *Giornale storico della letteratura italiana* 158 (1981): 77–101; idem, "L'Accademia Veneziana." Federico Badoer was imprisoned in 1561 on order of the Council of Ten for fraudulent speculation with the funds of the Academia della Fama. As Martin Lowry notes ("Reform of the Council of Ten"), Badoer found himself once again in serious trouble in 1568 for "illicit dealings with foreign powers" (297), when he tried to "secure a post for a dependent on the staff of Duke Henry of Brunswick without asking permission of the Ten to contact a foreign ruler. He was fined 500 ducats and banned from office for five years." On this ruling, see *Nunziature di Venezia,* ed. Aldo Stella (Rome: Istituto storico italiano, 1958–77), 8:464, 469.

82. The ceiling of the room, painted by Titian, portrays the figure of Sapienza (Wisdom). On the decorations of the room, see Nicolas Ivanoff, "I cicli allegorici della Libreria e del Palazzo Ducale di Venezia," in *Rinascimento europeo e rinascimento veneziano,* ed. Vittore Branca (Florence: G. C. Sansoni, 1967), 281-97; Bolzoni, "L'Accademia Veneziana," 154–56.

83. On Badoer's financial ruin, see Rose, *"Academia Veneziana,"* 210–15. See also the entry on "Badoer" in the *Dizionario biografico degli italiani* (Rome: Istituto della Enciclopedia Italiana, 1960–) 5:107–8.

84. See chap. 1 n. 94; chap. 2 nn. 78, 80, 85.

85. The only woman writer other than Veronica Franco to write capitoli is Gaspara Stampa, but hers are completely different; she composed five capitoli which were included in the 1554 posthumous edition of her *Rime d'amore.* See Maria Bellonci's edition and introduction to Stampa's *Rime* (Milan: Rizzoli, 1954), 230–41.

86. Girolamo Ruscelli (*Del modo di comporre in versi nella lingua italiana* [Venice: Giovanni Battista Sessa, 1582]) attests to the difficulty in using the "terzetto" form. I refer here to *Il rimario del Signor Girolamo Ruscelli* (Venice: Simone Occhi, 1750). This quotation comes from the heading entitled "Delle risposte" (91).

87. Ruscelli, *Il rimario,* 91–94.

88. See capitolo 15, "Signor, ha molti giorni, ch'io non fui" (Signor, for many days I have not come to pay you my respects), in which she explicitly refers to the gathering of friends for the purposes of literary exchange and conversation. The only book-length studies on Domenico Venier's literary activities and the group of poets that surrounded him are Taddeo, *Il manierismo letterario;* and W. Theodor Elwert, *Studi di letteratura veneziana* (Venice: Istituto per la Collaborazione Culturale, 1958).

89. The language of combat was very familiar to Venetian courtesans. In the trial against Isabella Bellocchio, a witness was asked whether Isabella kept any heretical books in her house, to which she responded that Isabella possessed only one book—a copy of Ariosto's *Orlando furioso*

which she had on display on her mantelpiece. See Milani, "La verità," 150 n. 59. Isabella, unlike Veronica Franco, was illiterate. That courtesans often kept books for display was a standard charge leveled against them by male satirists such as Pietro Aretino, but in this case it was to emphasize their posturing as cultivated women in order to lure men. This posture of sophistication, these satirists charged, was calculated to conceal their deceitful ways. For an example of a Venetian merchant also tried by the Inquisition, who owned a copy of the *Orlando furioso*, see Rossato, "Religione e moralità," 228. Paul F. Grendler (*Schooling in Renaissance Italy: Literacy and Learning, 1300–1600* [Baltimore: Johns Hopkins University Press, 1989]) claims that *Orlando furioso* was one of the texts most widely used in Venetian schools, because reading chivalric romances was fashionable. See also idem, "Chivalric Romances in the Italian Renaissance," *Studies in Medieval and Renaissance History* 10 (1988): 57–102.

The allusions to *Orlando furioso* are numerous throughout the *Terze rime*. Girolamo Ruscelli, a member of the Venier circle, published a commentary, *Le annotationi, gli avvertimenti et le dichiarationi . . . sopra i luoghi difficili et importanti del Furioso* (Venice: Valgrisi, 1556); and Alberto Lavezuola (*Le osservationi*, which was included in his edition *Orlando furioso . . . nuovamente adornato* [Venice: Francesco de' Franceschi Senese, 1584], 9), focuses on the moral and ethical implications of "il tenzonare con donna" (the [poetic] battling with a woman). This moralizing approach to *Orlando furioso*, informed by Horatian theories, is also evident in many of the commentaries and theoretical studies by the Venetian writers who frequented the Accademia della Fama. In the *Somma delle opere*, the academy's list of projected works, a study of Ariosto focuses on "delle bellezze dell'Ariosto . . . le allegorie morali" (the beautiful passages of Ariosto . . . the moral allegories).

90. On the erotic nature of sixteenth-century Venetian painting as influenced by Venetian "volgarizzamenti" (vernacular translations) by such writers as Ludovico Dolce and Francesco Sansovino, see Carlo Ginzburg, "Tiziano, Ovidio, e i codici della figurazione erotica del Cinquecento," *Paragone* 339, no. 29 (1978): 3–24; Charles Hope, *Titian* (New York: Harper and Row, 1980), 135, 142 n. 18. For a new critical edition of Romano's engravings with Aretino's accompanying sonnets, see Lynne Lawner, *I modi: The Sixteen Pleasures—An Erotic Album of the Italian Renaissance* (Evanston, Ill.: Northwestern University Press, 1988).

91. This echoes Castiglione's *Il libro del cortegiano*, book 3, where the Magnifico Giuliano quotes Saint Paul, "Si non caste, tamen caute," in his larger denunciation of religious hypocrisy among friars who in turn corrupt women. See Charles S. Singleton's translation, *The Book of the Courtier* (New York: Doubleday, 1959), 221.

92. On the transformation in Petrarch's sonnets 90 and 45 of an idolatrous icon of worship which has both human and divine attributes, and on the function of a proper name (Laura) in his lyrics, see Giuseppe Mazzotta, "The *Canzoniere* and the Language of the Self," *Studies in Philology* 75 (1978): 271–96; John Freccero, "The Fig Tree and the Laurel," *Diacritics* 5 (1975): 34–40; and Nancy J. Vickers, "Diana Described: Scattered Woman and Scattered Rhyme," in *Writing and Sexual Difference*, ed. Elizabeth Abel (Chicago: University of Chicago Press, 1982), 95–109; Fiora A. Bassanese, "What's In a Name? Self-Naming and Renaissance Women Poets," *Annali d'Italianistica* 7 (1989): 104–15.

93. Dazzi, *Il fiore della lirica veneziana*, 1:37–40. The manuscript source is Biblioteca Nazionale Marciana, MSS it. IX 217 (=7061), cc. 56r–59r. A "cartello di sfida" is defined in Fausto Sebastiano da Longiano, *Il duello* (Venice: Vincenzo Valgrisi, 1552), 14 and passim. See also Girolamo Muzio, *Il duello* (Venice: Gabriel Giolito de' Ferrari, 1564), especially book 1, chap. 13, "Della forma de' cartelli," 26–27, and chap. 15, "Del mandare i cartelli," 27–28.

94. On Aristotle's view of women, see Susan Moller Okin, *Women in Western Political Thought* (Princeton: Princeton University Press, 1973), 73–96; Maryanne C. Horowitz, "Aristotle and Women," *Journal of the History of Biology* 9 (1979): 183–213; and Katherine M. Rogers, *The Troublesome Helpmate* (Seattle: University of Washington Press, 1966); Ian Maclean, *The Renaissance Notion of Women* (New York: Cambridge University Press, 1980), 8–9, 36–38, 41–43, 48–49 and passim.

95. It is not clear exactly to which "lingua selvaghesca" poem she refers, but she is probably alluding to Maffio Venier's *canzone*, "La Strazzosa." On the recent critical edition of this poem, see n. 7 above.

CHAPTER FIVE: THE COURTESAN IN EXILE

1. On rhetorical devices in Ovid's *Heroides*, see Howard Jacobson, *Ovid's "Heroides"* (Princeton: Princeton University Press, 1974), 79–82, 87–89, 151–52. For a discussion of the plaintive lament and switches in address in Ovid's *Heroides*, see Linda S. Kauffman, *Discourses of Desire: Gender, Genre, and Epistolary Fictions* (Ithaca: Cornell University Press, 1986), 30–50; Joan DeJean, *Fictions of Sappho, 1546–1937* (Chicago: University of Chicago Press, 1989), 44–49. DeJean primarily discusses Ovid's authority over Sappho as registered in French writers and readers of the Renaissance.

2. Ovid's letter from Sappho to Phaon in the *Heroides* is often cited as an example of a male poet's appropriation of a woman's eroticism to satisfy his own erotic fantasies. Recent arguments surrounding Ovid's *Heroides* 15, however, vary considerably. Howard Jacobson (*Ovid's "Heroides,"* 277–99) sees Ovid as identifying psychologically with Sappho as lover and erotic poet; this often leads him to verbal excess and self-destruction. Florence Verducci (*Ovid's Toyshop of the Heart: Epistulae Heroidum* [Princeton: Princeton University Press, 1985], 156–63) claims that Ovid's appropriation of Sappho's poetic voice underscores his awareness that eroticism undoes a poet's mastery of his art. The recovery of Sappho for twentieth-century feminists also reveals a wide range of interpretations. See Kauffman, *Discourses of Desire,* 30–33, 50–61. Kauffman stresses Ovid's skepticism about the extent to which a person can ever know or represent another person (especially a man representing a woman), while DeJean (*Fictions of Sappho*) emphasizes a Freudian interpretation of Jacobson's argument. See also Lawrence Lipking, *Abandoned Women and Poetic Tradition* (Chicago: University of Chicago Press, 1988), 57–126; Lipking discusses Sappho as a model of a woman poet in relationship to a poetics of abandonment.

3. Randolph Starn (*Contrary Commonwealth: The Theme of Exile in Medieval and Renaissance Italy* [Berkeley: University of California Press, 1982], 24–28 and passim) discusses the connections between the theme of exile, real and fictional, and love elegy in Ovidian verse. He also examines the relationship of the works Ovid composed while in exile—the *De Tristia* and *Epistulae ex Ponto*—with the theme of banishment and attachment to one's homeland. See 25–26, 122, 126–27, for an exploration of the themes of unrequited love and banishment; Starn claims that the mournful poet often substitutes the homeland for the mistress as the object of his desire. The poet also defines his grief as the distance from a specific place, which then becomes, in turn, a separation from himself. For the many classical allusions to this theme, see 25.

4. It is important to note that not all elegies are conceived as laments or poems of mourning. Perhaps only Ovid's elegy on the death of Tibullus could be viewed as specifically a funereal lament, for even Catullus's *carme* 68 blended mourning with other themes. Many amorous elegiac poems, however, deplored the misfortunes of love. The conflation of forms in the ancient elegiac poets' works often confused sixteenth-century theorists; see J. C. Scaliger, *Poetics libri*

septem (Lugduni: Antonium Vicentium, 1561). For a discussion of the theoretical confusion of the nature and uses of classical elegy during the French Renaissance, see Gertrude S. Hanisch, *Love Elegies of the Renaissance: Marot, Louise Labé, Ronsard* (Saratoga, Calif.: Stanford French and Italian Studies, 1979), 10–29; Robert E. Hallowell, *Ronsard and the Conventional Roman Elegy* (Urbana and Chicago: University of Illinois Press, 1954).

Evaluations of women's subjective poetry traditionally collapse the real with the fictional representation of love's misfortunes. See Peter Dronke, *Women Writers of the Middle Ages* (Cambridge: Cambridge University Press, 1984), 84–143; Louise Labé, *Oeuvres complètes de Louise Labé*, ed. François Rigolot (Paris: Garnier Flammarion, 1986), 22; Helisenne de Crenne, *Renaissance Woman: Helisenne's Personal and Invective Letters*, trans. Marianna M. Mustacchi and Paul J. Archambault (Syracuse: Syracuse University Press, 1986), 8–33. Some critics have viewed Veronica Franco's poems as autobiographical confessions. See Arturo Graf, "Una cortigiana fra mille: Veronica Franco," in his *Attraverso il Cinquecento* (Turin: Chiantore, 1888), 232ff.; Giuseppe Tassini, *Veronica Franco: Celebre poetessa e cortigiana del secolo XVI* (Reprint, Venice: Alfieri, 1969), 99–105; Francesco Flora, "Veronica Franco" in his *Storia della letteratura italiana* (Milan: A. Mondadori, 1941), 11:517–20; Riccardo Scrivano, "Veronica Franco," in his *Cultura e letteratura del Cinquecento* (Rome: Ateneo, 1966), 197–228. Scrivano reviews the different critical evaluations of Franco's oeuvre and offers a more thorough stylistic assessment of her poetics. And see A. Giovanni Frugoni, "I capitoli della cortigiana Veronica Franco," *Belfagor* 3 (1948): 44–59.

5. Judith P. Hallett has argued persuasively that the women featured in the elegies of Propertius and Ovid "managed to attain a singularly exalted stature, to be appreciated as people in their own right. Their admirers, moreover, not only glorified them out of genuine adoration, they were also motivated by a powerful, often mischievously subversive desire to differentiate themselves and their own system of values from existing forms of conduct" ("The Role of Women in Roman Elegy: Counter-Cultural Feminism," *Arethusa* 6, no. 1 [1973]: 103–4). All references to Ovid's *Amores* are to John Barsby, ed. and trans., *Ovid: Amores Book I* (Oxford: Clarendon Press, 1973). For books 2 and 3, I cite the recent translation by A. D. Melville, with notes and introduction by E. J. Kenney: *Ovid: The Love Poems* (New York: Oxford University Press, 1990).

On Ovid's ventriloquized female voice in his elegies, especially in the *Heroides*, see Jacobson, *Ovid's "Heroides"*; Kauffman, *Discourses of Desire*, 17–61; Susan Lee Carrell, *Le Soliloque de la passion feminine ou le dialogue illusoire: Etude d'une formule monophonique de la litterature epistolaire* (Paris: Editions Jean-Michel Place, 1982); Janet Gurkin Altman, "Portuguese Writing and Women's Consciousness: The Loneliness of the Long-Distance Lover," *Degré Second* 7 (1983): 163–75; Elizabeth D. Harvey, "Ventriloquizing Sappho: Ovid, Donne, and the Erotics of the Feminine Voice," *Criticism* 31, no. 2 (1989): 115–38. For the view that this appropriation of the female voice was an indication of these poets' dissatisfaction with heroic epic, see Hallett, "Role of Women in Roman Elegy," 109, 111–18. For her examination of Propertius's Cynthia in book 4 of the *Elegies*—a female figure remarkably akin to Franco's self-representation in the *Terze rime*—see 120. All references to Propertius in English are to *The Poems of Propertius*, trans. John Warden (Indianapolis and New York: Bobbs-Merrill, 1972).

6. The Roman elegists' dissatisfaction with martial exploits is discussed in Hallett, "Role of Women in Roman Elegy," 109–17. For further studies that point to ancient authors collapsing political rhetoric with amorous elegy, see David O. Ross, *Style and Tradition in Catullus* (Cambridge: Harvard University Press, 1969), 85–89; Judith P. Hallett, "Book IV: Propertius' Recusatio to Augustus and Augustan Ideals" (Ph.D. diss., Harvard University, 1971).

7. Propertius protests to Maecenas, after his patron pleads with him to write in a loftier vein, "I'm not the one to spread my sails / and scud through the heavy swell. / I'm more at home in the shelter of a tiny stream." (Non ego velitera tumidum mare findo carina, / tota sub exiguo flumine nostra mora est). See *Poems of Propertius,* 3.9.2.

8. Propertius (book 4) presents several Roman women (Arethusa, Tarpeia, Acanthis, and Cornelia) other than his beloved Cynthia, who is more absent here than in the other books. As Judith P. Hallett argues ("Role of Women in Roman Elegy"), the contrast between the independent, intelligent, and faithful Cynthia and these women shows how "they embrace and even embody conventional Roman, that is to say Augustan, beliefs about woman's role" (117). For various depictions of Cynthia in book 4.7 and 8, in which she discredits luxury, infidelity, dishonesty, and materiality, see 120. For useful discussions regarding Propertius's conflicting positions on his attachments and obligations to his native city, see Steele Commager, *A Prolegomenon to Propertius* (Norman: University of Oklahoma Press, 1974); Hans-Peter Stahl, *Propertius: "Love" and "War": Individual and State Under Augustus* (Berkeley: University of California Press, 1985).

9. Howard Jacobson claims (*Ovid's "Heroides,"* 6–7) that Ovid "deheroiz[es] the male mythic hero when he adopts the passionate female monologue from Euripides in his elegiac verse epistles." For an examination of the nature of erotic discourse in Latin elegies, see Antonio La Penna, "Note sul linguaggio erotico dell'elegia latina," *Maia* 4 (1951): 208. On the role of women in ancient Roman society in relation to male elegists, see Hallett, "Role of Women in Roman Elegy," especially with reference to sexual mores and marriage conventions, 104–9; Sara Lilja, *The Roman Love Elegists' Attitude to Women* (Helsinki: Suomalainen Tiedeakatemia, 1965), 31–42. See also P. E. Corbett, *The Roman Law of Marriage* (Oxford: Oxford University Press, 1930), 68–106; J. A. Crook, *Law and Life of Rome* (Ithaca: Cornell University Press, 1967), 100 and passim; Sarah B. Pomeroy, *Goddesses, Whores, Wives, and Slaves: Women in Classical Antiquity* (New York: Schocken Books, 1975), especially 149–226, for an examination of Roman society; *Women's Life in Greece and Rome,* ed. Mary R. Lefkowitz and Maureen B. Fant (Baltimore: Johns Hopkins University Press, 1982); idem, *Heroines and Hysterics* (New York: Saint Martin's Press, 1981).

10. On the charge that women embody dissimulation, and in relation to Ovid's Sappho in the *Heroides,* see Kauffman, *Discourses of Desire,* 52–61. See also Elizabeth D. Harvey, "Ventriloquizing Sappho: Ovid, Donne, and the Erotics of the Feminine Voice," *Criticism* 31, no. 2 (1989): 115–38; she argues that Ovid's epistle subordinates the woman poet's voice to his own, thereby providing an "indelible legacy that displaced the authority of her own words, blurring the boundaries between 'authentic' and constructed discourse" (118). Susan Gubar ("Sapphistries," *Signs* 10 (1984): 43–62) focuses on Sappho as a powerful female precursor for women poets. See also Judith P. Hallett, "Sappho and Her Social Context: Sense and Sensuality," *Signs* 4 (1979): 447–64, and Eva Stehle Stiger's response, 465–71.

11. The concept of "amor mutuo" (mutual love) possibly echoes Venetian humanists' concerns with love in marriage as articulated by Francesco Barbaro in his 1416 treatise *De re uxoria,* part of which was written to celebrate the marriage of Lorenzo de' Medici and Ginevra Cavalcanti. Although he advocates the home as the woman's proper realm, and believes that all of her activities should concentrate on the well-being of her children and the comfort of her husband, Barbaro also believes that husband and wife should offer one another "mutual love . . . freely and diligently acquired, nurtured and preserved." On this treatise, and for an English translation, see *The Earthly Republic: Italian Humanists on Government and Society,* ed. Benjamin G. Kohl and Ronald G. Witt (Philadelphia: University of Pennsylvania Press, 1978),

198. On the bonds of love in marriage in the late fifteenth century in Venice, see Stanley Chojnacki, "The Power of Love: Wives and Husbands in Late Medieval Venice," in *Women and Power in the Middle Ages,* ed. Mary Erler and Maryanne Kowaleski (Athens: University of Georgia Press, 1988), 126–48.

12. On Ovid's break with poetic and rhetorical traditions, see Gordon Williams, *Tradition and Originality in Roman Poetry* (Oxford: Clarendon Press, 1968), and *Figures of Thought in Roman Poetry* (New Haven: Yale University Press, 1980). For Ovid's uses of monologue in his elegies, see Herbert Frankel, *Ovid: A Poet between Two Worlds* (Berkeley: University of California Press, 1945), 45 and passim; L. P. Wilkinson, *Ovid Recalled* (Cambridge: Cambridge University Press, 1955); Brooks Otis, *Ovid as an Epic Poet* (Cambridge: Cambridge University Press, 1970), 15–18; Jacobson, *Ovid's "Heroides,"* 7, 337–39, 346, and passim.

13. The *rimembranza* and *dipartita* themes in lyric poetry were popular among Italian quattrocento poets such as Tebaldeo, Serafino Aquilano, Panfilo Sasso, and Niccolo da Correggio, who carried on a Petrarchan lyric tradition which had its roots in classical elegy. Petrarch refers to the term "dipartita" in his *canzone* 37 ("Si è debile il filo a cui s'attene") which echoes Dante's "Amor, da che convien pur ch'io mi doglia." On the quattrocento poets, see *Poesia italiana: Il Quattrocento,* ed. Carlo Oliva (Milan: Garzanti, 1978), 219–77. And for examples of this theme in the classical tradition, see, among others, Ovid, *Amores* 1.15 and 2.16, and Propertius, *Elegies* 1.18 and 2.32. See also the informative essay on this quattrocento lyric tradition, with an emphasis on Ariosto, by Antonia Tissoni Benvenuti: "La tradizione della terza rima e l'Ariosto," in *Ludovico Ariosto: Lingua, stile e tradizione,* ed. Cesare Segre (Milan: Feltrinelli, 1976), 305–13. On the notion of a self-reflexive lament or *rimembranza* that precludes any possibility of an outside referentiality, most evident in pastoral elegy, see Ellen Z. Lambert, *Placing Sorrow: A Study of the Pastoral Elegy Convention from Theocritus to Milton* (Chapel Hill: University of North Carolina Press, 1976). On the compression of time and its use as a structural component in all lyrical sequences, see Roland Green, *Post-Petrarchism: Origins and Innovations of the Western Lyric Sequence* (Princeton: Princeton University Press, 1991), 22–58; on Petrarch's indebtedness to Ovid, Catullus, and especially Propertius, see 34–43. See also Thomas M. Greene, *The Light in Troy: Imitation and Discovery in Renaissance Poetry* (New Haven: Yale University Press, 1982), 138–41 and passim; Leonard Barkan, *The Gods Made Flesh: Metamorphosis and the Pursuit of Paganism* (New Haven: Yale University Press, 1986).

14. Amedeo Quondam (*Le "carte messaggiere": Retorica e modelli di communicazione epistolare* [Rome: Bulzoni, 1981], 57) suggests that Franco's letters are composed according to fictional thematic models, that is, *concetti,* rather than as "real" letters dispatched according to the *segretario* model. In this sense, Franco's letters offer glosses on themes or topics addressed in her *Terze rime.* For the view that Franco's letters combine to form an epistolary autobiography, see Marcella Diberti Leigh, *Veronica Franco: Donna, poetessa e cortigiana del Rinascimento* (Ivrea: Priuli and Verlucca, 1988), 219–23 and passim; Elvira Favretti, "Rime e Lettere di Veronica Franco," *Giornale storico della letteratura italiana* 163, no. 523 (1986): 358–61. Favretti defines the poems as "una raccolta di lettere in versi" (a grouping of letters in verse) that can be read in tandem with the letters.

15. For golden age themes in Latin poets and in Italian and English Renaissance poetry, see A. Bartlett Giamatti, *The Earthly Paradise and the Renaissance Epic* (Princeton: Princeton University Press, 1966), especially chap. 1; David Quint, *Origin and Originality in Renaissance Literature: Versions of the Source* (New Haven: Yale University Press, 1983), 43–81; Harry Levin, *The Myth of the Golden Age in the Renaissance* (New York: Oxford University Press, 1969), 1–57.

16. Much has been written about the genre of the English country-house poem in the sixteenth and seventeenth centuries. The works most useful to this study have been Don Wayne, *Penshurst: The Semiotics of Place and the Poetics of History* (Madison: University of Wisconsin Press, 1984); Heather Dubrow, "The Country-House Poem: A Study in Generic Development," *Genre* 12, no. 2 (1979): 153–79. For a recent sociohistorical and architectural evaluation of the development of the villa in Italy during the sixteenth century, see James Ackerman, *The Villa: Form and Ideology of Country Houses* (Princeton: Princeton University Press, 1990).

17. On the metonymic relation between the unknowable aspects of the plague as Boccaccio describes it in the introduction to the *Decameron*, and the distresses caused by unrequited passion because of its power to confuse and distort one's ability to reason, see Giuseppe Mazzotta, *The World at Play in Boccaccio's Decameron* (Princeton: Princeton University Press, 1986), 22–36. All references to the *Decameron*, unless otherwise stated, are taken from *Tutte le opere di Giovanni Boccaccio*, vol. 4, *Decameron*, ed. Vittore Branca (Milan: Mondadori, 1976). For the translation I refer to here, see Giovanni Boccaccio, *Decameron*, trans. G. H. McWilliam (New York: Penguin Books, 1972).

18. For bibliography on the plague in Venice in 1575–77, see chapter 1 nn. 37 and 123.

19. The writers who met in Domenico Venier's home in Santa Maria Formosa before the academy was formed most probably also frequented the academy's meetings in the Libreria Sansoviniana in Piazza San Marco. While there is no documented evidence to affirm that academy members were the same group who met at Ca' Venier, it is certain that the leading intellectuals in Venice, most of whom were patricians, met in Venier's salon after the academy's demise in 1561, a year after the meetings had transferred to Federigo Badoer's private house. For an overview of the academy, see chapter 2 above. See also Michele Maylender, *Storia della accademie d'Italia* (Bologna: 1926–30), 5:446; Pietro Pagan, "Sulla Accademia 'Venetiana' o della 'Fama,'" *Atti dell'Istituto Veneto di Scienze, Lettere ed Arti* 132 (1973–74): 359–92; Paul Lawrence Rose, "The *Accademia Venetiana*: Science and Culture in Renaissance Venice," *Studi veneziani* 11 (1969): 191–242; Lina Bolzoni, "L'Accademia Veneziana: Splendore e decadenza di una utopia enciclopedica," in *Università, accademie e società scientifiche in Italia e in Germania dal Cinquecento al Settecento*, ed. Laetitia Boehm and Ezio Raimondi (Bologna: Il Mulino, 1982), 117–69.

20. On late-sixteenth-century Venetian poets' insistence on widening Bembo's formal perimeters for the lyric, see Carlo Dionisotti, *Geografia e storia della letteratura italiana* (Turin: Einaudi, 1967), 169–77; Lina Bolzoni, "L'Accademia Veneziana," 120 n. 11, 135–36; Giancarlo Mazzacurati, *Conflitti di culture* (Naples: Liguori, 1977), 237 and passim. Mazzacurati studies the impact of Bembo's theories, especially with regard to Florentine poets of the period.

21. The importance of the academy's list of projected publications for understanding the relations between the press, nobility, and literary trends in Venice in this period was first discussed in depth by Lina Bolzoni ("L'Accademia Veneziana," 121–24, 128–46). She indicates that there were two versions printed, one in Latin and one in the vernacular. Both printed lists were circulated throughout Italy and in Germany, and a third one was printed especially for the Frankfurt book fair. See also Anna Laura Puliafito, "Due lettere del Pinelli e l'Accademia della Fama," *Studi veneziani* 18 (1989): 285–98. The full title is: *Somma delle opere che in tutte le scientie et arti più nobili, et in varie lingue ha da mandare in luce l'Accademia Venetiana, parte nuove et non più stampate, parte con fedelissime tradottioni, giudiciose corretioni et utilissime annotationi riformate* (1558). The Latin title reads: *Summa librorum quos . . . in lucem emittet Academia Venetiana* (1559). For this third list, see Puliafito, "Due lettere," 289 n. 17.

22. Federigo Badoer, the academy's principal founder, saw his mission as invoking the classical splendor of ancient Rome, a republic that was often compared to Venice. The publications sponsored by the academy therefore proposed classical editions in the vernacular, accompanied by commentaries. On the connections between a Christian interpretation of classical texts and the reemergence of ancient philosophy, see Bolzoni, "L'Accademia Veneziana," 154–59. Bolzoni also examines the decorations of the academy's rooms as emulating classical texts and architecture. On the classicizing decorations of the Libreria Sansoviniana, see Nicola Ivanoff, "Il ciclo allegorico della Libreria Sansoviniana," in *Arte antica e moderna* (Florence: Sansoni, 1961): 248–59. On the academy's motto, which depicts Fortune with one foot on the globe announcing with a trumpet the academy's *impresa*, see Pompeo G. Molmenti, *La storia di Venezia nella vita privata dalle origini alla caduta della repubblica*, 5th ed. (Bergamo: Istituto italiano d'arte grafiche, 1928), 308–9.

23. The *Somma* also lists Homer, Virgil, Lucretius, and Seneca as ancient authors to be studied and printed. For the resurgence of interest in Venice in Platonic hermeticism and Neoplatonism in a study of lyric poetry that echoes the fifteenth-century Florentine tradition of interpreting poetry in a philosophical vein, see Bolzoni, "L'Accademia Veneziana," 134–38.

24. Catullus played a part in the genesis of Roman elegy. Many of his more introspective poems are in elegiac couplets and are addressed to his *domina*, "Lesbia," with whom he professes he can live neither with nor without. The entry in the *Somma* reads: "Catullo, con un breve discorso innanzi del proprio stato dell'endecasillabo; dal quale si conoscerà per qual cagione l'endecasillabo di questo poeta avanzi di gran lunga tutti gli altri, che in questo genere di versi hanno scritto, con una dichiaratione de' maravigliosi aggiunti poetici usati da lui ne' versi heroici, e degli affetti grandissimi, che ha sparsi fra le sue elegie" (Catullus, with a brief introduction about the status of the hendecasyllable; from which it will be easily understood why this poet's hendecasyllable is so much superior to that written by many other poets in this genre; along with an exposition of the marvelous poetic additions used by him in heroic verses, and the grandest affects (emotions) he has scattered throughout his elegies.) (3)

25. The entry on Tibullus reads, "Tibullo con gli avvertimenti di tutte le sue bellezze, al quale anderà innanzi una dotta consideratione, onde sarà chiaramente dimostrato la sua candidezza, et il vero modo di comporre elegie" (Tibullus, with notes on all of his beautiful qualities, to be preceded by a learned comment that clearly demonstrates his candor, and the proper way of composing elegies.) (3)

26. Ibid., 3.

27. The entry in the *Somma delle opere* reads: "Tutte le opere di Ovidio, con un trattato innanzi in verso heroico: nel quale si dimostra il meraviglioso artificio da lui usato nella concatenazione di una favola con l'altra; e dichiaresi a parte a parte gli alti misteri nascosti sotto il velame di esse favole; et un altro innanzi alle compositioni fatte nel verso elego, dove si considera quanta forza habbia havuto nel muover gli affetti quasi in tutte queste opere; et poi quanto nelle epistole scritte sotto 'l nome delle donne heroine vaglia nella persuasione" (All of Ovid's works preceded by a treatise in heroic verse: in which will be demonstrated the marvelous skill used by him in linking one fable to the next; and, separately, will be explained the deep mysteries concealed behind the veil of these fables; and a further consideration prefacing the compositions written in elegiac verse, in which will be examined how strongly he has stirred the affects (emotions) in almost all of these works; and furthermore, how great is his ability to persuade in the letters written in the name of his heroic women.) (28).

28. Remigio Fiorentino's translation (*Epistole d'Ovidio di Remigio Fiorentino: Divise in due libri. Con le dichiarationi in margine delle favole e dell'historie* [Venice: Oratio de' Gobbi, 1581]) was also published earlier, in 1555. For Camilli's translation, see his *L'Epistole d'Ovidio* (Venice: Giovanni Battista Ciotti, 1587); and for information on his other translations and poetic works, see *Dizionario biografico degli italiani* 17:210. In a seminal essay, Carlo Dionisotti examines the impact that classical poets had on the Italian lyric in the fifteenth and sixteenth centuries (*Geografia e storia*, 156–63). For an analysis of the popularity of Ovid's *Heroides* during the Renaissance in France, see Anne Moss, *Ovid in Renaissance France: A Survey of the Latin Editions of Ovid and Commentaries Printed in France Before 1600* (London: Warburg, 1982). For a survey of the many translations of Ovid's texts into the vernacular during the sixteenth century in Italy and throughout Europe, and for a partial list of cinquecento vernacular versions of Ovid's *Metamorphoses*, see Nicolae Lascu, "La fortuna di Ovidio dal Rinascimento ai tempi nostri," *Studi Ovidiani* (1959): 81–95. See Bodo Guthmuller, *Ovidio Metamorphoseos Vulgare: Formen und Funktionen der volkssprachlichen Wiedergabe klassischer Dichtung in der italienischen Renaissance* (Boppard am Rhein: Harold Boldt Verlag, 1981), for translations in 1333–1561.

29. See below nn. 38–45.

30. The rediscovery of Provençal poetry in this period is discussed in Mazzacurati, *Conflitti di culture*, 136–38. See also Marianne Shapiro, "The Provençal *Trobairitz* and the Limits of Courtly Love," *Signs* 3, no. 31 (1978): 560–71. Shapiro suggests that Ovid's *Heroides* intersect with the women troubadours' lyric poems.

31. Dionisotti, *Geografia e storia*, 170–71.

32. On Bernardo Tasso's involvement and influence in the Accademia della Fama, see Edward Williamson, *Bernardo Tasso* (Rome: Edizioni di storia e letteratura, 1951), 30 and passim; Giorgio Cerboni Baiardi, *La lirica di Bernardo Tasso* (Urbino: Argaglia, 1966), 68 and passim. For the publication of his *Amadigi*, see Bolzoni, "L'Accademia Veneziana," 124–27. For this letter, see 127.

33. Bolzoni, "L'Accademia Veneziana," 157–58.

34. On Bernardo Tasso's departure from Venice and his renting a house on the island of Murano, see ibid., 158.

35. For a history and an explanation of the academy's failure, see ibid., 159–67.

36. Paolo Manuzio was the academy's official printer. When he left Venice for Rome in 1560, the academy was not able to recover from his absence. On this, see ibid., 159. For ties established between Venetian writers and the powerful printing industry in Venice during the sixteenth century, see Amedeo Quondam, "Nel giardino di Marcolini: Un editore veneziano tra Aretino e Doni," *Giornale storico della letteratura italiana* 157 (1980): 75–105; Paul F. Grendler, "Venetian Presses and *Poligrafi*," in his *Critics of the Italian World, 1530–1560: Anton Francesco Doni, Nicolò Franco, and Ortensio Lando* (Madison: University of Wisconsin Press, 1969), 3–20; idem, *The Roman Inquisition and the Venetian Press, 1540–1605* (Princeton: Princeton University Press, 1977), 3–16.

37. Torquato Tasso composed his youthful work, the *Rinaldo*, in Padua the same year his father printed his *Ragionamento della poesia* for academy members in Venice. Torquato Tasso refers to Domenico Venier's inspiration in *Rinaldo* 19.30. For a study of *Rinaldo*, see Michael Sherberg, "Epic and Romance in Tasso's *Rinaldo:* The Conflict of Genre," *Stanford Italian Review* 9, nos. 1–2 (1990): 67–85.

38. On Claudio Tolomei's *Versi et regole della nuova poesia toscana* (Rome: Antonio Blado d'Asola, 1539), see Dionisotti, *Geografia e storia*, 174. I refer here to the 1563 edition: (Venice:

Gabriel Giolito de' Ferrari), book 3, 208, 213–14. See also Lodovico Dolce, *I quattro libri delle osservationi* (Venice: Domenico Farri, 1566). Bernardo Tasso's *Rime* . . . *divise in cinque libri* (Venice: Gabriel Giolito de' Ferrari, 1560) is a notable example of a hybrid collection of lyrical forms (odes, pastoral eclogues, elegies) drawn from both antiquity and early romance genres. On the importance of "volgarizzamenti" (vernacular translations) in Italian poetic practices of the sixteenth century, see Dionisotti, *Geografia e storia*, 125–78.

39. Dolce, *I quattro libri delle osservationi*, 208.

40. Girolamo Muzio, *Rime diverse del Mutio* and *Dell'arte poetica* (Venice: Gabriel Giolito de' Ferrari, 1551), 72.

41. For a discussion of Bembo's rhetorical and poetic codification of the vernacular, in which he affirms his theory that the vernacular enjoyed equal dignity with Latin, and the impact that this had on the Venetian printing industry and Venetian literati such as those discussed here, see Pasquale Sabbatino, *La "scienza" della scrittura: Dal progetto del Bembo al manuale* (Florence: Leo S. Olschki Editore, 1988).

42. Giovan Battista Pigna, *I Romanzi* (Venice: Vincenzo Valgrisi, 1554), is dedicated to Luigi d'Este. See 54–55 for a discussion of the nature of terza rima verse. On the uses of terza rima for elegy, see 62. For an evaluation of Ariosto's uses of elegy, see 73.

43. Dolce, *I quattro libri delle osservationi*, 213–14.

44. On the appointment of Celio Magno as the academy's official translator, see Bolzoni, "L'Accademia Veneziana," 120–21 nn. 13, 14, and 137 n. 70. For contemporary treatises on the problems in translation from Latin into the vernacular, see Orazio Toscanella, *Per tradurre* (Venice: Pietro de' Franceschi, 1575); Fausto da Longiano, *Dialogo del modo de lo tradurre d'una in altra lingua* (Venice: Giovanni Griffo dell'Avanzi, 1556).

45. Sebastiano Erizzo (1525–85), one of the academy's most prominent members, characterizes the specific passions expressed in the classical elegiac lament, as well as in Petrarch's verses, in his *Espositione di M. Sebastiano Erizzo delle tre canzoni di Francesco Petrarca* (Venice: Andrea Arrivabene, 1561). For this passage, see 3. He speaks about how the elegiac love lyric must express the soul's conflicting passions. On passion as a philosophical principle in the sixteenth century, see Anthony Levi, *French Moralists: The Theory of the Passions, 1585 to 1649* (Oxford: Clarendon Press, 1964), 1–63.

46. Erizzo, *Espositione*, 3.

47. I cite from another edition of this often-printed work. See Girolamo Ruscelli, *Del modo di comporre in versi nella lingua italiana* (Venice: Giovanni Battista Sessa, 1582), 92.

48. Ibid., 140.

49. Dionisotti, *Geografia e storia*, 239.

50. Many of these observations refer to, and are indebted to, the discussion of the exordiums in Ovid's *Heroides* in Jacobson, *Ovid's "Heroides,"* 349–56, 365–66, 401–6. I first discussed these poems in "Veronica Franco: The Courtesan as Poet in Sixteenth-Century Venice" (Ph.D. diss., Yale University, 1985), 92–235; and "A Courtesan's Voice: Epistolary Self-Portraiture in Veronica Franco's *Terze Rime*," in *Writing the Female Voice: Essays on Epistolary Literature*, ed. Elizabeth C. Goldsmith (Boston: Northeastern University Press, 1989), 3–24. See also Ann Rosalind Jones, "City Women and Their Audiences: Louise Labé and Veronica Franco," in *Rewriting the Renaissance: The Discourses of Sexual Difference in Early Modern Europe*, ed. Margaret W. Ferguson, Maureen Quilligan, and Nancy J. Vickers (Chicago: University of Chicago Press, 1986), 299–316. According to the definition I propose here, a verse love letter (or *epistola amorosa*) differs from a capitolo that is merely elegiac (plaintive or deploring love's misfortunes) in

nature or theme. In the first type, the fiction claims that the poem is sent to a specific lover, who then responds in turn with another letter, whereas in the second, no answer is requested. These verse epistles represent both the speaker's inner psychological state and the interpersonal dynamic between lovers.

51. A comparison of the direct addresses in Veronica Franco's capitoli 3, 17, and 20 with the exordiums in *Heroides* 1, 2, and 4, as they appear in Camillo Camilli's translations, demonstrate the similarities between the two:

> *Penelope la Casta al tardo Ulisse*
> *senza aspettare altra risposta hormai,*
> *questa per far, ch'a lei ritorni, scrisse.* (1.1–3)

> *Fillide hospite tua son'io, ch'il giorno,*
> *Demofonte mi doglio esser passato,*
> *che da noi si prescisse al tuo ritorno.* (2.1–3)

> *La Guerrier Amazonio una cretese*
> *manda salute, e corre a mortal danno*
> *s'ei si salute a lei non è cortese.* (4.1–3)

52. On the double letters, see Jacobson, *Ovid's "Heroides,"* ix, 317. See also Marina Scordilis Brownlee, *The Severed Word: Ovid's Heroides and the Novela Sentimental* (Princeton: Princeton University Press, 1990), 23–36, for a discussion of the dialogic nature of the Ovidian epistle.

53. The musical force and rhythm of the elegiac lament was intended to move the reader (and the letter's recipient) to feel compassion and pity. Unlike a solitary and self-reflexive elegiac monologue that forbids any intimate communion with the reader because of its closed, circular system and its failure to make an authentic contact with an external person, the letter form allows the reader to participate in a silent dialogue with the letter writer. The letter functions not only as a dialogue with the self and the letter's interlocutor but as a dialogue with the imaginary reader. We can read ourselves into either the letter writer's role or into that of the mute recipient. Paradoxically, this affective state can be effected only if the pleasure imparted by the words, or the emotions they evoke, match the lack of pleasure, or denial of pleasure, that the speaker is forced to endure.

54. See Lambert, *Placing Sorrow.* It is important to note that not all elegies are conceived as laments, or poems of mourning. Perhaps only Ovid's elegy on the death of Tibullus could be specifically viewed as a funeral lament, for even Catullus's *carme* 68 blended mourning with other themes. Ovid, in his *Remedia Amoris* 379, proposed a new definition for elegy: "blanda pharetratos Elegia cantet Amores." Loeb Classical Library, trans. J. H. Mozley (Cambridge: Harvard University Press, 1929). For Catullus, see *Catullus, Tibullus, and Pervigilium Veneris,* Loeb Classical Library (Cambridge: Harvard University Press, 1956).

55. As in Boccaccio's *Elegia di Madonna Fiammetta* and Ariosto's love poems, the *Capitoli,* an exchange of voices, sometimes only in the lover's imagination, or sometimes as a dialogue, mirrors the conflicting emotions that the lover feels. For a discussion of the strategies used by Boccaccio in his solipsistic stream-of-consciousness narrative, see Janet Levarie Smarr, *Boccaccio and Fiammetta: The Narrator as Lover* (Urbana and Chicago: University of Illinois Press, 1986), especially 129–48; Smarr comments on the affinities between Boccaccio's work and Ovid's *Heroides,* as well as with Dante's *Inferno.* See also Brownlee, *Severed Word,* 58–69. Brownlee speaks of Ovid's *Heroides* in terms of the intended readers (women), and discusses the nature of the epistolary monologue conceived as a diary both inviting a female reader and preventing her from reading

what she has written. Brownlee sees Fiammetta's monologue as a "specular image of herself" which Boccaccio, as author, "voyeuristically" reveals to a reading public much as Ovid had. Ovid had exposed his heroines' intimate discourses to a male public. See Giovanni Boccaccio, *Elegia di Madonna Fiammetta,* in *Opere,* ed. Cesare Segre (Milan: Mursia, 1966), 943–1081; and see the recent translation, *The Elegy of Lady Fiammetta,* ed. and trans. Mariangela Causa-Steindler and Thomas Mauch (Chicago: University of Chicago Press, 1990).

56. The door, an extended symbol of sexual frustration and impenetrability, also acted as a foil for classical elegists' moral invectives against society's corrupt mores. Ovid went a step further than Propertius. He transformed the self-absorbed lover's address to the door into a comic parody of the lover's bondage and the doorkeeper's servility. Some of the sources for Propertius's lament in 1.16 are the plays of Plautus (*Curculio*), Terence (*Eunuctius*), and Aristophanes (*Lysistrata*). On the theme of the *exclusus amator,* see Frank O. Copley, *Exclusus Amator: A Study in Latin Love Poetry* (Madison, Wis.: American Philological Association, 1956), 20–85 and passim. I would like to thank Ann Rosalind Jones for pointing out to me the importance of this theme for Franco's capitolo 20. For examples in antiquity of a woman singing this kind of lament before the door, and for Ovid's parodic play with this theme, see Barsby, *Ovid,* 18–21.

57. On the uses of Plautus in cinquecento plays in Italy, see Giulio Ferroni, *Il testo e la scena: Saggi sul teatro del Cinquecento* (Rome: Bulzoni, 1980), 76–84. An interesting literary tradition in Venice (although of more popular origin) depicted female characters' conflicts in love. Among Venetian writers who dealt with this theme was Leonardo Giustinian (1388–1446), the author of *I Contrasti* and the anonymous author of the comedy in Venetian dialect, *La Venexiana.* For a discussion of this play and its references both to this popular literary tradition and to the importance of its female characters, see Giorgio Padoan, "La Venexiana 'non fabula non comedia ma vera historia,'" in *Momenti del rinascimento veneto* (Padua: Editore Antenore, 1978), 284–347; and Ludovico Zorzi, trans. and ed., *La Venexiana* (Turin: Einaudi, 1979). For a comprehensive bibliography on the play, see 101–19. On Leonardo Giustinian's poetry, see Manlio Dazzi, *Leonardo Giustinian poeta popolare d'amore* (Bari: Laterza, 1934).

58. On the Renaissance rhetorical tradition of praise and blame as also connected to oratory, see *Renaissance Eloquence: Studies in the Theory and Practice of Renaissance Eloquence,* ed. James J. Murphy (Berkeley: University of California Press, 1983), 199, 204, 239, 241, 377.

59. Some examples of some of the rhyme schemes proposed by Franco in capitolo 3 and then followed by the *incerto autore* in capitolo 4 are: *scrive/amante/vive; piante/core/sembiante; vigore/aspetto/dolore* (capitolo 3), and *s'ascrive/tante/descrive; sante/ardore/diamante; fore/petto/amore* (capitolo 4).

60. For this myth, see Ovid's *Metamorphoses* 3.359–98; for the myth as adopted by women writers, see Patricia Kleindienst Joplin, "The Voice of the Shuttle Is Ours," *Stanford Literature Review* 1 (1983): 25–53; Ann Rosalind Jones, "Surprising Fame: Renaissance Gender Ideologies and Women's Lyric," in *The Poetics of Gender,* ed. Nancy K. Miller (New York: Columbia University Press, 1986), 80–81; idem, "New Songs for the Swallow: Ovid's Philomela in Tullia d'Aragona and Gaspara Stampa," in *Refiguring Woman: Gender Studies and the Italian Renaissance,* ed. Marilyn Migiel and Juliana Schiesari (Ithaca: Cornell University Press, 1991), 263–77; idem, *The Currency of Eros* (Bloomington and Indianapolis: Indiana University Press, 1990), 115–16, 138–39, 212 n. 39; Wendy Pfeiffer, *The Change of Philomel* (New York: Peter Lang, 1985), especially 8–21 for classical sources. On the use of myth as a poetic device in Renaissance lyric poetry, with particular reference to the Petrarchan tradition's use of the Ovidian texts, see, among others, Nancy J. Vickers, "Diana Described: Scattered Woman and Scattered Rhyme,"

in *Writing and Sexual Difference,* ed. Elizabeth Abel (Chicago: University of Chicago Press, 1982), 95–111; Giuseppe Mazzotta, "The *Canzoniere* and the Language of the Self," *Studies in Philology* 75 (1978): 271–96.

61. For the topos of the tearstained letter, see Jacobson, *Ovid's "Heroides,"* 388–90; and Kauffman, *Discourses of Desire,* 36–37. Kauffman speaks of the tears as legal proof, that is, as evidence of physical and psychic suffering uniting the body and text into one form of grief. Examples in Ovid, Catullus, and Propertius are, respectively, Ovid, *Ars amatoria* 2.729–32, *Heroides* 3.3–4, 15.97–98, 178–79; Catullus, *carme* 68.1–2; Propertius, *Elegie* 4.3.3–4, 3.266–67. For other conventional themes of elegiac poetry, including the *exclusus amator* topos, see Hallowell, *Ronsard and the Conventional Roman Elegy.*

62. All references to the *Heroides* are to the Italian-Latin bilingual edition. See *Le eroidi,* trans. Gabriella Leto (Turin: Einaudi, 1966).

63. 1.75–76.

64. On the figure of the blind cupid, see Erwin Panofsky, *Studies in Iconology* (New York: Harper and Row, 1939), 95–128. On the role of "anteros" in the love relationship, see idem, *Problems in Titian: Mostly Iconographic* (New York: New York University Press, 1969), 129 and passim; Edgar Wind, *Pagan Mysteries in the Renaissance* (New York: W. W. Norton, 1958), 53–80.

65. For the entire elegy, see Propertius, *Poems of Propertius* 4.8.

66. For other scenes of male sexual betrayal in Propertius's text, where Cynthia berates him for his lack of fidelity and his drunkenness, and Propertius regards her anger as a form of sexual passion, see 1.3; 3.8; 4.7.

67. In the *commedia grave* tradition (made popular by Bernardino Pino, Luigi Pasqualigo, Girolamo Bargagli, Giambattista Della Porta and others), a product of the latter half of the sixteenth century and the Counter-Reformation, the courtesan was often portrayed comically and ironically, in contrast to the noble aristocratic woman and the unfaithful male lover, as the upholder of morality and the champion of scholarly pursuits. On the advent of this "good-natured whore" in the dramatic tradition, see Louise George Clubb, "Castiglione's Humanist Art and Renaissance Drama," in *Castiglione: The Ideal and the Real in Renaissance Culture,* ed. Robert W. Hanning and David Rosand (New Haven: Yale University Press, 1983), 191–208. A scene in Bernardino Pino's *Gli ingiusti sdegni* (Rome: 1553) clearly characterizes this ironic role reversal and helps identify the specific comic tone of betrayal in Veronica Franco's capitolo 17. In act 3.4, Aurelia the courtesan speaks with her maid Gianotta about the virtues of study and about how she has financially supported her lover's interest in acquiring knowledge. On the popularity of this type of "serious comedy" in Europe, a term, as Louise George Clubb notes, that was once applied to humanistic comedy, and on the courtesan as a "strikingly sympathetic figure," see Louise George Clubb, *Italian Drama in Shakespeare's Time* (New Haven: Yale University Press, 1989), 52–63, especially 56–57. On Pino da Cagli, see Walter Temelini, "The Life and Works of Bernardino Pino da Cagli" (Ph.D. diss., University of Toronto, 1969).

68. Throughout the *Terze rime,* Veronica Franco refers to her own name within the context of her argument for individual freedom, honesty, or liberation from male deception and treachery. For another example of this play on names, see capitolo 8.1–2, "Ben vorrei fosse, come dite voi, / Ch'io vivessi d'amor libera, e franca." On the semiotic value of a proper name in Renaissance poetry, see François Rigolot, *Poétique et onomastique: L'exèmple de la Renaissance* (Geneva: Droz, 1977). For the many definitions of *franco,* see *Vocabolario degli Accademici della Crusca* (Florence: 1889), 4:441–45. For the possible derivation from, or connection to, the Provençal

attributes for the epithet *franc,* see Glynnis M. Cropp, *Le vocabulaire courtois des troubadours de l'époque classique* (Geneva: Droz, 1975), 83–88.

69. The source for this theme comes from Ovid's *Ars amatoria* 2:523–28 and 3:579–88. I refer to the Italian-Latin edition, *Ovidio: L'arte di amare,* trans. Latino Maccari (Turin: Einaudi, 1969).

70. Veronica Franco's borrowing from an ancient theatrical tradition may be certainly linked to a resurgence of interest in Plautus's texts, which were translated into the vernacular in the cinquecento. The *Somma delle opere's* entry on Plautus reads: "Le commedie di Plauto purgate da molte errori, con alcuni avvertimenti delle usanze tenute da gli antichi nel recitar le commedie" (28). On this tradition, see Ferroni, *Il testo e la scena,* 76–84.

71. In Propertius 1.16, the door is the speaker throughout. As Catullus had done before him in *carme* 67 ("O dulce iocunda viro, iocunda parenti"), the door attests to the *domina's* lack of fidelity. In addition to the primary sources already cited, see Horace, *Carme* 1.25, trans. W. Bennet (London: Heinemann, 1934). On this point, see Barsby, *Ovid,* 71–81. For Ovid's treatment of this theme, see Kathleen Morgan, *Ovid's Art of Imitation: Propertius in the Amores* (Brill: Lugduni Bavatorum, 1977). Ovid parodies not only the self-absorbed lover's lament (as interpreted by the door) but also the moralistic tone traditionally expressed in the *paraclausithyron* in both Propertius 1.16 and Catullus, *Carme* 67. Ovid makes the doorkeeper an easily corruptible figure, capable of acquiescing to the lover's pleas.

72. *La Venexiana,* trans. and ed. Ludovico Zorzi (Turin: Einaudi, 1979). On the double roles of the women characters and on sexual doubling, see Franca Angelini, "La Venexiana: Spazi e tempi dello 'sperimentare,'" *Letteratura e società,* ed. G. Petronio (Palermo: Palumbo, 1980), 129–39.

73. The male lover's lament in Propertius 1.16 does not succeed, however, in softening the stern "ianua's" rigidity, for as the door reports, the lover scolds it for staying tightly shut before him. See Antonio La Penna, *L'integrazione difficile: Un profilo di Properzio* (Turin: Einaudi, 1977), 364–65.

74. In Ovid's text, the male lover believes the "ianator" does not keep his expected vigil of the door because *he* is making love to a woman. On this series of *captatio benevolentiae* in Ovid's text, see John Barsby, ed. and trans., *Ovid: Amores Book I* (Oxford: Clarendon Press, 1973), 71–81.

75. Dante, *The Divine Comedy,* trans. Charles S. Singleton (Princeton: Princeton University Press, 1970), *Purgatory,* 3:95.

76. On the servility of the doorkeeper, see Copley, *Exclusus Amator,* 126.

77. On Louise Labé and elegy, see Jones, *The Currency of Eros,* 173–78; Hanisch, *Love Elegies of the Renaissance,* 53–73.

78. On the myth of Echo, see Ovid's *Metamorphoses* 3.356–401. For a study of this myth as a theory of allusion, especially in English poetry, see John Hollander, *The Figure of Echo: A Mode of Allusion in Milton and After* (Berkeley: University of California Press, 1981).

79. There are many references to this theme in Ovid's elegies. See, among others, *Amores* 2.16.11–12 and 2.16.33. Also see Ariosto, *Rime,* ed. Segre, 175–77 (capitolo 5, "Meritamente ora punir mi veggio"), where this theme often appears. For an incisive analysis of Ariosto's use of the term "errore" in the *Orlando furioso* as signaling a deviation ("errare") from the epic norm in favor of romance, see Patricia Parker, *Inescapable Romance* (Princeton: Princeton University Press, 1983), 6–53, and 245–50. On the remedy of travel, see Ovid, *Remedia amoris* 2.237–48. For a sixteenth-century translation into the vernacular, see Angelo Ingegneri, *De rimedi contro l'amore* (Avignon: Pietro Rosso, 1576).

80. For the Petrarchan text, see *Petrarch's Lyric Poems*, ed. and trans. Robert M. Durling (Cambridge: Harvard University Press, 1976), 94–5.

81. Diane Owen Hughes has indicated in her studies of sumptuary laws in Italy in the early modern period that many of the regulations proposed against women's excessive spending were "issued by men who were fully implicated in female folly. They lived off the condemned dowries, they paid for the forbidden dresses whose splendour reflected their status, and they generally appeared in court and paid the fines demanded for contravention of the law by their women. In talking about women, their dress and comportment, men were talking about themselves and about their conflicting roles as fathers and husbands. But they did not just talk, they acted." For this view, one implied, I believe, in Franco's poem, see Diane Owen Hughes, "Sumptuary Laws and Social Relations in Renaissance Italy," in *Disputes and Settlements: Law and Human Relations in the West*, ed. John Bossy (Cambridge: Cambridge University Press, 1983), 96.

82. On switches in rhetorical tone, see Jacobson, *Ovid's "Heroides,"* 356. In the second letter in book 2.49–52 and 61–66, Phyllis remembers the force of Demophoon's words and the conviction with which he expressed them in his declarations of love for her. By reconstructing his discourse, first in her mind and then on the page, she uncovers the original language of deceit. Marina Scordilis Brownlee (*Severed Word*, 7–11, 22–36) points to Ovid's awareness in the *Heroides* of the essentially deceptive nature of all language.

83. Pastoral poetry offers poets an imaginative space where a particular version of social order is possible. As a highly eclectic form that proliferates into other literary genres, it also occupies a central position in social and class questions at the heart of Renaissance society. For a survey of the different approaches to the pastoral genre, especially among English critics, see Jonathan Goldberg, "The Politics of Renaissance Literature: A Review Essay," *ELH* 49 (1982): 514–42, especially 525–28. The critical works most useful are Louis Adrian Montrose, "Of Gentlemen and Shepherds: The Politics of Elizabethan Pastoral Form," *ELH* 50 (1983): 415–59; "'Eliza, Queene of shepheardes,' and the Pastoral of Power," *English Literary Renaissance* 10 (1980): 153–82; Jones, *Currency of Eros*, 118–41. Jones discusses the uses of pastoral poetry by another Venetian woman poet, Gaspara Stampa. See also the important study by William Kennedy (*Jacopo Sannazaro and the Uses of Pastoral* [Hanover, N. H.: University Press of New England, 1983]) of the pastoral tradition in Italy, with specific focus on Jacopo Sannazaro (1458–1530), the most influential poet of pastoral eclogues of the Italian Renaissance, and his connections to Italian humanism.

84. Many critics have commented on the poetic abilities that Franco reveals in this long *capitolo*. See Scrivano, "Veronica Franco," in *Cultura e letteratura del Cinquecento* (Rome: Edizione dell' Ateneo, 1966), 215; Luigi Baldacci, *Il petrarchismo italiano nel Cinquecento* (Milan: Riccardi, 1957), 167; Benedetto Croce, *Poeti e scrittori del pieno e tardo rinascimento* (Bari: Laterza, 1970), 419. A recent essay presents an illuminating reading of this poem and analyzes in groundbreaking ways Franco's reworking of the Petrarchan model in her *Terze rime*. See Sara Maria Adler, "Veronica Franco's Petrarchan *Terze rime*: Subverting the Master's Plan," *Italica* 65, no. 3 (1989): 213–33. For discussions of the uses of the Petrarchan model in Italy throughout the sixteenth century, see Amedeo Quondam, *La locuzione artificiosa: Teoria ed esperienza della lirica a Napoli* (Rome: Bulzoni, 1979); idem, *Il petrarchismo mediato* (Rome: Bulzoni, 1974); idem, *La parola nel labirinto: Società e scrittura del manierismo a Napoli* (Bari: Laterza, 1975).

85. The concept that the natural and human worlds are conjoined is central to the Renaissance view. In a garden the reciprocity of the natural world and human artifice is most pronounced. Claudia Lazzaro states ("The Visual Language of Gender in Sixteenth-Century Garden

Sculpture," in *Refiguring Woman: Gender Studies and the Italian Renaissance*, edited by Marilyn Migiel and Juliana Schiesari [Ithaca: Cornell University Press, 1991]) that in the Renaissance, "works of art were also termed a second or another nature. The garden, however, was described by contemporaries not as a second but as a third nature, because nature is also an active, shaping force. . . . Nature becomes the creator of art, and shares art's essence; it is not simply the object of the shaping human hand, but it also shares equally in the forming and ordering process" (72–73). See also Arthur Steinberg and Jonathan Wylie, "Counterfeiting Nature: Artistic Innovation and Cultural Crisis in Renaissance Venice," *Society for Comparative Study of Society and History* 32, no. 1 (1990): 54–88, for the concept of *natura artificialis* as a painterly term with regard to the use by Venetian of *colorito* rather than *disegno* for imitating or "counterfeiting" nature. Pastoral painting played a large role in early Venetian landscapes after the League of Cambrai (1509). On the crisis provoked by this league with regard to Venice's maritime dominion and its conquest of the mainland, see Felix Gilbert, "Venice in the Crisis of the League of Cambrai," in *Renaissance Venice*, ed. J. R. Hale (London: Faber and Faber, 1974), 274–92; Nicolai Rubinstein, "Italian Reactions to Terraferma Expansion in the Fifteenth Century," in Hale, *Renaissance Venice*, 197–217. When Venice reconquered its mainland dominion after 1516, there was again depiction of the countryside in Italian painting. See *Places of Delight: The Pastoral Landscape*, ed. Robert C. Cafritz, Lawrence Gowing, and David Rosand (London: Weidenfeld and Nicolson, 1988), especially "Giorgione, Venice, and the Pastoral Vision," (20–73), which links Venetian patricians' move to the *terraferma* and the decoration of their villas again with classical pictorial programs. Linda Carroll (*Angelo Beolco* [*Il Ruzante*] [Boston: Twayne, 1990]) argues that after Venice's defeat at Agnadello in 1509, Venice changed from "dominator to dominated. The prevalence of submissive figures, servants, and peasants in the painting and literature of Italy during the late fifteenth and early sixteenth centuries, when its city-states were enduring defeat at the hands both of other Europeans and of the Turks, points to a realization that, in the larger balance of power, Italian city-states' relations with European nation-states echoed those of peasants and servants with aristocrats" (11). See also 110 n. 11 for further bibliography on this issue.

On Della Torre's villa in the Roman style, situated in the Valpolicella valley, see *Palladio e Verona*, ed. Paola Marini (Vicenza: Neri Pozza, 1980), xvi, especially Lanfranco Franzoni, "Collezionismo e cultura antiquaria," 125–68. Franzoni uses records in the state archives in Verona to document the history of the ownership and decoration of Villa Della Torre in Fumane. He finds that the villa was divided among brothers and male relatives on 3 September 1573; one of the brothers was Marcantonio Della Torre, Franco's host. After the death of his uncle, Girolamo, in November 1573, the villa was passed on to Marcantonio. An inventory (only a segment of it remains) survives which records the many precious tapestries and their monetary value. The tapestries which depict Jupiter's amorous conquests are the ones which Franco describes in the poem.

86. For an examination of the garden setting as frame for the storytelling, and in particular the significance of the *brigata*'s move to the Valley of the Ladies, see Marshall Brown, "In the Valley of the Ladies," *Italian Quarterly* (1974–75): 33–52.

87. For the Valley of Ladies episode as the conclusion to day 6, I refer here to the English translation, Boccaccio, *Decameron*, trans. G. H. McWilliam (New York: Penguin, 1972), 514–20.

88. Ibid., 518.

89. Ibid., 64. Franco's reference to the palace of the sun alludes to Ovid's account of Phaethon's journey to find his true father (Sol) and to his overstepping his mortal boundaries in

the opening of book 2 in Ovid's *Metamorphoses*. I refer to *Ovid: The Metamorphoses*, trans. Horace Gregory (New York: Viking Press, 1958). The notion of attempting to compete with divinity as a transgressive act of hubris appears later in this *capitolo*, when Franco compares the splendor of Fumane to that of two villas often described in Neopolitan pastoral idylls of the period. For this, see Salza, *Rime*, 11.33–38. Elvira Favretti sees her allusion to the villas of Baia and Pozzuoli as "una proposta di gara con i poeti di scuola napoletana, e particolarmente con quell'effuso ma elegante descrittore di paradisi in terra che fu Luigi Tansillo" (a proposal for a competition with the poets of the Neopolitan school, and particularly with that effusive but elegant describer of earthly paradises, Luigi Tansillo) ("Rime e Lettere," 371). I might add to the list Boccaccio's *Elegia di Madonna Fiammetta*.

90. In 1563, Marcantonio Della Torre (1531–91) was the canon of the cathedral in Verona and protonotary apostolic, both extremely important ecclesiastical positions. In Verona he represented a style of life which brought together aristocratic traditions, ecclesiastical and landowning powers, and appreciation for aesthetics and literature, despite the pressures of the Counter-Reformation. Matteo Bandello in his novelle (11) points to Della Torre's villa as the most important meeting place for literati in Verona in the sixteenth century. On the Della Torre family and their villa in Fumane, see Scipione Maffei, *Verona illustrata*, part 3 (Milan: 1826), 239–40. Maffei claims that the Veronese painter Paolo Farinati (1524–1606) was responsible for the many frescoes in the villa, an opinion that Ridolfi recorded in 1648. See also Luciana Crosato, *Gli affreschi nelle ville venete del Cinquecento* (Treviso: Canova, 1962), 119. Pierpaolo Brugnoli (*La Chiesa e il priorato di Santa Maria del Degnano al Vaio di Fumane-Verona* [Verona: Centro per l'istruzione professionale grafica, 1968–69], 13ff.) argues that the architect of the villa was Sanmichele, who built over the existing structure in 1561. See also Giuseppe Mazzotti, *Le ville venete* (Rome: C. Bestetti, 1963), 369–70, 395–97; *La villa nel Veronese*, ed. Giuseppe Franco Viviani (Verona: 1975), 192.

91. On the tapestries in the Villa Della Torre, see n. 85 above. The archival document records "Li Razzi del Camerino pezzi 5, lire 223; Li Razzi del Camerone pezzi 7, lire 438."

92. See n. 89 above. Quintilian (*Institutione oratoriae* 3.7.27) discusses the poetics of poetry in praise of a specific place. This practice of poetic ecphrasis was common among Venetian poets of the period. Maffio Venier composed many sonnets in Italian in praise of the Medicis' villa of Pratolino and its statues by the sculptor Giambologna. Girolamo Fratta, one of the poets who frequented Ca' Venier, composed a poem in praise of Fumane (*L'amasio* [1581]), "Era ne la stagion, che 'l padre Autunno"; it ends with "Fumane si vedea, Fumane, ch'alta / Mente si loda per lo parte illustre." On this poetic tradition, see the classic study by Rensselaer W. Lee, *Ut Pictor Poesis: The Humanistic Theory in Painting* (New York: Norton, 1967). For Venetian painters, especially Titian's conversion of *poesie* into painted subjects, see David Rosand, "*Ut Pictor Poeta:* Meaning in Titian's *Poesie*," *New Literary History* (1971–72): 527–46; Giorgio Padoan, "'Ut Pictor Poesis': Le 'Pitture' di Ariosto, Le 'Poesie' di Tiziano," in *Tiziano e Venezia* (Vicenza: Neri Pozza, 1976), 91–102.

93. There has been considerable debate among art historians regarding the attribution of the portrait of Veronica Franco. Benedetto Croce was the first historian to isolate the question of iconographic representations of Veronica Franco in the concluding essay "Sulla iconografia della Franco," in his edition of her *Lettere* (1949), 75–83. A recent and very illuminating dissertation examines the iconography of representation of the Venetian courtesan in Renaissance painting. See Anne Christine Junkerman, "Bellissima Donna: An Interdisciplinary Study of Venetian Sensuous Half-Length Images of the Early Sixteenth Century" (Ph.D. diss., University of Califor-

nia, Berkeley, 1988). See also Carol M. Schuler, "The Courtesan in Art: Historical Fact or Modern Fantasy?" *Women's Studies* 19, no. 2 (1991): 209–22. A portrait, said to be of Veronica Franco, was acquired by the Worcester Art Museum from a private collection in Venice in 1948. On the painting, see Worcester Art Museum, *European Paintings in the Collection of the Worcester Art Museum,* Worcester, Mass.: Worcester Art Museum, 1974), 480–82. On the lining of the Worcester Art Museum's painting, Franco's name appears in block letters. The painting has been listed in the museum's catalog as by "a follower of Jacopo Tintoretto." As Lynne Lawner notes (*Lives of the Courtesans* [New York: Rizzoli, 1987], 205 n. 12), the portrait "has been lined onto another canvas, the signature visible only under ultraviolet light." Lawner concludes that the signature is impossible to date. Although we know that Franco had her portrait painted by Jacopo Tintoretto before 1580, because she writes a letter to him which she includes in her *Lettere familiari a diversi* (1580), it is not certain whether this is the Tintoretto portrait she refers to in her letter. The sitter of the Worcester portrait strikingly resembles, I believe, the facial features of the more rudimentary engraving of Veronica Franco for her *Terze rime* (1575) and includes the jeweled adornments and hair style of the engraving. Lawner suggests, also, that the sitter is the same woman who appears in a School of Tintoretto female bust portrait in the Museo del Prado, an observation with which I concur. For reproductions of these portraits, see Lawner, *Lives of the Courtesans,* 58. Paola Rossi ("I ritratti femminili di Domenico Tintoretto," *Arte illustrata* 30 [1970]: 92–99) argues that the Worcester portrait is by Domenico Tintoretto (1560–1635), and not his father, Jacopo (1518–94). Rossi compares this portrait on stylistic grounds with others by Domenico, most notably a Maddalena painting in the Church of San Bartolomeo in Pilsen (signed and dated 1586). A sixteenth-century manuscript in the Biblioteca Civico Correr in Venice lists portraits of "Cittadini Veneziani, li di cui ritratti furono esseguiti de seguenti valorosi Pittori," and the artists who painted them. The name "Veronica Franco" appears last on the list as "Veronica Franco dal Tintoretto." It is unclear if this means Domenico or Jacopo Tintoretto. See Cod. Gradenigo 192, c. 117 r and v. I thank Louisa Matthews for this source.

94. On the portraits of prelates in Della Torre's villa in Fumane, see n. 90 above, which gives bibliography on the decorations of the villa.

95. Sara Maria Adler, "Veronica Franco's Petrarchan *Terze Rime:* Subverting the Master's Plan," *Italica* 65, no. 3 (1988): 223, 228–29.

Works Cited

Ackerman, James. *The Villa: Form and Ideology of Country Houses*. Princeton: Princeton University Press, 1990.

———. "Geopolitics of Venetian Architecture." In *Titian: His World and His Legacy*, edited by David Rosand. New York: Columbia University Press, 1982.

Adler, Sara Maria. "Veronica Franco's Petrarchan *Terze Rime:* Subverting the Master's Plan." *Italica* 65, no. 3 (1988): 213–33.

Ageno, Franca. "A proposito del *Nuovo modo de intendere la lingua zerga.*" *Giornale storico della letteratura italiana* 135 (1958): 370–91.

degli Agostini, Giovanni. *Notizie istorico-critiche intorno la vita e le opere degli scrittori veneziani.* 2 vols. Venice: S. Occhi, 1752–54.

Aikema, B., and D. Meijers, eds. *Nel regno dei poveri*. Venice: Istituto di Ricovero e di Educazione, 1989.

Alonso, Damaso. *Pluralità e correlazione in poesia*. Translated by M. Rosataing and V. Minervini. Bari: Adriatica, 1971.

Altman, Janet Gurkin. *Epistolarity: Approaches to a Form*. Columbus: Ohio State University Press, 1982.

———. "Portuguese Writing and Women's Consciousness: The Loneliness of the Long-Distance Lover." *Degré Second* 7 (1983): 163–75.

———. "The Letter Book as a Literary Institution 1539–1789: Toward a Cultural History of Published Correspondences in France." *Yale French Studies* 71 (1986): 17–62.

Angelini, Franca. "La Venexiana: Spazi e tempi dello 'sperimentare.'" In *Letteratura e società*, edited by G. Petronio. Palermo: Palumbo, 1980.

Aquilecchia, Giovanni. "Pietro Aretino e altri poligrafi a Venezia." In *Storia della cultura veneta*, edited by G. Arnaldi and M. Pastore Stocchi. 4 vols. Vicenza: Neri Pozza, 1982.

Aquilecchia, Giovanni, ed. *Aretino: Sei giornate*. Bari: Laterza, 1975.

———. *Schede di italianistica*. Turin: Einaudi, 1976.

Aretino, Pietro. *Ragionamento nel quale M. Pietro Aretino figura quattro suoi amici che favellano delle corti del mondo e di quella del cielo*. Venice: Marcolini, [1538] 1539.

———. *Il terzo (quattro, quinto, sesto) libro delle lettere di M. Pietro Aretino*. Paris: Matteo il Maestro, 1608–9.

———. *Lettere*. 6 vols. Paris: Matteo il Maestro, 1609.

———. *Lettere, il primo e il secondo libro*. In *Tutte le opere*. Edited by Francesco Flora and Alessandro Del Vita. Milan: Mondadori, 1960.

———. *Aretino's Dialogues*. Translated by Raymond Rosenthal. New York: Stein and Day, 1971.

————. *Aretino: Sei giornate*. Edited by Giovanni Aquilecchia. Bari: Laterza, 1975.

Ariosto, Ludovico. *Tutte le opere di Ludovico Ariosto*. Edited by Cesare Segre. Milan: Mondadori, 1964–(84).

Arnaldi, G., and M. Pastore Stocchi, eds. *Storia della cultura veneta*. 4 vols. Vicenza: Neri Pozza, 1982.

Atanagi, Dionigi, ed. *Rime di diversi nobilissimi et eccellentissimi autori in morte della signora Irene delle signore di Spilimbergo*. Venice: Domenico and Giovanni Battista Guerra, 1561.

Baca, Murtha. "Aretino in Venice 1527–1537 and 'La Professione Del Far' Lettere." Ph.D. diss., UCLA, 1978.

Bakhtin, Mikhail M. *Rabelais and His World*. Translated by Helene Iswolsky. Cambridge: Harvard University Press, 1968.

————. *The Dialogic Imagination: Four Essays by M. M. Bakhtin*. Edited and translated by Michael Holquist. Austin: University of Texas Press, 1981.

Baldacci, Luigi. *Il petrarchismo italiano nel Cinquecento*. Milan: Riccardi, 1957.

Balduino, Armando. "Restauri e ricuperi per Maffio Venier." In *Medioevo e Rinascimento veneto: Con altri studi in onore di Lino Lazzarini*. 2 vols. Padua: Antenore, 1979.

Bardi, Girolamo. *Dichiaratione di tutte le historie che si contengono ne' quadri posti novamente nelle Sale del Scrutinio, e del Gran Consiglio del Palagio Ducale della Republica di Vinegia*. Venice: 1587 and 1607.

Barish, Jonas. *The Antitheatrical Prejudice*. Berkeley: University of California Press, 1981.

Barkan, Leonard. *The Gods Made Flesh: Metamorphosis and the Pursuit of Paganism*. New Haven: Yale University Press, 1986.

Barsby, John, ed. and trans. *Ovid: Amores Book I*. Oxford: Clarendon Press, 1973.

Barzaghi, Antonio. *Donne o cortigiane? La prostituzione a Venezia: Documenti di costume dal XVI al XVIII secolo*. Verona: Bertani, 1980.

Bassanese, Fiora A. *Gaspara Stampa*. Boston: Twayne, 1982.

————. "Private Lives and Public Lies: Texts by Courtesans of the Italian Renaissance." *Texas Studies in Language and Literature* 30, no. 3 (1988): 295–319.

————. "What's In a Name? Self-Naming and Renaissance Women Poets." *Annali d'Italianistica* 7 (1989): 104–15.

Bassi, Elena. *Ville della Provincia di Venezia*. Venice: Rusconi, 1987.

Beaujour, Michel. *Miroirs d'ancre: Rhétorique de l'auto-portrait*. Paris: Seuil, 1980.

Becker, Marvin B. *Civility and Society in Western Europe 1300–1600*. Bloomington and Indianapolis: Indiana University Press, 1988.

Bell, Rudolph M., and Judith C. Brown. "Renaissance Sexuality and the Florentine Archives: An Exchange." *Renaissance Quarterly* 40 (1987): 96–100.

Beloch, Karl Julius. *Bevolkerungsgeschichte Italiens*. 3 vols. Berlin: De Gruyter, 1937–61.

Beltrami, Daniele. *Storia della popolazione di Venezia dalla fine del secolo XVI alla caduta della Repubblica*. Padua: Cedam, 1954.

Benzoni, Gino. *Venezia nell'età della controriforma*. Turin: Mursia, 1973.

————. "Aspetti della cultura urbana nella società veneta del Cinquecento e Seicento: Le accademie." *Archivio veneto* 108 (1977): 87–159.

————. *Gli affanni della cultura: Intellettuali e potere nell'Italia della Controriforma e Barocca*. Milan: Feltrinelli, 1978.

Bertelli, Pietro. *Diversarum Nationum Habitus Centum*. Padua: Alciatum Alcia, 1589.

Bertolotti, Antonio. *Muzio Manfredi e Passi Giuseppe letterati in relazione col duca di Mantova.* Rome: Tipografia delle scienze matematiche e fisiche, 1888.

Bertoni, Giulio. *Le Rime di Giovanni M. Barbieri.* Modena: 1907.

Bistort, Giulio. *Il magistrato alle pompe nella repubblica di Venezia.* Venice: Emiliana, 1912; reprint, Bologna: Forni Editore, 1969.

Bloch, R. Howard. "Medieval Misogyny." *Representations* 20 (1987): 1–24.

Bloch, R. Howard, and Frances Ferguson, eds. *Misogyny, Misandry, and Misanthropy.* Berkeley: University of California Press, 1988.

Boccaccio, Giovanni. *La Genealogia de gli dei de gentili.* Venice: 1581.

————. *Elegia di Madonna Fiammetta.* In *Opere,* edited by Cesare Segre. Milan: Mursia, 1966.

————. *Decameron.* Translated by G. H. McWilliam. New York: Penguin Books, 1972.

————. *Tutte le opere di Giovanni Boccaccio.* Edited by Vittore Branca. Milan: Mondadori, 1976.

————. *The Elegy of Lady Fiammetta.* Edited and translated by Mariangela Causa-Steindler and Thomas Mauch. Chicago: University of Chicago Press, 1990.

Boerio, Giuseppe. *Dizionario del dialetto veneziano.* 2d ed. Venice: Giovanni Cecchini, 1856.

Bolgar, R. R. *The Classical Heritage and Its Beneficiaries.* Cambridge: Cambridge University Press, 1954.

Bolzoni, Lina. "Il 'Badoardo' di Francesco Patrizi e l'Accademia Veneziana della Fama." *Giornale storico della letteratura italiana* 158 (1981): 77–101.

————. "L'Accademia Veneziana: Splendore e decadenza di una utopia enciclopedica." In Laetitia Boehm and Ezio Raimondi, eds., *Università, accademie e società scientifiche in Italia e in Germania dal Cinquecento al Settecento.* Bologna: Il Mulino, 1982.

Borghesi, Diomede. *Rime.* 2 vols. Padua: Lorenzo Pasquati, 1566–67.

————. *Lettere.* 3 vols. Padua: Lorenzo Pasquati, 1574–1603.

Boucher, Jacqueline. *La cour de Henri III.* Rennes: Ouest-France, 1986.

Bouwsma, William J. *Venice and the Defense of Republican Liberty: Reniassance Values in the Age of the Counter Reformation.* Berkeley: University of California Press, 1968.

Braudel, Ferdinand. *The Mediterranean and Mediterranean World in the Age of Phillip II.* 2 vols. London: Collins, 1973.

————. "La vita economica di Venezia nel secolo XVI." In *Storia della civiltà veneziana,* edited by Vittore Branca. 3 vols. Florence: Sansoni, 1979.

Brown, Judith. *Immodest Acts: The Life of a Lesbian Nun in Renaissance Italy.* New York: Oxford University Press, 1986.

Brown, Marshall. "In the Valley of the Ladies." *Italian Quarterly* (1974–75): 33–52.

Brown, Patricia F. "Honor and Necessity: The Dynamics of Patronage in the Confraternities of Renaissance Venice." *Studi veneziani* 14 (1987): 179–212.

————. *Venetian Narrative Painting in the Age of Carpaccio.* New Haven: Yale University Press, 1988.

Brownlee, Marina Scordilis. *The Severed Word: Ovid's Heroides and the Novela Sentimental.* Princeton: Princeton University Press, 1990.

Brucker, Gene. "Sorcery in Early Renaissance Florence." *Studies in the Renaissance* 10–11 (1963–64): 7–25.

————. *Giovanni and Lusanna: Love and Marriage in Renaissance Florence.* Berkeley: University of California Press, 1986.

Brugnoli, Pierpaolo. *La Chiesa e il priorato di Santa Maria del Degnano al Vaio di Fumane-Verona.* Verona: Centro per l'istruzione professionale grafica, 1968–69.

Buccio, Pietro. *Le coronationi di Polonia et di Francia del Christianissimo Re Henrico III.* Padua: Lorenzo Pasquati, 1576.

Burke, Kenneth. *A Rhetoric of Motives.* 1950; reprint, Berkeley: University of California Press, 1969.

Burke, Peter. *The Historical Anthropology of Early Modern Italy: Essays on Perception and Communication.* Cambridge: Cambridge University Press, 1987.

Cafritz, Robert C., Lawrence Gowing, and David Rosand, eds. *Places of Delight: The Pastoral Landscape.* London: Weidenfeld and Nicolson, 1988.

Cagli, Corrado, and Francesco Valcanover. *L'opera completa di Tiziano.* Milan: Rizzoli, 1969.

Cairns, Christopher. *Domenico Bollani, Bishop of Brescia: Devotion to Church and State in the Republic of Venice in the Sixteenth Century.* Nieuwkoop: De Graaf, 1976.

———. *Pietro Aretino and the Republic of Venice: Researches on Aretino and His Circle in Venice, 1527– 1556.* Florence: Leo S. Olschki, 1985.

Calmo, Andrea. *Lettere.* Venice: Domenico Farri, 1580.

Calza, Carlo. *Documenti inediti sulla prostituzione tratti dagli archivi della repubblica veneta.* Milan: Tipografia della Società Cooperativa, 1869.

Camilli, Camillo, trans. *L'Epistole d'Ovidio.* Venice: Giovanni Battista Ciotti, 1587.

Canal, B. "Il collegio, l'ufficio e l'archivio dei Dieci Savi alle Decime in Rialto." *Nuovo archivio veneto* 16 (1908).

Carmichael, Ann G. *Plague and the Poor in Renaissance Florence.* Cambridge: Cambridge University Press, 1986.

Carrell, Susan Lee. *Le Soliloque de la passion feminine ou le dialogue illusoire: Etude d'une formule monophonique de la litterature epistolaire.* Paris: Editions Jean-Michel Place, 1982.

Carroll, Linda. *Language and Dialect in Ruzzante and Goldoni.* Ravenna: Longo Editore, 1981.

———. "Carnival Rites as Vehicles of Protest in Renaissance Venice." *Sixteenth Century Journal* 16, no. 4 (1985): 487–502.

———. "Who's on Top? Gender as Societal Power Configuration in Italian Renaissance Drama." *Sixteenth Century Journal* 20, no. 4 (1989): 531–38.

———. *Angelo Beolco (Il Ruzante).* Boston: Twayne, 1990.

Casagrande di Villaviera, Rita. *Le cortigiane veneziane del Cinquecento.* Milan: Longanesi, 1968.

Casali, Scipione. *Gli annali della tipografia veneziana di Francesco Marcolini,* no. 26. Forli: Matteo Casali, 1861.

Castiglione, Baldassare. *The Book of the Courtier.* Translated by Charles S. Singleton. New York: Doubleday, 1959.

Catullus. *Catullus, Tibullus, and Pervigilium Veneris.* Translated by F. W. Cornish and J. W. MacKail. Loeb Classical Library. Cambridge: Harvard University Press, [1913] 1962.

Cave, Terence. *The Cornucopian Text: Problems of Writing in the French Renaissance.* Oxford: Oxford University Press, 1979.

Cecchetti, Bartolomeo. "Testamenti fatti in tempo di peste." *Archivio veneto* 32 (1886).

Cerboni Baiardi, Giorgio. *La lirica di Bernardo Tasso.* Urbino: Argaglia, 1966.

Chartrou, Josephe. *Les entrées solennelles et triomphales à la Renaissance (1448–1551).* Paris: Les presses universitaires de France, 1928.

Chemello, Adrianna. "Donna di palazzo, moglie, cortigiana: Ruoli e funzioni sociali della donna in alcuni trattati del Cinquecento." In *La corte e il "Cortegiano,"* edited by Amedeo Quondam. Rome: Bulzoni, 1980.

———. "La donna, il modello, l'immaginario: Moderata Fonte e Lucrezia Marinella." In *Nel cerchio della luna: Figure di donna in alcuni testi del XVI secolo,* edited by Marina Zancan. Venice: Marsilio, 1983.

Chemello, Adrianna, ed. *Il merito delle donne.* Mirano: Eidos, 1988.

Cherchi, Paolo. *Enciclopedismo e politica della riscrittura: Tommaso Garzoni.* Pisa: Pacini Editore, 1980.

Cherchi, Paolo, and Beatrice Collina. "Esplorazioni preparatorie per un'edizione della "Piazza Universale" di Tomaso Garzoni." *Lettere Italiane,* no. 2 (1991): 250–66.

Chojnacki, Stanley. "Patrician Women in Early Renaissance Venice." *Studies in the Renaissance* 21 (1974): 176–203.

———. "Dowries and Kinsmen in Early Renaissance Venice." *Journal of Interdisciplinary History* 4 (1975): 571–600.

———. "La posizione della donna a Venezia nel Cinquecento." In *Tiziano e Venezia: Convegno Internazionale di Studi.* Vicenza: Neri Pozza, 1980.

———. "In Search of the Venetian Patriciate: Families and Factions in the Fourteenth Century." In *Renaissance Venice,* ed. J. R. Hale. London: Faber and Faber, 1974.

———. "Kinship Ties and Young Patricians in Fifteenth-Century Venice." *Renaissance Quarterly* 38 (1985): 240–70.

———. "Political Adulthood in Fifteenth-Century Venice." *American Historical Review* 91 (1986): 791–810.

———. "The Power of Love: Wives and Husbands in Late Medieval Venice." In *Women and Power in the Middle Ages,* edited by Mary Erler and Maryanne Kowaleski. Athens: University of Georgia Press, 1988.

———. " 'The Most Serious Duty': Motherhood, Gender, and Patrician Culture in Renaissance Venice." In *Refiguring Woman: Perspectives on Gender and the Italian Renaissance,* edited by Marilyn Migiel and Juliana Schiesari. Ithaca: Cornell University Press, 1991.

Ciammitti, Luisa. "Quanto costa essere normali: La dote nel Conservatorio femminile di Santa Maria del Baraccano (1630–1680)." *Quaderni storici* 53 (1983): 469–97.

Cicero, M. Tullius. *The Letters to His Friends.* Edited and translated by W. Glynn Williams. Loeb Classical Library. 3 vols. Cambridge: Harvard University Press, 1928.

———. *Letters to Atticus.* Translated by E. D. Winstedt. Loeb Classical Library. 3 vols. Cambridge: Harvard University Press, 1928.

———. *De oratore.* Edited and translated by E. W. Sutton and H. Rackham. Loeb Classical Library. 2 vols. Cambridge: Harvard University Press, 1948.

———. *Tusculan disputations.* Translated by J. E. King. Loeb Classical Library. Cambridge: Harvard University Press, 1966.

Cicogna, Emmanuele Antonio. *Delle inscrizioni veneziane.* 6 vols. Venice: Giuseppe Orlandelli, 1824–53.

Cipolla, Carlo M. *Public Health and the Medical Profession in the Renaissance.* Cambridge: Cambridge University Press, 1976.

———. *Fighting the Plague in Seventeenth-Century Italy.* Madison: University of Wisconsin Press, 1981.

Citolini, Alessandro. *La tipocosmia di Alessandro Citolini.* Venice: Vincenzo Valgrisi, 1561.

Clough, Cecil H. "The Cult of Antiquity: Letters and Letter Collections." In *Cultural Aspects of the Italian Renaissance: Essays in Honor of Paul Oskar Kristeller,* edited by C. H. Clough. Manchester: University of Manchester Press, 1976.

Clubb, Louise George. "Castiglione's Humanist Art and Renaissance Drama." In *Castiglione: The Ideal and the Real in Renaissance Culture*, ed. Robert Hanning and David Rosand. New Haven, Yale University Press, 1983.

―――. *Italian Drama in Shakespeare's Time*. New Haven: Yale University Press, 1989.

Cocchiara, Giuseppe. *Popolo e letteratura in Italia*. Turin: Einaudi, 1959.

Cohen, Elizabeth S. "Courtesans and Whores: Words and Behavior in Roman Streets." *Women's Studies* 19 (1991): 201–8.

Cohen, Sherrill. "Convertite e Malmaritate: Donne 'irregolari' e ordini religiosi nella Firenze rinascimentale." *Memoria: Rivista di storia delle donne* 5 (1982): 23–65.

―――. "Asylums for Women in Counter-Reformation Italy." In *Women in Reformation and Counter-Reformation Europe: Private and Public Worlds*, edited by Sherrin Marshall. Bloomington and Indianapolis: Indiana University Press, 1989.

Commager, Steele. *A Prolegomenon to Propertius*. Norman: University of Oklahoma Press, 1974.

Compagnon, Antoine. "A Long Short Story: Montaigne's Brevity." In *Montaigne: Essays in Reading*, in *Yale French Studies* 64 (1983): 24–50.

Cope, Maurice E. *The Venetian Chapels of the Sacrament in the Sixteenth Century*. New York: Garland, 1979.

Copley, Frank O. *Exclusus Amator: A Study in Latin Love Poetry*. Madison, Wis.: American Philological Association, 1956.

Corbett, P. E. *The Roman Law of Marriage*. Oxford: Oxford University Press, 1930.

Coryat, Thomas. *Coryat's Crudities*. London, 1611. Edited by James Maclehouse. 2 vols. Reprint, Glasgow: University of Glasgow Press, 1905.

Costa, Pietro. *Courtisanes et la police des moeurs à Venise*. Sauveterre: Imprimerie Chollet, 1886.

Cozzi, Gaetano. *Il doge Nicolo Contarini: Ricerche sul patriziato veneziano agli inizi del Seicento*. Venice: Istituto per la Collaborazione Culturale, 1958.

de Crenne, Helisenne. *Renaissance Woman: Helisenne's Personal and Invective Letters*. Translated by Marianna M. Mustacchi and Paul J. Archambault. Syracuse: Syracuse University Press, 1986.

Crescimbeni, Giovan Mario. *L'istoria della volgar poesia*. 6 vols. Venice: L. Basegio, 1730–31.

Croce, Benedetto. *Lettere dall' unica edizione del MDLXXX con Proemio e nota iconografica*. Naples: Ricciardi, 1949.

―――. *Poeti e scrittori del pieno e tardo rinascimento*. Bari: Laterza, 1970.

―――. "Pagine di Tommaso Garzoni." In Croce, *Poeti e scrittori*, 2:208–20.

―――. "Letterati poeti del Veneto e dell'Italia meridionale sulla fine del cinquecento." In Croce, *Poeti e scrittori*.

Crook, J. A. *Law and Life of Rome*. Ithaca: Cornell University Press, 1967.

Cropp, Glynnis M. *Le vocabulaire courtois des troubadours de l'époque classique*. Geneva: Droz, 1975.

Crosato, Luciana. *Gli affreschi nelle ville venete del Cinquecento*. Treviso: Canova, 1962.

Cruz, Anne J. "Sexual Enclosure, Textual Escape: The *Picara* as Prostitute in the Spanish Female Picaresque Novel." In *Seeking the Woman in Late Medieval and Renaissance Writings*, edited by Sheila Fisher and Janet E. Halley. Knoxville: University of Tennessee Press, 1989.

Dante. *The Divine Comedy*. 3 vols. Translated by Charles S. Singleton. Princeton: Princeton University Press, 1970.

Davidson, Nicholas S. "Il Sant'Uffizio e la tutela del culto a Venezia nel Cinquecento." *Studi veneziani* 6 (1982): 87–103.

Davis, James C. *A Venetian Family and Its Fortune*. Philadelphia: American Philosophical Society, 1975.

Davis, Natalie Zemon. *Society and Culture in Early Modern France*. Stanford: Stanford University Press, 1975.

———. "The Sacred and the Body Social in Sixteenth-Century Lyon." *Past and Present* 90 (1981): 40–70.

———. *The Return of Martin Guerre*. Cambridge: Harvard University Press, 1983.

———. *Il ritorno di Martin Guerre*. Turin: Einaudi, 1984.

———. "Scandale à l'Hotel-Dieu de Lyon (1537–1543)." In *La France d'Ancien Régime: Etudes réunies en l'honneur de Pierre Goubert*, edited by Pierre Goubert. 2 vols. Toulouse: Société de Démographie Historique Privat, 1984.

———. *Fiction in the Archives: Pardon Tales and Their Tellers in Sixteenth-Century France*. Stanford: Stanford University Press, 1987.

Dazzi, Manlio. *Leonardo Giustinian poeta popolare d'amore*. Bari: Laterza, 1934.

———. *Il fiore della lirica veneziana: Il libro segreto (chiuso)*, vol. 2. Vicenza: Neri Pozza, 1956.

———. *Aldo Manuzio e il dialogo veneziano di Erasmo*, vol. 26. Vicenza: Neri Pozza, 1969.

Debenedetti, Santorre. *Gli studi provenzali in Italia nel Cinquecento*. Turin: Loescher, 1911.

Defaux, Gerard, ed. *Montaigne: Essays in Reading. Yale French Studies* 64 (1983).

DeJean, Joan. *Fictions of Sappho: 1546–1937*. Chicago: University of Chicago Press, 1989.

De Lorenzi, G. Batta. *Leggi e Memorie Venete sulla prostituzione fino alla caduta della Repubblica*. Privately published for Lord Orford. Venice, 1870–72.

Delumeau, Jean. *Vie économique et sociale de Rome dans la seconde moitié du XVIe siècle*. 2 vols. Paris: De Boccard, 1957–59.

Demus, Otto. *The Church of San Marco in Venice: History, Architecture, Sculpture*, vol. 6. Washington: Dumbarton Oaks Studies, 1960.

De Nichilo, Adrianna. "La lettera e il comico." In *Le "carte messaggiere": Retorica e modelli di comunicazione epistolare per un indice di lettere del Cinquecento*. Rome: Bulzoni, 1981.

De Nolhac, Pierre, and Angelo Solerti. *Il viaggio in Italia di Enrico III Re di Francia e le feste a Venezia, Ferrara, Mantova e Torino*. Turin: 1890.

Derosas, Renzo. "Moralità e giustizia a Venezia nel '500–'600: Gli esecutori contro la bestemmia." In *Stato, società e giustizia nella Repubblica Veneta*, edited by Gaetano Cozzi. Rome: Jouvence, 1980.

Diberti Leigh, Marcella. *Veronica Franco: Donna, poetessa e cortigiana del Rinascimento*. Ivrea: Priuli and Verlucca, 1988.

Diefendorf, Barbara B. "Family Culture, Renaissance Culture." *Renaissance Quarterly* 40 (1987): 661–81.

Dionisotti, Carlo. *Geografia e storia della letteratura italiana*. Turin: Einaudi, 1967.

Dizionario biografico degli italiani. 19 vols. Rome: Istituto della Enciclopedia Italiana, 1960–.

Doglio, Maria Luisa. "La letteratura ufficiale e l'oratorio celebrativa." In *Storia della cultura veneta*, ed. G. Arnaldi and M. Pastore Stocchi. 4 vols. Vicenza: Neri Pozza, 1976–86.

———. "Scrivere come donna: Fenomenologia delle 'Lettere familiari' di Alessandra Macinghi Strozzi." *Lettere Italiane* 36, no. 4 (1984): 484–97.

Doglioni, Giovanni Nicolò. *Venetia trionfante, et sempre libera*. Venice: A. Muschio, 1613.

Dolce, Lodovico. *Paraphrasi nella sesta satira di Giuvenale*. Venice: Curtio Navo e fratelli, 1538.

———. *I quattro libri delle osservationi*. Venice: Domenico Farri, 1566.

Dolcetti, Giovanni. *Le bische e il giucco d'azzardo a Venizia, 1172–1807*. Venice: Manuzio, 1903.

Doni, Anton Francesco. *L'epistole di Seneca ridotte nella lingua toscana*. Venice: 1549.

————. *I Marmi*.

Douglas, Mary. *Purity and Danger: An Analysis of Concepts of Pollution and Taboo*. London: Routledge and Kegan Paul, 1969.

Dronke, Peter. *Women Writers of the Middle Ages*. Cambridge: Cambridge University Press, 1984.

Dubrow, Heather. "The Country-House Poem: A Study in Generic Development." *Genre* 12, no. 2 (1979): 153–79.

Edgerton, Samuel W. *Pictures and Punishment: Art and Criminal Prosecution during the Florentine Renaissance*. Ithaca: Cornell University Press, 1985.

Ellero, Giuseppe. *Archivio I.R.E.: Inventari di fondi antichi degli ospedali e luoghi pii di Venezia: Istituzioni di Ricovero e di Educazione*. Venice: 1984–87.

Elwert, W. Theodor. *Studi di letteratura veneziana*. Venice: Istituto per la Collaborazione Culturale, 1958.

————. "Pietro Bembo e la vita letteraria del suo tempo." In *La civiltà veneziana del Rinascimento*. Fondazione Giorgio Cini. Florence: Sansoni, 1958.

————. *Versificazione italiana: Dalle origini ai giorni nostri*. Paris: Le Monnier, 1973.

Epistole di G. Plinio, di M. Francesco Petrarca e del S. Pico della Mirandola, trans. Lodovico Dolce. Venice: Gabriel Giolito de' Ferrari, 1548.

Erasmus. *I Ragionamenti, overo colloqui famigliari di Desiderio Erasmo*. Translated by Pietro Lauro. Venice: Vincenzo Valgrisi, 1549.

Erizzo, Sebastiano. *Espositione di M. Sebastiano Erizzo nelle tre canzoni di M. Francesco Petrarca*. Venice: Andrea Arrivabene, 1561.

Erspamer, Francesco. *La biblioteca di Don Ferrante: Duello e onore nella cultura del Cinquecento*. Rome: Bulzoni, 1983.

————. "Petrarchismo e manierismo nella lirica del secondo cinquecento." In *Storia della cultura veneta: Il seicento*, ed. G. Arnaldi and M. Pastore Stocchi. Vicenza: Neri Pozza, 1983.

Essercizi accademici, traduzioni, discorsi et altre cose istruttive e piacevoli.

Fasoli, Gina. "Nascita di un mito." In *Studi storici in onore di Gioacchino Volpe*. Florence: Sansoni, 1958.

Favretti, Elvira. "Una raccolta di Rime del Cinquecento." *Giornale storico della letteratura italiana* 158 (1981): 543–72.

————. "Rime e Lettere di Veronica Franco." *Giornale storico della letteratura italiana* 163, no. 523 (1986): 355–82.

Fedalto, Giorgio. *Ricerche storiche sulla posizione giuridica ed ecclesiastica dei greci a Venezia nei secoli XV e XVI*. Florence: Leo S. Olschki, 1967.

Feldman, Martha. "Venice and the Madrigal in the Mid-Sixteenth Century." 2 vols. Ph.D. diss., University of Pennsylvania, 1987.

————. "The Composer as Exegete: Interpretations of Petrarchan Syntax in the Venetian Madrigal." *Studi musicali* 18, no. 2 (1989): 203–38.

————. "The Academy of Domenico Venier, Music's Literary Muse in Mid-*Cinquecento* Venice." *Renaissance Quarterly* 44, no. 3 (1991): 475–510.

Fenlon, Iain. *Music and Patronage in Sixteenth-Century Mantua*. 2 vols. New York: Cambridge University Press, 1980.

Ferguson, Margaret W. "A Room Not Their Own: Renaissance Women as Readers and Writers."

In *The Comparative Perspective on Literature: Approaches to Theory and Practice,* edited by Clayton Koelb and Susan Noakes. Ithaca: Cornell University Press, 1988.

Margaret W. Ferguson, Maureen Quilligan, and Nancy J. Vickers, eds. *Rewriting the Renaissance: The Discourses of Sexual Difference in Early Modern Europe.* Chicago: University of Chicago Press, 1986.

Ferrante, Lucia. "L'onore ritrovato: Donne nella Casa del Soccorso di San Paolo a Bologna." *Quaderni storici* 53 (1983): 499–527.

Ferro, Marco. *Dizionario del diritto comune, e veneto.* 10 tomes in 5 vols. Venice: Modesto Fenzo, 1778–81.

Ferroni, Giulio. *Poesia italiana: Il Cinquecento.* Milan: Garzanti, 1978.

———. *Il testo e la scena: Saggi sul teatro del Cinquecento.* Rome: Bulzoni, 1980.

Finlay, Robert. *Politics in Renaissance Venice.* New Brunswick: Rutgers University Press, 1980.

Fiorentino, Remigio. *Epistole d'Ovidio di Remigio Fiorentino: Divise in due libri. Con le dichiarationi in margine delle favole e dell'historie.* Venice: Oratio de' Gobbi, 1581.

Flora, Francesco. "Veronica Franco." In his *Storia della letteratura italiana.* Milan: Mondadori, 1941.

Foa, Anna. "The New and the Old: The Spread of Syphilis (1494–1530)." Translated by Carole C. Gallucci. In *Sex and Gender in Historical Perspective,* edited by Edward Muir and Guido Ruggiero. Baltimore: Johns Hopkins University Press, 1990.

Fonte, Moderata. *Il merito delle donne.* Edited by Adrianna Chemello. Mirano: Eiodos, 1988.

Foucault, Michel. *Discipline and Punish: The Birth of the Prison.* Translated by Alan Sheridan. New York: Vintage Books, 1979.

Fragnito, Gigliola. "Per lo studio dell'epistolografia volgare del Cinquecento: Le lettere di Ludovico Beccadelli." *Bibliothèque d'Humanisme et Renaissance* 43, no. 1 (1981): 61–87.

———. "L'Epistolario di Ludovico Beccadelli: Autoritratto e manuale epistolografico." In *La correspondance,* Actes du Colloque International. Aix-en-Provence: 1984.

Frame, Donald M. *Montaigne's Discovery of Man: The Humanization of a Humanist.* Westport, Conn.: Greenwood Press, 1983.

Franco, Giacomo. *Habiti delle donne venetiane intagliate in rame nuovamente di Giacomo Franco.* Venice: Ferdinando Ongania, 1610.

Franco, Veronica. *Terze rime.* Venice: 1575.

———. *Lettere dall'unica edizione del MDLXXX con Proemio e nota iconografica* (Venice: 1580), edited by Benedetto Croce. Naples: Ricciardi, 1949.

Frankel, Herbert. *Ovid: A Poet between Two Worlds.* Berkeley: University of California Press, 1945.

Frantz, David O. *Festum Voluptatis: A Study of Renaissance Erotica.* Columbus: Ohio State University Press, 1989.

Franzoi, Umberto. *Le prigioni della repubblica di Venezia.* Venice: Stamperia di Venezia, 1966.

Franzoni, Lanfranco. "Collezionismo e cultura antiquaria." In *Palladio e Verona,* ed. Paola Marini. Vicenza: Neri Pozza, 1980.

Freccero, John. "The Fig Tree and the Laurel." *Diacritics* 5 (1975): 34–40.

Frugoni, A. Giovanni. "I capitoli della cortigiana Veronica Franco." *Belfagor* 3 (1948): 44–59.

Fumaroli, Marc. "Genèse de l'épistolographie classique: Rhétorique humaniste de la lettre, de Petrarque à Juste Lipse." *Révue d'Histoire Littéraire de la France* 78, no. 4 (1978): 888.

———. *L'age de l'éloquence: Rhetorique et "res literaria" de la Renaissance au seuil de l'époque classique.* Geneva: Droz, 1980.

Gaeta, Franco. "Alcune considerazioni sul mito di Venezia." *Bibliothèque d'Humanisme et Renaissance* 23 (1961): 58–75.

———. "L'idea di Venezia." In *Storia della cultura veneta: Il seicento,* edited by G. Arnaldi and M. Pastore Stocchi. Vicenza: Neri Pozza, 1982.

Gamba, Bartolommeo. *Lettere di donne italiane del secolo XVI.* Venice: Alvisopoli, 1832.

Garimberto, Girolamo. *Concetti.* Venice: Vincenzo Valgrisi, 1553.

Garrard, Mary D. *Artemisia Gentileschi: The Image of the Female Hero in Italian Baroque Art.* Princeton: Princeton University Press, 1990.

Garzoni, Tomaso. *La Piazza universale di tutte le professioni del mondo.* Venice: Giovanni Battista Somasco, 1585.

Giamatti, A. Bartlett. *The Earthly Paradise and the Renaissance Epic.* Princeton: Princeton University Press, 1966.

Gianghian, Giorgio, and Paola Pavanini. *Dietro i palazzi: Tre secoli di architettura minore a Venezia, 1492–1803.* Venice: Arsenale, 1984.

Gilbert, Felix. "Venice in the Crisis of the League of Cambrai." In *Renaissance Venice,* ed. J. R. Hale. London: Faber and Faber, 1974.

———. *The Pope, His Banker, and Venice.* Cambridge: Harvard University Press, 1980.

Gilmore, Myron P. "Myth and Reality in Venetian Political Theory." In *Renaissance Venice,* edited by J. R. Hale. London: Faber and Faber, 1974.

Ginzburg, Carlo. *Il formaggio e i vermi: Il cosmo di un mugnaio del '500.* Turin: Einaudi, 1976.

———. "Tiziano, Ovidio, e i codici della figurazione erotica del Cinquecento." *Paragone* 339, no. 29 (1978): 3–24.

———. *The Cheese and the Worms.* Translated by John Tedeschi and Anne C. Tedeschi. Baltimore: Johns Hopkins University Press, 1980.

———. "Morelli, Freud, and Sherlock Holmes: Clues and Scientific Method." *History Workshop* 9 (1980): 5–36.

———. *Witchcraft and Agrarian Cults in the Sixteenth and Seventeenth Centuries.* Translated by John Tedeschi and Anne C. Tedeschi. New York: Penguin Books, 1985.

———. "The Inquisitor as Anthropologist." In *Clues, Myths, and the Historical Method,* translated by John Tedeschi and Anne C. Tedeschi. Baltimore: Johns Hopkins University Press, 1989.

Goffen, Rona. "Renaissance Dreams." *Renaissance Quarterly* 40 (1987): 682–706.

———. *Piety and Patronage in Renaissance Venice: Bellini, Titian, and the Franciscans.* New Haven: Yale University Press, 1987.

Gold, Penny Schine. *The Lady and the Virgin.* Chicago: University of Chicago Press, 1985.

Goldberg, Jonathan. "The Politics of Renaissance Literature: A Review Essay." English Literary History 49 (1982): 514–42.

———. *James I and the Politics of Literature: Jonson, Shakespeare, Donne, and Their Contemporaries.* Baltimore: Johns Hopkins University Press, 1983.

Goldsmith, Elizabeth C. *"Exclusive Conversations": The Art of Interaction in Seventeenth-Century France.* Philadelphia: University of Pennsylvania Press, 1988.

Goldsmith, Elizabeth C., ed. *Writing the Female Voice: Essays on Epistolary Literature.* Boston: Northeastern University Press, 1989.

Gradenigo, Pietro. *Lettere inedite di Pietro Gradenigo Patrizio Veneto Scritte a diversi.* Venice: Biblioteca Nazionale Marciana, MSS it. X, 23 (=6526).

Graf, Arturo. *Attraverso il Cinquecento.* Turin: Chiantore, 1888.

Grafton, Anthony, and Lisa Jardine. *From Humanism to the Humanities: Education and the Liberal Arts in Fifteenth- and Sixteenth-Century Europe.* Cambridge: Harvard University Press, 1986.

Greco, Aulo. "Tradizione e vita negli epistolari del Rinascimento." In *Civiltà dell'umanesimo,* edited by Giovannangiola Tarugi. Florence: Leo S. Olschki, 1982.

Green, Roland. *Post-Petrarchism: Origins and Innovations of the Western Lyric Sequence.* Princeton: Princeton University Press, 1991.

Greenblatt, Stephen. *Renaissance Self-Fashioning from More to Shakespeare.* Chicago: University of Chicago Press, 1969.

Greene, Thomas M. *The Light in Troy: Imitation and Discovery in Renaissance Poetry.* New Haven: Yale University Press, 1982.

Grendler, Paul F. *Critics of the Italian World, 1530–1560: Anton Francesco Doni, Nicolò Franco, and Ortensio Lando.* Madison: University of Wisconsin Press, 1969.

———. *The Roman Inquisition and the Venetian Press, 1540–1605.* Princeton: Princeton University Press, 1977.

———. "What Zuanne Read in School: Vernacular Texts in Sixteenth-Century Venetian Schools." *Sixteenth Century Journal* 13, no. 1 (1982): 41–53.

———. "The Organization of Primary and Secondary Education in the Italian Renaissance." *Catholic Historical Review* 71, no. 2 (1985): 185–205.

———. "Chivalric Romances in the Italian Renaissance." *Studies in Medieval and Renaissance History* 10 (1988): 57–102.

———. *Schooling in Renaissance Italy: Literacy and Learning, 1300–1600.* Baltimore: Johns Hopkins University Press, 1989.

Groto, Luigi. *Trofeo della vittoria sacra.* Venice: Sigismondo Bordogna, 1572.

———. *Lettere famigliari di Luigi Groto Cieco d'Adria.* Venice: Giovacchino Brugnolo, 1601.

Grubb, James S. "When Myths Lose Power: Four Decades of Venetian Historiography." *Journal of Modern History* 58 (1986): 43–94.

———. *Firstborn of Venice: Vicenza in the Early Renaissance State.* Baltimore: Johns Hopkins University Press, 1988.

Gubar, Susan. "Sapphistries." *Signs* 10 (1984): 43–62.

Guerrini, Paolo. *Una celebre famiglia lombarda, I Conti di Martinengo: Studi e ricerche genealogiche.* Brescia: Geroldi, 1930.

Guthmuller, Bodo. *Ovidio Metamorphoseos Vulgare: Formen und Funktionen der volkssprachlichen Wiedergabe klassischer Dichtung in der italienischen Renaissance.* Boppard am Rhein: Harold Boldt Verlag, 1981.

Hale, J. R. "Venice and its Empire." In *The Genius of Venice, 1500–1600,* edited by Jane Martineau and Charles Hope. New York: H. N. Abrams, 1984.

Hallett, Judith P. "Book IV: Propertius' Recusatio to Augustus and Augustan Ideals." Ph.D. diss., Harvard University, 1971.

———. "The Role of Women in Roman Elegy: Counter-Cultural Feminism." *Arethusa* 6, no. 1 (1973): 103–20.

———. "Sappho and Her Social Context: Sense and Sensuality." *Signs* 4 (1979): 447–64.

Hallowell, Robert E. *Ronsard and the Conventional Roman Elegy.* Urbana and Chicago: University of Illinois Press, 1954.

Hanisch, Gertrude S. *Love Elegies of the Renaissance: Marot, Louise Labé, Ronsard.* Saratoga, Calif.: Stanford French and Italian Studies, 1979.

Harvey, Elizabeth D. "Ventriloquizing Sappho: Ovid, Donne, and the Erotics of the Feminine Voice." *Criticism* 31, no. 2 (1989): 115–38.

Haselkorn, Anne. *Prostitution in Elizabethan and Jacobean Comedy.* Troy, N.Y.: Whitson, 1983.

Henderson, Judith Rice. "Erasmus on the Art of Letter-Writing." In *Renaissance Eloquence: Studies in the Theory and Practice of Renaissance Rhetoric,* edited by James J. Murphy. Berkeley: University of California Press, 1983.

Herlihy, David. "Tuscan Names, 1200–1530." *Renaissance Quarterly* 41, no. 4 (1988): 561–82.

Hollander, John. *The Figure of Echo: A Mode of Allusion in Milton and After.* Berkeley: University of California Press, 1981.

Hope, Charles. *Titian.* New York: Harper and Row, 1980.

Horace. *Carme.* Translated by W. Bennet. London: Heinemann, 1934.

Horowitz, Maryanne C. "Aristotle and Women." *Journal of the History of Biology* 9 (1979): 183–213.

Howard, Deborah. *Jacopo Sansovino: Architecture and Patronage in Renaissance Venice.* New Haven: Yale University Press, 1975.

Howell, Martha C. "Citizenship and Gender: Women's Political Status in Northern Medieval Cities." In *Women and Power in the Middle Ages,* edited by Mary Erler and Maryanne Kowaleski. Athens: University of Georgia Press, 1988.

Hughes, Charles, ed. *Shakespeare's Europe: A Survey of the Condition of Europe at the End of the Sixteenth Century* New York: Benjamin Blum, 1903; reprint, 1967.

Hughes, Diane Owen. "From Brideplace to Dowry in Mediterranean Europe." *Journal of Family History* 3 (1978): 262–96.

———. "Sumptuary Laws and Social Relations in Renaissance Italy." In *Disputes and Settlements: Law and Human Relations in the West,* edited by John Bossy. Cambridge: Cambridge University Press, 1983.

———. "Earrings for Circumcision: Distinction and Purification in the Italian Renaissance City." In *Persons in Groups: Social Behavior as Identity Formation in Medieval and Renaissance Europe,* edited by Richard C. Trexler. Binghamton, N. Y.: Medieval and Renaissance Texts and Studies, 1985.

———. "Representing the Family: Portraits and Purposes in Early Modern Italy." *Journal of Interdisciplinary History* 17 (1986): 7–38.

Huse, Norbert, and Wolfgang Wolters. *The Art of Renaissance Venice: Architecture, Sculpture, and Painting 1460–1590.* Chicago: University of Chicago Press, 1990.

Ingegneri, Angelo. *Versi alla vinitiana, zoé canzon, satire, lettere amorose, matinae, canzonette . . . .* Vicenza: Salvadori, 1617.

———. *De rimedi contro l'amore.* Avignon: Pietro Rosso, 1576.

———. *Del buon segretario: Libri tre.* Rome: Guglielmo Faciotto, 1594.

Ivanoff, Nicola. "Il ciclo allegorico della Libreria Sansoviniana." In *Arte antica e moderna.* Florence: Sansoni, 1961.

———. "I cicli allegorici della Libreria e del Palazzo Ducale di Venezia." In *Rinascimento europeo e rinascimento veneziano,* edited by Vittore Branca. Florence: G. C. Sansoni, 1967.

Jacobson, Howard. *Ovid's "Heroides."* Princeton: Princeton University Press, 1974.

Jacquot, Jean. *Les fêtes de la Renaissance.* 3 vols. Paris: Editions du centre nationale de la récherche scientifique, 1956.

Jardine, Lisa. *Still Harping on Daughters: Women and Drama in the Age of Shakespeare.* Totowa, N.J.: Barnes and Noble, 1983.

Javitch, Daniel. *Poetry and Courtliness in Renaissance England.* Princeton: Princeton University Press, 1978.

―――. "The Impure Motives of Elizabethan Poetry." In *The Power of Forms in the English Renaissance,* edited by Stephen Greenblatt. Norman, Okla.: Pilgrim Books, 1983.

Jones, Ann Rosalind. "Assimilation with a Difference: Renaissance Women Poets and Literary Influence." *Yale French Studies* 62 (1981): 135–53.

―――. "City Women and Their Audiences: Louise Labé and Veronica Franco." In *Rewriting the Renaissance: The Discourses of Sexual Difference in Early Modern Europe,* edited by Margaret W. Ferguson, Maureen Quilligan, and Nancy J. Vickers. Chicago: University of Chicago Press, 1986.

―――. "Surprising Fame: Renaissance Gender Ideologies and Women's Lyric." In *The Poetics of Gender,* edited by Nancy K. Miller. New York: Columbia University Press, 1986.

―――. "Nets and Bridles: Early Modern Conduct Books and Sixteenth-Century Women's Lyrics." in *Essays on Literature and the History of Sexuality,* edited by Nancy Armstrong and Leonard Tennenhouse. London: Methuen, 1987.

―――. *The Currency of Eros: Women's Love Lyric in Europe, 1540–1620.* Bloomington and Indianapolis: Indiana University Press, 1990.

―――. "New Songs for the Swallow: Ovid's Philomela in Tullia d'Aragona and Gaspara Stampa." In *Refiguring Woman: Gender Studies and the Italian Renaissance,* edited by Marilyn Migiel and Juliana Schiesari. Ithaca: Cornell University Press, 1991.

Jones, Ann Rosalind, and Peter Stallybrass. "The Politics of Astrophil and Stella." *Studies in English Literature* 24, no. 1 (1984): 53–68.

Joplin, Patricia Kleindienst. "The Voice of the Shuttle Is Ours." *Stanford Literature Review* 1 (1983): 25–53.

Jordan, Constance. "Feminism and the Humanists: The Case of Sir Thomas Elyot's *Defense of Good Women.*" In *Rewriting the Renaissance,* ed. Margaret W. Ferguson, Maureen Quilligan, and Nancy J. Vickers. Chicago: University of Chicago Press, 1986.

―――. "Boccaccio's In-Famous Women: Gender and Civic Virtue in the *De mulieribus claris.*" In *Ambiguous Realities: Women in the Middle Ages and Renaissance,* edited by Carole Levin and Jeanie Wilson. Detroit: Wayne State University Press, 1987.

―――. *Renaissance Feminism: Literary Texts and Political Models.* Ithaca: Cornell University Press, 1990.

Junkerman, Anne Christine. "Bellissima Donna: An Interdisciplinary Study of Venetian Sensuous Half-Length Images of the Early Sixteenth Century." Ph.D. diss., University of California, Berkeley, 1988.

Kahr, Madilyn Millner. "Danae: Virtuous, Voluptuous, Venal Woman." *Art Bulletin* 58 (1978): 43–55.

Kauffman, Linda S. *Discourses of Desire: Gender, Genre, and Epistolary Fictions.* Ithaca: Cornell University Press, 1986.

Kennedy, William. *Jacopo Sannazaro and the Uses of Pastoral.* Hanover, N. H.: University Press of New England, 1983.

Kernan, Alvin B. "Aggression and Satire: Art Considered as a Form of Biological Adaptation." In *Literary Theory and Structure: Essays in Honor of William K. Wimsatt,* edited by Frank Brady, John Palmer, and Martin Price. New Haven: Yale University Press, 1973.

Kieckhefer, Richard. *European Witch Trials: Their Foundations in Popular and Learned Culture, 1300–1500.* Berkeley: University of California Press, 1976.

King, Margaret L. "Personal, Domestic, and Republican Values in the Moral Philosophy of Giovanni Caldiera." *Renaissance Quarterly* 28 (1975): 535–74.

———. "Caldiera and the Barbaros on Marriage and the Family: Humanist Reflections of Venetian Realities." *Journal of Medieval and Renaissance Studies* 6 (1976): 19–50.

———. "Thwarted Ambitions: Six Learned Women of the Early Italian Renaissance." *Soundings* 76 (1976).

———. "Book-lined Cells: Women and Humanism in the Early Italian Renaissance." In *Beyond Their Sex: Learned Women of the European Past,* edited by Patricia H. Labalme. New York: New York University Press, 1980.

———. *Venetian Humanism in an Age of Patrician Dominance.* Princeton: Princeton University Press, 1986.

King, Margaret L., and Albert Rabil, Jr., eds. *Her Immaculate Hand: Selected Works by and about the Women Humanists of Quattrocento Italy.* Binghamton, N.Y.: Center for Medieval and Early Renaissance Studies, 1983.

Kirshner, Julius. "Pursuing Honor While Avoiding Sin: The Monte delle Doti of Florence." *Quaderni di "Studi senesi"* 41 (1978): 1–82.

Kirshner, Julius, and Anthony Molho, "The Dowry Fund and the Marriage Market in Early Quattrocento Florence." *Journal of Modern History* 50 (1978): 403–16.

Klapisch-Zuber, Christiane. *Women, Family, and Ritual in Renaissance Italy.* Translated by Eric Cochrane and Lydia Cochrane. Chicago: University of Chicago Press, 1985.

Kohl, Benjamin G., and Ronald G. Witt, eds. *The Earthly Republic: Italian Humanists on Government and Society.* Philadelphia: University of Pennsylvania Press, 1978.

Kritzman, Lawrence. *Destruction/Découverte: La fonctionnement de la rhétorique dans les Essais de Montaigne.* Lexington: University Press of Kentucky, 1980.

Kuehn, Thomas. "Reading Microhistory: The Example of *Giovanni and Lusanna.*" *Journal of Modern History* 61 (1989): 512–34.

Kuntz, Marion L. "The Virgin of Venice and Concepts of the Millenium in Venice." In *The Politics of Gender in Early Modern Europe,* edited by Jean R. Brink, Allison P. Coudert, and Maryanne C. Horowitz (Kirksville, Mo.: Sixteenth Century Journal Publishers, 1989).

Labalme, Patricia H. "Women's Roles in Early Modern Venice: An Exceptional Case." *In Beyond Their Sex: Learned Women of the European Past,* edited by Patricia H. Labalme. New York: New York University Press, 1980.

———. "Venetian Women on Women: Three Early Modern Feminists." *Archivio veneto,* 5th ser., 117 (1981): 81–109.

———. "Personality and Politics in Venice: Pietro Aretino." In *Titian, His World and His Legacy,* edited by David Rosand. New York: Columbia University Press, 1982.

———. "Sodomy and Venetian Justice in the Renaissance." *Legal History Review* 52 (1984): 217–54.

Labé, Louise. *Oeuvres complètes de Louise Labé,* edited by François Rigolot. Paris: Garnier Flammarion, 1986.

LaCapra, Dominique. *History and Criticism.* Ithaca: Cornell University Press, 1985.

Lambert, Ellen Z. *Placing Sorrow: A Study of the Pastoral Elegy Convention from Theocritus to Milton.* Chapel Hill: University of North Carolina Press, 1976.

Lami, Alessandro, and Franco Maltomini, translators and editors. *Dialoghi di dei e di cortigiane.* Milan: Rizzoli, 1986.

Lane, Frederick C. "The Enlargement of the Great Council Hall of Venice." In *Florilegium Histo-*

riale: Essays Presented to Wallace K. Ferguson, edited by J. G. Rowe and W. H. Stockdale. Toronto: University of Toronto Press, 1971.

―――. *Storia di Venezia.* Turin: Einaudi, 1978.

Larivaille, Paul. *La vie quotidienne des courtisanes en Italie au temps de la Renaissance.* Paris: Hachette, 1975.

―――. *Lettere di, a, su Aretino nel fondo Bongi dell'Archivio di Stato di Lucca.* Nanterre: Centre de Récherches de Langue et Litterature Italiennes, 1980.

―――. *Pietro Aretino: Fra rinascimento e manierismo.* Translated by Mariella Di Maio and Maria Luisa Rispoli. Rome: Bulzoni, 1980.

―――. *"La Venexiana* ou les ressources du langage honnête. Censure et théâtre à Venise." In *Le pouvoir et la plume: Incitation, contrôle, et répression dans l'Italie du XVIeme siècle.* Paris: Centre Interuniversitaire de Recherche sur la Renaissance italienne, 1982.

La Penna, Antonio. "Note sul linguaggio erotico dell'elegia latina." *Maia* 4 (1951): 208.

―――. *L'integrazione difficile: Un profilo di Properzio.* Turin: Einaudi, 1977.

Lasareff, Victor. "Studies in the Iconography of the Virgin." *Art Bulletin* 20 (1938): 26–65.

Lascu, Nicolae. "La fortuna di Ovidio dal Rinascimento ai tempi nostri." *Studi Ovidiani* (1959): 81–95.

Lavezuola, Alberto. *Le osservationi,* in *Orlando furioso . . . nuovamente adornato.* Venice: Francesco de' Franceschi Senese, 1584.

Lawner, Lynne. *Lives of the Courtesans.* Milan: Rizzoli, 1987.

―――. *I modi: The Sixteen Pleasures—An Erotic Album of the Italian Renaissance.* Evanston, Ill.: Northwestern University Press, 1988.

Lazzaro, Claudia. "The Visual Language of Gender in Sixteenth-Century Garden Sculpture." In *Refiguring Woman: Gender Studies and the Italian Renaissance,* edited by Marilyn Migiel and Juliana Schiesari. Ithaca: Cornell University Press, 1991.

Lee, Rensselaer W. *Ut Pictor Poesis: The Humanistic Theory in Painting.* New York: Norton, 1967.

Lenzi, Maria Ludovica. *Donne e madonne: L'educazione femminile nel primo rinascimento italiano.* Turin: Loescher, 1982.

Levi, Anthony. *French Moralists: The Theory of the Passions, 1585 to 1649.* Oxford: Clarendon Press, 1964.

Lettere amorose et sonetti familiari in diversi propositi: Confrontati alle lettere per poter scriver a casi occorrenti. Venice: Frezzaria al Segno della Regina, 1580.

Levarie Smarr, Janet. *Boccaccio and Fiammetta: The Narrator as Lover.* Urbana and Chicago: University of Illinois Press, 1986.

Levin, Harry. *The Myth of the Golden Age in the Renaissance.* New York: Oxford University Press, 1969.

Libro di Marco Aurelio con l'Horologio de' Principi, 3 vols. Venice: Francesco Portonaris, 1556.

Lichtenstein, Jacqueline. "Making Up Representation: The Risks of Femininity." *Representations* 20 (1987): 77–87.

Lilja, Sara. *The Roman Love Elegists' Attitude to Women.* Helsinki: Suomalainen Tiedeakatemia, 1965.

Lipking, Lawrence. *Abandoned Women and Poetic Tradition.* Chicago: University of Chicago Press, 1988.

Loi, Maria Rosa, and Mario Pozzi. "Le Lettere familiari di Sperone Speroni." *Giornale storico della letteratura italiana* 163, no. 523 (1987): 383–413.

Longhi, Silvia. *Lusus: Il capitolo burlesco nel Cinquecento.* Padua: Antenore, 1983.

da Longiano, Fausto Sebastiano. *Il duello.* Venice: Vincenzo Valgrisi, 1552.

———. *Dialogo del modo de lo tradurre d'una in altra lingua.* Venice: Giovanni Griffo dell'Avanzi, 1556.

Lowry, Martin. "The Reform of the Council of Ten, 1582–83: An Unsettled Problem?" *Studi veneziani* 13 (1971): 275–310.

———. *The World of Aldus Manutius: Business and Scholarship in Renaissance Venice.* Ithaca: Cornell University Press, 1979.

Lucian. *Dialoghi di dei e di cortigiane.* Translated and edited by Alessandro Lami and Franco Maltomini. Milan: Rizzoli, 1986.

MacKinnon, Catharine A. *Feminism Unmodified: Discourses on Life and Law.* Cambridge: Harvard University Press, 1987.

Maclean, Ian. *The Renaissance Notion of Woman: A Study in the Fortunes of Scholasticism and Medical Science in European Intellectual Life.* New York: Cambridge University Press, 1980.

Maffei, Scipione. *Verona illustrata.* Verona: Jacopo Vallarsi and Pierantonio Berni, 1731–32.

Magno, Celio, and Orsatto Giustinian. *Rime di Celio Magno et Orsatto Giustinian.* Venice: Andrea Muschio, 1600.

Malipiero, Angelo. *Notizie istoriche della Pia Casa di Santa Maria del Soccorso.*

Manfredi, Muzio. *Per donne romane: Rime di diversi.* Bologna: Alessandro Benacci, 1575.

———. *Cento donne cantate.* Mantua: Stamperia d'Erasmo, 1580.

———. *Cento madrigali.* Mantua: Francesco Osanna, 1587.

———. *La semiramis boscareccia.* Bergamo: Comino Ventura, 1593.

———. *Cento sonetti . . . in lode di cento donne di Pavia.* Pavia: Girolamo Bartoli, 1601.

———. *Lettere brevissime di Mutio Manfredi.* Venice: Francesco Rondinelli, 1606.

———. *Delle lettere volgari di diversi nobilissimi huomini, et eccellentissimi ingegni scritte in diverse materie, con la giunta del terzo libro.* Venice: Paolo Manuzio, 1567.

Manuzio, Paolo. *Tre libri di lettere volgari.* Venice: Aldus, 1556.

———. *Lettere volgari di Paolo Manutio.* Venice: Aldus, 1560.

Maranini, Giuseppe. *La costituzione di Venezia dopo la serrata del Maggior Consiglio.* 2 vols. 2d ed. Florence: La Nuova Italia, 1974.

Marcellino, Marco Valerio. *Il diamerone.* Venice: Gabriel Giolito de' Ferrari, 1564.

Marini, Paola, ed. *Palladio e Verona.* Vicenza: Neri Pozza, 1980.

Mariotti Masi, M. L. *Bianca Cappello: Una veneziana alla corte dei Medici.* Milan: Mursia, 1986.

Martelli, Nicolo. *Il primo libro delle lettere.* Florence: Anton Francesco Doni, 1546.

———. *Opere poetiche.* Florence: 1548.

Marti, Mario. "L'epistolario come 'genere' è un problema editoriale." In *Studi e problemi di critica testuale.* Convegno di Studi di Filologia italiana nel Centenario della Commissione per i testi di lingua, 7–9 april 1960. Bologna: 1961.

Martin, John. "Out of the Shadow: Heretical and Catholic Women in Renaissance Venice." *Journal of Family History* (1985): 21–33.

———. "L'Inquisizione romana e la criminalizzazione del dissenso religioso a Venezia all'inizio dell'età moderna." *Quaderni storici* 66, no. 3 (1987): 777–802.

———. "A Journeyman's Feast of Fools." *Journal of Medieval and Renaissance Studies* 17, no. 2 (1987): 149–74.

———. "Salvation and Society in Sixteenth-Century Venice: Popular Evangelism in a Renaissance City." *Journal of Modern History* 60, no. 2 (1988): 205–33.

Martin, Ruth. *Witchcraft and the Inquisition in Venice, 1550–1650.* Oxford: Basil Blackwell, 1989.

Maschio, Ruggero. "Le Scuole Grandi a Venezia." In *Storia della cultura veneta.* ed., Girolamo Arnaldi and Manlio Pastore Stocchi. 4 vols. Vicenza: Neri Pozza, 1981.

―――. *Motivi storici della educazione femminile: Scienza, lavoro, giouchi.* Naples: M. D'Aurio, 1982.

Masetti Zannini, Gian Ludovico. "Veronica Franco a Roma: Una pellegrina 'tra mille.'" *Strenna dei romanisti* (1982): 322–31.

Masson, Georgina. *The Courtesans of the Italian Renaissance.* London: Secker and Warburg, 1975.

Maylender, Michele. *Storia delle accademie d'Italia.* 5 vols. Bologna: 1926–30.

Mazzacurati, Giancarlo. *Misure del classicismo rinascimentale.* Naples: Liguori, 1977.

―――. *Conflitte di culture.* Naples: Liguori, 1977.

Mazzotta, Giuseppe. "The *Canzoniere* and the Language of the Self." *Studies in Philology* 75 (1978): 271–96.

―――. *The World at Play in Boccaccio's Decameron.* Princeton: Princeton University Press, 1986.

Mazzotti, Giuseppe. *Ville venete.* Rome: C. Bestetti, 1963.

Medin, Antonio. *Per la storia della Repubblica di Venezia nella poesia.* Milan: Ulrico Hoepli, 1904.

Menetto, L., and G. Zennaro, eds. *Storia del malcostume a Venezia nei secoli XVI e XVII.* Abano Terme: Piovan Editore, 1987.

Milani, Marisa. "Il caso di Emilia Catena, meretrice, 'striga et herbera.'" *Museum Patavinum* 4 (1985): 75–97.

―――. "L''Incanto' di Veronica Franco." *Giornale storico della letteratura italiana* 262: no. 518 (1985): 250–63.

―――. "La verità *ovvero* il processo contro Isabella Bellocchio." Venezia, 12 gennaio–14 ottobre 1589. 2 vols. Padua: Centrostampa, 1985.

Miles, Margaret R. *Image as Insight: Visual Understanding in Western Christianity and Secular Culture.* Boston: Beacon Press, 1985.

―――. "The Virgin's One Bare Breast: Female Nudity and Religious Meaning in Tuscan Early Renaissance Culture." In *The Female Body in Western Culture,* edited by Susan Rubin Suleiman. Cambridge: Harvard University Press, 1986.

Mitchell, Bonner. *The Majesty of the State: Triumphal Progresses of Foreign Sovereigns in Renaissance Italy, 1494–1600.* Florence: Leo S. Olschki, 1986.

Molmenti, Pompeo G. *La storia di Venezia nella vita privata dalle origini alla caduta della repubblica.* 7th ed. Bergamo: Istituto italiano d'arti grafiche, 1928.

Montaigne, Michel. *Discorsi morali, politici et militari del molto illustre Signor Michiel di Montagna Cavaliere dell'Ordine del Re Christianissimo . . . .* Translated by Girolamo Naselli. Ferrara: Benedetto Mamarello, 1590.

―――. *Saggi di Michel Signor di Montagna overo Discorsi naturali, politici, e morali.* Translated by Marco Ginammi. Venice: Marco Ginammi, 1633.

―――. *Journal de voyage en Italie,* edited by Maurice Rat. Paris: Editions Garnier, 1955.

―――. *The Complete Essays of Montaigne.* Translated by Donald M. Frame. Stanford: Stanford University Press, 1965.

―――. *Essais: Livre I.* Edited by Alexandre Micha. Paris: Garnier-Flammarion, 1969.

Monter, William. "Women and the Italian Inquisitions." In *Women in the Middle Ages and the Renaissance and Historical Perspectives,* edited by Mary Beth Rose. Syracuse: Syracuse University Press, 1985.

Montrose, Louis Adrian. "'Eliza, Queene of shepheardes,' and the Pastoral of Power." *English Literary Renaissance* 10 (1980): 153–82.

_____. "Of Gentlemen and Shepherds: The Politics of Elizabethan Pastoral Form." English Literary History 50 (1983): 415–59.

Morgan, Kathleen. *Ovid's Art of Imitation: Propertius in the Amores.* Brill: Lugduni Bavatorum, 1977.

Moss, Ann. *Ovid in Renaissance France: A Survey of the Latin Editions of Ovid and Commentaries Printed in France Before 1600.* London: Warburg, 1982.

Mueller, Reinhold C. "Procurators of San Marco." *Studi veneziani* 13 (1971): 190–220.

Muir, Edward. "Images of Power: Art and Pageantry in Renaissance Venice." *American Historical Review* 84, no. 1 (1979): 16–52.

_____. *Civic Ritual in Renaissance Venice.* Princeton: Princeton University Press, 1981.

_____. "The Virgin on the Street Corner: The Place of the Sacred in Italian Cities." In *Religion and Culture in the Renaissance and Reformation,* edited by Steven Ozment. vol. 11 (1987): 25–40.

Muir, Edward, and Ronald F. E. Weissman. "Social and Symbolic Places in Renaissance Venice and Florence." In *The Power of Place: Integrating Geographical and Sociological Imaginations,* edited by John Agnew and James Duncan. Boston: Unwin Hyman, 1989.

Mulier, Eco O. G. Haitsma. *The Myth of Venice and Dutch Republican Thought in the Seventeenth Century.* Translated by Gerard T. Moran. Assen: Van Gorcum, 1980.

Muraro, Michelangelo. "Venezia: Interpretazione del Palazzo Ducale." *Studi urbinati di storia, filosofia e letteratura* 45 (1971): 1160–75.

Murphy, James J., ed. *Renaissance Eloquence: Studies in the Theory and Practice of Renaissance Eloquence.* Berkeley: University of California Press, 1983.

Musatti, Eugenio. *La donna in Venezia.* Padua: Arnaldo Forni, 1892.

Mutinelli, Fabio. *Annali urbani di Venezia dall'anno 810 al 12 maggio 1797.* Venice: G. B. Merlo, 1841.

Muzio, Girolamo. *Rime diverse del Mutio* and *Dell'arte poetica.* Venice: Gabriel Giolito de' Ferrari, 1551.

_____. *Il duello.* Venice: Gabriel Giolito de' Ferrari, 1564.

_____. *Il gentiluomo.* Venice: Giovanni Andrea Valvassori, 1564.

_____. *Due discorsi.* Padua: Paolo Meietti, 1590.

Neff, Mary Frances. "A Citizen in the Service of the Patrician State: The Career of Zaccaria de' Freschi." *Studi veneziani* 5 (1981): 33–61.

_____. "Chancellery Secretaries in Venetian Politics and Society, 1480–1533." 2 vols. Ph.D. diss., UCLA, 1985.

Newcomb, Anthony. "Courtesans, Muses, or Musicians? Professional Women Musicians in Sixteenth-Century Italy." In *Women Making Music: The Western Art Tradition, 1150–1950,* edited by Jane Bowers and Judith Tick. Urbana and Chicago: University of Illinois Press, 1986.

Newett, Margaret. "The Sumptuary Laws of Venice in the Fourteenth and Fifteenth Centuries." In *Historical Essays by Members of the Owens College, Manchester,* edited by T. F. Tout and James Tait. Manchester: University Press of Manchester, 1907.

Newett, Margaret, ed. *Canon Pietro Casola's Pilgrimage to Jerusalem in the Year 1494.* Manchester: University Press of Manchester, 1907.

Newman, Karen. "City Talk: Women and Commodification in Jonson's *Epicoene.*" *English Literary History* 56, no. 3 (1989): 503–18.

Nordio, Tiziana Agostini. "Rime dialettali attribuite a Maffio Venier. Primo regesto." *Quaderni veneti,* no. 2 (1985): 7–23.

Nordio, Tiziana Agostini. "'La Strazzosa,' Canzone di Maffio Venier: Edizione critica." In Tiziana Agostini Nordio and Valerio Vianello, *Contributi Rinascimentali: Venezia e Firenze.* Padua: Francisci Editore, 1982.

Nussbaum, Felicity A. *The Brink of All We Hate: English Satires on Women 1660–1750.* Lexington: University Press of Kentucky, 1984.

———. *The Autobiographical Subject: Gender and Ideology in Eighteenth-Century England.* Baltimore: Johns Hopkins University Press, 1989.

Nutter, David. "A Tragedy for Henry III of France, Venice, 1574." In *Essays in Honor of Craig Hugh Smyth,* edited by Andrew Morrogh et al. 2 vols. Florence: Giunti Barbera, 1985.

Odorisio, Ginevra Conti. *Donna e società nel seicento.* Rome: Bulzoni, 1979.

Okin, Susan Moller. *Women in Western Political Thought.* Princeton: Princeton University Press, 1973.

Oliva, Carlo, ed. *Poesia italiana: Il Quattrocento.* Milan: Garzanti, 1978.

Olivieri, Achillo. "Erotisme et groupes sociaux a Venise au XVIe siècle: La Courtisane." *Communications* 35 (1982): 85–91.

O'Neil, Mary R. "*Sacerdote ovvero strione:* Ecclesiastical and Superstitious Remedies in Sixteenth Century Italy." In *Understanding Popular Culture,* edited by Steve Kaplan. New York: Mouton, 1984.

O'Neill, John. *Essaying Montaigne: A Study of the Renaissance Institution of Writing and Reading.* London: Routledge and Kegan Paul, 1982.

Ossola, Carlo, and Adriano Prosperi. *Le corte e il Cortegiano.* 2 vols. Rome: Bulzoni, 1980.

Otis, Brooks. *Ovid as an Epic Poet.* Cambridge: Cambridge University Press, 1970.

Otis, Leah Lydia. *Prostitution in Medieval Society: The History of an Institution in Languedoc.* Chicago: University of Chicago Press, 1985.

Ovid. *Remedia Amoris.* Translated by J. H. Mozley. Cambridge: Harvard University Press, 1929.

———. *Ovid: The Metamorphoses.* Translated by Horace Gregory. New York: Viking Press, 1958.

———. *Le eroidi.* Translated by Gabriella Leto. Turin: Einaudi, 1966.

———. *Ovidio: L'arte di amare.* Translated by Latino Maccari. Turin: Einaudi, 1969.

———. *Ovid: Amores Book One,* Edited and translated by John Barsby. Oxford: Clarendon Press, 1973.

———. *Ovid: The Love Poems.* Translated by A. D. Melville, with notes and introduction by E. J. Kenney. New York: Oxford University Press, 1990.

Padoan, Giorgio. "'Ut Pictor Poesis': Le 'Pitture' di Ariosto, Le 'Poesie' di Tiziano." In *Tiziano e Venezia.* Vicenza: Neri Pozza, 1976.

———. "La Venexiana 'non fabula non comedia ma vera historia.'" In his *Momenti del rinascimento veneto.* Padua: Editore Antenore, 1978.

———. "Maffio Venier. Tre liriche: I. Do donne me sè drio quasi ogni dì II. Amor, son co' xe un can da scoassera III. M'ho consumà aspettandote, ben mio." *Quaderni veneti,* no. 2 (1985): 7–30.

Padoan, Giorgio, ed. *Petrarca, Venezia e il Veneto*. Florence: Leo S. Olschki, 1976.

Pagan, Pietro. "Sulla Accademia 'Venetiana' o della 'Fama.'" *Atti dell'Istituto Veneto di Scienze, Lettere ed Arti* 132 (1973–74): 359–92.

Palladino, Lora. "Pietro Aretino: Orator and Art Theorist." Ph.D. diss., Yale University, 1984.

Pallavicino, Giuseppe. *Delle lettere del Signor Gioseppe Pallavicino da Varrano. Libri tre.* Venice: Francesco Rampazetto, 1566.

Palumbo-Fossati, Isabella. "L'interno della casa dell'artigiano e dell'artista nella Venezia del Cinquecento." *Studi veneziani* 8 (1984): 109–53.

Panegirico nel felice dottorato dell'Illustre, et Eccellentissimo Signor Gioseppe Spinelli, Dignissimo Rettor de legisti, et cavalier splendidissimo. Padua: Lorenzo Pasquati, 1575.

Panofsky, Erwin. *Studies in Iconology*. New York: Harper and Row, 1939.

——. *Problems in Titian: Mostly Iconographic*. New York: New York University Press, 1969.

Panrose, Boies. *Urbane Travelers, 1591–1635*. Philadelphia: University of Pennsylvania Press, 1942.

Parker, Patricia. *Inescapable Romance*. Princeton: Princeton University Press, 1983.

——. *Literary Fat Ladies*. London: Methuen, 1987.

Paschini, Pio. "I monasteri femminili in Italia nel 1500." In his *Problemi di vita religiosa in Italia nel Cinquecento*. Padua: Antenore, 1960.

Passe, Crispijn van de. *Le miroir des plus belles courtisannes de ce temps*. Printed for the author, 1631.

Paterno, ed. *Satire di cinque poeti illustri*. Venice: G. A. Valvassori, 1565.

Pavan, Elizabeth. "Police del moeurs, societé et politique à Venise à la fin du Moyen Age." *Révue Historique* 264 (1980): 244–66.

Pavanini, Paola. "Abitazioni popolari e borghesi nella Venezia cinquecentesca." *Studi veneziani* 5 (1981): 63–126.

Pavia, Mario N. *Drama of the Sigla de Oro: A Study of Magic, Witchcraft, and Other Occult Beliefs*. New York: Hispanic Institute in the United States, 1959.

Pelaez, Mario. "Nicolo Martelli." In *Enciclopedia Italiana*, vol. 22. Rome: Istituto della Enciclopedia Italiana, 1934.

Pellegrini, Domen Maria. "Breve dissertazione previa al Sommario dell'Accademia Veneta della Fama." *Giornale della italiana letteratura* 22–23 (1808).

Perry, Mary Elizabeth. "'Lost Women' in Early Modern Seville: The Politics of Prostitution." *Feminist Studies* 4, no. 1 (1978): 195–214.

——. "Deviant Insiders: Legalized Prostitutes and a Consciousness of Women in Early Modern Seville." *Comparative Studies in Society and History* 27 (1985): 135–58.

——. *Gender and Disorder in Early Modern Seville*. Princeton: Princeton University Press, 1990.

Petrarch, Francesco. *Petrarch's Lyric Poems*. Edited and translated by Robert M. Durling. Cambridge: Harvard University Press, 1976.

Pfeiffer, Wendy. *The Change of Philomel*. New York: Peter Lang, 1985.

Piejus, Marie-Françoise. "La première anthologie de poèmes féminins: L'écriture filtrée et orientée." In *Le pouvoir et la plume*. Paris: Université de la Sorbonne Nouvelle, 1982.

Pigna, Giovan Battista. *I Romanzi*. Venice: Vincenzo Valgrisi, 1554.

Pignatti, Terisio. *Veronese*. 2 vols. Venice: Alfieri, 1976.

Pilot, Antonio. "Di alcuni versi inediti sulla peste del 1575." *Ateneo veneto* 26 (1903): 350–58.

——. *Canzoni inediti di Maffio Venier*. Capodistria: 1906.

Pino, Bernardino. *Gli ingiusti sdegni*. Rome: 1553.

Piseztsky, Rosita Levi. *Storia del costume in Italia*. 5 vols. Turin: Einaudi, 1964–69.

Poli, Doretta D. "La moda nella Venezia del Palladio, 1550–1580." In *Architettura e utopia nella Venezia del Cinquecento*, edited by Lionello Puppi. Milan: Electa, 1980.

Pollak, Ellen. *The Poetics of Sexual Myth*. Chicago: University of Chicago Press, 1985.

Pomeroy, Sarah B. *Goddesses, Whores, Wives, and Slaves: Women in Classical Antiquity*. New York: Schocken Books, 1975.

———. *Heroines and Hysterics*. New York: Saint Martin's Press, 1981.

———. *Women's Life in Greece and Rome*. Edited by Mary R. Lefkowitz and Maureen B. Fant. Baltimore: Johns Hopkins University Press, 1982.

Pozzi, Mario. *Trattatisti del Cinquecento*. 2 vols. Milan and Naples: Ricciardi, 1978.

Preto, Paolo. *Peste e società a Venezia, 1576*. Vicenza: Neri Pozza, 1978.

———. "La società veneta e le grandi epidemie di peste." In *Storia della cultura veneta*. 4 vols.

Previtera, Carlo. *La poesia giocosa e l'umorismo*. Milan: Francesco Vallardi, 1939.

Procaccioli, Paolo. "Per una lettura del 'Ragionamento.'" *La Rassegna della letteratura italiana* 91 (1987).

Propertius. *The Poems of Propertius*. Translated by John Warden. Indianapolis and New York: Bobbs-Merrill, 1972.

Puliafito, Anna Laura. "Due lettere del Pinelli e l'Accademia della Fama." *Studi veneziani* 18 (1989): 285–98.

Pullan, Brian. *Rich and Poor in Renaissance Venice: The Social Institutions of a Catholic State, 1580 to 1620*. Cambridge: Harvard University Press, 1971.

———. "The Occupations and Investments of the Venetian Nobility in the Middle and Late Sixteenth Century." In *Renaissance Venice*, ed. J. R. Hale. London: Faber and Faber, 1974.

———. "The Old Catholicism, the New Catholicism, and the Poor." In *Timore e carità: I poveri nell'Italia moderna*, edited by Giorgio Politi et al. Cremona: Annali della Biblioteca Statale e Libreria Civica di Cremona, 1982.

———. *The Jews of Europe and the Inquisition of Venice, 1550–1670*. Oxford: Basil Blackwell, 1983.

Pullan, Brian, ed. *Crisis and Change in the Venetian Economy in the Sixteenth and Seventeenth Centuries*. London: Methuen, 1968.

La puttana errante. Venice: 1531; reprint, Paris: 1883.

Puppi, Lionello, ed. *Architettura e utopia nella Venezia del Cinquecento*. Milan: Electa, 1980.

Queller, Donald E. *The Venetian Patriciate: Reality versus Myth*. Chicago and Urbana: University of Illinois Press, 1987.

Quint, David. *Origin and Originality in Renaissance Literature: Versions of the Source*. New Haven: Yale University Press, 1983.

Quintilian. *Institutio oratoria*. 4 vols. Translated by H. E. Butler. Loeb Classical Library. Cambridge: Harvard University Press, [1920] 1969.

Quondam, Amedeo. *Il petrarchismo mediato*. Rome: Bulzoni, 1974.

———. *La parola nel labirinto: Società e scrittura del manierismo a Napoli*. Bari: Laterza, 1975.

———. "La scena della menzogna: Corte e cortigiano nel 'Ragionamento' di Pietro Aretino." *Psicon* nos. 8–9 (1976): 4–23.

———. *La locuzione artificiosa: Teoria ed esperienza della lirica a Napoli*. Rome: Bulzoni, 1979.

———. "Nel giardino del Marcolini: Un editore veneziano tra Aretino e Doni." *Giornale storico della letteratura italiana* 157 (1980): 75–116.

————. Le "carte messaggiere": Retorica e modelli di communicazione epistolare per un indice dei libri di lettere del Cinquecento. Rome: Bulzoni, 1981.

Rao, Cesare. L'argute et facete lettere di M. Cesare Rao. Pavia: G. Bartoli, 1580.

Reécritures 2: Commentaires, Parodies, Variations dans la literature italienne de la Renaissance. Paris: Université de la Sorbonne Nouvelle, 1984.

Regosin, Richard L. The Matter of My Book: Montaigne's "Essais" as the Book of the Self. Berkeley: University of California Press, 1977.

————. "Recent Trends in Montaigne Scholarship: A Post-Structuralist Perspective." Renaissance Quarterly 37, no. 1 (1984): 34–54.

Relatione di tutti il successo di Famagosta. Venice: Giorgio Angelieri, 1572.

Renouard, A. A. Annales de l'imprimerie des Aldes, ou histoire des trois Manuce. 3d ed. Paris: 1843.

Richlin, Amy. The Garden of Priapus: Sexuality and Aggression in Roman Humor. New Haven: Yale University Press, 1983.

Richter, Bodo L. O. "Petrarchism and Anti-Petrarchism among the Veniers." Forum Italicum 3 (1969): 20–42.

Rigolot, François. Poétique et onomastique: L'exèmple de la Renaissance. Geneva: Droz, 1977.

————. "Montaigne's Purloined Letters." Yale French Studies 64 (1983): 145–66.

————. "Gender vs. Sex Difference in Louise Labé's Grammar of Love." In Ferguson et al., Rewriting the Renaissance.

Rime diverse d'alcune nobilissime e virtuosissime donne, edited by Ludovico Domenichi. Lucca: Vincenzo Busdragho, 1559.

Rime diverse di molti eccellentissimi autori, edited by Ludovico Domenichi. Venice: Gabriel Giolito de' Ferrari, 1545.

Rinaldi, Stefania Mason. "Storia e mito nei cicli pittorici di Palazzo Ducale." In Architettura e utopia nella Venezia del Cinquecento, edited by Lionello Puppi. Milan: Electa, 1980.

Roberts, Alexander, and James Donaldson, eds. The Anti-Nicene Fathers: Translations of the Writings of the Fathers Down to A.D. 325. Grand Rapids, Mich.: Eerdmans, 1971–86.

Rogers, Katharine M. The Troublesome Helpmate. Seattle: University of Washington Press, 1966.

Romano, Dennis. "Charity and Community in Early Renaissance Venice." Journal of Urban History 2 (1984): 63–82.

————. Patricians and Popolani: The Social Foundations of the Venetian Renaissance State. Baltimore: Johns Hopkins University Press, 1987.

————. "Gender and the Urban Geography of Renaissance Venice." Journal of Social History 23, no. 2 (1989): 339–53.

Rosand, Ellen. "Music in the Myth of Venice." Renaissance Quarterly 30 (1977): 511–37.

Rosand, David. "Ut Pictor Poeta: Meaning in Titian's Poesie." New Literary History (1971–72): 527–46.

————. "Titian's Presentation to the Virgin in the Temple and the Scuola della Carità." Art Bulletin 58 (1976): 55–84.

————. Painting in Cinquecento Venice: Titian, Veronese, Tintoretto. New Haven: Yale University Press, 1982.

————. "Venetia Figurata: The Iconography of a Myth." In Interpretazioni veneziane: Studi di storia dell'arte in onore di Michelangelo Muraro, edited by David Rosand. Venice: Arsenale, 1984.

Rose, Mary Beth. The Expense of Spirit: Love and Sexuality in English Renaissance Drama. Ithaca: Cornell University Press, 1988.

Rose, Paul Lawrence. "The *Accademia Venetiana:* Science and Culture in Renaissance Venice." *Studi veneziani* 11 (1969): 191–242.

Rosenthal, Margaret F. "Veronica Franco: The Courtesan as Poet in Sixteenth-Century Venice." Ph.D. diss., Yale University, 1985.

————. "A Courtesan's Voice: Epistolary Self-Portraiture in Veronica Franco's *Terze Rime* (1575)." In *Writing the Female Voice: Essays on Epistolary Literature,* edited by Elizabeth C. Goldsmith. Boston: Northeastern University Press, 1989.

————. "Veronica Franco's *Terze Rime:* The Venetian Courtesan's Defense." *Renaissance Quarterly* 42, no. 2 (1989): 227–57.

————. "Venetian Women Writers and Their Discontents." In *Sexuality and Gender in Early Modern Europe: Institutions, Texts, Images,* edited by James Grantham Turner. Cambridge: Cambridge University Press, 1992.

Ross, Cheryl Lynn. "The Plague and the Figures of Power." Ph.D. diss., Stanford University, 1985.

Ross, David O. *Style and Tradition in Catullus.* Cambridge: Harvard University Press, 1969.

Rossetti, Giovanventura. *Plichto de l'arthe de tentori che insegna tenger pani telle bambasi et sede* . . . . Venice: Augustino Bindoni, 1548.

Rossi, Paola. "I ritratti femminili di Domenico Tentoretto." *Arte illustrata* 30 (1970): 92–99.

Rossiaud, Jacques. "Prostitution, jeunesse et société dans les villes du sud-est au XVe siécle." *Annales: Economies, Sociétés, Civilisations* 31 (1976): 289–325.

————. *Medieval Prostitution.* Translated by Lydia G. Cochrane. London: Basil Blackwell, 1988.

Roth, Cecil. *History of the Jews in Venice.* New York: Schocken Books, 1975.

Rubin, Gayle. "The Traffic in Women: Notes on the 'Political Economy' of Sex." In *Toward an Anthropology of Women,* edited by Rayna Reiter. New York: Monthly Review Press, 1975.

Rubinstein, Nicolai. "Italian Reactions to Terraferma Expansion in the Fifteenth Century." In *Renaissance Venice,* ed. J. R. Hale. London: Faber and Faber, 1974.

Rudmann, Valnea. "Lettura della canzone per la peste di Venezia di Maffio Venier." *Atti dell'Istituto Veneto di Scienze, Lettere, ed Arti* 121 (1963): 599–641.

Ruggieri, Nicola. *Maffio Venier: Arcivescovo e letterato veneziano del Cinquecento.* Udine: Tipografia Bosetti, 1909.

Ruggiero, Guido. "Modernization and the Mythic State in Early Renaissance Venice: The Serrata Revisited." *Viator* 10 (1979): 245–56.

————. *Violence in Early Renaissance Venice.* New Brunswick: Rutgers University Press, 1980.

————. *The Boundaries of Eros: Sex Crime and Sexuality in Renaissance Venice.* New York: Oxford University Press, 1985.

————. " 'Più che la vita caro': Onore, matrimonio, e reputazione femminile nel tardo rinascimento." *Quaderni storici* 66, no. 3 (1987): 753–75.

Ruscelli, Girolamo. *Le annotationi, gli avvertimenti et le dichiarationi* . . . *sopra i luoghi difficili et importanti del Furioso.* Venice: Valgrisi, 1556.

————. *Del modo di comporre in versi nella lingua italiana.* Venice: Giovanni Battista Sessa, 1582.

————. *Il rimario del signor Girolamo Ruscelli.* Venice: Simone Occhi, 1750.

Sabbatino, Pasquale. *La "scienza" della scrittura: Dal progetto del Bembo al manuale.* Florence: Leo S. Olschki Editore, 1988.

Sagredo, Agostino, and F. Berchet, *Il Fondaco dei Turchi in Venezia.* Milan: G. Civelli, 1860.

Salza, Abdelkader. "Madonna Gasparina Stampa, secondo nuove indagini." *Giornale storico della letteratura italiana* 62 (1913): 1–101.

———. *Rime: Gaspara Stampa e Veronica Franco.* Bari: Laterza, 1913.

Sansovino, Francesco. *Ragionamento di M. Francesco Sansovino nel quale brevemente s'insegna a giovani huomini la bella arte d'amore.* Venice: 1545.

———. *Delle cose notabili della città di Venetia.* Venice: Comin da Trino da Monferrato, 1561.

———. *Del secretario di M. Francesco Sansovino: Libri quattro.* Venice: Francesco Rampazetto, 1565.

———. *Dialogo del gentilhuomo venitiano.* Venice: 1566.

———. *Sette libri di satire.* Venice: Iacomo Vidali, 1573.

———. *Del secretario.* Venice: Vincenzo Valgrisi, 1580.

———. *Venetia città nobilissima et singolare.* Venice: Iacomo Sansovino, 1581.

———. *Della origine et de' fatti delle famiglie illustri d'Italia.* Venice: Altobello Salicato, 1582.

Santangelo, Salvatore. *Le tenzoni poetiche nella letteratura italiana dalle origini.* Geneva: Leo S. Olschki, 1928.

Santore, Cathy. "Julia Lombardo, 'Somtuosa Meretrize': A Portrait by Property." *Renaissance Quarterly* 41, no. 1 (1988): 44–83.

Santosuosso, Antonio. *Vita di Giovanni Della Casa.* Rome: Bulzoni, 1978.

Sanuto, Marin. *I diarii.* Edited by Rinaldo Fulin et al. 58 vols. Venice: 1879–1902.

Scaliger, J. C. *Poetices libri septem.* Lugduni: Antonium Vicentium, 1561.

Scarabello, Giovanni. "Paure, Superstizioni, Infamie." In *Storia della cultura veneta,* edited by G. Arnaldi and M. Pastore Stocchi. Vicenza: Neri Pozza, 1982.

———. "Devianza sessuale ed interventi di giustizia a Venezia nella prima metà del XVI secolo." In *Tiziano e Venezia.* Vicenza: Neri Pozza, 1980.

———. "Strutture assistenziali a Venezia nella prima metà del '500 e avvii europei della riforma dell'assistenza." In *"Renovatio urbis": Venezia nell'età di Andrea Gritti (1523–1538),* edited by Manfredo Tafuri. Rome: Officina, 1984.

Schiavon, Alessandra. "Per la biografia di Veronica Franco: Nuovi documenti." *Atti dell'Istituto Veneto di Scienze, Lettere, ed Arti* 137 (1978–79): 243–56.

Schuler, Carol M. "The Courtesan in Art: Historical Fact or Modern Fantasy?" *Women's Studies* 19, no. 2 (1991): 209–22.

Schulz, Juergen. *Venetian Painted Ceilings of the Renaissance.* Berkeley: University of California Press, 1968.

———. "The Houses of Titian, Aretino, Sansovino." In *Titian: His World and His Legacy,* edited by David Rosand. New York: Columbia University Press, 1982.

Schutte, Anne Jacobson. "The *Lettere Volgari* and the Crisis of Evangelism in Italy." *Renaissance Quarterly* 28 (1975): 639–88.

———. "Teaching Adults to Read in Sixteenth-Century Venice: Giovanni Antonio Tagliente's *Libro maistrevole.*" *Sixteenth Century Journal* 17, no. 2 (1986): 3–16.

———. "Irene di Spilimbergo: The Image of a Creative Woman in Late Renaissance Italy." *Renaissance Quarterly* 44, no. 1 (1991): 42–61.

Scrivano, Riccardo. *Cultura e letteratura del Cinquecento.* Rome: Edizioni dell'Ateneo, 1966.

———. *La norma e lo scarto: Proposte per il Cinquecento letterario italiano.* Rome: Bonacci, 1980.

Seidel, Michael. *Satiric Inheritance: Rabelais to Sterne.* Princeton: Princeton University Press, 1979.

Seidel-Menchi, Silvana. "L'Inquisizione come repressione o inquisizione come mediazione?" *Annuario dell'Istituto Storico Italiano per l'Età Moderna e Contemporanea* 35–36 (1983–84): 56–61.

———. *Erasmo in Italia, 1520–80.* Turin: Bollati Borenghieri, 1987.

Serassi, Pierantonio. *Rime di Domenico Veniero senatore viniziano raccolte ora per la prima volta ed illustrate.* Bergamo: Pietro Lancellotto, 1751.

Shapiro, Marianne. "The Provençal *Trobairitz* and the Limits of Courtly Love." *Signs* 3, no. 31 (1978): 560–71.

Shemek, Deanna. "Of Women, Knights, Arms and Love: The *Querelle des Femmes* in Ariosto's Poem." *Modern Language Notes* 104, no. 1 (1989).

Sherberg, Michael. "Epic and Romance in Tasso's *Rinaldo:* The Conflict of Genre." *Stanford Italian Review* 9, nos. 1–2 (1990): 67–85.

Sherr, Richard. "Guglielmo Gonzaga and the Castrati." *Renaissance Quarterly* 33, no. 1 (1980): 33–56.

Shiff, Jonathan. "'Lingua zerga' in the Grimani Banquet Plays." *Italica* 66, no. 4 (1989): 399–411.

Simonsfeld, Henry. *Der Fondaco dei Tedeschi in Venedig und die Deutsch-Venetianischen Handelsbeziehungen.* 2 vols. Stuttgart: Cotta, 1887.

Sinding-Larsen, Staale. *Christ in the Council Hall: Studies in the Religious Iconography of the Venetian Republic.* Rome: Institutum Romanum Norvegiae, 1974.

Smith, Logan Pearsall, ed. *The Life and Letters of Sir Henry Wotton.* Oxford: Oxford University Press, 1907.

Smith, Pauline. *The Anti-Courtier Trend in Sixteenth-Century French Literature.* Geneva: Droz, 1966.

Snyder, Jon R. *Writing the Scene of Speaking: Theories of Dialogue in the Late Italian Renaissance.* Stanford: Stanford University Press, 1989.

Somma delle opere che in tutte le scientie et arti più nobili, et in varie lingue ha da mandare in luce l'Academia Venetiana, parte nuove et non più stampate, parte con fedelissime tradottioni, giudiciose corretioni et utilissime annotationi riformate. Venice: 1558.

Speroni, Sperone. *Orationi del Sig. Speron Speroni Dottor et Cavalier Padovano.* Venice: Ruberto Meietti, 1596.

———. *Opere di M. Sperone Speroni degli Alvarotti: Tratte de' Mss. Originali,* 5 vols. Edited by Natal dalle Leste and Marco Forcellini. Venice: Domenico Occhi, 1740.

Spierenburg, Petrus Cornelis. *The Spectacle of Suffering: Execution and the Evolution of Repression from a Preindustrial Metropolis to the European Experience.* New York: Cambridge University Press, 1984.

Stahl, Hans-Peter, *Propertius: "Love" and "War": Individual and State Under Augustus.* Berkeley: University of California Press, 1985.

Stallybrass, Peter. "Patriarchal Territories: The Body Enclosed." In *Rewriting the Renaissance,* ed. Margaret W. Ferguson, Maureen Quilligan, and Nancy J. Vickers (Chicago: University of Chicago Press, 1986).

Stallybrass, Peter, and Allon White. *The Politics and Poetics of Transgression.* Ithaca: Cornell University Press, 1987.

Stampa, Gaspara. *Rime.* Edited by Maria Bellonci and Rodolfo Ceriello. 2d ed. Milan: Rizzoli, 1976.

Starn, Randolph. *Contrary Commonwealth: The Theme of Exile in Medieval and Renaissance Italy.* Berkeley: University of California Press, 1982.

Steinberg, Arthur, and Jonathan Wylie. "Counterfeiting Nature: Artistic Innovation and Cultural Crisis in Renaissance Venice." *Society for Comparative Study of Society and History* 32, no. 1 (1990): 54–88.

Stella, Aldo, ed. *Nunziature di Venezia.* 27 vols. Rome: Istituto storico italiano, 1958–77.

———. *Chiesa e stato nelle relazioni dei nunzi pontifici a Venezia: Ricerche sul giurisdizionalismo veneziano dal XVI al XVIII secolo.* Vatican City: 1964.

Strong, Roy. *Art and Power: Renaissance Festivals, 1450–1650.* Berkeley: University of California Press, 1984.

Taddeo, Edoardo. *Il manierismo letterario e i lirici veneziani del tardo Cinquecento.* Rome: Bulzoni, 1974.

Tafuri, Manfredo. *L'armonia e i conflitti: La chiesa di San Francesco della Vigna nella Venezia del Cinquecento.* Turin: Einaudi, 1983.

———. "Scuole Grandi." In his *Venezia e il Rinascimento.* Turin: Einaudi, 1985.

Tafuri, Manfredo, ed. *"Renovatio urbis": Venezia nell'età di Andrea Gritti (1523–1538).* Rome: Officina Edizione, 1984.

La tariffa delle puttane di Venegia. Venice: 1535.

Tassini, Giuseppe. *Alcune delle più clamorose condanne capitali eseguite in Venezia sotto la repubblica.* Venice: Filippi Editore, 1966.

———. *Veronica Franco: Celebre poetessa e cortigiana del secolo XVI.* 1874. Reprint, Venice: Alfieri, 1969.

———. *Curiosità veneziane.* 8th ed. Venice: Filippi Editore, 1970.

Tasso, Bernardo. *Rime . . . divise in cinque libri.* Venice: Gabriel Giolito de' Ferrari, 1560.

———. *Le lettere.* 2 vols. Venice: Cavalcalupo, 1580.

Tasso, Torquato. *Delle lettere familiari.* Venice: Lucio Spineda, 1605.

Tedeschi, John. "Preliminary Observations on Writing a History of the Roman Inquisition." In *Continuity and Discontinuity in Church History,* edited by F. Forrester Church and Timothy George. Leiden: E. J. Brill, 1979.

Temelini, Walter. "The Life and Works of Bernardino Pino da Cagli." Ph.D. diss., University of Toronto, 1969.

Tenenti, Branislava. "Noli ragusei per Venezia nella seconda metà del cinquecento." *Studi veneziani* 16 (1974).

———. "Venezia e il commercio raguseo delle carisee (1550c.–1620c.)." *Studi veneziani* 17–18 (1975–76).

Tertullian. "On the Apparel." In *The Anti-Nicene Fathers: Translations of the Writings of the Fathers Down to A.D. 325,* edited by Alexander Roberts and James Donaldson. 10 vols. Grand Rapids, Mich.: Eerdmans, 1971–86.

Tissoni Benvenuti, Antonia. "La tradizione della terza rima e l'Ariosto." In *Ludovico Ariosto: Lingua, stile e tradizione,* edited by Cesare Segre. Milan: Feltrinelli, 1976.

Toderini, Teodoro. *Genealogie delle famiglie Venete ascritte alla cittadinanza originaria.* 4 vols. Miscellanea codici, I.

Tolomei, Claudio. *Versi et regole della nuova poesia toscana.* Rome: Antonio Blado d'Asola, 1539.

Toscanella, Orazio. *L'Institutioni oratorie di Marco Fabio Quintiliano . . . .* Venice: Gabriel Giolito de' Ferrari, 1566.

———. *Discorsi cinque.* Venice: Pietro de' Franceschi, 1575.

————. *I modi più communi con che ha scritto Cicerone le sue epistole.* 1559; Venice: Bolognino Zaltieri, 1575.

Trafton, Dain A. "Politics and the Praise of Women: Political Doctrine in the *Courtier's* Third Book." In *Castiglione: The Ideal and the Real in Renaissance Culture,* edited by Robert Hanning and David Rosand. New Haven: Yale University Press, 1983.

Trexler, Richard C. *Public Life in Renaissance Florence.* New York: Academic Press, 1980.

————. "La prostitution florentine au XVe siécle: Patronage et clientèles." *Annales, Economies, Sociétés, Civilisations* 36 (1981): 983–1015.

Ulvioni, Paola. "Accademie e cultura in Italia dalla Controriforma all'Arcadia: Il caso Veneziano." In *Libri e documenti: Archivio storico civico e Biblioteca Trivulziana.* Milan: Archivio Storico Civico e Biblioteca Trivulziana, 1979.

Urban, Lina Padoan. "La festa della Sensa nelle arti e nell'iconografia." *Studi veneziani* 10 (1968): 291–353.

————. "Gli spettacoli urbani e l'utopia." In *Architettura e utopia nella Venezia del Cinquecento.* Milan: Electa, 1980.

Vecellio, Cesare. *Degli habiti antichi et moderni di diverse parti del mondo.* 2 vols. Venice: D. Zenaro, 1590.

Vedova, G. *Biografie degli scrittori padovani.* Bologna: 1836.

Vendramino, M. Federico, and Ludovico Dolce. *Opere morali di Marco Tullio Cicerone: Cioé tre libri de gli uffici.* Venice: Gabriele Giolito de' Ferrari, 1563.

Venezia e la peste, 1348–1797. Venice: Marsilio Editore, 1979.

Venier, Domenico. *Rime di Domenico Veniero, Senatore viniziano raccolte ora per la prima volta ed illustrate,* edited by Pierantonio Serassi. Bergamo: Pietro Lancelotto, 1751.

Verducci, Florence. *Ovid's Toyshop of the Heart: Epistulae Heroidum.* Princeton: Princeton University Press, 1985.

Vermeule, Cornelius C. *The Goddess Roma in the Art of the Roman Empire.* Cambridge: Harvard University Press, 1959.

Vickers, Nancy J. "Diana Described: Scattered Women and Scattered Rhyme." In *Writing and Sexual Difference,* edited by Elizabeth Abel. Chicago: University of Chicago Press, 1982.

Viviani, Giuseppe Franco, ed. *La villa nel Veronese.* Verona: 1975.

Vocabolario degli Accademici della Crusca. 11 vols. Florence: 1889.

von Pastor, Ludwig. *The History of the Popes from the Close of the Middle Ages.* 40 vols. Wilmington, N. C.: Consortium Books, 1978.

Walvoord, Laura. "A Whore's Vices Are Really Virtues: Prostitution and Feminine Identity in Sixteenth-Century Venice." Graduate seminar paper, Department of History, University of California, Berkeley.

Warner, Marina. *Alone of All Her Sex: The Myth and Cult of the Virgin Mary.* New York: Vintage Books, 1983.

Wayne, Don E. *Penshurst: The Semiotics of Place and the Poetics of History.* Madison: University of Wisconsin Press, 1984.

Weaver, Elissa. "Spiritual Fun: A Study of Sixteenth-Century Tuscan Convent Theater." In *Women in the Middle Ages and the Renaissance and Historical Perspectives,* ed. Mary Beth Rose. Syracuse: Syracuse University Press, 1985.

Weinberg, Bernard, ed. *Trattati di poetica e retorica del Cinquecento.* 4 vols. Bari: Laterza, 1970–74.

Weisbach, Werner. *Trionfi.* Berlin: G. Grote, 1919.

Weisner, Merry E. "Women's Defense of Their Public Role." In *Women in the Middle Ages and the Renaissance and Historical Perspectives,* ed. Mary Beth Rose. Syracuse: Syracuse University Press, 1985.

———. *Working Women in Renaissance Germany.* New Brunswick: Rutgers University Press, 1987.

———. "Paternalism in Practice: The Control of Servants and Prostitutes in Early Modern German Cities." In *The Process of Change in Early Modern Europe: Essays in Honor of Miriam Usher Chrisman,* edited by Phillip N. Bebb and Sherrin Marshall. Athens: Ohio University Press, 1988.

Whigham, Frank. "Interpretation at Court: Courtesy and the Performer-Audience Dialectic." *New Literary History* 14 (1983): 623–41.

———. *Ambition and Privilege: The Social Tropes of Elizabethan Courtesy Theory.* Berkeley: University of California Press, 1984.

Wilkinson, L. P. *Ovid Recalled.* Cambridge: Cambridge University Press, 1955.

Williams, Gordon. *Tradition and Originality in Roman Poetry.* Oxford: Clarendon Press, 1968.

———. *Figures of Thought in Roman Poetry.* New Haven: Yale University Press, 1980.

Williamson, Edward. *Bernardo Tasso.* Rome: Edizioni di storia e di letteratura, 1951.

Wind, Edgar. *Pagan Mysteries in the Renaissance.* New York: W. W. Norton, 1958.

Woodhouse, J. R. *Baldesar Castiglione: A Reassessment of "The Courtier."* Edinburgh: Edinburgh University Press, 1978.

Worcester Art Museum. *European paintings in the collection of the Worcester Art Museum.* Worcester, Mass.: Worcester Art Museum, 1974.

Wurthmann, William B. "The Council of Ten and the *Scuole Grandi* in Early Renaissance Venice." *Studi veneziani* 18 (1989): 15–66.

Yriarte, Charles. *La vie d'un patricien de Venise au seizième siécle.* Paris: E. Plon, 1874.

Zacco, Bartolomeo. *Storia di Padova sino alla estinzione dei principi Carraresi.*

Zorzi, Alvise. *Cortigiana veneziana: Veronica Franco e i suoi poeti.* Milan: Camunia Editrice, 1986.

Zorzi, Ludovico, ed. and trans. *La Venexiana.* Turin: Einaudi, 1979.

Zucchi, Bartolomeo, ed. *L'idea del secretario.* Venice: Compagnia Minima, 1606.

Index